New York Yankees
Openers

New York Yankees Openers

*An Opening Day History
of Baseball's Most Famous
Team, 1903–2017*

SECOND EDITION

LYLE SPATZ

McFarland & Company, Inc., Publishers
Jefferson, North Carolina

ISBN (print) 978-1-4766-6765-2
ISBN (ebook) 978-1-4766-3247-6

Library of Congress cataloguing data are available

British Library cataloguing data are available

Front cover photograph by Matt Brown (iStock)

Printed in the United States of America

*McFarland & Company, Inc., Publishers
Box 611, Jefferson, North Carolina 28640
www.mcfarlandpub.com*

In loving memory of Marilyn, 1939–2017

Table of Contents

Preface

Things are always at their best in the beginning.—Blaise Pascal

This volume is the second edition of New York Yankees Openers. The first, published by McFarland & Company in 1997, ended with the 1996 season, just as the Yankees were establishing a new dynasty. This second edition adds the years 1997 to 2017, all of which have greatly enriched the history of baseball's most famous team. It also updates the years 1903 to 1996. In reading through those years I found several errors that needed correcting. I also corrected statements pertaining to records set or tied that were true in 1997, but are no longer true.

Perhaps because it comes in the spring, the season of hope and renewal, Americans have always greeted the opening of a new baseball season with a euphoria that no other sport inspires. To baseball fans Opening Day is a kind of holiday, often the most eagerly anticipated one of the year. There was a time, particularly in the early years of the twentieth century, when major league cities actually did treat Opening Day like a holiday, a joyous celebration complete with flags, bands, parades, and speeches. Of course, Opening Day rituals have changed substantially since then. This book, while noting those changes, goes well beyond them to survey the more wide-ranging transformation of baseball, and even beyond that to the transformation of life in America.

The mechanism for examining these changes is the opening-day games of the New York Yankees. In reliving each Yankees' opener, we see how the game has evolved from the team's birth in 1903 to now. Opening Day gives us our first look at the significant changes in baseball as they occur—changes like the breaking of the color line, the expansion and shifting of franchises, the introduction of the designated hitter, interleague play, and the leagues splitting, first into two divisions and then into three. Investigating the additions to and deletions from each season's opening-day lineup enables us to track the effects of trades, injuries, and retirements on each player's career. We also get to look back at the major-league debuts of many players, some of whom were never heard from again, and some—like Ted Williams, Phil Rizzuto, and Mickey Mantle—who were on the way to a Hall of Fame career. Occasionally, there are particular opening-day events that we know in retrospect will influence or foreshadow a player's season, or sometimes his career.

However, baseball, as we know, is more than just the game and its players; it is a part of the social and cultural life of the nation. Whatever affects America affects baseball. The Yankees have played their openers while the country dealt with international incidents, wars, depression, labor strife, racial unrest, and the death of a president. Just as those events influenced the course of life in the United States, so they influenced the course of baseball.

Because I am a baseball fan as well as a baseball historian, there is a mixture of both opinion and fact in this book, although I do not think the reader will have any problem separating the two. The opinions, which deal primarily with how the game has changed, are of course my own. Nevertheless, I believe they reflect the feelings of many fans who first fell in love with baseball in that period roughly between Franklin D. Roosevelt's first term as president and Dwight D. Eisenhower's last. My own enchantment, which continues unabated despite the seemingly endless assaults on fandom, began in the final days of World War II. I overheard a group of adults trying to make sense of why the Yankees had sold Hank Borowy, their best pitcher, to the Chicago Cubs. Why this fascinated an eight-year-old more than the day's other topic of conversation—the crash of a military plane into the Empire State Building—I cannot say; however, I remain forever grateful that it did. Horace Greeley once said, "The illusion that times that were are better than those that are, has probably pervaded all ages." Greeley was not talking about baseball fans, but he could have been. So while there have been many things to complain about in baseball these last years, and I have complained about all of them, I remain optimistic. I am confident that the game will continue to incorporate the good changes and survive the bad ones, just as it always has.

My major sources of information for each Yankees' opening day game were the newspapers of the period. Newspapers are a treasure trove for the baseball researcher, but they are also much more. For in addition to telling us what was happening on the field that day, newspapers also give us a freeze-frame look at life in the city where the game took place. Obviously, for the purposes of this book, half the time that means New York. Before 1960, however, it's also Boston or Philadelphia or Washington; and after 1960, almost every other American League city. For some openers, the focus of the day's events is more national than it is local, and there are some years where the focus is strictly on baseball. In all cases, I have tried to convey to the reader the flavor of the period—what people were thinking, feeling, and saying then—while also attempting to add some historical perspective.

To that end, I have made the box score accompanying each game account reflective of the type of box score in use at the time. In some years I have combined box scores from different newspapers to make them as informative as possible. Much of the information in the post–World War II boxes comes from the wonderful work of a dedicated group of baseball researchers at *Retrosheet*, under the direction of Dr. David Smith.

Still, there are some things—perhaps arcane to some, but not to baseball fans—that one can't find in books, newspapers, or box scores. For those special facts, I turned to my colleagues at the Society for American Baseball Research. To them and to others both in and out of SABR who graciously answered my questions and provided advice and encouragement, I offer my thanks.

I would also like to thank the staffs at the Library of Congress, where I did almost all my research, the National Baseball Library and Archive in Cooperstown, which provided access to certain player files, and Stephan Saks, for locating newspapers I was unable to find.

Maury Bouchard, of Schenevus, New York, served as my fact-checker as he has done in the past, and as always saved me from numerous potential embarrassments. Like Maury, Rick Huhn of Westerville, Ohio, and Tom Bourke, of St. Petersburg, Florida, also read the entire original manuscript. Rick, a first-rate biographer himself, made several suggestions to make this a better book. Tom, the former Chief of the Microforms Division at the New York Public Library, was an enormous help with the history and geography of New York City.

Most of all, I want to thank my late wife, Marilyn, whose interest in baseball was mostly nonexistent, but who, nevertheless, good-naturedly tolerated my "first love" since the year Mickey Mantle won the Triple Crown.

Introduction

The Cincinnati peace agreement of January 10, 1903, made it possible for the American League to replace its defunct Baltimore franchise with one in New York. This placing of a second major-league team in New York is testimony to the political skills of American League founder and president Ban Johnson, who had to overcome the opposition of Tammany Hall operator Andrew Freedman, the owner of the National League's New York Giants. Johnson gladly agreed not to invade National League territory in Pittsburgh in exchange for a franchise in the nation's largest city.

The Greater New York Club of the American League, purchased for $18,000, was incorporated on March 18, 1903, with Joseph Gordon as president and Frank Farrell as treasurer. Gordon was chosen as president because he was a respectable businessman, but in reality he was only a figurehead. Ownership of the club was in the hands of Farrell and "Big Bill" Devery, each with enough Tammany Hall connections of his own to offset Freedman's opposition. Farrell was a major figure in the New York gambling trust whose syndicate operated more than two hundred betting parlors. Devery started as a bartender, but his Tammany Hall patrons got him appointed to the police force, and in 1898, Mayor Robert A. Van Wyck appointed him New York City's chief of police.

It was from these humble and somewhat disreputable beginnings that the Yankees would rise to become America's preeminent and most respected (although hardly most loved) team. For almost half a century, beginning just after World War I and lasting into the war in Vietnam, the Yankees were unrivaled in baseball, much the way America and its foremost city, New York, were unrivaled in the world. The Yankees dominated the game almost uninterruptedly from the arrival of Babe Ruth to the last days of Mickey Mantle. Moreover, they achieved their fame and success with a style and elegance admired by even the most ardent Yankee haters. For half a century, doing things the "Yankee way" was doing them the right way. Since then, the Yankees have lost, and regained, a good part of their grandeur. So too has baseball, New York City, and much else in America. As we progress through the twenty-first century, my hope is that the Yankees, baseball, New York City, and America will all be fully restored to their former glory.

I

1903–1909

Despite the efforts of American League president Ban Johnson to bring a championship team to New York, it was mostly failure and frustration for the Highlanders (the Yankees' original name) in their first seven seasons. They did make a serious run at the pennant in 1904 but lost it to Boston on the last day of the season; they finished second again two years later. Second place was also the Highlanders' position in the city's affections, which were lavished on John McGraw's highly successful New York Giants.

The Highlanders won no pennants under their original owners, Frank Farrell and William "Big Bill" Devery, but their fans got to cheer for some of the finest players of the century's first decade. Future Hall-of-Famers Jack Chesbro and Willie Keeler, along with lesser-known stars like Al Orth, Kid Elberfeld, Jimmy Williams, and the spectacular Hal Chase, all starred at Hilltop Park, the club's original home on Manhattan's Upper West Side. In 1904 Chesbro won 41 games, which remains the post-nineteenth-century major league record.

Pitcher Clark Griffith managed the team from its beginnings in New York until he quit during the 1908 season. Shortstop Kid Elberfeld replaced him but was a complete failure as a manager. New York lost 103 games, which remains a club record. In 1909 Elberfeld went back to being a player, and George Stallings took over as manager. The team climbed to fifth place and drew a record 501,000 fans to Hilltop Park, nearly 200,000 more than in 1908. Nevertheless, Stallings would be gone before the end of the 1910 season.

Wednesday, April 22, 1903
American League Park, Washington
Washington 3 New York 1

Our pastime and our happiness will grow. —William Wordsworth

In January 1903 representatives of the National and American Leagues met at the St. Nicholas Hotel in Cincinnati to sign a peace agreement. The settlement ended two years of expensive and disruptive cross-league player raids and confirmed the American League as a full and equal partner with the National League. In their first joint action, both leagues agreed to a new rule that limited rosters to 16 players after June 1, and the American League adopted the foul strike rule, which had been in use in the National League since 1901. (Under the foul strike rule, a foul ball, not caught, counts as a strike against the batter unless he already has two strikes against him.)

But the principal provision of the agreement was in awarding teams territorial rights. It allowed the National League to retain its exclusivity in Pittsburgh, while accepting the American League's entry into New York. American League president Ban Johnson quickly arranged for the creation of a new franchise in the nation's largest city to replace the defunct one in Baltimore. The peace agreement, along with the increased financial benefits and prestige of having another team in New York, would propel baseball into a period of unprecedented stability and prosperity. It would benefit from an American economy that was booming, especially in the cities. Even as the Highlanders (the most common of several appellations the press used as a nickname for the club) were making their official debut in Washington, the nation's capital was taking the first steps toward construction of its magnificent railroad hub, Union Station. And back in New York, Mayor Seth Low was dedicating the new Stock Exchange building at Broad and Wall Streets in lower Manhattan. Meanwhile, at the other end of Manhattan, at Broadway and 165th Street, the first carload of chairs for the grandstand arrived at Hilltop Park (officially called American League Park), the Highlanders' new home. After four games in Washington and three in Philadelphia, the Highlanders would play their first home game on April 30.

An overflow crowd of more than 11,500 (a record for Washington's American League Park) witnessed the Highlanders' first American League game, a 3–1 loss to the hometown Senators. It was a surprisingly large turnout for Washington, a city with a reputation as a poor baseball town. And though the weather was cold and unpleasant, a greater than usual number of women were at the game, wearing what the *Evening Star* called their "pretty costumes." The crowd was so huge that spectators completely covered the deepest parts of the outfield. They stood behind ropes that kept them off the playing field, making it necessary for a special grounds rule to govern balls hit into their midst.

Washingtonians were seeing a New York team that bore little resemblance to the Baltimore club it had replaced. The 1902 season had been a cataclysmic one for the Orioles, both on the field and off, as Johnson's desire to disband the club became apparent to both players and fans. When Orioles' manager John McGraw learned that Johnson's plans did not include him, he secretly signed a contract to manage the New York Giants of the National League. McGraw had come to hate Johnson and would have loved to wreck the new league in its infancy. He contrived a backdoor stock deal that allowed Giants owner Andrew Freedman to become the majority owner of the Orioles. Freedman and McGraw immediately began shifting several of Baltimore's best players—including Joe McGinnity, Roger Bresnahan, and Dan McGann—to the Giants.

Conversely, a considerable portion of the Highlanders' roster consisted of players obtained from National League franchises, including future Hall-of-Famers Willie Keeler and Jack Chesbro. In joining the Highlanders, Keeler, who began his big-league career with the Giants in 1892 and played the last four years for Brooklyn, became the first man to play for all three teams then in New York. At 31 he was among the game's best hitters, having batted .333 or higher in each of his nine full seasons in the National League. To lure him away from Brooklyn and into the American League, he was being paid a league-high $10,000 for the season.

Chesbro, a 29-year-old right-hander, pitched for the pennant-winning Pittsburgh Pirates in 1902, leading the National League in wins (28) and winning percentage (.824). Four of his Pittsburgh teammates were also with the Highlanders: pitcher Jesse Tannehill, catcher Jack O'Connor, third baseman Wid Conroy, and outfielder Lefty Davis. All but Tannehill were in the starting lineup, joining Chesbro, manager Clark Griffith's choice to pitch the opener. Griffith, 33, had pitched for and managed the American League's Chicago White Stockings in 1901–1902, guiding them to the pennant in 1901. Nevertheless, Johnson, recognizing the necessity of having a successful franchise in New York, prevailed upon his friend, White Stockings owner Charles Comiskey, to allow the transfer of Griffith to the Highlanders.

The pregame parade, an opening-day tradition carried over from the nineteenth century, began at two o'clock. Originating at the Ebbitt House in downtown Washington (where the Highlanders were staying), horse-drawn carriages transported the teams down K Street and across Pennsylvania Avenue to American League Park. Upon arriving at the park, situated at Florida Avenue and Trinidad Avenue Northeast, the Highlanders and the Senators lined up behind Haley's Band and marched to the music of "The Washington Post March" from the clubhouse to home plate. The Senators were wearing their home, white uniforms, which had a blue fold-down collar and a large blue ornamental "W" on the left breast. They wore white caps with blue bills and blue stockings. New York's visiting uniform was blue, with a large white "N" on the right breast and a large white "Y" on the left breast. The belts were white and the blue caps were trimmed with white piping. As was the custom, flowers were presented to Washington manager Tom Loftus (who managed in civilian clothes) and to popular hometown players. Two local politicians, District of Columbia Commissioner Henry L. West and Maryland Senator Arthur Pue Gorman, presided over the pregame formalities. Earlier in the day, Gorman, a staunch opponent of voting rights for Negroes, had won the endorsement of Democratic National Chairman James K. Jones as his party's 1904 presidential nominee. After West tossed the ceremonial first ball to umpire Tommy Connolly, the Senators came to bat. It was not unusual in this era for the home team to bat first, and Loftus chose to do so for the usual reason—to take advantage of the new ball.

Chesbro began the game and New York's American League presence by walking the first two Senators' batters, Rabbit Robinson and Kip Selbach. As Ed Delahanty, the American League's 1902 batting champion, approached the plate, umpire Connolly held up play and allowed a group of fans to present him with a beautiful horseshoe of roses. Delahanty, who would not survive the 1903 season (he fell or was pushed to his death on July 2 from a bridge over Niagara Falls), had "jumped" to the Senators in 1902 after a long and successful career with the National League's Philadelphia Phillies. However, when the season ended, he attempted to "jump back" to the National League by signing a three-year contract with the New York Giants. The committee that worked out the peace settlement resolved the Delahanty impasse a few days before the 1903 season began by awarding him to Washington. In return, Johnson authorized the American League to send a check for $4,000 (the amount the Giants had given to Delahanty as an advance) to National League Secretary John H. Heydler. Delahanty, noticeably overweight and out of shape, went down on strikes, but Chesbro walked the next batter, Jimmy Ryan, to load the bases. With the crowd roaring for a big inning, Chesbro got first baseman Scoops Carey to hit the ball back to him. He fielded it cleanly and threw to catcher O'Connor forcing Robinson. O'Connor then threw to first baseman John Ganzel to get Carey and complete the inning-ending double play.

Left fielder Lefty Davis became New York's first ever batter when he led off the bottom of the first against Washington's Al Orth, known as "The Curveless Wonder." Davis had been a promising player for the Pirates until he broke his leg in a game at Pittsburgh's Exposition Park in 1902. However, he would be a disappointment in New York, batting just .237 in 104 games in his only season with the Highlanders. Orth retired him on a ground ball to second baseman Gene DeMontreville, but then walked Keeler. Dave Fultz, purchased from the Philadelphia Athletics in March, followed with a single to left that sent Keeler to third. Actually, Delahanty's throw had beaten Keeler to the bag, but Willie used a beautiful fade-away slide to avoid third baseman Bill Coughlin's tag. When second baseman Jimmy Williams, the only Highlander from the 1902 Orioles in the starting lineup, went out on a slow roller to DeMontreville, Keeler came across with the Highlanders' first-ever run. It would be their only run today against Orth, a six-foot right-hander in his second year with the Senators following seven solid seasons with the Phillies. New York got just five well-spaced hits over the next eight innings, and came close to scoring again only in the sixth. With two out and runners at first and second, Fultz lined a ball to center field that Ryan pulled down with a good running catch.

Washington tied the score with a run off Chesbro in the fourth. Delahanty led off with a walk and went to second on a sacrifice by Ryan. When Carey singled to left, it appeared Delahanty would score easily. But DeMontreville, doing double duty as the third-base coach, held him at third. Coughlin followed with a bouncer that Chesbro snared, trapping Delahanty off third. A rundown ensued in which Delahanty was tagged out and Carey reached second. DeMontreville, a player again, atoned for his coaching misjudgment by driving a ball into the crowd in left for a ground-rule double that scored Carey. Washington staged their winning rally in the fifth, scoring two runs on singles by Robinson, Selbach, and Delahanty and an error by shortstop Herman Long. Long had signed with the Highlanders after 13 superb seasons with the National League's Boston Beaneaters. Before the ascent of Honus Wagner, Long, George Davis of the Giants, and Bill Dahlen of the Chicago Colts were baseball's best shortstops. However, at age 37 Long was clearly past his prime. He would play in only 22 games for the Highlanders before they traded him, along with infielder Ernie Courtney, to the Detroit Tigers on June 10. It was New York's first trade, and an excellent one. In return they received Norman "Kid" Elberfeld who was to be their shortstop for the next seven years.

New York would get its first league victory the following day, defeating the Senators 7–2.

The Highlanders finished fourth (72–62) in their first season, 17 games behind the pennant-winning Boston Americans. Jack Chesbro won 21 games (21–15) and Willie Keeler led the team in batting with a .313 average, his lowest full-season average to that time.

Wednesday, April 22, 1903

Washington	ab	r	h	po	a	e	New York	ab	r	h	po	a	e
Robinson ss	3	1	1	3	7	2	Davis lf	4	0	0	2	0	0
Selbach rf	3	1	1	0	0	0	Keeler rf	3	1	0	0	0	0
Delahanty lf	3	0	1	1	0	0	Fultz cf	4	0	2	0	0	0
Ryan cf	2	0	0	2	0	0	Williams 2b	3	0	0	0	3	1
Carey 1b	4	1	1	7	0	0	Ganzel 1b	4	0	1	14	1	0
Coughlin 3b	4	0	1	3	2	0	Conroy 3b	4	0	1	4	3	0
DeMontreville 2b	3	0	1	6	2	0	Long ss	4	0	1	1	4	1
Clarke c	4	0	0	3	2	0	O'Connor c	4	0	1	5	2	0
Orth p	4	0	0	2	2	1	Chesbro p	3	0	0	1	5	0
Total	30	3	6	27	15	3	ᵃCourtney	1	0	0	0	0	0
							Total	34	1	6	27	18	2

ᵃBatted for Chesbro in ninth.

Washington	000	120	000–3
New York	100	000	000–1

Left on bases—Washington, 6; New York, 9. First base on balls—off Orth, 3; off Chesbro, 4. Struck out—by Chesbro, 3; by Orth 2. Two-base hits—DeMontreville, Coughlin, Fultz. Sacrifice hits—DeMontreville, Ryan. Double play—Chesbro, O'Connor, and Ganzel. Wild pitches—Orth, 1; Chesbro, 1. Umpire—Mr. Connolly. Time—1 hr. 45 min.

Thursday, April 14, 1904
Hilltop Park, New York
New York 8 Boston 2

If you aspire to the highest place it is no disgrace
to stop at the second, or even the third place.—Cicero

By the spring of 1904, President Theodore Roosevelt had been in office for two and a half years and America, inspired by his dynamic leadership, was bursting with confidence and enthusiasm. Nowhere was this sense of optimism greater than in New York City. The byword for the new century was change, and in every way the city was changing. It also was growing. Fueled by the thriving economy and massive immigration, the city's population also was exploding. New York was obviously a city with room for two major-league baseball teams—three if you counted Brooklyn, which, of course, not many in Manhattan did. While most New Yorkers remained loyal to the Giants and the rough-and-tough National League style of play, an increasing number had been won over by the more "sportsmanlike" play of the new American League. Therefore, it was not surprising that in spite of a brief morning snowstorm and bitter cold weather, 15,842 fans were at Hilltop Park to witness the opening of the Yankees' second season. (It was during this season that many newspapers and fans began calling the team the Yankees rather than the Highlanders.) Such a large crowd on such a wintry day was convincing evidence that the American League was in New York to stay.

Hilltop Park, also known as American League Park or affectionately as "The Rockpile," was a single-deck, wooden structure located on Broadway between 165th and 168th Streets in the Washington Heights section of Manhattan. It sat on property that the club had leased from the New York Institute for the Blind for ten years at $10,000 per year. "When the grounds are completed, no field in the country will approach the American grounds in its scenic attractions," Henry Chadwick had written. "Looking to the Northwest, the view embraces the Hudson River and the Palisades; while on the other side are the Westchester Hills with the Long Island Sound in sight." Later this year, New York would open its first subway line, the Interborough Rapid Transit (IRT), running from City Hall to Broadway and 145th Street in Washington Heights. Beginning in 1905, millions of New Yorkers would use the IRT and subsequent subway lines to travel to baseball games. But that was still a year away. To make it easier to get to today's opener the Metropolitan Street Railway put on 200 extra surface cars that ran directly from 145th Street to the park.

When the fans arrived at the Hilltop, attendants handed them small American flags, which further heightened the prevailing holiday spirit. New York had had a very productive off-season, adding pitchers Long Tom Hughes and Jack Powell, and Norwegian-born John Anderson, a switch-hitting outfielder. The new additions led many Yankees fans to predict their team was now strong enough to replace today's opponents, the Boston Americans, as world champions. Last fall, Boston, led by manager/third baseman Jimmy Collins, defeated

Pittsburgh of the National League five games to three in the first modern World Series. After passing through the turnstiles, New Yorkers saw a Hilltop Park greatly improved from the substandard facility it had been in 1903. During the off-season, workmen had filled the ravine behind right field and placed rock fillings beneath the grandstand and bleachers, thus strengthening them. They also extended the outfield area, enlarged the scoreboard in left field, and installed a new carriage gate that included special provisions for those arriving by automobile.

Before the game the 69th Regiment Band entertained the crowd, which included many local officials. Former National League great Adrian "Cap" Anson was among the spectators, as was injured New York Giants star Roger Bresnahan. Anson predicted (correctly, as it turned out) that New York would be in the race all the way. "Griffith has a great team," he said, "one of the best I ever saw." Bresnahan wished the Yankees and the American League good luck, telling Frank Farrell, the team's treasurer and co-owner, "I am rooting for you, and I think you will beat these fellows, 3–0." For some unexplained reason Bresnahan was at this game rather than being with his teammates who were opening against the Superbas across the East River in Brooklyn. The Giants were playing in Brooklyn despite a request from Ban Johnson that the National League arrange its schedule so that the Giants not open the season in New York. Evidently the National League felt, as did many residents of Manhattan, that by having the Giants open in Brooklyn they were honoring that request.

The pregame ceremonies concluded at 3:30 P.M. with a presentation of American beauty roses, arranged as a horseshoe, to Yankees manager Clark Griffith. Then, William M. K. Olcott, substituting for Mayor George McClellan Jr., threw out the first ball. Olcott was among New York's most prominent Republican politicians, having served as a district attorney and a judge of the city court. He tossed a brand new white ball to umpire Frank Dwyer, and the 1904 season was under way. Dwyer was one of the two umpires Johnson provided for today's game; former National League umpire Bill Carpenter worked the bases. Oddly, this was the first American League game for both. For Dwyer, 1904 would be his only American League season, while Carpenter would last only until June 23, when Johnson dropped him. He was quickly rehired by the National League, stayed a few years, and then began a long umpiring career in the minor leagues.

The Yankees took the field wearing their white home uniforms, which had a blue collar and a large blue "N" on the right breast and a large blue "Y" on the left breast. Their stockings were blue and white, their belts were blue, and there was blue piping on their white caps. The visitors wore gray uniforms and caps, with blue stockings and blue trim and a blue, block-lettered "BOSTON" across the jersey front. The Americans and Boston's National League entry, the Beaneaters, were the only big-league teams still wearing the nineteenth-century style laced collar.

As Boston left fielder Patsy Dougherty stepped in to lead off the game, the band struck up "The Star-Spangled Banner." Although it was a popular tune, playing it before a baseball game was highly unusual; it was not until 1931 that an act of Congress made it the national anthem. Nevertheless, on hearing it, the crowd instantly came to their feet and waved their flags. Dougherty was among the league's best young players, having batted .342 as a rookie in 1902 and .331 the following year. Because of what he had accomplished in his first two seasons, baseball fans were astounded when the Americans traded him to the Yankees in June. Especially so considering what they got in return: Bob Unglaub, a rookie infielder who had played in only six games. There was a great outcry over the trade, and not only in Boston. Fans around the league understood that Johnson was trying to strengthen the Yankees in their battle with the Giants for the devotion and dollars of the New York fans. What bothered them was that he was doing it at the expense of their teams.

Thursday, April 14, 1904

Boston	ab	r	h	po	a	e	New York	ab	r	h	po	a	e
Dougherty lf	4	0	1	2	0	0	Conroy 3b	3	1	1	1	1	0
Collins 3b	4	0	2	0	2	1	Fultz cf	4	1	1	4	0	0
Stahl cf	4	0	0	1	0	0	Keeler rf	3	1	1	2	0	0
Freeman rf	4	1	1	0	0	0	Elberfeld ss	3	0	1	1	2	0
Parent ss	3	1	1	1	1	0	Anderson lf	4	2	2	0	0	0
LaChance 1b	4	0	0	13	2	1	Williams 2b	3	1	1	1	1	0
Ferris 2b	3	0	0	1	4	0	Ganzel 1b	4	0	1	11	0	0
Criger c	3	0	1	5	2	0	McGuire c	3	0	0	7	1	0
Young p	3	0	0	1	2	1	Chesbro p	3	2	2	0	3	0
Total	32	2	6	24	13	3	Total	30	8	10	27	8	0

```
Boston      000   000   101–2
New York    511   100   00X–8
```

First base on balls—off Chesbro, 1. Struck out—by Chesbro, 4; by Young 2. Left on bases—Boston, 4; New York, 2. Home runs—Chesbro, Freeman, Parent. Three-base hit—Conroy. Two-base hits—Keeler, Anderson, Chesbro, Dougherty, Criger. Sacrifice hits—Conroy, Keeler, Elberfeld, Williams. Stolen base—Ganzel. Double plays—Criger and LaChance; McGuire and Ganzel. Passed ball—McGuire. Umpires—Messrs. Carpenter and Dwyer. Time—1 hr. 35 min. Attendance—15,842.

Six months from the opener, on the last day of the season, the Americans defeated Jack Chesbro and the Yankees on this field to win the American League pennant. Today, however, it was an easy victory for Chesbro as he pitched and batted the New Yorkers to a resounding 8–2 victory. He allowed Boston only one walk and six hits, while contributing a double and a long inside-the-park home run to the Yankees' ten-hit attack. Anderson also had two hits, while each of his teammates had at least one except for 40-year-old catcher Deacon McGuire. Excellent fielding by his teammates aided Chesbro throughout the game, with especially fine performances by right fielder Willie Keeler, third baseman Wid Conroy, first baseman John Ganzel, and shortstop Kid Elberfeld. Both Boston runs came on inside-the-park home runs: one by American League home-run king Buck Freeman in the seventh, and one by Freddy Parent in the ninth. Freeman's drive landed near the newly installed carriage gate in right field. Keeler was unable to get to the ball because of the poor condition of the field in that area, and as it rolled toward the fence, Freeman completed his trip around the bases. Similarly, in the ninth, Parent circled the bases when his low-liner to center got by Dave Fultz who failed in his attempt at a shoestring catch. By that time, however, the New Yorkers already had scored eight runs, including five in the first inning. The assault came at the expense of the great Boston pitcher, Cy Young. Although Young's fastballs and curves seemed as commanding as ever, the Yankees hit him freely in that first inning. After Conroy led off with a long triple, Young threw wildly on Fultz's come-backer, allowing the first run to score. Four more came home on doubles by Keeler and Anderson, a single by Jimmy Williams, and an error by Boston first baseman Candy LaChance. That was all that Chesbro would need, although New York added single runs in the second (on Chesbro's home run), third, and fourth innings.

This was the first season of the 154-game schedule that would endure in the major leagues until the expansion of the American League in 1961. Jack Chesbro set a modern-day record for wins with 41 (41–12), but lost the first game of a doubleheader to Boston on the final day of the season. That clinched the pennant for the Americans as New York finished second (92–59), 1½ games behind. Willie Keeler batted .343 and had 186 hits, second in both categories to Cleveland's Nap Lajoie's .376 batting average and 208 hits.

Friday, April 14, 1905
American League Park, Washington
New York 4 Washington 2

There are certain things that cannot be bought: loyalty, friendship, health, love and an American League pennant. —Edward Bennett Williams

Two days before the Washington Nationals were to open the season against New York; they received an added incentive to do well. New owner Thomas C. Noyes promised each player a bonus of $1,000 if the team avoided the cellar in 1905 (they had finished there the last two seasons). He also promised an additional $500 for every position the Senators finished above seventh place. This was an extremely generous offer at a time when many players' salaries were not much higher than $1,000; nor were the salaries of many other working people. On the day of the opener, the New York City Department of Education announced its new wage schedule for teachers: the annual salary for women teachers would now start at $936 and go up to $1,440, while for men, the range would be from $1,500 to $2,400.

The Yankees' 1905 opener marked the major-league debut of Hal Chase, the charming, enigmatic Californian who would develop into perhaps the game's most fascinating character. Chase was the team's new first baseman, replacing John Ganzel who paid the club $3,000 to obtain his release. Ganzel wanted out so he could play for the Grand Rapids club of the Western League, a team he had recently purchased. New York paid the Los Angeles Angels of the Pacific Coast League a reported $2,700 for the 22-year-old Chase. They received a superbly gifted athlete whom, contrary to the statistical evidence, many old-timers still consider the greatest fielding first baseman ever. Unfortunately, Chase's sense of ethics would eventually prove to be far short of his physical abilities. In a generally impressive debut, he had a hit and fielded flawlessly in the Yankees' 4–2 victory.

The winning pitcher was Jack Chesbro and the loser Case Patten, both of whom made excellent use of the spitball. Patten had been Washington's best pitcher in 1904, winning 14 games for a team that won only 38. His 106 lifetime victories are still the most by a Senators' left-hander. Meanwhile, Chesbro's 1904 season ranks with the greatest pitching seasons ever. He led the league in several departments including games won, with a twentieth-century high of 41 (41–12). Chesbro tried for win number 42 against first-place Boston on the last day of the season, with New York needing a sweep of the doubleheader to win the pennant. But in the ninth inning of the first game, he threw a run-scoring wild pitch that gave Boston a 3–2 win and the flag. The pitch, a spitter, sailed over the head of catcher Red Kleinow, a rookie who split the catching duties that season with veteran Deacon McGuire. While Chesbro always claimed Kleinow should have caught the ball, most eyewitnesses disagreed.

Washington was beginning the second year of play in its new home, which—like its old one—was named American League Park (through 1906 it was also known as National Park). Its location at Florida Avenue and Seventh Street NW was on the site of the old Boundary Field, home of the National League Washington Senators from 1892 to 1899. Off-season patching work had covered over the many holes in the fences, making it no longer possible for fans to stand outside and watch the game through one of those holes without paying. Although it had rained steadily all morning, groundskeeper Shorty Brown had the field in good playing condition. By noon the rain had ended, giving way to sunny skies and chilly temperatures. Still, the combination of rain and cold had kept many fans away, limiting the attendance to less than ten thousand. Yankees president Joseph Gordon was among the team's many followers who came down from New York to see the game and join in the festivities. Gordon, a former state assemblyman, was president in name only; his true role was to serve as the front man for co-owners Bill Devery and Frank Farrell.

Haley's Band had been playing for 45 minutes when at 3:45, to great applause, they began the pregame parade from the clubhouse. Behind the band, marching in lines of four, were the visitors wearing their gray coats trimmed in scarlet. And behind them was the home team, wearing double-breasted gray coats trimmed in blue, with a "W" on the right sleeve above the elbow. Each team had adopted a precedent-setting new uniform for the 1905 season. In late March, Washington officials had chosen "Nationals" as the new name for the club, hoping to change the losing image associated with the old name, "Senators." On this day, their black-trimmed, home-whites would have the word "NATIONALS" spelled in block letters across their shirt fronts, marking the first time a team had used its nickname on its game uniforms. For the Yankees, traditional gray replaced the dark blue road uniforms they had worn in their first two seasons. Also, the "N" and "Y" were no longer separated on the right and left breasts, but merged on the left breast in the first incarnation of the emblem that would later become the most famous in sports.

After the parade pregame practice began, first for the Yankees and then for the Nationals. Maryland senator Arthur Pue Gorman was to have thrown out the first ball but was away on business. Gorman had long been associated with baseball in the nation's capital. In 1859 he helped form one of the first amateur teams in the District of Columbia, also called the Nationals, for whom he played shortstop and served as team secretary. He later became the president of the National Association of Professional Baseball Players. Because Gorman's substitute, District of Columbia commissioner Henry L. West, was nowhere to be found, umpire Tom Connolly just handed the ball to catcher Mal Kittridge and the game began. Kittridge had been the Senators' manager on Opening Day last year, but after getting off to a 1–16 start the club replaced him with Patsy Donovan. After Washington finished the season with a record of 38–113, the worst in either league, they fired Donovan and appointed Jake Stahl, a college-educated, 26-year-old first baseman, as the new manager. For New York, Clark Griffith was beginning his third year at the helm.

Just as they had done in last year's opener against Boston, the Yankees scored enough runs in their first at-bat to win the game. Patsy Dougherty led off the first inning with a routine ground ball to second base. Jim Mullen fielded the ball, but his throw to first pulled Stahl off the bag and the runner was safe. Dougherty went to third on Willie Keeler's single and came home on Kid Elberfeld's squeeze bunt. Second baseman Jimmy Williams followed with a two-run inside-the-park home run to deep left field, giving New York a 3–0 lead. Williams had begun his major-league career in 1899 with a spectacular rookie season. He played in 153 games at third base for Pittsburgh, which at the time was the most games ever played by a rookie at any position. He batted .354, fifth highest in the National League. He also had nine home runs (his career high) and led the league in triples with 27. After moving to Baltimore, Williams was the American League's triples leader in 1901 and 1902, getting 21 each season. Although he never again reached the level of his early years, Williams had a fine 11-year major-league career, including five years in New York.

After his first-inning single, Keeler twice was the victim of a stellar defensive play. In the sixth, he led off with a long drive that center fielder Charlie Jones raced back and caught with a sensational barehanded grab. And earlier, in the third inning, third baseman Hunter Hill charged in to field Willie's well-placed bunt and made an off-balance throw to nip him at first. Hill sparkled on defense all afternoon, contributing several outstanding plays. Elberfeld scored the Yankees' fourth run after drawing a two-out walk in the sixth inning. He came all the way around on a scratch single by John Anderson, with the help of errors by shortstop Joe Cassidy and catcher Kittridge. Cassidy had joined the Washington club in 1904 without having played in the minor leagues. Although erratic, he was developing into an exciting player when he was stricken with typhoid fever. He died on March 25, 1906, at the age of 23.

Chesbro allowed only two walks and struck out seven. The Nationals scored their first run against him in the fifth when right fielder Harry Cassady walked, went to third on Patten's single, and came home as Jones hit into a force play. That was the only time in the game that Jones put the ball in play. In his other three at-bats, Chesbro fanned him each time. Washington made it 4–2 in the ninth, scoring on an error by Elberfeld and two-out singles by Mullen and Cassady. Then, with the tying runs aboard and the crowd up and cheering, Chesbro retired Kittridge on a force-play grounder to Elberfeld to end the game.

It was a season marred by injuries, as every Yankees' regular except Willie Keeler missed multiple games. New York did lead the league in stolen bases with 200, and Dave Fultz was the individual leader with 44, but the team finished a disappointing sixth (71–78), 21½ games behind Philadelphia. The Washington Nationals took advantage of their owner's preseason proposition by finishing seventh.

Friday, April 14, 1905

New York

	ab	r	h	po	a	e
Dougherty lf	4	1	2	0	0	0
Keeler rf	3	1	1	4	0	0
Elberfeld ss	2	1	0	2	6	2
Williams 2b	4	1	1	6	2	0
Anderson cf	4	0	3	2	0	0
Conroy 3b	4	0	1	0	2	0
Chase 1b	4	0	1	6	0	0
Kleinow c	3	0	0	7	1	0
Chesbro p	3	0	0	0	1	0
Total	31	4	9	27	12	2

Washington

	ab	r	h	po	a	e
Jones cf	4	0	0	2	0	0
Hill 3b	3	0	0	2	6	0
Stahl 1b	4	1	0	13	1	0
Huelsman lf	4	0	1	2	0	1
Cassidy ss	4	0	1	1	4	2
Mullen 2b	4	0	1	2	0	1
Cassady rf	3	1	2	2	0	0
Kittridge c	4	0	0	3	2	0
Patten p	3	0	1	0	1	0
Total	33	2	6	27	14	4

New York	300	001	000–4
Washington	000	010	001–2

Left on bases—Washington, 6; New York, 4. First base on balls—off Patten, 1; off Chesbro, 1. Struck out—by Patten, 3; by Chesbro, 7. Home run—Williams. Two-base hit—Chase. Sacrifice hits—Keeler, Elberfeld, Kleinow. Hit by pitcher—Cassady. Double plays—Elberfeld to Williams to Chase; Stahl to Cassidy. Umpire—Mr. Connolly. Time of game—1 hr. 35 min.

Saturday, April 14, 1906
Hilltop Park, New York
New York 2 Boston 1 (12 Innings)

What's in a name?—William Shakespeare

No matter what name one chose to call them, and most newspapers and fans were now calling New York's American League team the "Yankees" rather than the "Highlanders," all who saw their 2–1 opening-day victory against Boston agreed that it was as exciting and well-played an opener as ever seen in this city. Even as the Hilltop Park crowd rejoiced over the triumph, the game's two principal combatants were standing together down on the field. Boston's Cy Young and New York's Jack Chesbro were chatting, shaking hands, and congratulating each other for a job well done. "I'm glad we won, but you are certainly a tough proposition," said Chesbro to Young. "No, not tough," Young replied, "just a trifle difficult, you know."

For 12 innings these two distinguished veterans had waged a memorable battle before the Yankees took advantage of a Boston error to score the winning run. Young allowed seven hits, struck out seven, and walked one; Chesbro was touched for eleven hits, struck out three, and walked no one. With better defense, "Happy Jack," making his fourth consecutive opening-day start, might have had a shutout and a 1–0 nine-inning victory. Catcher Charlie Graham scored the lone Boston run in the fifth inning with the aid of errors by third baseman Frank LaPorte and shortstop Kid Elberfeld. LaPorte had played in 11 games for New York in September 1905, but was still a rookie. Except for the error, he played a fine third base, and judging by the applause he received appeared to win the admiration of the fans. LaPorte was replacing Wid Conroy, whom manager Clark Griffith had moved to center field to fill the void left by Dave Fultz's retirement. Fultz was only 31, and still a fine athlete; his 44 stolen bases in 1905 set the still-existing, post-1900 record for a player in his final year. But a broken nose and jaw suffered in a late September collision with Elberfeld convinced Fultz, a Columbia University graduate who had passed the New York Bar exam, to leave baseball and begin the practice of law. In 1912 Fultz would reappear in baseball to organize and lead the Players Fraternity.

A crowd of about 15,000 was on hand for the Saturday opener. Sunday, of course, would be an off day because of the New York State blue laws prohibiting Sunday baseball. Not until 1919, when Governor Al Smith signed the legislation lifting the ban, would any of the New York teams play regularly scheduled Sunday home games. Yet while no one at Hilltop Park could have guessed it, just two weeks later, on April 29, the state would temporarily lift the prohibition and the Yankees would play a Sunday home game against the Philadelphia Athletics. The exception was made for a good cause: to benefit victims of the April 18 San Francisco earthquake and fire.

Though the weather was reminiscent of March, with gray skies, chill winds, and a threat of rain, Hilltop Park looked magnificent. It was a newly painted apple green and bedecked with colorful flags and bunting, with the banners of many nations flying from dozens of poles set atop the fences surrounding the park. The spectators, too, looked wonderful. As described in the *New York Press*, "the men looked prosperous, and the women were dressed in the height of metropolitan fashion." Getting to Hilltop Park should have been easier today. The subway was now running to the West 168th Street station, only a short walk from the park. However, an accident at the station made it necessary for the fans to get off the train where they formerly did, at 157th Street. It was a public relations fiasco for the transit company, which had been advertising the "convenience" of the new stop at Hilltop Park. Many subway riders showed their displeasure by refusing to pay the 25 cents for the carriage ride from 157th Street to the park, choosing instead to walk. Upon arriving, some fans elected to watch the game from alternate sites. Men and boys, gladly willing to suffer some discomfort, filled the two trees that stood beyond center field, while less agile fans used the roofs and windows of the nearby buildings. During the pregame parade, the Boston players marched wearing gray sweaters over their blue-trimmed, gray road uniforms. The Yankees wore blue coats with pearl buttons over their home whites. They had separated the interlocking "NY," again placing the "N" on the right breast and the "Y" on the left. After the parade both teams practiced for 30 minutes, first Boston and then New York. When the home team began their warm-ups, the band played "Yankee Doodle Dandy," a further indication that "Yankees" was rapidly becoming the name of choice. Then it was time for John Montgomery Ward to throw out the first ball. Ward, now a flourishing lawyer, had played for the Giants and Brooklyn and was among the most popular players ever to perform in New York. As both teams' managers and starting batteries and home plate umpire Jack Sheridan gathered around him, Ward removed his hat, gave a short speech, and then handed the ball to Griffith. An interested onlooker was Dan Brouthers, the great nineteenth-century slugger who had been a teammate of Ward's with Brooklyn in 1892. However, Brouthers had also played for Boston teams in the National League, the Players League, and the American Association and informed everyone that he was rooting for the Americans.

Two years earlier, in 1904, these teams had engaged in a season-long struggle for the pennant, eventually won by Boston on the last day. But both teams slipped badly in 1905, Boston finishing fourth and New York sixth. Chesbro's win total dropped from 41 to 19, and Young, with a record of 18–19, experienced the first losing season of his 16-year career. Things would get worse for Young and Boston this year. The 39-year-old pitcher would have his poorest season ever (13–21), and the Americans, after five consecutive first-division finishes, would fall to last place.

New York broke on top in the second inning, scoring when Young allowed a single by Conroy, hit Deacon McGuire with a pitch, and was touched for a two-out double to right by Chesbro. Conroy scored easily on Chesbro's drive, but a fine relay from right fielder Buck Freeman to second baseman John Godwin to catcher Graham cut down McGuire, who also was trying to score. Godwin was substituting for regular second baseman Hobe Ferris, out with an ankle injury, while Graham was one of several catchers the Americans used in 1906 to replace Lou Criger. Because of illness, Criger would play in only seven games this season. From the third through the eighth innings Young was perfect, setting the Yanks down in order each time. When he batted in the twelfth inning, the knowledgeable New York crowd showed their appreciation by giving him a great and well-deserved ovation. Meanwhile, Chesbro struggled. Boston had at least one hit in every inning except the eighth and the tenth, yet they could score only in the fifth, and that was a result of two Yankees' errors. Graham was on second with a one-out double when LaPorte misplayed Young's grounder, allowing the pitcher to reach first and Graham to go to third. When Kip Selbach grounded to second baseman Jimmy Williams, it should have been the third out. Instead Williams started what should have been an inning-ending double play by flipping the ball to Elberfeld for the force on Young. But Elberfeld, who had three errors on the day, made a bad throw to first baseman Hal Chase allowing Graham to score.

Saturday, April 14, 1906

Boston	ab	r	h	po	a	e	New York	ab	r	h	po	a	e
Selbach lf	6	0	1	3	0	0	Dougherty lf	5	0	2	3	0	0
Collins 3b	6	0	2	1	1	1	Keeler rf	5	0	0	0	0	0
Stahl cf	6	0	0	4	0	0	Elberfeld ss	5	0	0	4	10	3
Parent ss	5	0	1	2	2	0	LaPorte 3b	5	0	0	1	4	1
Freeman rf	5	0	1	2	1	0	Williams 2b	5	1	1	4	6	0
Grimshaw 1b	5	0	2	9	0	0	Conroy cf	5	1	1	0	0	0
Godwin 2b	5	0	1	1	3	0	Chase 1b	5	0	1	19	0	0
Graham c	5	1	2	13	0	0	McGuire c	3	0	0	5	1	0
Young p	5	0	1	0	3	1	Chesbro p	4	0	2	0	2	0
Total	48	1	11	35	10	2	Total	42	2	7	36	23	4

*Two out when winning run was scored.

Boston	000	010	000	000–1
New York	010	000	000	001–2

Struck out—by Young, 8; by Chesbro, 3. Left on bases—Boston, 11; New York, 6. Stolen bases—Collins, Conroy. Double play—Elberfeld, Chase. Two-base hits—Chesbro, Dougherty, Williams, Young, Graham, Freeman. Umpires—Messrs. Sheridan and Evans. Time of game—2 hrs. 10 min. Attendance—15,000.

The Yankees looked as if they would win the game in the ninth, an inning in which Patsy Dougherty went from almost-hero to almost-goat in the space of a few pitches. Dougherty led off the inning with a long double over the head of center fielder Chick Stahl, but then got picked off by Young after wandering too far off second. Billy Evans, umpiring in his first major-league game, made the out call on Dougherty. Evans, 22, the youngest man ever to umpire in the big leagues, would have a 22-year career and in 1973 be elected to the Hall of Fame. After Dougherty was picked off, Willie Keeler reached second when Jimmy Collins, Boston's manager/third baseman, threw his bunt into right field. That of course magnified the significance of Dougherty's blunder. Had he not been picked off, he would have scored easily. Still, New York had the winning run at second with only one out. Young, however, was unyielding. He retired Elberfeld on a grounder to first baseman Moose Grimshaw and LaPorte on a fly to Freeman, sending the game into the tenth inning. It was the first Yankees' opener to go into extra innings.

Both teams threatened in the 11th; each had the potential winning run in scoring position with less than two outs. However, neither could score, and the game went on. It was close to six o'clock when Williams doubled to left with one out in the home 12th. After Young got Conroy to foul out to catcher Graham, Chase hit a 1–1 pitch on the ground to short. The ball bounded off the foot of shortstop Freddy Parent who then ran it down and threw home, but too late. Williams, running with two outs, had gotten a good jump and just beat Parent's throw to give the Yankees the win. The victory set off a raucous celebration as fans yelled, waved handkerchiefs and flags, did war dances, and tossed their hats in the air.

For Boston, it was the beginning of what would be a 100-loss season and a personal tragedy. When Collins gave up managing late in the season, Chick Stahl took over, but the pressure of managing would prove too much for him. On March 28, 1907, during spring training, Stahl committed suicide in West Baden Springs, Indiana. He was 34 years old.

The Yankees' Al Orth led the American League in wins with 27 (27–17), complete games (36), and innings-pitched (338⅔). Jack Chesbro also was a 20-game winner, while Willie

Keeler, Kid Elberfeld, and Hal Chase all hit above .300. Still the Yanks finished second (90–61), three games behind the Chicago White Sox.

Thursday, April 11, 1907
American League Park, Washington
New York 3 Washington 2

It couldn't have happened anywhere but in little old New York.—O. Henry

Opening Day has always been a time when baseball captures the attention of a large portion of the American public, including that of even the "casual fan," the one you are not likely to hear from again until the World Series. While that sense of celebration surrounding the return of "the game" still exists, it was decidedly more pronounced in the years before World War I. Then, only an event of major significance could turn the conversation of baseball fans away from the opening of a new season. Just such an event was taking place in a New York City courtroom on Opening Day 1907; an event newspapers were calling "the most sensational murder trial in American history." Ten months earlier, on June 25, 1906, Harry K. Thaw, an erratic millionaire playboy, shot and killed the noted American architect Stanford White. Thaw committed the murder as White dined in the rooftop dinner theater of the original Madison Square Garden, a building White had designed. But what set the incident apart and sparked nationwide interest was what Thaw had said before pulling the trigger. He accused White of "ruining his wife." Thaw's wife was Evelyn Nesbit, a beautiful young woman, who as a teenager had spent time with White at his West 24th Street studio. Testimony given in the trial revealed that White had engaged in similar dalliances with many young girls. However, Miss Nesbitt, whom according to witnesses White often asked to pose naked on a red velvet swing, was a particular favorite. It was a tale of sex, murder, and depravity among the rich and famous. The press loved it and so did the public. By Opening Day the sequestered jury had passed a second night without reaching a verdict. After 49 hours of debate they remained deadlocked, with seven voting for conviction and five for acquittal. The next day the judge dismissed them, declaring it a hung jury.

Meanwhile, away from the frenzy in New York, the Yankees were opening the season with a 3–2 victory at Washington's American League Park. Al Orth, the league's leading winner a year ago (27), pitched for the Yankees, the first time that manager Clark Griffith gave the opening-day assignment to a pitcher other than Jack Chesbro. Some of the same fans in the record-breaking crowd of 12,902 may have also been at the 1903 opener when Orth, a Yankee since July 1904 but then pitching for the Senators, defeated New York in its first league game. Joe Cantillon, Washington's new manager, chose Long Tom Hughes as his opening-day pitcher. Hughes, who along with pitcher Barney Wolfe, were the players the Yankees had traded to Washington to get Orth. He pitched a fine game against his old mates, although it was in a losing cause. He had five strikeouts, including one against Willie Keeler who rarely struck out. Umpire Tom Connolly remarked after the game that it was the best he had ever seen Hughes pitch.

Because the crowd was so large—the largest crowd ever at an athletic event in the nation's capital—many fans watched the game while standing in rows that completely ringed the outfield. The standees necessitated a grounds rule covering balls hit in among them; they would be two-base hits, a ruling that was to play a critical part in the game's outcome. The Washington weather, cold but sunny, was a vast improvement over the previous day's weather when snow forced the umpires to call off the Yankees last exhibition game in nearby Baltimore after five innings. Unlike previous years, many of the standard opening-day pregame festivities were omitted today. There was no parade by the teams through the city, nor was there a first-ball ceremony. However, both teams, with the band leading them, did parade across the field. The visiting Yankees were again wearing gray, following a one-year return to their dark road uniforms, while Washington had abandoned "NATIONALS" across their shirt fronts and returned the large blue "W" to the left breast. (*Nationals* was the official team name, but *Senators* remained the name of choice among the fans.) When the Washington players received their new uniforms at practice on the day before the game, several of them discovered they had been issued the wrong size. That began a general swapping of shirts, pants, caps, etc., which must have worked. By game time, most of the players appeared to have found their correct sizes.

In keeping with the opening-day custom, as each of the hometown Senators made his first plate appearance the fans greeted him with a resounding cheer. Third baseman Lave Cross, a popular veteran in his 21st major-league season, received the largest ovation. Cross had begun his big-league sojourn with Louisville of the American Association (then a major league) back in 1887. But he had spent most of his career in Philadelphia, where he played for teams in four different major leagues: the American Association, the Players League, and both the National and American Leagues. He was in his second year at Washington, as was second baseman Larry Schlafly and center fielder Dave Altizer. And they were the veterans. No one in the Senators' starting lineup had been with them more than three years, and three starters were making their Washington debuts. Two had played briefly in the National League, right fielder Bob Ganley and catcher Cliff Blankenship, and the third, shortstop John Perrine (whose major-league career would consist of the 44 games he played this year), was up from the minors. So complete was the Senators' turnover in personnel, not one player that started against the Yankees on Opening Day two years earlier was starting today.

The Yankees were opening the season without first baseman Hal Chase, who was unhappy with the contract the club offered him for 1907. Chase felt it was an insufficient reward after he batted .323 in 1906, third-best in the league. Refusing to sign, the always-unpredictable Chase decided to go home to San Francisco several days before the opener. Since then, he had settled his dispute with the club and was on his way back East. Chase had not arrived in time to play this afternoon, so George Moriarty, normally a third baseman, substituted for him at first. Moriarty, a slick fielder but a weak hitter, would play in the major leagues for 13 years. He then became an American League umpire, from 1917 to 1926, managed the Detroit Tigers in 1927–1928, and returned as an American League umpire from 1929 to 1940. Then, after managing the Tigers in 1927–1928, spend many more years as an American League umpire.

After umpire Connolly called "Play ball!" promptly at four o'clock, center fielder Danny Hoffman stepped in for the Yankees. Hoffman, traded from the Philadelphia Athletics in May 1906, lined Hughes's first pitch into right field for a single, and when Ganley's throw back to the infield was wild, he took second. Ganley's error would be the only one of the game, but it proved a costly one for Washington. It allowed Hoffman to reach third on a sacrifice by Keeler, and then score on Kid Elberfeld's single to center. New York increased its lead to 3–0 in the fourth, but not without controversy. Elberfeld was on first with a walk, when Frank LaPorte hit a low liner toward left-center that rolled to the edge of the crowd standing in the outfield. Elberfeld came all the way around to score, and LaPorte was at third with a triple. The Washington players argued that the ball had gone into the crowd and therefore should be a grounds-rule double with Elberfeld held at third. Their protest was unsuccessful, as umpire Connolly held fast to his ruling. Elberfeld was involved in several other close calls, in all of which Connolly ruled against him, but the hot-tempered shortstop held his tongue. At least for this one game, the man called "The Tabasco Kid" for his volatile outbursts was keeping his promise to "lay off the umpires this year." Elberfeld's most recent eruption had come last September 3, when the police had to forcibly remove him from a game at Philadelphia after he assaulted umpire Silk O'Loughlin.

Moments after Connolly decreed that LaPorte was entitled to be at third, Wid Conroy's single to left scored him with New York's third run. Conroy was out trying to steal, but Moriarty singled and Red Kleinow doubled, and now there were two runners in scoring position with Orth coming up. However, Hughes kept the game close by getting Orth, an excellent hitting pitcher, on a fly to another former Yankee, John Anderson.

Conroy, playing left field, made the defensive play of the game on Anderson's long drive in the seventh inning. He went way back, leaped at the final second to catch the ball one-handed, and then tumbled head over heels. It turned out to be an extremely important play. Perrine and Blankenship followed with singles, and then Hughes doubled into the crowd bringing Perrine home with the Senators' first run. Because it was a grounds-rule double, Blankenship was forced to remain at third. Had Conroy not made his spectacular catch, this could have been a disastrous inning for Orth. Washington made it 3–2 in the eighth, but again a fine fielding play from the New York outfield prevented more runs from scoring. The run came on Altizer's two-out single that brought Cross home, but one batter earlier, Keeler had gone into deep right field to catch a drive by Charley Hickman. Washington rooters came alive again in the ninth when Perrine led off with a single. The tying run was aboard with nobody out, but Orth retired Blankenship, Hughes, and Ganley to nail down the win.

The Yankees fell into the second division early in the race and finished fifth (70–78), 21 games behind Detroit. Hal Chase led the team with a .287 average, but Willie Keeler had the worst year of his career batting a lowly .234. Al Orth went 14–21, going from the league's leading winner in 1906 to tying the St. Louis Browns Barney Pelty as the leading loser in 1907.

Thursday, April 11, 1907

New York	ab	r	h	po	a	e	Washington	ab	r	h	po	a	e
Hoffman cf	3	1	1	1	0	0	Ganley rf	5	0	0	2	0	1
Keeler rf	3	0	0	4	0	0	Schlafly 2b	3	0	0	2	2	0
Elberfeld ss	3	1	1	1	2	0	Cross 3b	4	1	2	1	3	0
Williams 2b	4	0	0	3	2	0	Hickman 1b	4	0	1	14	0	0
LaPorte 3b	4	1	3	1	0	0	Altizer cf	4	0	1	0	0	0
Conroy lf	4	0	1	5	1	0	Anderson lf	4	0	1	1	0	0
Moriarty 1b	4	0	1	6	0	0	Perrine ss	4	1	2	2	3	0
Kleinow c	4	0	1	6	0	0	Blankenship c	4	0	2	5	3	0
Orth p	3	0	1	0	1	0	Hughes p	4	0	1	0	4	0
Total	32	3	9	27	6	0	Total	36	2	10	27	15	1

New York   100   200   000–3
Washington   000   000   110–2

Earned runs—New York, 2; Washington, 1. Left on bases—New York, 5; Washington, 8. First base on balls—off Hughes, 1; off Orth, 1. Struck out—by Hughes, 5; by Orth, 3. Three-base hit—LaPorte. Two-base hits—Kleinow, LaPorte, Hughes, Cross. Sacrifice hit—Keeler. Stolen bases—Schlafly, Altizer, Hoffman. Hit by pitcher—by Hughes, Hoffman. Wild pitches—Orth, 1. Umpire—Mr. Connolly. Time of game—1 hr. 55 min.

Tuesday, April 14, 1908
Hilltop Park, New York
New York 1 Philadelphia 0 (12 Innings)

We were a ghastly crew.—Samuel Taylor Coleridge

Despite the occasional successes of civic-minded New Yorkers trying to reform the political system, the Democratic Party machine, Tammany Hall, controlled New York City. Tammany was a powerful, often unscrupulous organization whose approval was needed before anything important happened in New York. When the Highlanders entered the American League in 1903, it was the Tammany connections of co-owners Bill Devery and Frank Farrell that secured the land for Hilltop Park, offsetting the objections of the Giants' Tammany-backed owner, Andrew Freedman. And it was Tammany that two years later engineered the reelection of Democratic mayor George McClellan, the son of the Civil War General. Although McClellan himself was not corrupt, he had needed all the customary illegal maneuvering that Boss Charles Murphy could muster to withstand the independent challenge of newspaper publisher William Randolph Hearst. Even with Murphy's help, McClellan won the election by fewer than 4,000 votes out of a total of more than 700,000 cast. William M. Ivins, the Republican candidate, finished a distant third. Hearst's supporters, aware that Tammany had cheated their man out of winning, sued for a recount. This afternoon the selection of a jury to hear the case was underway. That jury would eventually uphold the election results, deciding that the problem had been not with the vote totals, but with the fraudulent voter lists that went into assembling those totals. Proving those lists fraudulent, they claimed, was much too difficult. Meanwhile, McClellan, who was still the mayor, was at Hilltop Park for the Yankees' season-opener against the Philadelphia Athletics. He sat with Devery and Farrell, who early last year had removed Joseph Gordon as team president and made public their true positions as owners of the franchise. When it came time to throw out the first ball, McClellan made the toss from the owners' box, throwing it to plate umpire Tim Hurst.

The 1908 season would be among the worst in Yankees history, a season full of turmoil and discord, culminating in 103 losses and a last-place finish. That, however, was in the future. Because Opening Day is a day of hope, the crowd of more than 20,000 (the biggest crowd so far at Hilltop Park), arrived with great expectations. And their optimism soared after Harry Niles, in his first game as a Yankee, hit a 12th-inning sacrifice fly to give the Yanks a 1–0 victory over the powerful Athletics. New York had acquired Niles in an off-season multiplayer trade with the St. Louis Browns.

"Slow Joe" Doyle, who pitched a complete-game shutout, the first thrown by a Yankee on Opening Day, was the winner. In several ways the game was much like the one that opened the season here in 1906. Jack Chesbro defeated Cy Young and Boston 2–1 in that one, a game in which the Yanks also scored the winning run with two outs in the last of the 12th inning.

As often happens on Opening Day, especially when the weather is good, a carnival-like atmosphere infused the pregame activities. Hilltop Park had been well decorated for its previous openers, but this year the adornments were even more elaborate. Flags and bunting appeared everywhere, with particularly colorful shield-like arrangements of American flags draping the box seats and grandstand. New York was enjoying a delightful spring day, and never, it seemed, had a more cheerful or enthusiastic crowd attended an opener. The mood of the fans was so good they even displayed affection for their haughty intra-city rivals, the Giants. When the scoreboard showed McGraw's team leading in their opener at Philadelphia, they responded with a resounding cheer. Although the crowd was predominantly male, it did contain many women, many more than would be present at the average mid-season game. The fans had begun arriving early, quickly filling all the available space in the bleachers. Some who were unable to get a seat began to destroy the barricade in front of the left-field stands and rush onto the field. Their action served as a signal to those without seats in right field, and they too took up positions on the outfield grass. Before long, there was a cordon of fans 15 feet deep surrounding the entire outfield.

The Old Guard Band, dressed in blue jackets and white trousers with a red stripe, led the pregame parade across the field. Marching on their left was the Philadelphia team, wearing colorful green jackets. Under the jackets the A's wore their gray road uniforms, with a large red "A" on the left breast and red stockings. Among the marchers was Jimmy Collins, still looking very much out of place in a Philadelphia uniform. Collins, obtained in a June 1907 trade with the Boston Red Sox, had been a star with Boston teams in the National and American Leagues. He managed the Americans (as the Red Sox were called from 1901 to 1907) from their birth in 1901 through 1906, and in 1903 was the winning manager in the first modern World Series. Now, in his final season as a player, Collins was Philadelphia's starting third baseman. In late September the Athletics would call up Frank Baker, who soon succeeded Collins as the league's best third baseman. Eventually Collins and Baker would be the first two third basemen elected to the Hall of Fame, Collins in 1945, and Baker in 1955. The Yankees marched to the band's right, wearing their home whites. The black "N" and "Y" on their right and left breasts were of a more ornamental design than previously, and their hats were now black rather than white. New York had made significant roster changes since the end of the 1907 season. Gone were pitcher Earl Moore, backup catcher Ira Thomas, and three regulars: outfielder Danny Hoffman, infielder-outfielder Frank LaPorte, and second baseman Jimmy Williams. Williams had been the starting second baseman every Opening Day since the team's first year in New York in 1903. New Yankees besides Niles included first baseman Jake Stahl, outfielders Birdie Cree and Charlie Hemphill, and pitcher Fred Glade. On July 10, the Yanks would sell Stahl to the Red Sox, and on August 17, trade Niles to Boston to reacquire LaPorte.

Manager Clark Griffith's selection of Doyle to pitch the opener surprised Yankees-followers expecting to see either Glade, the newcomer, or the veteran Al Orth. Doyle had come up from the Wheeling (West Virginia) Stogies in August 1906 and quickly distinguished himself by being the first major-leaguer to throw shutouts in his first two starts. His nickname "Slow Joe" came not from the velocity of his pitches but from the torpid pace at which he worked. On May 3, 1907, against the Athletics, Doyle's deliberate manner caused a ten-inning game to last a record three hours and seven minutes.

After finishing only 1½ games behind Detroit in 1907, Philadelphia figured to again be a strong challenger for the pennant. Connie Mack was the manager, just as he had been since the origin of the American League in 1900, and before that for the three years that the A's were the Milwaukee club of the Western League. Mack, who managed from the bench in civilian clothes, was the only manager still leading the same club he had led in 1901, the American League's first year as a major league. His choice of Nick Carter to pitch the opener was even more surprising than Griffith's choice of Doyle. Carter, a 28-year-old right-hander who pitched for the Syracuse Stars of in the New York State League in 1907, had never before appeared in a major-league game.

Working at his usual laggardly pace, Doyle pitched a magnificent game. Over the 12 innings he allowed only three singles, a double, and two walks. The first hit off him was by left fielder Topsy Hartsel, the game's first batter. That Hartsel was even in the lineup was a tribute to his fortitude. During pregame practice, a wild toss by Yankees pitcher Joe Lake struck him in the face and broke his nose. The A's trainer patched the wound with adhesive plaster and Hartsel played the whole game, seemingly unaffected. Philadelphia threatened to score only once, in the tenth inning, but right fielder Willie Keeler snuffed out the bid with a sensational catch and throw. There was one out when Doyle hit ex–Yankee Rube Oldring with a pitch, sending the Philadelphia center fielder to first base. Catcher Syd Smith, who like his battery mate was making his major-league debut, got his first big-league hit, a double into the crowd that sent Oldring to third. Carter followed with a fly to deep right that looked like it would fall for extra bases and produce two runs for the visitors. However, Keeler, running at full speed, pulled it down with a fine catch, then turned and made a perfect throw to the plate. Catcher Red Kleinow put the tag on Oldring trying to score after the catch to complete a spectacular inning-ending double play.

Carter matched Doyle's shutout pitching for eleven innings, despite giving up nine hits—including three by Kleinow and two by Hal Chase—and having second baseman Danny Murphy make three errors behind him. Finally, in the 12th, the Yankees managed to push across the game's only run. With one out, Kleinow hit a fly ball into the crowd in center field for a grounds-rule double. Doyle got a big hit, a single to left that sent Kleinow to third. Niles followed with a drive to right fielder Jack Coombs, a pitcher who was playing in right for the injured Socks Seybold. The ball was hit deep enough to allow Kleinow to beat Coombs's throw to the plate and score the game-winning run.

Doyle's opening-day win would be his only one of the year (1–1), although he came back to win eight games for New York in 1909. He would win only 22 games in his career, but seven would be shutouts. Carter won two games and lost five in 1908, his only major-league season.

After going 24–32, Clark Griffith resigned as manager on June 24, claiming interference by the owners. The Yankees had a horrendous 27–71 record under his replacement, Kid Elberfeld, and finished last (51–103), 39½ games behind the Detroit Tigers.

Tuesday, April 14, 1908

Philadelphia	ab	r	h	po	a	e	New York	ab	r	h	po	a	e
Hartsel lf	3	0	1	0	0	0	Niles 2b	5	0	0	1	6	1
Nicholls ss	4	0	0	1	3	0	Keeler rf	5	0	1	5	1	0
J. Collins 3b	5	0	0	1	4	0	Stahl lf	4	0	0	0	0	0
Davis 1b	5	0	1	15	0	0	Elberfeld ss	3	0	1	4	2	0
Murphy 2b	5	0	0	3	3	32	Chase 1b	4	0	1	14	0	0

Philadelphia	ab	r	h	po	a	e	New York	ab	r	h	po	a	e
Coombs rf	5	0	2	6	0	0	Hemphill cf	4	0	0	2	0	0
Oldring cf	4	0	0	2	0	1	Conroy 3b	5	0	0	3	4	0
Smith c	5	0	1	6	3	0	Kleinow c	5	1	3	7	1	0
Carter p	4	0	0	1	3	0	Doyle p	4	0	1	0	0	0
Total	40	0	5	35	16	3	Total	39	1	7	36	14	1

*Two out when winning run scored.

Philadelphia	000	000	000	000–0
New York	000	000	000	001–1

Two-base hits—Smith, Kleinow. Sacrifice hits—Nicholls, Doyle, Niles, Chase. First base on balls—off Doyle, 2; off Carter, 3. Struck out—by Carter, 4; by Doyle, 3. Stolen bases—Stahl (2), Kleinow (2). Double plays—Keeler and Kleinow; Collins and Davis. Left on bases—New York, 10; Philadelphia, 8. Hit by pitcher—Elberfeld, Oldring. Time of game—2 hrs. 25 min. Umpires—Messrs. Hurst and Connolly. Attendance—20,000.

Monday, April 12, 1909
American League Park, Washington
Washington 4 New York 1

The game begins in the spring, when everything
else begins again.—A. Bartlett Giamatti

The Yankees opened the 1909 season in Washington, and for the first time in their seven-year history it was under a manager other than Clark Griffith. Griffith, now the manager in Cincinnati, had resigned in June 1908 after accusing owners Frank Farrell and Bill Devery of interference and an unwillingness to spend money for players. Shortstop Kid Elberfeld replaced Griffith, but the team played terribly under Elberfeld, whose abrasive style and personality alienated many of his teammates. After deciding Elberfeld was a better player than he was a manager, the Yankees signed George Stallings, a 41-year-old former major-league manager with the Philadelphia Phillies (1897–1898), and the Detroit Tigers (1901), to lead the club in 1909. Stallings took over a team badly demoralized by the managerial turmoil of 1908 and the self-indulgence of Hal Chase, its star first baseman. Disappointed by the choice of Elberfeld to replace Griffith rather than him, Chase left the team late in the year to join the Stockton Millers of the California State League. The Yankees coaxed him into rejoining them for the 1909 season, but he would not be in the lineup for the opener. Chase's absence resulted from a spring training illness that was first thought to be smallpox. However, to everyone's relief, or at least most everyone, doctors later diagnosed his ailment as a mild form of the disease. When the club first suspected Chase might have smallpox they had all the players vaccinated, which caused many of them to have sore arms. Then, at the end of spring training, just as their arms were beginning to heal, they were revaccinated in Lynchburg, Virginia. As a final precaution, medical authorities in Richmond examined the whole team, declared them free from smallpox, and allowed them to cross the state line into the District of Columbia.

So, as his teammates prepared to open the season in Washington, Chase was recuperating in Augusta, Georgia. Joe Ward, purchased from the Altoona (Pennsylvania) Mountaineers of the Class B Tri-State League in March, replaced him at first base. This would be Ward's only appearance at first base for New York. After playing in nine games, the Yankees sold him to the Phillies on June 7. Ward was part of an opening-day infield that was very different from the one that started last year's opener. Only Elberfeld was a repeater, and he was at a different position. Leg injuries had limited him to just 19 games in 1908; but now, after regaining his health and being relieved of his managing duties, Elberfeld was ready to again become a full-time player. He was at third base today, while John Knight, acquired the previous August from the Eastern League's Baltimore Orioles, was at shortstop. The second baseman was Neal Ball, who last year had been the full-time shortstop in Elberfeld's absence.

Six weeks earlier, when the United States inaugurated William Howard Taft as its new president, a late winter blizzard had clobbered the nation's capital. But by Opening Day the Washington winter was just a memory. The season began on a perfect spring afternoon, the kind for which this beautiful city is famous. Old-time Washingtonians could not recall a baseball season ever beginning on a lovelier day. People all around the city were enjoying the outdoors this Easter Monday. At the National Zoo, a record crowd of 30,000 passed through the gates, while on the White House lawn, close to 10,000 children frolicked at the traditional Easter egg rolling. Inspired by the beautiful weather and the return of baseball, several thousand people arrived early at American League Park, some showing up even before the park opened. A new crosstown trolley line running from Southeast Washington brought 500 Washington Navy Yard employees to the game, most of who headed for the bleachers. Soon, all the available seats in the park were filled, and those who had a ticket but not a seat were standing a dozen deep around the rim of the outfield. The attendance, estimated at 15,000 paid admissions, was a record for a baseball game in Washington. Pistori's Band entertained the early arrivals, who also amused themselves while waiting by singing "*Down Went McGinty*" and other familiar classics.

The crowd was disappointed that neither President Taft nor Vice President James S. Sherman—both ardent baseball fans—were there to throw out the first ball. Sherman was addressing the Chamber of Commerce in his hometown of Utica, New York, and the president was otherwise engaged. Taft did have one sports-related activity on his schedule this day. He accepted an invitation that day to start the June 1 New York-to-Seattle auto race for the Guggenheim Cup. He would press a button at the White House, after which New York mayor George McClellan would fire a pistol to start the race. A year from now, President Taft *would* throw out the first ball at the Senators' opener against Philadelphia, beginning a cherished Washington tradition that with rare exceptions endured until baseball deserted the Capital in 1972. After the police, fearing a riot from fans unable to get in, stopped the sale of tickets, Senators' officials instructed umpire Billy Evans to start the game immediately. Thus, the season began without a first-ball ceremony, even though the crowd contained the usual number of high government officials and celebrities willing to do the honors. Among those spotted in the better seats were Samuel Gompers, president of the American Federation of Labor, and "Diamond Jim" Brady, the famous New York sportsman.

The Senators had not won an opener since their victory over New York in 1903, and when Washington manager Joe Cantillon selected Charlie Smith (9–13 in 1908) as his pitcher, the hometown fans anticipated the five-game losing streak would likely reach six this afternoon. The half-hearted cheers that accompanied the announcement of Smith's name were in marked contrast to those usually given by the home crowd to their opening-day pitcher. A sore arm that was now healed had been responsible for much of Smith's ineffectiveness in 1908, but to the fans that was irrelevant. It was not so much Smith's presence on the mound that accounted for their lack of enthusiasm; it was Walter Johnson's absence. The 21-year-old Johnson was now the fans' favorite player. Last September he had electrified the baseball world and given it an indication of his future greatness by shutting out these same Yankees three times in four days. Johnson would have been the starter today had he not been recuperating from an illness, although he was well enough to watch the game from the grandstand. Johnson would not make his first start of the season for another two weeks. Not yet fully recovered, he started against the Yankees at Hilltop Park on April 24 and lasted only two innings in a 17–0 loss.

Once again, the Senators were wearing a new home uniform, abandoning the block-lettered "WASHINGTON" they wore in 1908 and returning the blue "W" to the left breast. However, the stockings were now gray, the fold-down collar white rather than blue, and the blue cap with the white piping no longer had a "W" on it. The Highlanders too had a new look in 1909. Gone were the "N" and "Y" from the shirt fronts of both the home-whites and the road grays, leaving them bare. There was an interlocking blue "NY" on the left sleeve, at the level of the biceps, and an interlocking red "NY" on the blue cap. Also, two thick, red horizontal stripes had been added to their blue stockings.

Monday, April 12, 1909

New York	ab	r	h	po	a	e	Washington	ab	r	h	po	a	e
Hemphill cf	4	0	1	1	0	0	Clymer rf	3	0	1	0	0	0
Keeler rf	4	0	0	3	0	0	Milan cf	4	1	1	0	0	0
Elberfeld 3b	4	1	2	2	2	0	Unglaub lf	4	1	1	1	0	0
Engle lf	3	0	0	4	1	0	Delahanty 2b	4	2	1	2	2	1
Ward 1b	3	0	0	5	0	1	Conroy 3b	4	0	2	2	1	0
Ball 2b	4	0	0	1	0	0	Freeman 1b	3	0	1	9	0	0
Knight ss	2	0	1	3	2	0	McBride ss	2	0	0	2	3	0
Kleinow c	3	0	0	5	4	1	Street c	3	0	0	11	2	0
Newton p	1	0	0	0	1	1	Smith p	3	0	1	0	2	0
aDemmitt	1	0	0	0	0	0	Total	30	4	8	27	10	1
Brockett p	1	0	0	0	0	0							
Total	30	1	4	24	10	3							

aBatted for Newton in fifth.

New York	000	100	000–1
Washington	301	000	00X–4

Earned runs—Washington, 2. Left on bases—Washington, 7, New York, 5. First base on balls—off Smith, 2; off Newton, 1; off Brockett, 1. Hits made—off Newton, 6 in 4 innings; off Brockett, 2 in 4 innings. Struck out—by Smith, 10; by Newton, 3; by Brockett, 3. Three-base hit—Knight. Two-base hits—Unglaub and Elberfeld. Sacrifice hits—McBride and Ward. Sacrifice fly—Street. Stolen bases—Conroy and Freeman. Double play—Engle and Knight. Hit by pitcher—by Newton, 1. Balk—Smith. Umpires—Messrs. Evans and Egan. Time of game—2 hrs. Attendance—15,000.

Stallings chose Doc Newton, a 31-year-old journeyman in his final major-league season, to pitch the opener. The best of Newton's eight big-league seasons had been 1902, when he won 15 games for Brooklyn. Stallings picked him because Newton was left-handed, and the Senators had been especially futile against left-handers in 1908. Newton would make four starts for the Yankees in 1909 and was winless with three losses when they released him. Washington's 1908 difficulties with left-handers notwithstanding, they pushed across three runs against Newton in the first inning, which would be all the runs the rejuvenated Smith would need. A walk, a double by Bob Unglaub, and consecutive errors by catcher Red Kleinow (on a throw to the plate from Newton) and Newton himself (on a slow roller by ex-Yankee Wid Conroy) scored one run and left the bases loaded. First baseman Jerry Freeman followed with a single to left that scored Unglaub and Jim Delahanty. Washington got their fourth run in the third inning, and only a spectacular catch by left fielder Clyde Engle prevented them from getting more. Singles by Delahanty and Conroy and a Newton pitch that hit George McBride loaded the bases with one out. Catcher Gabby Street followed with a long drive to left field that looked to be a grand-slam home run. Engle, in his first major-league game, raced back and made a one-handed diving catch while falling into the crowd. His throw to Elberfeld doubled up Conroy who was already around third, but not before Delahanty had tagged up and scored.

Lew Brockett came on to pitch for New York in the fifth, and though he held the Senators scoreless the rest of the way, it was too late. The Yankees were no match for Smith, who allowed only four hits and struck out ten. New York's only run came in the fourth, when Elberfeld opened with a double and eventually scored on Ball's ground out. In the ninth, Smith got Engle on a grounder, and then fanned Ward and Ball to end both the game and the Yankees five-game opening-day winning streak. The crowd let out a mighty cheer, and the band played "Ain't Dat a Shame," but the celebrations were to be few in Washington in 1909. The team set two American League records for futility that still stand: their 380 runs (in 156 games) is the fewest one-season total ever, and they were shut out a record 30 times (one game was a tie).

New York improved under manager George Stallings, finishing fifth (74–77), 23½ games behind the Detroit Tigers. It was the last year in a Yankees uniform for the team's first two great stars: on September 11, the club sent Jack Chesbro to the Boston Red Sox for the waiver price, and in February 1910 it released Willie Keeler.

II

1910–1919

The Yankees (the name became official in 1913) abandoned Hilltop Park after the 1912 season and moved into the Polo Grounds as tenants of the New York Giants. From 1911 to 1914 they had four managers and four second-division finishes, but their fortunes began to change when Colonel Jacob Ruppert and Captain Til Huston purchased the club in January 1915.

The new owners began spending money to bring quality players to New York, purchasing pitchers George Mogridge and Bob Shawkey, first baseman Wally Pipp, and third baseman Frank "Home Run" Baker. Mogridge, before he was traded, and Baker, before he retired, each gave the Yankees several excellent seasons. Meanwhile, Shawkey and Pipp, both of whom would have long and productive careers in New York, became stars on joining the Yankees. Shawkey led the club in wins in 1916, 1917, and 1919 (he was in the U.S. Navy in 1918), while Pipp became the first Yankee to win a home run crown, leading the league in both 1916 and 1917.

Former Detroit Tigers pitcher Bill Donovan, brought in to manage when Ruppert and Huston bought the club, was fired after three mediocre seasons and was replaced by Miller Huggins in 1918. The Yankees finished fourth and third in Huggins's first two seasons, 1918 and 1919, closing out their second decade without a pennant. Then, in January 1920, the Yankees bought Babe Ruth from Boston and baseball changed forever.

Thursday, April 14, 1910
Hilltop Park, New York
New York 4 Boston 4 (14 Innings)

Give me the clear blue sky over my head,
and the green turf beneath my feet.—William Hazlitt

By the time the American League began its tenth major-league season, it had long resolved any questions concerning its equality with the older, more established National League. However, if any lingering doubts remained about the league's status, President William Howard Taft ended them on Opening Day. Taft not only threw out the first ball at Washington's opener against Philadelphia, he stayed for the entire game—a game in which Walter Johnson one-hit the Athletics, 3–0. Baseball has often paid tribute to President Taft for this act, one that most fans know better than any other during his presidency. However, Taft took part in another ceremonial act that evening—one that is less celebrated. In his welcoming address to the National American Women's Suffrage Convention, the President of the United States told the women he opposed giving them the right to vote, an opinion that earned him prolonged hissing from the disappointed delegates. The battle for women's rights in America has been an ongoing struggle. In the years before World War I it consisted of many crushing defeats, such as Taft's speech, and an occasional small victory, such as the one taking place this day in New York City. Counting for the thirteenth U.S. Census had begun, and as they had since 1880, women were serving as enumerators.

Had any of those census takers been at Hilltop Park for the Yankees' opener with Boston, they could have quickly tallied 25,000 people, the approximate number of fans who saw the Yanks and Red Sox battle to a 14-inning, 4–4 tie. It was then the largest crowd ever to see a game at Hilltop Park, and the length of the game they saw (14 innings) is still the Yankees' record for most innings played on Opening Day. The game began in brilliant sunshine, but by the time umpire Tom Connolly stopped play two hours and forty-five minutes later, it had gotten so dark players could barely see balls hit in the air. For New York, it was the third consecutive season they had played an extra-inning game as opening-day hosts. In 1908 they beat the Philadelphia Athletics 1–0 in 12 innings, and two years earlier it also took 12 innings to defeat the Boston Americans (the Red Sox former name) 2–1.

Changing the team's name from Americans to Red Sox came in a roundabout way, the result of a decision made by Fred Tenney, manager of the National League's Boston Doves. In 1907, Tenney switched the Doves from red stockings to white, fearing the colored stockings might cause leg injuries to his players. Boston newspapers criticized the move as a serious break with tradition, reminding Tenney that in their long history the Boston National League club had always worn red stockings. The Doves' switch gave John Irving Taylor, president of the Boston American League club, an opportunity to score a victory over his National League rival in the battle for the allegiance of Boston fans. Swiftly taking advantage of the situation, Taylor announced, "I am going to grab the name Red Sox and the Boston American League club will wear red stockings," which they did, both in 1908 and 1909. However, this year the Red Sox stockings were not red, they were gray, though they did have a thick red stripe. They did retain the color red for the block-lettered "BOSTON" across the front of their jerseys, a change they had introduced last season. The Red Sox were now the only major-league team that still wore the laced collar, but this would be the last year they did so. New York's home uniform, with the interlocking "NY" on the left sleeve, was only slightly changed from 1909. The cap, formerly all blue, now had a red bill, and the old fold-down collar had given way to the new, short, stand-up "cadet style" collar, in blue.

Since the end of the 1909 season the Yankees had released Willie Keeler, the last remaining starter from the Highlanders first opening-day game, and sold Kid Elberfeld to Washington, leaving the team without anyone who had played for them in that first season of 1903. Even more indicative of the way the team was changing was the composition of their 1910 opening-day lineup. Only two of the men who started the 1909 opener were playing today: left fielder Clyde Engle and center fielder Charlie Hemphill. And the noticeably overweight Engle was starting only because Birdie Cree's injured hand prevented him from playing.

Hilltop Park's gates opened at one o'clock, and by three, fans completely occupied the grandstand and bleachers. Those who could not get seats spread out on the outfield grass in front of the fences, obscuring the whiskey, automobile, and other sundry advertisements usually seen there. Mayor William Gaynor bypassed the opener, choosing instead to spend the day at City Hall. Two days earlier, the mayor had entertained Charles M. Frey, the champion rat-catcher of Greater New York. Gaynor and Frey reportedly discussed such topics as rats, jury duty, and the sayings of the Greek philosopher Epictetus. On the day of the game, Gaynor sent an 11:00 A.M. message to the Yankees informing them of a change in security procedures for the opener. City policemen would be on duty outside Hilltop Park as usual, but unlike past years they would not be on duty inside. Fortunately for all, the crowd was well behaved, with the standees generally finding places that were out of the way of the action. In particular, they did not congregate behind the catcher as overflow crowds sometimes did. Along with being well behaved, the crowd was also well dressed, as was typical of New Yorkers. (Perhaps they were well behaved because they were well dressed.) Many, both men and women, were wearing the latest spring fashions, and almost everyone wore a hat. For the men it was mainly derbies, but the women displayed varying styles of headgear, with those decorated with flowers the most prevalent. The setting at Hilltop Park, the emerald green grass of the playing field under blue skies and a bright sun, was such a beautiful sight the fans could not help but be in a merry mood. Adding to the festive atmosphere were the brightly colored flags and bunting that always adorned Hilltop Park on Opening Day. It had been a long, cold winter, and like people all around the country, New Yorkers were rejoicing in the return of baseball. Shortly after 3 P.M., new captain (and new father) Hal Chase led the Yankees onto the field through a door in the right-field fence to begin their pregame workout. The fans loudly saluted Captain Chase as he hit practice grounders to his infielders. After the band played "The Star-Spangled Banner" and Chase had shaken hands with Boston's captain, third baseman Harry Lord, Yankees co-owner Bill Devery tossed out the first ball. The recipient, home-plate umpire Connolly, shouted out the names of the two batteries, and then "Play ball!"

On the mound for the Yankees was Jim Vaughn, a massive six-foot-four, rookie left-hander with the nickname "Hippo." Vaughn, who had celebrated his 22nd birthday only a few days earlier, is still the youngest pitcher ever to start an opener for the Yankees. Manager George Stallings made his selection just before game time, switching to Vaughn from Jack Quinn, his intended starter. Vaughn had impressed Stallings in his final spring training appearance on April 11 with eight strikeouts in six innings against Princeton University. Although he had appeared briefly for New York in June of 1908, pitching two and one-third innings in two relief appearances, this would be his first major-league start. Boston's starter was also something of a surprise. The consensus of opinion was that manager Patsy Donovan would use 20-year-old Joe Wood, but instead he was going with right-hander Ed Cicotte, a 14-game winner (14–5) with a 1.94 earned run average in 1909. Donovan was managing his first game for the Red Sox after having previously managed at Pittsburgh, St. Louis (NL), Washington, and Brooklyn.

The Red Sox got away to a 1–0 lead in the first inning. Leadoff batter Amby McConnell reached first when Yankee third baseman Jimmy Austin, after fielding his ground ball, pulled Chase off the bag with a high throw. After Lord forced McConnell at second base, Tris Speaker, doubled to deep right field bringing Lord home. Boston added two more runs in the third. A walk to Cicotte and a triple by Lord scored one, and then Lord came home when shortstop Eddie Foster's throw to the plate on Speaker's grounder sailed over the head of catcher Jeff Sweeney. This was Foster's first big-league game, and although he made two errors, he had eight assists and showed a powerful throwing arm. Nevertheless, he would get into only 30 games in 1910, hitting a lowly .133. The Yankees released him to Rochester of the Eastern League, where he batted a respectable .288 in 1911. Washington purchased his contract in 1912, and Foster went on to play 12 more seasons as a second and third baseman in the American League.

New York got its first run in the bottom of the third on a double by Sweeney and a single by Hemphill. Boston added a run in the fifth on singles by Cicotte and Lord and Sweeney's passed ball, which the Yankees matched in the sixth on a double by Chase and a single by Engle. So as they came to bat in the eighth, the Yanks were trailing 4–2. Hemphill, trying to bounce back from a subpar 1909, opened the inning with his third hit of the game, a line-drive double to right. Harry Wolter's single moved Hemphill to third. Wolter, a 25-year-old, left-handed hitter had come over from the Red Sox for the $1,500 waiver price to replace Willie Keeler. With Chase at the plate, one of Cicotte's pitches got away from catcher Bill Carrigan, allowing Hemphill to score and Wolter to go all the way to third. Boston's lead was down to one, and to protect it, Donovan removed Cicotte and brought in Wood.

Wood threw nothing but fastballs to Chase, high-velocity fastballs. But Chase connected with one, sending it to the deepest part of center field, where after a long run Speaker caught up with it. As the crowd roared its approval for both the hit and the catch, Wolter scored easily from third to tie the game at 4–4. When Engle followed with a sharply hit, low liner, Speaker, who was beginning to establish his reputation as a great center fielder, further displayed his range by racing in to make a shoestring catch.

Thursday, April 14, 1910

Boston	ab	r	h	po	a	e	New York	ab	r	h	po	a	e
McConnell 2b	5	0	1	2	2	0	Hemphill cf	6	1	3	0	0	0
Lord 3b	6	2	3	4	3	0	Wolter rf	4	1	1	3	1	0
Speaker cf	6	0	2	4	0	0	Chase 1b	5	1	2	21	1	0
Stahl 1b	6	0	0	17	1	0	Engle lf	6	0	1	0	0	0
Wagner ss	6	0	2	3	5	0	Gardner 2b	6	0	1	5	3	0
Niles rf	5	0	0	2	0	0	Foster ss	6	0	1	3	8	2
Hooper lf	6	0	1	1	0	0	Austin 3b	5	0	1	2	3	1
Carrigan c	5	0	1	8	1	0	Sweeney c	5	1	1	8	4	0
Cicotte p	2	2	1	0	7	0	Vaughn p	5	0	0	0	7	0
Wood p	2	0	0	1	0	0	Total	48	4	11	42	27	3
Total	49	4	11	42	19	0							

Game called at end of fourteenth inning on account of darkness.

Boston	102	010	000	000	00–4
New York	001	001	020	000	00–4

Two-base hits—Speaker, Sweeney, Hemphill, Chase. Three-base hit—Lord. Sacrifice hits—Wolter, McConnell, Austin. Sacrifice fly—Chase. Stolen base—Hooper. Left on bases—Boston, 6; New York, 5. First base on errors—Boston, 2. Double play—Foster, Gardner, and Chase. Struck out—by Vaughn, 7 (Niles, Harper, Stahl (3), Carrigan, Speaker); by Cicotte, 1 (Sweeney); by Wood, 6 (Chase, Sweeney, Vaughn, Hemphill, Foster, Austin). Bases on balls—off Vaughn, 2 (Cicotte, Niles); off Cicotte, 1 (Wolter). Wild pitch—Wood. Passed ball—Sweeney. Hits—off Cicotte, 9 in 7 innings; off Wood 2 in 7 innings. Time of game—2 hrs. 45 min. Umpires—Messrs. Connolly and Dinneen. Attendance—25,000.

For the next six innings Vaughn and Wood were in complete control, and neither team could mount a serious threat. Vaughn, who needed only four pitches to retire the Red Sox in the fourth inning, needed only three in the tenth, and four again in the 12th. Wood struck out six in his seven innings, including the last two batters in the 14th. By now it was getting dark, although very few fans had left. However, after watching the Yankees flail away at Wood's fastball in the 14th, umpire Connolly wisely called a halt before anyone was seriously injured. The tie was the first of the record 19 ties that the American League played in 1910.

Late in the season, with the Yankees at 78–59, Hal Chase told Frank Farrell he would leave the team if they did not fire manager George Stallings. However, Stallings, like Clark Griffith before him, had become fed up with front office meddling. Furthermore, he suspected that Chase was "throwing" games, so he quit. Farrell then named Chase the manager for the season's final 14 games (10–4). The Yankees combined record of (88–63) was good for second place, although a distant 14½ games behind the Philadelphia Athletics. Rookie Russ Ford, with 26 wins (26–6), and an .813 winning percentage, finished second in the league in both categories.

Wednesday, April 12, 1911
Shibe Park, Philadelphia
New York 2 Philadelphia 1

Few, save the poor, feel for the poor.—Letitia Elizabeth Landon

During America's Civil War, baseball began its progression from a diversion played mostly by members of elite gentlemen's clubs to a game enjoyed by Americans of every social class. By Opening Day 1911, the eve of the 50th anniversary of the bombardment of Fort Sumter that started the war, the game had established its place as a staple of American culture. This was certainly so in New York City, which had three teams beginning the new season today: the Giants at home, the Dodgers in Boston, and the Yankees in Philadelphia. That may have been the reason the city's Department of Parks chose this day to issue its first annual report, one that further illustrated the game's popularity. It said that while girls had a fondness for dancing, "the prime interest of all boys more than six years old during the summertime is baseball." It recommended the city build two hurdy-gurdies for the girls, with folk-dance tunes on the rolls, and proposed making places other than Central Park available for the boys to play baseball. The Parks Department recognized that playing on the city's streets was getting increasingly dangerous. Another report, also distributed today, emphasized that danger; the Manhattan Board of Coroners reported machines (automobiles) had killed 62 people in New York City in 1910. Although that was still fewer than the 93 killed by horse-drawn vehicles, the combined 155 people killed in traffic accidents for the year confirmed that life on the street was indeed hazardous. However, as New Yorkers were learning, it was not as hazardous as life in the city's hundreds of "sweatshops." It was in one of those factories that a fire less than a month ago, on March 25, had killed 146 people. The dead were mostly young Jewish and Italian immigrant girls, employees of the Triangle Shirtwaist Company. They were unable to escape the conflagration in the Asch Building, located in Manhattan's Greenwich Village section, because someone had illegally locked the doors. This morning Isaac Harris and Max Blanck, the two proprietors of the company, were being indicted for manslaughter.

Although unsafe working conditions for immigrants were generally ignored by the public even more than they are now, this particular tragedy was so horrendous it would eventually lead to workplace reform. Nevertheless, the safety of New York factory workers was far from the minds of the people who had come out to Philadelphia's magnificent Shibe Park, now in its third year of operation. They were there on this cold and windy day to see the Athletics begin the defense of their world championship. The only New Yorkers that concerned them were the New York Yankees baseball team, who were in town to furnish the opposition. Having New York as the opponent heightened the crowd's excitement. Despite finishing 14½ games behind the Athletics in 1910, the Yankees represented a major obstacle to Philadelphia repeating as champions. An opportunity to get a first look at the potential challengers drew more than 18,000 fans on this dreary, dismal day. They were rewarded with an exceedingly well-pitched game, although one with a disappointing result—a 2–1 Yankees victory. The Athletics did not go down easily. They even got the tying run into scoring position with two outs in the ninth inning, but Danny Murphy grounded out to manager/first baseman Hal Chase to end the game.

Chase was beginning his first full season as the Yankees' manager after replacing George Stallings last September. He selected as his starting pitcher left-hander Jim Vaughn (13–11 in 1910), just as Stallings had done last year. Philadelphia's Connie Mack chose right-hander Chief Bender (23–5). Both men pitched excellent games: Bender allowed seven hits and one walk and Vaughn just three hits, while also issuing one walk. Better defense could have prevented Philadelphia's fifth-inning run, but conversely, only a sparkling play by third baseman Roy Hartzell kept the A's from scoring an inning earlier. New York was ahead, 1–0, when Eddie Collins smashed a hard ground ball between short and third. Hartzell, moving to his left, knocked it down, picked it up, and made a hurried throw to first to nip the speedy Collins by a step. The importance of this play became obvious when Frank Baker followed with a double and Harry Davis flied deep to right. It was an impressive Yankees' debut for Hartzell, who had come, along with $5,000, from the St. Louis Browns in February in exchange for Jimmy Austin and Frank LaPorte. A .218-hitter for the 1910 Browns, he batted a career-high .296 in 1911, with 91 runs batted in. On July 12, Hartzell knocked in eight runs in a game against his old team, an American League record that stood until Jimmie Foxx broke it with nine in a game in 1933.

The crowds began to gather at Shibe Park at noon, arriving on foot or by taxicab or trolley. The gates opened at one o'clock, and by two thirty fans had filled the bleachers and lower grandstand. Although the Athletics were the world champions, there was no special pregame ceremony to honor their triumph over the Chicago Cubs the previous fall. There would be one, but it would be later in the season. However, there were many of the other festivities fans in every city loved and had come to expect on Opening Day. When Kendle's First Regiment Band began their march to the flagpole, people throughout the stands stood and cheered. The band marched four abreast with both teams (21 from each club) following. They headed toward deepest center field, where Chase and Davis, the A's captain, raised the American flag. As the band struck up *The Star-Spangled Banner*, everyone removed their hats and sang along. Then the teams gathered at home plate for a presentation by Henry Clay, Philadelphia's Director of Public Safety. The Athletics were in their home-whites, with the large blue "A" on the left breast and the blue horizontal stripes on their white pillbox caps. The Yankees still had the interlocking "NY" on their left sleeves and no designation on the front of the jersey, but had replaced the two red stripes on their blue stockings with one thick white one. Later this season, they would wear a road uniform that for the first time had the words "NEW YORK" printed in blue across their shirt fronts. With the players looking on, Clay presented second baseman Collins with a new automobile. Collins, the A's best player, gave a short thank you speech as he watched someone drive the new auto around the field. Shortly after that, Clay, seated in Athletics president Ben Shibe's box in the upper pavilion by third base, threw out the first ball to umpire Billy Evans. Evans tossed it to Bender as leadoff batter Harry Wolter stepped in and the season began.

New York scored first, reaching Bender for a run in the third inning. With two outs,

Wolter doubled to right, took third when right fielder Murphy's return throw to the infield went astray, and scored on Charlie Hemphill's single. Murphy's error must have brought on a sense of déjà vu to both teams. In the 1908 opener between the two, Murphy, then playing second base, made three errors on the day. Fittingly, Collins, his replacement at second, made three outstanding plays in this game. In each, he threw out the batter after using his great speed to get to ground balls that looked like sure hits. The 1911 season would be the one during which Philadelphia's legendary "$100,000 infield" came together. Besides Collins, the other members were third baseman Baker, shortstop Jack Barry, and first baseman Stuffy McInnis. The 20-year-old McInnis was on the bench for the opener as Davis made the start, but he would soon become the regular first baseman. McInnis had played briefly for the Athletics in each of the past two seasons, but never at first base. He was most often a shortstop, with some games at second and third, and even one in the outfield.

Through four innings, the A's had only two hits: a scratch single by Collins in the first inning and Baker's double in the fourth. But after retiring the first two batters in the fifth, Vaughn got Bender to hit a routine fly ball to Wolter in right that Wolter misjudged and after catching up with it, dropped it. Left fielder Willie Hogan, playing in his first major-league game, followed with a long double down the left-field line that easily scored Bender, who was running on the pitch. Although Hogan was a right-handed hitter, Yankees left fielder Birdie Cree was playing him well off the line, assuming that the rookie would be unable to pull the ball against Vaughn. Hogan played only six more games for the Athletics, with only one additional hit, before Mack sold him to the Browns in May.

Vaughn ended the inning by getting Rube Oldring to ground out to Otis Johnson at short. From that point on, only one other Philadelphia batter reached base, and that was on Chase's error with two outs in the ninth. The score remained tied until the eighth inning when Bender's defense betrayed him, allowing New York to score its second run. Cree led off by drawing Bender's only walk. Johnson, attempting to sacrifice, laid down a bunt and reached first when catcher Ira Thomas threw high, pulling Davis off the bag. With runners at first and second and no one out, catcher Walter Blair also attempted a sacrifice. Davis, charging in, grabbed his bunt in the air and then threw to shortstop Barry doubling Cree off second. Blair, a graduate of Bucknell University, was starting his fifth season with the Yankees, but this was his first opening-day appearance. He was out of the major leagues in 1912–1913, but returned with Buffalo of the Federal League in 1914–1915. Davis's fine play drew a loud cheer from the appreciative crowd. They sensed that with two down, a runner at first, and the pitcher coming up, Bender would keep the visitors from scoring. But the tension began to mount again when Vaughn poked a single to left, moving Johnson to second. The crowd breathed easier when Wolter smacked a routine grounder to short; however, Barry booted the ball, and as it rolled into short center field, Johnson came around with what would be the winning run. For Johnson, who died at age 32 in 1915, this was his first game in his only major-league season.

Wednesday, April 12, 1911

New York							Philadelphia						
	ab	r	h	po	a	e		ab	r	h	po	a	e
Wolter rf	4	1	1	3	0	1	Hogan lf	4	0	1	3	0	0
Hemphill cf	4	0	2	1	0	0	Oldring cf	4	0	0	1	0	0
Chase 1b	4	0	1	12	2	1	Collins 2b	4	0	1	5	4	0
Hartzell 3b	4	0	1	2	2	0	Baker 3b	3	0	1	1	1	0

New York	ab	r	h	po	a	e		Philadelphia	ab	r	h	po	a	e
Knight 2b	4	0	0	2	4	0		Davis 1b	4	0	0	10	1	0
Cree lf	3	0	1	1	0	0		Murphy rf	4	0	0	1	0	1
Johnson ss	2	1	0	1	4	1		Barry ss	3	0	0	2	0	1
Blair c	3	0	0	3	0	0		Thomas c	3	0	0	4	4	1
Vaughn p	3	0	1	2	1	0		Bender p	3	1	0	0	3	0
Total	31	2	7	27	13	3		Total	32	1	3	27	13	3

```
New York        001    000    010–2
Philadelphia    000    010    000–1
```

Earned runs—New York, 1; Philadelphia, 1. Two-base hits—Wolter, Baker, Hogan. Sacrifice hit—Johnson. Stolen bases—Chase, Collins. Left on bases—New York, 3; Philadelphia, 5. Struck out—by Bender, 4; by Vaughn, 3. Double plays—Davis to Barry. First base on errors—New York, 2; Philadelphia, 1. First base on called balls—off Bender, 1; off Vaughn, 1. Umpires—Messrs. Evans and Egan. Time of game—1 hr. 55 min.

The Athletics gave the fans a last bit of hope in the ninth. Vaughn got Philadelphia's two most dangerous hitters, Collins and Baker, but then Chase fumbled Davis's potential game-ending ground ball. After regaining possession, his throw to Vaughn covering first was wild. Blair, backing up the play, also had trouble picking up the ball, and Davis easily made it to second. The fans were on their feet pleading with Murphy to deliver the tying run. However, this time Chase cleanly handled his ground ball and the game was over.

Although the Yankees swept the opening three-game series in Philadelphia, they lost 15 of the remaining 18 games to the Athletics and finished sixth (76–76), 25½ games behind them. Birdie Cree batted .348, breaking Willie Keeler's club record of .343 set in 1904. That remained the Yankees team record until Babe Ruth hit .376 in 1920. The five-foot-six, 150-pound Cree also led the team in hits (181), runs (90), triples (22), and stolen bases (48). He finished fourth in the league in slugging percentage (.513), and fifth in total bases (267). After completing his first full season as manager, Hal Chase resigned the position on November 21.

Thursday, April 11, 1912
Hilltop Park, New York
Boston 5 New York 3

The Valley of Humiliation.—John Bunyan

On Opening Day 1912, the Yankees made their first appearance in the uniform that eventually would become the most recognizable in sports. Over the ensuing decades, the pinstripes with the interlocked "NY" on the left breast would become synonymous with baseball's greatest franchise. How paradoxical then, that the first Yankees' team to wear this uniform would not only lose its first game, but do so by squandering a ninth-inning lead. In retrospect, the 5–3 loss to the Red Sox served as an omen for what would be a disastrous season, at least in a baseball sense. The origin of a true disaster had begun a day earlier, on April 10, when the White Star liner RMS Titanic left Southampton, England on her maiden voyage.

Those who believed in bad omens could find an abundance of them associated with the Yankees this spring. They began with a series of mishaps at training camp in Atlanta and continued right up to the floral horseshoe that co-owner Frank Farrell presented to his new manager, Harry Wolverton, before the game. According to superstition, for horseshoes to bring good luck they must be displayed with the two ends facing up—which was not the case with Wolverton's wreath. As described in the *New York Press*, "the assistant florist had mounted it upside-down, thus letting all the day's luck run out of the ends." The presentation of the wreath, which had the word "Success" written on a silk ribbon across it, was part of the ceremony welcoming Wolverton to New York. Following the floral gift, Assemblyman Alfred E. Smith handed the manager a loving cup donated by the Board of Trade of Oakland, California, where Wolverton had managed the previous two seasons.

A disappointing crowd of barely 12,000 attended what would be the last opener played at Hilltop Park. Only the 25¢ seats in the right-field corner appeared filled, while many sections in the outer reaches of the park remained completely unoccupied. The two most likely reasons for the poor showing were the chilly weather and the competition from the Giants, who were opening against Brooklyn before a turn-away crowd at Washington Park. The crowd in Brooklyn was so large that fans were standing only 15 feet from the base lines. Finally, after six innings, with the Giants ahead 18–3, the umpires called a halt to the game. Rube Marquard was the winning pitcher, the first of his record-setting 19 consecutive victories to start the 1912 season.

A comparison of the attendance for the Yankees-Red Sox and Giants-Dodgers openers clearly showed that despite the inroads made by the American League, New York was still a National League city. It was also a city that was continuing to grow in population and influence. There were now close to five million people living in the five boroughs, making it ever more difficult to govern. The man who had that responsibility was Mayor William Gaynor, a decent, honest public servant who had been supported by the Tammany bosses but then turned against them. Gaynor would turn out to be among the best mayors in the city's history, but still he had his critics. On Opening Day a year ago, the Grand Jury investigating the crime wave then sweeping New York City heard testimony that placed part of the blame on him. The mayor, they said, was at fault for allowing the criminals to charge the police with brutality. And even this day, Professor Howard A. Kelly of Johns Hopkins University, speaking in New York, said, "The moral rottenness of New York City is a stench in the nostrils of the whole country." Therefore, Kelly continued, "no matter how praiseworthy Mayor Gaynor might be, he could never ascend to the Presidency."

While the opening-day crowd was smaller than usual, there was the normal lavish display of flags and a band to keep the fans entertained until the game began. Prince's Military Band provided the music, playing a series of popular songs such as Irving Berlin's "Everybody's Doing It Now," but once the game started, they limited their playing to between innings only. Typical of Opening Day, there was a good turnout of women, many with bouquets of flowers pinned to the furs they wore to protect against the cold. About 5,000 people were in the stands at five minutes to two when the Red Sox, led by manager/first baseman Jake Stahl, came from their clubhouse onto the field. Despite being the enemy, the fans cheered the Bostonians, happy just to see baseball players again after the long off-season. Like the Yankees, the Sox had also adopted pinstripes, but unlike the New Yorkers, they had them on their home and road uniforms. In a change of more lasting significance to their home and road attire, they replaced the block-lettered "BOSTON" on their shirt fronts with the block-lettered "RED SOX," the first time that name had ever appeared on their uniform. At two o'clock, the Yankees appeared and the cheers, of course, grew noticeably louder, with the loudest ones going to Wolverton. Hal Chase, ever the individualist, made his entrance 15 minutes later. The New York fans still adored Chase and greeted his appearance with great applause and affectionate shouts.

Stahl and Wolverton chose a pair of right-handers to pitch the opener; Smoky Joe Wood for Boston and Ray Caldwell for New York. Wood had established his place among the league's premier pitchers by winning 23 games (23–17) in 1911, while Caldwell, a rookie, won 14 and lost 14 for the sixth-place Yankees. New York State Supreme Court Justice Edward Everett McCall, who was not only a big fan but had been a renowned sandlot player in his youth, threw out the first ball.

Harry Hooper opened the game with a sharp single to left field. The Sox tried to move him to second with a sacrifice, but failed; Steve Yerkes, after twice bunting foul, took a called third strike. But with Tris Speaker at the plate, Hooper got there on his own, stealing second as catcher Gabby Street's high throw sailed into center field. Speedy center fielder Bert Daniels quickly recovered Street's errant toss and threw to third baseman Al "Cozy" Dolan, but not in time to get the sliding Hooper. Street, Daniels, and Dolan were all playing in their first openers as Yankees. Street had come to New York for infielder John Knight in a preseason trade with Washington. He was behind the plate this afternoon because regular catcher Jeff Sweeney was still a holdout. Daniels, in his third year with the club, replaced Charlie Hemphill, the opening-day center fielder the previous four years whose big-league career was now over. Dolan, up briefly with the 1909 Reds and the 1911 Yanks, would play in only 18 games before being sold to the Rochester Hustlers of the International League in May. In 1924, while Dolan was a coach for the Giants, Commissioner Kenesaw M. Landis banned him from baseball for his part in attempting to fix games that season. Wolverton would use several players at third base in 1912, including himself. Although he was 38 years old and had not faced major-league pitching in seven years, Wolverton played in 34 games for the Yankees, mostly as a pinch hitter, and batted .300 (15 for 50).

With Hooper now at third and Speaker, who had walked, at first, Stahl went after Caldwell's first pitch. He lifted a fly ball that left fielder Birdie Cree caught, but Hooper scored after the catch. The crowd sensed that this could be a very important run because Wood, in his still young career, had been particularly effective against New York. Therefore, they were pleasantly surprised when the Yankees reached the Boston fireballer for two runs in their first at-bat. Harry Wolter started the inning with a walk and took second on Daniels's single. Both men moved up a base on Chase's sacrifice bunt. When Cree grounded out to second baseman Yerkes, Wolter scored and Daniels moved to third. Roy Hartzell drew Wood's second walk of the inning and promptly took off for second base. Boston backstop Les Nunamaker ignored Hartzell and threw to third thinking he could catch Daniels wandering off that base. It was a good idea, but badly executed. Nunamaker's throw got by third baseman Larry Gardner and went into left field, allowing Daniels to score easily. Hartzell continued to circle the bases as he too attempted to come home, but a good throw by left fielder Duffy Lewis retired him on a close play at the plate.

Although both teams had opportunities over the next seven innings, neither could score, and New York retained its 2–1 lead into the ninth. Caldwell and Wood benefitted from outstanding fielding plays by their teammates: Chase and Cree for New York, and Hooper for Boston. Caldwell, mixing his spitball and fastball, limited the Red Sox to just three singles through eight innings. However, in the ninth he made the mistake of walking the leadoff batter, Stahl, on a 3–2 pitch. The Red Sox, playing for the tie, had Gardner sacrifice, which he did successfully, moving Stahl to second. Lewis then raised a high pop foul that Street just missed catching, the ball bouncing out of his mitt when he bumped against the stands. It was Street's second error; the only two the Yankees made in the game. Had he held the ball it might have finished the Sox, but given another chance Lewis slashed a single to right field scoring Stahl with the tying run. Shortstop Heinie Wagner reached base on an infield single, which was followed by Nunamaker's single to center that scored Lewis and put Boston ahead, 3–2. Daniels showed poor judgment on Nunamaker's hit, pointlessly throwing home in an attempt to get Lewis, allowing Nunamaker and Wagner to take second and third.

Bill Carrigan had been on deck, preparing to pinch-hit hit for Wood, but now that Boston had the lead he handed Wood the bat and headed back to the dugout. Wood, a very good hitter, lined a single to center that brought Wagner and Nunamaker home, making the score 5–2. With the damage done, Wolverton replaced Caldwell with Jim Vaughn who got the final two outs. Hartzell and Dolan opened the last of the ninth, with singles, giving the fans hope that the Yankees might stage a dramatic comeback. It was not to be. They could manage only one run as Wood easily retired the bottom third of the batting order: Earle Gardner, Street, and Hack Simmons, batting for Vaughn.

On June 24, when he was 2–8 with an ERA of 5.14, the Yankees gave up on Vaughn and sold him to Washington for the waiver price. In late August, the Senators traded him to the Kansas City Blues of the American Association. A year later in August 1913, Kansas City Traded him to the Chicago Cubs where he spent the next nine years, becoming a standout pitcher and a five-time 20-game winner.

Joe Wood went on to win 34 games this season (34–5), and added three more wins against the Giants in the World Series. For the Yankees, the loss was the first of six straight defeats. The sixth was an 11-inning 7–6 loss to the Red Sox on April 20 in the first major league game played at Boston's Fenway Park.

Thursday, April 11, 1912

Boston	ab	r	h	po	a	e	New York	ab	r	h	po	a	e
Hooper rf	4	1	1	3	0	0	Wolter rf	3	1	2	1	0	0
Yerkes 2b	5	0	0	3	2	0	Daniels cf	3	1	1	1	0	0
Speaker cf	3	0	0	1	0	0	Chase 1b	3	0	0	7	2	0
Stahl 1b	2	1	0	11	4	0	Cree lf	3	0	0	5	0	0
L. Gardner 3b	2	0	0	1	3	0	Hartzell ss	3	1	1	4	5	0
Lewis lf	4	1	1	0	1	1	Dolan 3b	4	0	1	0	2	0
Wagner ss	4	1	2	1	2	0	E. Gardner 2b	4	0	1	4	1	0
Nunamaker c	3	1	1	3	1	1	Street c	4	0	0	5	2	2
Wood p	4	0	2	4	3	0	Caldwell p	3	0	1	0	1	0
Total	31	5	7	27	16	2	Vaughn p	0	0	0	0	0	0
							ªSimmons	1	0	0	0	0	0
							Total	31	3	7	27	13	2

ªBatted for Vaughn in the ninth inning.

Boston	100	000	004–5
New York	200	000	001–3

First base on errors—New York, 1; Boston, 1. Sacrifice hits—Chase, Daniels, L. Gardner. Sacrifice fly—Stahl. Stolen bases—Hooper, Hartzell, E. Gardner, Wolter. Left on bases—New York, 6; Boston, 6. Double play—Street and E. Gardner. Struck out—by Caldwell, 5 (Yerkes, Lewis, Wagner, Nunamaker,

Speaker); by Vaughn, 1 (Hooper); by Wood, 2 (Dolan, Caldwell). Bases on balls—off Caldwell, 5 (Nunamaker, Speaker, L. Gardner, Hooper, Stahl); off Wood, 3 (Wolter, Hartzell, Cree). Passed ball—Street. Hits—Off Caldwell, 7 in 8⅓ innings; off Vaughn, 0 in ⅔ of an inning. Time of game—2 hrs. 2 min. Umpires—Messrs. Connolly and Hart.

The worst record in team history (50–102), and a last-place finish, 55 games behind the Boston Red Sox, was more than enough to make Harry Wolverton a one-year manager. On January 8, 1913, the Yankees signed Frank Chance as their new leader.

Thursday, April 10, 1913
National Park, Washington
Washington 2 New York 1

A name to all succeeding ages curst.—John Dryden

In April 1911, after a fire destroyed the Polo Grounds' stands, Yankees co-owners Frank Farrell and Bill Devery invited the Giants to play their home games at Hilltop Park. The Giants accepted, playing 28 games at the Hilltop over six weeks while construction crews rebuilt the Polo Grounds. In late June they moved back, even though the new steel and concrete structure, built at a cost of $500,000, was not completely finished. Two years later, when Farrell's and Devery's lease of Hilltop Park was not renewed, Harry Hempstead, who had succeeded his father-in-law John T. Brush as the Giants' president, returned the gesture of cooperation. He made the Polo Grounds available to the Yankees for a yearly rental fee of $50,000. The Yanks agreed to become the Giants' tenants, and after ten years of playing at quaint, sometimes ramshackle Hilltop Park, they moved into the stately Polo Grounds. Following season-opening visits to Washington and Boston, they would debut in their new home on April 17. But after going winless in their first 18 games at the Polo Grounds (17 losses and a tie), they might have wondered why they ever left Hilltop Park. It was not until June 7 when they defeated the Chicago White Sox, 3–2, that the Yankees finally got their first home win. And it was indisputably the Yankees who won that game. With the move from Hilltop Park, the club discarded "Highlanders" completely, and they were officially the Yankees, beginning with their 2–1 opening-day loss at Washington's National Park.

President Woodrow Wilson attended the game and threw out the first ball, following the precedent established by President William Howard Taft three years earlier. Washington area fans loved the new custom and now had come to expect it from the chief executive. Wilson, a Democrat, had been inaugurated just five weeks earlier after winning the presidency in a three-way contest with Taft and Taft's predecessor, Theodore Roosevelt. Attending a baseball game, even on a chilly overcast day, would be a pleasant respite for him, a chance to spend a few hours away from the tariff battles that he was currently fighting with the Congress. Wilson also was confronting two other major issues this spring: the Income Tax Bill, under consideration in the House of Representatives, and the nagging question of "naval preparedness." Elsewhere in Washington, not far from National Park, a pair of little-known Americans were addressing these problems. Representative Cordell Hull of Tennessee, chairman of the subcommittee that prepared the Income Tax Bill, said his goal was "to remove from the collection of the tax all of the distasteful features so as to enable the Collectors of Internal Revenue to draw the money into the Treasury with as little disturbance to the individual and to business as possible." Meanwhile, Assistant Secretary of the Navy Franklin Delano Roosevelt welcomed delegates to the annual convention of the Navy League, where the general feeling among the delegates was that the U.S. Navy was too small to "compel peace" or "fight a war." As Roosevelt spoke in Washington, Europeans were making preparations for the next international peace conference. They scheduled it for 1915 in The Hague, but by then, of course, there would be no peace in Europe.

Questions of war and taxes notwithstanding, President Wilson, accompanied by his daughter Eleanor and several aides, arrived at the ballpark just before game time. When the crowd spotted the president, dressed in a fur-lined overcoat and brown fedora, they greeted him with riotous cheering. Wilson and his party sat in a box behind the Senators dugout, while Vice President Thomas R. Marshall, a rabid baseball fan, sat nearby. Assorted Congressmen and Cabinet officers were scattered throughout the better seats.

The gates had opened at noon with the fans ready and waiting. After they occupied every available seat and packed the aisles, the remaining fans found places on the fringes of the playing field. The Pistori Band provided pregame entertainment, and the Senators' two baseball clowns, 36-year-old pitcher Nick Altrock and 37-year-old infielder Germany Schaefer, performed skits that helped pass the time. The many women in the crowd wore assorted gowns and suits, with red and blue being the most popular colors for their spring bonnets. As the *Washington Post* reported; "The grey day only served to set off by contrast more sharply the gay colors of the gowns and millinery of the women in the double-decked stands. Washington 'rooters' are not confined to its male population, by any means, and the number of women who came to cheer the home city's champions to victory compared very favorably with the number of men supporters present." Washington's leading newspaper, *The Evening Star,* said that "Hundreds of women helped to make up the record-breaking crowd, and the brilliant tints of their costumes and hats made vivid splashes of color against the somber background of masculine raiment."

Clark Griffith was beginning his second year in Washington, having managed the Senators to their first winning season, a second-place finish in 1912. Led by first baseman Chick Gandil, center fielder Clyde Milan, and pitcher Walter Johnson, Washington appeared to be even stronger this year. Strong enough, Griffith believed, to bring the nation's capital its first American League pennant. The key to their success was Johnson, baseball's best pitcher, coming off a 1912 season in which he won 33 games (33–12), with a 1.39 earned run average. Griffith, who managed the Yankees for the first five and a half years of their existence, and now particularly enjoyed beating them, naturally chose his ace to pitch the opener.

New York was opening the season under a different manager for the third consecutive year. This time it was Frank Chance, ex-manager of the Chicago Cubs, who released him late in 1912. The Yankees made a lucrative offer to Chance, winner of four National League pennants and two world championships. To take over their lowly club, they gave him a three-year contract reportedly worth $25,000 per year, plus 5 percent of any profit the team might make. American League president Ban Johnson, still working to shore up the New York franchise, brokered the deal. Johnson remained concerned that continued weak performances in New York could cause major financial problems and possibly doom the whole league. Actually, everything about his league concerned the micro-managing Johnson, even the length of its games. Believing they lasted too long, he ordered that players were no longer to chase foul balls unless they had a chance of making an out. Those balls would be retrieved and returned to the umpires between innings.

The speculation in the press was that Chance would open with Ray Caldwell, the team's most effective pitcher this spring. On April 5, Caldwell concluded his preseason efforts by pitching six strong innings against Brooklyn in the first game played at Ebbets Field. However, in a last-minute change of mind, Chance named George McConnell (8–12 as a 34-year-old rookie in 1912) as his starter. Big George—he was six-feet-three and 190 pounds—came through with an outstanding game, allowing only six hits, but he had one bad inning and that was one too many against Walter Johnson.

President Wilson officially opened the season by tossing out the ceremonial first ball to Johnson, who had walked to within 50 feet of his box. Johnson then handed the ball to Griffith, who gave it to the president to autograph. The cheers for Johnson from the crowd were even louder than those for Wilson, evidence of the love the people of Washington had for their great pitcher. The autographed ball was safely in the Senators dugout as Johnson, equipped with a fresh one, hit leadoff batter Bert Daniels in the back with his second pitch. Harry Wolter followed with a twisting ground ball to the right side. First baseman Gandil fumbled it as Daniels, who had stolen second, rounded third and headed for home. George McBride, the American League's best defensive shortstop, went way over into short right-center field, retrieved the ball, and threw to the plate. It was a close play, but Daniels, with a perfect slide, beat catcher Eddie Ainsmith's tag.

The Yankees should have scored a second run this afternoon, but after today Johnson would not allow another run until May 14. By the time the St. Louis Browns scored against him in the fourth inning of that game in St. Louis, Johnson had pitched 55⅔ consecutive scoreless innings, which is still the American League record. Catcher Jeff Sweeney was the Yankees' player responsible for losing that second run. In the seventh inning he led off with a low line drive that got past center fielder Milan for what should have been an easy double. However, halfway between first base and second, Sweeney heard shouting from Ezra Midkiff, a utility infielder who was coaching at first. Midkiff was yelling for him to "come back and touch first base." Sweeney, realizing he had missed the bag, hustled back, forced to settle for a single instead of the sure double. The next batter was Ralph Young, a five-foot-five, switch-hitting shortstop playing in his first major-league game. Claud Derrick had come north as the Yanks' first-string shortstop, but was unavailable today. Brooklyn's Zack Wheat had spiked him on his throwing hand in an exhibition game three days before the opener. Young would play only seven games, getting one hit in 15 at-bats, before the Yanks sent him to Sacramento of the Pacific Coast League.

Young forced Sweeney at second, and then McConnell forced Young; so when Daniels followed with a single, no run scored. Johnson ended the inning by getting Wolter to hit back to him. Manager Chance gave Sweeney a stern talking-to when the catcher returned to the bench, no doubt instructing him in the necessity of touching each base as he made his way around them. Chance had wanted to play in the opener, but a leg injury incurred during spring training in Bermuda had not completely healed. (In going to Bermuda, the Yankees became the first major-league team to hold spring training outside the United States.) Charlie Sterrett, a student of President Wilson when both were at Princeton, played first in Chance's absence. Hal Chase had been the Yankees' first baseman since 1905, his rookie year, but after Chance joined the club, Chase volunteered to cede the job to the new manager and move to second base. Chase was a magnificent athlete who, despite being left-handed, sometimes played other infield positions, not only second base as he did this afternoon, but also third base and shortstop.

Thursday, April 10, 1913

New York	ab	r	h	po	a	e	Washington	ab	r	h	po	a	e
Daniels rf	3	1	1	0	0	0	Moeller rf	3	0	2	2	0	0
Wolter cf	3	0	1	8	0	0	Foster 3b	4	0	2	0	1	0
Hartzell 3b	4	0	2	2	1	0	Milan cf	4	0	0	1	0	0
Cree lf	4	0	2	1	0	0	Gandil 1b	4	0	0	10	0	1
Chase 2b	4	0	0	1	0	0	Morgan 2b	3	0	1	4	4	0
Sterrett 1b	4	0	1	7	1	0	Ainsmith c	1	1	0	5	0	0
Sweeney c	4	0	1	3	2	0	Shanks lf	3	1	2	1	1	0
Young ss	3	0	1	2	0	0	McBride ss	1	0	0	4	1	0
aLelivelt	1	0	0	0	0	0	Johnson p	3	0	0	0	4	0
McConnell p	3	0	0	0	6	1	Total	26	2	7	27	11	1
Total	33	1	9	24	10	1							

aFlied out for Young in ninth inning.

```
New York      100    000    000–1
Washington    000    000    20X-2
```

Sacrifice hits—McConnell, McBride (2). Stolen bases—Daniels, Moeller (2), Foster. Double play—Young and Hartzell. Left on bases—New York, 8; Washington, 5. First base on balls—by McConnell, 2; by Johnson, 1. Hit by pitcher—by McConnell, Ainsmith; by Johnson, Daniels. Struck out—by McConnell, 2; by Johnson, 3. Passed ball—Ainsmith. Umpires—Messrs. Connolly and McGreevy. Time of game—Two hrs. 5 min.

McConnell nursed his slim lead through six innings, with the biggest threat against him coming in the fourth. With the bases loaded and two men out, Howard Shanks ripped a ball down the third-base line that Roy Hartzell smothered and just beat the runner, Eddie Foster, to the bag. McConnell rescued himself in the fifth inning; with runners at second and third and two outs, he picked Danny Moeller off third. Moeller, unlike Sweeney, would make amends for his careless base running and emerge as the game's hero. As the Senators came to bat in the home seventh, the fans, as was the custom, stood and cheered. President Wilson smiled and seemed amused at all the cheering, but remained seated. Washington got the leadoff man aboard when McConnell, who had relied almost exclusively on his spitball, hit Ainsmith for the second time. Now that the tying run was on base, the significance of Sweeney's mental error in the top of the inning became even more apparent. Shanks bunted, attempting to get Ainsmith to second. McConnell fielded the ball and though he had plenty of time, he rushed his throw, pulling Sterrett off the bag at first. McBride, the number-eight hitter, moved the runners to second and third with a perfect sacrifice bunt. Johnson was among the game's best-hitting pitchers, but McConnell fanned him on three swinging strikes for the second out. The groans of the crowd had barely subsided when Moeller lashed McConnell's first pitch on a line into right field. It scored both Ainsmith and Shanks to give the Senators a 2–1 lead. The fans erupted in a frenzy of cheers and, for the first time in the game, even the president applauded.

After Sterrett led off the Yankee's ninth with a single, Chance chose to play for the win rather than the tie and ordered Sweeney to swing away. The big catcher bounced one down to third baseman Foster, who threw to second baseman Ray Morgan to force Sterrett. Jack Lelivelt, batting for Young, poked a short fly ball to left that got caught up in the wind, but Shanks stayed with it for out number two. The next scheduled batter was McConnell, another good-hitting pitcher, who last season batted .297. Chance allowed him to bat, but

McConnell grounded weakly to second to end the game. Johnson had the first of his 36 wins (36–7), and the first of the five he would have against the Yankees this year.

The Yankees (57–94) finished in seventh place, one game better than the cellar-dwelling St. Louis Browns, and 38 games behind the champion Philadelphia Athletics. They had eight home runs for the season, the fewest in the major leagues. It did not take long for Frank Chance to sour on Hal Chase. When he began to suspect, as had George Stallings before him, that Chase was "throwing" games, he got rid of him. On June 1, the Yankees traded Chase to the Chicago White Sox for first baseman Babe Borton and infielder Rollie Zeider.

Tuesday, April 14, 1914
Polo Grounds, New York
New York 8 Philadelphia 2

I established law and justice in the land.—Hammurabi

At a time when people got their news from newspapers, the competition for readers was intense, particularly in New York, which had more newspapers and more readers than any other American city. Each paper sought to establish its own niche by developing a distinctive relationship with different segments of the public. However, when an important story came along, all competed to be the first to get it on the street, preferably with the most lurid details. And when the stories dealt with especially stirring topics like tales of revenge and honor, journalistic ethics were pushed to their limits. Two such stories filled the papers on the Opening Day of the 1914 baseball season. The revenge involved the previous day's execution in Sing Sing prison's electric chair of four young men for the murder of gambler Herman Rosenthal. The four, all from New York City and all in their early 20s, were Louis Rosenberg (Lefty Louie), Jacob Seidenshner (Whitey Lewis), Frank Cirofici (Dago Frank), and Harry Horowitz (Gyp the Blood). Newspapers reported as much of the sordid details of the executions as the prevailing standards would allow, but while the public took perverse pleasure in reading them, it is not likely that many people outside their families wept for these young killers. Of greater concern to Americans was the news that the country was now close to a war with Mexico over a matter of "honor." President Wilson had ordered a large portion of the Atlantic fleet to Mexican waters in an attempt to force the government of General Victoriano Huerta to make a public salute to the Stars and Stripes. The salute would serve as an apology for the arrest of American Marines at Tampico a week earlier. It seemed that only an apology by General Huerta could stop United States Marines from invading Mexico.

For that matter, a tale of honor and revenge, albeit on a much smaller scale, could also be found in today's season opener at the Polo Grounds. The Yankees provided the city of New York with a bit of both when they easily defeated the world champion Philadelphia Athletics, 8–2. Philadelphia had won that championship six months earlier, defeating the Giants' Christy Mathewson on this field to win their third World Series in four years. For New Yorkers, having a team from Philadelphia thrash a team from New York in two of the last three World Series (they also beat the Giants in 1911) was a blow to civic pride. While Yankees fans normally did not root for the Giants, this was different; the average New Yorker believed his city should be the best in everything, including baseball. To make the

Yankees' victory even sweeter, they beat an A's team that used a lineup and batting order identical to the one they used last fall. The starting pitcher for Connie Mack's champions was second-year man Bullet Joe Bush, an 8–2 winner in Game Three of the Series, also played here. By contrast, the Yankees—as bad teams do—had made many changes. Catcher Jeff Sweeney was the lone man playing the same position he had played on Opening Day in 1913. The only other holdover from that lineup was Roy Hartzell, who played third base then but was now at second base. Hartzell was the shortstop in the 1912 opener, making this his third opening-day position in three years.

Not surprisingly, the Athletics, who finished 38 games ahead of the Yankees in 1913, also won the season series from them 17 games to 5. However, that was last year; so far this year, or at least for this one frosty April day, the Yankees were the better team. They scored four first-inning runs against Bush, drove him from the mound after two innings, and won the game by the same 8–2 score that Bush had beaten the Giants last fall. Only third baseman Fritz Maisel among the Yankees' starters failed to get at least one hit. The beneficiary of this unusual display of Yankees offense was pitcher Marty McHale. Manager Frank Chance had considered three choices for his starting pitcher—McHale, Ray Caldwell, and Ray Keating—deciding on McHale shortly before game time. McHale's ethnicity and pleasant singing voice had earned him the nickname, "The Irish Thrush." He would eventually gain greater fame as a singer than he had as a pitcher, teaming with Giants' star Mike Donlin on the vaudeville circuit. McHale had signed with the Red Sox in 1910 after pitching for the University of Maine, where he threw three consecutive no-hitters. Yet going into today's opener, his major-league experience consisted of six games for Boston in 1910–1911, seven for the Yankees in 1913, and an unimposing lifetime win-loss record of two wins and six losses.

The damp, chilly weather helped limit the crowd to about 15,000, most of whom, ignoring the cold, were dressed for more spring-like temperatures. This was primarily true of the women, who appeared to be freezing in their spring gowns and hats. Aside from Prince's Band, which serenaded the crowd with all the latest tunes (with a special emphasis on the tango), there was little of the traditional hoopla usually seen on Opening Day. After the band played "America," Robert F. Wagner, New York's acting lieutenant governor, threw out the first ball. McHale caught it and the 1914 season began. Judge Edward B. McCall, "Diamond Jim" Brady, and New York City Fire Commissioner Robert Adamson were among the many celebrities in the Polo Grounds' crowd. Also there were Harry Payne Whitney, railroad magnate O. H. Harriman, A's owner Ben Shibe, and former heavyweight champion Jim Corbett. Corbett, who did not arrive until after the first inning, may have wondered as he made his way to his seat why the fans seemed so happy. The scoreboard read Athletics 4, Yankees 0—surely not a score to please the hometown crowd. Someone sitting nearby gladly informed "Gentleman Jim" that the scoreboard boy must have posted it that way from force of habit; he assured the champ that it really was the Yankees who had scored the four runs.

New York's first-inning uprising began after Bush fanned Maisel, the leadoff batter. Hartzell lined a double into the left-field corner and scored on Jimmy Walsh's single. Walsh, a former Athletic who would be traded back to Philadelphia in June, became the second out when a fine throw by catcher Wally Schang cut him down as he tried to steal second. But before Bush could get the third out, the Yankees added three more runs. Harry Williams walked and stole second; Bill Holden walked; and Doc Cook singled sharply to right, scoring Williams. When the A's failed to cut off Eddie Murphy's throw to the plate, Holden took third and Cook second. Both came home on Roger Peckinpaugh's single, and it was 4–0 as the crowd roared its approval.

First baseman Williams, center fielder Holden, and right fielder Cook all had made their major-league debuts with the Yankees in 1913. All had seen limited action, and only Cook would stay in the major leagues past the 1914 season. Shortstop Peckinpaugh had come from Cleveland in a May 1913 trade for outfielder Jack Lelivelt and infielder Bill Stumpf. He soon became the everyday shortstop the club had been seeking ever since they sold Kid Elberfeld to Washington after the 1909 season. Peckinpaugh was the Yanks' seventh opening-day shortstop in seven years, but he solidified the position and would retain it through the 1921 season.

Chance, coaching at third base, was extremely active all afternoon, imploring his boys with cries of "Be alive!" However, despite his admonitions, it was Chance himself who was guilty of the team's one mental lapse. In the second inning, he tried physically to help Sweeney get back to third base after he fell during a rundown. Under a new rule, base coaches were no longer allowed to help runners in this way, and umpire Billy Evans quickly ruled that Sweeney was out. The A's got their first run in the third inning, and they did it without a base hit. Jack Barry reached on an error by Maisel and stole second. McHale struck out Schang and then got pinch-hitter Tom Daley, batting for Bush, to ground to Hartzell. But Hartzell was unable to make the play and there were now runners at first and third. Barry scored the unearned run as Murphy grounded into a force play at second.

With Bush removed for a hitter, Mack put in a new battery. He replaced Schang with veteran catcher Jack Lapp and sent Charlie Boardman to the mound. Because there was no listing in the program for Boardman, a 21-year-old left-hander, it took a while for the crowd to identify the new Philadelphia pitcher. Boardman got through the third and fourth innings, but in the fifth New York broke the game open. After Holden, who had three hits in the game, singled, Cook forced him at second. Cook went to third on Peckinpaugh's double to left, and both runners scored on Sweeney's single to right. A passed ball allowed Sweeney to take second, and a single by McHale moved him to third. To the delight of the fans, catcher and pitcher then pulled a double steal; McHale swiped second as Sweeney slid home with his second stolen base of the day. Shortly before the start of the season, Sweeney accepted a bet from Yankees scout Arthur Irwin, who claimed that Sweeney would not steal 15 bases this year. Sweeney won the bet, finishing with 19, which is still the record for most stolen bases in one season by a Yankees' catcher. Maisel also had two steals on the day; both came in the fourth when he stole second and third after drawing a walk. He would steal 74 bases this season, the most in the American League and a team record that endured until Rickey Henderson stole 80 in 1985. Maisel also qualified as the most brazen of the Yankees, deriding Eddie Collins when the A's great second baseman had trouble handling a low throw from Schang in the second inning.

Tuesday, April 14, 1914

Philadelphia	ab	r	h	po	a	e	New York	ab	r	h	po	a	e
E. Murphy rf	3	0	0	3	1	0	Maisel 3b	3	0	0	0	4	1
Oldring lf	4	0	0	1	0	0	Hartzell 2b	5	2	2	3	1	1
Collins 2b	3	1	1	8	1	0	Walsh lf	2	0	1	0	0	0
Baker 3b	4	0	2	3	0	1	Williams 1b	4	1	1	15	0	0
McInnis 1b	4	0	2	1	0	0	Holden cf	4	1	3	1	0	0
Strunk cf	4	0	0	2	1	0	Cook rf	3	2	1	2	0	0
Barry ss	4	1	0	2	1	0	Peckinpaugh ss	4	1	2	1	6	0

Philadelphia   New York

	ab	r	h	po	a	e
Schang c	1	0	0	1	2	1
Lapp c	3	0	0	3	1	0
Bush p	0	0	0	0	1	0
ªDaley	1	0	0	0	0	0
Boardman p	2	0	0	0	0	0
ᵇKopf	1	0	0	0	0	0
Total	34	2	5	24	8	2

	ab	r	h	po	a	e
Sweeney c	4	1	2	5	0	1
McHale p	4	0	1	0	5	0
Total	33	8	13	27	17	3

ªSafe on error for Bush in the third inning.
ᵇBatted for Boardman in the ninth inning.

Philadelphia	001	000	010–2
New York	400	030	01X–8

Two-base hits—Peckinpaugh, Hartzell. Three-base hit—Holden. Stolen bases—Maisel (2), Hartzell, Williams, Sweeney (2), McHale. First base on errors—New York, 1; Philadelphia, 2. Left on bases—New York, 9; Philadelphia, 7. Double play—Murphy, Collins and McInnis; Strunk and Collins. Struck out—by McHale, 6; by Bush, 1; by Boardman, 2. Bases on balls—off McHale, 2; off Bush, 4; off Boardman, 4. Wild pitch—Boardman. Passed ball—Lapp. Hits—off Bush, 5 in 2 innings; off Boardman, 8 in 6 innings. Time of game—2 hrs. 56 min. Umpires—Messrs. Evans and Egan.

McHale held the Athletics hitless through five innings, but with two gone in the sixth, Collins, Frank Baker, and Stuffy McInnis hit consecutive singles to load the bases. The threat ended when Amos Strunk flied out to Cook, but those same three came back in the eighth inning to produce Philadelphia's second run. Again there were two men out and no one on when Collins walked, took third on a single by Baker, and scored on a single by McInnis. McHale again ended the inning by retiring Strunk. New York got its final run in the eighth on a single by Hartzell, a steal of second (the Yankees' seventh stolen base of the game), and a single by Williams. The A's went quietly in the ninth to send the crowd home happy. It was cold and it had been a long game—the first three innings took an hour to play—but the home team had won.

The Yankees finished in a sixth-place tie with the Chicago White Sox (70–84), 30 games behind the Athletics. Although the team showed improvement, Frank Chance was unhappy in New York, particularly with the owners. With 20 games left in the season, he quit and went back to California. Roger Peckinpaugh, only 23, led the team for those last 20 games (10–10), becoming the youngest manager in big-league history. The Yankees continued to be a weak-hitting team, batting a major-league low .229, with just 12 home runs. For Philadelphia it was their fourth pennant in five years, but in the World Series the Boston Braves, managed by ex–Yankees skipper George Stallings, upset them, winning in a four-game sweep.

Wednesday, April 14, 1915
National Park, Washington
Washington 7 New York 0

All things have second birth.—William Wordsworth

Although a fourth consecutive second-division finish made 1914 another disappointing season for the Yankees, things were about to change for the better. On January 11, 1915, Bill Devery and Frank Farrell, who purchased the club for $18,000 in 1903, sold it to Colonel

Jacob Ruppert and Captain Tillinghast Huston for $460,000, a price possibly reduced or offset by liabilities the club carried on its books. The arrival of Ruppert and Huston (especially Ruppert) began the Yankees' ascent from also-rans to baseball's greatest franchise, and the impetus for it came from an unexpected source—John McGraw. Like everyone else, the Giants' manager knew that besides their personal disagreements, Devery and Farrell were having serious financial problems and were anxious to sell the club. When McGraw learned that Ruppert and Huston, whom he earlier had introduced to one another, were interested in buying a team, he suggested that they speak to American League President Ban Johnson about buying the Yankees, even though Johnson remained his bitter enemy. That McGraw would do something to help his American League tenants suggests just how secure he was in presuming that his Giants would always be New York's most popular team. This year's Polo Grounds attendance figures would only strengthen that presumption; the Yankees drew just 256,035, the lowest total during their ten-year stay at the Polo Grounds. Meanwhile, the Giants, although suffering through McGraw's only full-season last-place finish, drew 391,850, confirming that they were undeniably still number one in New York.

Ruppert and Huston's first move was to appoint Harry Sparrow, a close friend of McGraw, to be the team's business manager. They then went after Detroit Tigers manager Hughie Jennings to be the new field boss, but Tigers owner Frank Navin refused to let Jennings go. As a second choice, Jennings recommended "Wild Bill" Donovan, one of his star pitchers at Detroit and more recently the manager of the International League's Providence Grays. The Yankees accepted Jennings's advice and hired Donovan, who, like every previous Yankees' manager except George Stallings, assumed the role of player/manager. Donovan had not pitched in the major leagues since 1912, yet he would put himself into nine games for New York in 1915, losing his only three decisions. He also would pitch one game in 1916, which would be the last time a Yankees' manager would play in a league game until catcher Bill Dickey in 1946.

The club's debut under its new ownership was in Washington, where Walter Johnson shut them out, 7–0, allowing just two hits. Johnson was baseball's greatest pitcher, yet after slipping a bit in 1914, he looked at this season as one of redemption. The extent of Johnson's "slippage" was this: although his 28 victories again led the American League, it was the first time in three years his win total had slipped below 30; and his earned run average, which at 1.72 was third best in the league, was the highest it had been since 1911. After the season ended, Johnson became baseball's biggest off-season story when he turned down a 1915 salary offer he felt was below his worth and signed to play for the Federal League's Chicago Whales. The Federal League had been offering huge salaries in an attempt to sign established major-league stars for the past two years, and now they had landed one of the biggest—or so it seemed. Clark Griffith, Johnson's friend and manager, acted quickly. After contemplating the potential loss to Washington and the American League of one of its biggest stars (and biggest drawing cards), Griffith persuaded Senators president Benjamin Minor to make Johnson a new offer. Minor may also have been pushed to do so—and perhaps even helped financially—by Chicago White Sox owner Charles Comiskey, who feared competing at the gate against a team that included Walter Johnson.

After receiving Washington's new proposal, Johnson reneged on his contract with Chicago and re-signed with the Senators. Johnson, an inordinately decent and honorable man, felt that he had done wrong by backing out of his Federal League contract. Still, he considered it a lesser wrong than it would have been to abandon Washington. Throughout the off-season, the Federal League threatened legal action, but in the end they did nothing further to prevent Johnson from playing with the Senators. If he had illegally violated his contract, the Feds were not pursuing it. While Johnson had no legal problems, he still had to wonder what the fan reaction would be to his Federal League adventure. Today's crowd quickly dispelled any uncertainties he may have had. They began to cheer him the moment he walked on the field and continued to do so all afternoon.

A recent study by the Census Bureau had concluded that Washington, D.C., was among the few American municipalities whose revenues exceeded its costs. Most other cities, said the Bureau, were living beyond their means. Yet despite their obvious dedication and austerity, it was not unusual for some of Washington's government employees and schoolchildren to forego their duties on Opening Day and head for the ballpark, just like folks in the less fiscally responsible municipalities. Today, however, the government workers and schoolchildren among the 15,556 fans at National Park were there legitimately. All government offices and schools in the District of Columbia were closed in memory of the 50th anniversary of Abraham Lincoln's assassination. The recollection of that tragic event did not prevent the hometown fans from enjoying themselves. And they had much to cheer about, for after the first inning a Washington win was never in doubt.

Even with the game being so one-sided, the guest of honor, President Woodrow Wilson, stayed for the full nine innings. Accompanying Mr. Wilson, a widower since the previous August, were his first cousin, Miss Helen Woodrow Bones, Mrs. Norman Galt (who would become Wilson's second wife), Captain Cary Grayson, USN, and Secretary to the President Joseph P. Tumulty. Sitting nearby was the usual turnout of high government officials. Today they included Secretary of the Navy Josephus Daniels, Secretary of the Interior Franklin K. Lane, Secretary of War Lindley M. Garrison, and Secretary of State William Jennings Bryan, a man who rarely attended baseball games. The president chatted with his companions throughout the afternoon and displayed his knowledge of baseball by explaining to them what was happening on the field. He also showed his growing familiarity with the game's customs by being among the first to rise to his feet in the home seventh. Wilson had spent the morning reading reports of what was so far the biggest battle of the war in Europe; more than a million men had fought for a ridge that separated Galicia from Hungary. Now that the war was intensifying, he also had to consider the proper response to Germany's request that the United States decide whether it was neutral or an enemy of Germany. But he put the affairs of state aside temporarily and arrived at the park at 2:40 P.M. The Marine Band struck up "The Star-Spangled Banner" as the crowd stood and removed their hats. Griffith and Minor welcomed Wilson, while motion picture and still photographers recorded the event. Wilson made the first-ball toss, intending it for Johnson, who was standing with the other players in front of the presidential box. However, as he released the ball, umpires Billy Evans and Dominic Mullaney (in his only American League season) walked in front of the players. Evans, surprised to see the ball coming at him, caught it and quickly flipped it to Johnson.

The Yankees best scoring opportunity against Johnson came in the first inning, the only inning in which they got a runner as far as third base. With two men out and Hugh High on second base via a walk and a steal, Wally Pipp lined a single to left. Howard Shanks, the left fielder, got to the ball quickly and threw it home, holding High at third as Pipp took second. The chance to get an early lead on Johnson, usually something you had to do to beat him, ended as Doc Cook grounded to shortstop George McBride. Jeff Sweeney's two-out single in the second inning would be the Yankees' only other hit. Left fielder High and first baseman Pipp, both obtained on waivers from Detroit on February 4, were impressive in their Yankees' debuts. High walked in his first three at-bats, stole two bases, and exhibited excellent speed in the outfield. Pipp, along with his first-inning single, showed fine defensive work at first base. A few years earlier, Pipp had attended nearby Catholic University, which today was celebrating its 25th anniversary, though it had opened officially in November 1889. Among the dignitaries in Washington for the festivities were James Cardinal Gibbons of Baltimore, John Cardinal Farley of New York, and William Cardinal O'Connell of Boston.

Ray Caldwell was the Yankees best pitcher and the logical opening-day starter. However, because of his wife's illness Caldwell was back in New York, so Donovan opened with veteran right-hander Jack Warhop. Known as "Crab" for his surly disposition, Warhop was beginning the eighth and final year of his major-league career, all with the Yankees. He would establish his place in baseball history three weeks later in a game against Boston when he yielded Babe Ruth's first big-league home run.

The Senators scored the only run Johnson would need today in their first at-bat. Danny Moeller walked and Eddie Foster singled, putting runners at first and second with no one out. After Clyde Milan moved the runners up with a sacrifice, Alva Williams drove a ball high and deep to left field. It had the look of a home run, but the wind held it up allowing High, with his great speed, to make the catch. Moeller tagged up and trotted home with the run. A walk to Ray Morgan and a double by Eddie Ainsmith made it 2–0 in the fourth inning. The Senators added three more in the fifth. Moeller and Foster opened with infield singles, and one out later Williams singled to load the bases. Morgan hit a liner to right field that Cook started in on and then watched sail over his head for a bases-clearing triple. Washington added single runs in the seventh and eighth innings against Warhop, who pitched the entire game.

The Yankees had only one scoring opportunity after the first inning. In the fifth, Sweeney was on second and High on first with two out when Birdie Cree lined a ball waist-high between first baseman Williams and second baseman Morgan. Williams, normally a catcher, was playing first base because of an injury to Chick Gandil. He dove to his right, the glove on his left hand extended across his body, and snared the ball. Johnson needed no further help as he retired the last nine batters consecutively. When the game was over, Griffith presented President Wilson with a bat and ball for his grandson, Francis Sayre. Sayre, the last child born in the White House, would grow up to become dean of the Episcopal Cathedral in Washington.

For the first time ever, the Yankees led the American League in home runs with 31, but still finished in fifth place (69–83), 32½ games behind the Boston Red Sox. Shortstop Roger Peckinpaugh and second baseman Luke Boone led the team in home runs with five each.

Wednesday, April 14, 1915

New York

	ab	r	h	po	a	e
Maisel 3b	4	0	0	1	2	1
High lf	1	0	0	5	0	1
Cree cf	4	0	0	3	0	0
Pipp 1b	4	0	1	7	0	0
Cook rf	4	0	0	1	1	0
Peckinpaugh ss	4	0	0	4	1	0
Boone 2b	3	0	0	0	3	0

Washington

	ab	r	h	po	a	e
Moeller rf	3	2	2	2	0	0
Foster 3b	4	1	2	1	3	0
Milan cf	2	1	1	2	0	0
Williams 1b	4	1	2	14	0	0
Morgan 2b	1	1	1	1	1	1
Shanks lf	3	0	0	3	0	0
McBride ss	3	0	1	1	4	0

New York	ab	r	h	po	a	e		Washington	ab	r	h	po	a	e
Sweeney c	3	0	1	3	0	0		Ainsmith c	4	1	2	3	0	0
Warhop p	3	0	0	0	4	0		Johnson p	4	0	1	0	4	0
Total	30	0	2	24	11	2		Total	28	7	12	27	12	1

New York	000	000	000–0
Washington	100	130	11X–7

Two-base hit—Ainsmith. Three-base hit—Morgan. Sacrifice hits—Milan, Shanks, Moeller. Sacrifice flies—Foster, Williams, Morgan. Stolen bases—High (2). Double play—Cook and Pipp. Left on bases—Washington, 9; New York, 6. First base on balls—off Warhop, 4; off Johnson, 3. First base on errors—New York, 1; Washington, 2. Hit by pitcher—by Warhop (Morgan). Time of game—1 hr. 42 min. Umpires—Messrs. Evans and Mullaney.

Wednesday, April 12, 1916
Polo Grounds, New York
Washington 3 New York 2 (11 Innings)

It is our true policy to steer clear of permanent alliance
with any portion of the foreign world.—George Washington

In his 1796 Farewell Address, President George Washington had warned Americans about the dangers of "permanent alliances" with foreign powers. His countrymen heeded that advice and for the next 120 years avoided the seemingly never-ending European conflicts—including the one currently devastating the continent. While the old men of the warring nations talked of glory and national honor, the young men of those nations continued to senselessly slaughter each other. Three days earlier, 3,000 British soldiers died in a battle with Turkish forces near Fallahiya, Mesopotamia, while in France, the French government, safely ensconced in Paris, ordered their defenders at Verdun "to stand firm and die rather than yield." This morning, a less war-like speech by British prime minister Herbert Asquith raised hopes throughout the world for an early peace settlement. But there would be no quick end to the war, and by Opening Day 1917, the United States, too, would be involved. However, this was Opening Day 1916 and most Americans were more interested in the return of baseball than they were in the war in Europe. They were optimistic we would stay out of that war, and those who were baseball fans were optimistic about the new season. But then, baseball fans are optimistic at the start of every new season; all it takes are a few new faces in the lineup to convince them this year's team is better than last year's. Typically, this is just the normal enthusiasm born of spring and Opening Day. When it becomes apparent that this year's players are no better than last year's, the excitement begins to fade. Although that sometimes happens as early as Opening Day, the "hope springs eternal" attitude remains at the heart of fan involvement. Should it ever disappear, the grip that baseball has had on the American public for more than a century would be lost.

That invigorating sense of opening-day optimism was discernible in the faces of the more than 20,000 Yankees fans at the Polo Grounds this pleasantly cool day. It was there when they started lining up long before the gates opened, and was still there after the 11-

inning, 3–2 loss to Walter Johnson and the Senators. Despite five consecutive finishes in the second division, the fans realized, as did the rest of the league, that the Yankees' fortunes would soon be on the rise. The club's new owners were determined to have a winning team, and more important, they were willing to spend money to get one. Since buying the Yankees, Jacob Ruppert and Til Huston had acquired several players in cash transactions. First came Bob Shawkey, purchased from Connie Mack, who had begun to dismantle his great Philadelphia Athletics team to build up his treasury. In July 1915 the Yankees paid Mack $3,000 for the promising young pitcher. Then in early 1916 they added Lee Magee and Frank "Home Run" Baker. Magee, the ex-player/manager for the Brooklyn Tip-Tops of the now defunct Federal League, was the first player who had jumped to the Federal League to be welcomed back to "organized baseball." The Yankees paid the Athletics $37,500 for Baker, despite his absence from the game in 1915. Baker, in protest against Mack's player sales and the salary offered him, had spent the entire season at his farm in Trappe, on Maryland's Eastern Shore. More than anything, it was the arrival of Baker that raised the fans' expectations. Even with the one-year layoff (he did play some semi-pro ball in Pennsylvania), he was still among the game's biggest stars. Prior to his sit-out, Baker had won or tied for the league home-run crown for four consecutive years (1911–1914), a title no Yankees' player had ever won even once. Foremost among those gone from New York to make room for the new acquisitions was the popular Birdie Cree. The tiny outfielder batted .292 in his eight-year major-league career, all spent with the Yankees.

As the players came out for batting practice, the fans greeted them warmly, saving their loudest cheers for Baker. The Yankees were in the pinstriped home uniforms they had started wearing again in 1915 (after abandoning them in 1913–1914), but the stripes were now blue instead of black. When the home-team players first stepped onto the field, Frank's Brass Band, which had entertained Senators' manager Clark Griffith with Scottish tunes, switched to Irish melodies in honor of Yankees manager Bill Donovan. The band later concluded their day's work with a rousing rendition of *The Stars and Stripes* that brought everyone in the park to his feet. There were noticeably fewer women in the crowd this year. Perhaps, as Heywood Broun speculated in the *New York Tribune*, it was because "women were growing increasingly frank and were no longer afraid to say that they don't care about baseball."

Ruppert and Huston walked Al Smith, the sheriff of New York County, across the field to the box seats where he threw out the first ball. Smith, who 12 years later would be the Democratic Party's candidate for president, shook hands with everyone nearby, both before and after the ceremony. His throw, as poor as any seen at the Polo Grounds in recent years, took several bounces before it reached catcher Les Nunamaker. Jeff Sweeney, the opening-day catcher for the previous three years, was now with the Toledo Iron Men of the American Association. His absence prompted Irvin S. Cobb of the *New York American* to write, "any team missing Sweeney had to be better."

New York was drawing Johnson as its opening-day opponent for the third time in four years. Donovan responded by choosing his best pitcher, Ray Caldwell, a 19-game winner (19–16) in 1915. Caldwell came through with a tough, gritty performance, but like George McConnell's effort on Opening Day 1913, it was not good enough to beat Johnson. The Senators' ace allowed only five hits, did not walk anyone, and struck out ten. Caldwell began the game by walking leadoff batter Ray Morgan on four pitches. Eddie Foster followed with a smash down the third base line that Baker turned into a snappy double play via second baseman Joe Gedeon and first baseman Wally Pipp. The fans had no sooner stopped applauding this fine play by their new hero when veteran center fielder Clyde Milan hit a slow curve ball into the seats in right for a home run. Through six innings, Johnson protected the 1–0 lead provided by his longtime roommate and best friend. He had shut out the Yanks in the opener at Washington a year ago, and the crowd seemed resigned to seeing him do it again. To this point he had faced only 19 batters, one above the minimum, and held them to just two hits. Baker, in his first at-bat as a Yankee, got the first hit, a single to left leading off the second. He tried to stretch it into a double, but was out on a good throw by left fielder Howard Shanks. The other hit was a one-out single by Nunamaker in the sixth.

When New York came to bat in the seventh, their prospects looked even bleaker. The Senators had added a run in their half on George McBride's double to left, a sacrifice bunt by Johnson, and Morgan's single to center. Now trailing 2–0, right fielder Frank Gilhooley led off the home seventh with a hit on a little squibber that shortstop McBride could not handle. McBride, quite a popular player in Washington, was in his ninth and final season as the Senators' everyday shortstop. A weak hitter but an outstanding defensive player, he had led the league in fielding in each of the four previous seasons. Magee followed with an infield hit on a ground ball inside the first base bag. Joe Judge came up with the ball, and though Johnson was late in getting to first, he appeared to have beaten Magee. Umpire Brick Owens, in his American League debut, called the runner safe. Owens, who was early in an umpiring career that would last for 25 years, later admitted that he blew the call. First baseman Judge was in his first full year with Washington, where he would remain through the 1932 season. A Brooklyn native, he had honed his skills in New York playing for the Edison Company team.

The two infield hits put Yankees' runners at first and second with nobody out and the dangerous "Home Run" Baker coming up. McBride, the Washington captain, called time and went to the mound to discuss the situation with Johnson. The fans were imploring Baker to hit one into the seats, but Johnson was a difficult man to hit home runs against. He would pitch a league-leading 369⅔ innings in 1916 and not allow even one. Baker did manage to get around on a fastball, lashing a sharp single to right that scored Gilhooley and sent Magee to third. The next batter was Gedeon, purchased in January from Salt Lake City of the Pacific Coast League. Gedeon, who had brief stints with the Senators in 1913–1914, hit a fly ball to Milan in center field deep enough to allow Magee to score after the catch. People in the streets blocks away from the Polo Grounds could hear the cheers that erupted as the tying run came across the plate. That, however, was the end of the Yankees' offense for the day. From then on, Johnson did not allow a single base runner.

Washington threatened to go ahead in the tenth, but Caldwell showed great tenacity in pitching his way out of a first-and-third, none-out situation. Morgan was at third and Foster at first, both with singles, when Pipp turned Milan's grounder into a rundown play that retired Morgan. Caldwell then fanned Judge on a 3–2 pitch and got Shanks on a pop to Nunamaker. It had been a difficult inning for Caldwell, one that seemed to take a lot out of him. Nevertheless, Donovan sent him out to pitch the 11th. Caldwell allowed leadoff batter Charlie Jamieson to reach base with an infield single that he got a glove on but could not hold. Seeking greater speed on the bases, Griffith had Danny Moeller run for Jamieson. After Alva Williams fouled out to Nunamaker, McBride hit a sharp grounder to third. It looked like a sure double play, but Gedeon dropped Baker's quick throw to second and both runners were safe. It was Gedeon's second error of the day, and the Yankees' third. Caldwell got Johnson on a fly to Magee for the second out; however, he could not get by

Morgan. The Senators' second baseman got his third hit of the day, a single to center that easily scored Moeller with the game-winning run. Although disappointed at losing, the fans were pleased with the spirit of the team and the performances of the new players. Hope was very much alive.

> *New York had its first winning season in five years, finishing fourth (80–74), 11 games behind the Boston Red Sox. Wally Pipp became the first Yankee to lead the league in home runs, with 12. Frank Baker was the runner-up with ten. The Yankees hit 35 home runs to again lead the American League. Bob Shawkey's 24 wins were only one behind the leader, Walter Johnson.*

Wednesday, April 12, 1916

Washington

	ab	r	h	po	a	e
Morgan 2b	5	0	3	3	3	0
Foster 3b	6	0	1	0	2	0
Milan cf	5	1	1	5	0	0
Judge 1b	4	0	0	7	1	0
Shanks lf	5	0	1	3	1	0
Jamieson rf	5	0	1	2	0	0
Moeller pr, rf	0	1	0	0	0	0
Williams c	5	0	2	10	0	0
McBride ss	5	1	1	3	0	0
Johnson p	2	0	0	0	2	0
Total	42	3	10	33	9	0

New York

	ab	r	h	po	a	e
Maisel cf	5	0	0	3	0	0
Gilhooley rf	4	1	1	2	0	0
Magee lf	4	1	1	4	0	0
Baker 3b	4	0	2	3	2	0
Gedeon 2b	3	0	0	5	3	2
Pipp 1b	4	0	0	6	2	0
Peckinpaugh ss	4	0	0	1	1	0
Nunamaker c	4	0	1	9	2	1
Caldwell p	4	0	0	0	1	0
Total	36	2	5	33	11	3

Washington	100	000	100	01–3
New York	000	000	200	00–2

Two-base hits—Williams, McBride. Home run—Milan. Stolen bases—Morgan, Baker. Sacrifice hit—Johnson. Sacrifice fly—Gedeon. Double play—Baker, Gedeon, and Pipp. Left on bases—New York, 2; Washington, 11. First base on error—Washington, 1. Bases on balls—off Caldwell, 4. Earned runs—off Caldwell, 2; off Johnson, 2. Struck out—by Caldwell, 5; by Johnson, 10. Wild pitch—Caldwell. Umpires—Messrs. Connolly and Owens. Time of game—2 hrs. 30 min.

Wednesday, April 11, 1917
Polo Grounds, New York
Boston 10 New York 3

> *The world must be made safe for democracy.*—Woodrow Wilson

Pregame parades had been an integral part of opening-day ceremonies for as long as most fans could remember. The march of the players across the newly grown grass to raise the flag was symbolic of the American people's love of country and of their joy at the return of spring and baseball. However, no baseball fan had ever seen a pregame parade like the one that preceded the 1917 Yankees–Red Sox season opener at the Polo Grounds. Instead of the usual disorganized stroll to the flagpole by players and dignitaries, the crowd of approximately 20,000 saw squads of Yankees' players parade around the field while executing a precise set of military drills. It was a sight they would remember long after they had forgotten today's final score, a 10–3 Boston victory. The motivation for this display of martial posturing had occurred the previous week, on April 6, when the United States officially declared war on Germany. Since the outbreak of the European war in August 1914, President Woodrow Wilson, reflecting the wishes of most of his fellow citizens, had kept America neutral. Even after 128 Americans died when a German submarine torpedoed the British passenger liner RMS Lusitania on May 7, 1915, Wilson withstood the calls for revenge and maintained our neutrality. Then, in March 1917, there occurred a combination of events that persuaded the president to issue his declaration of war. First, the sinking of several American merchant ships by German submarines began to move public opinion away from neutrality and toward supporting Great Britain. The second impetus to war was the revelation that the German government had attempted to get Mexico to join with them in an alliance against the United States.

Much like people all over America, the crowd at the Polo Grounds was flushed with patriotism and supremely confident that our entry on the side of the Allies would assure a quick victory. Just this morning, Secretary of State Robert Lansing had announced that British Foreign Minister Arthur Balfour and Marshal of France Joseph Joffre would lead their nation's delegations to the United States for a Joint War Council. But while these aged leaders planned and talked, young British, French, and German soldiers were fighting and dying along a 120-mile front east of Rheims, France. Meanwhile, from Russia came news that seemed insignificant, but would eventually alter the course of the twentieth century: the anti-czarist Council of Workmen and Soldiers had suggested their country should exit the war.

While the death and maiming of America's young men had yet to begin, people were beginning to see signs that their lives would be changing. There was an announcement today by the National Defense Council that Herbert Hoover, who had been heading the American Commission for Relief in Belgium, had accepted their offer to be chairman of a newly created Food Board in the United States. And here in New York, Governor Charles S. Whitman announced the formation of a Division of Aliens in the adjutant-general's office. Its job would be to keep track of aliens and to shift alien workers from strategic to nonstrategic industries. Even the nation's sporting calendar would be affected: Vanderbilt University and the University of Florida joined many other schools in announcing that because of the war they were canceling all 1917 athletic events. By 1918 the war's influence would spread to baseball's schedule and personnel, but for this season the game remained largely unchanged.

The Polo Grounds looked wonderfully inviting this Opening Day, a warming sight after a long winter without baseball. It was, of course, completely decorated with American flags, and thanks to the work of groundskeeper Henry Fabian and his crew, the grass was a perfect shade of green. Even the advertisements on the outfield fences were new, with the only discordant note the clock in right field, which was not working. There had been a spring snowstorm in New York two days earlier and a chill from the storm remained in the air through the morning. However, by one o'clock, when the gates to the park opened, the temperature had warmed considerably, and people began shedding their heavy coats. As the Yankees, led by a United States Army sergeant, emerged from a gate under the Polo Grounds bleachers, the fans greeted them with a raucous cheer. The players, marching in perfect formation, were smartly dressed in their home-whites with blue pinstripes. (The "NY" logo had been removed from the left breast during the 1916 season and would not reappear for 20 years.) Each player carried a bat on his shoulder as if it were a rifle. Following their series of drills, the columns passed in review before Major General Leonard Wood. To conclude their exercises, the players "presented arms" with their bats while Frank's Band played "The Star-Spangled Banner." At the suggestion of their co-owner, Captain Til Huston, the players had been practicing these drills for more than a month. So, in varying degrees, had most other teams. Among American League clubs, only the champion Red Sox failed to have an Army NCO drill and instruct them in military formations. The Boston players, who watched the Yankees while standing in ragged disorder around the plate, seemed dejected at not having taken part and enthusiastically joined the crowd in applauding the New Yorkers.

After the Yankees broke ranks, Huston and Jacob Ruppert introduced each player to General Wood. Earlier, the general had been telling reporters and anyone else who would listen how disturbed he was by the failure of the Army's volunteer system. He was calling for the nation to implement some type of universal military service. Once the assembly of photographers, loaded down with their cameras and tripods, left the field, General Wood threw out the first ball. It was high, but umpire Tom Connolly leaped and grabbed it, saving the general some embarrassment. Connolly tossed it to Ray Caldwell, who was again manager Bill Donovan's opening-day pitcher. Connolly's umpiring partner this day was Barry McCormick. The former 10-year big league infielder was making his American League debut after serving two years as an umpire in the Federal League. It would be his only season in the AL.

The Red Sox got right at it, jumping on Caldwell for two first-inning runs. Leadoff batter Harry Hooper, with two strikes on him, took a very close pitch that Connolly called a ball. Caldwell glared down at the umpire, visibly upset, and on the next pitch Hooper singled to right. He moved to second on a sacrifice by Boston's new manager, Jack Barry, and to third on an infield single by Dick Hoblitzell. Caldwell whiffed Duffy Lewis, but Tilly Walker hit a long drive over the head of center fielder Lee Magee for a two-run triple. Barry, the managerial replacement for Bill Carrigan, had come to the Red Sox in 1915 in one of Connie Mack's player sales. Despite leading the team to two successive world championships, Carrigan had quit the game to take up a financial career in Maine. Although Barry had been the shortstop in Philadelphia's $100,000 infield, the Red Sox had young Everett Scott playing short, so Barry moved to second.

In just over six years from this day, on Opening Day 1923, Babe Ruth would hit the first home run in the newly opened Yankee Stadium. However, for his first opener in New York, Ruth, 22, was Boston's starting pitcher and already recognized as the best left-hander in baseball. He had capped a 23–12 year in 1916 by winning the longest game in World Series history, a record later equaled twice. In Game Two of Boston's five-game Series triumph, Ruth beat Brooklyn's Sherry Smith 2–1 in 14 innings. He began the 1917 season by exhibiting that same form, setting the Yankees down on three singles. His only difficulty came in the fourth inning when a walk, a hit batter, Barry's error, and a single led to the Yankees three runs. Fritz Maisel opened the inning by drawing a walk. Maisel, who in previous openers had played third base and center field, was at second base today. The Yankees weren't sure if he could play the position, but Donovan wanted his speed in the lineup and was giving him the opportunity to take the job away from Joe Gedeon. A year earlier, at the 1916 winter meetings, the Yankees seemingly had a chance to acquire either Joe Jackson from the White Sox or Tris Speaker from the Red Sox. Both clubs wanted Maisel included in the deal, and in each case the Yankees, believing Maisel had more productive years remaining than either Jackson or Speaker, refused to make the trade. Following the season, they included both Maisel and Gedeon in a deal that brought second baseman Del Pratt from the Browns.

Wednesday, April 11, 1917

Boston	ab	r	h	po	a	e	New York	ab	r	h	po	a	e
Hooper rf	5	3	3	1	0	0	Gilhooley rf	4	0	1	1	0	0
Barry 2b	3	2	2	2	4	1	High lf	4	0	0	2	0	0
Hoblitzell 1b	3	2	2	12	0	0	Maisel 2b	3	1	0	2	2	0
Lewis lf	5	1	2	2	0	0	Pipp 1b	3	1	0	10	1	0
Walker cf	5	0	3	3	0	0	Baker 3b	4	1	0	2	2	0
Gardner 3b	4	0	1	1	3	0	Magee cf	3	0	0	3	0	0
Scott ss	4	0	0	5	2	0	Peckinpaugh ss	4	0	1	2	2	0
Thomas c	3	1	0	1	1	0	Nunamaker c	4	0	0	4	0	0
Ruth p	4	1	1	0	4	0	Caldwell p	2	0	1	1	4	0
Total	36	10	14	27	14	1	Total	31	3	3	27	11	0

```
Boston        200    001    403–10
New York      000    300    000–3
```

Two-base hits—Walker, Lewis. Three base hits—Walker, 2. Home run—Hoblitzell. Stolen base—Hoblitzell. Sacrifice hits—Barry, Hoblitzell, 2. Sacrifice fly—Barry. Double play—Maisel, Peckinpaugh, and Pipp. Left on bases—New York, 5; Boston, 5. First base on error—New York, 1. Bases on balls—off Caldwell, 2; off Ruth, 3. Earned runs—off Caldwell, 10; off Ruth, 2. Hit by pitcher—by Ruth (Pipp). Struck out—by Caldwell, 3; by Ruth, 1. Wild pitch—Caldwell. Umpires—Messrs. Connolly and McCormick. Time of game—2 hrs. 3 min.

With Maisel on first, one of Ruth's pitches grazed the arm of Wally Pipp, sending him to first and Maisel to second. Ruth and catcher Pinch Thomas argued vociferously that the ball had not touched Pipp, but Connolly stuck to his call. Frank Baker followed with a ground ball to Barry at second. Barry tried to tag Pipp, but the runner stopped after a few steps and began retreating to first base. Barry started to chase him before finally throwing the ball. The throw was wild, high over first baseman Hoblitzell's head, allowing Maisel to score, Pipp to take third, and Baker to take second. After Magee made the second out, Roger Peckinpaugh lined a single to center scoring Pipp and Baker, and the Yankees had a 3–2 lead.

When Boston came to bat in the seventh inning, the score was 3–3. The Sox had tied it in the sixth on a single by Barry, a sacrifice by Hoblitzell, and a double by Walker. Caldwell walked Thomas to begin the seventh and then fanned Ruth. Hooper topped a ball down the third base line that third baseman Baker could only watch and wish to go foul. It didn't, and the Red Sox had runners at first and second. Barry followed with a slow roller to the right side that Pipp fielded but was forced to hold as Caldwell failed to cover first base. Thomas, running full out, came all the way around to score. Hoblitzell then unloaded a home run into the right field seats, scoring Hooper and Barry ahead of him and giving Boston a 7–3 lead. Caldwell was still on the mound in the ninth when singles by Ruth and Hooper, a double by Lewis, and a triple by Walker led to three additional Boston runs. Walker, with a double, two triples, and four runs batted in, and Hoblitzell, with a three-run home run, were the batting stars for Boston. Walker was the player the Red Sox purchased from the St. Louis Browns in 1916 to replace Tris Speaker. Following the end of this season, the Sox sent him to Philadelphia as part of a four-man trade that brought Stuffy McInnis to Boston. For Hoblitzell, the home run was his only one this year and the last of his career, which ended during the 1918 season.

After improving their position in the standings in each of the previous four years, the Yankees (71–82) fell to sixth place, 28½ games behind the Chicago White Sox. Wally Pipp won his second straight home-run crown, although he had only nine, and the Yankees led the league in home runs for the third consecutive year. Following their disappointing finish, Colonel Ruppert fired manager Bill Donovan and hired Miller Huggins.

Monday, April 15, 1918
National Park, Washington
New York 6 Washington 3

When a true genius appears in the world, you may know him by this sign,
that the dunces are all in confederacy against him. —Jonathan Swift

Colonel Jacob Ruppert's October 25, 1917 announcement that he had given Miller Huggins a two-year contract to manage the Yankees ignited a wave of criticism in the New York press. The writers had expected the club to go after a "bigger" name, for although Huggins had played for 13 years in the National League and managed the St. Louis Cardinals since 1913, he was relatively unknown in New York. Co-owner Til Huston found Ruppert's choice of Huggins particularly distressful; he wanted to replace Bill Donovan with an old friend, Brooklyn manager Wilbert Robinson. However, Huston, a Spanish-American War veteran, was away in France serving with the American Expeditionary Forces. Huston had enlisted the day after Congress had declared war. Meanwhile, American League president Ban Johnson—still trying to make a winner of the New York franchise—persuaded Ruppert to select Huggins. Johnson, upset that Huggins's former team, the Cardinals, had signed Branch Rickey away from the American League's St. Louis Browns the year before, could not pass up an opportunity to lure a good man away from the National League. Huston, who already had a low opinion of Johnson, was extremely disappointed when he learned his partner had selected Johnson's man rather than his. The New York sportswriters, who by their sheer numbers wielded a great deal of power—Washington Senators manager Clark Griffith still believed they were responsible for many of his problems when he managed the Yankees—also were disappointed, but for another reason. They had been fond of Donovan and would have preferred someone like him, someone who was more outgoing and gregarious. In Huggins they were getting a quiet, introspective man who had a law degree and was not likely to become their drinking buddy. Most of what they wrote about Huggins in the winter of 1917–1918 compared him unfavorably to Giants manager John McGraw, the Lord of Baseball in New York.

The Yankees' "Huggins era," among the most successful in club history, began appropriately enough with a win. On a lovely day in Washington, George Mogridge and Allen Russell pitched the Yanks to a 6–3 victory over the Senators and Walter Johnson. The United States was now a fully committed participant in the European War and its citizens had become accustomed to reading daily reports from the battlefront. This morning's story told of how U.S. forces, although outnumbered two-to-one, had repelled a German attack on the right bank of the Meuse River north of St. Mihiel, France. Yet, not all the news was good; the Germans had captured Helsingfors (Helsinki), the Finnish capital. Also there were the latest casualty lists from France. Today that list included 20 New Yorkers from the 69th Infantry Regiment, which had been sent to France in October 1917 as part of the

42nd Rainbow Division. On another page of their morning newspaper (as the wheels of commerce rolled on), New Yorkers could read an advertisement for "the most approved and smart spring styles and materials for the various periods of mourning." These styles were on display in the private salon of the Stern Brothers Department Store on West 42nd Street, across from the majestic New York Public Library.

The war's impact on baseball would be much stronger this season. Before it was over, Provost Marshal Enoch Crowder's "work or fight order" would force many players to leave their teams to either enter the military or take a job in a defense-related industry. Even the ritual appearance of the president to throw out the first ball in Washington's opener had to be canceled. Because of the constant demands that the war made on his time, President Wilson was unable to attend. The president also had to forgo another of his traditional duties this day. Secretary of State Robert Lansing substituted for Wilson at the opening of the Daughters of the American Revolution's 27th Continental Congress. While the president was absent this afternoon, there was the usual assembly of important government officials present. Also on hand, as they always were at Senators' openers, were delegations from the Board of Trade, the Chamber of Commerce, and other Washington area civic associations. The lovely spring weather helped attract a crowd of close to 13,000, one of the largest in Washington in recent years. Patches of empty seats were visible only in the upper grandstand on the third-base side and in the pavilion. The crowd was particularly enthusiastic, and though many Yankees fans were here, one that was overwhelmingly rooting for the Senators. This was not always the case in Washington, whose population included many transplants. More people cheered for the visiting team here than in any other major-league city.

In keeping with the times, the pregame activities included Army sergeant Harry Marshall soliciting subscriptions for U.S. bonds, while a biplane scattered thousands of liberty loan cards. There were other martial aspects to the festivities; military music accompanied the flag raising in center field as players from both clubs stood at attention in front of their benches. The Yankees' uniforms included red, white, and blue armbands on their left sleeves. The only major league team to commemorate the war in this way, they would wear the armband all season. Louis Brownlow, a commissioner of the District of Columbia, substituted for the president in throwing out the first ball.

Walter Johnson was making his eighth opening-day start for Washington, the last seven consecutively. Johnson's win-loss record in his previous openers was 6–1, with four shutouts. To oppose him, Huggins had planned to use Ray Caldwell, but after watching Caldwell warm up, he changed his mind. He decided to hold Caldwell out for one more day and use Mogridge, a tall, thin left-hander who had won nine games and lost 11 in 1917. In their three previous openers against Johnson, all of which they lost, the Yankees had scored just three runs in 29 innings. This afternoon, they almost matched that in their first at-bat, scoring twice. It looked to be a routine inning for Johnson; there were two out and a runner at first (Elmer Miller's infield single) as he faced Wally Pipp. But second baseman Ray Morgan played Pipp's slowly hit grounder too casually, and Pipp, running hard all the way, beat it out. Frank Baker followed by lining a full-count fastball into right field to score Miller and send Pipp to third. Pipp scored the second run when third baseman Eddie Foster booted Ping Bodie's easy ground ball. Bodie, born Francesco Pezzolo, was the first of a succession of San Francisco area players, many of Italian heritage, who would find their way to the Yankees. He had come to New York during spring training in a three-team deal in which the Yankees purchased George Burns from the Tigers and then traded him to the Athletics for Bodie. Earlier, in his first major move as manager, Huggins traded five players to the St. Louis Browns for second baseman Del Pratt and pitcher Eddie Plank. The Yankees gave up infielders Joe Gedeon and Fritz Maisel; catcher Les Nunamaker; pitchers Nick Cullop and Urban Shocker; as well as $15,000. Plank, as expected, immediately retired. Huggins would come to regret the trading of Shocker (he became a four-time 20-game winner for the Browns) and would bring him back to New York in 1925.

Pratt opened the third inning with a bloop single to right. He moved to second on Pipp's single to center, and when Baker followed with his second line single to right, Pratt scored. Later in the inning, Roger Peckinpaugh's fly ball brought Pipp home with New York's fourth run.

Washington rallied against Mogridge in the fourth inning, scoring three runs and knocking him out of the game. With one down, they filled the bases: Clyde Milan walked, Howard Shanks got his second single, and Joe Judge hit a pop-fly single to left. Morgan's little tapper was turned into an out as Milan was forced at home, but Doc Lavan got an infield single to score Shanks with the Senators' first run. Two more came across on catcher Eddie Ainsmith's solid hit to left, making the score 4–3 and finishing Mogridge. Huggins brought in right-hander Allen Russell, who walked Johnson to reload the bases but allowed no further scoring.

Monday, April 15, 1918

New York	ab	r	h	po	a	e	Washington	ab	r	h	po	a	e
Gilhooley rf	5	1	1	2	0	0	Shotton rf	4	0	0	1	0	0
Miller cf	4	1	3	2	0	0	Foster 3b	5	0	0	2	2	1
Pratt 2b	4	1	1	1	5	0	Milan cf	3	0	0	1	0	0
Pipp 1b	5	2	2	13	0	0	Shanks lf	4	1	3	6	1	0
Baker 3b	3	0	2	0	3	0	Judge 1b	3	1	1	9	0	0
Bodie lf	4	0	0	1	0	0	Morgan 2b	3	1	0	5	0	0
Peckinpaugh ss	3	0	0	1	1	0	Lavan ss	4	0	1	0	4	1
Hannah c	3	1	1	7	0	0	Ainsmith c	3	0	1	3	1	0
Mogridge p	1	0	0	0	4	0	Johnson p	1	0	0	0	6	0
Russell p	2	0	1	0	2	0	ᵃAcosta	1	0	0	0	0	0
Total	34	6	11	27	15	0	Total	31	3	6	27	14	2

ᵃBatted for Johnson in ninth.

New York	202	000	020–6
Washington	000	300	000–3

Two-base hit—Gilhooley. Sacrifice hits—Mogridge, Bodie, Pratt, Johnson. Double play—Baker, Pratt, and Pipp. Left on bases—New York, 9; Washington, 8. First base on errors—New York, 1. First base on balls—off Mogridge, 1; off Russell, 5; off Johnson, 5. Hits—off Mogridge, 5 in 3⅔; off Russell, 1 in 5 ⅓. Struck out—by Johnson, 2; by Russell, 2. Passed ball—Ainsmith. Winning pitcher—Mogridge. Losing pitcher—Johnson. Time of game—1 hr. 45 min. Umpires—Messrs. Evans and Nallin.

Johnson settled down through the middle innings, although he was wilder than usual. In the eighth, catcher Truck Hannah led off by drawing Johnson's fifth walk of the game. Having traded Nunamaker, the Yankees were counting on Roxy Walters to do most of the catching this season. But Walters was out with a sore thumb, so Hannah, after nine years in the minor leagues, was making his big-league debut. After three years in New York, Hannah returned to the Pacific Coast League where he remained through the 1938 season. With Hannah at first, Russell dropped a perfect bunt down the third-base line and beat it out for a hit. Frank Gilhooley followed by grounding a double past third baseman Foster that scored Hannah. Huggins, coaching at third, sent Russell home too, but he was out on a fine relay from Shanks to shortstop Lavan to Ainsmith, as Gilhooley took third. Miller's third hit brought Gilhooley home and the Yankees now had a more comfortable 6–3 lead.

Lavan and right fielder Burt Shotton were making their debuts with the Senators after being traded from the Browns. Each would lead the American League in errors at their respective positions in 1918; shortstop Lavan had 57 errors, while Shotton led all outfielders with 18.

The Senators mounted their final threat in the eighth. Shanks, who had an outstanding game in the field and at the bat, got his third hit of the day, a one-out single. It was just the first hit off Russell, but when he followed it by walking Judge and Morgan to load the bases, Caldwell hurriedly began to warm up. However, Russell ended the uprising by getting Lavan on a short fly and fanning Ainsmith with a spitball. Although Mogridge pitched only three and two-thirds innings, the official scorer, following the scoring rules of the day, awarded him the win. It was the first of Mogridge's team-leading 16 wins (16–13) in 1918.

> In deference to the war, the regular season was shortened, ending on September 2. Military service took Yankees pitcher Bob Shawkey for almost the entire season (he pitched in three games) and first baseman Wally Pipp for part of the season. The club finished fourth (60–63), 13½ games behind the Boston Red Sox.

Wednesday, April 23, 1919
Polo Grounds, New York
Boston 10 New York 0

Thence we came forth to see the stars again.—Dante Alighieri

The winter of 1918–1919 had been catastrophic, among the deadliest in human history. Mankind had barely finished commemorating the end of the gruesome war in Europe when a horrendous influenza epidemic swept the world, killing 30–50 million people, including 675,000 in the United States. The epidemic had been especially severe in New York City, but by this sunny late-April day it had subsided and with war and pestilence behind them, New Yorkers were celebrating. For one, the city was welcoming home the USS Harrisburg, with 1,962 officers and men of New York's own Fighting 69th Infantry Regiment, led by Colonel William J. "Wild Bill" Donovan and Chaplain Father Francis P. Duffy. Up at Coogans Bluff the Yankees were playing host to the world champion Boston Red Sox. Opening Day's association with spring, the season of rebirth, made the return of the game particularly welcome this year. While most of the 30,000 fans would leave the Polo Grounds disappointed after Boston's Carl Mays shut out the Yanks 10–0, all were happy to have baseball back. The crowd was the largest ever to see the Yankees play at home, which thrilled business manager Harry Sparrow and his assistants, Mark Roth and Charlie McManus, who watched with smiling faces as the fans passed through the turnstiles. The crowd was typical of those that showed up at big events in New York, full of local politicians, movers and shakers from Wall Street, theater people, and sports celebrities. Lightweight champion Benny Leonard and his upcoming opponent, Willie Ritchie, were there, as was Broadway's George M. Cohan and America's leading jockey, Tod Sloan. Former Yankees manager Bill Donovan (now managing the Jersey City Skeeters of the International League) watched his old team from Colonel Ruppert's box. Two of the country's leading military men, Major General Thomas Barry and Rear Admiral Harry Huse occupied boxes nearby. Franklin P. Adams and Grantland Rice were among the throng of reporters covering the game for the various New York newspapers, and baseball statistician Al Munro Elias was around to inform everyone that Boston shortstop Everett Scott would be playing in his 387th consecutive game this afternoon. To feed the big crowd, as always, was concessionaire Harry M. Stevens, in his 26th consecutive Opening Day at a New York ballpark. Of course, the overwhelming majority of spectators at the Polo Grounds (or Brush Stadium as some called it in honor of Giants' owner John T. Brush) were just average New Yorkers, mostly men, but also women and children. All morning, the subways heading for Harlem had been bursting with these baseball-starved fans. Unfortunately for the New York City transit system, it had failed in its recent attempt to raise the fare from five cents to seven cents. Had the measure been approved, the fares paid by those bound for today's game would have resulted in several hundred additional dollars for the system. There was, however, some bad news for subway riders this morning, at least for those living or working on Staten Island. Mayor John F. Hylan had declared his opposition to a proposed independent subway route to this remote borough, and so the ferry would remain the only way to get to Manhattan.

Til Huston (now a colonel) had as his guests a group from the Sixteenth Engineers with whom he had served in France during the war. There were also thousands of other soldiers and sailors in the crowd. Their uniforms, and the brightly colored gowns and bonnets of the female fans, added to the widespread feeling of gaiety in the park. So too, did the festive tunes played by Frank's Band. The first straw hat sighted on a male patron got the traditional bashing, a ritual that had been a part of Polo Grounds' openers since before the turn of the century. The grass, under the care of groundskeeper Henry Fabian, looked beautiful, and there was a fresh coat of green paint on the walls. Even the oft-broken clock in right field was working, its hands painted a bright red. One notable difference from previous years was the disappearance of liquor advertisements from the outfield walls. Although the 18th amendment (Prohibition) would not become law in the United States until January 16, 1920, there had been no legal manufacture of whiskey here since September 8, 1917. Another difference was the huge 20 by 10-foot banner that appeared on the center field fence. It belonged to the Liberty Loan Committee, which was trying to raise money to pay the nation's war debts. The banner, which was lowered between innings and pulled up once play started, read, "It's Our War, Our Victory, Our Debt of Honor, Play Ball!"

Robert Moran, president of the New York City Board of Aldermen, had the honor of throwing out the first ball. After he made the ceremonial toss to plate umpire Tom Connolly, George Mogridge took the mound as his teammates ran to their positions. The infield, with Wally Pipp at first, Del Pratt at second, Roger Peckinpaugh at short, and Frank Baker at third, was the same as it was on Opening Day a year ago—the first time the Yankees had started the same infield in two consecutive openers. Mogridge also had the same catcher, Truck Hannah, and the same left fielder, Ping Bodie, he did on Opening Day 1918. Bodie had been ill with the mumps, and manager Miller Huggins planned to start 22-year-old Bill Lamar in his place. But when Bodie showed up this morning and pronounced himself cured, Huggins put him in the lineup.

Replacing Elmer Miller in center field was Duffy Lewis, the former Red Sox star who had missed the entire 1918 season serving in the military. Miller was at St. Paul and would not return to the Yankees until 1921. When Lewis was with Boston, he, Tris Speaker, and Harry Hooper comprised one of baseball's great outfields. Lewis had become a Yankee in last December's multiplayer trade that also brought pitchers Ernie Shore and Dutch Leonard to New York. (Leonard and Ruppert could not agree on a salary and Leonard's contract was sold to Detroit, where he played three seasons.) The Yanks gave up outfielder Frank Gilhooley, catcher Roxy Walters (who served as Boston's third-base coach today), pitchers Ray Caldwell and Slim Love, and $15,000. With Gilhooley traded, Sammy Vick, a rookie with only 12 games of major-league experience, was starting in right field. Vick, a decent hitter but a poor fielder, won the assignment when George Halas, another rookie, was sidelined with a charley horse. Halas was a speedy youngster who had played with the Great Lakes Naval Station team and before that the University of Illinois. His major-league career would consist of 22 at-bats in 1919 with an .091 batting average. Halas later went on to a successful career as the owner and head coach of the National Football League's Chicago Bears.

With Mogridge starting, Huggins had every reason to expect an opening-day victory. The slender left-hander had beaten the Red Sox six straight times and had not lost to them since September 4, 1917. Also, the Yankees entered the season in the midst of a hot streak; their 5–2 win over Brooklyn at Ebbets Field in their final exhibition game was their tenth straight victory. Mogridge's first pitch to Hooper, the only remaining member of Boston's great outfield of earlier times, was a strike, but on the next pitch, Hooper singled to right. After Jack Barry forced him at second, Mogridge threw a wild pitch with Amos Strunk at bat that allowed Barry to take second. Strunk popped out to Peckinpaugh and that brought Babe Ruth to the plate. When Barry, who managed the Sox in 1917, went into the Navy, Boston replaced him with Ed Barrow, former president of the International League. It was during Barrow's tenure as manager that Ruth began the transformation from one of baseball's greatest *pitchers* to its greatest *slugger*. In the shortened season of 1918, Ruth hit 11 home runs, tying Philadelphia's Tilly Walker for the league lead. Now he was a full-time outfielder, and his reputation as a home-run hitter was growing. Reporters were coining nicknames for him, such as the "Maryland Mauler" and "Tarzan of the Apes" in recognition of his great strength, and fans attending Red Sox games often did so just to see the Babe "hit one." While Mogridge pondered what kind of pitch to throw Ruth, many in the crowd pleaded for an intentional walk. They had watched in batting practice as the Babe put one long drive after another into the right field seats. Mogridge went to his curve ball, which the Babe lined viciously into right center field. Lewis moved to cut it off, but the ball skipped over his shoulder and rolled to the wall as Ruth legged out a two-run inside-the-park home run. Red Sox owner Harry Frazee, from his box seat, led the cheers.

Wednesday, April 23, 1919

Boston	ab	r	h	po	a	e	New York	ab	r	h	po	a	e
Hooper rf	5	1	2	1	0	0	Vick rf	4	0	0	3	1	1
Barry 2b	5	3	2	1	2	0	Peckinpaugh ss	2	0	1	6	1	3
Strunk cf	4	1	0	1	0	0	Pipp 1b	4	0	2	4	0	0
Ruth lf	4	2	2	2	0	0	Baker 3b	4	0	0	2	1	0
McInnis 1b	4	0	0	9	0	0	Pratt 2b	4	0	1	1	2	0
Vitt 3b	4	1	0	3	2	0	Lewis cf	4	0	0	4	1	0
Scott ss	5	1	2	1	1	0	Bodie lf	4	0	0	1	0	0
Schang c	5	1	4	9	1	0	Hannah c	3	0	0	5	0	0
Mays p	3	0	1	0	1	0	Mogridge p	1	0	0	1	2	0
Total	39	10	13	27	7	0	Total	30	0	4	27	8	4

| Boston | 210 | 000 | 016–10 |
| New York | 000 | 000 | 000–0 |

Two-base hits—Pratt, Schang (3). Home run—Ruth. Stolen bases—Hooper, Peckinpaugh. Sacrifice hit—Strunk. Sacrifice flies—McInnis, Mays. Double play—Vick to Pipp. Left on bases—New York, 8; Boston, 7. First base on error—Boston, 3. Bases on balls—off Mogridge, 2; off Mays, 4. Hit by pitcher—Hannah (by Mays). Struck out—by Mogridge, 2; by Mays, 8. Wild pitches—Mogridge (2). Umpires—Messrs. Connolly and Nallin.

Mays took over from there. The closest New York came to scoring off his underhand tosses was in the seventh. With two out, he hit Hannah and walked Mogridge, but kept his shutout intact by striking out Vick. The lineup that the *New York Tribune* called "Murderers Row" looked completely helpless against Mays, who struck out eight and allowed just four hits. Pipp had two of the hits, while Pratt and Peckinpaugh each had one. Boston scored again in the second on a walk to Ossie Vitt and singles by Wally Schang and Mays. Vitt, after seven years with Detroit, came to Boston in January in a three-way deal that included the Washington Senators. Schang was another of the former Philadelphia Athletics Boston had gotten from Connie Mack. There were four former A's in their lineup today: catcher Schang, center fielder Strunk, second baseman Barry, and first baseman Stuffy McInnis; ex–A's pitcher Joe Bush served as the first-base coach.

The score remained 3–0 until the Red Sox added a fourth run in the eighth and then blew the game open with a six-run ninth. The run in the fourth was scored without the benefit of a base hit. Barry reached base on an error by Peckinpaugh, took second on a sacrifice by Strunk, third on a wild pitch, and came home on McInnis's sacrifice fly. Peckinpaugh, the usually sure-handed Yankees' captain, had a terrible last two innings. His error in the eighth was the first of the three he made, and he also committed a mental error; after Mays walked him in the home eighth, he allowed himself to be picked off first base. Then he made two errors in the ninth that helped Boston score six runs and turn the game into a rout. By the time the Yankees went quietly in the ninth, many in the big crowd had already headed back to the subways.

In a season shortened to 140 games, the Yankees finished third (80–59), 7½ games behind the Chicago White Sox. Despite the reduced schedule, they drew 619,164 to the Polo Grounds, their largest home attendance to date. Babe Ruth hit 29 home runs for Boston, a new major-league record. Before the season was over Carl Mays would be a Yankee, and before the next season began, Ruth would be, too.

III

1920–1929

The arrival of Babe Ruth from the Boston Red Sox in 1920 signaled the first great decade in Yankees history. But Ruth, of course, did not do it alone; throughout the 1920s the club signed and brought to the major leagues a supporting cast of great players. Bob Meusel, who also joined the team in 1920, was followed by Earle Combs in 1924, Lou Gehrig and Mark Koenig in 1925, and Tony Lazzeri in 1926. Ed Barrow, who left the Red Sox to become the Yankees' general manager in 1921, was responsible for acquiring most of those men. Barrow also raided his old club for many of their stars; between 1921 and 1923 he brought pitchers Waite Hoyt, Joe Bush, Sam Jones, Herb Pennock, and George Pipgras; catcher Wally Schang; and infielders Everett Scott and Joe Dugan to New York.

After finishing third in Ruth's first year, manager Miller Huggins's club won pennants in 1921 and 1922 but lost to the Giants in the World Series both years. In 1923 they won a third consecutive pennant and this time beat the Giants to win their first world championship. In Ruth's first three seasons the Yankees outdrew the Giants, their Polo Grounds landlords, each year. However, their success led to their eventual eviction. Colonels Ruppert and Huston bought property for a new ballpark in the Bronx, and Yankee Stadium opened in 1923. Ruppert bought out Huston that year and became sole owner of the club.

Ruth continued to set batting records throughout the decade. He was joined by Gehrig in the latter half to form baseball's greatest one-two punch ever. The Yankees failed to win the pennant in 1924, and in 1925 tumbled all the way to seventh place. But they bounced back to win another three pennants in a row in 1926–1928, winning the World Series in four-game sweeps in '27 and '28. The decade ended with a second-place finish to the rising Philadelphia Athletics and the death, on September 25, 1929, of Miller Huggins, the Yankees' first great manager.

Wednesday, April 14, 1920
Shibe Park, Philadelphia
Philadelphia 3 New York 1

Go where glory waits thee.—Thomas Moore

We can never know how much of the post–1920 successes of the New York Yankees and failures of the Boston Red Sox trace back to Boston's sale of Babe Ruth to New York. Still, it is safe to say that nearly a century later it remains the most significant player transaction in sports history. The deal was actually consummated in December 1919; however, both teams withheld the announcement until January 5, 1920, when the Yankees got Ruth to sign a contract. The terms called for him to receive $20,000 per year for two years, double his 1919 salary with the Red Sox. Colonels Jacob Ruppert and Til Huston paid Boston owner Harry Frazee a reported $125,000 for Ruth, more than twice the amount ever paid for a player previously. They also gave Frazee, a theatrical producer more interested in Broadway than baseball, a $350,000 loan, which to the dismay of the fans in Boston was not used to enhance the fortunes of the Red Sox. At the time of the sale, the 24-year-old Ruth had already established himself as baseball's greatest slugger; in 1919 he led the league in runs batted in (113) and runs scored (103), and set major-league records in slugging percentage (.657) and home runs (29). Local fans recalled that home run number 28, the one that broke Ned Williamson's long-forgotten 1884 one-season mark, was among the longest ever hit at the Polo Grounds. So, from the moment they got the news Ruth was coming to New York, Yankees fans could barely wait for the season to begin; nor, so it seemed, could the players. The team was scheduled to open in Philadelphia on Wednesday, April 14, but the public was enduring another of the periodic work stoppages that had disrupted the nation's major industries since the end of the war. This one was an outlaw railroad strike, an action Attorney General A. Mitchell Palmer charged was engineered by the Industrial Workers of the World (IWW) as part of a worldwide Communist conspiracy. The strike interfered with the shipment of goods, especially food and coal, and caused chaos among travelers. With that in mind, the Yankees arrived at New York's Pennsylvania Station at five o'clock Tuesday evening. Not only did they leave earlier than they would have normally, they took the further precaution of hiring 12 automobiles and a baggage truck to stand by in case they were unable to get a train. There was some delay with the schedule, but the team checked into Philadelphia's Aldine Hotel with plenty of time to rest and prepare for the opener.

In contrast to the optimism in New York, A's fans had little to hope for in the new season. Since winning the pennant in 1914, Philadelphia had finished last for five consecutive years and would again this year and next. Yet despite this long period of mediocrity and the discomfort of an unseasonably chilly day, more than 12,000 fans were at Shibe Park for the game. Three months after it happened, the sale of Ruth to New York was still the biggest news in baseball, and many Philadelphians had come out just to see his Yankees' debut. For the privilege of doing so, almost all were paying higher ticket prices. At a joint meeting in February, the baseball establishment had decreed a new price structure for all parks: bleacher seats would now cost 50 cents, pavilion seats 75 cents, and grandstand seats one dollar. Even with the increase, it's unlikely that any of the fans exiting the park after the game felt they had not gotten their money's worth. Added to the joy of a home-team victory was an error by Ruth that decided the game. The Babe, playing center field, dropped an eighth-inning fly ball that allowed two runs to score and give the A's a 3–1 win.

Ruth's miscue made a winner of Philadelphia's Scott Perry and a loser of New York's Bob Shawkey, although the performance of the two pitchers was remarkably similar. Each allowed seven hits, one home run, one walk, and each struck out six and stranded six. Perry was in his third year with the A's after having previously pitched in a combined total of nine games for the 1915 St. Louis Browns, the 1916 Chicago Cubs, and the 1917 Cincinnati Reds. And while Shawkey missed almost all of the 1918 season serving in the navy, Perry had won a remarkable 20 games (20–19) for an Athletics team that won only 52. The Boston Braves, who had Perry briefly but traded him to Atlanta of the Southern Association, who in turn traded him to Philadelphia in late April 1918, claimed he still belonged to them. A's manager Connie Mack and American League president Ban Johnson went to court and won the battle that allowed Philadelphia to retain him. Perry slipped to 4–17 in 1919, with his best effort of the year coming on Opening Day in Washington, a 13-inning 1–0 loss to Walter Johnson. Meanwhile, Shawkey had come out of the navy to win 20 games (20–11) in 1919 and reclaim his role as the ace of the Yankees' staff.

Because the weather was so cold, the crowd, protectively dressed in heavy coats and furs, was not disappointed at the absence of the normal pregame parade and ceremonies. The throwing out of the first ball by mayor J. Hampton Moore was the only traditional opening-day ritual observed. The fans did get to see the unveiling of the A's new home uniforms. For the first time since 1917 they were wearing pinstripes (blue), and the blue elephant, added to the left sleeve in 1918, was now on the left breast. The elephant supplanted the large "A" that had been on the left breast since the Athletics began play in 1901.

Frank Gleich, a left-handed-hitting rookie, was the game's first batter. Gleich, playing right field, was replacing Ping Bodie, whom manager Miller Huggins benched because of a personal disagreement. After Gleich went out on a ground ball and Roger Peckinpaugh did the same, Wally Pipp blasted one of Perry's curve balls over the right field wall. It was the first opening-day home run by a Yankee since Jimmy Williams hit one off Case Patten in Washington 15 years earlier. Ruth was the next batter, and as he approached the plate the crowd began to tease him about Pipp "stealing his thunder." The Babe, in his first at-bat as a Yankee, tried to meet the challenge but had to settle for a single. He would not get his first home run as a Yankee until May 1, when he hit one over the right-field roof at the Polo Grounds against Boston's Herb Pennock.

Wednesday, April 14, 1920

New York	ab	r	h	po	a	e	Philadelphia	ab	r	h	po	a	e
Gleich rf	4	0	0	2	0	0	Witt cf	4	0	2	3	0	0
Peckinpaugh ss	4	0	0	1	1	0	Strunk rf	2	0	0	2	0	0
Pipp 1b	3	1	2	8	1	0	T. Walker lf	4	1	3	2	0	0
Ruth cf	4	0	2	4	0	1	Griffin 1b	3	1	1	8	0	0
Lewis lf	4	0	1	1	0	0	Dugan 2b	4	0	0	2	3	0
Meusel 3b	4	0	0	0	4	0	Galloway ss	4	0	0	1	2	1
Pratt 2b	4	0	2	0	1	0	Dykes 3b	3	0	0	3	2	0
Ruel c	3	0	0	7	0	0	Perkins c	3	1	1	6	0	0
Shawkey p	2	0	0	1	3	0	Perry p	3	0	0	0	1	0
Total	32	1	7	24	10	1	Total	30	3	7	27	8	1

New York   100   000   000–1
Philadelphia   000   010   02X–3

Home runs—Pipp, Perkins. Sacrifices—Griffin, Strunk. Double plays—Dugan and Galloway; Dykes and Griffin. Left on bases—New York, 6; Philadelphia, 6. Bases on balls—off Shawkey, 1; off Perry, 1. Hit by pitcher—by Perry (Shawkey) Struck out—by Shawkey, 6; Perry, 6. Umpires—Dinneen and Nallin. Time—1 hr. 35 min.

The Yankees 1–0 lead looked to be short-lived when the Athletics loaded the bases with nobody out in their half of the first inning. After Whitey Witt singled and Amos Strunk (back with Philadelphia) walked, Tilly Walker beat out a bunt when catcher Muddy Ruel's throw glanced off Walker's head. But Shawkey used both his pitching and his fielding skills to get out of this predicament without allowing a run. He pounced on Ivy Griffin's roller and threw home to force Witt, then struck out Joe Dugan and got Chick Galloway on a fly to Gleich. Philadelphia eventually tied the score in the fifth on a home run by catcher Cy Perkins. It remained tied until the fateful eighth, which the pesky Witt opened with a sharp single through Shawkey's legs. After Strunk sacrificed Witt to second, Walker hit a line drive up the middle that second baseman Del Pratt, lunging to his right, knocked down. Pratt had no play on Walker, but his effort saved a run as Witt was forced to hold at third. Witt did try to score on Griffin's grounder to third baseman Bob Meusel, but the rookie's throw to Ruel nailed him at the plate. When Dugan lifted a routine fly ball to center, it appeared that Shawkey had again worked his way out of trouble. Although the ball was over Ruth's head, he had plenty of time to get under it and make the catch. Instead, he tried to take it while slowly drifting back. The ball glanced off his glove, and Walker and Griffin, running with two out, scored easily. With one out in the Yankees' ninth, Lewis reached first on an infield single. Pratt followed with a well-hit ball, but third baseman Jimmy Dykes snared the liner and threw to Griffin for the game-ending double play.

Ruth was not the only notable player making his first appearance as a Yankee this afternoon. Meusel was beginning what would be an outstanding 11-year career as an outfielder, the first ten of those years as a Yankee. He was playing third this afternoon because Aaron Ward, a promising rookie infielder, was still nursing a knee injury. Huggins had chosen Ward to be his third baseman because of the absence of Frank Baker. Baker's wife, Ottalee, had died in February, leaving him unsure of his desire to play in 1920. He told Huggins that after the loss of their mother he was reluctant to leave his two children at home when the team was on the road. Baker, who was at today's game, promised his manager that he would reach a decision within a week, which he did, deciding, as he had in a salary dispute in 1915, to sit out the year.

> After a season-long three-way race with the Cleveland Indians and the Chicago White Sox, New York finished third (95–59), three games behind the champion Indians. In addition to leading the league in runs scored (158) and runs batted in (135), Babe Ruth established a new major-league high in walks (150) and broke the major-league record in slugging percentage (.847)—still the American League's all-time high—and home runs (54). With a team total of 115 home runs, the Yankees became the first major-league team to exceed 100. The purchase of Ruth was paying off not only on the field but also at the box office. The Yankees, outdrawing the Giants for the first time, set a major-league attendance record of 1,289,422, a total they would not surpass until 1946.

Wednesday, April 13, 1921
Polo Grounds, New York
New York 11 Philadelphia 1

An institution is the lengthened shadow of one man.—Ralph Waldo Emerson

Team owners were ecstatic when more than 160,000 fans turned out for the seven major-league opening-day games. (Chicago at Detroit was rained out.) The strong attendance was an early indication that their campaign to sell the 1921 season as "the comeback of baseball" and to make fans forget the charges surrounding the 1919 World Series would be successful. Late in the 1920 season, the country had been shocked to learn that gamblers had paid several members of the heavily favored Chicago White Sox to deliberately lose specific prearranged games of the 1919 Series to their opponents, the Cincinnati Reds. Baseball officials worried about the reaction to the scandal by the ticket-buying public. They decided that to restore the fans' confidence and loyalty, the game needed a strong-willed outsider to govern it. Led by the old ruling body, the Three Man Commission, baseball created the position of Commissioner and in November 1920 elected Kenesaw Mountain Landis, a federal judge, to fill it. Landis acted quickly and resolutely by suspending eight of the offending players, including such stars as Joe Jackson, Ed Cicotte, and Buck Weaver. He also banished permanently several other of the game's questionable characters. To the owners' relief, Landis's swift and decisive actions evidently had renewed the people's faith in baseball's integrity. Moreover, as it always seems to do when its approval slumps, baseball got lucky. As it fought to overcome the stain on its reputation, Babe Ruth came along to lift it, almost singlehandedly, to new heights of popularity. Ruth's sensational home-run hitting was not only altering the style of play, it was fast making him the biggest drawing card in sports history. His unprecedented 54 home runs in 1920, his first year in New York, guaranteed the Yankees would attract large crowds wherever they appeared.

The Babe helped draw 37,000 people to the Polo Grounds for the Yankees' season-opener against Philadelphia, almost one-fourth of the major league's total attendance that day and one of baseball's largest crowds ever. Then he treated them to a five-for-five performance in leading the Yanks to an 11–1 trouncing of Connie Mack's hapless Athletics. The winning pitcher was Carl Mays, who two years earlier on Opening Day 1919 had shut out the Yankees, 10–0, in this same park. Mays was a member of the Boston Red Sox then, but he left the Red Sox that July complaining of a lack of batting and fielding support. The Sox were by now fed up with Mays, one of the least-liked players ever, and traded him to New York for pitchers Allen Russell and Bob McGraw and $40,000. American League president Ban Johnson disapproved of the trade and demanded the Yankees suspend Mays. But Jacob Ruppert and Til Huston believed that they had made a binding deal and Mays continued to pitch for them. Eventually, the directors of the American League and the courts sided with the Yankees' co-owners and overruled Johnson. The case signaled the beginning of the end of Johnson's autocratic rule of the American League.

Mays's manager in Boston, Ed Barrow, was now the Yankees' business manager. Barrow, who replaced the deceased Harry Sparrow, wasted no time in making a trade with his old club. On December 15 he sent catcher Muddy Ruel, pitcher Hank Thormahlen, outfielder Sammy Vick, and second baseman Del Pratt to the Red Sox in exchange for catcher Wally Schang, infielder Mike McNally, and pitchers Waite Hoyt and Harry Harper. The addition of Hoyt and Schang, plus the return of Frank Baker, made the Yankees the choice of many experts to finally win their first pennant. That is, forecasters were quick to add, only if the team played up to its ability. Prohibition may have been the law of the land, but throughout the spring New York newspapers had reported on the heavy drinking and riotous activities of many Yankees' players, particularly Ruth. The partying had begun at spring training in Shreveport, Louisiana, and continued uninterrupted as the team played its way north. The Yankees had exhibited similar rowdy behavior at spring training in Jacksonville, Florida, in 1920—behavior that led manager Miller Huggins to move the team's training camp to Shreveport this year. But when the change in location did not lead to a change in conduct, some in the press began to question Huggins's ability to control and lead this Yankees team.

The Great War, as wars always do, had significantly changed many traditional mores and habits. These changes harmed some segments of American society, while benefitting others. Clearly, a major beneficiary was any endeavor associated with the public's entertainment, particularly spectator sports. Veteran baseball watchers, who could recall when

Yankees' openers drew much smaller gatherings, were aware of this change. They attributed today's huge turnout partly to Ruth and partly to the warm weather, but believed it was mainly due to the tremendous increase in popularity currently affecting all sports. By two o'clock, only an hour after the gates to the Polo Grounds had opened, there were close to 20,000 people already seated, about a quarter of them women. Though game time was not until three-thirty, the early arriving fans had filled the entire lower stands. From that point on there was a steady stream of people entering the park, many trickling in after the game had started. The crush of the crowd at the 155th Street el station was so great that several window panes in the ticket booths were broken. Seeking to prevent similar problems at the park, the police stationed themselves close to the stadium and allowed no one without a ticket to approach the gates; they turned away an estimated 15,000 fans.

A thunderous cheer welcomed the home team when they came out on the field to begin pregame practice. The Yankees were wearing their home-whites with the blue pin-stripes and the blue and white stockings. There was no lettering of any kind on their uni-form. Only the blue interlocked "NY" on their pinstriped caps (the bills were solid blue) indicated they represented New York. The crowd applauded and encouraged each Yankee player as he came on the field, with an especially warm greeting for Baker, returning from his self-imposed one-year exile. Still, their loudest cheers went to the Babe, who was also the main target of the many photographers that followed him around the field snapping pictures of his every move. Following Ruth was no easy task; he seemed to be everywhere, even taking time to chat with spectators, including Jackie Coogan, child star of the hit movie *The Kid*. Later, the Athletics appeared, dressed in visitors' gray trimmed in blue. The blue elephant on the left breast of their jerseys, depicted in a standing position in 1920, was now seen rearing up on its hind legs.

At the conclusion of batting practice, Colonels Ruppert and Huston and Mayor John F. Hylan made their way across the field to the owner's box. Hylan was playing to the crowd, doffing his hat and waving in every direction. This morning, Republican governor Nathan L. Miller had proposed that the heavily Republican New York State Senate begin an inves-tigation into corruption in New York City under Hylan, its Democratic mayor. With a may-oral election scheduled for November, the fans at the Polo Grounds recognized the investigation to be simply a case of "politics as usual." New Yorkers understood this; and to let Hylan know they understood, they gave him a long ovation. Hylan's constituents rec-ognized that the mayor was a plodder, and not exceedingly bright, but they did think him honest. At 3:30, Hylan arose from his box along the first-base line and launched the season with a shaky toss to catcher Schang.

Mays's pitching opponent was Scott Perry, the right-hander who had beaten the Yanks in the opener a year ago. Perry pitched well again today; for six innings he battled Mays in a tense pitchers' duel before the Yanks pulled away in the late innings. Going into the seventh New York led only 2–0, having taken the early lead with two second-inning runs. Third baseman Aaron Ward had followed Ping Bodie's double over the head of center fielder Frank Welch with a home run to left. Bodie was starting in center field only because new Yankee Braggo Roth was still having a problem with his knee. Roth had come from Washington in January, with the Yanks giving up Duffy Lewis and George Mogridge to get him. It was Barrow's second major off-season trade, but unlike the deal that brought Hoyt and Schang to New York, the Roth trade would not be a good one for the Yankees. Although he was only 29 years old, the 43 games Roth played for New York in 1921 were the last of his major-league career.

For the first six innings, Philadelphia's offense against Mays's submarine deliveries consisted of a first-inning single by Tilly Walker. In innings two through six, Mays retired the A's in one-two-three order. Walker got his second single in the seventh, and one out later Joe Dugan hit a liner to left on which Ruth attempted to make a shoestring catch. However, he could not quite reach the ball, which bounced in front of him and rolled by for a run-scoring triple. It was now a one-run game, but not for long. In the home seventh the Yanks scored three runs to stretch the lead to 5–1 and relieve some of the pressure on Mays. Schang led off by drawing Perry's first walk. Mays, with three hits on the day—the same number as he allowed—followed with a looping bunt single over the mound. After second baseman Chick Fewster successfully sacrificed the runners along, Roger Peckinpaugh's infield hit scored Schang. Ruth chipped in with a pop-fly single over the head of shortstop Chick Galloway that scored Mays and sent Peckinpaugh to third. Wally Pipp's ground out brought Peckinpaugh home with the Yankees' fifth run.

Glenn Myatt batted for Perry in the top of the eighth, so Bob Hasty was on the mound as New York batted in their half of the inning. Ward welcomed the young right-hander with a sharp single past rookie first baseman Frank Brazill. Schang reached base with a little tapper back to the box on which Hasty made a wild throw, helping to open the way for a six-run inning. Ward and Schang moved up a base as Mays grounded out, and then both scored on Fewster's single to center. Peckinpaugh's double sent Fewster to third and brought Ruth to the plate. Ruth, who already had two singles and two doubles in the game, hit a slow ground ball to the right side. Second baseman Jimmy Dykes, playing deep, as was the entire Philadelphia defense, charged in and made a good throw, but it was not in time. The Babe beat it out for his fifth hit as Fewster came home with New York's eighth run. For Ruth, it was the third time in his career he had collected five hits in a game.

After Pipp's grounder resulted in Peckinpaugh being thrown out at the plate, Hasty hit Bob Meusel to load the bases. Bodie quickly cleared them with a triple against the right-field wall, scoring Ruth, Pipp, and Meusel, and making the score 11–1. That last trio of Yankees to score meant each member of the team had scored at least one run. Philadelphia went quietly in the ninth, with Fewster making a fine play on Brazill's ground ball for the final out. Mays had the first victory of what would be his league-leading total of 27 (27–9), while extending his long winning streak against the Athletics. The streak, begun on August 30, 1918, when he was with Boston, eventually would reach 24 games, before losing to the A's on October 4, 1923.

New York won its first American League pennant (98–55), finishing 4½ games ahead of the defending champion Cleveland Indians. In the World Series, played entirely at the Polo Grounds, the Yankees lost to the New York Giants five games to three in the third and final year of the nine-game World Series. The Yankees led the league in runs (948), runs batted in (875), home runs (134), and slugging percentage (.464). Babe Ruth had what many consider his best offensive year. He had 204 hits, batted .378, had 59 home runs, 168 runs batted in, 177 runs scored, an .846 slugging percentage, and 457 total bases. He also drew 145 walks and stole 17 bases.

Wednesday, April 13, 1921

Philadelphia	ab	r	h	po	a	e	New York	ab	r	h	po	a	e
Dykes 2b	4	0	0	2	2	0	Fewster 2b	4	1	1	0	4	0
Witt rf	4	0	0	1	0	0	Peckinpaugh ss	5	1	2	1	4	0

Philadelphia	ab	r	h	po	a	e	New York	ab	r	h	po	a	e
T. Walker lf	4	1	2	2	0	0	Ruth lf	5	1	5	2	0	0
Brazill 1b	4	0	0	7	1	0	Pipp 1b	4	1	2	14	0	0
Dugan 3b	3	0	1	2	2	0	Meusel rf	4	1	0	0	0	0
Perkins c	3	0	0	8	0	0	Bodie cf	5	1	2	3	0	0
Welch cf	3	0	0	2	1	0	Ward 3b	5	2	2	2	3	0
Galloway ss	2	0	0	0	2	0	Schang c	3	2	0	4	0	0
Perry p	2	0	0	0	1	0	Mays p	4	1	3	1	4	0
ªMyatt c	1	0	0	0	0	0	Total	39	11	17	27	15	0
Hasty p	0	0	0	0	2	1							
Total	30	1	3	24	11	1							

ªGrounded out for Perry in the eighth inning.

Philadelphia	000	000	100–1
New York	020	000	36X–11

Runs batted in—by Dugan, 1; by Fewster, 2; by Peckinpaugh, 1; by Pipp 1; by Ruth, 2; by Bodie, 3; by Ward, 2. Left on bases—Philadelphia, 3; New York 8. First base on error, New York. Two-base hits—Peckinpaugh, Bodie, Pipp, Ruth (2). Three-base hits—Dugan, Bodie. Home run—Ward. Sacrifice hits—Pipp, Fewster. Bases on balls—off Perry, 1; Mays, 1. Hit by pitcher—by Hasty, (Meusel). Hits—off Perry, 12 in 7 innings; off Hasty 5 in 1 inning. Earned runs—off Perry 6; off Hasty, 2; off Mays, 1. Struck out—by Perry, 5, Mays, 2. Losing pitcher—Perry. Umpires—Dinneen, Nallin, and Wilson. Time of game—1 hr. 30 min.

Wednesday, April 12, 1922
Griffith Stadium, Washington
Washington 6 New York 5

Any excuse will serve a tyrant.—Aesop

Neither the absence of Babe Ruth nor their team's dismal past could detract from the joy 25,000 Senators' fans felt following their team's exciting come-from-behind, 6–5, victory against the American League champion Yankees. Even President and Mrs. Warren G. Harding, who were part of the record-breaking crowd that packed Griffith Stadium for the season opener, greeted the win with a spirited show of emotion. The Senators were now under the complete command of former Yankees manager Clark Griffith. Griffith had purchased 10 percent of the stock when he became Washington's manager in 1912 and had acquired a controlling interest in the team in November 1919. He was now the Senators' president and the principal owner, and as such had renamed the park after himself. He had also expanded its seating capacity, extending the upper deck from first and third bases all the way to the foul poles. But even the added seats could not accommodate all the people attending this afternoon's opener. A large group of spectators watched the action from the playing field; several rows of them completely encircled the outfield.

More than in other cities, Opening Day in Washington was a social occasion, which accounts for nearly half of today's crowd being female. Many women were wearing what the *Washington Post* called, "gayly decked hats and clothing," in a combination of colors that the *Post* predicted were "what the 'flapper fan' will wear to games this year." The huge turnout was evidence of high expectations in the nation's capital, where, except for Walter Johnson, baseball fans had never had much to cheer about. In 21 years of play in the American League, they had watched their team finish in the second division 15 times. The Senators and the St. Louis Browns were the only two American League clubs that had never won a pennant. However, the Senators and the Browns were fielding potent teams in 1922, and either one seemed strong enough to dethrone the defending champion Yankees. Interest in the Senators was so intense this season; the club was making efforts to have the daily baseball results and also the play-by-play of important games given on the radio. Washingtonians based their confidence on the team's strong showing in 1921 (80–73), as well as the additions of shortstop Roger Peckinpaugh and outfielder Goose Goslin to a lineup that already had Sam Rice, Joe Judge, and Bucky Harris. The Senators obtained Peckinpaugh from the Boston Red Sox in January, just a month after the Yankees traded him there. Goslin, a rookie, had an impressive spring and won the opening-day start in right field.

In addition to Ruth's absence, the Yankees were also playing without Bob Meusel, whose 24 home runs in 1921 tied St. Louis' Ken Williams for second place in the league. Ruth, of course, led with 59, breaking his record of 54 set the year before. Besides revolutionizing baseball with his phenomenal batting feats, Ruth was also revolutionizing the game's salary structure. He had recently signed a three-year contract at $52,000 per year, three times the salary of longtime star Frank Baker, the next highest paid Yankee at $16,000. Ruth and Meusel were out of the lineup because Commissioner Landis had suspended them for "barnstorming" following the 1921 season. They had violated the commissioner's edict that World Series participants were not to appear in post-season exhibition games. When Ruth and Meusel, attempting to earn some extra money, ignored Landis's warning to stop the tour, the commissioner ordered them suspended until May 20, 1922.

Meusel had tonsillitis and probably would have been unable to play in the opener anyway. But Ruth, wearing street clothes, was at Griffith Stadium to lend support to his teammates. He even took part in the pregame parade before joining Yankees co-owner Til Huston and American League president Ban Johnson in a box behind the New York dugout. The fans applauded Ruth warmly; nevertheless, he was clearly disappointed at not being in the lineup. Ruth, Meusel, and Whitey Witt (purchased from the Philadelphia A's in April) would eventually make up New York's regular outfield this season, but none of the three was playing today. Manager Miller Huggins was starting three second-stringers: Norm McMillan, playing in his first major-league game, was in right; Elmer Miller, a journeyman playing in his final season, was in center; and Chick Fewster, a utility player, was in left. The Yanks would soon trade all three to the Red Sox, Miller and Fewster in July and McMillan following the season.

For Washington fans, the absence of Ruth was not nearly as disappointing as that of their beloved Walter Johnson. Johnson had been ill for most of the spring, and Washington's rookie manager, Clyde Milan (he replaced George McBride) felt that his longtime friend and teammate was not yet ready to pitch. It was only the second time in 13 years that Johnson had not pitched the Senators' opening game. In his place, Milan chose left-hander George Mogridge, the pitcher the Yankees had traded with Duffy Lewis to Washington for Braggo Roth in January 1921. Mogridge, who won 18 games for Washington in 1921, was the only one of the three still in the big leagues.

At the first sight of President Harding, the crowd stood and cheered for the entire five minutes it took him to cross the field and reach his seat. Some of those sitting with or near the president and Mrs. Harding were Vice President Calvin Coolidge, Secretary of State

Charles Evans Hughes, Secretary of War John W. Weeks, General John J. Pershing, Secretary of the Navy Edwin Denby, and Mr. and Mrs. Charles Dawes. Admiral Robert E. Coontz, the Chief of Naval Operations, marching right behind the Meyer Goldman Band, led a parade out to the flag-raising ceremony. Both clubs marched behind Coontz, followed by a high school squad of cadets and a Boy Scout troop. The Yankees' caps were a solid navy blue with a white interlocked "NY" on the crown. Their stockings, too, were now a solid navy blue. Washington wore blue pinstripes with a blue "W" on the left sleeve. Their caps were blue with a white "W" on the crown, and their stockings were blue and white.

As the admiral raised the flag and the crowd stood bareheaded for "The Star-Spangled Banner," to everyone's delight the sun broke through. When the teams returned to their dugouts, the Harmony Lodge of the Masons presented Griffith with a large basket of flowers. While Griffith accepted his gift, Ruth and Ban Johnson were in the presidential box being introduced to President Harding. The president also met six-year-old Walter Johnson Jr., who was wearing a miniature Senators uniform. Harding spent the first three innings holding the youngster on his lap and later told the great pitcher, "You have a fine boy." Manager Milan presented Harding with a brand new baseball that the president threw to Mogridge as the crowd roared their approval. Milan retrieved the ball and handed it back to Harding, who in turn gave it to Mrs. Harding. The president wanted his hands free so he could keep score. Harding was a knowledgeable fan, who while puffing on a cigar, watched the game carefully and kept a detailed scorecard.

After Mogridge retired the Yankees in the first inning, Washington came to bat against Sam Jones, making his Yankees' debut. In 1921, as a member of the Red Sox, Jones had beaten the Senators on Opening Day and continued to pitch well against them throughout the year. A right-hander, as were all the Yankees starters, Jones came to the team in the Peckinpaugh trade. New York also received pitcher Joe Bush and shortstop Everett Scott in that transaction, while pitchers Jack Quinn, Rip Collins, and Bill Piercy accompanied Peckinpaugh to Boston. Jones gave up a leadoff single to Judge, who later took second on a passed ball by catcher Wally Schang. Two outs later, Rice ripped a double to left to score Judge and put Washington ahead.

The Yankees roared back to take a 4–1 lead in the second, reaching Mogridge for all four runs after two were out. With Wally Pipp who had walked at third, and Schang who had singled at first, Jones hit a fly ball that landed in the overflow crowd in center field for a ground-rule double. Pipp scored and Schang took third. Miller brought both runners home with a double over Rice's head, and then Fewster singled to score Miller. After Fewster's hit, pitcher Tom Phillips hurried down to the Washington bullpen to warm up, but Mogridge fanned Baker to end the inning.

Washington retaliated in its half of the second. Harris led off with a double, and reached third as Patsy Gharrity was grounding out. Gharrity's ball was hit between third and short, requiring Scott, the Yanks' new shortstop, to go deep in the hole and make a strong throw to get the out. Harris scored on Mogridge's bloop single into left. A double by Judge scored Mogridge, making the score 4–3, but Scott ended the inning and saved a run by making another great play on Peckinpaugh's bid for a base hit. Scott, playing his first game as a Yankee, was appearing in his 833rd consecutive game. Later in the season Huggins would make him the team captain after stripping Ruth of that title following the Babe's fifth suspension.

The visitors upped their lead to 5–3 in the third on a single by Scott that scored Pipp. Schang followed with a double, but Scott was out attempting to score on a strong relay from left fielder Elmer Smith to third baseman Shanks to catcher Gharrity. Although it was only the third inning, that run was the end of the Yankees' offense. Mogridge would allow them only two hits over the final six innings. Harris started another Senators' rally with a double in the fourth, a routine fly ball to left that Fewster lost in the sun. It was the second ball Fewster had lost that way, evidence enough for Huggins to switch him to center field and let center fielder Miller, a more experienced outfielder, try to deal with the sun in left. Harris was still at second with two outs, and Gharrity, who had walked, was at first when Judge came to the plate. The veteran first baseman came through with his third hit of the game, a double into the crowd that scored Harris and moved Gharrity to third. Once more it was Scott who preserved the Yankees' lead as he again robbed Peckinpaugh of a hit with a spectacular play.

The Senators finally drew even in the seventh. With one out, Peckinpaugh hit a ground ball in the hole that even Scott could not reach; third baseman Baker knocked it down but had no play. After reaching second on a wild pitch, Peckinpaugh scored on Smith's single to right. Rice followed with a single off Jones's glove, but Scott killed the uprising with another terrific stop, turning rookie Goslin's ground ball into a double play. Scott's defense was keeping the Yankees in the game, but in the eighth, Washington scored on a double by Shanks and a single by Gharrity. When Shanks crossed the plate with what would prove to be the winning run, it set off a demonstration as loud as any in the memory of local fans. Included among the demonstrators was Mr. Harding, who was slapping Mr. Hughes—the frock-coated Secretary of State—on the back, and Mrs. Harding, who was applauding with great enthusiasm. The celebrations continued as the Yankees batted in the ninth, causing a halt in play for several minutes. Some fans in the pavilion and upper deck started throwing the air cushions—provided by Griffith for their seating comfort—at one another. However, the disturbance was slight and quickly over. Not until Mogridge got the final three outs did anyone leave the park, and that included the president and his party.

New York and St. Louis battled the whole season before the Yankees (94–60) won their second straight pennant. They finished one game ahead of the Browns, while Washington was a disappointing sixth. In the World Series the Yanks again lost to the New York Giants, failing to win a single game; one game ended in a tie. Babe Ruth played in only 110 games and hit just 35 home runs, third in the league behind Ken Williams and Tilly Walker. The American League reintroduced a Most Valuable Player Award, absent since 1914. The Brown's George Sisler won it, with Joe Bush, who led Yankees' pitchers with a record of 26–7, finishing fourth.

Wednesday, April 12, 1922

New York	ab	r	h	po	a	e	Washington	ab	r	h	po	a	e
Miller cf, lf	5	1	2	0	0	0	Judge 1b	5	1	3	11	1	0
Fewster lf, cf	4	0	1	2	1	0	Peckinpaugh ss	4	1	1	3	1	1
Baker 3b	5	0	0	1	3	0	Smith lf	4	0	1	3	1	1
McMillan rf	4	0	0	1	0	0	Rice cf	4	0	3	2	0	0
Pipp 1b	4	2	1	13	0	0	Goslin rf	4	0	0	0	0	0
Ward 3b	3	0	1	3	3	0	Harris 2b	4	2	2	2	2	0
Scott ss	3	0	1	2	4	0	Shanks 3b	4	1	2	0	2	1
Schang c	3	1	2	2	1	0	Gharrity c	3	0	1	6	0	0
Jones p	3	1	1	0	3	0	Mogridge p	4	1	2	0	2	0
Total	34	5	9	24	15	0	Total	36	6	15	27	9	3

New York	041	000	000–5
Washington	120	100	11X–6

Two-base hits—Rice, Jones, Miller (2), Harris (2), Schang, Judge (2), Ward, Shanks. Sacrifices—Fewster, Ward, Schang. Double play—Scott to Pipp. Left on bases—New York, 9; Washington, 7. Base on balls-off Mogridge, 3; Jones, 1. Struck out—by Mogridge, 4; Jones, 2. Hit by pitcher—by Mogridge, (Jones). Wild pitch—Jones. Passed ball—Schang, (2). Umpires—Owens and Chill. Time of game—2 hrs. 8 min.

Wednesday, April 18, 1923
Yankee Stadium, New York
New York 4 Boston 1

May it live and last for more than a century.—Catullus

On a glorious spring day in the Bronx, New York City unveiled the latest monument to its power and prestige with the opening of the magnificent new Yankee Stadium. Appropriately, Babe Ruth hit the Stadium's first home run, a three-run blast that led the Yankees to a 4–1 victory over the Boston Red Sox. Ruth, of course, was the man most responsible for the Yankees' new home. His extraordinary home-run feats and exuberant personality had made him the greatest gate attraction in sports history. As a result, the Yankees had drawn more than a million fans to the Polo Grounds in each of the three years since he joined them. No other team in baseball had ever drawn a million even once. The Yankees' unparalleled success upset their landlords, the New York Giants, whose owner Charles Stoneham and manager John McGraw still believed that the city belonged to them (although it would be another 23 years and both would be long gone before the Giants would draw a million people to the Polo Grounds). Understandably dismayed at being outdrawn in their own park, Stoneham and McGraw had decided not to renew the Yankees' lease when it expired following the 1922 season. They informed co-owners Jacob Ruppert and Til Huston the American Leaguers would have to find another place to play. The Colonels quickly selected a ten-acre lot in the Bronx, just across the Harlem River from the Polo Grounds as the site for their new park. Jake Weber, Fordham University's athletic trainer, had suggested the location to Ruppert while giving him his regular massage. The Yankees bought the land from the estate of William Waldorf Astor for $625,000 in February 1921, and the White Construction Company began construction in May 1922. Eleven months and $2,500,000 later the park opened.

Yankee Stadium was the biggest, most lavish ballpark ever built. It had three concrete decks that extended from home plate to the left and right field corners, with a single deck in left-center and wooden bleachers around the rest of the outfield. To erect this extraordinary structure, it took 600,000 lineal feet (two million board feet) of lumber, 2,500 tons of structural steel, 1,000 tons of reinforcing steel, 500 tons of iron, and four miles of piping. Forty-five thousand cubic yards of earth were needed to fill and level the ground, and then more than 100,000 square feet of sod was trucked in from Long Island to create the playing surface. Head groundskeeper Phil Schenck and his crew did a terrific job getting the field in excellent condition for the opener and justifiably received many compliments for their work.

The opening-day attendance was reported as exceeding 74,000, though that was likely too generous an estimate. Still, it was by far the largest crowd ever to have seen a baseball game, surpassing the previous record of 42,620 set at Braves Field in the fifth game of the 1916 World Series between Brooklyn and the Boston Red Sox. (The Red Sox used Braves Field, opened in 1915, as the home of the National League's Boston Braves, in the 1915 and 1916 World Series and on various other occasions when they expected big crowds.) In spite of the enormous turnout and the unfamiliarity people had with the new stadium, there were no major complications. Everyone involved handled the logistics of getting the fans to the stadium, getting them around inside, and then getting them out with great skill. Subway transportation was exceptionally heavy coming and going (even Commissioner Landis arrived by subway), but there were no breakdowns and no unusually long delays. Having 36 ticket booths and 40 turnstiles available at the Stadium allowed the fans to buy their tickets and enter without difficulty. Two days before the game the Yankees announced they had sold all the reserved seats but would put 30,000 grandstand seats and 22,000 bleacher seats on sale at noon on the day of the game. By two o'clock on game day, those 52,000 seats were gone and "standing room only" signs went up. The New York City police, who did an outstanding job of controlling the crowd, estimated that more than 25,000 disappointed fans failed to get in. Surprisingly, the police reported only two arrests for ticket scalping outside the Stadium; one man tried to sell his $1.10 grandstand ticket for $1.25, and another man tried to sell a similar priced ticket for $1.50. Ruppert, Huston, Ed Barrow, and everyone associated with the business end of the Yankees operation was overjoyed at the sight of so many paying customers. Concessionaires Harry M. Stevens and his brother Frank were also having a big day as fans spent their money not only on food but also on first-game mementoes. The Stevens's had expanded the information in the scorecards, which normally sold for a nickel, renamed them "souvenir programs," and were selling them for 15 cents.

The biggest park in the biggest city called for the biggest pregame celebration, and that is precisely what the fans got. Promptly at one o'clock, the Seventh Regiment Band, wearing long gray coats and white trousers, began entertaining the crowd. Shortly after three, the band set off on the parade to the flagpole with the two teams close behind. Guest conductor John Philip Sousa, dressed in his formal military uniform, led the march. Because of the chilly early spring weather, the parading players were wearing sweaters over their uniforms, grey for the Yankees and bright red for Boston. At the flagpole in center field, Yankees manager Miller Huggins and new Red Sox skipper Frank Chance raised the American flag as the band played "The Star-Spangled Banner." Then, to the cheers of the crowd, the two managers raised the flag signifying the Yankees' 1922 American League championship. The parade back across the field, with Governor Al Smith and Commissioner Landis at its head, included a whole slew of high-ranking military people, all of whom had been waiting in center field. When they returned to the area in front of the Yankees dugout, Huggins was presented with a large horseshoe of roses, one of which Colonel Ruppert plucked and wore in his lapel throughout the game. Red Sox owner Harry Frazee, the man who sold Ruth to the Yankees three years earlier, was at the game as was just about every politician in New York who could get a ticket or a free pass. A notable exception was Mayor John F. Hylan. The mayor was too ill to attend, as was Ban Johnson, the man who had tried so long to make the Yankees a success. Colonel Ruppert stood next to Smith as the governor threw out the first ball to catcher Wally Schang, and then it was time to play ball. Calling balls and strikes was Tom Connolly, the same umpire who had been behind the plate 20 years earlier when the Yankees played their first league game at Washington.

Huggins gave the honor of pitching the Yankee Stadium opener to Bob Shawkey, the senior member of the staff. Shawkey had been with the Yankees since June 28, 1915, and was second, by five months, only to Wally Pipp in length of service. Chick Fewster, traded by the Yankees to Boston in mid–1922, was the first official batter. He took Shawkey's initial pitch for a ball before grounding out to Everett Scott at short. Scott, despite a sore ankle, was playing in his 987th consecutive game. This season he would lead American League shortstops in fielding for the eighth consecutive year. Red Sox first baseman George Burns got the first hit in the new stadium, a single in the second inning. It was one of only three hits Shawkey allowed in a very strong performance. Pitcher Howard Ehmke had a single in the sixth, and in the seventh Norm McMillan, another former Yankee, tripled home Burns, who had walked. That was Boston's only run and by that time the Yankees had four.

Ehmke, making his Boston debut after six years with the Detroit Tigers, was joining a club that had been in decline since winning the World Series in 1918. A last-place team in 1922, the Sox would finish last again in 1923, winning only 61 games, of which Ehmke won 20. Ehmke started well. He retired the first six batters before Aaron Ward led off the third with the Yankees' first hit in their new stadium. Ward smacked a single to left and went to second on Scott's sacrifice bunt. But he got caught in a rundown on Shawkey's come-backer and was tagged out by third baseman Howard Shanks, playing his first game for Boston after spending 11 years with the Washington Senators. Shawkey wound up on second in the rundown, and after Whitey Witt drew a walk, Shawkey scored on Joe Dugan's single to center. Dugan had taken over from Frank Baker as the regular third baseman after coming from Boston in the Fewster trade of July 1922. Following that season Baker retired, and the Yankees made two more deals with Boston, acquiring pitchers George Pipgras, still a minor leaguer, and Herb Pennock.

With two runners on, the stage was set for Ruth. The Babe had capped his tumultuous 1922 season, which included five suspensions, with a disastrous .118 batting average in the World Series. He had vowed to make amends for what he considered a poor season, saying before the game he would give a year of his life to hit a home run today. In the Series, Giants' pitchers had stopped Ruth with an assortment of off-speed pitches. Ehmke had done the same in the Babe's first at-bat, so with the count two balls and two strikes, he tried another off-speed pitch. This time Ruth was ready and with a mighty swing deposited it ten rows deep in the lower right-field seats for a three-run homer. Grinning as he followed Witt and Dugan around the bases, he waved his cap at the crowd, which responded with the loudest roar of the day. Given the size of the crowd, the ovation Ruth received following his home run may have been the biggest yet heard at a ballgame.

Babe's blast made the score 4–0, a sufficient lead for Shawkey, who stifled all of Boston's potential uprisings. One came in the fifth, when with Joe Harris on second courtesy of a dropped fly ball by Ruth and McMillan on first with a walk, he struck out Shanks and got catcher Al DeVormer—yet another ex–Yankee—to ground to first-baseman Pipp. Ruth, in his third opener as a Yankee, had played center field in the first one (1920), left field in the second (1921), and was playing right field today. (He was on suspension for the 1922 opener.) His error, like his home run, was the first committed at Yankee Stadium. After McMillan's triple in the seventh drove in Burns with Boston's only run, Shawkey again got out of trouble by retiring Shanks and DeVormer. He did it the same way, fanning Shanks and getting DeVormer on a grounder—this time to third baseman Dugan, who made a good play on the ball.

Shawkey's excellent pitching notwithstanding, as the tremendous crowd departed the

Stadium the talk was primarily of Ruth and the marvelous new ballpark he had made possible. To end the spectators' perfect day, exiting was mostly trouble-free. Double ramps brought upper-deck patrons down to street level where they joined the flow onto the surrounding streets. Only at the Jerome Avenue subway station was there a delay. There, the crowd waiting to board the trains was so large the police had to hold them back and let them enter the station in shifts. Despite the huge throng, the stadium emptied in less time than it took for a big crowd to do so at the Polo Grounds.

The Yankees (98–54) breezed to their third straight pennant, winning by 16 games over the Detroit Tigers, and for the third straight year they met the New York Giants in the World Series. This time they won the "Battle of Broadway," defeating their intracity rivals in six games for their first world championship. Babe Ruth hit .393 with 41 home runs and was unanimously chosen the league's Most Valuable Player. Home attendance in the first year of Yankee Stadium was 1,007,066, less than in any of the three preceding years at the Polo Grounds.

Wednesday, April 18, 1923

Boston	ab	r	h	po	a	e	New York	ab	r	h	po	a	e
Fewster ss	3	0	0	2	6	0	Witt cf	3	1	1	3	0	0
Collins rf	4	0	0	2	1	0	Dugan 3b	4	1	1	1	1	0
Skinner cf	4	0	0	0	0	0	Ruth rf	2	1	1	3	0	1
Harris lf	4	0	0	0	0	0	Pipp 1b	3	0	0	12	0	0
Burns 1b	3	1	1	9	2	1	Meusel lf	4	0	1	0	0	0
McMillan 2b	2	0	1	2	0	0	Schang c	4	0	0	4	2	0
Shanks 3b	3	0	0	3	0	0	Ward 2b	3	0	1	3	5	0
DeVormer c	3	0	0	6	2	0	Scott ss	2	0	1	1	4	0
Ehmke p	2	0	1	0	4	0	Shawkey p	3	1	1	0	0	0
aMenosky	1	0	0	0	0	0	Total	28	4	7	27	12	1
Fullerton p	0	0	0	0	0	0							
Total	29	1	3	24	15	1							

aGrounded out for Ehmke in eighth inning.

Boston	000	000	100–1
New York	004	000	00X–4

Two-base hits—Meusel, Scott. Three-base hit—McMillan. Home run—Ruth. Sacrifice hit—Scott. Double play—Scott, Ward, and Pipp. Left on bases—New York, 5; Boston, 4. Bases on balls—off Shawkey, 2; Ehmke, 3; Fullerton, 1. Struck out—by Shawkey, 5; Ehmke, 4; Fullerton, 1. Hits—off Ehmke 7 in 7 innings; Fullerton, none in 1 inning. Hit by pitcher—by Shawkey, (Fewster). Losing pitcher—Ehmke. Umpires—Connolly, Evans, and Holmes. Time of game—2 hrs. 5 min. Attendance—74,000.

Tuesday, April 15, 1924
Fenway Park, Boston
New York 2 Boston 1

All men are liable to error.—John Locke

As the Yankees began their quest to win a fourth consecutive pennant—something no major-league team had ever done—business manager Ed Barrow saw no reason to significantly alter the team that had won the last three. He made only two moves of note during the off-season, purchasing outfielder Earle Combs from the Louisville Colonels of the American Association and selling veteran pitcher Carl Mays to the Cincinnati Reds. The Yankees envisioned Combs, who batted .380 in 1923, with 241 hits and 145 runs batted in, as the successor to Whitey Witt in center field. Eventually he would be, but not this year; Combs broke his ankle early in the 1924 season and played in only 24 games. Manager Miller Huggins strongly supported the dumping of Mays, whom he disliked intensely. Huggins had not forgiven Mays for what he felt was a questionable pitching performance in the fourth game of the 1921 World Series. He used him in only 23 games in 1923, mostly in relief, even though Mays was completely healthy. On December 11, after all American League teams had passed on him, the Yankees sold Mays to the Reds for the waiver price. For Huggins it was the type of transaction that Branch Rickey defined as "addition by subtraction."

Huggins's on-field control of his players had increased after Jacob Ruppert paid Til Huston $1.5 million for his share of the club and became the Yankees' sole owner. Before then, some players, knowing Huston had never been happy with Huggins, may have doubted the manager's authority. By buying out Huston, Ruppert was sending a message to the players, and particularly to Babe Ruth, that Huggins was his manager and would continue to be his manager. Huggins, appreciative and reassured by the confidence showed in him, rewarded Ruppert with the Yankees' third straight pennant in 1923 and their first World Series victory.

The Yanks began their pursuit of that fourth straight flag at Boston's Fenway Park. They left Grand Central Station for Boston the evening before the game, minus two young players sent back to the minor leagues earlier that day. Both were former collegians who had made brief appearances with the Yankees in 1923: infielder Mike Gazella from Lafayette College, who went to the Minneapolis Millers of the American Association, and first baseman Lou Gehrig from Columbia University, who went to the Hartford Senators of the Eastern League. Gehrig in particular had attracted considerable attention in college. Just a year ago, on the day Yankee Stadium opened, he had struck out 17 Williams College batters in a 5–1 Columbia loss.

The 1924 opener drew more than 25,000 (23,856 paid) to Fenway, the largest crowd ever for an Opening Day in this city. Although this would be the eighth opening-day meeting between the Yanks and Red Sox, it was the first one played at Boston. Howard Ehmke pitched a superb game for the Red Sox, but the "breaks of the game" were with the New Yorkers today. Two ninth-inning errors by Boston second baseman Bill Wambsganss led to two unearned runs and a 2–1 Yankees victory. Yet, despite the bone-chilling cold weather and the ninth-inning collapse, it had been a most enjoyable day for Red Sox fans. That was unusual. With the Sox coming off two consecutive last-place finishes, joyful days at Fenway Park had been rare in recent years. Attendance in 1923 had slipped to 229,688, the lowest in the team's history. But in July of that year, despairing Boston fans happily learned that Red Sox owner Harry Frazee, the most hated man in New England, the man who sold Babe Ruth to New York, was selling the team. A group of businessmen including former St. Louis Browns President Bob Quinn bought the Red Sox for more than a million dollars. The group named Quinn president and chose Lee Fohl as the new manager. Quinn was pleasantly surprised by the record turnout today. Boston, where April weather was only intermittently Spring-like, had never been among the league's more enthusiastic opening-day cities. Once the grandstand sold out, fans headed for the bleachers and the pavilion and quickly filled large parts of those venues. Over the past several years, the few fans that came to Fenway Park had taken great delight in belittling the home team, but at least for this one day the fans put their bitterness aside and offered the Red Sox players only cheers and words of encouragement.

Ruppert and Barrow braved the cold to be at the game, as did Governor Channing Cox of Massachusetts, American League president Ban Johnson, and Bill Carrigan, who had played and managed for Boston back when they were among the league's elite. Carrigan, down from his home in Lewiston, Maine, chatted before the game about the "old days" with several of his former players, including Ruth and Everett Scott of the Yankees. He remarked that Scott, preparing to play in his record-extending 1,139th consecutive game, looked much the same as he had when Carrigan managed him as a Boston rookie in 1914. Jimmy Coughlin's Veterans Band led the pregame parade, followed by Quinn, Boston mayor James M. Curley, a squad of Marines from the Boston Navy Yard, and the two ball clubs. The Yankees wore their road-grays, with blue caps and stockings and the block-lettered "NEW YORK" on their jersey fronts. The Red Sox wore their home-whites, with no trim or lettering, red and white stockings, and a white cap with a red bill. At the flagpole, managers Huggins and Fohl raised the American flag along with the new Red Sox flag, a pair of red stockings on a white background. Mayor Curley amused the crowd when he went to the pitcher's mound to make the traditional opening-day throw. On the receiving end, stationed behind the plate, was Quinn, wearing equipment borrowed from Boston's new catcher Steve O'Neill. Witt, the Yankees' leadoff batter (Combs would not make his debut until tomorrow), had taken his place in the batter's box, but had to jump out quickly when Curley's throw nearly plunked him in the ribs.

Ehmke replaced the mayor on the mound and threw four more wide ones to Witt, but then got Joe Dugan to hit into a double play. Ruth, batting in his customary number three slot, was next. He ran the count full against Ehmke before plate umpire Tom Connolly called him out on strikes. The Yankees repeated that offensive pattern through the next seven innings. They would get a hit here and a walk there, but Ehmke with his off-speed underhand deliveries kept them scoreless. Yankees pitcher Bob Shawkey, who had defeated Ehmke and Boston 4–1, in last season's opener at Yankee Stadium, was almost as effective. Shawkey allowed only two singles before leaving for pinch-hitter Harvey Hendrick in the eighth. He left trailing 1–0, as the Red Sox had used their two hits to produce a fifth-inning run. Howard Shanks got the first hit, a leadoff single. Fohl, noting how effectively both Shawkey and Ehmke were pitching, chose to play for one run. He had shortstop Dud Lee, playing his first big-league game since a brief trial with the St. Louis Browns in 1920–1921, sacrifice Shanks to second. When O'Neill grounded out to second baseman Aaron Ward, Shanks moved to third. He came home when Ehmke went after the first pitch and drove it into left field for a run-scoring single.

Ehmke took the 1–0 lead he had provided himself into the ninth, but to preserve it he would have to get past the heart of the Yankees lineup: Ruth, Wally Pipp, and Bob Meusel. After hosting a team party at his Sudbury (Massachusetts) farmhouse the previous night, Ruth had not looked good in his previous three at-bats, but he led off with a sharply lined single. Huggins, playing for the tie, had Pipp lay down a bunt that Ehmke fielded and threw to Wambsganss covering first for the out. Meanwhile, Ruth, sliding hard into second, had twisted his right ankle. Doc Wood, the Yankees' trainer, treated the injury—a slight sprain— and play resumed. Meusel smashed a ground ball right at Wambsganss, who fumbled it, permitting Meusel to reach first and Ruth to go to third. With the potential tying run now at third base, the Red Sox had a choice of how to play their infield. They could play in to prevent the run from scoring on a ground ball, or they could play back and turn that ground ball into a game-ending double play. Fohl elected to play his infield in, which turned out to be the wrong decision. Ward hit a routine ground ball that eluded both shortstop Lee and third baseman Shanks and brought Ruth home with the tying run. Wally Schang followed with a ground ball to second that Wambsganss, playing his first game for Boston after ten years with the Cleveland Indians, again had trouble picking up. While he tried to come up with the ball, Meusel, who had gotten a good lead off second, came tearing around third to score the go-ahead run. After Scott fouled out, Lee made a sensational play behind second base to take a hit away from Waite Hoyt and end the inning. Although disappointed at having lost the lead, the crowd stood and applauded their new shortstop. Hoyt, who had come on to pitch in the eighth inning and set the Sox down in order, quickly got the first two batters in the ninth: former longtime Detroit Tigers outfielder Bobby Veach and first baseman Joe Harris. Rookie Ike Boone kept the fans' hopes alive by drawing a walk, but Shanks's hard smash was right back at Hoyt, who fielded it and threw to Pipp for the final out.

Tuesday, April 15, 1924

New York	ab	r	h	po	a	e
Witt cf	3	0	1	3	0	0
Dugan 3b	4	0	1	2	2	0
Ruth lf	3	1	1	0	0	0
Pipp 1b	2	0	0	9	0	0
Meusel rf	4	1	0	2	0	0
Ward 2b	4	0	1	4	1	0
Schang c	4	0	0	5	1	0
Scott ss	4	0	0	2	3	0
Shawkey p	2	0	0	0	1	0
ªHendrick	1	0	1	0	0	0
Hoyt p	1	0	0	0	2	0
Total	32	2	5	27	10	0

Boston	ab	r	h	po	a	e
Flagstead cf	3	0	0	0	0	0
Wambsganss 2b	4	0	0	5	1	2
Veach lf	3	0	0	0	0	0
Harris 1b	3	0	0	11	1	0
Boone rf	2	0	0	2	0	0
Shanks 3b	4	1	1	1	5	1
Lee ss	2	0	0	2	3	0
O'Neill c	2	0	0	6	0	0
Ehmke p	3	0	1	0	2	0
Total	26	1	2	27	12	3

ªSingled for Shawkey in eighth inning.

New York	000	000	002–2
Boston	000	010	000–1

Stolen bases—Ruth, Witt. Sacrifices—Pipp, Lee. Double plays—Scott and Pipp; Scott, Ward, and Pipp; Lee, Wambsganss, and Harris; Wambsganss and Harris. Left on bases—New York, 7; Boston, 5. Base on balls-off Shawkey, 5; Hoyt, 1; Ehmke, 3. Struck out—by Shawkey, 3; Hoyt, 1; Ehmke, 4. Hits—off Shawkey, 2 in 7 innings; Hoyt, none in 2 innings. Passed ball—O'Neill. Winning pitcher—Hoyt. Umpires—Connolly and Dinneen. Time of game—2 hrs. Attendance—25,000.

Under their new leadership the Red Sox would show limited improvement in 1924, finishing seventh. However, because Quinn persuaded the fans he was trying to make the team a winner again, they ended their boycott and home attendance nearly doubled.

The Yankees were unable to win their fourth consecutive pennant, finishing second (89–63), two games behind the Washington Senators. (In the National League, the New York Giants did win a fourth consecutive pennant.) Babe Ruth led the league in batting (.378), home runs (46), runs (143), slugging percentage (.739) and walks (142). His 121 RBIs were second to Goose Goslin of the Senators, who had 129, thereby preventing Ruth from winning the Triple Crown.

Tuesday, April 14, 1925
Yankee Stadium, New York
New York 5 Washington 1

*I look upon it, that he who does not mind his
belly will hardly mind anything else.* —Samuel Johnson

After completing their first spring training in St. Petersburg, Florida, the Yankees were playing their way north when Babe Ruth collapsed in Asheville, North Carolina. Team officials rushed Ruth by train to St. Vincent's Hospital in Manhattan where doctors discovered he had an intestinal abscess. They scheduled him for surgery on April 17, which would be three days after the Yankees' opener against the defending champion Washington Senators. Although Ruth realized he would be unable to play on Opening Day, he still wanted to be at Yankee Stadium for the game. He argued that just his presence would lend moral support to his teammates, but his physician, Dr. Edward King, refused permission. However, Ruth's absence did not prevent his wife Helen from being there, taking notes for a local newspaper column that ran under the Babe's byline. When Ruth, in his bed at St. Vincent's, learned Urban Shocker had pitched the Yanks to a 5–1 victory and his substitute, rookie Ben Paschal, had contributed a two-run homer, he said smilingly, "They don't seem to miss me much."

The Babe remained at St. Vincent's until May 26, and did not play his first game until June 1. He played in only 98 games in 1925, batting .290 with 25 home runs—second in the league to teammate Bob Meusel. In the years since 1925, historians have attributed Ruth's affliction to various causes, ranging from eating too many hot dogs to venereal disease. Nevertheless, whereas he may have suffered the effects of both those indulgences during his lifetime, the intestinal abscess story was more than likely the truth.

A crowd of about 50,000 came out for the opener in spite of the Babe's absence and the cold, gloomy weather. The Yankees, along with Ty Cobb's Detroit Tigers, were thought to be Washington's strongest challengers this season, which made this opening four-game series between the Yanks and Senators particularly important. New York fans, noted for their fairness, greeted the Senators with a burst of applause when they took the field for batting practice. It was their way of acknowledging Washington's thrilling seven-game triumph over the New York Giants last fall. The Senators were led by second baseman Bucky Harris, baseball's youngest manager, who was just 27 when Clark Griffith chose him to replace Donie Bush in February 1924. The Senators responded to the "Boy Wonder" by producing Washington's first championship season.

As Harris and his players—wearing their gray road uniforms with the blue "W" on the left sleeve—went through their drills, coaches Al Schacht and Nick Altrock entertained the fans. Schacht and Altrock, both former pitchers, went through their comedy act that included making circus catches in the outfield and acting out a slow-motion boxing match. The official pregame ceremonies began later when three brass bands marched onto the stadium grass. The three—the Sixteenth Infantry First Division Band, the Marine Band from the Brooklyn Navy Yard, and the Seventh Regiment Band—marched to the flagpole along with Colonel Ruppert, detachments of soldiers and sailors, and the two ball clubs. At 3:30, Rear Admiral Charles P. Plunkett, commander of the Third Naval District and the Brooklyn Navy Yard, tossed the ball to Yankees catcher Steve O'Neill, who handed it back to the

Admiral as umpire Tom Connolly shouted, "Play ball!" Jack Lentz, using his megaphone, announced the batteries: Mogridge and Ruel for Washington, Shocker and O'Neill for New York.

Shocker was back with the Yankees after seven years with the St. Louis Browns. Miller Huggins, in his first move as manager, had traded him to St. Louis in the Del Pratt deal. The stockily built Shocker won 20 games four times with the Browns and blossomed into one of the league's best pitchers. His general success and his many victories against the Yankees led Huggins to reacquire him in a December 1924 trade for pitchers Joe Bush, Milt Gaston, and Joe Giard. Harris had planned to pitch Walter Johnson today, but changed his mind because of the cold weather. Johnson, beginning his 19th season with the Senators, had pitched 12 of the last 13 openers, missing only 1922 when he was ill. Coincidentally, that game too had been against a Yankee team that was playing without Babe Ruth; and George Mogridge, who substituted for Johnson that day, was doing so again today. Mogridge, who won that '22 opener, 6–5, was an ex–Yankee who had been Huggins's opening-day starter in each of his first two seasons as manager. This afternoon, he retired the side in order in the first inning and got two quick outs in the second before running into trouble. He gave up singles to Aaron Ward and Everett Scott and then had a temporary wild spell, which was unusual for the 36-year-old left-hander whose success depended on guile and good control. First he walked catcher O'Neill, the number-eight hitter, obtained on waivers from the Boston Red Sox. O'Neill was catching the opener only because Shocker, among the last of the legal spitballers, was pitching. O'Neill had experience handling the pitch, having caught Stan Coveleski in Cleveland and Jack Quinn in Boston.

Mogridge, who now had loaded the bases, then committed one of baseball's unpardonable sins; he walked the pitcher. The free pass to Shocker forced Ward in with New York's first run. As Paschal faced Mogridge for the second time, he had his first opportunity to be a hero, but he failed, fouling out to catcher Muddy Ruel. Washington tied the game in the fourth inning, also scoring after two were out and the bases empty. Goose Goslin singled to left, stole second, and scored when Ossie Bluege followed a walk to Joe Judge with a single to center. Shocker ended the inning by getting Roger Peckinpaugh to swing and miss at a full-count spitter.

In the Yankees' fifth, Shocker, a good-hitting pitcher, led off with a drive over the head of left fielder Goslin. By the time Goslin retrieved it, Shocker, huffing and puffing all the way, was at third base. He barely had regained his breath when Paschal lined a single to left to send him home and put the Yanks ahead, 2–1. Mogridge then bobbled Joe Dugan's attempted sacrifice, and the Yanks had two on with nobody out. Earle Combs, starting his first opener, tried to move both runners up, but this time Mogridge fielded the ball cleanly and threw to Bluege at third to force Paschal. After Meusel lined a single off Bluege's glove to load the bases, the crowd, sensing a big inning, was roaring. However, Mogridge, a veteran who did not ruffle easily, stranded the three runners by fanning Wally Pipp and Ward, his only two strikeouts of the game.

Scott opened the home sixth with his second single of the day. Though bothered by bad legs, Scott was intent on stretching his consecutive games played streak to 1,300, now only nine games away. His streak would end early in May at 1,307, and a month later the Yankees would sell him to Washington. Two outs later, with Scott at second, Paschal drove one of Mogridge's off-speed pitches into the left-field bleachers, increasing the lead to 4–1. The vast majority of those in Yankee Stadium would have preferred that Ruth hit the season's first home run. Yet it seemed only appropriate to them that if the Babe couldn't do it, at least it was his substitute who did. Paschal, a 29-year-old right-handed-hitter, had first appeared in the major leagues ten years earlier, playing nine games with the 1915 Cleveland Indians. Five years later he played nine games with the Red Sox, and then in September 1924 four games with the Yankees. Paschal would remain in New York through 1929, but on a team that had an outfield of Ruth, Meusel, and Combs, he would never be a regular.

Tuesday, April 14, 1925

Washington	ab	r	h	po	a	e	New York	ab	r	h	po	a	e
McNeely cf	4	0	0	2	0	0	Paschal rf	4	1	2	0	0	0
Harris 2b	4	0	1	1	2	0	Dugan 3b	3	0	0	0	3	0
Rice cf	4	0	0	1	0	0	Combs cf	4	0	0	1	0	0
Goslin lf	4	1	1	0	0	0	Meusel lf	4	1	2	3	0	0
Judge 1b	3	0	1	14	0	0	Pipp 1b	4	0	0	12	1	0
Bluege 3b	2	0	2	1	5	0	Ward 2b	4	1	2	3	4	0
Peckinpaugh ss	3	0	0	0	1	0	Scott ss	4	1	2	5	4	0
Ruel c	3	0	0	5	1	0	O'Neill c	3	0	0	3	1	0
Mogridge p	2	0	2	0	3	1	Shocker p	2	1	1	0	2	0
ªLeibold	1	0	0	0	0	0	Total	32	5	9	27	15	0
Russell p	0	0	0	0	2	0							
Total	30	1	7	24	14	1							

ªBatted for Mogridge in eighth inning.

Washington	000	100	000–1
New York	010	012	10X–5

Three-base hit—Shocker. Home runs—Paschal, Meusel. Stolen base—Goslin. Sacrifices—Shocker, Dugan. Double plays—Shocker, Scott, and Pipp; Scott, Ward, and Pipp; Pipp and Scott. Left on bases—New York, 7; Washington, 4. Bases on balls—off Shocker, 2; Mogridge, 2. Struck out—by Shocker, 3; Mogridge, 2. Hits—off Mogridge, 9 in 7 innings; Russell, none in 1 inning. Losing pitcher—Mogridge. Umpires—Connolly and Nallin. Time of game—1 hr. 50 min.

Meusel completed the scoring with a one-out home run in the seventh, a blow that landed in the same area of the left-field bleachers that Paschal's had an inning earlier. Even before Meusel was back in the dugout, many spectators began to make their way to the exits, certain of a Yankees' victory. Shocker had been far from overpowering this afternoon. He allowed the Senators seven hits and two walks, but his infield helped him with three double plays. Meusel made the individual defensive play of the game in the fifth when he pulled Ruel's potential home run out of the first row of seats in left. With today's victory, Shocker continued his career-long effectiveness against Washington, raising his record against them to 27–9. He would finish at 12–12, the only Yankees' starter not to have a losing record this dreadful season. Mogridge's lifetime mark versus his former team slipped to 8–10. Washington came back to win the remaining three games of the series and went on to repeat as American League champions.

Bob Meusel led the league in home runs (33) and runs batted in (134). Earle Combs batted .342, earning him unofficial recognition as the American League's best rookie. Nevertheless, the Yankees had a horrendous year. They experienced their only second-division finish under Huggins, plummeting to seventh place (69–85), 28½ games behind Washington. The Yankees would not end a season in the second division again until 1965, 40 years later.

Tuesday, April 13, 1926
Fenway Park, Boston
New York 12 Boston 11

And this is good old Boston.—John Collins Bossidy

Frigid Fenway Park was the setting for the Yankees' first game using the lineup that many historians would later call the greatest ever. The Yanks won the game, but not easily. Boston battled back from a ten-run deficit and had the tying run in scoring position before the visitors escaped with a 12–11 victory. The bitterly cold weather kept the crowd to about 12,000, many of whom were already gone when the Red Sox staged their late-inning comeback. Managers Miller Huggins of the Yankees and Lee Fohl of the Red Sox used a total of nine pitchers in the three-hour, 29-hit marathon. Each Yankee position player had at least one hit in the game, and so did six of the Boston starters. Strangely, there were no home runs hit, but the two teams did combine for nine doubles and two triples. It was the type of slugfest that helped establish Fenway Park's reputation as a place where no lead was ever safe.

The Yankees had spent the off-season making the moves they felt necessary to bounce back from 1925's seventh-place finish. In scrutinizing the team's needs, Huggins and business manager Ed Barrow were satisfied the pitching was strong; and that in Babe Ruth, Bob Meusel, and Earle Combs, they had the game's best outfield. However, they did set about to revamp their inner defense, which was now beginning to show signs of age. When they were finished, only third baseman Joe Dugan remained from the infield that started the opener a year ago. Two San Francisco-born rookies, second baseman Tony Lazzeri and shortstop Mark Koenig, replaced the double-play combination of Aaron Ward and Everett Scott, opening-day starters since 1922. Huggins had first handed the shortstop job to 22-year-old Pee Wee Wanninger last June after selling Scott to Washington. But Wanninger, who never before had played above Class B, was not ready for major-league pitching and batted only .236. Koenig, 21, who had been up briefly last September, won the position with an excellent spring training, during which he compiled an 18-game hitting streak. Second baseman Lazzeri, 22, had played with Salt Lake City of the Pacific Coast League in 1925, attracting the attention of the baseball world with 222 runs batted in, 60 home runs, and 202 runs scored.

The Pacific Coast League played a 200-game schedule; nevertheless, all of those totals were new highs for organized baseball. The new first baseman was Lou Gehrig, also 22, who had supplanted 32-year-old Wally Pipp during the calamitous 1925 season. Pipp, a Yankee since 1915, had been New York's opening-day first baseman for each of the last 11 years. However, Gehrig's youth and power—he hit 20 home runs in 437 at-bats in 1925—made Pipp expendable, and in January the Yanks sold him to the Cincinnati Reds for $7,500. Huggins's new lineup had been almost unbeatable in spring training. They won their final 18 games, and also swept a 12-game series with the Brooklyn Robins.

Huggins selected Bob Shawkey to pitch the opener, while Boston went with Howard Ehmke. It was Shawkey's fourth opening-day start for the Yankees, which at the time tied him with Jack Chesbro for the most in club history. And for the third time in four years, he was opposing Ehmke in the season-opener. In 1923, Shawkey had three-hit the Red Sox, 4–1, in the first game played at Yankee Stadium. A year later at Fenway Park, New York scored two unearned runs in the ninth inning to defeat Ehmke 2–1. Waite Hoyt, with two scoreless innings in relief, was the winner in that one. Like Shawkey, Ehmke also had some newcomers playing behind him. Fohl was opening the season with three rookies: outfielders Tom Jenkins and Si Rosenthal and Cuban-born second baseman Mike Herrera.

In an act of compassion, given the freezing temperatures, Red Sox officials kept the pregame ceremonies short. Both clubs even chose to skip the march to the flagpole, preferring to watch it from their dugouts. Only the politicians took part, not willing to give up an appearance before 13,000 potential voters. Massachusetts governor Alvan T. Fuller and lieutenant governor Frank G. Allen, Boston mayor Malcolm E. Nichols, and Red Sox president Bob Quinn led a detachment of marines and a local band in the flag raising and the playing of "The Star-Spangled Banner." Standing on the mound, Mayor Nichols, the last of the Boston Brahmins to hold that position, threw the first ball to Governor Fuller, stationed at home plate. Umpires Bill Dinneen and Bill McGowan took up their positions, and the game began. Earlier, when the umpires made their first appearance on the field, Dinneen said, "These are our special occasion suits." He was referring to the new uniforms all American League umpires were now wearing: gray pants and coats, black ties, and blue caps. This was the only American League game played today that used just two umpires, and would be the last Yankees' opener that did so.

The Yanks set the tone for the afternoon when they jumped in front with four first-inning runs off Ehmke. After Koenig opened with a bunt single and Combs walked, Huggins ordered Gehrig to lay down a sacrifice. Ehmke fielded the bunt, but his throw to third base trying to force Koenig was late, loading the bases for Ruth. The Babe had been at the State House's taxation office that morning in response to an arrest warrant charging him with failure to pay Massachusetts state income tax for 1923 and 1924. (Henry F. Long, Commissioner of Corporations and Taxation, granted him one week to prove he had not been a Massachusetts resident in those years.) Working carefully, Ehmke got Ruth to hit a ground ball to second base. But Herrera booted what might have been a rally-killing double play, permitting Koenig to score, and keeping the bases loaded. Meusel, in the lineup despite a bad cold, followed by lifting a high twisting foul ball along the first base line. Phil Todt, the first baseman, caught up with it, but Combs scored after the catch. New York reloaded the bases on a double steal by Gehrig and Ruth and a walk to Lazzeri. Dugan's infield single scored Gehrig, and Ehmke walked catcher Pat Collins to send Ruth home with the fourth Yankee run. Collins, playing with a badly bruised forefinger on his throwing hand, was in his first game as a Yankee. He was returning to the major leagues after an outstanding season at St. Paul in the American Association, which followed six years with the St. Louis Browns. The bases were still loaded, but Ehmke fanned Shawkey and got Koenig on another foul ball to Todt, limiting the damage to four runs.

A double by veteran outfielder Ira Flagstead and two ground balls got Boston a run in their first at-bat. The Yankees countered with a run in the third when Collins singled home Lazzeri, who had been hit by a pitch. Back-to-back triples by Combs and Gehrig and run-scoring singles by Ruth and Collins made it 8–1 in the fourth. Gehrig's blast, which sailed over center fielder Flagstead's head, landed in the deepest part of the park. No one present could recall a longer hit ball at Fenway that had stayed in play.

Rudy Sommers, a 39-year-old left-hander with very limited major-league experience, replaced Ehmke in the fifth. This was Sommers's first big league appearance in 12 years; he had pitched one game for the Chicago Cubs in 1912 and 23 games for Brooklyn Tip-Tops of the Federal League in 1914. He lasted one inning—one of the two innings he pitched for the Red Sox before they released him. A walk to Koenig, opposite field doubles by Gehrig and Ruth, and a single by Dugan led to three more runs and an 11–1 Yankees' lead.

Boston began their long climb back with two runs in the bottom of the fifth. Catcher Alex Gaston and pinch hitter Sam Langford (in his only at-bat of the season) reached base on errors by Dugan and Shawkey. Gaston scored on a hit by Flagstead, and Langford came home on Todt's grounder to Lazzeri. An inning later, a five-run outburst brought the Sox to within three, 11–8. A pop-fly double by Herrera and a walk to Gaston put two men on with one out. German-born Tony Welzer, who had pitched a scoreless sixth in his big-league debut, was the due batter, but Fohl sent Roy Carlyle up to bat for him. Carlyle came through with a single to right that scored Herrera. Flagstead followed with a double to left that scored Gaston, sent Carlyle to third, and Shawkey to the showers. Urban Shocker took over and gave up a run-scoring single to Fred Haney, the third baseman the Red Sox had gotten in a December trade with the Detroit Tigers. A wild pitch by Shocker and a double by Todt accounted for two more Boston runs.

New York got its 12th and final run in the seventh against Del Lundgren, another Boston newcomer. It came on Ruth's double to right, a sacrifice by Meusel, and Lazzeri's infield single. Meusel was the American League's defending home-run champion, yet Huggins, just as he had done with Gehrig in the first inning, had Meusel lay one down. The resulting run, which stretched New York's lead to 12–8, proved to be the game-winner. Boston got a run in their half of the seventh, again reducing New York's margin to three runs. Herrera was hit by a pitch, went to second on a passed ball, and scored on a pinch-hit double by Jack Rothrock, batting for Lundgren. In the eighth, the Red Sox warmed the crowd by scoring two more runs to make it a one-run game at 12–11. Facing Sam Jones, who relieved Shocker in the seventh, Rosenthal, Jenkins, Herrera, and Fred Bratschi all singled to account for the two scores. The hit by Bratschi, another newcomer playing his first game for Boston, gave the Sox three successful pinch hits on the day.

Tuesday, April 13, 1926

New York	ab	r	h	po	a	e	Boston	ab	r	h	po	a	e
Koenig ss	5	2	1	2	1	1	Flagstead cf	6	2	4	4	0	0
Combs cf	5	2	2	1	0	0	Haney 3b	5	1	2	1	0	0
Gehrig 1b	4	3	2	11	0	0	Rosenthal rf	5	1	1	0	0	0
Ruth lf	6	3	3	0	0	0	Todt 1b	5	0	1	12	3	0
Meusel rf	3	1	1	1	0	0	Jenkins lf	5	1	1	1	0	0
Lazzeri 2b	4	1	1	1	5	0	Herrera 2b	4	1	2	1	3	1
Dugan 3b	5	0	3	3	1	1	Lee ss	4	1	0	3	1	0
Collins c	3	0	2	8	2	0	aBratschi	1	0	1	0	0	0
Shawkey p	3	0	0	0	1	1	McCann ss	0	0	0	2	0	0
Shocker p	1	0	0	0	2	0	Gaston c	3	2	0	3	0	0
Jones p	0	0	0	0	2	0	Ehmke p	1	0	0	0	1	0
Total	39	12	15	27	14	3	Sommers p	0	0	0	0	1	0
							bLangford	0	1	0	0	0	0
							Welzer p	0	0	0	0	0	0
							cCarlyle	1	1	1	0	0	0
							Lundgren p	0	0	0	0	1	0
							dRothrock	1	0	1	0	0	0
							Wiltse p	0	0	0	0	0	0

Boston

	ab	r	h	po	a	e
ᵉGeygan	1	0	0	0	0	0
Kiefer p	0	0	0	0	2	0
Total	42	11	14	27	12	1

ᵃSingled for Lee in eighth inning.
ᵇReached base on error for Sommers in fifth inning.
ᶜSingled for Welzer in sixth inning.
ᵈDoubled for Lundgren in seventh inning.
ᵉStruck out for Wiltse in eighth inning.

New York	401	330	100—12
Boston	100	025	120—11

Two-base hits—Flagstead (2), Gehrig, Ruth (2), Herrera, Todt, Rothrock, Meusel. Three-base hits—Combs, Gehrig. Sacrifice hits—Gehrig, Meusel, Haney. Sacrifice flies—Meusel, Rosenthal. Stolen bases—Ruth, Gehrig. Double play—Todt and Lee. Left on bases—New York, 13; Boston, 11. Bases on balls—Off Ehmke, 4; Shawkey, 3; Sommers, 2; Welzer, 1; Shocker, 1; Lundgren, 1; Wiltse, 1. Struck out—by Shawkey, 4; Ehmke, 2; Jones, 2. Hits—off Ehmke, 8 in 4 innings; Sommers, 3 in 1 inning; Welzer, 1 in 1 inning; Lundgren, 2 in 1 inning; Wiltse none in 1 inning; Kiefer, 1 in 1 inning; off Shawkey, 6 in 5 ⅓ innings; Shocker, 3 in 1 inning; Jones, 5 in 2⅔ innings. Passed ball—Collins. Wild pitch—Shocker. Hit by pitched ball—by Ehmke (Lazzeri); by Shocker (Herrera). Winning pitcher—Shawkey. Losing pitcher—Ehmke. Umpires—Dinneen and McGowan. Time of game—3 hrs.

The Yankees wasted a leadoff double against Joe Kiefer, Boston's sixth pitcher, in the ninth. Kiefer, like the four pitchers that followed Ehmke, and preceded him—Sommers, Welzer, Lundgren, and Hal Wiltse—was making his first appearance in a Red Sox uniform. Flagstead buoyed the hopes of the hometown fans when he singled to lead off the last of the ninth, his fourth hit of the game. Haney successfully moved him along, and Boston had the tying run at second base. However, Jones got Rosenthal and Todt, allowing the Yanks to eke out the victory.

Fohl had led Boston to seventh- and eighth-place finishes in his first two seasons as manager, and when the Sox finished last again this year, with more losses (107) than they had ever had in a single season, he resigned.

The Yankees (91–63) rebounded from their seventh-place finish in 1925 to win the pennant by three games over the Cleveland Indians, but lost the World Series to the St. Louis Cardinals in seven games. Babe Ruth had another magnificent season, batting .372 and leading the league in home runs (47), RBIs (153), runs (139), walks (144), and slugging percentage (.737). Tony Lazzeri hit 18 home runs, a new high for an American League rookie.

Tuesday, April 12, 1927
Yankee Stadium, New York
New York 8 Philadelphia 3

What men or gods are these?—John Keats

Only half the nation's sportswriters polled in the spring of 1927 thought the Yankees would win the American League pennant. Most of the others picked the defending champions' opening-day opponents, Connie Mack's Philadelphia Athletics. Mack had slowly brought his team back to respectability after they went from first place in 1914 to last in 1915, and remained there through 1921. This year he had added three all-time greats whom he hoped had enough talent left to bring Philadelphia its first pennant in 13 years. It was the addition of these veterans—outfielders Ty Cobb and Zack Wheat, and second baseman Eddie Collins—to a team with such young stars as outfielder Al Simmons, catcher Mickey Cochrane, and pitcher Lefty Grove that made the A's the pennant choice of so many experts. That such a strong team would finish in second place, 19 games behind them, suggests how great a team the 1927 Yankees were.

Mack and the Yankees' Miller Huggins, the league's two longest-serving managers, had been opposing each other since 1918, the year Huggins replaced Bill Donovan. Mack, of course, was the only manager the Athletics had ever had. He, Huggins, and Bucky Harris, beginning his fourth year in Washington, were the only American League managers opening the season with the same club with which they finished the 1926 season. Four of the others were making their major-league managerial debuts: Ray Schalk at Chicago, Jack McCallister at Cleveland, George Moriarty at Detroit, and Dan Howley at St. Louis, while in Boston, Bill Carrigan was returning as the manager after a 10-year absence.

In 1921, when the A's last opened the season in New York, the Yankees crushed them, 11–1, before a record-breaking crowd of 37,000 at the Polo Grounds. Now, just six years later, an immense, swarming throng nearly three times as great was attempting to make its way into Yankee Stadium. Unfortunately for the fans and the Yankees' coffers, the Stadium could not hold them all. Those who got in—estimated at about 72,000—made for an even larger crowd than the one that witnessed the stadium's opening in 1923, and that had been baseball's greatest gathering ever. The entire block of reserved seats had been sold by yesterday and all the unreserved seats were gone an hour before game time, including the standing-room tickets for the lower deck and the mezzanine. It would be another highly profitable day for Harry M. Stevens, the Yankees' concessionaire. Stevens had been part of the New York baseball scene since 1894 when he began printing and selling scorecards at the old Polo Grounds. Now, 33 years later, he and his sons controlled the catering at four major-league parks and six racetracks. There was some consolation for the nearly 30,000 unhappy patrons denied admission; they could follow the game, play-by-play, on the radio. Graham McNamee, the premier sports announcer of the time, was broadcasting the day's events over two New York radio stations, WEAF and WJZ. Whether watching in person or listening on the radio, it was a happy day for Yankees' enthusiasts as the team won its fifth consecutive opener, beating Philadelphia and Grove, 8–3.

At this point in baseball history, Ty Cobb, after 22 years with the Detroit Tigers, was recognized universally as the greatest player in American League history, and by most fans as the greatest player ever. He had signed with the Athletics following an unpleasant incident the previous winter in which former pitcher Hubert "Dutch" Leonard had accused Cobb and the Cleveland Indian's Tris Speaker of "game-fixing." Commissioner Landis cleared the two stars, both of whom were then managing their respective clubs, but suggested they find new teams to play for in 1927. Speaker chose the Washington Senators and Cobb the Athletics. Mack was paying him $60,000 for his services this season, about a quarter of which the A's earned today as their share of the gate receipts. Even at age 40, Cobb was still a great player; he would appear in 133 games in 1927 and bat .357. Yet despite his unequaled ability, Cobb had never been a popular player with the fans in New York, or, for that matter, anywhere else but Detroit, and not always there. Nevertheless, the local fans greeted him warmly when he came out for fielding practice, which Cobb acknowledged by doffing his cap. As part of the pregame ceremonies, Bayard J. Budds, representing the Georgia Society in New York, presented him with a beautiful floral arrangement.

At 3:15 P.M., with the sun shining brightly, Colonel Jacob Ruppert and Mayor James J. Walker led the Seventh Regiment Band and the two clubs on the parade to the flagpole. As the band played "The Star-Spangled Banner," the Stars and Stripes was raised. So too was the Yankees' 1926 pennant, a white flag that said "Champions, American League, 1926," in red and blue letters. The photographers had been taking endless pictures of Cobb and Babe Ruth all afternoon; but when Mayor Walker got ready to throw out the first ball, they turned their attention to him. Among those seated near the mayor were British yachtsman Sir Thomas Lipton, former chancellor of the German Republic Dr. Wilhelm Cuno, and Broadway's George M. Cohan. After a few practice throws for the cameramen's benefit, the mayor made his official throw to catcher Johnny Grabowski. Grabowski was new to the Yankees, having come in a January trade with the White Sox (with second baseman Ray Moreheart) in exchange for second baseman Aaron Ward. After ten years with the Yankees, Ward was expendable, having lost his job to Tony Lazzeri in 1926.

For four innings the two pitchers, Grove and New York's Waite Hoyt, kept these two powerful teams scoreless. The Yankees finally broke through with four runs in the fifth, and then four more in the sixth to coast to the victory. Defense helped make the difference; the Athletics committed five errors behind Grove, including some very costly ones. With his blazing fastball, Grove had looked nearly invincible early on. Then, in the fifth, the Yankees got to him. After Joe Dugan singled and Grabowski walked, Hoyt attempted to bunt them over. First baseman Dud Branom, a 29-year-old rookie playing his first major-league game (he would only play 30), fumbled the ball and the bases were loaded. The hot-tempered left-hander was clearly upset at Branom's error. He became more perturbed when Earle Combs sliced a double over the head of left fielder Bill Lamar. Comb's two-bagger scored Dugan and Grabowski and sent Hoyt to third. Grove got Mark Koenig to ground out as the runners held, and then fanned Ruth. But Lou Gehrig's grounder to the right side got by second baseman Collins for a double, scoring Hoyt and Combs to make the score 4–0. Gehrig had his first two runs batted in for 1927, a season in which he would drive in 173, breaking Ruth's major-league record of 168 set in 1921.

Ruth's strikeout this inning was his second of the game. Grove fanned him in the first, but not before home-plate umpire Billy Evans stopped play for a little ceremony. As the Babe (with a noticeable potbelly) approached the plate, Mayor Walker came out of the stands and presented him with a silver loving cup. The cup, donated by newspaper publisher William Randolph Hearst, was in recognition of Ruth's popularity with the fans. In his second at-bat, in the fourth inning, he popped out with Koenig at third when a fly ball would have meant a run. When Ruth, with two strikeouts and a pop-up, was due to bat in the sixth, Huggins sent up right-handed-hitting Ben Paschal to pinch-hit. The Babe later claimed he was suffering from indigestion and dizzy spells, although the more cynical fans present believed it was Grove's fastballs and curves that had caused his departure. Ruth would have his most memorable season in 1927, but on Opening Day, whatever the cause, Grove simply overmatched him. Grove was in only his third big-league season, but baseball people were comparing his fastball to Walter Johnson's. He had already established himself as Johnson's successor to the title of baseball's strikeout king by leading the league in batters fanned as a rookie in 1925, and repeating in 1926. Grove would lead again in 1927 and every year after that through 1931.

Philadelphia reached Hoyt for two runs in the sixth on a bunt single by Cobb, a single by Sammy Hale, an infield out by Branom, and an infield hit by Cochrane. But in the bottom of the sixth, five hits and an error produced four more Yankees' runs. Lazzeri led off with a double and went to third when Grove was slow in getting to a tapper by Dugan that went for a hit. Dugan tried to advance on what he thought was a wild pitch; it wasn't, and Cochrane threw him out at second. Lazzeri stayed at third, but scored on Grabowski's single to left. After taking second on Hoyt's sacrifice, Grabowski came home when Combs's grounder went through the legs of shortstop Joe Boley. Koenig's long triple to left made it 7–2. Then Paschal, pinch-hitting for the "ailing" Ruth, singled to drive Koenig across with run number eight. Two errors and a hitless day made for a disappointing debut for the 30-year-old Boley, who was making his major-league debut after a long and successful career (1919–1926) with the Baltimore Orioles. During his stay in Baltimore; the Orioles won seven consecutive International League pennants (1919–1925). Mack finally paid Orioles owner Jack Dunn $65,000 to get Boley, a considerable amount of money for a minor leaguer.

Tuesday, April 12, 1927

Philadelphia	ab	r	h	po	a	e	New York	ab	r	h	po	a	e
E. Collins 2b	4	0	0	3	0	1	Combs cf	4	2	1	3	1	0
Lamar lf	5	0	0	0	0	0	Koenig ss	3	1	2	2	5	0
Cobb rf	4	1	1	1	0		Ruth rf	3	0	0	1	0	0
Simmons cf	4	1	2	1	0	0	Paschal ph, rf	2	0	1	1	0	0
Hale 3b	3	1	2	1	4	0	Gehrig 1b	4	0	1	12	0	0
Branom 1b	3	0	1	10	2	1	Meusel lf	4	0	0	2	0	0
Cochrane c	3	0	2	7	1	0	Lazzeri 2b	3	1	1	1	2	0
Boley ss	3	0	0	1	4	2	Dugan 3b	4	1	3	1	0	0
aFrench	1	0	0	0	0	0	Grabowski c	3	2	1	4	2	0
Grove p	2	0	0	0	4	1	Hoyt p	2	1	0	0	2	0
bBishop	1	0	0	0	0	0	Total	32	8	10	27	12	0
Quinn p	0	0	0	0	0	0							
cWheat	1	0	1	0	0	0							
Total	34	3	9	24	15	5							

aStruck out for Boley in ninth inning.
bGrounded out for Grove in seventh inning.
cSingled for Quinn in ninth inning.

Philadelphia	000	002	010–3
New York	000	044	00X–8

Two-base hits—Combs, Gehrig, Lazzeri, Simmons. Three-base hit—Koenig. Sacrifices—Koenig, Hoyt (2), Hale. Double play—Branom, Boley, and Branom. Left on bases—New York, 8; Philadelphia, 8. Bases on balls—off Hoyt, 3; Grove, 3; Quinn, 2. Struck out—by Hoyt, 3; Grove, 6. Hits—off Grove, 9 in 6 innings; Quinn, 1 in 2 innings. Passed ball—Cochrane. Losing pitcher—Grove. Umpires—Evans, Hildebrand, and McGowan. Time of game—2 hrs. 7 min.

Grove went out for a pinch-hitter in the seventh, and Mack brought Jack Quinn in to replace him. Quinn, now 43 years old, was one of a dwindling group of pitchers still permitted to throw a spitball. When the pitch was outlawed before the 1920 season, the league allowed certain designated pitchers to continue to use it; Quinn, then with the Yankees, was one of those pitchers. Actually, he had done two tours of duty with the Yankees, 1909–1912 and 1919–1921. Now in his 17th big-league season, Quinn pitched a scoreless seventh and eighth, allowing just one hit.

The Athletics got their final run in the eighth on a double by Simmons and a single by Hale. Hale foolishly tried to stretch his hit into a double—his team was down by five runs—but was out on a good throw by Combs. With one out in the ninth, Mack sent Wheat, a longtime Brooklyn Robins' hero, up to hit for Quinn. Wheat had spent 18 years in Brooklyn before his release, and the New York fans gave him an appreciative round of applause. He punched a single into center field and took second unopposed, but got no farther as Hoyt retired Collins and Lamar.

The Yankees, never out of first place, set an American League record for most wins in a season (110–44) and won the pennant by 19 games over Philadelphia. In the World Series they swept the Pittsburgh Pirates in four games. Their offense dominated the league, highlighted by Babe Ruth's 60 home runs, which broke his own record. Lou Gehrig (.373 BAV, 47 HR, and 173 RBI) won the league's Most Valuable Player Award. The only offensive categories in which the team did not lead the league were doubles and stolen bases. Batting average and stolen bases were the only individual offensive categories in which a Yankee did not lead. Waite Hoyt's 22 wins (22–7) and .759 winning percentage led all American League pitchers in those departments. (Ted Lyons of the Chicago White Sox also had 22 wins.) Hoyt and teammates Urban Shocker and rookie Wilcy Moore had the three lowest earned run averages in the league.

Wednesday, April 11, 1928
Shibe Park, Philadelphia
New York 8 Philadelphia 3

Our severest winter, commonly called the spring.—William Cowper

Among the stout-hearted fans at Shibe Park who shivered through the hometown Athletics 8–3 opening-day loss to the Yankees were Earl Staddon and George Young. While it's unlikely that many outside their immediate circles had ever heard of Earl Staddon or George Young, these two Philadelphians illustrated the singular relationship baseball fans once had with their teams. Staddon, a 22-year-old house painter, arrived at the park at 7:45 in the morning and became the first person in line for admission. He said he had skipped a day's work and come early in hopes of getting a good seat behind first base. Young, president of the First Gamer's Club, had been at every A's home-opener since 1901. Staddon and Young represented fans everywhere who wanted to share in that special enchantment of Opening Day, no matter how bad the weather. And the weather was bad this day, the coldest Opening Day on record in Philadelphia. Still, 25,000 hardy souls braved freezing temperatures, howling winds, and a forecast that called for rain and sleet to be at the game. The forecast for rain and sleet, incidentally, was correct; late in the day both forms of precipitation did begin to fall. Certainly a postponement seemed in order, but the revenue from 25,000 paying customers was too much for A's manager (and controller) Connie Mack and president Tom Shibe to resist. The inclement weather severely curtailed the festivities that normally surround the season opener. There was no parade to the flagpole, and the members of the band, with lips and fingers frozen, eventually gave up trying to play any music. Even the flags and decorations, usually omnipresent on Opening Day, were missing. That, however, may have been less a function of the weather than it was the Athletics' budget. The only visible flag was the Stars and Stripes in center field being whipped about in the almost gale-like winds.

A tradition that *was* maintained was the pregame presentation of gifts to selected home-team players. This year they included a travel bag to first baseman Joe Hauser, a new saxophone for catcher Mickey Cochrane, and radios provided by the Atwater Kent Manufacturing Company for the two great veterans, Tris Speaker and Ty Cobb. Speaker, signed by Philadelphia in the off-season after the Washington Senators released him, was entering his 22nd major-league season. Both he and Cobb, beginning his 24th, were in the starting lineup as they began their final campaigns as active players. Speaker was substituting for Al Simmons, the team's best hitter, who was in Pennsylvania Hospital recovering from a tonsillectomy. Mule Haas, a rookie who had won an outfield position that spring, had leg problems and was also sitting out the opener. Mayor Harry A. Mackey was there to throw out the first ball, looking not at all like the football lineman he had been for the University of Pennsylvania back in the 1890s. Wearing a blue overcoat, with gray trousers, pearl spats, and a soft gray hat, Mackey passed the time chatting with Tom Shibe and Ernest S. Barnard, Ban Johnson's successor as American League president. After posing for the cameramen, he threw the ball to plate umpire Bill Dinneen.

Lefty Grove, 20–13 in 1927, his first 20-win season, took the mound for Philadelphia wearing a uniform that brought back memories of his team's gloried past. After an eight-year absence, the Athletics had returned the capital "A" to the left breast of their jerseys. It replaced the elephant (either in blue or white) that had occupied that space from 1920 through 1927. Philadelphia players had first worn an elephant in 1918–1919, wearing it on their left sleeve before it was moved to their jerseys in 1920. Now the elephant, the A's long-time symbol, was visible only on the team windbreaker. The Athletics had also restored the two blue stripes to their white stockings. Leadoff batter Earle Combs stepped in against Grove dressed in the road uniform the Yankees had introduced a year ago. On his jersey, in place of "NEW YORK," which had appeared there since 1913, was the word "YANKEES." The Yanks would wear this uniform on the road through the 1930 season.

Grove had pitched well all spring, right through the city series against the Phillies. He continued to look sharp in the first inning, retiring Combs, Mark Koenig, and Babe Ruth. Yankees starter Herb Pennock (19–8 in 1927) had a more difficult first inning as the Athletics threatened, but did not score. With Cobb, who had singled, at third and Bing Miller, who had doubled, at second, Pennock ended the threat by getting Cochrane on a come-backer. Manager Miller Huggins had chosen the stylish left-hander for the opener following a spring of transition and uncertainty for the team's pitching staff. Wilcy Moore, the rookie sensation of 1927, had a sore arm, and the club had released veterans Bob Shawkey and Dutch Ruether. Another veteran pitcher, Urban Shocker, was still holding out. (Shocker would pitch in only one game after signing, and in September would tragically die of mitral valve failure.) But Huggins knew he could always depend on Pennock, a pitcher with excellent control of himself and the baseball. Pennock's success did not come from intimidating hitters; it came primarily from his knowledge of pitching and the good fortune of having a great team behind him. He was only 18 when the Athletics signed him in 1912, but in 1915, a season after he went 11–4, Mack sold him to the Red Sox on waivers. Over the years Philadelphia had many opportunities to regret that decision, as Pennock, first with Boston and then with the Yankees, piled up victory after victory against his original club.

Grove had a temporary loss of control in the second inning, which cost him two runs. He walked Bob Meusel, Leo Durocher, and Pat Collins to fill the bases, and Pennock brought Meusel and Durocher home with a two-out single to left. Durocher, a rookie, was at second base this afternoon while Tony Lazzeri was home in New York recovering from a muscle strain in his back. The other half of the Yankees' double-play combination, shortstop Koenig, was playing with a spike wound in his left hand that had not completely healed. His first-inning fly ball to Speaker was the first time he had batted since suffering the injury in an exhibition game in Knoxville. Had Koenig been unable to play today, Durocher would have played shortstop, his normal position, with newcomer Gene Robertson, formerly of the St. Louis Browns, playing second. Durocher, who had one at-bat in 1925, got his first big-league hit in the third inning, and it was a big one as the Yankees jumped on Grove for three more runs and a 5–0 lead. Ruth drew a one-out walk and went to third on Lou Gehrig's single. Meusel singled to center, scoring Ruth and sending Gehrig to third. Speaker's throw to third base, attempting to get Gehrig, was late, allowing Meusel to take second. Grove fanned Joe Dugan for the second out, but Durocher punched a single to right to score Gehrig and Meusel.

A base on balls to second baseman Max Bishop led to Philadelphia's first run in their half of the third inning. Bishop, one of baseball's best ever at drawing walks, was nicknamed "Camera Eye" for obvious reasons. He took second when Durocher booted Speaker's ground ball and scored on Miller's sharp single to right. Jimmie Foxx, batting for Cochrane, ended the rally by grounding into a double play, Koenig to Durocher to Gehrig. Foxx, still only 20 years old, was in his fourth season with Philadelphia, but the first in which he would play at least 100 games. He played in 118, split among first base, third base, and catcher. The A's scored two more runs in the sixth, cutting the Yankees' lead to 5–3.

Wednesday, April 11, 1928

New York	ab	r	h	po	a	e	Philadelphia	ab	r	h	po	a	e
Combs cf	5	0	0	3	1	0	Bishop 2b	4	1	0	2	4	0
Koenig ss	4	1	1	2	2	0	Cobb rf	3	0	1	0	0	0
Ruth lf	3	3	1	0	0	0	Speaker cf	4	0	0	3	0	0
Gehrig 1b	5	1	2	11	0	0	Miller lf	3	1	3	2	0	0
Meusel rf	4	2	2	3	0	0	Cochrane c	1	0	0	1	0	0
Dugan 3b	5	0	1	0	1	0	Foxx c	3	1	1	6	1	0
Durocher 2b	3	1	1	3	3	1	Hauser 1b	4	0	1	11	0	0
P. Collins c	2	0	0	4	1	0	Dykes 3b	4	0	0	0	1	0
ªDurst	1	0	0	0	0	0	Boley ss	4	0	1	1	4	0
Grabowski c	0	0	0	1	0	0	Grove p	1	0	0	0	1	0
Pennock p	3	0	2	0	4	0	Shores p	2	0	0	0	2	0
Total	35	8	10	27	12	1	Powers p	0	0	0	1	1	0
							ᵇHale	0	0	0	0	0	0
							Total	33	3	7	27	14	0

ªFouled out into a double play for Collins in seventh inning.
ᵇBatted for Powers in ninth inning.

New York   023   000   201–8
Philadelphia   001   002   000–3

Runs batted in—Pennock 2, Meusel 2, Gehrig 2, Durocher 2, Miller 1, Hauser 1, Boley 1. Two-base hit—Miller. Three-base hit—Ruth. Double plays—Koenig, Durocher, and Gehrig (2); Foxx and Powers; Powers, Boley, and Hauser; Boley, Bishop, and Hauser. Left on bases—New York, 7; Philadelphia, 8. Bases on balls—off Pennock, 5; Grove, 4; Shores, 2; Powers, 1. Struck out—by Pennock, 4; Grove, 1; Shores, 3; Powers, 2. Hits—Off Grove, 4 in 3 innings; Shores, 5 in 3 (none out in seventh); Powers, 1 in 3. Losing pitcher—Grove. Umpires—Dinneen, Nallin, and Barry. Time of game—2 hrs. 25 min.

Grove left after three innings, saddled with his second consecutive opening-day loss to New York. Bill Shores, a right-hander pitching in his first major-league game, came on and for three innings kept the Yankees scoreless. But in the seventh, he was touched for two runs and left with nobody out and the bases loaded. An outstanding relief job by Ike Powers, another youngster, prevented the Yanks from scoring any more runs. Koenig had led off the inning with a single, and Ruth, after taking two strikes, walked. Gehrig singled to right, scoring Koenig and sending Ruth to third. Meusel singled to left to score Ruth, and when Dugan followed with a bunt single, the bases were loaded. At that point Powers replaced Shores. Powers got out of the inning with good pitching and his own alert fielding. After he fanned Durocher, Huggins sent up left-handed hitter Cedric Durst to bat for Collins. Durst lifted a foul behind the plate that Foxx ran down and caught at the edge of the seats. Gehrig took off from third trying to score after the catch, but Powers, covering the plate, took Foxx's throw and tagged the sliding Gehrig to complete the double play.

The Yankees got their final run in the ninth when Ruth drove a Powers fastball far over the head of center fielder Speaker for a triple. The Babe scored on a ground ball by Gehrig as he beat Bishop's throw to the plate. Meanwhile, Pennock offered the frostbitten fans no further reason to come out from under their blankets and cheer. He kept the A's scoreless in the last three innings, and the Yankees had their sixth consecutive opening-day victory. The convincing win against the league's second-best team helped reassure those Yankee fans back home, troubled by the club's many spring training losses. Now that the games counted, the world champions were ready to resume their winning ways.

The Yankees (101–53) got off to a great start, winning 33 of their first 40 games, and threatened another runaway. However, the Athletics persevered, and on September 7 tied New York for the lead only to fall back and finish 2½ games behind. New York swept its second consecutive World Series, this time against the St. Louis Cardinals, avenging the seven-game loss of 1926. Babe Ruth and Lou Gehrig had sensational years, but because of a rule then in effect barring previous winners neither was considered for the Most Valuable Player Award, which was won by Mickey Cochrane.

Thursday, April 18, 1929
Yankee Stadium, New York
New York 7 Boston 3

Whose little body lodg'd a mighty mind. —Homer

Remarkably, given the capriciousness of springtime weather in the East, the Yankees had never failed to begin their season on schedule. Their string of good fortune ended this year when cold, rain, and high winds in the New York area twice forced them to cancel the season opener against the Boston Red Sox. Finally, on the third day the weather cleared, and the Yankees launched the 1929 campaign by downing the Sox, 7–3. It was their seventh consecutive opening-day victory, but because of the two postponements and today's overcast skies, fewer than 40,000 fans were there to see it, well below the 50,000-plus that the club had expected two days earlier. The wintry weather affected all the major-league openers, which drew roughly 169,500—the lowest opening-day attendance in years. In New York, it had taken some time for fans around the city to realize there really would be a game played this afternoon. However, once they did they began to head for the Stadium, and while at 2:15 P.M. there appeared to be more ushers than spectators in the park, by game time there were still lines of people waiting to get in.

There was an additional consequence of the two-day delay; Jimmy Walker, New York's fashionable mayor, was not at Yankee Stadium to throw out the first ball. Walker had been ready to do so Tuesday and Wednesday, but had a full schedule of city-related business to deal with today. One item on his agenda would greatly influence the city's social and economic future. The mayor and the Board of Estimate approved a new "retail district" in the once exclusively residential section of Murray Hill in Manhattan. They did so over the bitter objections of several of Murray Hill's wealthy property owners, including J. P. Morgan, Jr., and the Rockefeller family.

Perhaps it was Mayor Walker's absence, or it might just have been the gloomy weather, but the pregame ceremonies lacked the excitement usually associated with both the mayor and with Opening Day. Lieutenant Francis Sutherland of the Seventh Regiment Band began the festivities, such as they were, at three o'clock. He led both teams on the parade to the center field flagpole, where Commissioner Landis, American League president Ernest S. Barnard, and Colonel Jacob Ruppert joined them. The three dignitaries, who had been waiting in the warmth under the left-field bleachers, took part in the raising of Old Glory and the Yankees' world championship banner. When they returned to home plate, Judge Landis presented the Yankees with diamond-studded wristwatches. The watches were a remembrance of last fall's World Series victory over the St. Louis Cardinals, but while Landis handed them out, many spectators were directing their attention elsewhere. Jack Dempsey had just taken his seat in a box behind third base, and fans in the surrounding sections were straining to get a look at the popular former heavyweight champion. Joseph V. McKee, president of the New York City Board of Aldermen, substituted for Mayor Walker in throwing out the first ball. The crowd greeted him with lukewarm applause as he made the toss from Colonel Ruppert's box alongside the Yankees' dugout. McKee was a protégé of Edward J. Flynn, the Bronx Democratic boss, and would temporarily serve as mayor when Walker resigned under fire in 1932.

Right-hander George Pipgras, who had emerged as the Yankees' leading pitcher in 1928, got the starting assignment for New York. Pipgras led the league in innings pitched (300⅔), and tied Philadelphia's Lefty Grove for the most games won, with 24. However, he also allowed the most hits (314), and his 103 walks were second only to teammate Hank Johnson who walked 104 in 199 innings. Although Pipgras earned the win in this game, journeyman Fred Heimach, who turned in an outstanding relief effort, was the day's best pitcher. While Pipgras allowed the Red Sox only three hits in his 5⅓ innings, he was extremely wild, issuing nine walks. His control was off from the very beginning; he walked the bases full in the first inning, but escaped by retiring third baseman Bobby Reeves.

In contrast to Pipgras's tying for the most wins in 1928, Boston starter Red Ruffing had endured the most losses; 25 (10–25). Ruffing, however, was pitching for a Red Sox team that finished in last place, a position they had occupied in each of his four full seasons with them. He got two quick outs in the last of the first, but then Babe Ruth thrilled the crowd by lining a 2–2 curve ball 402 feet away into the lower left-field seats. Ruth, a widower, had taken advantage of yesterday's second postponement to marry Mrs. Claire Hodgson, a widow, at St. Gregory the Great Catholic Church in Manhattan. Now, as he rounded second base with the Yankees' first opening-day home run in four years, he raised his cap to his new bride. Mrs. Ruth, wearing a fur coat to protect her from the cold, enthusiastically waved back from her seat in Box 173 behind third base. As the Babe made his way around the bases a large number three was clearly visible on his broad back. Ruppert had decreed that every Yankees' player would wear a number on the back of his uniform this season. The numbering system was simple. Each member of the starting lineup, excepting pitcher Pipgras, wore a number consistent with his place in the batting order. Thus, Earle Combs wore No. 1, Mark Koenig No. 2, Ruth No. 3, Lou Gehrig No. 4, and so on through catcher Johnny Grabowski, batting eighth and wearing No. 8. Pipgras wore No. 14. All of the 30 players on the opening-day roster wore numbers, ranging from Combs's No. 1 to rookie catcher Arndt Jorgens's No. 32. Numbers 13 and 23 were omitted. Wearing uniform numbers proved so popular with the fans, within a few years all major-league teams had adopted the practice. Now when fans plunked down five cents for a scorecard, they would be better able to identify the players. The sale of scorecards increased, which made the companies that advertised in them happy: companies like Regal Shoes, who had an ad in each Yankees scorecard for their $6.60 men's dress shoes.

Although putting numbers on uniforms was a break with tradition, it did not affect the actual play of the game. The same cannot be said for National League president John Heydler's proposal last December to institute a rule allowing a "designated hitter" to bat for the pitcher. New York joined other American League clubs in voting down this radical alteration to the way the game is played. Because the American League rejected it, the season opened without its use in either league.

After going out in order in the second inning, the Red Sox again loaded the bases in the third, this time with nobody out. They did it on a Jack Rothrock single and walks to shortstop Hal Rhyne and right fielder Russ Scarritt. Rhyne and Scarritt were each playing their first game for Boston. Rhyne had been with Pittsburgh in 1926–1927, and Scarritt was making his major-league debut. Pipgras got Ira Flagstead to bounce to third baseman Koenig, who started a double play while Rothrock scored the tying run. Bill Regan followed with a line-drive single over Pipgras's head that brought Rhyne home and gave Boston a 2–1 lead. The double play started by Koenig was one of five chances he had at third base today. He handled all of them cleanly, although this was his first big-league game at the position. Joe Dugan, the Yankees' third baseman for the past seven years, was gone. The Yanks sold him to the Boston Braves last December, two weeks after they sold catcher Pat Collins to the same team. Leo Durocher, a .270-hitter as a rookie in 1928, replaced Koenig at shortstop, while Tony Lazzeri, fully recovered from the crippling arm injury that limited him to 116 games in 1928 and almost ended his career, was back at second base. Eventually Koenig would share the shortstop job with Durocher, while Gene Robertson and rookie Lyn Lary would see much of the action at third base.

New York regained the lead in the fourth. Working cautiously, Ruffing walked the inning's first two batters, Ruth and Gehrig. Bob Meusel's double to right scored Ruth and sent Gehrig to third. After Lazzeri fanned for the first out, Durocher grounded to third baseman Reeves. Gehrig made it back to the bag, but Meusel running from second was an easy out. When Reeves also fielded Grabowski's grounder and threw across to first, the inning looked to be over. But first baseman Phil Todt mishandled the throw, allowing the ball to get by him as Gehrig scored to put the Yanks ahead, 3–2. When the ball continued to roll, Grabowski headed for second. Catcher Charlie Berry, backing up the play, threw Grabowski out, but not before Durocher scored all the way from first with the Yankees' fourth run.

Pipgras managed to escape the fifth inning despite walking two more, but his wildness undid him in the sixth. With one out and Todt, who had singled, at first, he walked both Berry and pinch- hitter Elliot Bigelow. (Bigelow, in his first big-league appearance, replaced Ruffing with a count of 2–1.) Bill Carrigan, who had come out of retirement in 1927 to again manage the Sox, sent another youngster playing in his first big-league game, Bill Narleski, in to run for Bigelow. When Pipgras's first two pitches to Rothrock were out of the strike zone, Yankees manager Miller Huggins went to his bullpen. He summoned Heimach, a veteran left-hander who joined the Yanks from St. Paul of the American Association late in 1928 to help in the pennant drive. Heimach got the switch-hitting Rothrock to fly to Meusel—Todt scoring to make it 4–3—and then retired Rhyne to end the inning. The Sox did no better against him in the seventh, eighth, or ninth, as he disposed of them in order each time.

Thursday, April 18, 1929

Boston	ab	r	h	po	a	e	New York	ab	r	h	po	a	e
Rothrock cf	4	1	1	2	0	0	Combs cf	4	0	1	4	0	0
Rhyne ss	3	1	0	2	1	0	Koenig 3b	4	0	0	1	5	0
Scarritt rf	1	0	0	2	1	0	Ruth rf	2	2	1	1	0	0
Flagstead lf	1	0	0	1	0	0	Gehrig 1b	3	2	2	12	1	0
aK. Williams lf	2	0	0	0	0	0	Meusel lf	4	0	2	2	0	0
Regan 2b	3	0	1	3	2	0	Lazzeri 2b	4	1	1	3	2	0
Reeves 3b	4	0	0	0	3	0	Durocher ss	3	2	0	0	5	0
Todt 1b	3	1	1	3	2	1	Grabowski c	3	0	1	3	1	0
Standaert 1b	1	0	0	0	0	0	Pipgras p	1	0	0	1	0	0
Berry c	3	0	0	10	0	0	Heimach p	2	0	0	0	0	0
Ruffing p	2	0	0	0	1	0	Total	30	7	8	27	14	0
bBigelow	0	0	0	0	0	0							
cNarleski	0	0	0	0	0	0							
M.Gaston p	0	0	0	1	0	0							
dBarrett	1	0	0	0	0	0							
Total	28	3	3	24	10	1							

aPopped out for Flagstead in fifth inning.
bWalked for Ruffing in sixth inning.
cRan for Bigelow in sixth inning.
dGrounded for M. Gaston in ninth inning.

Boston	002	001	000–3
New York	100	303	00X–7

Runs batted in—Ruth, Meusel, Flagstead, Regan, Gehrig, Rothrock, Combs(2). Two-base hit—Meusel. Home runs—Ruth, Gehrig. Sacrifice—Rothrock. Double plays—Koenig, Lazzeri, and Gehrig; Rhyne, Regan, and Todt. Left on bases—New York, 5; Boston, 8. Bases on balls—off Pipgras, 9; Ruffing, 3; Gaston, 3. Struck out—by Pipgras, 2; Heimach, 1; Ruffing, 5; Gaston, 2. Hits—Off Pipgras, 3 in 5⅓ innings; Heimach, none in 3⅔; Ruffing, 3 in 5; Gaston, 5 in 3. Winning pitcher—Pipgras. Losing pitcher—Ruffing. Umpires—McGowan, Van Graflan, and Connolly. Time of game—2 hrs. 25 min.

Meanwhile the Yankees padded their lead by adding three runs in the last of the sixth against Milt Gaston, Ruffing's successor. Gehrig led off with a long home run into the right-field seats, and having no wife, raised his cap to the entire crowd as he made his way around the bases. The home-run twins, Ruth and Gehrig, had finished one-two in the league for the last two years. Now, as the 1929 home-run race began, each had one.

After Meusel went out, Lazzeri singled and Durocher and Grabowski walked to load the bases. Heimach fanned for out number two, but Combs singled sharply past Reeves, driving in two more runs. The Yanks threatened again in the seventh when they loaded the bases with one out, but Gaston got Lazzeri to hit into an inning-ending double play. Heimach did the rest, retiring all 11 batters he faced with an excellent curve ball and the aid of some fine fielding by Koenig and Durocher.

> *Although Ruth (46) and Gehrig (35) were again one-two in home runs, New York (88–66) finished second, a distant 18 games behind the Philadelphia Athletics. On September 22, coach Art Fletcher took over as the Yankees interim manager, relieving the ailing Miller Huggins. Three days later, at age 51, Huggins died at St. Vincent's Hospital in New York from pyemia, a form of blood poisoning.*

IV

1930–1939

After a transitional year under Bob Shawkey, Joe McCarthy became the Yankees' manager in 1931 and led the team to five world championships in the decade. Babe Ruth left after the 1934 season, but Joe DiMaggio arrived in 1936 and soon took over the Babe's place as baseball's greatest star. The Yankees won the World Series in each of DiMaggio's first four seasons. They would win ten pennants and nine World Series in DiMaggio's 13 seasons as an active player.

Bill Dickey and Lou Gehrig, both of whom had come up under Miller Huggins, continued their great careers under McCarthy until illness forced Gehrig to retire in 1939. Meanwhile, the Yankees continued to replenish themselves with outstanding young players, mainly from their farm system. Among those joining the club in the early '30s were George Selkirk, Frank Crosetti, and Red Rolfe, while the late '30s brought Tommy Henrich, Charlie Keller, and Joe Gordon. Through it all McCarthy relied on a solid pitching staff, anchored by Lefty Gomez and Red Ruffing. Each had four 20-win seasons during the decade, and between them they started every Yankees' opener from 1931 to 1940.

In January 1939 Colonel Jacob Ruppert died, ending his quarter-century ownership of the club. It passed to three women: Ruppert's two nieces and Helen Weyant, a friend, while Ed Barrow took over as president. That spring the club began regular radio broadcasts of their games with lead announcer Arch McDonald, assisted by Mel Allen.

Tuesday, April 15, 1930
Shibe Park, Philadelphia
Philadelphia 6 New York 2

He that would govern others, first should be master of himself.—Philip Massinger

Following Miller Huggins's death in September 1929, business manager Ed Barrow asked Yankees coach Art Fletcher to succeed his old boss. Fletcher seemed the logical choice. He had managerial experience, having led the Phillies from 1923 to 1926, and as the Yanks' interim manager for the last 11 games of 1929. However, to Barrow's dismay, Fletcher had no desire to manage again. He refused the offer, telling Barrow he preferred to remain with the club as a coach, which he would do through the 1945 season. Barrow had another problem, Babe Ruth, now 35 years old, and with the end of his playing days in sight, believed he was the rightful successor to Huggins. Ruth campaigned openly for the job but never received serious consideration from Barrow, who doubted the Babe's qualifications to be manager. In mid-October Barrow selected former Yankees' pitcher Bob Shawkey, who had coached under Huggins in 1929 and impressed the late manager with his ability to help the team's young pitchers.

Shawkey made his managerial debut at Shibe Park against Connie Mack's Philadelphia Athletics, the defending world champions. It had taken Mack 16 years, but as he began his 30th season in Philadelphia he was again leading a championship team. Beginning in 1915, after the A's had won four pennants in five years, financial considerations had forced him to trade or sell many of his best players. That year the Athletics went from pennant winners to cellar dwellers, and remained there for the next six years. But throughout the mid–1920s the Athletics got a little better each year before finally reaching the summit in 1929. After dethroning the Yankees for the American League pennant, they beat the Chicago Cubs for their first World Series championship since 1913. Philadelphia showed its appreciation by awarding Mack the distinguished Edward W. Bok Prize. Given to the person who had done the most for Philadelphia in the preceding year, the prize had never before gone to a sports figure.

As often happens in baseball, the two best teams—then the Athletics and the Yankees—were in the same league. In 1930, however, the A's and Yanks were more than just the two best teams of the day, they were two of the best ever. Of the 18 men in the opening-day starting lineups, nine were future Hall-of-Famers: Babe Ruth, Lou Gehrig, Earle Combs, Tony Lazzeri, and Bill Dickey for New York; Lefty Grove, Mickey Cochrane, Al Simmons, and Jimmie Foxx for Philadelphia. (Future Hall-of-Fame pitchers Herb Pennock, Waite Hoyt, and Lefty Gomez were on the Yankees' bench.) These two magnificent ball clubs began the season on a chilly, overcast day before a capacity crowd estimated at 38,000. The Shibes had enlarged and remodeled their eponymous park several times since its opening in 1909. In 1929 they added a mezzanine and for this season raised the roof of the original grandstand, which allowed for the addition of 3,000 extra seats and a new press box. Radio station WIP in Philadelphia broadcast the game, the only scheduled regular-season home broadcast they would do in 1930. Sixty-year-old Monte Cross, who played shortstop for Mack and the Athletics from 1902 through 1907, was the announcer.

A few hours before game time, while A's shortstop Joe Boley was taking his batting practice cuts against pitcher Jack Quinn, a great cheer unexpectedly rose from the spectators seated near the Philadelphia dugout. They had noticed Simmons, the A's leading hitter in 1929, emerge from the dugout in uniform and make his way to the batting cage. When fans in other parts of the then half-full park spotted him, they too joined in the applause. Simmons had been holding out all spring, while working out on his own in Hot Springs, Arkansas. Philadelphians seeing him on the field dressed to play surmised that his holdout was over. It was; Simmons, who had been asking for $35,000, had signed his 1930 contract just minutes earlier. Subsequent reports said he settled for $30,000, but whatever Simmons's salary was, he more than earned it. He followed a spectacular 1929 season (.365 average, 34 home runs, and a league-leading 157 runs batted in) by leading the American League in batting (.381) and runs scored (152) in 1930, while finishing second in runs batted in (165).

Meanwhile, Ruth, still disappointed at not being a playing manager, had signed a two-year contract on March 8 calling for a mind-boggling $80,000 per year. This was just five months after the stock market crash that would lead the United States into the worst economic depression in its history. The story goes that when Ruth learned he was making more money than President Herbert Hoover, he supposedly replied, "I had a better year than he did." While that may have been true, the crusty Barrow's comment on the signing was a good deal less insightful. Presumably speaking only of ballplayers, the Yankees' normally astute business manager said, "No one will ever be paid more than Ruth."

Philadelphia Mayor Harry A. Mackey led the pregame parade, marching at the head of the two teams. Behind them, dressed in flashy red uniforms, were 60 members of the American Legion's Frankford Post Drum and Bugle Corps. For some unexplained reason, the Athletics had decided a few years back to not decorate Shibe Park in the traditional manner for Opening Day. That policy continued, and the park looked no different today than it would on any other afternoon of the regular season. The only decorations to be seen were some light blue and gold bunting and the city flag of Philadelphia. Both adorned the mayor's box in the lower deck behind home plate, the site from which Mackey later threw out the first ball. The crowd came to their feet for "The Star-Spangled Banner" as Shawkey and Eddie Collins, captain of the Athletics, raised the American flag. The music, however, was not coming from anywhere on the field, but from a set of loud speakers that were sitting atop the scoreboard in right-center field. In the third inning those loud speakers would cost Ruth a home run.

Although Mack made it a practice never to reveal his starting pitcher beforehand, to no one's surprise he chose Grove. A 20-game winner for the past three seasons, Grove would win 28 games in 1930 and follow that with win totals of 31, 25, and 24. He was baseball's dominant pitcher between 1927 and 1933, winning 172 games and losing only 54 for a majestic winning percentage of .761. This afternoon the A's furnished him an early 2–0 lead, thanks to a two-run first-inning home run by Simmons off Yankees starter George Pipgras. Simmons's blow followed a Mule Haas walk and precipitated the largest ovation of the day. The Yanks rallied against Grove to tie the score in the third inning, amid a controversial ruling on what seemed to be a Ruth home run. Mark Koenig, who walked, was on first with one out when Ruth clubbed a long drive to right that seemed destined for 20th Street and a game-tying two-run homer. However, instead of clearing the wall, the ball hit the loud speakers on top of the scoreboard and bounced back onto the field. Neither Ruth nor Koenig was running very hard—each assumed it was a home run—and by the time they realized the ball was still in play, Ruth was only at second and Koenig at third. The umpires ruled that because the amplifiers overhung the field, and because there was no grounds rule covering them, they should be considered an extension of the scoreboard. That meant that balls hitting them were in play. Home-plate umpire Bill McGowan listened to the Yankees' complaints, but stayed with his call. Thus, instead of his first home run of the year (and two runs batted in), Ruth had to settle for a double. McGowan's decision, however, did not cost the Yankees any runs. Gehrig, the next batter, hit a ground ball to first baseman Foxx whose throw to Grove covering first was wide, allowing both Koenig and Ruth to score. The official scorer charged the error to Foxx, though Grove was slow in getting to first. Grove, notoriously short tempered, knew he should have been in position to catch the throw, and he was clearly irritated at his own lack of hustle. He ended the inning by fanning the next two batters, second baseman Lazzeri and right fielder Dusty Cooke, a rookie playing in his first major-league game. Cooke was replacing Bob Meusel, a Yankees' star since 1920 but only a .261-batter in 1929. Aware that his best days had passed and needing to make room for Cooke after his outstanding year in the American Association with St. Paul, the Yanks sold Meusel to the Cincinnati Reds for the waiver price.

New York had another highly touted rookie in its lineup; third baseman Ben Chapman. Like Cooke, Chapman was making his big-league debut after a strong year at St. Paul. Never before had the Yankees opened a season with two such novices in their starting lineup. Yet when the A's retook the lead with two runs in the bottom of the third, it was due in part to misplays not by the rookies, but by veteran Yankees. The errors were both of omission and commission. Max Bishop led off with a line drive that Gehrig knocked down, but his throw to first was too late after Pipgras was slow in covering. Then Dickey allowed a pitch to get away from him and Bishop moved to second. Last year, in his first full season, Dickey had established himself as the Yankees' first-string catcher by batting .324 in 130 games. Haas's single to center brought Bishop home, giving the Athletics a 3–2 lead. One out later came the oddest play of the game. Simmons rapped a hard grounder to short, an apparent double-play ball. Koenig fielded it cleanly and flipped it to second baseman Lazzeri for the force on Haas. But Lazzeri apparently thought that Haas was the third out. Instead of throwing the ball to Gehrig to complete the double play, he rolled it to the mound, tossed his glove away, and headed for the Yankees dugout. (Prior to 1954, players left their gloves on the field between innings.) Koenig retrieved the ball but, inexplicably, chased Haas, whom he had just forced at second base, toward third. While that futile chase was taking place, Simmons took second. When Foxx followed with a single to center, Simmons scored run number four. Koenig, who had regained the shortstop job following the February sale of Leo Durocher to Cincinnati, would be unable to hold it. He batted just .230 in 21 games, and on May 30 the Yanks sent him to Detroit and installed second-year man Lyn Lary at short.

Tuesday, April 15, 1930

New York	ab	r	h	po	a	e	Philadelphia	ab	r	h	po	a	e
Combs cf	4	0	1	2	0	0	Bishop 2b	2	3	1	2	4	0
Koenig ss	3	1	1	0	4	0	Haas cf	2	1	2	3	0	0
Ruth lf	4	1	1	3	0	0	Cochrane c	4	0	1	10	0	0
Gehrig 1b	4	0	2	7	0	0	Simmons lf	4	2	1	1	0	0
Lazzeri 2b	4	0	0	3	2	1	Foxx 1b	4	0	1	6	2	1
Cooke rf	3	0	0	3	0	0	Miller rf	4	0	0	1	0	0
Chapman 3b	4	0	0	1	3	0	Dykes 3b	4	0	2	0	0	0
Dickey c	4	0	1	5	0	1	Boley ss	4	0	0	3	2	1
Pipgras p	1	0	0	0	2	0	Grove p	3	0	0	1	2	0
ªHargrave	1	0	0	0	0	0	Total	31	6	8	27	10	2
Johnson p	0	0	0	0	0	0							
ᵇLary	1	0	0	0	0	0							
Total	33	2	6	24	11	2							

ªStruck out for Pipgras in seventh inning.
ᵇFouled out for Johnson in ninth inning.

New York	002	000	000–2
Philadelphia	202	010	10x–6

Runs batted in—Simmons 2, Haas, Foxx, Cochrane, Gehrig. Two-base hit—Ruth. Home run—Simmons. Sacrifices—Haas. Double plays—Boley, Bishop, and Foxx; Bishop, Boley, and Foxx. Left on bases—New York, 7; Philadelphia, 5. Bases on balls—off Grove, 3; Pipgras, 2; Johnson, 1. Struck out—by Grove, 9; Pipgras, 2; Johnson, 3. Hits—off Pipgras, 6 in 6 innings; Johnson, 2 in 2. Wild pitch—Johnson. Passed ball—Dickey. Losing pitcher—Pipgras. Umpires—McGowan, Connolly, and Van Graflan. Time of game—1 hr. 53 min.

The Athletics scored again in the fifth on a Cochrane single that brought home Bishop. Their sixth and final run came in the seventh against Hank Johnson, who had just taken over from Pipgras. Back in 1928 Johnson, pitching mainly as a starter, had won 14 games, including four (without a loss) against Grove, which constituted half of Grove's eight losses that year. Johnson struck out the side, but between the strikeouts he walked Bishop, gave up a single to Haas, and then wild-pitched Bishop home. Grove's fastball, difficult to hit at any time, was particularly effective on this cold, hazy day. He struck out nine batters—all in the last seven innings—in handing the Yankees their first opening-day loss since 1922. By the time he got pinch-hitter Lary to foul out to Foxx to end the game, most of the chilled patrons had already departed.

> A "juiced-up" ball produced unusually high offensive statistics throughout the major leagues in 1930. The Yankees (86–68) scored an American League record-setting 1,062 runs but finished in third place, 16 games behind the Athletics. Babe Ruth led the league in home runs (49), while batting .359. Lou Gehrig led in runs batted in with 173 and finished second in batting (.379) and home runs (41). After the season the Yankees fired Bob Shawkey and hired Joe McCarthy as their new manager.

Tuesday, April 14, 1931
Yankee Stadium, New York
New York 6 Boston 3

Tower'd cities please us then, and the busy hum of men.—John Milton

By the end of the 1920s, New York, driven by a decade of economic expansion, had solidified its position as the unchallenged business capital of America and reigned as corporate headquarters for most of the nation's major financial, communications, and entertainment enterprises. Throughout the '20s new skyscrapers had gone up in Manhattan, one after another, with each seeming to rise higher than the one before. When the 77-story Chrysler Building was completed in 1930, it was hailed as the world's tallest structure; it would be so only until May 1931, when the Empire State Building officially opened several blocks away. Unfortunately, by the time the Empire State Building opened, the "good times" in New York—and America—had ended. Since the devastating October 1929 stock market crash, construction in the city had all but ceased, many businesses had gone bankrupt, and hundreds of thousands of people had lost their jobs. At one point, 25 percent of New York City's working residents were unemployed. People standing in breadlines and living in shacks in Central Park, the city's magnificent urban oasis, had become a common sight. If there was a positive effect of the economic difficulties, it was the increased attention it brought to city government. Many New Yorkers were already aware that some city officials received payoffs and kickbacks and that companies often obtained contracts for city projects illegally. They also knew about the crooked judges and policemen and about the ties Mayor Jimmy Walker's administration had to underworld figures like Arnold Rothstein. In 1929, Congressman Fiorello La Guardia had made corruption in the Walker administration the central issue of his campaign against the mayor.

Of course, there has always been some degree of corruption in the governance of New York City; it in no way makes the city unique. Whether it was worse now under Mayor Walker than it had been under previous Tammany-dominated administrations is irrelevant. Most New Yorkers accepted political corruption as a necessary part of doing business in the city. If things were going well, the average person was content to look the other way. This was especially true if they did not perceive the illegal activities as affecting them directly—which of course they did. Now, however, things were not going well for most New Yorkers. Nor were they going well for Mayor Walker. As he traveled to Yankee Stadium for the Yankees' 1931 season opener against the Boston Red Sox, City Hall was under special police guard. An anonymous caller had phoned in a bomb threat to "protest against official inactivity in behalf of the unemployed." The mayor was also a primary target of former Judge Samuel Seabury's series of state-ordered investigations into racketeering in New York City. Earlier this morning, Governor Franklin D. Roosevelt had written to Seabury requesting the minutes of the public hearings relating to the investigation.

However, in attending the opener, Mayor Walker was joining 70,000 other fans who preferred, at least for today, not to concern themselves with things like racketeering, or corruption, or the Depression. They were there to watch baseball and to see Joe McCarthy in his first game as the Yankees' manager. Many in the crowd, inspired by yesterday's warm, sunny weather and a forecast for the same today, had rushed to the Yankees midtown ticket office on 42nd Street to buy their tickets. They were the wise ones. So too were those who came to the Stadium early. There were lines at the gates well before noon, and by one o'clock spectators had filled half the seats. As late as a few minutes before game time, automobile traffic was tied up on all the nearby streets leading to the Stadium. Economic hard times were everywhere, but it was hard to tell at Yankee Stadium. The expansion of the Stadium's seating capacity in the winter of 1927–1928—second and third decks were added in left-center field—would help to hold the enormous crowd.

McCarthy, who was replacing the fired Bob Shawkey, was the only current big-league manager without big-league playing experience. He had spent the last five years managing the Chicago Cubs, leading them to a pennant in 1929. But he had become unhappy with what he saw as a lack of support from owner William Wrigley and resigned late in the 1930 season. Jacob Ruppert and Ed Barrow quickly signed him, even though he was such a stranger to the American League that today he would be seeing his first game ever at Yankee Stadium. The only other new manager in the American League was Boston's Shano Collins, McCarthy's opponent this afternoon. Last year's manager, Heinie Wagner, had been unable to prevent Boston's sixth consecutive last-place finish, and like Shawkey was gone after just one year.

Although the usual assortment of recognizable faces from New York's social, political, business, and entertainment worlds were among those scattered throughout the huge throng, one familiar face was missing. Colonel Ruppert was recovering from bronchitis, and his doctors insisted that he stay home. This was the first opener Ruppert had missed since buying the club in 1915. There was also a group sitting in the box next to Mayor Walker's that was clearly not part of the usual Yankee Stadium crowd. Grover Whalen, the city's official greeter, and his wife were playing host to a party of titled visitors: the Duke and Duchess of Sutherland, the Count and Countess di Frasso, and Lord Wavertree.

As the two teams began the pregame ceremonies with their march to the flagpole, the visiting Red Sox displayed their redesigned uniforms. A navy blue outline now surrounded the red block letters spelling "RED SOX" on their jerseys. Their stockings had gone from red and white to all red, and their team symbol, a pair of those red stockings, appeared on their left sleeves and on their hats. After the flag was raised, it was then lowered to half-mast in honor of Ernest S. Barnard, the former American League president. Barnard had died on March 27, one day before Ban Johnson, his predecessor and the founder of the league. Mayor Walker led the parade back to the plate, bowing in every direction while receiving a standing ovation from his forgiving constituents. The mayor returned to his box and, after some posing for photographers, threw out the first ball (oddly no one caught it) and the season began. Red Ruffing walked to the mound to make the first of what would be five opening-day starts for the Yankees. Ruffing had been Boston's starting (and losing) pitcher when the Red Sox opened here two years ago. But in May 1930, Barrow had given up Cedric Durst and $50,000 to bring him to New York. Winless with three losses when he came over, Ruffing went 15–5 as a Yankee.

Boston shortstop Rabbit Warstler got the attention of the crowd immediately by leading off with a triple to left field. One out later, first baseman Bill Sweeney singled and the Sox had a 1–0 lead. After being touched for that quick run, Ruffing settled down. He limited Boston to two singles over the next six innings, did not walk a man all afternoon, and struck out seven. Meanwhile, the Yankees came back to bang out 11 hits, including a Babe Ruth home run. By the time the Red Sox rallied to score their final two runs in the eighth on a single by Charlie Berry and a pinch-hit home run by rookie Tom Winsett, New York had moved to a comfortable 6–1 lead. Catcher Bill Dickey led several of his teammates in claiming that Winsett's drive had curved foul, but the home-run call stood.

Wilcy Moore (an ex–Yankee in his Boston debut) kept his old mates scoreless in the first inning, despite a two-out single by Ruth. The Babe, as if trying to prove true the spring-time stories of his rejuvenation, then stole second, but Moore got Lou Gehrig on a come-backer to the mound. Gehrig was playing in his 888th consecutive game, a streak that began on June 1, 1925, when he pinch-hit for Pee Wee Wanninger. Only two other major leaguers had played in more consecutive games: his new teammate Joe Sewell with 1,103, and former Yankee Everett Scott with a record 1,307.

In the second inning, Ben Chapman, playing second base while Tony Lazzeri shifted to third, forced Lazzeri who had reached base on a throwing error by Warstler. When Dusty Cooke, Ruffing, and Earle Combs all followed with singles, the Yankees had a 2–1 lead. Lazzeri would soon return to second base and Chapman to center field as Sewell, picked up in January after his release by the Cleveland Indians, took over at third base. New York drove Moore out in the fourth inning, scoring three runs on a single by Chapman, a walk to Cooke, and singles by Dickey, Combs, and Lyn Lary. McCarthy, coaching at third and the only Yankee not wearing a number, just kept waving the runners home. Back in 1928 the Yankees purchased Lary and his double-play partner, Jimmy Reese, from the Oakland Oaks of the Pacific Coast League for $125,000. They gave Lary the shortstop job after trading Mark Koenig (along with Waite Hoyt) to the Detroit Tigers on Memorial Day, 1930. He batted a respectable .289 (the Yankees hit .309 as a team in offense-crazy 1930), but still had to withstand a spring training challenge from rookie Bill Werber to keep his job. Lary would knock in 107 runs this season, which is still the one-season high for a Yankee shortstop.

For anyone who attended a Yankees game between 1920 and 1934, no matter their age, the day would not be complete unless he or she saw Babe Ruth hit a home run. So, in the seventh inning, when the Babe smashed reliever Ed Durham's first pitch into the right-field seats, it generated the most excitement of the afternoon. It was the 566th career home run for Ruth, now in the second and final season of his $80,000 per-year contract. To put Ruth's salary in perspective, the State of New Jersey unanimously passed a pension bill this day that would give a dollar a day to people who were above the age of 70, had lived in the state for 15 years, and owned less than $3,000 in real estate. To put it in further perspective, John D. Rockefeller Jr. chose this day to announce a one-million-dollar *improvement* plan for his Pocantico Hills estate in Tarrytown, New York.

Following Winsett's two-run homer in the eighth, Russ Scarritt hit a two-out double. Then after Sweeney singled, Earl Webb, Boston's clean-up hitter, came to the plate representing the tying run. However, Ruffing calmed whatever anxiety the crowd and his manager might have had by getting Webb to hit into a force-play grounder. The Sox went quietly in the ninth and Joe McCarthy had his first Yankees win.

Despite scoring 1,067 runs, breaking the major-league record they set a year ago, the Yankees (94–59) finished in second place, 13½ games behind the Athletics, who won their third straight pennant. Babe Ruth and Lou Gehrig tied for the home run title with 46, and Gehrig broke his own one-season American League runs batted in record with 185. Ben Chapman led the league in stolen bases with 61. Gehrig finished second to Lefty Grove as the league's Most Valuable Player, an award that the Baseball Writers Association of America was now administering.

Tuesday, April 14, 1931

Boston	ab	r	h	po	a	e	New York	ab	r	h	po	a	e
Warstler ss	3	1	1	2	5	1	Combs cf	4	0	2	3	0	0
aCreeden	1	0	0	0	0	0	Lary ss	4	0	1	0	3	0
Marquardt ss	0	0	0	0	0	0	Ruth rf	3	1	2	2	0	0
Scarritt lf	4	0	1	0	0	0	Gehrig 1b	4	0	1	8	0	0
Sweeney 1b	4	0	2	6	0	0	Lazzeri 3b	3	0	0	0	0	0
Webb rf	4	0	0	2	0	0	Chapman 2b	4	2	1	4	4	0
Rothrock 3b	4	0	0	1	2	0	Cooke lf	3	1	2	2	0	0
Reeves 2b	4	0	0	6	0	0	Dickey c	4	1	1	8	1	0
Oliver cf	4	0	0	2	0	0	Ruffing p	4	1	1	0	2	0
Berry c	3	1	2	5	1	0	Total	33	6	11	27	10	0
Moore p	1	0	1	0	3	0							
Durham p	1	0	0	0	0	0							
bWinsett	1	1	1	0	0	0							
Morris p	0	0	0	0	0	0							
Total	34	3	8	24	11	1							

aBatted for Warstler in eighth inning.
bHomered for Durham in eighth inning.

Boston	100	000	020–3
New York	020	300	10X–6

Runs batted in—Sweeney, Ruffing, Combs (2), Dickey, Lary, Ruth, Winsett (2). Two-base hit—Scarritt. Three-base hit—Warstler. Home runs—Ruth, Winsett. Stolen bases—Ruth, Cooke. Double plays—Warstler and Sweeney. Left on bases—New York, 6; Boston, 4. Bases on balls—off Moore, 2; Durham, 1. Struck out—by Ruffing, 7; Durham, 2; Morris, 1. Hits—off Moore, 7 in 3⅓ innings; Durham, 4 in 3⅔ innings; Morris, none in 1 inning. Losing pitcher—Moore. Umpires—McGowan, Van Graflan, and Connolly. Time of game—1 hr. 55 min.

Tuesday, April 12, 1932
Shibe Park, Philadelphia
New York 12 Philadelphia 6

When society requires to be rebuilt, there is no use in attempting to rebuild it on the old plan.—John Stuart Mill

Between them, the Philadelphia Athletics and the New York Yankees had won the last six American League pennants; Philadelphia had taken the last three, and New York the previous three. Although the Yankees figured to be the major obstacle to a fourth-straight Philadelphia pennant, the first meeting of these two marvelous teams attracted a meager 16,000 fans to Shibe Park. The size of the crowd for the season opener was disappointing, yet it was not unexpected. For most people, baseball is entertainment, and in April 1932 money for entertainment was extremely limited. It would remain that way for a long time. At Shibe Park, home attendance this season would be down by more than 200,000 from 1931, itself a year in which most people struggled financially. But the economic situation would grow even worse in 1932 as increasing numbers of Americans lost their jobs, businesses, and savings. Just three years earlier, on Opening Day 1929, the number of shares traded on the New York Stock Exchange totaled 3,768,650; the closing average was $150.79 for 25 railroad stocks and $311.87 for 25 industrial stocks. On Opening Day 1932, only 1,553,160 shares were traded, the 25 railroad stocks closed at $21.73, and the 25 industrial stocks at $62.33. In Washington this morning, politicians searched for solutions to the crisis. The 12 presidents of the Federal Reserve Banks reviewed the nation's monetary policy, while in the Senate two committees held hearings designed to deal with America's economic predicament. The Banking and Currency Committee heard testimony from Richard Whitney, the president of the New York Stock Exchange, who reported the value of stocks and bonds had declined $6 billion just in the last two weeks. Meanwhile, the Finance Committee was debating a proposed billion-dollar tax bill.

Nor was much help coming from the White House. President Herbert Hoover spoke of "keeping in contact" with the nation's business and financial leaders, but the public needed the president to take bold action to raise their morale; Hoover failed to do so. He did, however, find the time to send a telegram to John McGraw, congratulating him on beginning his 30th year as manager of the New York Giants. Both McGraw and Hoover would be gone before the year was over; McGraw would retire in June and Hoover would lose the presidency in November. By the time McGraw stepped down on June 3, McCarthy's Yankees were well on their way to the American League pennant. They had begun their rampage through the league on Opening Day, smashing five home runs in a 12–6 rout of the A's. Babe Ruth and fourth-year outfielder Sammy Byrd had two home runs each, and Lou Gehrig had one. Gehrig, playing in consecutive game number 1,043, also had a triple and a single. A's starter George Earnshaw gave up ten of the Yankees' runs and four of their home runs in his four innings of work.

Earnshaw, as do many ballplayers, had an odd superstition—one he shared with teammate Lefty Grove. Both pitchers felt it was bad luck for them to take the mound unless A's coach Kid Gleason had given them a handshake and a pat on the shoulder. Gleason was a former major-league player and manager; however, he was no longer a "kid." He was now 65 years old and in poor health, which had prevented him from being with the Athletics at their Fort Myers, Florida, training camp. Nevertheless, despite today's bitter cold and gusty winds, Gleason, aware of Earnshaw's superstition, was at the game. He left his sick bed wrapped in sweaters and came to the park to give his pitcher the required handshake and pat. Unfortunately for Earnshaw, Gleason's courageous gesture proved to be no protection against today's Yankees onslaught.

Earnshaw had been a 20-game winner for the Athletics in each of their three pennant-winning seasons, yet this was his first opening-day start as it was for the Yanks' Lefty Gomez. New York had paid the San Francisco Seals a reported $45,000 for the 20-year-old

Gomez in 1929, but they sent him to the St. Paul Saints of the American Association after he lost five of his first seven decisions as a Yankee in 1930. He returned to New York in 1931 and became the club's best pitcher, winning 21 games (21–9) and compiling an ERA of 2.67, second in the league to Grove. Gomez also pitched 17 complete games in 1931 but, despite being staked to a big lead, could not get one today. When the A's rallied with two out in the ninth, McCarthy, sensing his young pitcher was tiring, brought in Red Ruffing to get the final out.

Several hours earlier, precisely at 2:40 P.M., the American Legion's Houston Post Bugle Corps—led by a drum major dressed in white—gathered the two teams for the march to the center field flagpole. Once there, McCarthy and A's coach Eddie Collins (substituting for manager Connie Mack) had the honor of raising Old Glory. After the official party led by Mayor J. Hampton Moore, the mayor's cabinet and A's president Tom Shibe took their seats in a box near the Athletics dugout, the crowd stood and removed their hats as the amplifiers broadcast "The Star-Spangled Banner," officially the national anthem since 1931. When the music ended, Mayor Moore aimed the opening toss at catcher Mickey Cochrane. The throw did not quite make it that far, but Cochrane quickly retrieved it and threw it to Earnshaw.

The Yankees were opening this season with two starters who were playing in their first big-league game, just as they had here in Philadelphia two years earlier. In 1930 it had been Ben Chapman and Dusty Cooke; now it was second baseman Jack Saltzgaver and third baseman Frank Crosetti. Saltzgaver, 29, who played for the American Association St. Paul Saints in 1931, soon yielded second base back to Tony Lazzeri. He would play in only 20 games in 1932, then do a stint in the minors before returning to the Yankees in 1934 to serve as a utility infielder for the next four years. Crosetti, like Gomez a native of the San Francisco Bay area, had been Yankees' property since they purchased him from the Seals in August of 1930. Because he was only 19 years old at the time, they allowed him to play in San Francisco through the 1931 season. Crosetti had played shortstop during spring training, while last year's shortstop Lyn Lary played third base. But in the final preseason game at Ebbets Field against Brooklyn, McCarthy switched Crosetti to third and Lary to short, and that's where they were for the opener. Crosetti eventually overcame the Yankees' doubts about his ability to play shortstop in the major leagues and went on to play more than 1,500 games there. He would wear a Yankees' uniform, as a player and a coach, for the next 37 years.

New York got off to a quick four-run lead against Earnshaw highlighted by Ruth's tremendous first-inning home run with Byrd and Saltzgaver aboard. The drive sailed over the wall in right field and landed on a roof across 20th Street. Gehrig followed by hitting the first pitch for a long triple off the center-field wall; Chapman's fly to Mule Haas scored him, and the Yanks were up 4–0 before Philadelphia had even batted. The Athletics cut the lead in half in the bottom of the first on Bing Miller's bloop double that scored Haas and Al Simmons. Each team added a run in the third inning; the Yankees on a Gehrig home run and Philadelphia on a triple by Cochrane and a single by Simmons. The Yanks let loose on Earnshaw in the fourth, battering him for five more runs to extend their lead to 10–3. All the runs came after he had retired the first two batters. Lary doubled off the scoreboard in right and came home on a single to center by Gomez. Byrd followed with a home run into the upper deck in left field. Then, after Saltzgaver walked (Saltzgaver and A's second baseman Max Bishop each had four walks on the day), Ruth hit another home run over the right-field wall. The Babe's second blast, which traveled even farther than the first, increased his lifetime home run total to 613.

Jimmie DeShong, a 22-year-old right-hander making his major-league debut, came on for Philadelphia in the fifth and held the Yanks to two runs and four hits the rest of the way. One was Byrd's second home run of the game, a sixth-inning drive into the seats in left. That gave Byrd, who had homered in each of the last four spring training games, six home runs in five games. However, it was not enough to earn him a regular position. Earle Combs would reclaim center field, and Byrd would spend most of the year—as he did in each of his six years with the Yankees—serving as a late-inning replacement for Ruth.

Adhering to the theory that a team should always try to score as many runs as possible, the Yankees, with an 11–4 lead, added another run in the ninth on Gehrig's steal of home. It was the 11th time Gehrig had stolen home, always as part of a double steal—as was this one with Chapman stealing second. Over the next three years, Gehrig would steal home four more times, each as the front end of a double steal. Chapman's steal was the first of his league-leading 38 in 1932, as he retained the American League stolen-base crown.

The A's got a run in the seventh on a Jimmie Foxx home run that cleared the center-field wall and was the longest drive of the day. Foxx would hit a league-leading 58 home runs this season to end Ruth's six-year hold on the American League home run title. In the ninth, after Gomez quickly disposed of Bishop and Haas, many remaining fans began heading for the exits. They stopped momentarily when the home team scored two quick runs. Veteran catcher Johnnie Heving, a fifth-inning replacement for Cochrane, singled and Simmons homered into the upper deck in left, the third hit of the day for the league's defending batting champion. Simmons's home run was the seventh of the game, one short of what was then the two-team American League record of eight set by the Athletics and Detroit Tigers in 1921. Gomez appeared to have gotten the final out when Foxx lifted a seemingly playable, high pop foul near home plate. However, after getting under the ball, catcher Bill Dickey dropped it for an error. Taking advantage of a second chance, Foxx singled. So did Miller, and when Jimmy Dykes walked to load the bases, the departing fans hurried back. McCarthy, meanwhile, hurried to the mound and brought in Ruffing to pitch to shortstop Dib Williams. Ruffing vanquished any dreams Philadelphians may have had of a miracle finish when he got Williams on a game-ending liner to Byrd.

Joe McCarthy captured his first American League pennant as the Yankees (107–47) won easily, finishing 13 games ahead of the A's and ending Philadelphia's streak of three consecutive titles. They swept the Chicago Cubs in the World Series, giving New York sweeps in each of its last three series (1927, 1928, 1932). Lefty Gomez led Yankees' pitchers with 24 wins (24–7), including seven against the second-place A's. Lou Gehrig again finished second in the MVP voting, this time to Jimmie Foxx; Gomez was fifth.

Tuesday, April 12, 1932

New York	ab	r	h	po	a	e	Philadelphia	ab	r	h	po	a	e
Byrd cf	5	3	3	4	0	0	Bishop 2b	1	0	0	1	4	0
Saltzgaver 2b	1	2	0	2	2	0	Haas cf	5	1	1	3	0	0
Ruth lf	5	2	3	1	0	0	Cochrane c	3	1	1	2	0	0
Gehrig 1b	4	3	3	6	0	0	Heving c	2	1	1	3	1	0
Chapman rf	5	0	1	2	0	0	Simmons lf	4	2	3	2	0	0
Crosetti 3b	5	0	0	1	1	0	Foxx 1b	5	1	3	12	0	0
Dickey c	5	0	0	9	0	1	Miller rf	5	0	2	0	0	0
Lary ss	4	1	1	2	0	0	Dykes 3b	4	0	0	3	0	0

New York   Philadelphia

	ab	r	h	po	a	e
Gomez p	4	1	1	0	2	0
Ruffing p	0	0	0	0	0	0
Total	38	12	12	27	5	1

	ab	r	h	po	a	e
Williams ss	5	0	0	1	3	1
Earnshaw p	1	0	0	0	1	0
[a]McNair	1	0	0	0	0	0
DeShong p	2	0	0	0	3	0
Total	38	6	11	27	12	1

[a]Fouled out for Earnshaw in fourth inning.

New York	401	501	001–12
Philadelphia	201	000	102–6

Runs batted in—Ruth 5, Chapman, Gehrig, Gomez, Byrd 3, Miller 2, Simmons 3, Foxx. Two-base hits—Miller, Lary, Simmmons. Three-base hits—Gehrig, Cochrane, Chapman. Home runs—Ruth 2, Gehrig, Byrd 2, Foxx, Simmons. Stolen bases—Gehrig, Chapman. Double plays—Williams, Bishop, and Foxx; Heving and Williams. Left on bases—New York, 5; Philadelphia, 11. Bases on balls—off Gomez, 5; Earnshaw, 2; DeShong, 4. Struck out—by Gomez, 7; Earnshaw, 1; DeShong, 3. Hits—off Gomez, 11 in 8⅔ innings; Ruffing, none in ⅓; Earnshaw 8 in 4; DeShong 4 in 5. Hit by pitcher—by Gomez (Simmons). Winning pitcher—Gomez. Losing pitcher—Earnshaw. Umpires—Hildebrand, Moriarty, and Dinneen. Time of game—2 hrs 3 min.

Thursday, April 13, 1933
Yankee Stadium, New York
New York 4 Boston 3

The only thing we have to fear is fear itself.—Franklin Delano Roosevelt

By the time the 1933 baseball season opened, the fans heading out to the nation's ballparks, like most Americans, sensed (prematurely, as it would turn out) that the worst days of the economic depression were over. President Franklin D. Roosevelt had begun the difficult task of restoring confidence from the moment he took the oath of office on March 4, 1933 (the last presidential inauguration held in March). Two days after the swearing-in, Roosevelt ordered all the banks in the country closed to prevent the outflow of gold, silver, and other currency for foreign exchange. Three days later he called for a special session of Congress and began submitting a myriad of bills, the National Industrial Recovery Act, the Agricultural Adjustment Act, and the Tennessee Valley Authority Act, all aimed at bringing economic reform and stimulating recovery. Today's news from Washington further reassured the average American that Roosevelt was acting to alleviate his worst fear—the fear of losing his home or farm. The president was urging passage of refinancing legislation that would protect from foreclosure all homes worth less than $10,000.

Nevertheless, "happy days" were not quite yet "here again." Nineteen thirty-three would be another dismal year for much of the American economy, including baseball. Major-league attendance would fall to 6,089,031, a post–World War I low, and while the Yankees, as usual, would lead both leagues, they would do it with almost a quarter-million fewer fans than the previous year. Opening Day, naturally, attracted one of the season's larger gatherings to Yankee Stadium. Actually, the Yanks and Red Sox were supposed to open yesterday, but an unexpected spring storm that passed through New York pelted the city with a mixture of rain and snow and forced a postponement. It was still raw and chilly for today's rescheduled opener, but Lou Gehrig warmed the crowd of nearly 40,000 (36,221 paid) with a first-inning three-run homer that propelled the Yankees to a 4–3 victory.

Just as FDR was doing for the nation, Boston fans hoped their new leader, Tom Yawkey, would do for the Red Sox; lift them from the depths. Yawkey, a 30-year-old heir to a lumber and iron fortune, had bought the team from Bob Quinn in February for $1.25 million. He promptly chose former Philadelphia A's and Chicago White Sox great, Eddie Collins, as his general manager, and the two set about to revive the franchise. Boston had finished last in nine of the previous 11 years and had not finished in the first division since their world championship year of 1918. Moreover, because an inevitable repercussion of bad teams is poor attendance, the Red Sox had drawn only 182,150 fans to Fenway Park in 1932, which remains their all-time low. In the coming years, Yawkey would spend millions of dollars to buy players he hoped would again make the Red Sox a winning team. However, on Opening Day 1933, those transactions were still in the future. The team that took the field on Opening Day 1933 greatly resembled the losing teams of the recent past, except for their new uniforms; they looked completely different from any Boston teams had worn before. For the first time Red Sox players were wearing solid navy blue caps, and also for the first time, there was the letter "B" on the cap. On the front of the jersey, in red letters outlined in blue, was "RED SOX," which had been there since 1912.

The traditional opening-day parade to the flagpole began at three o'clock with Jacob Ruppert, Mayor John P. O'Brien, and the Seventh Regiment Band leading the players from both teams. As the band played the national anthem, the Stars and Stripes was raised, as was New York's 1932 world championship flag. Once back at home plate, with the band playing "My Hero," Ruppert and the mayor handed out watches or rings to the Yankees' players to commemorate last fall's sweep of the Chicago Cubs. Yawkey and Collins watched the gift giving from a box near the visiting dugout, undoubtedly hoping that such ceremonies were in their team's future. Among the celebrities seated near the two dugouts were former heavyweight champion Jack Dempsey, heavyweight contender Max Baer, and wrestling star Jumping Joe Savoldi. With the recent repeal of Prohibition, Yankee Stadium vendors again were selling beer. That not only pleased the fans (at least a large segment of them), it absolutely delighted Ruppert, who besides owning the Yankees also owned several large breweries. However, because of the cold weather, more patrons were drinking coffee than they were the Colonel's beer. Mayor O'Brien threw a few practice tosses and then made the official first pitch. O'Brien had been elected mayor in November 1932 in a special election held to fill the last year of Jimmy Walker's term (Walker had resigned under pressure on September 1). O'Brien, a political hack in the Tammany machine, would lose to Republican Fiorello La Guardia in the mayoralty election of November 1933.

After Lefty Gomez (24–7 in 1932) retired leadoff batter Rabbit Warstler, manager/third baseman Marty McManus lined a double to left. McManus, a longtime American League infielder with the St. Louis Browns and Detroit Tigers, had come to Boston for catcher Muddy Ruel in an August 1931 trade with Detroit. When manager Shano Collins resigned in June 1932, the Red Sox replaced him with McManus. Gomez got the next batter, Johnny Watwood, on a ground ball, but Dale Alexander followed with the first of his three hits, a run-scoring single to center. A year ago, Alexander was batting .250 for Detroit when on June 12 the Tigers traded him to Boston. After joining the Red Sox, he hit .372 in 101 games and won the American League batting championship with a combined average of .367. Recently, some have challenged the validity of Alexander's batting title because he had only 392 official at-bats. However, the rule in effect at the time required that a player need only have played in 100 games to be eligible. Because Alexander played in 124 games (he had played in 23 for the Tigers), the American League continues to recognize him as their 1932 batting champion. Alexander, Harry Walker, who played for the St. Louis Cardinals and Philadelphia Phillies in 1947, and Nap Lajoie, who played one game for the Philadelphia A's and 86 for Cleveland in 1902, are the only batting champions to have won the title while playing for two different teams in their championship season.

Boston's starting pitcher was Ivy Andrews, a former Yankee traded to Boston last June with Hank Johnson and $50,000 for Danny MacFayden. Andrews had good success in Boston; he won eight and lost six (10–7 total) and was second on the club in earned run average (3.81). Eagle-eyed Joe Sewell, the Yankees' regular third baseman since joining them in 1931, drew a one-out walk. This season he would strike out just four times in 524 at bats, an amazing ratio even for Sewell, who struck out only 114 times in 7,132 career at-bats. When the season ended, Sewell retired as an active player, but stayed with the Yankees as a coach for two more years.

Babe Ruth followed Sewell's walk with a line single to right. Ruth, beginning his 20th big-league season, had signed a one-year contract for $52,000, well below the $75,000 he earned in 1932. The Yankees explained that besides the general cost-cutting made necessary by the depression, Ruth's production had declined. In 1932, the year of his "decline," Ruth batted .341, with 41 home runs and 137 runs batted in. Gehrig came to the plate with two on and one out, and drove an Andrews pitch far up into the right-field bleachers for a three-run homer. For Gehrig, playing in his 1,199th consecutive game, it was the 268th home run of his spectacular career and gave the Yankees a 3–1 lead. Later in the season, on August 17 at St. Louis, Gehrig would play in consecutive game 1,308, breaking the record of former teammate Everett Scott. By scoring, the Yankees stretched their streak of consecutive games without being shut out to 212. No pitcher had blanked them since Boston's Wilcy Moore did it, 1–0, in the second game of a doubleheader on August 2, 1931. The streak would reach a record 308 before Lefty Grove ended it with a 7–0 victory on August 3 of this season.

In the fourth the Yanks stretched their lead to 4–1 when Tony Lazzeri singled, Bill Dickey doubled (one of his three hits), and Frank Crosetti singled Lazzeri home. Dickey also tried to score, but his entanglement with shortstop Warstler between second and third held him up sufficiently to allow the Red Sox to throw him out at the plate. Andrews kept New York scoreless in the fifth and sixth, then turned it over to relievers Bob Kline and Johnny Welch who retired the Yanks in order in the seventh and eighth. Meanwhile, Boston continued to get their hits against Gomez; they would outhit the Yankees 12–9. Three of their hits, eighth-inning singles by Johnny Hodapp, Merv Shea, and pinch-hitter Bob Fothergill, followed a walk to Alexander who was forced by Smead Jolley and helped narrow the Yankee lead to 4–3. Manager Joe McCarthy had relieved Gomez with the Yanks holding a six-run lead and two out in the ninth inning of last year's opener. But this time, even with the potential go-ahead run on base, McCarthy stayed with his ace. Gomez repaid the confidence, getting Warstler to fly to Ben Chapman in left to strand Shea and Fothergill and end the inning. Left fielder Chapman was making his fourth consecutive opening-day start at a different position. In 1930 he had been at third base, in 1931 at second base, in 1932 in right field, and now in left field. He would be back in right on Opening Day 1934 and in center for the 1935 and '36 openers.

Boston got the tying run aboard again in the ninth, but McCarthy again stayed with Gomez, who got the complete game and his second straight opening-day win. While Gomez fanned only four batters this afternoon, he would top the league with 163 strikeouts in 1933, averaging a league-high 6.25 per game.

Lefty Gomez (16–10) and Red Ruffing (9–14) combined for just 25 wins as the Yanks (91–59) finished second, seven games behind the Washington Senators. Lou Gehrig scored 138 runs, the most in the league, and Babe Ruth led in walks (114) for the 11th time. It was the last time Ruth led the American League in any offensive category.

Thursday, April 13, 1933

Boston	ab	r	h	po	a	e		New York	ab	r	h	po	a	e
Warstler ss	5	0	1	2	3	0		Combs cf	4	0	0	2	0	0
McManus 3b	5	1	2	0	0	0		Sewell 3b	3	1	0	1	3	0
Watwood lf	5	0	0	3	0	0		Ruth rf	4	1	1	1	0	0
Alexander 1b	4	0	3	9	1	0		Gehrig 1b	4	1	2	9	2	0
Jolley rf	4	0	0	0	0	0		Chapman lf	3	0	0	2	0	0
bMulleavy	0	1	0	0	0	0		Lazzeri 2b	4	1	1	2	3	0
Welch p	0	0	0	0	0	0		Dickey c	3	0	3	5	0	0
cFriberg	1	0	0	0	0	0		Crosetti ss	3	0	2	3	2	0
Hodapp 2b	4	0	2	1	4	0		Gomez p	2	0	0	2	1	0
R. Johnson cf	3	1	2	5	1	0		Total	30	4	9	27	11	0
Shea c	4	0	1	2	1	0								
Andrews p	2	0	0	1	1	0								
aSeeds	0	0	0	0	0	0								
Kline p	0	0	0	1	1	0								
dFothergill rf	1	0	1	0	0	0								
Total	38	3	12	24	12	0								

aBatted for Andrews in seventh inning.
bRan for Jolley in eighth inning.
cBatted for Welch in ninth inning.
dSingled for Kline in eighth inning.

Boston	100	000	020–3
New York	300	100	00X–4

Runs batted in—Alexander, Gehrig 3, Crosetti, Shea, Fothergill. Two-base hits—Dickey, McManus, R. Johnson. Home run—Gehrig. Double plays—Hodapp, Warstler, and Alexander; Sewell, Lazzeri, and Gehrig. Left on bases—New York, 5; Boston, 11. Bases on balls—off Andrews, 3; Gomez, 3. Struck out—by Gomez, 4; Andrews, 1. Hits—off Andrews, 9 in 6 innings; Kline, 0 in 1; Welch, 0 in 1. Wild pitch—Gomez. Losing pitcher—Andrews. Umpires—Moriarty and Geisel. Time of game—1 hr. 56 min.

Tuesday, April 17, 1934
Shibe Park, Philadelphia
Philadelphia 6 New York 5

By the time a man gets well into the seventies his continued existence is a mere miracle.—Robert Louis Stevenson

History was repeating itself in Philadelphia. Just as he had done 20 years earlier, Connie Mack, now 71 years old, was in the process of tearing down a dynasty. However, he had not torn it down completely. And while his 1934 Athletics were clearly no longer the star-studded club that had won three consecutive pennants from 1929 to 1931, they had not yet become the dreadful aggregation that would finish last seven times and seventh twice in the nine years between 1935 and 1943. Nonetheless, they were going in that direction. In return for several hundred thousand dollars and a few marginal players, Mack had traded or sold many of the players responsible for the Athletics' recent championship seasons. He blamed the dismantling of the A's on the economic hardship caused by the depression, which he claimed was forcing him to sell his stars to keep the franchise afloat. During a period of 18 months, Lefty Grove, the league's best pitcher, and George Earnshaw and Rube Walberg, two other pitching mainstays, had left Philadelphia. Gone, too, was most of Mack's pennant-winning lineup: Al Simmons, Mickey Cochrane, Mule Haas, Jimmy Dykes, and Max Bishop. Philadelphia's financial situation was so bad that Jimmie Foxx, who won the Triple Crown in 1933, had been forced to hold out before finally settling for a 1934 salary of $18,000.

Having depleted his lineup, Mack was depending on outfielder Bob Johnson and third baseman Pinky Higgins, two youngsters who were coming off great rookie years, to fortify the A's offense. The two would get off to a fine start, combining for five of Philadelphia's ten hits this afternoon. But it was Bing Miller, a 39-year-old veteran who had been a starting outfielder on the three pennant-winning teams, who was Philadelphia's opening-day hero. Although Miller was now primarily a backup player, it was his two-out, ninth-inning pinch-single that gave the A's a 6–5 come-from-behind victory over the Yankees. The blow delighted the small gathering (fewer than 10,000) that sat through the long contest on a gloomy, overcast day. Miller, the A's captain, had been sitting on the bench since he and Yankees manager Joe McCarthy had hoisted the flag during the pregame activities. As they did, the Nineteenth Marine Reserve Band, which was returning live music to a Shibe Park opener after an absence of several years, played the national anthem. The band also marched in the pregame parade along with the two teams, A's president Tom Shibe, and first-ball thrower Mayor J. Hampton Moore. In a ceremony held in the Athletics dugout, Judge Harry McDevitt, a local politician with eyes on the governor's mansion, presented Mack with the Harry Mackey Trophy. The trophy, named for a former Philadelphia mayor, was in recognition of the A's victory over the Phillies in the recently concluded Philadelphia city series. That series included a Sunday game, which was now possible because Pennsylvania had recently repealed the "blue law" that prohibited Sunday baseball.

Throughout the spring, Mack had praised left-hander Merritt "Sugar" Cain, his opening-day starter, predicting he soon would replace Grove as the A's best pitcher. That may have been wishful thinking by Mack, or simply his attempt to placate the fans, but in either case, it did not turn out that way. Cain, 13–12 in 1933, would win only nine games in 1934 (9–17) and was 0–5 when Mack traded him to the St. Louis Browns in May 1935. However, for the first four innings this afternoon, Cain may have reminded some of Grove as he and the Yankees' Lefty Gomez (making his third straight opening-day start) kept the game scoreless. The Yanks finally broke through against him with two runs in the fifth, the first on rookie Don Heffner's double that followed Bill Dickey's single. With Heffner at second and Gomez at the plate, Cain threw a pitch in the dirt. Catcher Charlie Berry, whom the A's got from the White Sox to replace Cochrane, prevented it from being a wild pitch, but in doing so suffered a split finger. Berry left for backup Ed Madjeski. After Gomez sacrificed Heffner to third, Earle Combs hit a bouncer back to Cain that trapped Heffner midway between third and home. However, in the rundown Madjeski made a terrible throw to third that went into left field and allowed Heffner to come home with the Yankees' second run. Rookie Red Rolfe drew a walk, but Cain avoided further scoring by getting Babe Ruth to hit into a double play.

Second baseman Heffner, purchased from the Baltimore Orioles of the International League, and shortstop Rolfe, a graduate of Dartmouth College, had been the most talked about players at the Yankees' St. Petersburg training camp. Particularly touted was Rolfe, who batted .409 in the spring (second only to Ruth's .415) and made a very strong impression on McCarthy and many of the team's veterans. Still, cynics remembered that two years earlier Jack Saltzgaver had inspired similar raves. Saltzgaver never lived up to his promise, becoming another example of the foolhardiness of making premature judgments about rookies based on their spring training performances. But while Heffner, like Salzgaver, never became more than a run-of-the-mill player, Rolfe did. He took over as the Yankees' third baseman in 1935 and remained a fixture there until 1942.

Philadelphia got a run back in their half of the fifth on Madjeski's single and Rabbit Warstler's double. Warstler, who came to the A's from the Boston Red Sox in the Grove deal, was playing second for the injured Dib Williams. The Athletics went ahead, 3–2, in the bottom of the sixth on shortstop Eric McNair's upper-deck home run to left field with Foxx aboard. Foxx, the lone remaining starter from Philadelphia's glory days, had reached base on a walk, one of three issued to him by prudent Yankees' pitchers. When Johnson followed McNair's homer with another walk, and then Higgins singled, McCarthy summoned rookie Johnny Murphy from the bullpen. Murphy, from Fordham University, had been a 1933 teammate of Rolfe's with the Newark Bears, the International League franchise Colonel Ruppert had purchased in 1931. Murphy got the side out without any further scoring, the first of many times in their careers that Murphy would bail Gomez out of a troublesome situation.

New York tied the score in the seventh on singles by Dickey and Heffner and a long double by Combs that brought Dickey home. Heffner attempted to score from first but was out on a fine relay from center fielder Doc Cramer to second baseman Warstler to catcher Frankie Hayes. Hayes, a 19-year-old rookie, had replaced Madjeski—who was obviously not yet in top playing shape—an inning earlier. The Yankees went ahead, 5–3, in the eighth on Ben Chapman's single that scored Ruth, who had walked, and Lou Gehrig, who had singled. Ruth was playing left field today in what was his last opening-day appearance as a Yankee. In the latter years of his career, Ruth would play right field in Yankee Stadium and left field on the road, except for League Park in Cleveland and Griffith Stadium in Washington, both of which were deeper in left field than in right. Ruth, who made no secret about his desire to manage, preferably the Yankees, had signed for $35,000—a $17,000 pay cut. He was earning more than that for a 13-week stint he was doing on radio. For a thrice-weekly 15-minute show on NBC, Quaker Oats was paying him $39,000.

Tuesday, April 17, 1934

New York	ab	r	h	po	a	e	Philadelphia	ab	r	h	po	a	e
Combs cf	3	0	1	3	0	0	Warstler 2b	4	0	1	1	8	0
Rolfe ss	4	0	0	2	5	0	Cramer cf	2	0	0	2	1	0
Ruth lf	3	1	0	2	0	0	Coleman rf	5	0	0	1	0	0
Hoag lf	0	0	0	0	0	0	Foxx 1b	2	1	0	10	0	0
Gehrig 1b	3	1	2	7	1	0	McNair ss	5	2	2	5	3	0
Chapman rf	4	0	1	1	0	0	Johnson lf	4	1	3	0	0	0

New York	ab	r	h	po	a	e
Lazzeri 3b	2	0	0	1	4	0
Dickey c	4	2	2	7	0	0
Heffner 2b	4	1	2	3	1	0
Gomez p	1	0	0	0	2	0
Murphy p	1	0	0	0	1	0
Smythe p	1	0	0	0	0	0
Uhle p	0	0	0	0	0	0
Total	30	5	8	26	14	0

Philadelphia	ab	r	h	po	a	e
Higgins 3b	3	1	2	1	2	0
Berry c	1	0	0	2	1	0
Madjeski c	1	1	1	0	0	1
Hayes c	3	0	0	5	1	0
Cain p	3	0	0	0	1	0
ªFinney	0	0	0	0	0	0
Cascarella p	0	0	0	0	0	0
ᵇMiller	1	0	1	0	0	0
Total	34	6	10	27	17	1

*Two out when winning run scored.
ªWalked for Cain in eighth inning.
ᵇSingled for Cascarella in ninth inning.

New York	000	020	120–5
Philadelphia	000	012	012–6

Runs batted in—Heffner, Combs, Chapman 2, Warstler, McNair 2, Cramer, Johnson, Miller. Two-base hits—Heffner, Warstler, Combs, Higgins, Johnson. Home run—McNair. Stolen base—Hayes. Sacrifices—Gomez, Lazzeri. Double plays—Berry and McNair; Higgins, Warstler, and Foxx; Warstler, McNair, and Foxx; Gomez, Rolfe, and Gehrig; Lazzeri, Heffner, and Gehrig. Left on bases—New York, 7; Philadelphia, 13. Bases on balls—off Gomez 6, Murphy 4, Smythe 1, Cain 6, Cascarella 1. Struck out—by Gomez 3, Murphy 1, Smythe 1, Cain 4, Cascarella 2. Hits—off Gomez, 5 in 5 innings (none out in sixth); Murphy 2 in 2⅔ innings; Smythe 2 in ⅔ inning; Uhle 1 in ⅓ inning; Cain 8 in 8 innings; Cascarella 0 in 1 inning. Wild pitch—Murphy, Cain. Winning pitcher—Cascarella. Losing pitcher—Smythe. Umpires—Dinneen and Summers. Time of game—2 hrs. 40 min.

After keeping the Athletics scoreless in the seventh, Murphy quickly ran into trouble in the eighth. A single by Johnson and a double by Higgins put runners at second and third with nobody out. Johnson tried to score on Hayes's come-backer but was out on Murphy's throw to Dickey. Lou Finney batted for Cain and drew a walk to load the bases. Murphy got a big second out when he induced Warstler to foul out to Dickey, but then walked Cramer forcing Higgins home with Philadelphia's fourth run. With left-handed hitter Ed Coleman at the plate, McCarthy yanked Murphy and brought in left-hander Harry Smythe, who fanned Coleman to end the rally.

Right-hander Joe Cascarella, a native Philadelphian in his major-league debut, kept the Yankees from scoring in the ninth, thus setting the stage for the A's dramatic finish. The three scheduled batters for Philadelphia were all right-handed: Foxx, McNair, and Johnson. Foxx was the most feared right-handed hitter in the game; McNair had already homered against the left-handed Gomez; and Johnson had hit 21 home runs as a rookie. Nevertheless, McCarthy stayed with Smythe, whose only previous major-league experience was with the Phillies back in 1929–1930. Smythe retired Foxx, but McNair beat out a grounder to deep short. McCarthy allowed Smythe to pitch to Johnson, who doubled off the center-field wall, sending McNair home with the tying run. It was Johnson's third hit of the day and just missed clearing the fence for a game-winning home run. After an intentional walk to Higgins (the 11th walk issued by Yankees' pitchers, and the 18th in the game), McCarthy removed Smythe and brought in veteran right-hander George Uhle to pitch to right-handed hitter Hayes. Uhle got the youngster to hit an apparent double-play grounder to Rolfe at short, but Higgins's hard slide into second prevented Heffner from getting off a throw. Hayes was safe at first as Johnson took third. With Cascarella due up, Mack called on Miller, who lined Uhle's first pitch into center field to bring Johnson home with the game-winning run.

The Detroit Tigers won their first pennant since 1909, finishing seven games ahead of the second place Yankees (94–60). Lou Gehrig won the Triple Crown with a .363 batting average, 49 home runs, and 166 runs batted in. Lefty Gomez led the league in wins (26–5), winning percentage (.839), ERA (2.33), complete games (25), and strikeouts (158). Gomez finished third and Gehrig fifth (despite the Triple Crown) in the voting for the Most Valuable Player Award, won by Detroit's Mickey Cochrane.

Tuesday, April 16, 1935
Yankee Stadium, New York
Boston 1 New York 0

You have delighted us long enough.—Jane Austen

Babe Ruth hit a home run and drove in three runs as he led his team to an opening-day, 4–2, victory. Unfortunately for the Yankees, he did it not for them but for his new team—the National League's Boston Braves. While Ruth was at Braves Field pounding Carl Hubbell and the New York Giants, at Yankee Stadium Red Sox right-hander Wes Ferrell was shutting out the Yanks, 1–0, on just two hits. Ruth had become an ex–Yankee as a result of the plotting and machinations between New York's business manager Ed Barrow and the Braves' financially strapped owner, Judge Emil Fuchs. After the Yankees released Ruth in February, Fuchs signed him immediately. His salary would be a lowly (for him) $20,000, but Fuchs sweetened the deal with a vague promise that the Babe would be the Braves' next manager. Until then, he would serve as the assistant manager to current skipper Bill McKechnie.

After his opening-day heroics, Ruth faded quickly—but not without one last great day. On May 25 he hit the final three home runs of his career—numbers 712, 713, and 714—against the Pirates at Forbes Field. A week later, on June 2, the Babe retired as an active player. Baseball had lost not only its greatest performer, but also its biggest drawing card. The effect of Ruth's departure on attendance was most clearly felt in New York. Only 657,508 fans would come out to Yankee Stadium in 1935, the lowest for any season since the Stadium opened 12 years earlier. The pattern was set in the opener, which attracted 32,000 (just 29,287 paid). It was the smallest opening-day crowd yet at the Stadium, but it's unlikely that even Ruth's presence could have boosted it much. With early morning temperatures hovering near the 32-degree mark, and with the sighting of occasional snow flurries around the city, it was a tribute to the fans that so many did attend.

The winter-like weather did not deter New York's number one citizen, Mayor Fiorello La Guardia. When the clock struck three, there he was, taking part in all the usual pregame celebrations. First he joined in the march to the flagpole with Colonel Ruppert, Lieutenant Francis Sutherland's Seventh Regiment Band, and the two teams. Then he watched managers Joe Cronin and Joe McCarthy raise the flag, made the return march, and threw out the ceremonial first pitch. When La Guardia finally sat down it was in a box alongside the Yankees dugout, where he joined his guest, Governor Harry Nice of Maryland. Despite the mayor's great popularity, the fans showed greater interest in the boxes nearby where George Raft, Carole Lombard, and Eddie Cantor sat. The Hollywood stars were in town for the Al Jolson celebration, held the night before, at the Casino de Paree, on 54th Street, West of Broadway. No one in the crowd paid much attention to an unoccupied seat the club had reserved for Jim Mutrie. In fact, it's unlikely that many people in the Stadium had ever even heard of Jim Mutrie. Yet half a century earlier, he had been among the most prominent baseball figures in New York. In 1883 Mutrie helped found, and was the manager of, the New York Metropolitans of the American Association, then a major league. He also helped to organize a New York franchise in the National League, managed them from 1885 to 1891, and was responsible for their name: Giants. But the 83-year-old Mutrie was in declining health, and the bitterly cold weather prevented him from making the trip from his home on Staten Island.

The visiting Red Sox were an almost entirely different team from the one that opened the season here two years earlier. Backed by owner Tom Yawkey's money—he had spent close to a million dollars in the past two years—General Manager Eddie Collins had bought and traded players freely. None of the Boston starters on Opening Day 1933 were in the starting lineup today, and of the 15 players the Sox used that day, only outfielder Roy Johnson and pitcher Johnny Welch were still with the team. There was also a new look to the Red Sox uniforms, or a new-old look. They had eliminated the blue outline around the red-lettered "BOSTON" on their road jersey fronts, and their socks were all red again, having ditched the white and blue stripes from the previous season.

Under new manager Bucky Harris, the Sox had moved up to fourth place in 1934; the first time they had been in the first division since 1918. Nevertheless, they fired Harris and replaced him with Cronin, acquired from the Washington Senators for Lyn Lary and $225,000. That was then the highest amount ever paid for a single player, which no doubt helped Senators owner Clark Griffith rationalize the sale of the man married to his niece, Mildred. Cronin, still only 28 years old, had been a pennant-winning manager with the Senators and also the American League's All-Star shortstop. For his Red Sox debut he was opening with Ferrell, who at 14–5 was Boston's best pitcher in 1934. Before coming to the Red Sox from the Cleveland Indians, Ferrell had been a 20-game winner in each of his first four major-league seasons (1929–1932). A sore arm ended his streak of 20-win seasons in 1933, when he slipped to 11–12. Cleveland responded to Ferrell's long holdout in the spring of 1934 by first suspending him, and in May trading him to Boston.

Lefty Gomez, the league's top pitcher in 1934 (26–5), was making his fourth consecutive opening-day start for the Yankees, tying the club record set by Jack Chesbro (1903–1906). Bob Shawkey also made four opening-day starts for the Yankees, but they were not consecutive. Gomez had not pitched particularly well in any of his three previous openers, though he won two of them and had a no-decision in the other. This afternoon he did pitch well, allowing only six hits and a walk. However, the one run he did allow was enough to tag him with his first opening-day defeat. Boston's run came as the result of some daring sixth-inning base running by third baseman Bill Werber (a throw-in in the Yankees' May 1933 sale of George Pipgras to Boston) and two throwing errors.

Max Bishop, the former Philadelphia Athletic, opened the sixth with a single to center, but catcher Bill Dickey threw him out trying to steal second. Werber lined a hit to left, rounded first at full speed, and beat left fielder Earle Combs's throw to second. Werber took a long lead, but when Gomez attempted to pick him off, he made the Yankees' first bad throw of the inning. His high toss caromed off second baseman Tony Lazzeri's glove, allowing Werber to go to third. Carl Reynolds went down swinging, but the ball got away from Dickey, requiring a throw to first. As Dickey released the ball, Werber took off from third heading for the plate. Reynolds was out at first, but Lou Gehrig's return throw to Dickey was high and Werber came home with the game's only run.

The Sox just missed scoring an additional run, or maybe more, in the seventh. With two out and Rick Ferrell, Wes's brother and battery mate, on second, Babe Dahlgren drove a ball to deep left center. Left fielder Combs raced back and made a great running catch at the wall. The fans responded with the longest and loudest ovation of the day, even exceeding the one he had gotten when he was introduced as the Yankees' leadoff batter. Combs was playing his first league game since last July 24 when he suffered a fractured skull colliding with a wall in Sportsman's Park, St. Louis. His excellent catch prevented Dahlgren, playing his first major-league game, from getting his first major-league hit. Dahlgren did, however, play a very impressive game defensively at first base. Three times he turned potential throwing errors by shortstop Cronin into outs.

Tuesday, April 16, 1935

Boston	ab	r	h	po	a	e	New York	ab	r	h	po	a	e
Bishop 2b	3	0	1	1	4	0	Combs lf	4	0	0	4	0	0
Werber 3b	4	1	2	0	0	0	Rolfe 3b	4	0	0	2	2	0
Reynolds rf	4	0	1	1	0	0	Selkirk rf	3	0	1	0	0	0
Cronin ss	4	0	1	0	6	0	Gehrig 1b	3	0	1	14	0	1
R. Ferrell c	4	0	1	1	0	0	Dickey c	3	0	0	2	2	0
Solters lf	3	0	0	6	0	0	Chapman cf	3	0	0	0	0	0
Almada cf	3	0	0	4	0	0	Lazzeri 2b	3	0	0	3	3	0
Dahlgren 1b	3	0	0	14	0	0	Crosetti ss	3	0	0	2	6	0
W. Ferrell p	3	0	0	0	2	0	Gomez p	2	0	0	0	2	1
Total	31	1	6	27	12	0	ªWalker	1	0	0	0	0	0
							Total	29	0	2	27	15	2

ªGrounded out for Gomez in ninth inning.

Boston	000	001	000–1
New York	000	000	000–0

Two-base hits—Reynolds, Werber, R. Ferrell, Gehrig. Double play—Rolfe, Lazzeri, and Gehrig. Left on bases—New York, 2; Boston, 4. Bases on balls—off Gomez, 1. Struck out—by Gomez, 2. Umpires—Dinneen, Kolls, and Donnelly. Time of game—1 hr. 35 min.

Although Ferrell did not strike out anyone, he used his curves to offset a lively fastball that had the Yankees' hitters off balance all afternoon. Brother Rick said he had not seen such speed and good stuff from Wes in three years. The two hits the Yankees had constituted their only base runners, as Ferrell faced just 29 batters. George Selkirk got the first one, a single to center in the fourth inning. Selkirk, a second-year man, had the unenviable assignment of succeeding Ruth. In that capacity he was batting third, playing right field, and wearing No. 3. Gehrig, whose consecutive-game streak had now reached 1,505, got New York's second hit, a line-drive double to center field in the seventh. The Yankees' newly appointed team captain began the season with 348 lifetime home runs, which would make him the major league's active home-run leader after Ruth retired in June. Dickey followed Gehrig's double with another long drive to center, but Boston center fielder Mel Almada ran it down and made the catch. Almada, from Huatabampo, Mexico, had joined the Sox in 1933, becoming the first Mexican-born player in the major leagues.

The game was a quick one, played in just over an hour and a half. It was the first time the Yankees had been shut out on Opening Day since 1919 when Carl Mays of Boston blanked them, 10–0, at the Polo Grounds. Ferrell went on to lead the American League in wins with 25 (25–14) and finish second to the Detroit Tiger's Hank Greenberg as the league's

Most Valuable Player. Gomez, the tough-luck loser, suffered his first loss ever to the Red Sox after 11 straight wins. He would win only 12 games this season and lose 15, his worst full season as a Yankee. Despite the loss, Mayor La Guardia, ever the optimist, commented: "It was an interesting, close game and we are going to have one pennant, if not both in New York at the end of the season." Then La Guardia, his wife Marie, and Lester Stone, his secretary, got into the mayor's official car for the trip home. On the way they encountered a police emergency truck at St. Nicholas Ave. and 152nd Street in upper Manhattan, which the mayor had his chauffeur follow, ending up at a fire on 126th Street. It was the type of stunt that would make La Guardia New York's best and most beloved mayor.

> *Mayor La Guardia was wrong; there were no pennants in New York in 1935. The Giants finished third, while the Yankees (89–60) finished second, three games behind the Detroit Tigers (93–58). There is no telling what the final standings would have been if the league had required both teams to make up their postponed games.*

Tuesday, April 14, 1936
Griffith Stadium, Washington
Washington 1 New York 0

The way to resumption is to resume. —Salmon P. Chase

Three years after President William Howard Taft opened Washington's baseball season by throwing out the first ball, the Yankees played in their first "presidential opener." That was in 1913; Woodrow Wilson was in the White House and they lost to Walter Johnson, 2–1. Two years later, President Wilson watched as Johnson blanked the Yankees, 7–0. The Yanks did win the season opener here in 1918, but Wilson, occupied with the war in Europe, missed that one. By 1922, Warren Harding was the president and Johnson was ill, but still the Yankees lost, this time to George Mogridge, 6–5. By Opening Day 1936, 14 years had passed since their last "presidential opener," and Franklin D. Roosevelt was now the guest of honor, but the result remained the same—a Yankees' loss. They fell to the Senators, 1–0, the victims of a heroic effort by Bobo Newsom, who pitched a complete game despite receiving a fearful blow to his head from a thrown ball. Washington scored the game's only run in the ninth inning, sending Lefty Gomez to his second straight opening-day defeat.

For Newsom it was, in a way, a compensatory victory. A year earlier, while with the St. Louis Browns, he had lost the opener, 2–1, in 14 innings to the Cleveland Indians' Mel Harder. Newsom also lost his next five decisions and was 0–6 when the Browns sold him to the Senators in May for $40,000. He pitched well for Washington, winning 11 games and losing 12, although his combined 18 losses were the most in the league. Newsom had gotten the opening-day start only because manager Bucky Harris was unhappy with the condition of his ace, Earl Whitehill. Newsom, a colorful, gregarious right-hander, relished pitching in front of a big crowd, especially one that included the president of the United States. FDR had left the White House for Griffith Stadium at 2:30 P.M., after arranging to have all his work and meetings concluded by then. His son Elliott and his daughter-in-law Mrs. James Roosevelt were with him. The chauffeur drove the president's limousine through a special entrance gate and proceeded onto the field before coming to a stop in front of the Washington dugout. The capacity crowd cheered Mr. Roosevelt and so did the Yankees and

Senators players who had lined up to greet him. Senators owner Clark Griffith escorted FDR to the presidential box situated above the home-team dugout. There his son James joined him, as did his physician, his military and naval aides, and assistant White House secretary Marvin H. McIntyre. Former first lady Edith Wilson and former Senators owner Benjamin Minor, two distinguished guests from an earlier era in the nation's capital, sat nearby.

Vice President John Nance Garner substituted for the president on the march to the flagpole and the accompanying flag-raising ceremonies. That completed, Mr. Roosevelt was helped to his feet, and with Harris and Yankees manager Joe McCarthy standing alongside him and more than 40 photographers gathered around his box, he threw out the first ball. His throw, however, did not land among the Washington players as it was supposed to; it landed off to the side, setting off a scramble among the players for the presidential souvenir. After finishing his first-ball duties, the president picked a rose from a basket of flowers presented to him, put it in the lapel of his coat, and took his seat. He had with him a five-cent scorecard and a bag of peanuts. Roosevelt was a "good luck charm" for the Senators; he had yet to see them lose in five visits to Griffith Stadium, dating from 1917 when he was Assistant Secretary of the Navy. This afternoon the president and his party remained for the entire game, not even leaving their seats in the fifth inning when it began to rain—a passing shower on an otherwise beautiful day. The previous evening, he had spoken at a Jefferson Day dinner in Baltimore, where he confessed that unemployment was higher than he had hoped and proposed a shorter workweek with no cut in wages.

It was in the fifth inning that Newsom had his near-fatal accident. He had been nearly flawless through four, allowing only one Yankees' base runner, Gomez, who reached on an error by shortstop Cecil Travis. But in the fifth, Bill Dickey led off with an easy ground ball that Travis booted for his second error. Ben Chapman followed with an attempted sacrifice, dropping a bunt down the third-base line. Third baseman Ossie Bluege scooped it up and fired the ball across the diamond toward first baseman Joe Kuhel. It never got there. The ball, thrown at full speed from only 30 feet away, hit Newsom, who was standing on the mound, just below the right ear. While Kuhel retrieved the ball to keep the Yankees' runners from advancing, Newsom took several staggering steps toward third base. Still on his feet, with his hands to his head, he bent over as teammates rushed to his assistance. The incident quickly transformed the always festive and holiday-like atmosphere of Opening Day into one of sobering anxiety. As the president and the huge crowd waited, Senators trainer Mike Martin examined Newsom in the Washington dugout, checking for a possible broken jaw or worse. Anticipating the need for a new pitcher, Harris, in the second season of his second stint as manager of the Senators, sent Jack Russell to the bullpen to warm up. However, after a five-minute delay, to the crowd's surprise and delight, and contrary to medical advice, Newsom came bounding out of the dugout and sprinted back to the mound. Led by President Roosevelt, the largest crowd ever to see a baseball game in Washington, more than 31,000, greeted him with a standing ovation. Newsom's dugout examination had revealed no serious injury, nor did a more thorough inspection at a hospital that evening. However, for the rest of the game the imprint of the ball was visible on his neck and right ear.

Undoubtedly Bluege, who had not expected to be in the opening-day lineup, felt relieved. A veteran of 14 seasons with Washington, he had lost his job to 19-year-old Buddy Lewis, who had a sensational spring training. But Lewis had tailed off in the last few exhibition games, and Harris wanted to protect the teenager from all the tumult surrounding Opening Day. Rather than subject him to unnecessary pressure, he would allow Lewis to ease his way into the lineup. The stratagem proved successful as Lewis had a strong rookie year, batting .291 in 143 games. "Buddy has 12 or 14 years ahead of him," predicted Harris. It was an accurate prediction. Lewis would play 11 years for the Senators, compiling a lifetime batting average of .297 despite missing three and a half years in the middle of his career for service in World War II.

Following the accident Newsom lost some of his effectiveness; he walked six and allowed three more hits. (Chapman's attempted sacrifice was ruled a hit.) Nevertheless, he survived every threat as he stranded 11 New York base runners. The always boastful Newsom had predicted he would win the game by a score of 5–1 and hold the Yankees to five or six hits, but even he had not been bold enough to forecast a four-hit shutout. Newsom's courage in finishing the game was matched to a lesser extent by Yankees second baseman Tony Lazzeri. While trying unsuccessfully to steal second in the seventh inning, Lazzeri injured his leg. He lay on the ground for several minutes before limping off the field, but he too stayed in the game. Lazzeri's keystone partner, shortstop Frank Crosetti, was also playing with some discomfort. Crosetti had a broken nose and a blackened right eye, but refused to miss the opener.

For Gomez, making his record fifth consecutive opening-day start for the Yankees, it was the second straight opener in which he allowed only one run, yet lost the game. Last year he was the loser when Boston's Wes Ferrell beat the Yankees with a two-hitter. Gomez had thrown exceptionally well in his last preseason outing, pitching five hitless innings against Brooklyn on April 10, but he was not nearly as sharp today. He gave up seven hits and four walks and frequently left runners in scoring position. He worked out of trouble in the third inning, when the Senators had runners at second and third with one out, and again in the sixth, when they had the bases loaded with one out. It was a resolute performance by Gomez that ended with dramatic swiftness in the ninth. Travis, who had doubled in the second but was out attempting to stretch the hit into a triple, led off with a single to right. The next batter, in an obvious bunt situation, was right fielder Carl Reynolds. With Yankees third baseman Red Rolfe moved well up on the infield grass, Reynolds bunted Gomez's first pitch foul. Rolfe remained just a few yards from home plate as Reynolds checked the sign with Harris, coaching at third. The manager, in a bold move, switched off the bunt and signaled Reynolds to hit away, which he did. He lined the next pitch to the base of the left center-field wall for a double that sent Travis home with the winning run.

Reynolds no doubt felt more than the usual satisfaction that comes from driving in a game-winning run. Back on July 4, 1932, here at Griffith Stadium, Dickey, the Yankees' catcher, cut Reynolds's season short when he broke his jaw with a punch following a play at home plate. It cost the normally gentlemanly Dickey a $1,000 fine and a 30-day suspension. After the 1932 season the Senators traded Reynolds to the Browns, who after the 1933 season traded him to the Red Sox. On December 17, 1935, Reynolds, along with outfielder Roy Johnson, was traded back to Washington in exchange for Heinie Manush. Johnson never got to play for the Senators. A month later they sent him to the Yankees along with pitcher Bump Hadley for pitcher Jimmie DeShong and outfielder Jesse Hill. Johnson was in left field for the Yanks today, replacing the retired Earle Combs. Combs was serving as a Yankees' coach, a position he would hold for the next nine years. Besides the skull fracture he had suffered crashing into the wall in St. Louis in 1934, the Yankees gave Combs further impetus to retire when they signed Joe DiMaggio, the much-heralded outfielder from the Pacific Coast League's San Francisco Seals. DiMaggio was with the team in Washington.

He even took batting practice, although he knew he would not be playing (he wore No. 9—catcher Arndt Jorgens had switched to No. 18). On March 22, after going 12 for 20 in his first few exhibition games, DiMaggio was spiked on his left instep by infielder Joe Coscarart in a game against the Boston Bees. The next day, during treatment for the injury, an attendant left a diathermy machine on too long, causing burns to the foot. DiMaggio missed the rest of spring training and the first 17 games of the regular season. He did not make his Yankees' debut until May 3. The Joe DiMaggio era had begun, but without Joe DiMaggio.

After three consecutive second-place finishes, the Yankees (102–51) won their second pennant under Joe McCarthy. They clinched it on September 9, the earliest pennant-clinching ever, and finished a league-record 19½ games ahead of the Detroit Tigers. The Yanks went on to defeat the New York Giants in six games to win the World Series. Joe DiMaggio lived up to his advance notices, batting .323 with 29 home runs and 125 runs batted in. His 132 runs scored set an American League rookie record. Lou Gehrig hit .354, batted in 152 runs and led the league in home runs with 49. He also led in walks (130) and runs scored (167) and for the second time won the league's Most Valuable Player Award.

Tuesday, April 14, 1936

New York	ab	r	h	po	a	e	Washington	ab	r	h	po	a	e
Rolfe 3b	4	0	0	1	1	0	Hill lf	2	0	1	1	0	0
Johnson lf	3	0	0	0	0	0	Bluege 3b	2	0	1	1	3	0
Selkirk rf	3	0	0	1	0	0	Myer 2b	2	0	0	5	1	0
Gehrig 1b	4	0	1	10	0	0	Powell cf	3	0	0	2	0	0
Dickey c	2	0	0	6	1	0	Travis ss	4	1	2	2	4	2
Chapman cf	4	0	1	2	1	0	Reynolds rf	4	0	1	0	0	0
Lazzeri 2b	3	0	1	2	3	0	Kuhel 1b	3	0	0	13	1	0
Crosetti ss	3	0	1	1	2	0	Bolton c	3	0	1	3	2	0
Gomez p	2	0	0	1	3	0	Newsom p	3	0	1	0	2	0
Total	28	0	4	24	11	0	Total	26	1	7	27	13	2

*None out when winning run scored.

New York	000	000	000–0
Washington	000	000	001–1

Run batted in—Reynolds. Two-base hits—Travis, Reynolds. Stolen base—Bluege. Sacrifices—Hill, Lazzeri, Myer, Gomez 2, Selkirk, Bluege. Left on bases—New York 11; Washington 8. Bases on balls—off Gomez 4, Newsom 6. Struck out—by Gomez 6, Newsom 3. Umpires—Ormsby, McGowan, and Quinn. Time of game—2 hrs. 13 min.

Tuesday, April 20, 1937
Yankee Stadium, New York
Washington 3 New York 2

All baseball fans can be divided into two groups: those who come to batting practice and the others. Only those in the first category have much chance of amounting to anything.—Thomas Boswell

A disputed home run by Washington outfielder Al Simmons as well as physical and mental errors by the Yankees contributed to a disappointing opening-day loss for the defending champions. The Senators spoiled an otherwise beautiful day at Yankee Stadium by scoring single runs in the first, sixth, and eighth innings to defeat Lefty Gomez, 3–2. Senators pitcher Monte Weaver allowed the Yankees ten hits, but his ability to pitch out of tight spots resulted in ten runners left on base. It was a tenacious effort by Weaver, a 30-year-old right-hander who was not your typical ballplayer; Weaver had a master's degree in mathematics from the University of Virginia and taught at Virginia's Emory and Henry College during the off-season. However, as a pitcher he had never fulfilled the promise of his rookie year when he won 22 games (22–10). That was in 1932 and since then, partially due to an illness and a sore arm, he had won only 28 more.

The crowd, which eventually totaled 45,850, had begun streaming in to the freshly painted stadium when the gates opened at noon. Those heading for the bleachers discovered that the old wooden benches had been replaced by concrete ones. Everything in the park looked spectacular in the bright sunshine of this warm spring day. Even the groundskeepers were resplendent in their new white uniforms with flowing blue ties. Red, white, and blue bunting was everywhere, including the steel girders of the soon-to-be completed second and third decks in right field. Technology, however, had removed one familiar landmark from Yankee Stadium. Gone was the man with the megaphone who had announced the lineups to the crowd for as long as anyone could remember. In his place was a modern public address system. The club had installed the system for the 1936 World Series, and it would now become a permanent part of the Stadium scene.

Many early arrivals took the opportunity to watch batting and fielding practice, as discerning fans often like to do. This is especially true on Opening Day as it affords them a first look at their team's newcomers. Today those fans were studying Tommy Henrich, the 24-year-old outfielder "freed" by Commissioner Landis from the Cleveland Indians farm system six days earlier. New York had outbid seven other clubs to sign Henrich, a .346 hitter for the Southern Association's New Orleans Pelicans in 1936. He would not make his debut until May 11, but the knowledgeable New York crowd seemed to like what they saw, applauding many of Henrich's catches and throws.

The ever-present duo of Colonel Ruppert and Mayor La Guardia led the players in the pregame parade, accompanied by the martial music of Captain Francis Sutherland's Seventh Regiment Band. The Senators had gone through similar ceremonies yesterday in the "presidential opener" in Washington, a game they lost in ten innings to Philadelphia, 4–3. It was the first time President Roosevelt had seen them lose at home. This afternoon, however, they were the visitors and were in their road uniforms, which were completely gray except for a red "W" on the left sleeve and the blue cap, and their red and blue stockings. The Yankees were wearing their familiar pinstripes, which now bore the interlocked "NY" on the left breast. They had returned the hallmark "NY" to their jerseys last season after an absence of 20 years. As the band played the national anthem, managers Joe McCarthy of New York (one day shy of his 50th birthday) and Bucky Harris of Washington raised the Stars and Stripes and the Yankees' world championship flag. These ceremonies did not get the undivided attention that usually attends them. For just as the parade started, the fans spotted Babe Ruth and his wife Claire taking their seats in a box near the Yankees dugout. Ruth, retired just two years, remained incredibly popular in New York, and those nearby greeted him with heartfelt cheers and applause. As fans in other parts of the Stadium realized what the cheering was about, they too joined in, completely drowning out the music coming from the field. Autograph seekers and picture takers besieged Ruth throughout the game, while a steady stream of people came by just to get a look at him. The crowd gave the Babe a good-natured cheer when he caught a foul ball hit by Frank Crosetti in the fourth inning, a catch Ruth seemed to enjoy even more than the fans did.

Following the raising of the flag, the parade swung by the bleachers where the fans rose and began chanting, "We want Ruffing," "We want Ruffing," at Ruppert. But Ruffing, as they all knew, was not in Yankee Stadium; he was home in Illinois holding out for a salary of $16,000, which, despite his 20–12 record in 1936, was a thousand dollars more than the Yankees wanted to pay him. Ruffing was the lone member of the team still unsigned, although several other Yankees, including Lou Gehrig and Joe DiMaggio had threatened business manager Ed Barrow with holdouts before finally capitulating. Ruppert himself had countered Gehrig's request for $40,000 by pointing out that the Red Sox were paying his contemporary, Jimmie Foxx, only $18,000. Ruppert also argued that Mickey Cochrane, who not only *played* for the Detroit Tigers but also *managed* them, was making only $28,000.

Gehrig, who settled for $36,000 and a $750 signing bonus, was playing today despite a severely strained ligament in the middle finger of his left hand. The injury, which made it difficult for him to throw or grip a bat, caused him to miss the final three preseason games with Brooklyn. However earlier today, Dr. Robert Emmet Walsh, the Yankees' new team physician, removed the splint that had been on the finger and Gehrig's consecutive-game streak continued. It now had reached 1,809.

Although Ruffing, DiMaggio, and Gehrig each signed for something less than what they were asking, the club had at least offered them raises. Their original salary offer to Gomez, 13–7 in 1936, was $7,500, a $12,500 *cut*. DiMaggio eventually agreed to $15,000, an increase of $6,500 over 1936 and the highest salary ever paid to a second-year player. Regrettably, he would miss the opener, just as he had in his rookie year. The chronology of DiMaggio's absence began on April 2 when he strained his arm making a throw in an exhibition game at Tallahassee, Florida. A week later, with the arm still sore, a doctor in Knoxville, Tennessee, traced the problem to DiMaggio's enlarged tonsils. Joe left the team in Knoxville and took the train to New York, where Dr. Girard Oberrender, Colonel Ruppert's personal physician, examined him and agreed the enlarged tonsils were indeed responsible for the sore arm. Dr. Oberrender recommended their removal, which took place at Lenox Hill Hospital on April 16, just four days before the opener. Athough DiMaggio was unable to play, he was at the game, stylishly dressed in a blue suit. He joined his teammates at home plate when Judge Landis handed the players their World Series watches or rings (player's choice). DiMaggio played his first game ten days later, an April 30 pinch-hitting appearance in Washington.

After Mayor La Guardia threw out the first ball, Ben Chapman, a former Yankee, began the game with a single. New York had traded Chapman to Washington for Jake Powell on June 14, 1936, a trade of one notorious bigot for another. Buddy Lewis followed with a fly ball to Myril Hoag, substituting for DiMaggio in center field. Hoag tried to double-up Chapman returning to first but threw the ball past Gehrig, and before catcher Bill Dickey could retrieve it the speedy Chapman was at third. Gomez struck out Joe Kuhel, but Simmons hit the first pitch into center field for a run-scoring single. The Yankees had second and third with two out against Weaver in the bottom of the first, but second baseman Buddy Myer made a diving one-handed grab of Dickey's liner to end the inning. New York took the lead in the third, scoring two runs on four hits. Red Rolfe opened with an infield single and went to third on a single by Roy Johnson. Gehrig lashed a hit into right field that scored Rolfe and sent Johnson to third. Gehrig roared around first, trying to stretch his hit into a double, but shortstop Ossie Bluege put the tag on him after receiving a perfect throw from right fielder John Stone. Bluege, a third baseman for most of his 16 years with the Senators, was at shortstop today substituting for Cecil Travis, who was still recovering from a spike wound suffered three days earlier. A single by Dickey scored Johnson and put the Yanks ahead, 2–1.

In the sixth, Simmons, whom the Senators purchased two weeks earlier from the Tigers, homered into the first row of the bleacher seats in right. The Yankees protested that a fan had reached over and touched the ball, and therefore Simmons should not have a home run, only a grounds rule double. However, first-base umpire Brick Owens, in the final year of his 25-year umpiring career, stood by his call and the score was tied at 2–2. The Yankees threatened to recapture the lead in the seventh. They reached Weaver for two singles, a double, and a walk, but a busted hit-and-run play kept them from scoring. Crosetti singled to open the inning. With Rolfe at the plate, McCarthy signaled for the hit-and-run. But Rolfe swung and missed at a Weaver fastball and catcher Shanty Hogan threw out Crosetti at second. Rolfe eventually fouled out. Johnson singled, and then Gehrig doubled, his third hit and second double of the game. With runners at second and third and two outs, Weaver intentionally walked Dickey to get to George Selkirk. It was Weaver against Selkirk with the game on the line, and Weaver won. He got Selkirk to foul out to Hogan for the third out.

Selkirk may have been still pondering his failed at-bat in the top of the eighth when his lack of concentration helped the Senators score the winning run. After Simmons singled and was forced at second by Stone, Bluege sliced a fly ball down the right-field line, headed for the corner where the low screen and the foul line came together. Selkirk went after it, but the ball glanced off his glove in fair territory, hit the screen, and then caromed back to him. However, instead of getting the ball back to the infield and arguing afterwards, Selkirk charged in, claiming he had caught the ball cleanly. But while Selkirk argued, Stone, who had stopped at second, took advantage of the situation and moved down to third. After Gomez walked Myer, Hogan, beginning his final major-league season, brought Stone home with a long fly ball to left fielder Johnson.

The Yankees got the tying run on in the eighth, but Powell, batting for Gomez, hit into a double play. Johnny Murphy pitched the ninth for New York, giving up a single to Chapman before retiring the next three batters. In the last of the ninth, Weaver got Crosetti, Rolfe, and Johnson to send the Yanks down to their fourth straight opening-day defeat. For Gomez, making his sixth consecutive opening-day start, it was the third year in a row that he lost by a single run. Gomez would not start another opener in his five remaining years in New York.

The Yankees (102–52) won the pennant by 13 games over the Detroit Tigers. They defeated the New York Giants in the World Series again, winning in five games. Lefty Gomez (21–11) and Red Ruffing (20–7) were the American League's only 20-game winners. Joe DiMaggio had a .346 batting average, 167 runs batted in, and led the league in home runs (46), slugging percentage (.673), runs scored (151), and total bases (418). Lou Gehrig had his last great year, batting .351 with 37 home runs and 158 RBIs. DiMaggio finished second and Gehrig fourth as Detroit's Charlie Gehringer won the Most Valuable Player Award.

Tuesday, April 20, 1937

Washington	ab	r	h	po	a	e	New York	ab	r	h	po	a	e
Chapman cf	4	1	2	0	0	0	Crosetti ss	5	0	2	5	2	1
Lewis 3b	5	0	1	0	1	0	Rolfe 3b	4	1	1	2	2	0

Washington

	ab	r	h	po	a	e
Kuhel 1b	5	0	0	10	0	0
Simmons lf	5	1	3	3	0	0
Stone rf	4	1	1	2	1	0
Bluege ss	4	0	1	1	3	0
Myer 2b	3	0	1	5	6	0
Hogan c	4	0	1	6	1	0
Weaver p	3	0	0	0	1	0
Total	37	3	10	27	13	0

New York

	ab	r	h	po	a	e
Johnson lf	5	1	2	2	0	0
Gehrig 1b	4	0	3	4	1	0
Dickey c	3	0	1	9	0	0
Selkirk rf	3	0	0	1	1	0
Lazzeri 2b	2	0	0	1	2	0
Hoag cf	4	0	0	3	1	1
Gomez p	3	0	1	0	1	0
aPowell	1	0	0	0	0	0
Murphy p	0	0	0	0	0	0
Total	34	2	10	27	10	2

aHit into double play for Gomez in eighth inning.

Washington	100	001	010–3
New York	002	000	000–2

Runs batted in—Simmons 2, Gehrig, Dickey, Hogan. Two-base hits—Gehrig 2. Home run—Simmons. Double play—Myer and Kuhel. Left on bases—New York 10; Washington 10. Bases on balls—off Gomez 3, Weaver 5. Struck out—by Gomez 6, Weaver 3. Hits—off Gomez 9 in 8 innings, Murphy 1 in 1. Losing pitcher—Gomez. Umpires—Dinneen, Owens, and Hubbard. Time of game—2 hrs. 35 min.

Monday, April 18, 1938
Fenway Park, Boston
Boston 8 New York 4

Look with favor on bold beginnings.—Virgil

On a cold, raw, rainy day in Boston, Jim Bagby Jr. of the Red Sox became only the seventh major-league pitcher in the twentieth century to make his debut as an opening-day starter. Win Kellum of the Boston Americans, Roy Patterson of the Chicago White Sox, and Roscoe Miller of the Detroit Tigers all did it in 1901, the year the American League achieved major-league status. The other three were Henry Schmidt of the Brooklyn Superbas in 1903, Nick Carter of the Philadelphia Athletics (against the Yankees) in 1908, and Lefty Grove of the Athletics in 1925. Since 1938 it has been done only once, by the Philadelphia Phillies' Al Gerheauser five years later. Given the circumstances, Bagby did a decent job, allowing four runs in his six innings of work. He left trailing 4–2, but thanks to a sixth-inning, six-run rally that gave Boston an 8–4 victory, he emerged as the winning pitcher. Manager Joe Cronin had chosen Bagby on a hunch, bypassing Jack Wilson, a veteran right-hander who was 16–10 in 1937. It was an especially unorthodox choice, for although Bagby was the son of Jim Bagby Sr., a 31-game winner for the 1920 world champion Cleveland Indians, he had never *seen* a major-league game. With that in mind, Cronin protected his young pitcher from excessive worry and the possible loss of a night's sleep by not revealing his plans until the morning of the game. Bagby took the news with relative calm; nevertheless, Cronin assigned veteran catcher Moe Berg to warm him up before the game and to counsel him between innings. The 21-year-old right-hander was in his fourth year as a professional, but had never pitched above the Class A level. He was making the jump from the Hazleton (Pennsylvania) Red Sox, where he had a 21–8 record in 1937 and won the New York-Pennsylvania League's Most Valuable Player Award.

Bagby's opponent was Red Ruffing, who was also right-handed, but aside from that there was a world of difference between the two pitchers. Ruffing was 32 years old and in his 15th big-league season. His 20–7 record in 1937 made him one of only two 20-game winners in the American League; his teammate Lefty Gomez was the other. Gomez had pitched the last six Yankee season openers, but with most of Boston's power coming from the right side, manager Joe McCarthy chose to go with Ruffing.

The small crowd, only 10,700, was a result of the miserable weather, which also limited the pregame festivities. When Jimmy Coughlin's Veterans Band and a detachment of marines from the Charlestown Navy Yard paraded to the flagpole, the players remained behind, restricting their activity to lining up along the foul lines. Even Fenway Park's new public address system broke down shortly before game time, although that can't be blamed on the bad weather. The more perceptive fans noticed a slight change in the appearance of the words "RED SOX" on the jerseys of the Boston players. They were a little smaller than they had been in previous years, assuming the shape, color, and size that for the most part they retain to the present. The Yankees were in their familiar road-grays, trimmed in blue, with "NEW YORK" on their shirt fronts. Each Yankee had on his left sleeve an orange patch emblazoned with an orange trylon and perisphere and the blue numerals "1939," symbols of next year's New York World's Fair. Players on New York City's other two teams, the Giants and the Dodgers, also wore these patches.

While the Red Sox are officially Boston's team, in spirit they have always belonged to all of New England, as today's gathering of politicians from throughout the region illustrated. Along with Boston mayor Maurice J. Tobin and Massachusetts governor Charles F. Hurley, there were former Massachusetts governor Frank G. Allen, New Hampshire governor Francis P. Murphy, Robert E. Quinn, the governor of Rhode Island, and Lewis O. Barrows and Louis J. Brann, the present and former governors of Maine. It had rained most of the morning and did so again briefly just after Governor Hurley threw out the first ball. Showers fell again in the second inning and in the eighth, when umpire-in-chief Bill Summers halted play for ten minutes, but for much of the afternoon it stayed dry. Bagby, showing no signs of nervousness, retired the Yankees in the first, striking out Frank Crosetti and, after a single by Red Rolfe, inducing George Selkirk to hit into a double play. In the bottom of the inning, his teammates staked him to a quick one-run lead. Doc Cramer doubled off the left-field wall on Ruffing's first pitch and scored when Jimmie Foxx drilled a one-out single over the head of third baseman Rolfe. Foxx, in his third year in Boston, was on his way to a prodigious offensive year. He would lead the league in batting (.349) and runs batted in (175), and hit 50 home runs. However, the Detroit Tiger's Hank Greenberg would hit 58, preventing Foxx from winning his second Triple Crown, although not his third Most Valuable Player Award.

While Bagby *appeared* stoic, he could be forgiven a feeling of trepidation as he looked in to begin the second inning and saw Lou Gehrig standing at the plate. Gehrig was playing in his 2,000th game as a Yankee, the last 1,966 consecutively. He had batted .347 over the last 12 years, and entered the 1938 season as the major league's active leader in home runs, doubles, runs batted in, and total bases. Bagby walked him on four pitches. Bill Dickey followed with a double off the wall in left center sending Gehrig to third. Then, Bagby hung a high curve that Henrich ripped into right field, scoring Gehrig. Moments later, Dickey scored when Myril Hoag's ground ball went through the legs of shortstop Cronin. Hoag was the center fielder today, again replacing Joe DiMaggio who was missing his third consecutive opener. However, unlike the previous two the reason this time was not physical but financial. DiMaggio, who made $15,000 in 1937, was asking for $40,000. The Yankees would not budge from their offer of $25,000, so DiMaggio waited at home in San Francisco, losing $162 in salary each day.

If Cronin's error had unnerved Bagby, he did not show it. He kept Hoag at first by striking out rookie second baseman Joe Gordon, then Ruffing, and getting Crosetti on a force play. Gordon, playing in his first major-league game, had batted .280 for the Yankees' Newark Bears farm team that won 109 games and the Little World Series in 1937. Three pitchers from that team, a team that ranks among the best minor-league clubs ever, were on the Yankees' opening-day roster: Atley Donald, Steve Sundra, and Joe Beggs. Newark manager Oscar Vitt had used Gordon primarily in the leadoff spot, but McCarthy, after considering his 26 home runs, 70 strikeouts, and only 50 walks, decided to bat him lower down in the lineup. Gordon took over the second-base spot long held by Tony Lazzeri, whom the Yanks had released five days after winning the 1937 World Series. Lazzeri had been a major contributor to their success for 12 years—he even batted .400 in the '37 Series to lead all hitters—but he was 34 years old and his skills were diminishing. Gordon, only 23, was a much better second baseman and the Yankees had to make room for him.

Ben Chapman, who would bat .340 this year, his first full season in Boston, tied the score with a second-inning home run; but the Yanks regained the lead with two runs in the third. Bagby hit Rolfe in the leg to open the inning, and then walked Selkirk. After Gehrig's infield out moved the runners up, he walked Dickey intentionally to load the bases. The runners held as Tommy Henrich made the second out on a short fly to Cramer, but Hoag's single to left scored Rolfe and Selkirk, putting New York ahead, 4–2. Ruffing protected the lead through five, but in the sixth the Red Sox pounded him and his successor Joe Vance for six runs, all charged to Ruffing. A leadoff single by Cronin, a walk to Pinky Higgins (acquired from the Philadelphia Athletics in December 1936), and a sacrifice by Chapman put the tying runs in scoring position. The next batter was second baseman Bobby Doerr, just 11 days past his 20th birthday and beginning his second season with the Red Sox. Starting today and continuing through the 1940s, Doerr and Gordon—both future Hall of Famers—would be the dominant second basemen in the American League.

After just missing a home run on a ball that went foul by two feet, Doerr smacked a double high off the wall in left. Cronin and Higgins scored and the game was tied at 4–4. Following a walk to catcher Gene Desautels, Cronin sent reserve outfielder Leo Nonnenkamp up to bat for Bagby. The crowd reacted negatively to Bagby's removal, but Cronin later explained he felt Bagby had done enough for one game and that a pinch hitter might bother Ruffing. Nonnenkamp, whose only previous major-league experience was one at-bat with the 1933 Pirates, also walked, loading the bases. When Cramer followed with his third hit, a two-run single to left, McCarthy replaced Ruffing with Vance, a journeyman right-hander. Vance got Vosmik to fly out, but a single by Foxx scored Nonnenkamp and a double by Cronin, his second hit of the inning, scored Cramer. Vance pitched a scoreless seventh and eighth, but after one more relief appearance and one start, his abbreviated big-league career came to an end.

To protect Boston's 8–4 lead, Cronin called on left-hander Archie McKain, 8–8 as a rookie in 1937. Despite being a left-hander (often a problem in Fenway Park) and pitching against the feared "Bronx Bombers," McKain turned in a superb relief effort. He breezed through the final three innings, which included the ten-minute rain delay in the eighth, allowing only one hit. Boston had their fourth consecutive opening-day win under Cronin, while the Yankees now had not won an opener since 1933. Bagby went on to have a fine rookie year. Working as a starter and reliever, he pitched in 43 games in 1938, third most in the league, winning 15 and losing 11. While Bagby did not face DiMaggio in his debut, a dramatic confrontation awaited the two men three years later. On July 17, 1941, Bagby was the Cleveland pitcher who got DiMaggio to hit into an eighth-inning double play that ended Joe's record hitting-streak at 56 consecutive games.

DiMaggio finally agreed to a salary of $25,000 and for the second year in a row played his first game of the season on April 30 in Washington. The fans were not happy with DiMaggio's holdout. Most of them sided with Yankees owner Jacob Ruppert and business manager Ed Barrow, both of whom also voiced displeasure with DiMaggio. However, they were not displeased enough to accept an overture from President Don Barnes of the St. Louis Browns, who offered them $150,000 to take DiMaggio off their hands.

New York (99–53) finished 9½ games ahead of the second-place Red Sox, who had their best season in 20 years. They then swept the Chicago Cubs to win their third consecutive World Series. Although his production was below that of 1937, Bill Dickey hit .313, with 27 home runs, and 115 RBIs and finished second to Jimmie Foxx in the Most Valuable Player balloting. Red Ruffing, who led the league in wins and was second in winning percentage, finished fourth. Joe DiMaggio played in 145 games and batted .324, with 32 home runs and 140 runs batted in. He finished sixth in the voting.

Monday, April 18, 1938

New York	ab	r	h	po	a	e	Boston	ab	r	h	po	a	e
Crosetti ss	4	0	0	3	2	1	Cramer cf	5	2	3	3	0	0
Rolfe 3b	3	1	1	0	1	0	Vosmik lf	5	0	1	1	0	0
Selkirk lf	4	1	0	3	0	1	Foxx 1b	5	0	2	9	2	0
Gehrig 1b	2	1	0	7	0	0	Cronin ss	4	1	2	2	2	1
Dickey c	3	1	2	4	0	0	Higgins 3b	3	1	0	1	4	1
Henrich rf	4	0	1	2	0	0	Chapman rf	3	1	1	1	0	0
Hoag cf	4	0	2	4	0	0	Doerr 2b	4	1	2	3	3	0
Gordon 2b	4	0	0	1	3	0	Desautels c	3	1	0	7	0	0
Ruffing p	3	0	0	0	2	0	Bagby p	2	0	0	0	1	0
Vance p	0	0	0	0	0	0	[b]Nonnenkamp	0	1	0	0	0	0
[a]Knickerbocker	1	0	0	0	0	0	McKain p	1	0	0	0	0	0
Total	32	4	6	24	8	2	Total	35	8	11	27	12	2

[a]Popped out for Vance in ninth inning.
[b]Walked for Bagby in sixth inning.

New York	022	000	000–4	
Boston	110	006	00X–8	

Runs batted in—Hoag 2, Henrich, Foxx 2, Chapman, Cramer 2, Doerr 2, Cronin. Two-base hits—Dickey, Hoag, Cramer, Cronin, Doerr. Home run—Chapman. Sacrifice—Chapman. Double plays—Higgins, Foxx, and Cronin; Foxx, Cronin, and Foxx; Doerr and Foxx. Left on bases—New York 8; Boston 7. Bases on balls—off Ruffing 3, Bagby 6. Struck out—by Ruffing 3, Vance 1, Bagby 5, McKain 2. Hits—off Ruffing 8 in 5 ⅓ innings, Vance 3 in 2⅔, Bagby 5 in 6, McKain 1 in 3. Hit by pitcher—By Bagby (Rolfe). Winning pitcher—Bagby. Losing pitcher—Ruffing. Umpires—Summers, Quinn, and Rue. Time of game—2 hrs. 10 min. Attendance—10,700.

Thursday, April 20, 1939
Yankee Stadium, New York
New York 2 Boston 0

He whom the Gods favor dies in youth.—Plautus

Long after the memory of Red Ruffing's 2–0 shutout of the Red Sox had faded, the 30,278 fans at Yankee Stadium would remember this Opening Day as something special. They had witnessed the first game of what would become the legendary rivalry between Ted Williams and Joe DiMaggio, and, on a sadder note, the final Opening Day for Lou Gehrig. While Williams and DiMaggio would play against one another many times, this would be the only game in which Williams and Gehrig appeared together. The Yankees were to play at Boston later in the month, on April 27 and 28, but those games were postponed due to cold weather. By the time the teams next met on May 29, Gehrig was no longer playing.

Inclement weather had already taken its toll on the schedule. When rain canceled New York's opener in Washington three days ago, Manager Joe McCarthy switched from Lefty Gomez to Ruffing for the next day's game at the Stadium against Boston. But rain washed out that game and also the next day's. Still, McCarthy held to his plan; he would start Ruffing whenever the opener came. Ruffing had lost the opener to Boston rookie Jim Bagby Jr. last year, but this time his opening-day adversary was a contemporary, Lefty Grove. Like Ruffing, Grove had won his first American League game back in 1925. However, 1938 had been a difficult year for the 38-year-old Grove. He missed most of the second half of the season with a mysterious arm injury, although it did not prevent him from leading the league in earned run average for the eighth time. Grove had not tested the arm much this spring, pitching only ten innings as Red Sox manager Joe Cronin allowed him to prepare at his own pace.

Opening Day 1939 was special in another way. Millions of Yankee fans would remember it as the first game they listened to on the radio. The Dodgers' new president, Larry MacPhail, had broken the agreement by the New York clubs to ban radio broadcasts and his doing so had forced the Yankees and Giants to go along. Arch McDonald, former (and future) broadcaster for the Washington Senators, was the Yankees' lead announcer on station WABC. Six weeks into the season, he would be joined by 26-year-old Mel Allen.

New Yorkers were particularly eager to get a look at (or a listen to) Williams, whose sensational hitting (and brashness) made him the most talked about rookie of the spring. Last season, as a 19-year-old playing for the Minneapolis Millers, Williams won the American Association's Triple Crown with a .366 batting average, 43 home runs, and 142 runs batted in. The crowd cheered when Ruffing fanned him in his first major-league at-bat, and again later, but Williams caught their attention with the longest hit of the day. His fourth-inning double hit the bleacher wall in right-center field just to the right of the 407-foot sign—a most impressive blow. At six-foot-three, the slender Williams reminded many in the crowd of two former left-handed Dodgers hitters; Babe Herman and Tom Winsett. Those comparisons were short-lived. Before long, as he progressed through his extraordinary rookie season, the only player Williams was reminding anybody of was Babe Ruth. And, as the "baseball Gods" would have it, Ruth was at the Stadium for Williams's debut. He appeared at a quarter of three, dressed in his familiar tan overcoat and, as always, received the loudest ovation of the day. On June 12, the Babe would be in Cooperstown, New York, for the dedication of the new Baseball Hall of Fame. There he would be honored along with the four other original inductees: Ty Cobb, Walter Johnson, Honus Wagner, and the late Christy Mathewson. Eventually, ten of the players on the field today: Williams, Cronin, Grove, Bobby Doerr, and Jimmie Foxx for Boston; Ruffing, Gehrig, DiMaggio, Joe Gordon, and Bill Dickey for the Yankees would join those five in the Hall of Fame. Also Cooperstown bound were Yankees manager McCarthy and coach Earle Combs, as well as Red Sox coaches Herb Pennock and Hugh Duffy.

DiMaggio was making his first opening-day start after being absent each of the three previous years. Myril Hoag, his substitute in center in the 1937 and '38 openers, was gone. He and catcher Joe Glenn (Dickey's backup since 1932) had been traded to the St. Louis Browns last October for pitcher Oral Hildebrand and outfielder Buster Mills. Buddy Rosar, whose .387 batting average with the Newark Bears led the International League in 1938, replaced Glenn. Given the luxury of retaining two additional players this season (the owners had voted to increase major-league rosters from 23 to 25), the Yankees kept two rookie outfielders, Joe Gallagher and Charlie Keller. Gallagher, a product of New York's Manhattan College, batted .343 for the Kansas City Blues in 1938, second in the American Association to Williams. As a right-handed hitter, he got the start in right field against Grove today, but was hitless in three at-bats. On June 13, after batting .244 in 14 games, the Yanks traded Gallagher to the Browns for second baseman Roy Hughes and cash. Keller, 22, was also a college man, from the University of Maryland. Playing for the powerful 1937 Newark Bears, he batted .353, but was unable to stick with the Yankees in 1938. McCarthy sent him back to Newark where he hit .365 with 22 home runs and 129 RBIs. Keller would have an outstanding rookie season, even outhitting Williams, .334 to .327, although Williams's run production was appreciably higher.

Following the three days of rain, the sun had come out briefly in the early morning. However, by the time the gates opened, it had disappeared, not to return until the eighth inning. Even with Boston and their heralded rookie furnishing the opposition, the dampening effect of the two rainouts limited the crowd. The Yankees had expected a much larger gathering; last season's Memorial Day doubleheader against the Red Sox drew 83,533 (81,891 paid), the largest crowd in Yankee Stadium history. This much cozier crowd was mostly in place when at 3 P.M., Captain Francis Sutherland and the gray-clad Seventh Regiment Band gathered at home plate for the annual march to the flagpole. Last season, the Red Sox home uniform had taken on the look that has in most part endured down to the present time. Their road uniform had changed, too, and would remain the same for several decades. The blue cap had an ornamental red "B," and the stockings were red at the bottom with blue and white stripes at the top. A blue, block-lettered "BOSTON" was on the jersey. As did all professional teams in 1939, major league and minor, the Sox wore a patch on the left sleeve to commemorate the 100th anniversary of the supposed "invention" of baseball by Abner Doubleday. It was the first time in any season that all 16 major-league teams were wearing the same patch on their uniforms.

At the flagpole, the players and the band were met by Mayor Fiorello La Guardia, George Ruppert, the brother of Jacob Ruppert, and Ed Barrow, the team's new president. Barrow had replaced Colonel Ruppert who died in January at age 71. Ownership of the Yankees was now in the hands of three women: two of the Colonel's nieces and Helen Weyant, a former friend of Ruppert's. George Weiss took over some of Barrow's former duties while continuing in his position as general manager of the Yankees' farm teams.

Ruppert had been a colonel in the Seventh Regiment and always had his old outfit perform at Stadium openers. This afternoon, as so often in the past, they accompanied the raising of the American flag and the Yankees' 1938 world championship flags by playing "The Star-Spangled Banner." Following the march back to home plate, the schedule called for the Yanks to receive World Series mementos from Commissioner Landis. However, Landis had been called back to Chicago, and when an adequate substitute could not be found, the ceremony was canceled. La Guardia went ahead and tossed out the first ball (after warming up with Yankees bat boy Tim Sullivan), but none of the players seemed ready for the throw. The ball landed in the hands of plate umpire Red Ormsby, who graciously returned it to the mayor. The American League assigned four umpires to work this game instead of the usual three. One of them, working at third base, was George Pipgras, the former Yankees' pitcher who ten years earlier, on Opening Day 1929 here in Yankee Stadium, defeated the Red Sox, 7–3. Boston's losing pitcher that day was Red Ruffing.

Grove seemed shaky at the start, allowing two runners in the first before getting Gehrig on a fly ball to end the inning. The public address announcer's introduction of Gehrig as the next batter had set off a prolonged ovation from a crowd that sensed the "Iron Horse's" fabulous career was nearing its end. His millions of fans were hoping that Gehrig's 1938 season, in which he batted .295, hit 29 home runs, and had 114 runs batted in, was just an "off-year." But anyone looking beyond the statistics recognized that Gehrig was deteriorating. Though only 35, he looked old and slow at first base, and the ball no longer seemed to "jump" off his bat. Often he seemed awkward and unsure of himself, and his increasing lack of coordination was becoming increasingly obvious.

In the second inning, Grove, behind 2–0 on Dickey leading off, came in with a fastball that the Yankees' catcher lined into the lower right-field seats for a home run. Gallagher, the next batter, reached base on an error by shortstop Cronin, and Joe Gordon singled to left. But again Grove stranded two runners as he fanned Ruffing and Frank Crosetti and got Red Rolfe on a fly ball. The Yanks scored their second run in the fifth with the aid of an error by Foxx. After the big first baseman let Rolfe's one-out grounder go through his legs, Jake Powell followed with a looping fly ball into the right-field corner. The ball bounced against the railing, and as the rookie Williams attempted to figure out which way it would carom, Powell reached third with a run-scoring triple. Attempting to prevent a third run from scoring, Grove intentionally walked DiMaggio to get at Gehrig. Lou had already grounded into one double play following DiMaggio's single in the third inning. This time he hit the ball hard but it was a liner right at second baseman Doerr who turned it into another double play.

Meanwhile, Ruffing was pitching a remarkable game. He allowed seven hits, walked one, and one got aboard on an error by Gehrig. The Red Sox had nine base runners, one in every inning, and each of them was left on base. Ruffing's shutout was only the second ever thrown by a Yankee on Opening Day. The first was by Joe Doyle, who in 1908 blanked the Philadelphia Athletics, 1–0, in 12 innings. Fortunately for Ruffing, he had DiMaggio in center field. Joe made two spectacular catches, and since both were followed by doubles, he clearly saved at least two runs. In the fourth, he made a shoestring catch of a low liner by rookie Jim Tabor, and in the sixth he raced to the bleacher wall in right to rob Cronin of a possible triple.

Grove recovered from 1938's arm problems and had his final Grove-like season. He went 15–4, second in the league in winning percentage (.789) for the fifth time. It was the tenth time Grove was in the top ten in that pitching category, including five firsts. His 2.54

earned run average was also the league's best; the ninth time he had won the ERA title. Gehrig went hitless in the opener and made a ninth-inning error while extending his consecutive games played streak to 2,123. He would play in seven more games before asking McCarthy to take him out of the lineup on May 2 in Detroit. Gehrig, batting just .143, said it was "for the good of the team." Babe Dahlgren, whom the Yanks had purchased from the Red Sox in February 1937, replaced him. On June 17, after learning that he was suffering from amyotrophic lateral sclerosis, a disease to which his name would become forever attached, Gehrig retired, although he remained with the team as its captain.

New York (106–45) completely dominated the league, both in batting and pitching. They finished 17 games ahead of Boston to become the first American League team to win four consecutive pennants. And when they swept the Cincinnati Reds, they became the first major-league team to win four consecutive World Series. The Yankees' record in those four series was 16–3. Red Ruffing (21–7) was a 20-game winner for the fourth consecutive year. He finished second in the league in wins, to Bob Feller, and third in winning percentage, behind Lefty Grove and teammate Atley Donald. Despite missing 32 games with a leg injury, Joe DiMaggio, still only 24, won the batting championship with a .381 average, had 30 home runs, 126 runs batted in, and earned the league's Most Valuable Player Award. The 1939 Yankees are the only major league team to score 400 more runs than they allowed (967–656).

Thursday, April 20, 1939

Boston	ab	r	h	po	a	e	New York	ab	r	h	po	a	e
Cramer cf	4	0	1	2	0	0	Crosetti ss	4	0	0	0	0	0
Vosmik lf	4	0	2	3	0	0	Rolfe 3b	4	1	0	0	2	0
Foxx 1b	4	0	0	5	0	1	Powell lf	4	0	3	4	0	0
Cronin ss	4	0	0	2	1	1	DiMaggio cf	2	0	1	3	0	0
Tabor 3b	4	0	1	0	1	0	Gehrig 1b	4	0	0	6	0	1
Williams rf	4	0	1	3	0	0	Dickey c	3	1	2	7	0	0
Doerr 2b	4	0	1	4	3	0	Gallagher rf	3	0	0	3	0	0
Desautels c	3	0	0	5	1	0	Gordon 2b	3	0	1	4	3	0
ᵃNonnenkamp	1	0	0	0	0	0	Ruffing p	3	0	0	0	3	0
Grove p	2	0	1	0	1	0	Total	30	2	7	27	8	1
ᵇPeacock	1	0	0	0	0	0							
Total	35	0	7	24	7	2							

ᵃHit into a force play for Desautels in ninth inning.
ᵇGrounded out for Grove in ninth inning.

Boston	000	000	000–0
New York	010	010	00X–2

Runs batted in—Dickey, Powell. Two-base hits—Williams, Dickey, Tabor, Vosmik. Three-base hit—Powell. Home run—Dickey. Double plays—Doerr, Cronin, and Foxx; Doerr and Foxx. Left on bases—New York 6; Boston 9. Bases on balls—off Grove 2, Ruffing 1. Struck out—by Grove 5, Ruffing 5. Umpires—Ormsby, Summers, Basil, and Pipgras. Time of game—1 hr. 47 min. Attendance—30,278.

V

1940–1949

The Yankees began the decade under one managerial legend, Joe McCarthy, and ended it under another, Casey Stengel. McCarthy won pennants in 1941, 1942, and 1943, with world championships in '41 and '43, before resigning in May 1946. Bucky Harris took over in 1947 and won a World Series, but George Weiss, the new general manager, fired him after the Yanks finished third the next year. Casey Stengel arrived in 1949 and won the first of what would be five consecutive World Series.

World War II affected the Yankees (as it did all teams) as they were forced to scrape for the best available players not in the military. Some, like Johnny Lindell and George Stirnweiss, did well and stayed on to contribute after the war. But only Phil Rizzuto, who came up in 1941, Tommy Henrich, and Joe DiMaggio of the prewar Yankees made significant postwar contributions to the team. DiMaggio, who won his second Most Valuable Player Award in 1941, served three years in the Army and came out to win his third MVP in 1947.

In the late '40s, the Yankees' farm system produced players like Yogi Berra, Hank Bauer, Jerry Coleman, Joe Collins, and pitcher Vic Raschi. They and pitchers Allie Reynolds and Ed Lopat (acquired by Weiss in trades) would all play a significant role in the glory years of the early '50s.

Yankees' ownership passed in 1945 from Colonel Ruppert's heirs to a three-man partnership comprised of Del Webb, Dan Topping, and Larry MacPhail, but MacPhail left after the 1947 season. Attendance boomed after the war; in each of the five years beginning in 1946, Yankees' attendance passed the 2 million mark.

Tuesday, April 16, 1940
Shibe Park, Philadelphia
Philadelphia 2 New York 1 (10 Innings)

There are so few who can grow old with a good grace.—Sir Richard Steele

When Connie Mack first learned his Philadelphia Athletics would open the 1940 season at home against the New York Yankees, the four-time defending world champions, he made a bold prediction. Mack said that despite the A's seventh-place finish last year, his club would defeat the Yanks on Opening Day. At Shibe Park on the morning of the opener, Mack repeated his prediction, evidently discounting that the Yankees had finished 51½ games ahead of Philadelphia in 1939 and had won 18 of the 22 games played between them. The records of the opening-day pitchers, which accentuated the contrasting abilities of the two clubs, made Mack's prognostication seem even less likely to come true. Philadelphia was starting left-hander Chubby Dean, 5–8 in 1939 and the loser of his only two career decisions against New York. Moreover, the 24-year-old Dean had never pitched a complete game in the major leagues. Mack chose him because the Yankees' lineup contained five left-handed hitters, and Dean was the team's only left-handed starter. And while he had never gone nine innings in a regular-season game, he had been the only A's pitcher to do so in spring training this year. Dean had gone the distance in his last start against the Philadelphia Phillies in Atlanta, holding them to one run and seven hits.

Joe McCarthy's opening-day pitcher, for the third consecutive year, was his ace, Red Ruffing, 21–7 in 1939. Yet in spite of the obvious disparities between the teams and the starting pitchers, the Athletics fulfilled Mack's prophesy. Dean outlasted Ruffing and pitched his first complete game, a ten-inning, 2–1 victory. And to the further delight of the 20,187 victory-starved Athletics' fans, it was Dean's long fly ball in the tenth inning that drove in the winning run. The effort was obviously the best of Dean's career, but it got eclipsed nationally by pitching performances in Washington and Chicago that were even better. At Griffith Stadium, with President Roosevelt in attendance, Lefty Grove of the Boston Red Sox pitched a two-hitter to defeat the Senators, 1–0. But the big news was at Comiskey Park. Cleveland's Bob Feller pitched the only opening-day no-hitter in major-league history, beating the White Sox, 1–0.

Joe DiMaggio's younger brother Dominic made his big-league debut in the Boston-Washington game, playing right field for the Red Sox. However, for the fourth time in his five years in the league, big brother Joe was missing from the Yankees' opening-day lineup. The reason for his absence this year was a twisted right knee. Two days earlier, in the final exhibition game at Brooklyn, DiMaggio doubled with two out in the ninth inning and injured the knee sliding into second base. Heeding the advice of Yankees team physician Dr. Robert Emmet Walsh, he remained at home in New York. Tommy Henrich took DiMaggio's place in center field as part of an all left-handed hitting Yankees' outfield; although one that had no repeat starters from Opening Day 1939. George Selkirk was back in right field replacing the long-departed Joe Gallagher, and Charlie Keller, last year's rookie sensation, was in left, where Jake Powell had been a year ago. Powell was in an Ashland, Kentucky, hospital, recovering from a brain concussion. Six days before the opener he had crashed into an outfield wall, chasing a drive hit by Brooklyn's Ernie Koy. The most glaring absence in the Yankees' lineup was at first base, where Babe Dahlgren occupied the spot that had been Lou Gehrig's since 1926. Actually, Dahlgren was only the third Yankee to open the season at first base since 1915, Wally Pipp having been there for the 11 seasons preceding Gehrig.

Mack, beginning his 40th year in Philadelphia, watched the pregame parade and the raising of the flag from the comfort of the dugout on this bleak, overcast day. He did emerge to greet Mayor Robert E. Lamberton before Lamberton threw out the first ball. These were not happy times for the 77-year-old owner/manager. Following the breakup of his great teams of 1929–1931, the Athletics had suffered in the standings and at the gate. Over the previous five years, they had finished last three times and seventh twice. Plagued by poor attendance even in their best years, the Athletics had not drawn as many as half a million since 1931. Mack, who was soon to gain controlling interest in the club from the Shibe family, knew that Opening Day would be among the best attended games of the season—especially so because it was against New York, baseball's best attraction. For Philadelphia, like several other teams in the American League, the season's most important games were against the Yankees. The significance of these games transcended the pennant race. Wherever the Yankees played, the large crowds they drew were often the difference in whether these teams made a profit in any one season. If Mack could draw a few more fans by predicting an A's victory, so much the better.

Had it not been for a Philadelphia error that gave the Yankees an unearned run in the third inning, Dean would have had a nine-inning, 1–0, shutout. But then he would not have had the thrill of driving in the winning run. The Yanks lone tally was set up on a third-inning error by second baseman Benny McCoy. McCoy had been the most sought after of the 91 players under contract to the Detroit Tigers (four major-leaguers and 87 minor-leaguers) recently declared free agents by Commissioner Landis. Mack had uncharacteristically outbid ten other teams to sign McCoy. Besides giving him a $5,000 signing bonus, Mack also signed him to a two-year contract at $10,000 per year. The Philadelphia fans did their best to make McCoy feel welcome; only onetime idol Al Simmons, back with the Athletics after eight years, elicited more cheers. McCoy would bat .257 and .271 in his two years in Philadelphia, enter the navy, and never play again. His misplay came after Henrich walked to open the third. Dahlgren's hard-hit grounder was fielded cleanly by shortstop Bill Lillard, who tossed it to McCoy. In his anxiety to get the ball to first baseman Dick Siebert, McCoy dropped the ball. Instead of two out and no one on, the Yankees had nobody out and runners at first and second. They each moved up a base on Ruffing's sacrifice. When Frank Crosetti flied out to center fielder Bob Johnson, Henrich scored after the catch, while Crosetti was charged with an official at-bat. After a one-year trial, baseball had abandoned the "no at-bat for a sacrifice fly" rule.

Philadelphia tied the game with two down in the fourth when Johnson homered off the facade of the upper deck in left. Bob Johnson was an excellent hitter modern fans often overlook. He was overshadowed during his career by the many great players who were his contemporaries. He broke in with the A's in 1933, replacing Simmons, and played ten seasons in Philadelphia before finishing with a year with the Senators and two with the Red Sox. In his 13-year career, all spent with bad teams, Johnson drove in more than 100 runs eight times and scored more than 100 six times. He had at least 20 home runs in each of his first nine years in the league and a lifetime total of 288. When his big-league career ended, he was number eight on the all-time home-run list.

From the fifth through the ninth innings, pitchers Dean and Ruffing were in control, as neither team mounted a serious threat. Wally Moses twice stirred the crowd with long drives off Ruffing, but both times right fielder Selkirk raced back to pull them down at the wall. Dean had pitched in 62 major-league games, but this was only his fourth start. The longest he had ever gone in an official game before today was six innings in his first big-league start in 1937, a game in which he defeated Feller. Now he had matched Ruffing for nine innings and took the mound for the tenth. Dahlgren led off with a single, which brought Ruffing to the plate and forced McCarthy to make a decision. Should he sacrifice an out and move the runner into scoring position, or should he allow Ruffing, one of the best-hitting pitchers ever, to swing away? McCarthy chose to play for the big inning, but his decision backfired. Ruffing grounded sharply to the left side, where third baseman Al Rubeling smartly turned it into a 5–4–3 double play. It was a crucial play. Crosetti followed with a single and Red Rolfe walked, but Dean got Selkirk to pop out to catcher Frankie Hayes to end the inning.

There was some surprise among the spectators when Ruffing came out to pitch the last of the tenth. Yesterday, in the Yankees final preseason workout, a line drive by Keller had struck him squarely on his right elbow, putting his opening-day start in doubt. McCarthy alerted Monte Pearson that the start might be his, but Ruffing had awoken this morning with no ill effects. The crowd had been quiet for most of the afternoon, but stopping the Yanks in the tenth had energized them. Now they were calling for the home team to push across a run and end the game. After getting Siebert to pop to second baseman Joe Gordon, Ruffing walked Hayes. Rubeling, playing his first big-league game, got his first hit. He poked a little pop fly into short right field, and as right fielder Selkirk came charging in and second baseman Gordon went racing out, they collided. The ball fell between them for a double as Hayes raced around to third. McCarthy ordered an intentional walk to Dee Miles, whom Mack sent up to bat for Lillard. Loading the bases in this situation was the time-tested maneuver to set up either a double play or a force play at the plate.

Dean was the next scheduled batter, and when the crowd saw him making his way to the plate they let out a deafening roar. Philadelphia had signed Dean out of Duke University as a first baseman, a position he played for the Blue Devils for two years before Mack transformed him into a pitcher. And though Mack often used him as a pinch hitter, the fans feared that with the game on the line, he might go to his bench for a more experienced batter. But Mack stayed with Dean, perhaps reasoning that he did not have another pitcher who would be as effective as Dean had been. Apparently McCarthy believed that he too did not have a better pitcher than Ruffing to call on in this circumstance. He allowed Ruffing to pitch to the left-handed Dean, while ordering his outfielders to play shallow to catch any liners hit over the infield. However, Dean foiled the strategy as he drove the ball over the head of left fielder Keller. While the usual procedure for an outfielder in this situation is to concede the hit, and the run, Keller raced back and made a one-handed over-the-shoulder catch. He turned and threw home, but Hayes scored easily with the game-winner. As their teammates milled joyously around Hayes and Dean to offer their congratulations, groups of excited fans rushed onto the field to join them.

After the game, Mack spoke of his prediction of victory and further predicted the Yankees would not win a fifth consecutive pennant in 1940. He picked them to finish third. Yet as pleased as he was with the win and the pitching of Dean, Mack could not stop talking about the fielding performance of Joe Gordon. Although he was still recovering from a charley horse that caused him to miss ten days of spring training, Gordon had handled 12 chances flawlessly. Included among them were several of what Mack called the most acrobatic plays he had ever seen around second base. His play was so spectacular, even old-timers were calling it the best defensive performance ever in Shibe Park—at any position. Some of the plays, said Mack, "just aren't a part of baseball as we know it."

Just as Connie Mack predicted, the Yankees (88–66) did finish third, one game behind the second-place Cleveland Indians and two behind the pennant-winning Detroit Tigers. Joe DiMaggio batted .352 to win his second consecutive batting title, and finished third in the Most Valuable Player voting behind Bob Feller and the winner, Hank Greenberg.

Tuesday, April 16, 1940

New York	ab	r	h	po	a	e	Philadelphia	ab	r	h	po	a	e
Crosetti ss	5	0	1	0	0	0	McCoy 2b	4	0	1	4	3	1
Rolfe 3b	4	0	0	1	0	0	Moses rf	4	0	0	3	0	0
Selkirk rf	5	0	0	4	0	0	Simmons lf	4	0	1	3	0	0
Keller lf	4	0	1	2	0	0	Johnson cf	4	1	2	4	0	0

New York

	ab	r	h	po	a	e
Dickey c	4	0	1	6	0	0
Gordon 2b	4	0	0	6	6	0
Henrich cf	3	1	2	1	0	0
Dahlgren 1b	3	0	1	9	0	0
Ruffing p	3	0	0	0	4	0
Total	35	1	6	29	10	0

Philadelphia

	ab	r	h	po	a	e
Siebert 1b	4	0	1	10	0	0
Hayes c	3	1	0	2	1	0
Rubeling 3b	4	0	1	2	3	0
Lillard ss	2	0	0	2	2	0
aMiles	0	0	0	0	0	0
Dean p	4	0	0	0	4	0
Total	33	2	6	30	13	1

*Two out when winning run scored.
aDrew intentional walk for Lillard in tenth inning.

New York	001	000	000	0–1
Philadelphia	000	100	000	1–2

Runs batted in—Johnson, Dean, Crosetti. Two-base hits—McCoy, Rubeling. Home run—Johnson. Stolen base—Henrich. Sacrifice—Ruffing. Double plays—Gordon and Dahlgren; Ruffing, Gordon, and Dahlgren; Rubeling, McCoy, and Siebert. Left on bases—New York 8; Philadelphia 5. Bases on balls—off Ruffing 3, Dean 3. Struck out—by Ruffing 5, Dean 2. Umpires—Summers, Quinn, and Pipgras. Time of game—1 hr. 58 min. Attendance—20,187.

Monday, April 14, 1941
Griffith Stadium, Washington
New York 3 Washington 0

Let him who desires peace, prepare for war.—Vegetius

The Yankees' 1941 "presidential opener" at Washington, the only game scheduled in either league, began one of the most fondly remembered seasons in baseball history. It was the year of Joe DiMaggio's 56-game hitting streak, Ted Williams's .406 batting average, and the first of the many exciting Yankees-Dodgers World Series. However, the major reason the 1941 season evokes so many happy memories in those that remember it is that it played out over the last summer of peace. Yet as memorable as the 1941 season was, it did lack one thing: an American League pennant race. The Yankees would make a shambles of it, and they began with Marius Russo's, 3–0, opening-day shutout, the only shutout ever thrown by a Yankees' left-hander on Opening Day. President Franklin D. Roosevelt was part of the sweltering Easter Monday crowd at Griffith Stadium that saw the New Yorkers win the "presidential opener" by scoring single runs off Senators pitcher Dutch Leonard in the first, fifth, and sixth innings. Losing to New York was nothing new to Leonard; last season he lost six of his seven decisions against them. Meanwhile, Russo, a 26-year-old Brooklyn native, limited the home team to just three singles.

War would not come for America until December. Yet as the season began the likelihood of our eventual involvement was growing stronger. President Roosevelt had won an unprecedented third term last November, defeating Republican Wendell Willkie in an election centered on which candidate was most likely to keep us out of the war. On the other hand, many Americans had voted for FDR expecting the United States would eventually be drawn in and were reluctant to change leaders at such a critical period. Since that election, Germany had conquered more of the European continent, and ever-larger segments of the American public were questioning our neutrality. Even the president was obviously favoring Britain over Germany, just as President Woodrow Wilson had done a quarter-century earlier.

Roosevelt's first two administrations had stimulated a substantial population increase in the Washington area as government workers, needed to implement all the New Deal legislation, moved into the city and nearby suburbs. Now, with the threat of war escalating, even more bureaucrats had descended on the capital. The presence of all these new arrivals combined with the usual crush of springtime tourists made hotel space impossible to find this Easter weekend. The police reported that many visitors were spending nights in their cars. Washington is America's loveliest city, especially in the spring when its beauty attracts people from around the world. Besides the traditional sightseeing, they come for such cherished springtime events as the annual Cherry Blossom Festival and the Easter egg roll on the White House lawn. This year was no exception. The egg roll alone drew a record-breaking crowd of 53,258 adults and children. That only 32,000 fans were at Griffith Stadium was simply because that was the park's capacity. Had the park been larger, so too would have been the crowd.

Russo, a 14-game winner in 1940 (14–8), was the first Yankees' pitcher other than Lefty Gomez or Red Ruffing to start an opener since 1930, the year before Joe McCarthy became the manager. But Gomez, who started six openers for McCarthy, had missed most of last season with a sore arm; and Ruffing, who started the other four, fell to 15–12 in 1940 after four straight 20-win seasons. Still, neither Gomez nor Ruffing at their best could have improved on Russo's overall performance today. In addition to his excellent pitching, Russo also excelled at bat and in the field; he doubled home the Yankees' second run, and twice started rally-killing double plays. But as well as Russo played his position, fielding honors for the day went to Phil Rizzuto, the Yanks' rookie shortstop who was making his major-league debut. Although he went hitless, Rizzuto fielded his position flawlessly and served as the middleman in two of the team's three double plays. Like Russo, he too was a native New Yorker; in fact both Russo and Rizzuto had attended the same high school—Richmond Hill High in Queens. Earlier in his career, some baseball people (including then Brooklyn manager Casey Stengel) questioned whether the five-foot-six, 150-pound Rizzuto was big enough to play at the major-league level. No one questioned his size any longer. The only concern the Yankees had about Rizzuto was whether they would lose him to the military. The recently passed Selective Training and Service Act was beginning to have an impact on baseball. On March 8, Phillies' pitcher Hugh Mulcahy became the first major-leaguer drafted under the new law. Rizzuto, at 23, was the right age for a call-up, but as he provided the major support for his parents, his draft status—at least for now—was 3-A: deferred for dependency.

Rizzuto joined the Yankees in tandem with his minor-league double-play partner, Jerry Priddy. In the four years the two had been in the Yankees' system, the last three as teammates, their teams had won the pennant each year. Last season, playing for the American Association's Kansas City Blues, Rizzuto batted .347, while Priddy hit .306 with 112 runs batted in. After watching the two rookies shine in spring training, McCarthy decided to revamp the Yankees' infield to make room for both of them. He would stay with Red Rolfe at third (although Rolfe's batting average had fallen to .250 in 1940), but planned to use different players at the other three positions. Rizzuto would be the shortstop, replacing Frank Crosetti. Crosetti had been there since 1932, but in three of the previous four seasons he had hit below .250, and in 1940, he batted only .194. Rizzuto's double-play partner, just as he had been the last three years, would be Priddy, who would replace Joe Gordon at second base. Gordon would move to first to fill the spot Babe Dahlgren had occupied since the retirement of Lou Gehrig. Dahlgren had proved to be too weak a hitter to play first base for the Yankees, and so in late February they sold him to the Boston Braves.

The idea of moving Gordon, voted the major leagues' best second baseman the last two years, to make room for a rookie was not the way McCarthy usually did things. Yet this was the lineup he used throughout spring training, and it was the one he was ready to go into the season with. The only reason he didn't was that three days before the opener, Priddy twisted his ankle in an exhibition game against Brooklyn. With Priddy out of the opening-day lineup, McCarthy returned Gordon to second and put Johnny Sturm—another rookie from the Kansas City Blues—at first. When Priddy healed, he did take over at second, with Gordon moving to first. Gordon played first base for 30 games, but Priddy failed to hit and McCarthy moved Gordon back to second and Sturm became the fulltime first baseman.

Although he was injured, Priddy was in uniform when a delegation of fans from Norfolk, Virginia presented Rizzuto and him with a large yellow-flowered horseshoe. In 1938, their first year together, Rizzuto and Priddy played for the Yankees' Piedmont League team, the Norfolk Tars, and many of their old fans had come to Washington to wish them luck. The presentation took place in the middle of the infield at 2:30 P.M. and set in motion the pregame activities. But, of course, the highlight of any Washington opener was the appearance of the president, and this year it occurred at the conclusion of the Rizzuto-Priddy ceremonies. First, the United States Army Band took up positions in the infield, while players from both teams lined up in front of their dugouts—the Yanks on the third-base side and the Senators on the first-base side. From down the right-field line strolled a group that included Senators' owner Clark Griffith wearing his opening-day best, including a pearl gray hat. A contingent of secret service men and special police followed, walking before, behind, and alongside a big touring car. FDR was in the car, waving his hat and smiling to the crowd. As he took his place in the presidential box next to the Washington dugout, the band struck up "The Star-Spangled Banner." Applause for the president, making his ninth opening-day appearance at Griffith Stadium, seemed less vigorous than in his previous appearances, perhaps the result of the midsummer-like weather. Game-time temperature was in the high 80s, which led most of the men to take off their coats. However, the women, and there were lots of them, seemed intent on not removing what was described as their new-style, smooth-fitting jackets. They continued to wear them throughout the game, although the Easter orchids pinned to those jackets began to wilt before the first pitch. In a break with opening-day ritual, the players remained standing at attention along the foul lines instead of marching to the flagpole. They were content to watch as the band, along with Griffith, McCarthy, Washington manager Bucky Harris, and Henry A. Wallace, the new vice-president, made the long trek to center field.

Washingtonians were getting their first look at the Senators' redesigned home uniforms. Beginning in 1912, and for most of the next quarter-century, Washington players wore a small "W" on their left sleeves while their jersey fronts remained blank. In 1938, they had enlarged the "W" (in blue outlined in red) and moved it to the left side of the jersey front. The following year they switched the "W" back to the sleeve, which, with the change from buttons to a zipper, made the blank jerseys appear even starker. Now the blue "W" was again on the left breast, this time without the red piping. Following the march back to home plate, the players gathered around the presidential box where the president was preparing to throw out the first ball. This year's winner of the prized keepsake was Arnold "Red" Anderson, a rookie Washington pitcher.

The next pitch, the "real" first pitch of the season, was from Leonard to Rizzuto, and the obviously anxious rookie went after it and grounded out to shortstop Cecil Travis. After Rolfe lined a fastball into right field for a single, Tommy Henrich followed with a sharply hit bouncer to Buddy Myer. The veteran second baseman tossed it to Travis to force Rolfe, but Travis, attempting to complete the double play, threw wildly to first baseman George Archie, allowing Henrich to continue on to second. DiMaggio brought Henrich home with a booming triple to center field as he continued his torrid spring hitting streak. DiMaggio had hit safely in the last 19 exhibition games, a preview of the great streak that was to come.

Washington got the leadoff man aboard against Russo in each of the first three innings, but could not bring him around. In the first, Russo walked leadoff batter George Case on four pitches, but easily handled Doc Cramer and Ben Chapman, two outfielders the Senators had traded for in the off-season. Washington had two runners on in the second inning on Buddy Lewis's leadoff single and Myer's one-out walk, when Archie grounded to Rolfe at third. Rolfe stepped on the bag to force Lewis but threw wildly to Sturm, leaving the Senators still with two runners on. Russo ended the threat by striking out catcher Rick Ferrell. In the third, Leonard opened with a line single to center, but Russo snared Case's hard smash back to the box and turned it into a double play via Rizzuto and Sturm.

By the time the Senators threatened again, they were three runs down. The Yankees had scored in the fifth on doubles by Bill Dickey and Russo, who clubbed a 3–1 fastball off the wall in left. In the sixth, singles by Henrich and DiMaggio and a scoring fly by Charlie Keller brought home the final run. DiMaggio was the only player to have two hits on the day as he began his quest for a third straight American League batting championship. With two gone in the Washington seventh, Travis's ground ball went through Rolfe's legs for a two-base error. Rolfe was still rounding into shape. He had played in the Yanks' final exhibition game against the Dodgers, but that was his first action in two weeks. Myer's bloop single to left moved Travis to third, but Archie, having a painful debut in Washington, forced Myer at second for the third out. Myer, the American League batting champion in 1935, in his 17th and final big-league season, was playing in place of Jimmy Bloodworth. After playing superbly all spring, Bloodworth was beaned the day before the opener in a game in Baltimore against the International League Orioles. Although Baltimore's Union Memorial Hospital held him overnight for observation, Bloodworth was at the park in uniform and participated in the pregame activities. Later he complained of dizziness, and in the third inning changed back into his street clothes.

Hope stirred again for the hometown fans when Ferrell led off the eighth by drawing Russo's third walk. It quickly ended when Johnny Welaj, whom Harris sent in to bat for Leonard, grounded into the Senators third double play, Rizzuto to Gordon to Sturm. It was particularly vexing for the Washington fans that the team's three fastest runners, Case, Chapman, and Welaj, had hit into the three double plays.

After the game, manager Harris said that Leonard did not have his good knuckleball today, noting that none of the normally difficult pitches to handle got away from catcher Ferrell. Even without his best weapon, Leonard, pitched a fine game. He went eight innings, allowing six hits, no walks, and three earned runs before Ken Chase took over in the ninth. The lack of opening-day support was becoming familiar to him. Washington's three hits were one more than the Senators had gotten for him in last year's opener, a 2–0 loss to Boston's Lefty Grove. Leonard, who went on to win 18 games (18–13) for the sixth-place

Senators this season, would be the starting pitcher here in the first game of a June 29 doubleheader against New York. In that game, he yielded the double with which DiMaggio tied George Sisler's American League record of hitting safely in 41 consecutive games, a record DiMaggio broke in the second game.

The Yankees (101–53) won the pennant by 17 games over the Boston Red Sox, clinching on September 4, the earliest 154-game-season clinching date in major-league history. They won a hard-fought World Series over the Brooklyn Dodgers in five games. Joe DiMaggio batted .357, with 30 home runs and a league-leading 125 runs batted in. That, and his record-breaking 56-game hitting streak, earned him his second Most Valuable Player Award in a very close contest with Ted Williams. Williams batted .406 with 37 home runs (both league highs) and had 120 RBIs.

Monday, April 14, 1941

New York	ab	r	h	po	a	e	Washington	ab	r	h	po	a	e
Rizzuto ss	4	0	0	1	4	0	Case rf	3	0	0	4	0	0
Rolfe 3b	4	0	1	1	3	1	Cramer cf	4	0	0	4	0	0
Henrich rf	4	2	1	3	0	0	Chapman lf	4	0	0	2	0	0
DiMaggio cf	4	0	2	4	0	0	Lewis 3b	4	0	1	0	0	0
Keller lf	4	0	0	1	0	0	Travis ss	3	0	0	3	7	1
Gordon 2b	4	0	0	4	2	0	Myer 2b	2	0	1	2	3	0
Dickey c	3	1	1	2	0	0	Archie 1b	3	0	0	9	1	0
Sturm 1b	3	0	0	11	0	0	Ferrell c	2	0	0	2	0	0
Russo p	3	0	1	0	5	0	Leonard p	2	0	1	0	0	0
Total	33	3	6	27	14	1	ªWelaj	1	0	0	0	0	0
							Chase p	0	0	0	1	0	0
							Total	28	0	3	27	11	1

ªHit into double play for Leonard in eighth inning.

New York	100	011	000–3
Washington	000	000	000–0

Runs batted in—DiMaggio, Russo, Keller. Two-base hits—Dickey, Russo. Three-base hit—DiMaggio. Stolen base—DiMaggio. Double plays—Russo, Rizzuto and Sturm; Russo, Gordon, and Sturm; Rizzuto, Gordon, and Sturm. Left on bases—New York 3; Washington 4. Bases on balls—off Russo 3. Struck out—by Russo 1, Leonard 1. Hits—off Leonard 6 in 8 innings, Chase 0 in 1. Losing pitcher—Leonard. Umpires—Ormsby, McGowan, Summers, and Quinn. Time of game—1 hr. 47 min. Attendance—32,000.

Tuesday, April 14, 1942
Griffith Stadium, Washington
New York 7 Washington 0

I am always conscious of an uncomfortable sensation now and then when the wind is blowing in the east.—Charles Dickens

A month after America's entry into the war against Germany, Japan, and Italy, in December 1941, baseball commissioner Kenesaw Landis wrote to President Roosevelt asking for directions on how, or if, baseball should operate in 1942. Roosevelt answered on January 15, with his famous "green light" letter. "I honestly feel," said the president, "that it would be best for the country to keep baseball going." So it was that when the 1942 baseball season opened, it did so with the blessings of the president of the United States, albeit without his presence. FDR could not spare the time to attend the Senators' opener at Griffith Stadium; but aside from his not being there, the 1942 season began much the same as the 1941 season had. On Opening Day 1941, the Yankees' Marius Russo had shut out the Senators, 3–0, allowing three hits; this year Red Ruffing shut them out, 7–0, also allowing just three hits.

As at all parks on the East Coast, Griffith Stadium had a supply of sand and fire extinguishers available and instructions on what to do in case of an air raid. Other than that, evidence of the war was limited to the larger than usual number of servicemen in the capacity crowd and the pennant that read "Buy Defense Bonds" flying below Old Glory on the center-field flagpole. However, the most obvious effect of the war in the minds of the 31,000 fans present was the absence of the president. It was only the second time in his ten years as chief executive that FDR had missed a Senators' opener; but then this was the first time in 24 years that the baseball season had opened with the United States at war. Only four months had passed since the attack on Pearl Harbor, and despite the president's prediction that we would win the war in two to three years, the news from the various war fronts remained grim. The Japanese government reported today that 6,700 Americans, including 15 generals, were among the 40,000 captives taken on Bataan; meanwhile, Japanese forces continued their relentless assault on Corregidor. Roosevelt also had to deal with yesterday's shakeup in the French Cabinet, in which pro–Nazi Pierre Laval was about to return to take control of the Vichy Government. It would be seven long months before Winston Churchill could say that the Allies, while not having reached "the beginning of the end," had reached "the end of the beginning."

Vice President Henry Wallace substituted for the president in performing the opening-day ceremonies. The people's representatives who found the time to get away from their duties and attend the game included Senate Majority Leader Alben Barkley of Kentucky, Senate Minority Leader Charles McNary of Oregon, Senator Tom Connally of Texas (chairman of the Foreign Relations Committee), and Congressman Joe Martin of Massachusetts (chairman of the Republican National Committee). To free the regular police for more pressing duties, 80 auxiliary police, "40 whites and 40 Negroes," from Washington's 13th precinct were on duty at the ballpark.

While Cleveland's Bob Feller and Detroit's Hank Greenberg were the biggest stars baseball had lost to the military so far, Washington appeared to be the club most hurt by the mobilization. Their two best players, outfielder Buddy Lewis, 25, and shortstop Cecil Travis, 28, were already serving in the armed forces and each would see heavy combat. Lewis, with a lifetime .304 batting average for his six big-league seasons, was with the 1st Air Commando Group, US Army Air Force in Asia, where he would win a Distinguished Flying Cross. Travis, the American League's 1941 hit leader and runner-up to batting champion Ted Williams, was with the Army and would participate in the Battle of the Bulge. Neither Travis nor Lewis, both of whom had been among the best young players in the league, ever regained their prewar form after returning to the game late in 1945.

Attempting to make up for the loss of his two stars, Clark Griffith made numerous off-season personnel moves, resulting in 12 new players on Washington's opening-day roster. Outfielder George Case, acknowledged to be the fastest man in the game, was the only repeat starter from last year's opening-day lineup. Case would steal 44 bases (in 50 attempts) in 1942, the fourth consecutive year in which he led the American League. Even the Senators' home uniforms were new. They had added blue pinstripes to their pants and jerseys and a red stripe to their blue and white stockings, making them a patriotic red, white, and blue. That matched the red, white, and blue patch that adorned all major-league uniforms in 1942. The patch depicted a shield with three stars on top and the word *HEALTH* written within. All teams were wearing it on their left sleeves except the sleeveless Chicago Cubs, who wore it on their right breast.

The pregame ceremonies featured the 75-piece United States Army Band, which played the national anthem and participated in the traditional parade and flag raising. Among those in the parade were Griffith, American League president Will Harridge, and managers Joe McCarthy of New York and Bucky Harris of Washington. Buddy Hassett, a native New Yorker, emerged from the mass of assembled players to catch Vice President Wallace's season-opening throw. Hassett, after three years each with the Brooklyn Dodgers and the Boston Braves, came to the Yanks along with outfielder Gene Moore in an off-season trade. As part of the deal the Yankees gave up outfielder Tommy Holmes, who had been a .300 hitter in each of his five seasons in their farm system. It turned out to be among the worst trades the Yankees ever made. Moore stayed with them for only 19 days before they sold him to Brooklyn. Hassett, although he did not play in the opener, soon became the team's regular first baseman, playing in 132 games and batting .284. However, he entered military service in 1943 and never again played in the major leagues. Holmes, meanwhile, went on to have an excellent career with the Braves. He batted over .300 five times and twice led the National League in hits. In 1945, he set a twentieth-century National League record when he hit safely in 37 consecutive games, a record that lasted until Pete Rose broke it with 44 straight in 1978.

New York was beginning its 40th season in the American League, and beginning it in the same city where they had played—and lost—their first game back on April 22, 1903. Since then, the Yankees had won 12 American League pennants and nine World Series, including last year's. They were fielding a lineup today much like the one that opened the 1941 season. Baseball's best outfield—Tommy Henrich, Joe DiMaggio, and Charlie Keller— remained intact, but there were changes at the corners of the infield. At third base, second-year man Jerry Priddy was filling in for the ailing Red Rolfe, ending a streak of eight consecutive openers for Rolfe, the last seven at third base. And at first base, Ed Levy was replacing Johnny Sturm, now a member of the U.S. Army. On a sad note, Sturm had two joints of his right index finger amputated this day after being involved in a tractor accident at the Jefferson Barracks in Missouri.

Because Spud Chandler had been the Yankees' most effective pitcher in spring training, McCarthy's choice of Ruffing to pitch the opener was something of a surprise. For Ruffing, it was his fifth (and final) opening-day start for the Yankees. Yet while he was nearing his 38th birthday and had pitched just 16 innings during the exhibition season, he showed no lack of stamina or ability. Through the first seven innings he allowed only one hit—a single by Bruce Campbell leading off the second—and faced just 22 batters, one over the minimum. Ruffing's own two-run single was the big blow in New York's three-run second that gave him the early lead. Sid Hudson, a 27-year-old right-hander making his first opening-day start, had retired the Yanks in order in the first, but with one out in the second, an infield single by Keller and walks to Joe Gordon and Bill Dickey loaded the bases. Levy's infield out scored Keller, and then Ruffing's single to center brought Gordon and Dickey home. The Yankees made it 4–0 in the sixth on a run-scoring single by Gordon before adding their final three runs in the ninth. Hudson's own error was largely responsible for that outburst. Levy was at second and Priddy at first when Phil Rizzuto hit a one-out bouncer back to the mound. Hudson, eager to start a double play, threw wildly past short-stop Bob Repass, allowing Levy to score. A double by Henrich scored Priddy, and Rizzuto tallied on DiMaggio's ground out. Despite the trade for Hassett, Levy, whose only previous major-league experience was one at-bat with the Phillies in 1940, won the first-base job in spring training. He did it by outhitting Hassett, but soon lost it back, and after he played in only 13 games the Yankees sent him to their Kansas City farm team. The next year, 1943, Levy batted .322 for the Newark Bears—second in the International League to the Rochester Red Wings' Red Schoendienst—and returned to New York in 1944 as an outfielder.

Only in the eighth inning did the home crowd get a chance to express their emotions. First, in the top half, they cheered center fielder Stan Spence when he made two great catches that prevented any more Yankees' runs from scoring. With Henrich, who had singled, on first, Spence, acquired in an off-season trade with the Red Sox, ran down consecutive 400-foot drives by DiMaggio and Keller. Then, in the bottom of the eighth, the Senators mounted their only threat, and that a small one. Cuban-born Bobby Estalella drew a one-out walk, the only one Ruffing issued. Repass, making his Washington debut, moved Estalella to second with a single to left. Another new Senator, Jose Gomez, followed with a looping fly ball to right field on which Henrich made a fine shoestring catch. Repass was running, expecting the ball to drop, and Henrich's quick throw to Levy completed the inning-ending double play. Gomez, who played with the Phillies in 1935–1936, was the National League's first Mexican-born player and the second, after Mel Almada, to reach the majors.

Ruffing's win was the 245th of his career (now in its 18th full season), tying him with Ted Lyons of the Chicago White Sox for the most wins among active American League pitchers.

That night, at 10:27 P.M., the nation's capital experienced its first air-raid drill and blackout.

The Yankees (103–51) won the pennant by nine games over the Boston Red Sox. But after defeating the St. Louis Cardinals in the first game of the World Series, they lost the next four. Despite leading the league in strikeouts, double plays grounded into, and making more errors than any other American League second baseman, Joe Gordon won the league's Most Valuable Player Award. Gordon, who batted .322, with 18 home runs and 103 runs batted in, finished just ahead of Triple Crown winner Ted Williams. It was the second straight year Williams, after an exceptional season, had been beaten out in a close vote, calling into question the whole voting procedure.

Tuesday, April 14, 1942

New York	ab	r	h	po	a	e	Washington	ab	r	h	po	a	e
Priddy 3b	5	1	2	2	0	0	Case lf	4	0	1	3	0	1
Rizzuto ss	5	1	0	3	1	0	Spence cf	4	0	0	4	0	0
Henrich rf	5	0	2	2	1	0	Vernon 1b	4	0	0	13	3	0
DiMaggio cf	5	1	1	4	0	0	Campbell rf	3	0	1	0	0	0
Keller lf	5	1	1	1	0	0	Early c	3	0	0	5	1	0
Gordon 2b	3	1	2	1	1	0	Estalella 3b	2	0	0	0	0	0
Dickey c	3	1	0	8	0	0	Repass ss	3	0	1	0	3	1
Levy 1b	3	1	0	5	1	0	Gomez 2b	3	0	0	0	9	0
Ruffing p	4	0	2	1	1	0	Hudson p	2	0	0	2	2	1
Total	38	7	10	27	5	0	[a]Galle	1	0	0	0	0	0
							Total	29	0	3	27	18	3

[a]Batted for Hudson in ninth.

New York	030	001	003–7
Washington	000	000	000–0

Runs batted in—Levy, Ruffing 2, Gordon, Henrich, DiMaggio. Two-base hits—Priddy, Henrich. Double play—Henrich and Levy. Left on bases—New York 7 Washington 3. Bases on balls—off Hudson 3, Ruffing 1. Struck out—by Hudson 6, Ruffing 5. Umpires—Summers, Rommel, and Pipgras. Time of game—2 hrs 7 min. Attendance—32,000.

Thursday, April 22, 1943
Yankee Stadium, New York
New York 5 Washington 4

We will grieve not, rather find strength in what remains behind.—William Wordsworth

With every major-league team having lost key players to the armed forces, the 1943 season began with each club fielding lineups largely unfamiliar to their fans. Among the opening-day absentees who had played in 1942 were some of the game's greatest players, including Joe DiMaggio, Ted Williams, Johnny Mize, Pete Reiser, and Enos Slaughter. But it was not only the biggest stars that were missing. The Yankees, for example, had also lost from their 1942 team Tommy Henrich (he actually entered the Coast Guard late in the '42 season), Phil Rizzuto, George Selkirk, Buddy Hassett, and Red Ruffing. Ruffing was drafted in January despite his age—he was four months shy of 38—and having only one toe on his left foot. He had lost the other four in a mine accident as a youngster. Also gone, but not to the military, were two other longtime Yankees. During the off-season, Red Rolfe retired and Lefty Gomez—a Yankee since 1930—was sold to the Boston Braves. After Boston released Gomez in May without his ever pitching for them, he signed with Washington, lost the one game he pitched for the Senators, and then he too retired. The Yanks were also opening without Frank Crosetti, who had recently signed his 1943 contract and was on his way from California. Crosetti was serving a 30-day suspension for pushing umpire Bill Summers during an argument in the third game of the 1942 World Series and would be unable to play until May 21.

Yet even without all the familiar faces, this would be the first season opener at Yankee Stadium in four years, and the club was expecting a crowd upwards of 40,000 to be there. But then the rains came, washing out the game and any hopes of a big crowd. The next day, under still threatening skies—it had rained all morning—the Yankees did open, scoring two ninth-inning runs to win a come-from-behind, 5–4, decision over the Washington Senators. However, only 7,057 showed up, the smallest opening-day crowd in the team's history. The war had made missing work—or rescheduling days off—something that was not only frowned upon, but considered unpatriotic. This morning, the Office of War Information had issued the official government policy for wartime vacations. They recommended that every war worker should take a vacation, but that they should spend it as close to home as possible, preferably gardening or helping on a farm.

Johnny Murphy, who relieved starter Ernie Bonham in the ninth inning and threw only one pitch, got the win for New York, but the hero of the day was Yankees center fielder Roy Weatherly. Playing his first game as DiMaggio's wartime replacement, Weatherly hit a ninth-inning double that drove in the tying and winning runs. The victory ended what had been an eight-game home losing streak at Yankee Stadium. Because of wartime restrictions on travel, the government had asked all major-league teams to conduct their 1943 spring training activities somewhere close to home. Naturally, all complied, with the Yankees choosing Asbury Park, New Jersey. They played only six games against other big-league teams and lost them all—five to Brooklyn and one to the Braves. The loss to the Braves, and four of the losses to the Dodgers were in games played at the Stadium. That followed three home losses to the Cardinals in the 1942 World Series. New York had not won at home since last September 23 when Bonham beat the Senators 4–1. It was Bonham's 21st victory (21–5) of 1942, a year in which he led the American League in winning percentage (.808) and shutouts (6). He entered 1943 as the Yanks' best pitcher, and manager Joe McCarthy rewarded him with his first (and only) opening-day start. (Though Bonham was only 29, he had chronic back problems that had kept him out of the military.)

Earlier this spring, the Yankees announced that they would make 3,000 free seats available for servicemen and servicewomen at each of their 1943 home games. More than 300 uniformed men and women took advantage of that offer today, coming to the opener as guests of Yankees president Ed Barrow. Enlistments and the draft had taken so many men that it was becoming necessary to use women in jobs that had previously been off limits to them. Women not only took jobs in factories, where they made a major contribution to the war effort, but also those of a more mundane nature. For the first time ever, the Stevens Brothers had hired women to work in the commissary at Yankee Stadium. Because of the meat shortage, no vendors walked among the crowd selling hot dogs; however, they were available at the concession stands. Otherwise, things appeared normal at the Stadium. It was decorated in the red, white, and blue bunting as it always is for the opener, and pregame rituals were conducted just as they always had been. First came Captain Francis Sutherland and the Seventh Regiment Band leading both ball clubs and a group of dignitaries on the march to the center-field flagpole. After the American flag was raised, McCarthy and Senators' manager Ossie Bluege attempted to raise the Yankees' 1942 American League championship flag. As Mayor Fiorello La Guardia, Bronx borough president James Lyons, American League president Will Harridge, Senators president Clark Griffith, and Yankees vice president George Ruppert stood watching, the pennant came loose and landed on the screen in front of the center-field bleachers. While a couple of groundskeepers ran to retrieve it, all the marchers headed back toward home plate. It never did get raised, which the more superstitious fans saw as a bad omen.

Traditionally, the public address announcer at Yankee Stadium would make a pregame announcement to the crowd notifying them of the opposing batteries. However, beginning today he would now be informing them of each team's entire batting order. The small crowd gave the announcement of Bill Dickey's name their greatest applause, while also giving hearty cheers to other well-known Yankees like Joe Gordon, Charlie Keller, and Bonham. Mayor La Guardia threw out the first ball but left after three innings. Normally the mayor would stay for the whole game, but these were not normal times and he felt it necessary to get back to the city's business. Before the game, a telegram arrived at the Stadium from an army base in Santa Ana, California. It was from Joe DiMaggio, wishing his former teammates good luck in the pennant race. DiMaggio, who made $43,500 in 1942, had enlisted in February and was now an army sergeant making $50 a month. Only three of the Yankees that took the field with Bonham this afternoon had been regulars in 1942: catcher Dickey, second baseman Gordon, and left fielder Keller. Center fielder Weatherly (the Cleveland Indians) and first baseman Nick Etten (the Philadelphia Phillies) had come in trades, while

Billy Johnson at third and George Stirnweiss at shortstop were rookies playing in their first major-league game. Johnny Lindell, who had been with the team in 1942 as a pitcher was in right field. McCarthy believed Lindell was a better hitter than he was a pitcher and switched him to the outfield to get his powerful bat in the lineup.

By contrast, Washington was the one American League team that was as strong, or stronger, than it had been in 1942. Stars Cecil Travis and Buddy Lewis had already begun serving in '42, and since then they had lost only one significant player to the draft—pitcher Sid Hudson. The Senators had begun their season two days earlier, defeating the Philadelphia Athletics in the presidential opener. It was their first game under Bluege, who was replacing Bucky Harris as manager. Bluege had been with Washington since 1922, 18 years as a player and the last two as a coach. His starting pitcher today was 23-year-old right-hander Early Wynn. Both pitchers were in complete control for four innings as neither team came close to scoring. Bonham had allowed only one hit, to Wynn, and Wynn had allowed none. The Senators broke the drought in the fifth. Bonham walked first baseman Mickey Vernon to lead off the inning, and after he retired ex–Yankee Jerry Priddy, catcher Jake Early singled Vernon to third. Vernon scored when Gordon, attempting to complete the double play on John Sullivan's grounder, threw wildly past Etten at first. The Yankees came right back to take a 2–1 lead in their half of the fifth. They did it on a single by Etten, a walk to Johnson, a single by Lindell that scored Etten, and a single by Stirnweiss that scored Johnson.

It remained that way until the eighth, when the Senators' George Case, the league's best base stealer, reached base on an error by Stirnweiss, stole second, and scored on a single to center by Stan Spence. Gordon's solo home run deep into the left-field seats with two out in the eighth put the Yanks in the lead again, 3–2. With both leagues using the new "balata ball," made from materials that were not needed for the war effort, home runs were rare in the first days of the 1943 season. However, after a week of many shutouts and little power hitting, Commissioner Landis ordered the immediate return of the "rabbit ball" to the major leagues.

Bonham, needing just three outs for the win, began the ninth inning by walking Vernon, just as he had done in the fifth. He retired Priddy and Early and was now only one out away from victory, but he never got it. He gave up a single to Sullivan that moved Vernon to second, and then Gene Moore, batting for Wynn, singled to center and Vernon came home with the tying run. Ellis Clary followed with a ground ball that bounded off third base and went for a double, and Sullivan scored to put Washington ahead. That was all for Bonham. McCarthy summoned Murphy, his ace fireman, from the bullpen. Murphy retired Case with his first pitch, but as the Yankees came to bat in the last of the ninth, they were trailing, 4–3. Bluege called on Mickey Haefner, a 30-year-old left-hander, to nail down the win. Haefner, in his major-league debut, walked Dickey, the first man he faced. Lindell bunted, but Haefner's throw to second hit Tuck Stainback, running for Dickey, on the wrist and both runners were safe. The official scorer ruled it a sacrifice, with no error to Haefner. McCarthy sent reserve catcher Rollie Hemsley, a right-handed batter, up to hit for Murphy. Hemsley's assignment was to bunt the runners over to second and third, but Haefner's 1–1 pitch was wild, and the runners got there without the bunt. Bluege had seen enough of Haefner. He brought in Owen Scheetz, a 29-year-old right-hander who had pitched for the Minneapolis Millers of the American Association in 1942. Scheetz, appearing in his first major-league game, got Hemsley, who was now free to swing away, on a pop fly but walked Stirnweiss to load the bases. Then came Weatherly's game-winner, a blooper into left field that easily scored Stainback. Lindell, the runner from second, rounded third on his way home, but before he could get there, he slipped and fell. Then, when he got up and started back to third, third base coach Art Fletcher—seeing that left fielder Bob Johnson was having trouble picking the ball up—waved him home with the winning run. The official scorer gave Weatherly a double and two runs batted in. Johnson, in his first game for Washington after ten years with the A's, was not charged with an error. Murphy, who faced only one batter, got the win, and Haefner, who faced only two, got the loss.

New York (98–56) finished 13½ games ahead of Washington to give Joe McCarthy his eighth and final pennant with the Yankees. The Yanks avenged their 1942 World Series loss to the St. Louis Cardinals, defeating them in five games. Spud Chandler was the league's best pitcher, leading or tying in wins (20–4), winning percentage (.833), ERA (1.64), complete games (20), and shutouts (5). He won the Most Valuable Player Award, the third consecutive Yankee—following Joe DiMaggio and Joe Gordon—to do so.

Thursday, April 22, 1943

Washington

	ab	r	h	po	a	e
Clary 3b	5	0	1	0	1	0
Case rf	5	1	1	1	0	0
Spence cf	4	0	1	1	0	0
R. Johnson lf	4	0	0	1	0	0
Vernon 1b	2	2	0	10	2	0
Priddy 2b	4	0	1	1	5	0
Early c	3	0	1	6	1	0
Sullivan ss	4	1	1	3	5	0
Wynn p	3	0	1	2	0	0
ªMoore	1	0	1	0	0	0
Haefner p	0	0	0	0	0	0
Scheetz p	0	0	0	0	0	0
Total	35	4	8	25	14	0

New York

	ab	r	h	po	a	e
Stirnweiss ss	4	0	1	2	2	1
Weatherly cf	4	0	1	4	0	0
Keller lf	4	0	0	2	0	0
Gordon 2b	3	1	1	3	2	1
Etten 1b	3	1	1	8	0	0
W. Johnson 3b	3	1	0	1	3	0
Dickey c	3	0	1	6	1	0
ᵇStainback	0	1	0	0	0	0
Lindell rf	3	1	1	1	0	0
Bonham p	3	0	0	0	2	0
Murphy p	0	0	0	0	0	0
ᶜHemsley	1	0	0	0	0	0
Total	31	5	6	27	10	2

*One out when winning run scored.
ªSingled for Wynn in ninth inning.
ᵇRan for Dickey in ninth inning.
ᶜPopped out for Murphy in ninth inning.

Washington   000   010   012–4
New York   000   020   012–5

Runs batted in—Sullivan, Lindell, Stirnweiss, Spence, Gordon, Moore, Clary, Weatherly 2. Two-base hits—Clary, Weatherly. Home run—Gordon. Stolen base—Case. Sacrifice—Lindell. Double play—W. Johnson, Gordon, and Etten. Left on bases—New York 8; Washington 7. Bases on balls—off Bonham 3, Wynn 4, Haefner 1, Scheetz 1. Struck out—by Bonham 4, Wynn 4. Hits—off Wynn 5 in 8 innings, Haefner 0 in 0 (pitched to two batters), Scheetz 1 in ⅓, Bonham 8 in 8⅔, Murphy 0 in ⅓. Wild pitch—Haefner. Winning pitcher—Murphy. Losing pitcher—Haefner. Umpires—McGowan and Grieve. Time of game—2 hrs. 15 min. Attendance—7,057.

Tuesday, April 18, 1944
Fenway Park, Boston
New York 3 Boston 0

Man's inhumanity to man makes countless thousands mourn.—Robert Burns

For the first time in his 14 seasons as Yankees' manager, Joe McCarthy was not with the club on Opening Day. McCarthy, who had been ailing all spring, skipped the trip to Boston where the Yanks were opening against the Red Sox and flew home to Buffalo with his wife Elizabeth. Dr. Arthur J. Burkel, his personal physician, met them at the airport and later diagnosed McCarthy with both respiratory and gall bladder problems. Coach Art Fletcher managed the club in the opener and continued to manage them until McCarthy returned on May 10. Fletcher led the Yanks to a 9–4 record, but he could take little credit for today's victory. All he had to do was sit back and watch as Hank Borowy began New York's quest for a fourth consecutive American League pennant with a five-hit, 3–0, shutout.

By Opening Day of this third wartime season, the tide of battle had shifted heavily in favor of the Allies. Americans no longer wondered if we would win the war—only when. For most Americans, it could not come soon enough, regardless of the consequences. In a Gallup Poll published this morning, 74 percent of them said they would agree to bombing religious buildings in Rome and elsewhere if it would save the lives of American soldiers. This was not an idle question; U.S. bombers were now inflicting heavy damage on the Axis powers everywhere. Today in Berlin, 2,000 American planes, including nearly 1,000 Flying Fortresses and Liberators, bombed the Nazi capital. And in the Pacific, Admiral Chester W. Nimitz announced the aerial war against the Japanese in the Marshall and Caroline Islands was "hitting new highs," while Secretary of the Navy Frank Knox revealed that American submarines had sunk 532 Japanese ships since the attack on Pearl Harbor.

With a few exceptions, like the Boston Red Sox's Bobby Doerr and the St. Louis Cardinals' Stan Musial, most of the younger stars of baseball were now in the service and rosters consisted primarily of 4-F's, teenagers, and aging veterans. Players who did not fully possess major-league skills permeated both leagues. While some had possessed those skills in the past, and some would in the future, for all too many the war had given them the only opportunity they would ever have to play in the big leagues. Still, it was baseball, and a crowd of 9,973 (including 1,453 servicemen and women) came out to Fenway Park in perfect springtime weather to see the opener. The Coast Guard Band entertained them before the game, playing both popular tunes and military ones. There was a patriotic parade and pageant, featuring WAVES, WACS, SPARS, and women marines. The spectacle concluded with a detail of male marines raising the flag as the band played the national anthem. Leverett Saltonstall, the patrician governor of Massachusetts, threw out the first ball. The left-handed governor made a perfect throw to Red Sox catcher Roy Partee.

Johnny Lindell, batting clean-up, gave the Yankees a 1–0 lead when he led off the second inning with a long opposite-field home run. Lindell, now wearing Bill Dickey's No. 8 (Dickey was in the navy), blasted Yank Terry's second pitch into the Boston bullpen in right field. Terry, a 33-year-old right-hander whose given name was Lancelot, had been the Pacific Coast League's Most Valuable Player in 1941. His 26–8 record for the San Diego Padres earned him a promotion to Boston, where, because he was 4-F, he had been ever since. A year ago, when the Red Sox lost 17 of 22 to the Yankees, Terry had only one decision against New York—a loss. His season's record of 7–9 evened his career mark to 14 wins and 14 losses. Lindell, Nick Etten, and George Stirnweiss were the only Yankees' starters who had played in the 1943 opener against Washington. Lindell had been in right field then, but had since become the club's regular center fielder. (Roy Weatherly, the opening-day center fielder in 1943, was in the Army.) Flanking Lindell in the outfield was Ed Levy in left and Bud Metheny in right. Levy, the opening-day first baseman in 1942, was back in

New York as an outfielder after a big year with the Triple A Newark Bears. The left-handed Metheny, the archetypal wartime major-leaguer, was in his second year with the Yankees. Only Etten, the first baseman, was starting at the same position as he had in 1943. Etten would continue as the Yanks' first baseman throughout the war years and even into 1946. He, Lindell, and Stirnweiss were the only position players left from the team that faced the Cardinals in last fall's World Series. Stirnweiss, then a rookie, had played in 83 games in 1943, mostly at shortstop, but he batted just .219, and his only appearance in the Series was as a pinch hitter. McCarthy used the veteran Frank Crosetti against St. Louis, but Crosetti was no longer available. He was now working in a shipyard in California, as was another Yankee, pitcher Butch Wensloff. Stirnweiss, who played shortstop in the '43 opener, was at second base today. The shortstop was Oscar Grimes, a utility infielder who came with Weatherly from the Cleveland Indians in December 1942. With Billy Johnson in the army, rookie Don Savage was starting at third base.

Savage was up from Newark, where he batted .258 in 1943 but had shown some power, hitting 16 home runs. He would share third base this season with Grimes, while rookie Mike Milosevich, and later Crosetti when he came off the voluntary retired list, split time at shortstop.

Besides Johnson and Dickey, Joe Gordon (army air force), Charlie Keller (merchant marine), and Marius Russo (army) were other members of the 1943 world championship team now serving in the military. Borowy's batterymate, replacing Dickey, was Mike Garbark, a 28-year-old rookie. Ken Sears, who as a rookie had served as Dickey's backup in 1943, was, like Dickey, in the navy. Earlier in the day, the Yankees had signed two additional catchers: 36-year-old Rollie Hemsley, who had been with them since mid–1942, and rookie Bill Drescher, from their Newark farm team. Three Yankees—Joe DiMaggio (army), Tommy Henrich (coast guard), and Phil Rizzuto (navy)—would be missing their second full season. Of course, Red Sox manager Joe Cronin was without many of his best players, too: chiefly left-fielder Ted Williams (marines), the game's best hitter, shortstop Johnny Pesky (navy), who hit .331 with 205 hits in 1942, his rookie year, and center-fielder Dom DiMaggio (navy), who had a .289 batting average for his first three seasons.

Tuesday, April 18, 1944

New York	ab	r	h	po	a	e	Boston	ab	r	h	po	a	e
Stirnweiss 2b	5	0	1	1	2	0	Newsome ss	4	0	0	3	2	0
Metheny rf	4	0	0	2	0	0	Metkovich 1b	3	0	1	8	1	0
Etten 1b	3	0	0	13	1	0	Garrison rf	4	0	0	4	0	0
Lindell cf	3	1	1	0	0	0	Johnson lf	3	0	0	0	0	0
Savage 3b	3	0	0	2	5	0	Doerr 2b	3	0	0	6	2	1
Levy lf	4	1	2	2	0	0	Tabor 3b	4	0	1	2	3	0
Grimes ss	4	1	2	3	3	0	Culberson cf	4	0	2	1	0	0
Garbark c	3	0	1	3	0	0	Partee c	3	0	1	2	0	0
Borowy p	2	0	1	1	5	0	Terry p	2	0	0	0	2	0
Total	31	3	8	27	16	0	[a]Lazor	1	0	0	0	0	0
							Ryba p	0	0	0	1	0	0
							Total	31	0	5	27	10	1

[a]Batted for Terry in seventh inning.

New York	010	000	200–3
Boston	000	000	000–0

Runs batted in—Lindell, Grimes, Garbark. Two-base hits—Grimes, Partee. Three-base hit—Metkovich. Home run—Lindell. Stolen base—Culberson. Sacrifices—Metheny, Etten, Borowy, Doerr. Double plays—Tabor, Doerr, and Metkovich; Newsome, Doerr, and Metkovich. Left on bases—New York 8; Boston 8. Bases on balls—off Borowy 3, Terry 2, Ryba 2. Struck out—by Borowy 2, Ryba 2. Hits—off Terry 7 in 7 innings, Ryba 1 in 2. Losing pitcher—Terry. Umpires—Summers, Rue, and Boyer. Time of game—1 hr. 52 min. Attendance—9,973.

Although this was the first time all spring Borowy had pitched nine innings, he seemed stronger in the second half of the game than he did in the first. Several times in the early innings Boston seemed ready to take the lead, or at least tie the game, but each time Borowy got away without yielding a run. In the first, with two out and George Metkovich aboard, Levy made a fine running catch of Bob Johnson's drive to deep left center. An inning later, Leon Culberson singled and Partee walked after two were out, but Terry grounded out to Grimes. The Red Sox threatened again in the third on Metkovich's one-out triple off the right-field fence. This time Borowy had to get Boston's number three and four hitters, Ford Garrison and Johnson, to preserve the lead, which he did. In the fourth inning Jim Tabor and Culberson singled with one out, but Borowy retired Partee on a come-backer to the mound and struck out Terry. From then on, Borowy mowed down the Red Sox batters with great efficiency. Over the last five innings, he allowed just two more runners: Johnson walked to lead off the sixth, and Partee led off the seventh with a pop-fly double that landed on the foul line in right. In all, the Red Sox stranded eight men, including three at third base.

Meanwhile, Terry kept New York off the board until the seventh inning. They had come close in the sixth, loading the bases with one out, but Terry escaped by getting Savage to bounce into a double play. Levy opened the seventh with a single, his second hit of the day. Grimes's double off the wall in right scored Levy, and when second baseman Doerr's relay throw to the plate went astray, Grimes raced to third. It was a bad play by Doerr, who had no chance to get Levy, and he was charged with an error. Grimes scored on Garbark's first big-league hit, a single to left. The two runs stretched the lead to 3–0, and greatly reduced the pressure on Borowy.

With today's victory, Borowy raised his lifetime record to an imposing 30–13 (.698) since joining the Yankees in 1942. The win was his eighth straight in league play, dating back to August 16, 1943. During that span, Borowy also had a victory over the Cardinals in the 1943 World Series, and two spring training wins. He later recalled that six years earlier, almost to the day, he had pitched Fordham University to a victory against Boston College in nearby Chestnut Hill.

After staying in the race all season, the Yankees (83–71) finished third, six games behind the St. Louis Browns, who won their first and only pennant. Nick Etten led the American League in home runs, with 22, joining Wally Pipp and Lou Gehrig as Yankees' first baseman to win the home-run title. George Stirnweiss had a magnificent year, batting .319 and leading the league in hits (205), runs (125), triples (16), and stolen bases (55). He finished fourth to Detroit Tigers pitcher Hal Newhouser in the Most Valuable Player voting.

Tuesday, April 17, 1945
Yankee Stadium, New York
New York 8 Boston 4

As long as he lived, he was the guiding star
of a whole brave nation.—John Lothrop Motley

There were good reasons for the low level of enthusiasm with which the nation welcomed the opening of the 1945 season, reasons that went beyond the fans' recognition that the quality of play in this fourth year of wartime baseball would be the worst of the twentieth century. It was simply that much more important things were happening. The new season was beginning amid the earthshaking events that were taking place almost every day this spring. The day before the opener, American soldiers from the Ninth Army, advancing from the west, had pushed five miles past the Elbe River and were within 85 miles of linking up with Russian soldiers advancing from the east. With such momentous news, who cared that the Yankees were rained out of their "presidential opener" in Washington? And even today, while Yankees fans were pleased their team had won the opener, defeating the Red Sox 8–4 at Yankee Stadium, the news paled next to the increasingly encouraging reports coming from Europe. The American Ninth Army was now less than 50 miles southwest of Berlin, while the First Army was in Wurzen, ten miles east of Leipzig, and the Seventh Army was in Nuremberg. In less than two weeks, Adolf Hitler would commit suicide, and a week after that Germany would surrender.

Yet the public's rejoicing at the events in Europe was tempered by the news from the Pacific, which was much less euphoric. Although American infantrymen had met little resistance when they landed on Ie Shima, a small island three miles west of Okinawa, military experts predicted a fierce battle ahead. They were right; thousands would die on both sides before American soldiers and marines finally secured Okinawa. One casualty of the landing was popular newsman Ernie Pyle, who after traveling with the troops throughout the war was killed by a Japanese machine gunner. As the ground troops prepared to invade Okinawa, B-29 Superfortresses continued to bomb airbases on Kyushu, one of Japan's main islands. With a Japanese surrender unlikely, the Allies still faced the grisly task of invading the home islands. The casualty estimates for Operations Olympic and Coronet—the invasion of Japan—were reportedly as high as one million.

But even the war news, good or bad, was dwarfed by the shocking death of President Franklin Delano Roosevelt, who had succumbed to a cerebral hemorrhage five days ago at his vacation home in Warm Springs, Georgia. His passing had stunned the nation, most of whose citizens had been unaware of FDR's deteriorating physical condition. There were millions of younger Americans, including many serving in the military, who could not recall a president other than Roosevelt. Adding to the public's sense of estrangement was their apprehension about his successor, Vice President Harry S Truman. They questioned whether Truman, a nondescript former senator from Missouri, was competent to lead the nation at such a critical time. Would he be capable, they wondered, of representing America's interests in dealing with such powerful men as Britain's Winston Churchill and the Soviet Union's Josef Stalin?

The steady rain that washed out yesterday's game in Washington had also postponed the tributes and ceremonies scheduled in honor of the late president. They were rescheduled for April 20, when after three games at home with Boston, the Yankees would again be in town. By then the Yanks would be 3–0, having swept the series with the Red Sox. In the opener, a crowd of 13,923 (including 1,674 members of the armed forces) saw Russ Derry's two home runs lead New York to its fifth consecutive opening-day win. Derry's second homer was a grand slam that came in a seven-run seventh inning that broke a, 4–4, tie and finished Boston starter Rex Cecil. Atley Donald, who pitched a creditable game after a shaky first inning, got the win, with relief help from 41-year-old Jim Turner. The Red Sox out-hit the Yankees, nine to six, but their defense committed four errors—all in the seventh inning. The victory was New York's first under their new ownership triumvirate of Del Webb, Dan Topping, and Larry MacPhail. Webb, a real estate developer, Topping, a wealthy playboy and currently a marine captain, and MacPhail, a former president of the Brooklyn Dodgers, had in partnership purchased the team from Colonel Jacob Ruppert's heirs during the off-season. It cost them $2.8 million, but the three partners now owned the contracts of more than 400 ballplayers, Yankee Stadium, and the ballparks in Newark and Kansas City. MacPhail's addition to the Yankees, where he assumed the duties of general manager, displeased both chairman of the board Ed Barrow and manager Joe McCarthy. Barrow believed the boisterous MacPhail was too flamboyant for the Yankees, but he was powerless to prevent the sale from going through. All three of the new owners were at the opener.

Fans making their way toward the Stadium had to pass through a picket line of about twenty Negroes carrying signs that read, "If We Can Pay, Why Can't We Play?" or "If We Can Stop Bullets, Why Not Balls?" James E. Pemberton, the Democratic leader of the 14th Assembly District in Harlem, led the demonstrators. Pemberton, who was also president of The League for Equality in Sports and Amusements, said the picketing was a protest against "Jim Crowism in baseball." He pointed out that although Negroes comprised 25 percent of Yankees' attendance (or so he claimed), there were no Negro employees at the Stadium. While Pemberton did not even mention the obvious absence of Negro major-leaguers, the Red Sox had actually held a tryout yesterday for three Negro players at Fenway Park. They looked at outfielder Sam Jethroe and infielders Marvin Williams and Jackie Robinson, and though Robinson impressed manager Joe Cronin, Boston management gave no serious thought to signing any of them. Less than three years earlier, in August 1942, *The Sporting News* had published an editorial defending segregation in baseball. They argued that members of each race "prefer to draw their talents from their own ranks," and that "both groups know their crowd psychology and do not care to run the risk of damaging their own game." However, much had changed since then; the war made many Americans aware of the immorality of segregation, and Commissioner Kenesaw Landis, allegedly the staunchest defender of segregated baseball, had died in November 1944. Six months after Robinson's "tryout" with the Red Sox, Branch Rickey signed him to a contract with the Brooklyn Dodgers organization. Later, Rickey would also sign Jethroe.

The gloomy weather, along with the recent death of the president, had a sobering effect on the crowd. Despite the red, white, and blue banners that decorated the Stadium, the pregame exhilaration routinely evident on Opening Day was just not there. Even the ceremonies preceding the game were understandably subdued. Captain Francis Sutherland, among the few remaining links to the prewar years, was there to lead his Seventh Regiment Band on a march to the center-field flagpole. Also on hand was Mel Allen. Allen had become a Yankees' broadcaster in 1939, but he was still in the service, so Bill Slater and Al Helfer did today's game for radio station WINS. As the players from both teams took positions along the foul lines, the band played the national anthem. The American flag was raised to the top of the pole. Then, with the crowd standing silently, the bugles played "Taps" in memory of President Roosevelt as the flag was lowered to half-mast.

Mayor Fiorello La Guardia threw out the first ball, an honor he had performed so often, both at Yankee Stadium and the Polo Grounds. Sitting with La Guardia was Colonel Fulgencio Batista, the former president of Cuba. Batista had learned about American base-ball from prewar spring training appearances in Havana by the Giants and the Dodgers. Seated in a box behind La Guardia was another politician with a connection to baseball— James A. Farley, the former postmaster general. Farley, a longtime fan, was rumored to be among those under consideration to replace Judge Landis as baseball commissioner. However, one week after the opener, on April 24, the owners elected a different politician— Kentucky senator A. B. "Happy" Chandler—to succeed Landis. Other notables at the Stadium today included New York City police commissioner Lewis J. Valentine, New York City fire commissioner Patrick Walsh, Bronx borough president James J. Lyons, Manhattan borough president Edgar Nathan, and Tom Yawkey, the owner of the Red Sox with his new bride, Jean. Yankees pitcher Ernie Bonham was also a spectator. Bonham had arrived from California shortly before game time but was ineligible to be in uniform because he had not yet signed a contract for 1945. Yet no matter how many other celebrities were at the game, the one drawing the most attention, as he always did, was Babe Ruth. The Babe, now 50 years old, was shaking hands with everyone who came by. To those who asked, Ruth made it clear that in the future he would no longer be refereeing wrestling matches.

Boston jumped on Donald quickly; four of their first five batters singled as they scored three first-inning runs. Base hits by rookie second baseman Ben Steiner, first baseman George Metkovich, and outfielder Pete Fox produced the first run. Then, after getting Bob Johnson, Donald yielded a single to Cronin that scored Metkovich. When Derry failed to handle the ball cleanly, Fox continued to third and later scored on Leon Culberson's fly ball. The Red Sox scored their fourth run in the seventh when Steiner pulled a Donald pitch into the seats in right. Steiner, playing his first major-league game, was replacing Bobby Doerr, who was now in the Army. Only 23, he had batted .316 in a full season with the Louisville Colonels of the American Association in 1944.

Cecil, a six-foot-three right-hander, got the start for Boston although he had been a major-leaguer only since last August. The Red Sox had called him up from the San Diego Padres of the Pacific Coast League, where he was 19–11. He won four of his nine American League decisions, with a win and a loss against the Yankees. Through the first six innings this afternoon, Cecil did an outstanding job of protecting the lead. He allowed only two hits and one run—Derry's third-inning home run. Johnny Lindell had gotten New York's first hit, a second-inning single, but was later thrown out at the plate despite his hard slide into Boston catcher Fred Walters. Walters, a former blocking back at Mississippi State, held the ball and made the tag. (Lindell was playing only because his preinduction physical had been postponed.) The Yanks were still trailing, 4–1, when they came to bat in the seventh. However, before the inning was over, the fans would see not only a seven-run rally, but also a record-setting performance by Boston's Metkovich—albeit a negative one. In that fateful seventh, the Red Sox first baseman made three errors to set an American League record for errors by a first baseman in one inning. He also tied the major-league record set by the Philadelphia Phillies' Dolph Camilli in 1935.

Nick Etten, the league's defending home-run champion, led off the inning with a double. Shortstop Joe Buzas followed with a run-producing single to make the score, 4–2. Buzas, making his major-league debut, made the team in spring training by hitting safely in 13 of the 14 exhibition games and leading the club in batting. However, his big-league career would last for only 30 games before the Yankees returned him to Newark of the International League. After a Don Savage single that moved Buzas to second, and with catcher Mike Garbark at the plate, Cecil tried to pick off Buzas. His throw was wild, landing in center field as the tying runs moved into scoring position. It was the first of the four errors Boston would make in the inning; Metkovich had the next three. His troubles began when he fielded Garbark's ground ball and started to throw home to get Buzas. However, Buzas held at third until Metkovich made a move toward first; then he took off. Metkovich, after missing the tag on Garbark (error number one), threw wildly to the plate. The ball got past Walters (error number two), allowing Savage to score behind Buzas and make it a 4–4 game. After Bud Metheny, batting for Donald, sacrificed and George Stirnweiss walked, Metkovich misplayed Hershel Martin's ground ball (error number three) to load the bases. That set the stage for Derry's grand slam, a drive into the seats in right that put New York ahead, 8–4. Derry had missed the first half of the 1944 season while working on his Missouri farm. He joined the club on July 4 and hit .254 with four home runs in 38 games. After Derry's blast, Otis Clark came on and held the Yankees hitless the rest of the way, but it was much too late. Coincidentally, Clark would also make a relief appearance here at the Stadium on the last day of the season and yield the hit that gave Stirnweiss the 1945 batting championship.

Tuesday, April 17, 1945

Boston	ab	r	h	po	a	e	New York	ab	r	h	po	a	e
Steiner 2b	4	2	2	1	0	0	Stirnweiss 2b	3	1	0	3	2	0
Metkovich 1b	3	1	1	7	2	3	Martin lf	4	1	0	5	0	0
Fox rf	4	1	2	2	0	0	Derry rf	4	2	2	1	0	1
R. Johnson lf	4	0	0	1	0	0	Lindell cf	4	0	1	5	0	0
Cronin 3b	3	0	2	1	3	0	Etten 1b	3	1	1	7	0	0
Culberson cf	4	0	0	1	0	0	Buzas ss	4	1	1	3	4	0
Newsome ss	4	0	0	1	2	0	Savage 3b	4	1	1	1	1	1
Walters c	3	0	0	8	0	0	Garbark c	3	1	0	2	3	0
Cecil p	3	0	2	2	3	1	Donald p	2	0	0	0	1	0
Clark p	0	0	0	0	0	0	aMetheny	0	0	0	0	0	0
bLazor	1	0	0	0	0	0	Turner p	0	0	0	0	0	0
Total	33	4	9	24	10	4	Total	31	8	6	27	11	2

aLined out for Clark in ninth inning.
bSacrificed for Donald in seventh inning.

Boston	300	000	100–4
New York	001	000	70X–8

Runs batted in—Fox, Cronin, Culberson, Derry 5, Steiner, Buzas, Garbark. Two-base hit—Etten. Home runs—Derry 2, Steiner. Stolen base—Steiner. Sacrifice—Metheny. Double play—Buzas, Stirnweiss, and Etten. Left on bases—New York 3; Boston 5. Bases on balls—off Donald 3, Cecil 3. Struck out—by Donald 2, Cecil 5 Clark 1. Hits—off Donald 9 in 7 innings, Turner 0 in 2, Cecil 6 in 6 ⅓, Clark 0 in 1⅔. Wild pitch—Cecil. Winning pitcher—Donald. Losing pitcher—Cecil. Umpires—Grieve, Rommel, Pipgras, and Weafer. Time of game—2 hrs. 8 min. Attendance—13,923.

Rain, which had been threatening all afternoon, finally, began to fall in the home eighth causing a 16-minute delay. The sun did come out in the ninth, by which time Turner was pitching his second perfect inning in relief. It would be more than 20 years before baseball would introduce the "save" for relief pitchers, but had it been in effect in 1945, the one Turner earned today would have been the first of the league-leading ten saves he would have. Turner's big-league career ended after this season. But after managing in the minor leagues for three years, he returned to the Yankees in 1949 as a pitching coach under Casey Stengel. Nineteen-forty-five would also be the final season for Donald, who had joined the Yankees in 1938 and spent his entire big-league career with them. With today's win, he now had a lifetime record of 61 wins and 29 losses, a winning percentage of .678. The end was even closer for two future Hall-of-Famers here today. Although he had two hits this afternoon, it would be the last Opening Day as an active player for 38-year-old Joe Cronin. Now in his 20th season, he would play in only two more games and get one more hit before retiring. It was also the end of the line for Paul Waner, a fellow rookie with Cronin on the 1926 Pittsburgh Pirates. Waner, a day past his 42nd birthday, sat on the Yankees' bench the entire game and would get only one plate appearance before he too retired.

> *On July 27, the Yankees sold their best pitcher, Hank Borowy (10–5), to the Chicago Cubs for $97,500. Borowy helped pitch Chicago to the National League pennant, while the Yanks (81–71) finished fourth, 6½ games behind the Detroit Tigers. Nick Etten, with 111, was the only American Leaguer with more than 100 runs batted in. George Stirnweiss was the league's best position player. He won the batting championship (.309) and led the league in slugging percentage (.476), total bases (301), runs (107), triples (22), stolen bases (33), and hits (195). He remains the only Yankee to lead the league in hits in consecutive seasons, having also led in 1944. Stirnweiss finished third in the Most Valuable Player voting as Hal Newhouser, who won 25 games for the pennant-winning Tigers, won for the second consecutive season. Newhouser's teammate, second baseman Eddie Mayo, who failed to finish in the top five in any offensive category, was second.*

Tuesday, April 16, 1946
Shibe Park, Philadelphia
New York 5 Philadelphia 0

What a time! What a civilization!—Cicero

The United States emerged from World War II as the world's preeminent military and economic power. Beyond being the sole possessor of the atomic bomb, we were the only major participant in the war that had not experienced its devastation within our own country. All of our infrastructure and transportation systems were intact—and most often even stronger than they were before the war. American industry, which had turned out the planes, ships, and tanks so instrumental to the Allied victory, was now converting back to peacetime production. Businesses old and new, competing to satisfy the public's pent-up demand for goods and services, would launch the country on an extended period of unprecedented growth. Baseball, too, was entering one of its greatest eras—perhaps the greatest. After four years in which the quality of play had steadily worsened, the fans were eager to welcome back the game's returning heroes. Some, like Hank Greenberg, had already returned. Greenberg rejoined the Detroit Tigers during the second half of the 1945 season and was a major factor in their capturing the pennant and World Series. Now, as baseball's first postwar season got underway (and its last in which all the players were white), they were all back, including the game's biggest star, Joe DiMaggio.

The fans responded with the second-highest combined opening-day attendance to date. Only in 1931 (249,010) had the eight major-league openers attracted more than today's 236,730. In Philadelphia, where the Yankees were opening, a crowd of 37,472—the largest opening-day attendance in the city's history—jammed their way into Shibe Park. The size of the turnout, and the degree of fan interest, surprised even Connie Mack. The A's had sold all their box and reserved seats weeks ago, but despite windy, chilly weather, fans seeking the remaining tickets began arriving early in the morning. They soon grabbed every available seat and all the available standing room. With the large, spirited crowd and the nippy autumn-like weather, it seemed like a World Series game. While Shibe Park had not seen such an enthusiastic gathering in years, the crowd would not have much to cheer about. Yankees right-hander Spud Chandler, making his first opening-day start, allowed the Athletics only five hits and fanned six in chalking up a 5–0 shutout. Chandler, the league's Most Valuable Player in 1943, had been in the Army for most of the past two seasons, appearing in only one game in 1944 and four games in 1945. Today he had the backing of DiMaggio, who celebrated his return with a two-run homer, and another returning Yankees' stalwart, Tommy Henrich, who had a two-run double. The Yanks got all their runs off six-foot-three Russ Christopher, the A's starter who worked the first six innings. Christopher, a right-hander, had been Mack's best pitcher during the last two wartime seasons, with records of 14–14 in 1944 and 13–13 in 1945. Mack was hoping he had a pennant contender this year after struggling through 12 consecutive seasons in the second division. But the A's, who finished last in eight of those years, would do so again this year.

The Yankees were coming off an exhibition season that had been an artistic and financial success. Following three years of spring training on the New Jersey shore, the team had returned to St. Petersburg, Florida, their springtime home since 1925. However, before encamping in St. Pete, they worked out in Panama, their first visit outside the United States since the 1913 club trained in Hamilton, Bermuda. They won 28 of their 42 games, most of which they played before overflow crowds as attendance records were set throughout the Grapefruit League. Leading them, just as he had before the war, was DiMaggio, who pounded opposing pitchers for a .370 average, 19 home runs, and 54 runs batted in. Despite missing three prime years, DiMaggio at 31 seemed ready for his greatest season. Joe had even reclaimed his No. 5 that first baseman Nick Etten had worn for the last three years. With the "big boys" back, Etten (now wearing No. 9), George Stirnweiss, and Johnny Lindell were the Yankees' only repeat starters from the 1945 opener. Even so, three key regulars from the prewar days were missing: shortstop Phil Rizzuto, outfielder Charlie Keller, and second baseman Joe Gordon; all were out with injuries sustained during spring training. Both Rizzuto and Keller were nursing pulled leg muscles (Keller's occurring when he tried to avoid spiking rookie catcher Ferrell Anderson of Brooklyn), and Gordon was recovering from a spiking that had severed a tendon on a finger of his left hand. Thirty-five-year-old Frank Crosetti replaced Rizzuto, Oscar Grimes replaced Gordon, and Lindell replaced Keller. Stirnweiss, who had played shortstop and second base in previous openers, was at third base. Joe Buzas and Don Savage, the left side of the Yankees' infield on Opening Day 1945, were with the Newark Bears, never to return to the big leagues.

Philadelphia's Police and Firemen's Bugle and Drum Corps appeared just before game time to parade to the flagpole and conduct the flag-raising ceremonies. Teams were gradually abandoning the old custom of marching behind the band as part of the opening-day festivities. At most parks, they were replacing it with the more staid practice of standing at attention along the foul lines, as the players were doing here. Although the mayor of Philadelphia, Bernard Samuel, was at the game, he gladly relinquished the honor of throwing out the first ball. That distinction went to Pfc. Roy E. Heikkinen of the U.S. Army's 43rd Division, wounded in the South Pacific. Heikkinen, of Waskish, Minnesota, won the privilege in a poll conducted at the Valley Forge General Hospital where he was undergoing plastic surgery to repair his wounds. The war had been over for only eight months, still too soon for the public to forget those who had fought it, so throughout baseball this Opening Day, clubs were bestowing first-ball honors on wounded veterans. From his box seat behind home plate, with a nurse at his side, Heikkinen tossed the ball to Buddy Rosar, the A's catcher, who caught it and immediately returned it to the bandaged veteran. Rosar would catch everything this year. He was the first major-leaguer to catch in at least 100 games in a season (he caught in 117) and not make an error.

After Christopher set down the first six batters, 38-year-old Bill Dickey led off the third inning with a double down the left-field line. Dickey was in his 17th year with the Yankees, the longest tenure on the team. He would continue to play some after succeeding manager Joe McCarthy in May; however, this would be his final year as an active player. Dickey went to third on Grimes's high chopper that went for an infield single. Second baseman Gene Handley, making his major-league debut at age 31, did well to field the ball, but could not make a play on Grimes. Chandler also hit a high chopper, but this time Handley, skidding on his belly, made the putout at second as Dickey came home with the season's first run. Crosetti reached base on a single between first and second that Handley again did an excellent job getting to, but slipped on the grass and could not make a throw. The runners moved to second and third as Stirnweiss tapped out to Christopher, and both scored easily when Henrich blasted a first-pitch double over the head of right fielder Hal Peck.

DiMaggio's sixth-inning home run with Henrich aboard, extended the Yankees' lead to 5–0. Christopher had retired Joe in his first two at-bats, which pleased the crowd immensely. Now that the war was over and their players were back, the Yankees were again looking like the powerhouses of old. Therefore, it was again okay for the anti–Yankee hatred—and the anti–New York hatred—to resurface around the country. The fans had booed DiMaggio in his earlier appearances—this was, after all, Philadelphia—and as he approached the plate in the sixth, the booing began again. This time Joe silenced it by driving a fastball that sailed between two public address speakers and over the right field wall for the 220th home run of his career. Dick Fowler and Lum Harris kept the Yanks in check over the final three innings.

Tuesday, April 16, 1946

New York	ab	r	h	po	a	e	Philadelphia	ab	r	h	po	a	e
Crosetti ss	4	1	2	3	3	2	Garrison lf	4	0	1	1	0	0
Stirnweiss 3b	4	0	0	2	4	0	Peck rf	3	0	1	4	0	0
Henrich rf	3	1	1	1	0	0	Wallaesa ss	4	0	0	1	1	0
DiMaggio cf	4	1	1	2	0	0	Chapman cf	4	0	0	1	0	1
Etten 1b	4	0	0	8	1	0	McQuinn 1b	4	0	0	11	0	0
Lindell lf	4	0	0	2	0	0	Rosar c	4	0	1	7	0	0
Dickey c	4	1	2	6	1	0	Kell 3b	3	0	1	0	2	0
Grimes 2b	4	0	1	2	2	0	Handley 2b	3	0	1	2	3	0
Chandler p	3	1	0	1	0	0	Christopher p	2	0	0	0	3	0
Total	34	5	7	27	11	2	Fowler p	0	0	0	0	0	0
							ªKonopka	1	0	0	0	0	0
							Harris p	0	0	0	0	0	0
							Total	32	0	5	27	9	1

ªGrounded out for Fowler in eighth inning.

New York	003	002	000–5
Philadelphia	000	000	000–0

Runs batted in—Chandler, Henrich 2, DiMaggio 2. Two-base hits—Dickey, Henrich, Crosetti, Handley. Home run—DiMaggio. Double play—Crosetti, Grimes, and Etten. Left on bases—New York 3; Philadelphia 6. Bases on balls—off Chandler 1, Christopher 1. Struck out—by Chandler 6, Christopher 3, Fowler 4. Hits—off Christopher 6 in 6 innings, Fowler 1 in 2, Harris 0 in 1. Losing pitcher—Christopher. Umpires—Rommel, Boyer and Jones. Time of game—2 hrs. 3 min. Attendance—37,472.

Chandler, 38, used his guile and ability to keep the Athletics' hitters off balance all afternoon. He did his best pitching in the fourth, when the A's loaded the bases with none out. Chandler was in that precarious position mainly because Crosetti, in his haste to make a double play, made one of his two errors on the day. Chandler, the former football player at the University of Georgia, got the first out by retiring center fielder Sam Chapman, the former football All-American from the University of California, on a pop to Grimes. George McQuinn, an always dangerous left-handed hitter, was next. Philadelphia had sent their longtime first baseman Dick Siebert to the Browns to get McQuinn at the close of the 1945 season. Siebert never played for the Browns, or ever again in the major leagues, while McQuinn—after one year in Philadelphia—would join the Yankees. Chandler got McQuinn to bounce to Crosetti, who started an inning-ending double play. After that, the A's came close to scoring only one other time. Rosar and third baseman George Kell hit back-to-back singles with two out in the seventh, the only inning in which Chandler allowed more than one hit. One month into the season, on May 18, Mack would trade Kell, a future Hall-of-Famer, to Detroit for outfielder Barney McCosky.

For Yankee pitchers, who had thrown only one opening-day shutout in the team's first 36 years, this was their fifth in the last eight years. Chandler would finish second in the league in ERA (2.10) and fourth in winning percentage (.714) in 1946. His record of 20–8 gave him a lifetime mark of 100–38 (.725), at that time the highest percentage ever for any pitcher with at least 100 wins.

On May 24, with the Yankees' record at 22–13, manager Joe McCarthy resigned. McCarthy had won eight pennants and seven world championships in his 15 years, but his health was poor and he had never gotten on well with co-owner and general manager Larry MacPhail. Dickey took over and led the club to a 57–48 mark before he too quit. Coach Johnny Neun (8–6) finished out the season.

Joe DiMaggio batted .290, falling below .300 for the first time in his career, as the Yankees (87–67) finished a disappointing third, 17 games behind the champion Boston Red Sox. Nevertheless, they drew 2,265,512 fans to Yankee Stadium, becoming the first team to exceed 2 million in home attendance in a season. Over the objections of team president Ed Barrow, the Yankees' owners installed lights and the first night game at Yankee Stadium was played on May 28, a 2–1 loss to the Washington Senators.

Tuesday, April 15, 1947
Yankee Stadium, New York
Philadelphia 6 New York 1

I have always thought that all men should be free.—Abraham Lincoln

In the week before the 1947 season began, two baseball-related announcements transported the game from the sports pages of the nation's newspapers to its front pages. The first, a one-year suspension of Brooklyn Dodgers manager Leo Durocher for conduct detrimental to baseball, would significantly alter the future course of the game in New York City. The second, Brooklyn's signing of Jackie Robinson to a major-league contract, would immediately change baseball, and ultimately help to transform life in the United States. Commissioner Happy Chandler's suspension of Durocher on April 9 was the culmination of a feud between the Yankees and Dodgers that had simmered throughout spring training. The fracas generated charges and countercharges by Durocher, Brooklyn's Branch Rickey, and the Yankees' Larry MacPhail, Rickey's former friend and protégé and Durocher's one time boss. Durocher and MacPhail made the most damaging allegations, accusing each other of gambling and consorting with known underworld characters. Brooklyn also claimed that MacPhail was tampering when he signed two of Durocher's coaches, Charlie Dressen and John Corriden, to Yankees contracts for 1947. Besides suspending Durocher, Chandler also suspended Dressen for the season's first 30 days and fined both clubs $2,000. The next day, while everyone contemplated the implications of Durocher's suspension, the Dodgers quietly announced they had purchased Robinson's contract from their Montreal Royals farm team in the International League. He would be the first black man in the major leagues since 1884, when catcher Fleetwood Walker played for the Toledo Blue Stockings of the American Association, then a major league. Over the years, race relations would alternately improve and deteriorate in America, but from April 11, 1947, when Robinson trotted out to first base at Ebbets Field for an exhibition game against the Yankees, they would never again be what they had been.

While Robinson was understandably the focus of the media's attention in his first game as a Dodger, the game was also an opportunity for Yankees fans to see their team's new manager, Bucky Harris. MacPhail had signed the veteran Harris on November 5, 1946, following the managerial merry-go-round of 1946 when three different men led the team. Actually, Durocher claimed in his testimony before Commissioner Chandler that MacPhail had attempted to hire him to manage the Yankees, a charge MacPhail emphatically denied. (Conversely, following Durocher's suspension, Rickey offered the Brooklyn managerial job to former Yankees manager Joe McCarthy, who rejected the offer.) The 50-year-old Harris was second in managerial experience only to 84-year-old Connie Mack, having previously managed the Washington Senators (twice), the Detroit Tigers, the Boston Red Sox, and most recently, the Philadelphia Phillies. He was to have made his official Yankees' debut in Washington, where he had won back-to-back pennants in his first two seasons as manager, 1924 and 1925. However, when an all-day rain canceled the game, the Yanks took the train back to New York where they would open at Yankee Stadium against Mack's Philadelphia Athletics—the first time they had opened at home against the A's in 20 years. The cancellation cost Bill Bevens an opening-day start, even though he had a 4–1 record against Philadelphia a year ago. Harris switched to his ace Spud Chandler, who also had a 4–1 mark against the A's in 1946 when the Yanks beat them in 16 of 22 games.

Mack started Canadian-born Phil Marchildon, a 33-year-old right-hander who, during the war, served three years as a gunner with the Royal Canadian Air Force. Marchildon took part in 26 missions against the Nazis before he was shot down over Denmark and spent nine months in a prisoner-of-war camp. He was Philadelphia's biggest winner in 1946 with 13 victories (13–16), although he lost three of his four decisions to the Yankees. Today, however, he pitched an outstanding game against a team expected to be a strong pennant contender. Making strategic use of an excellent curve ball, he beat the Yanks, 6–1, limiting them to just six hits. The Stadium crowd of 39,344 sat mostly silent, as in only one inning could the home team manage more than one hit. New York left nine runners on base, and scored their lone run after the A's had already gotten their six.

The Yankees' lackluster performance followed opening-day ceremonies that were as brief and deficient of color as anyone could remember, literally and figuratively. Even the red, white, and blue bunting, always on display at Stadium openers, was absent, as was much enthusiasm from the crowd. Captain Francis Sutherland and the Seventh Regiment Band did their marching and flag raising, and Dorothy Sarnoff of the New York City Center Opera sang "The Star-Spangled Banner," but it was nevertheless a subdued beginning to what would be a most exciting season. Sergeant Anthony Guzzetta, a Bronx native and a wounded veteran stationed at Fort Jay Hospital, threw out the first ball. It was unusual for the mayor of New York not to perform this task at the season opener, but Mayor William O'Dwyer begged off, citing important city business. In 1946, his first year in office, O'Dwyer, an admitted Dodgers' fan, had attended only their opener. Many suspected that he boycotted the Yankees that year in response to a protest by the Catholic War Veterans. The New York chapter had objected to the Yanks playing their home opener on Good Friday. O'Dwyer did, however, arrange to have 26 guests at this game, all related to the United Nations Security Council. They included Secretary-General Trygve Lie and his daughter Guri, Alexei N. Krasilnikov, the stand-in for Russia's Andrei Gromyko, and Warren Austin, the American ambassador to the United Nations. Also on hand but shunning the spotlight were former president Herbert Hoover and former Yankees president Ed Barrow. After being relegated to a strictly honorary role by MacPhail, Barrow had retired in January. When the Yankees took the field, fans seated near third base were surprised to see umpire Hal Weafer wearing pinstripes on his blue coat. Weafer and first-base umpire Cal Hubbard were to work the opener in Washington but their suitcases, containing their uniforms, were stolen. Hubbard found a spare, but Weafer had to settle for the pinstripes.

Most of the foreign diplomats O'Dwyer invited found the game confusing and boring, saying they would much prefer to see soccer, cricket, or jai alai. While most Americans would find such an idea heretical (and even more so in 1947), from an action standpoint this particular game was a bit boring, especially for Yankees fans. The Yanks pitched, hit, and fielded poorly, and their two biggest stars, Joe DiMaggio and Tommy Henrich, were not in the starting lineup. Only the gentle spring weather prevented the day from being a total loss.

Henrich was out with a sprained wrist, although he was one of the three pinch-hitters Harris employed in an attempt to break through against Marchildon. None of the three—Henrich, rookie third baseman Bobby Brown, or veteran outfielder Frank Colman—was successful. DiMaggio, who missed most of spring training because of problems with his left heel, did participate in pregame fielding and batting practice while wearing a specially constructed shoe. His six batting-practice home runs would be among the few positive events of the afternoon for the home crowd. Henrich and DiMaggio would soon return, but gone permanently was second baseman Joe Gordon. On October 11, 1946, after a poor season in which he batted just .210, MacPhail traded Gordon to the Cleveland Indians for pitcher Allie Reynolds.

Johnny Lindell was in center field replacing DiMaggio, and in right field, in place of Henrich was rookie Yogi Berra. As a late season call-up from the Newark Bears last year, Berra, a left-handed hitter, batted .364 with two home runs in just 22 at-bats. He came to camp as a catcher/outfielder, and while Harris had not yet decided what position he wanted Berra to play, he knew he wanted his bat somewhere in the lineup. The Yankees already had a good left-handed-hitting catcher: Aaron Robinson. Robinson had won the job after returning from the service in mid–1945, hitting .297 in 100 games in 1946 to earn a place on *The Sporting News* combined major-league All-Star team.

One of Chandler's four wins against Philadelphia last year was an opening-day shutout, but this year the A's got on the board early, scoring two runs in the second. After Sam

Chapman beat out an infield single, Barney McCosky, attempting to sacrifice, forced Chapman at second. A single by Buddy Rosar moved McCosky to second and brought to the plate third baseman Hank Majeski, purchased from the Yanks last June. Chandler got Majeski to hit what looked like an inning-ending double play grounder to short. But as Phil Rizzuto bent to field it, the ball went through his legs as McCosky came home. The error proved to be worth two runs as Pete Suder followed with a run-scoring single to left. Philadelphia made it 3–0 in the fifth. Shortstop Eddie Joost singled with one out and went to third as second baseman George Stirnweiss mishandled Elmer Valo's twisting ground ball. Chandler fanned rookie first baseman Ferris Fain, but on the third strike the A's executed a double steal. Joost came home with the unearned run as catcher Robinson tried unsuccessfully to get Valo at second. Fain was making his major-league debut after batting .301 for San Francisco in the Pacific Coast League in 1946. Joost was also new to the Athletics, but he was a veteran who had spent eight years in the National League with the Cincinnati Reds and the Boston Braves. Fain, Joost, second baseman Suder, and third baseman Majeski, playing their first game as a unit today, would in 1949 spark the A's to a record-setting 217 double plays.

Marchildon was pitching so well that whatever hope the Yankees had of catching up vanished when Philadelphia added three more runs in the seventh. A single by Suder, a sacrifice by Marchildon, and Joost's third hit, a double to left, produced one run. Then, after Valo doubled to right to score Joost, Harris made his first pitching change. He brought in Randy Gumpert, who had been with the Athletics as a teenager between 1936 and 1938 before spending four years in the minors and three in the Coast Guard. He reappeared with the Yanks in 1946, winning 11 and losing three. Gumpert allowed a bunt single by Fain and walked Chapman to load the bases. McCoskey's long fly ball scored Valo with the A's sixth and final run. Al Lyons pitched the final two innings for New York, allowing one hit.

The Yanks avoided the ignominy of an opening-day shutout by scoring a hard-earned run in the eighth. Stirnweiss led off by drawing one of Marchildon's five walks. He was forced at second by George McQuinn, signed in the off-season following his release by the Athletics. Philadelphia had to make room at first base for Fain, so they had no problem in releasing McQuinn, who was almost 37 and had batted only .225 in 1946. McQuinn hit well in spring training and won the first base job from Nick Etten, whom the Yankees dropped the day before the opener. Along with Etten, they also released Johnny Murphy, their longtime relief ace who signed with the Red Sox. Charlie Keller's double sent McQuinn to third, and Berra's long fly to McCosky brought him home. It was the only activity of the day for Frank Crosetti, coaching at third in place of the suspended Dressen. Crosetti, who made his debut with the Yanks in 1932, would serve as a player-coach in 1947 and 1948 (he played in only three games in '47 and 17 in '48) before coming a full-time coach in 1949. He would remain a coach through the 1968 season, setting the record for the longest continuous service with the team—37 years.

Tuesday, April 15, 1947

Philadelphia	ab	r	h	po	a	e	New York	ab	r	h	po	a	e
Joost ss	5	2	3	4	1	0	Rizzuto ss	5	0	2	2	1	1
Valo rf	5	1	1	1	0	0	Stirnweiss 2b	2	0	0	2	5	1
Fain 1b	4	0	1	10	0	0	McQuinn 1b	4	1	1	7	1	0
Chapman lf	4	0	1	1	0	0	Keller lf	3	0	1	2	0	0

Philadelphia

	ab	r	h	po	a	e
McCosky cf	4	1	0	3	0	0
Rosar c	4	1	1	8	0	0
Majeski 3b	4	0	0	0	3	0
Suder 2b	4	1	2	0	2	0
Marchildon p	3	0	1	0	2	0
Total	37	6	10	27	8	0

New York

	ab	r	h	po	a	e
Berra rf	4	0	0	1	0	0
Lindell cf	4	0	0	5	0	0
Johnson 3b	2	0	0	1	1	0
ªBrown	1	0	0	0	0	0
Robinson c	3	0	1	6	1	0
Chandler p	2	0	1	0	2	0
Gumpert p	0	0	0	0	0	0
ᵇHenrich	1	0	0	0	0	0
Lyons p	0	0	0	1	0	0
ᶜColman	1	0	0	0	0	0
Total	32	1	6	27	11	2

ªFlied out for Johnson in ninth inning.
ᵇFlied out for Gumpert in seventh inning.
ᶜStruck out for Lyons in ninth inning.

Philadelphia	020	010	300–6
New York	000	000	010–1

Runs batted in—Suder, Joost, Valo, McCosky, Berra. Two-base hits—Joost, Valo, Keller. Stolen bases—Valo, Joost. Sacrifice—Marchildon. Double plays—Rizzuto, Stirnweiss, and McQuinn; Suder, Joost, and Fain. Left on bases—Philadelphia 7; New York 9. Bases on balls—off Chandler 1, Gumpert 1, Marchildon 5. Struck out—by Chandler 4, Marchildon 6, Lyons 2. Hits—off Chandler 8 in 6⅓ innings, Gumpert 1 in ⅔, Lyons 1 in 2. Losing pitcher—Chandler. Umpires—Berry, Hubbard, and Weafer. Time of game—2 hrs. 18 min. Attendance—39,344.

Chandler, a 20-game winner a year ago (20–8), was 9–5 when he developed bone chips in his elbow that ended his career. He was two months short of his 40th birthday when he defeated Washington, 7–3, on July 4 for his final major-league victory. Nevertheless, under the rules of the day that made any pitcher with at least ten complete games eligible for the ERA title, Chandler, with 13 complete games, won the title with an earned run average of 2.46.

In contrast to a dull afternoon at Yankee Stadium, there was plenty of excitement over at Ebbets Field, where the Dodgers, managed by coach Clyde Sukeforth, defeated the Boston Braves, 5–3. Jackie Robinson played first base and went 0–3 with a run scored in his major-league debut.

Powered by a 19-game winning streak, the Yankees (97–67) rolled to their 15th American League pennant, winning by 12 games over the Detroit Tigers. In one of history's most exciting World Series, they defeated the Brooklyn Dodgers in seven games. When the series was over, Larry MacPhail announced he was selling his shares in the club and leaving baseball. Allie Reynolds (19–8) led the team in wins and was second in the American League in winning percentage (.704)—teammate Frank Shea was first. Joe Page had the most saves in the league, with 17, although of course no one knew it at the time. Joe DiMaggio won his third Most Valuable Player Award, again beating out Triple-Crown winner Ted Williams.

Monday, April 19, 1948
Griffith Stadium, Washington
New York 12 Washington 4

A baseball season never really begins; it just sort of emerges out of the accumulated yesterdays.—Lonnie Wheeler

Joe Gordon had been very popular in New York, and Yankees fans reacted angrily to the October 1946 trade that sent him to the Cleveland Indians for pitcher Allie Reynolds. However, the fans would soon change their minds, for the deal would prove to be among the best the club ever made. Gordon, two years older than Reynolds, did have a fine season for the Indians in 1947, and an even better one the next year. In 1948 he teamed with manager/shortstop Lou Boudreau to lead Cleveland to the world championship. However, in 1949 both his batting and fielding skills declined noticeably and, following a mediocre 1950 season, Gordon retired. Meanwhile, Reynolds would have eight rewarding seasons in New York, helping pitch the Yankees to World Series victories in six of them. Overall, he won 131 regular-season games for the Yankees (131–60) and added seven more (7–2) in the Series. In 1947, Reynolds's first year with the team, he had a 19–8 record and pitched more than 240 innings. He was now recognized as the ace of the pitching staff, a designation that earned him the opening-day start at Washington. The Yanks had been rained out of the "presidential opener" in 1945 and 1947, but this year the weather cooperated, and a sellout crowd of 31,728 poured into Griffith Stadium. However, this would be a game that was, in effect, over after the Yankees batted in the first inning. Even before Reynolds made his first pitch, home runs by Tommy Henrich and Reynolds himself had powered the visitors to a seven-run lead, after which they coasted to a 12–4 victory. It was the Yankees' most productive first at-bat of a season ever, topping the five runs they scored against Boston's Cy Young at Hilltop Park in 1904.

For those in the Washington area with access to a television set, WTTG-TV (Channel 5) was televising the game, as they would all of the Senators' 1948 home games. Bob Wolff and Howard Williams were the telecasters. The game was also being televised back to New York over WABD-TV (Channel 5). However, because the overwhelming majority of fans were still getting their baseball via the radio in 1948, three Washington radio stations were broadcasting the game. Fans had a choice of hearing the play-by-play of Arch McDonald and Ray Morgan on WPIK-AM, WWDC-FM, or WASH-FM. In New York, Mel Allen and Russ Hodges could be heard on WINS.

The one-sidedness of today's game was an early indication to Washingtonians that although they had a new manager and some new players, they did not have a club that had improved much over last year's seventh-place bunch. Joe Kuhel, who retired as an active player in 1947 after an 18-year career with the Senators and Chicago White Sox, was the new manager. Kuhel succeeded Ossie Bluege, who had held the job since 1943 when replaced Bucky Harris, who was now the Yankees' manager. After the Senators finished seventh again this season, and eighth in 1949, owner Clark Griffith replaced Kuhel with—Bucky Harris. The biggest change in the Senators was in their outfield, which they had revamped after trading Stan Spence to the Boston Red Sox and losing Buddy Lewis to retirement. (In 1949, Lewis would come out of retirement and play one more year.) Leon Culberson, acquired from Boston in the Spence trade, was now the center fielder, with Sherry Robertson, a converted third baseman, in right. The left fielder was Gil Coan, a youngster who had played a total of 70 games for Washington in 1946–1947. Coan spent most of 1947 with the Chattanooga Lookouts of the Southern Association, batting .340, with 22 home runs and 42 stolen bases. He was among the fastest men in baseball, and the Washington organization expected great things from him.

Yesterday, the Yankees had played and lost their final preseason game to the Brooklyn Dodgers, 5–3, before what was then the largest crowd ever to see an exhibition game. The attendance at Yankee Stadium, on a beautiful Sunday afternoon, was 62,369. Fans of both teams left the park confident that their next game against one another would be in October. A few hours later, the Yanks took the 6:25 train from Pennsylvania Station to Washington. A "presidential opener" was still the biggest baseball event of the year in the Capital, attracting many high-ranking government officials. One interested onlooker this afternoon was Justice Thomas Alan Goldsborough of the United States District Court. Earlier that morning, Goldsborough had found John L. Lewis and his union, the United Mine Workers of America, guilty of civil and criminal contempt for refusing to obey a court order to end their strike. With his work done for the day, Judge Goldsborough was out at the park to enjoy baseball.

At 2:30 P.M. the U.S. Army Band struck up "Hail to the Chief" as President Harry Truman moved into the flag-bedecked presidential box. Accompanying the president were First Lady Bess Truman and their daughter Margaret, while waiting to greet the First Family were Griffith, Commissioner Happy Chandler, and Yankees co-owner Del Webb. American League president Will Harridge, who was supposed to be at the game, was still in Chicago recovering from influenza. Washington pitcher Marino Pieretti joined the group once the game began, sitting in front of Mr. Truman to protect him from foul balls. As the players awaited the president, they lined up along the foul lines, the home team on the first-base side and the visitors on the third-base side. The Senators were sporting their newly designed home uniforms, which featured Yankee-like pinstripes with a large blue "W" outlined in red on the left breast. After a four-year absence, color had returned to their blue stockings with the addition of red and white stripes. With Speaker of the House Joe Martin, the 78-year-old Griffith, and Chandler leading the way, the Army Band marched to the flagpole in center field. There, as the band played the national anthem, managers Harris and Kuhel raised the American flag. After the field was cleared, the president prepared to throw out the first ball. After several feints with his right hand, the ambidextrous Mr. Truman switched and made the toss with his left. Senators pitcher Sid Hudson emerged from the crowd to catch the eagerly sought souvenir just before it hit the ground.

Right-hander Early Wynn was making his second opening-day start for Washington. Last year he pitched a complete game in the Senators' opener at Boston, but lost 7–6. He also started against the Yankees in New York's 1943 opener, although for Washington it had been their second game of the season. Wynn left that game after eight innings with a 4–3 lead, but the Yanks scored two in the last of the ninth against the Senators' bullpen to win the game, 5–4. By 1947, when he won 17 games (17–15) for the seventh-place Senators, Wynn was showing signs of the exceptional pitcher and future Hall of Famer he eventually would become.

George Weiss, the former director of the Yankees' farm system and a member of the organization since 1932, was now the general manager, having succeeded Larry MacPhail. Weiss, an excellent judge of talent, felt that for the Yankees to repeat they needed another starting pitcher, and he was seeking to trade for Wynn. In return, Washington hoped to choose from a group that included infielder (and 1947 World Series hero) Bobby Brown, young pitcher Tommy Byrne, rookie outfielder Cliff Mapes, and minor-league outfielder Hank Bauer. The Yanks specifically balked at trading Bauer, a 25-year-old former marine. Although they had sent him to the American Association's Kansas City Blues and would not recall him until September, Weiss and Harris suspected Bauer one day would be an outstanding player.

However, Wynn did little this afternoon to boost his stock. The Yankees mauled him for 16 hits and all 12 runs. He fell behind, 2–0, after facing just two batters—a walk to

George Stirnweiss and a home run by Henrich—and never recovered. Henrich, a left-handed hitter who normally pulled the ball, lined a fastball over Coan's head into the temporary seats in left field. (The new seats, installed during the off-season, reduced the home-run distance in Griffith Stadium's cavernous left field from 405 feet to 375 feet.) Wynn got Charlie Keller to ground out, but then yielded back-to-back singles to Joe DiMaggio and George McQuinn. Following his third Most Valuable Player Award last year, DiMaggio, who had earned $43,750 for each of his last three active seasons (1942, 1946, and 1947), negotiated a salary increase to $70,000 for 1948. The only player ever to command a higher sum was Babe Ruth; the Yanks paid Ruth $80,000 in 1931. Billy Johnson's infield single brought DiMaggio home to make it 3–0, and after Phil Rizzuto grounded into a force play, Gus Niarhos, the catcher, singled to right scoring McQuinn with the fourth run.

Weiss had traded the Yankees' former number-one catcher, Aaron Robinson, in February. Robinson and pitchers Fred Bradley and Bill Wight went to the White Sox for left-handed pitcher Ed Lopat, another deal that would turn out very beneficially for New York. With Robinson gone, Harris planned to platoon the right-hand hitting Niarhos, a 27-year-old rookie who lost three years to the military, with second-year man Yogi Berra, a left-handed hitter. But Berra was still recovering from a split finger, so Niarhos was behind the plate in the opener. With Rizzuto on third and Niarhos on first, Reynolds stepped in and blasted the first and only home run of his major-league career. It too landed in the newly installed temporary seats, and it raised New York's lead to 7–0. After the game, Kuhel said "Wynn didn't have bad stuff. The Yankees just jumped on him quick, but they're liable to do that to any team." The next day Clark Griffith, who had approved of the shortening of the left field fence very reluctantly, had the temporary seats removed.

In their first at-bat, the Senators pounced on Reynolds for four hits and three runs to cut the lead to 7–3. The first two batters, third baseman Eddie Yost and second baseman Al Kozar, both singled. Yost, a former star at New York University, was in his second full season with Washington; Kozar, who like Culberson came to the Senators in the Spence trade, was playing in his first major-league game. Coan doubled for the third consecutive hit off Reynolds as Yost scored and Kozar held at third. First baseman Mickey Vernon, hoping to make 1948 a comeback season, was next. Vernon had batted just .265 in 1947, a drop of 88 points from his 1946 league-leading .353 average. He hit a long fly ball, but DiMaggio ran it down in deep center field, turned, and threw a perfect strike to the plate. However, it was not in time to get Kozar, who scored Washington's second run. Culberson's single to left brought Coan home with run number three. It would be the closest this game would get. Reynolds got the first two batters in the second, but then walked Yost and Kozar. That got relief ace Joe Page up and throwing in the Yankees' bullpen, situated in foul territory down the left-field line. (Unlike today, managers then felt free to use their best relief pitcher at any time.) Reynolds ended the threat by catching Coan's line drive that was hit head-high right back at him.

The Yanks made it 9–3 in the fourth on a single by Henrich, a long double by Keller, and a single by McQuinn. This was Keller's first game since undergoing surgery for the back problems that had limited him to just 45 games in 1947. He would play in 83 this season, but that would be the highest total he would reach for the remainder of his career.

An outstanding fielding play by McQuinn shut down a Washington rally after they scored their fourth and final run in the fifth inning. The run came on a walk to Vernon, a passed ball by Niarhos, and a single by Culberson. Culberson's single was one of the four he had on the day, which must have impressed Weiss. Three weeks later the Yankees traded outfielder Bud Stewart to Washington to get him, although after the trade Culberson never again played in a big-league game. After Robertson fouled out, Mark Christman had an infield single and the Senators had runners at first and second. Catcher Jake Early followed with a sharply hit ground ball between first and second that the left-handed McQuinn, ranging to his right, speared one-handed and threw to Rizzuto for the force on Christman. Wynn, a good hitting pitcher, batted for himself and fanned.

Monday, April 19, 1948

New York	ab	r	h	po	a	e	Washington	ab	r	h	po	a	e
Stirnweiss 2b	4	1	0	2	1	0	Yost 3b	3	1	2	1	3	2
Henrich rf	5	2	2	3	0	0	Kozar 2b	4	1	1	1	0	0
Keller lf	5	1	2	1	0	0	Coan lf	5	1	1	2	0	1
DiMaggio cf	4	2	2	3	0	0	Vernon 1b	4	1	2	11	2	0
McQuinn 1b	5	1	2	8	1	0	Culberson cf	5	0	4	2	0	0
Johnson 3b	5	1	2	1	2	0	Robertson rf	5	0	0	2	0	0
Rizzuto ss	5	2	2	2	1	0	Christman ss	4	0	1	3	2	0
Niarhos c	5	1	3	6	0	0	Early c	4	0	0	4	1	0
Reynolds p	5	1	1	1	2	0	Wynn p	3	0	0	1	3	0
Total	43	12	16	27	7	0	Garcia p	0	0	0	0	0	0
							Total	37	4	11	27	11	3

```
New York      700    200    003—12
Washington    300    010    000—4
```

Runs batted in—Henrich 2, Johnson 2, Niarhos 2, Reynolds 3, Coan, Vernon, Culberson 2, Keller, McQuinn, Rizzuto. Two-base hits—Yost, Coan, DiMaggio, Niarhos, Keller, Johnson. Home runs—Henrich, Reynolds. Double plays—Vernon, Christman, and Vernon; Johnson, Stirnweiss, and McQuinn. Left on bases—New York 6; Washington 11. Bases on balls—off Wynn 2, Reynolds 5. Struck out—by Wynn 1, Reynolds 5. Hits—off Wynn 16 in 8⅓ innings, Garcia 0 in ⅔. Passed balls—Niarhos, Early. Losing pitcher—Wynn. Umpires—Grieve, Berry, and Hurley. Time of game—2 hrs. 17 min. Attendance—31,728.

Two hits and two Washington errors gave New York their final three runs in the ninth. DiMaggio opened with an easy grounder to Yost who fielded it, but threw wildly past Vernon. Joe continued to second and then scored on a double by Johnson. Rizzuto singled Johnson home and raced around to third when Coan could not come up with the ball. At this point Kuhel mercifully relieved Wynn and brought in Cuban right-hander Ramon Garcia, who was making his major-league debut. Garcia, who spent 1947 pitching for the Havana telephone company, got Niarhos on a fly ball that scored Rizzuto with the 12th and final run. It had been an outstanding opener for Niarhos, three hits and two runs batted in. Six other Yankees had two hits on the day, and only Stirnweiss failed to have at least one. All nine Yankees scored.

Although they stayed in the race almost to the end, the Yankees (94–60) finished third, 2½ games behind Cleveland. The Indians had ended the season in a tie with the Boston Red Sox before defeating them in a one-game play-off, the first play-off in American League history. The close pennant race helped draw a record 2,373,901 to Yankee Stadium. Tommy Henrich led the league in runs (138) and triples (14), and four of his 25 home runs were grand slams—the first he had ever hit in the majors. Joe DiMaggio had another splendid season, batting .320 and leading the league in home runs (39) and RBIs (155). He finished second to Cleveland's Lou Boudreau in the voting for the Most Valuable Player Award. After the season, George Weiss fired Bucky Harris and on October 12 hired Casey Stengel to be the Yankees' new manager.

Tuesday, April 19, 1949
Yankee Stadium, New York
New York 3 Washington 2

All human things are subject to decay,
And, when fate summons, monarchs must obey.—John Dryden

The paths of two baseball legends intersected at Yankee Stadium on Opening Day 1949 when the Yankees said goodbye to Babe Ruth and hello to Casey Stengel. The day began with the dedication of a memorial to Ruth, who died of throat cancer on August 16, 1948, and ended with Tommy Henrich, playing Ruth's old position, hitting a ninth-inning home run to give the Yanks a dramatic, 3–2, victory over the Washington Senators. Henrich's two-out blast thrilled a Stadium crowd of 40,075 that included Ruth's widow Claire and his old boss Ed Barrow, and it made for a successful debut for Stengel. The Yankees' new manager survived the "jinx" of being presented with flowers before the game to begin the most successful managerial tour in baseball history. In his 12 years with the Yankees, he would win ten pennants and seven world championships.

Stengel's appointment to manage the Yankees last fall had surprised the baseball world, despite frequent rumors that it was going to happen. What many of the surprised failed to realize was that general manager George Weiss had wanted Stengel for the position ever since the final years of Joe McCarthy's reign. He tried to hire him in 1947, but Larry MacPhail, then the general manager (and co-owner), wanted Bucky Harris. MacPhail retired after the '47 season, but because the Yankees had won the World Series under Harris's leadership, Weiss felt obliged to retain him. But when the team fell to third in 1948, Weiss fired Harris and brought Stengel to New York. The announcement on October 12 came exactly 25 years after one of Stengel's finest moments as a player. It was on October 12, 1923, that Stengel's seventh-inning home run off the Yanks' Sam Jones at Yankee Stadium gave his Giants a 1–0 victory in game three of the World Series.

Following his retirement as an active player, Stengel had served two mediocre managerial stints in the National League, with Brooklyn (1934–1936) and Boston (1938–1943), never finishing in the first division. However, since 1944 he had been managing successfully in the minor leagues, and in 1948 led the Oakland Oaks to the Pacific Coast League pennant. Still, Stengel's reputation was that of a loser and a clown. Even on his memorable 1923 home run he had thumbed his nose at Colonel Jacob Ruppert as he rounded the bases, upsetting not only the Yankees' dignified owner, but also his team and its fans. Several New York sportswriters openly criticized Weiss's choice. They were of the opinion that Stengel, a lifetime National Leaguer, had neither the ability, the temperament, nor the *gravitas* to manage the legendary New York Yankees. Stengel had signed a two-year contract, but few expected him to last beyond that, if even that long. He was thought of as an interim manager whose club would finish well behind the favored Boston Red Sox.

On the advice of Jim Turner, his new pitching coach, Stengel chose veteran left-hander Ed Lopat to pitch the opener. Lopat, who won 17 games (17–11) in 1948, his first with the Yankees, had started one other opener. In 1947, pitching for the White Sox, he shut out Cleveland and Bob Feller, 2–0. Ray Scarborough had pitched the Senators' opener at home yesterday, defeating Philadelphia, 3–2. This afternoon, manager Joe Kuhel was going with right-hander Sid Hudson, who started and lost the 1942 opener to the Yankees at Griffith

Stadium, a 7–0 shutout by Red Ruffing. Last year, in the second game of the season, Hudson beat the Yanks, 9–1, in Washington, spoiling Lopat's Yankees' debut.

Stengel's club entered the season after compiling a lackluster 13–14–1 record in the Grapefruit League. Through it all, the 58-year-old manager often appeared unsure of himself as he attempted to evaluate his personnel and put together a starting lineup. It was a task made more difficult by a stream of injuries that had team physician Dr. Sidney Gaynor and trainer Gus Mauch continually ministering to the sick and wounded. Injuries would remain an obstacle for the Yankees throughout the tumultuous 1949 season, a season in which every regular but Phil Rizzuto would miss a significant amount of playing time. Foremost among their spring injury problems was the one to Joe DiMaggio's right heel. Although Dr. George Bennett of Baltimore's Johns Hopkins Hospital had removed a bone spur from the heel in November, it began causing DiMaggio pain from the first day of training camp. Finally, on April 10, after a game at Greenville, Texas, DiMaggio left the club and returned to Johns Hopkins. Because of the discomfort in the heel, he had batted just 31 times with seven hits for a .226 average. After spending a week in the hospital, DiMaggio rejoined the club and was at the opener, although not in uniform. Dressed in a blue suit and camel's hair coat, he sat in the dugout before the game, surrounded as always by a huge crowd of reporters and photographers. He had now missed six Opening Days in his 11 years with the Yankees, but this absence, which would be a long one, was particularly disturbing to him. DiMaggio, whose 1949 contract for $100,000 made him the game's highest-paid player ever, was aware of what he meant to the Yankees and how much the other players depended on him. He was more than just their leader; as his ex-manager Bucky Harris once said, "Since DiMaggio has been with the Yankees, he has been the Yankees." Bob Porterfield, a highly regarded young pitcher injured in the final weekend series with the Brooklyn Dodgers, was another Yankee casualty watching the game in civilian clothes.

Johnny Lindell was to be DiMaggio's replacement in center field, but because he was still nursing a swollen ankle, newcomer Gene Woodling got the start. New York's outfield situation became even more critical during batting practice when left fielder Charlie Keller pulled a muscle in his right side while swinging at a pitch. Stengel scratched Keller from the lineup and replaced him with rookie Hank Bauer. Keller's ongoing back problems limited him to just 144 plate appearances in 1949 and led to his release after the season ended. He would play with Detroit for the next two years, but then finish his career as a Yankee, playing two games in 1952.

The Yankees were starting an all-veteran infield, except for first base, where left-hand hitting Dick Kryhoski, up from the Kansas City Blues, was making his major-league debut. Rizzuto and George Stirnweiss were the double-play combo, as they had been since 1947; and at third was Bobby Brown, a .300 hitter in each of the last two seasons. Brown, who was attending medical school in the off-season, would become a noted cardiologist and then, in 1984, president of the American League. Stengel had planned to open with veterans at all the infield positions as far back as training camp in St. Petersburg. However, his notion of converting right fielder Henrich to first base was temporarily negated by DiMaggio's injury. (Stengel would make the switch later in the season.)

Fans arriving at the game by car discovered the cost of parking in the lots outside Yankee Stadium had doubled from 50 cents in 1948 to a dollar this year. Those who spent ten cents for the Yankees' official program and scorecard found much more information contained within. One welcome innovation was a list of all American League pitchers, with their uniform numbers, which would help the scoreboard watchers find who was pitching in the league's other games. The fans were delighted to see former catcher Bill Dickey back in uniform. Stengel had hired him to tutor Yogi Berra in the intricacies of the catching position, and to serve as the first-base coach. Frank Crosetti, another fan favorite and Dickey's former longtime teammate, was the third-base coach.

The pregame ceremonies began with Captain Eugene Labarre leading the New York City Police Department Band on a march from the left-field bullpen to home plate. From there they began the parade to the center-field flagpole accompanied by an entourage that included New York governor Thomas E. Dewey, his secretary Paul E. Lockwood, Mayor William O'Dwyer, Bronx borough president James J. Lyons, Yankees co-owners Del Webb and Dan Topping, and Bishop Stephen J. Donohue, who was representing Francis Cardinal Spellman. Following this distinguished group, in columns of two, were the Yankees and the Senators.

The tributes to Ruth began after a marine color guard raised the flag and Lucy Monroe sang the national anthem. Mel Allen served as master of ceremonies as wreaths were placed at the monuments and plaques to Jacob Ruppert, Miller Huggins, and Lou Gehrig, located in the deepest part of center field. Webb and Topping put a wreath at the plaque of their predecessor, Colonel Ruppert, while Ed Barrow and Mr. Lyons placed wreaths in front of the monuments to Huggins and Gehrig. Then Claire Ruth, with her daughters Dorothy and Julia at her side, unveiled the monument to the Babe. Bishop Donohue blessed it, and Governor Dewey and Mayor O'Dwyer laid wreaths from the American and National Leagues at its base. Dan Daniel of the *New York World-Telegram,* representing the New York sportswriters, made a short speech about what Ruth had meant to baseball, and then Miss Monroe sang "Auld Lang Syne" to conclude the unveiling ceremonies. Just before game time, J. Paul Carey II, the treasurer of the Babe Ruth Foundation, presented a check for $107,500 to Mayor O'Dwyer. The mayor immediately turned it over to Mefford Runyon, the vice president of the American Cancer Society. As a final salute to the Babe, Allen introduced the current baseball team at St. Mary's Industrial School in Baltimore. The crowd gave a vigorous cheer for the school where Ruth had learned the game as a boy. Gary Simpson, the St. Mary's captain, had the honor of throwing out the first ball, and then at 2:30 P.M. on this bright but cool afternoon, the game began.

Both Hudson and Lopat pitched effectively, if not efficiently, throughout. Hudson, who allowed runners in every inning except the fifth, gave up nine hits and walked seven, while stranding 11. Lopat was touched for eight hits—three by Gil Coan—but walked only two. The Yankees got the game's first run in the third inning. Rizzuto led off with a single, his second of the game, and went to third on Woodling's single. After Henrich failed to deliver for the second time—he struck out with two on in the first—Bauer hit a scoring fly ball to Coan in left. Although the right-hand hitting Bauer and the left-hand hitting Woodling were both in the starting lineup today, it would not often be that way. Over the next six years they frequently would have to share playing time in Stengel's platoon system. Both hated it and both constantly complained about it, but it was a system under which both prospered. Woodling had been playing professionally since 1940, with two years out (1944–1945) for service in the U.S. Navy. He had been an outstanding minor league hitter, yet had played in fewer than a hundred major-league games with the Cleveland Indians and Pittsburgh Pirates. In eight minor-league seasons, Woodling won four batting crowns: with Mansfield of the Ohio State League in 1940 (.398), Flint of the Michigan State League in 1941 (.394), Wilkes-Barre of the Eastern League in 1943 (.344), and with the Pacific Coast League's San Francisco Seals (.385) last year.

Washington tied the score in the fifth with the help of an outfield that was still wet from the rain that had fallen earlier in the week. A slippery spot caused Bauer to skid while fielding Al Evans's hit, which was scored a double. Evans came home on Hudson's single to center. The Senators went ahead, 2–1, in the sixth when after Lopat retired the first two batters, newly acquired first baseman Eddie Robinson homered into the right-field seats. Robinson had come from the world champion Indians in December, along with pitchers Joe Haynes and Ed Klieman. In return, the Indians received Early Wynn and Mickey Vernon. It was a poor deal for Washington, one that contributed to the Senators losing 104 games and finishing last this year.

Yogi Berra's two-out pinch single in the home seventh brought the Yankees even at 2–2. Berra, suffering from the flu, had been sitting on the bench all afternoon before Stengel sent him up to hit for Bauer. This was the second consecutive year Berra had not caught the opener; he sat out the 1948 inaugural with a split finger. Gus Niarhos, his replacement in both games, had three hits in the '48 opener, and had a perfect afternoon today—a single and three walks. Berra batted with Rizzuto on second and Woodling on first. Each had walked, although both Hudson and Evans thought the full-count pitch to Woodling was a strike. When plate umpire Ed Rommel called it ball four, Evans loudly disagreed while Hudson slammed his glove to the ground. Hudson recovered his composure to get Henrich on a fly to Clyde Vollmer and had two strikes on Berra before Yogi lined a single to center that scored Rizzuto.

Tuesday, April 19, 1949

Washington	ab	r	h	po	a	e	New York	ab	r	h	po	a	e
Coan lf	4	0	3	2	0	0	Stirnweiss 2b	4	0	1	3	0	0
Dente ss	4	0	1	4	2	0	Rizzuto ss	4	2	2	4	5	0
Lewis rf	3	0	0	1	0	0	Woodling cf	4	0	1	2	0	0
Vollmer cf	4	0	0	2	0	0	Henrich rf	5	1	1	1	0	0
Yost 3b	3	0	0	0	1	0	Bauer lf	3	0	0	1	0	0
Robinson 1b	4	1	1	10	1	0	ªBerra	1	0	1	0	0	0
Kozar 2b	4	0	1	1	0	0	Lindell lf	0	0	0	1	0	0
Evans c	4	1	1	5	2	0	Brown 3b	3	0	1	0	2	0
Hudson p	3	0	1	1	1	0	Kryhoski 1b	4	0	1	10	1	0
Total	33	2	8	26	7	0	Niarhos c	1	0	1	4	1	0
							Lopat p	4	0	0	1	1	0
							Total	33	3	9	27	10	0

*Two out when winning run scored.
ªSingled for Bauer in seventh inning.

Washington	000	011	000–2
New York	001	000	101–3

Runs batted in—Bauer, Hudson, Robinson, Berra, Henrich. Two-base hit—Evans. Home runs—Robinson, Henrich. Stolen base—Coan. Double plays—Kryhoski, Rizzuto, and Lopat; Kozar and Robinson. Left on bases—Washington 6; New York 11. Bases on balls—off Lopat 2, Hudson 7. Struck out—by Lopat 3, Hudson 5. Umpires—Rommel, Passarella, Boyer, and Hurley. Time of game—2 hrs. 23 min. Attendance—40,075.

Lopat did his best pitching in the final three innings with help from Henrich, who made a marvelous running catch in front of the bleachers against Buddy Lewis leading off the eighth. (Lewis, a longtime Senator (1935–1941, 1945–1947), had been out of baseball in 1948 building up his automobile agency in Gastonia, North Carolina.) The game seemed destined for extra innings when Hudson retired the first two Yankees in the ninth. Evans threw out Rizzuto, trying to bunt his way on, and first baseman Robinson took care of Woodling's foul pop. That brought up Henrich, who had failed to deliver in his three previous at-bats, each one with two runners on base. But he didn't fail this time. After taking a strike and then a ball, Henrich deposited Hudson's next pitch into the lower deck in right to give the Yankees the victory—an appropriate ending for this memorable occasion. It was an extremely tough loss for Hudson, the first of his 17 for the season that tied him for the league high with teammate Paul Calvert and the St Louis Browns' Ned Garver. Henrich would continue to deliver in the clutch all season, earning the name given to him by Mel Allen: "Old Reliable." Allen, incidentally, had a new sidekick on his broadcasts this season. Curt Gowdy had replaced Russ Hodges, who was now calling games for the New York Giants.

After missing the first 65 games of the season, Joe DiMaggio made a spectacular comeback and helped lead New York (97–57) to a dramatic pennant victory over the Boston Red Sox. The Yankees beat the Red Sox in the final two games of the season to finish one game ahead of them. They won the first of what would be five consecutive World Series, defeating the Brooklyn Dodgers four games to one. Game One, just like the season's opening game, was won on a ninth-inning home run by Tommy Henrich. Boston's Ted Williams won the Most Valuable Player Award, with Yankees' Phil Rizzuto finishing second, Joe Page third, and Henrich sixth.

VI

1950–1959

The New York Yankees dominated baseball in the 1950s like no team had done before or is likely ever to do again. They won eight pennants and six World Series in that ten-year span, all under the leadership of Casey Stengel. While prewar Yankees such as Tommy Henrich (in 1950) and Joe DiMaggio (in 1951) retired early in the decade, Phil Rizzuto continued to star at shortstop until the mid–50s. Of the postwar Yankees, Hank Bauer, Joe Collins, Johnny Mize, and Gene Woodling contributed to each of the five consecutive pennants from 1949 to 1953, while Yogi Berra was a major force in those five, and also the four from 1955 to 1958.

Mickey Mantle came up in 1951, replaced DiMaggio in 1952, and eventually succeeded him as the team's leader and biggest star. Whitey Ford had joined the team in mid-1950, but missed the next two seasons while serving in the army during the Korean War. He came back in 1953 to join the rotation of accomplished but aging veterans Allie Reynolds, Vic Raschi, and Ed Lopat. Soon the three old-timers were gone, and Ford assumed the role of staff ace.

Later in the decade, trades brought Bob Turley, Don Larsen, Clete Boyer, Bobby Shantz, and Hector Lopez to New York. Meanwhile, the Yankees' ever-productive farm system sent them Elston Howard, Bill Skowron, Billy Martin, Bobby Richardson, and Tony Kubek. With the 1955 arrival of Howard, their first black player, the Yankees left the dwindling group of non-racially integrated teams.

In 1958, the Dodgers and the Giants deserted New York for California, leaving the Yankees as the only team in town. Nevertheless, attendance continued to decline as it had done since the Yanks drew more than 2 million for each of the five years from 1946 to 1950.

Tuesday, April 18, 1950
Fenway Park, Boston
New York 15 Boston 10

Baseball is only dull to dull minds.—Red Smith

Some baseball games have an impact on the players and the fans that extends far beyond the final score. The ebb and flow of the game, its shifting momentum, and the manner in which it is decided can have lasting consequences—especially for the players. The Yankees and Red Sox played such a game at Fenway Park to open the 1950 season. Trailing 9–0 after five innings, the Yanks staged a sensational comeback (which included a nine-run eighth inning) to stun the Red Sox, 15–10. When co-owner Dan Topping congratulated Casey Stengel on his team's stirring comeback, the Yankees' manager said, "We got a good ball club. But the Sox have a good ball club, too. When two good clubs play this game, some amazing things can happen." Some amazing things surely did happen in this three-and-a-half-hour battle in which Stengel and Boston's Joe McCarthy made liberal use of their rosters. Stengel used five pinch hitters among the 20 players he employed, while McCarthy called on six different pitchers in an attempt to stop the New York onslaught. The game was the first of a three-day, four-game series (including a Patriots' Day double-header) that was Boston's most eagerly anticipated season-opening series in memory. Besides their normal hatred for the Yankees, Bostonians were still resentful at the manner in which the New Yorkers had "stolen" the 1949 pennant from them. The Red Sox had needed just a split in the season's final two games at Yankee Stadium to win the flag, but lost both games. Because these two teams again figured to wage a season-long battle for the American League title, today's defeat had to have a psychologically adverse effect on the Red Sox, who may have wondered just what it took to beat these Yankees.

Midway through the game, when the score was 9–0, it appeared the Yankee record for a lopsided shutout defeat was in jeopardy. Back on July 15, 1907, the Chicago White Sox had crushed them 15–0. (Coincidentally, just 16 days into this season, on May 4, Chicago would again beat them, 15–0.) For the 31,822 fans at Fenway, Boston's huge lead had made it a marvelous afternoon. Moreover, in addition to their pleasure at watching what portended to be a humiliating defeat for the despised invaders, they were watching it in weather that was absolutely balmy. However, it was not balmy enough for some Bostonians—women especially—who remained distrustful of the New England spring. Most of the women in the more expensive seats carried fur capes and jackets or spring topcoats. This was not so in the bleachers, where the fans of both genders were generally younger and there were very few coats or jackets of any kind. The beautiful weather was also perfect for the citywide cleanup that was beginning in Boston today. It was even warm enough for the female models recruited to publicize the event by scrubbing the pavements of Boston Common to wear bathing suits. Sailors stationed in the area were also out scrubbing the Common, although not in bathing suits.

Billy Boyle's Cloverleaf Club Band entertained the crowd prior to the game before taking their seats behind the visitor's bullpen in right field. Massachusetts Governor Paul A. Dever threw out the first ball; however, the highlight of the pregame ceremonies came when Commissioner A. B. "Happy" Chandler presented Ted Williams with his 1949 Most Valuable Player Award. Williams, who with his reported $125,000 salary had replaced Joe DiMaggio as baseball's highest-paid player, received a thunderous ovation from the adoring crowd. For the Yankees, the most memorable pregame occurrence resulted in a potentially disastrous blow to their pennant hopes. While throwing batting practice, pitcher Bob Porterfield, whom Stengel counted on to be in the starting rotation this year, was hit on the left shin by Bobby Brown's line drive. Trainer Gus Mauch immediately began to apply hot and cold compresses to the shin, which was badly bruised but, as X-rays later revealed, had no break in the bone.

The Red Sox ripped into Yankees starter Allie Reynolds for three runs in the first inning, with five of their first six batters hitting safely. After Dom DiMaggio and Johnny Pesky singled, Williams—who rarely hit to left—doubled off the wall out there to score DiMaggio. Run-scoring singles by Vern Stephens and Bobby Doerr followed. Boston stretched their lead to 4–0 on Williams's RBI single in the second, and then drove Reynolds out with a five-run fourth. The final two runs came on first baseman Billy Goodman's long home run into the right-field bleachers off reliever Fred Sanford. Although Goodman had batted .310 and .298 in his first two seasons, this was only his second major-league home run—not the kind of home-run production teams expected from a first baseman. So when Goodman suffered an injury on May 1, the Red Sox recalled slugger Walt Dropo from the American Association's Louisville Colonels. Dropo, a powerful right-handed batter, fit well in Boston's power-packed lineup and continued as their first baseman even after Goodman's return. He led the club in home runs with 34, and his 144 runs batted in tied teammate Stephens for the major-league high. Dropo easily outdistanced Yankees pitcher Whitey Ford to win the league's Rookie of the Year Award. Meanwhile, Goodman went on to lead the league in batting (.354) while playing at each of the other infield positions and in the outfield. Goodman, whose opponents in 1950 referred to him as a "one-man bench," is still the only non-designated hitter ever to win a batting title without having a regular fielding position.

While Boston was pounding Reynolds and Sanford for nine runs, left-hander Mel Parnell, 25–7 in 1949, had limited the Yanks to just one hit through five innings. That was by Joe DiMaggio, who led off the second with a triple on a long drive to center beyond the reach of his brother Dom. But, with a man on third and nobody out, Parnell demonstrated why he was the league's leading winner a year ago. It took him half an hour, but he got out of the inning without DiMaggio moving off third base. First he struck out Yogi Berra. Then, trying to be too careful, he walked third baseman Billy Johnson and left fielder Johnny Lindell to load the bases. The next batter was Jerry Coleman, who a year ago as a rookie had supplanted George Stirnweiss at second base; Parnell got him on a pop-up. Although it was only the second inning, the Yankees, trailing, 4–0, had the bases loaded with two outs and the pitcher due up. Yet Stengel allowed Reynolds to bat and Parnell easily retired him on a ground ball, stranding the three runners.

Despite Fenway Park's reputation as a place where no lead was ever thought to be "safe," the Yanks, trailing Boston's best pitcher by nine runs, looked like a beaten team. Even when they broke through for four runs in the sixth, it appeared to be too little too late. Tommy Henrich started the sixth-inning uprising with a triple and scored on a single by Hank Bauer. Parnell retired DiMaggio, but one of his pitches to Berra came too far inside and hit Yogi. Johnson lashed a run-scoring double, and Lindell brought Berra and Johnson home with a single. The year 1950 would be the last active season for Henrich, a player who exemplified everything admirable about the Yankees of his era. Because of his bad knees, he was now strictly a first baseman, and was even wearing a new mitt. It was a George McQuinn model, which conformed with the recently introduced restriction that limited the spread between the thumb and palm of a first baseman's mitt to four inches. Today was also the first day that another edict from the league office would be in effect. This one, which called for the umpires to more strictly enforce the balk rule, was much more controversial than the design of a first baseman's glove. However, despite the fears of many pitchers, umpires quickly reverted to calling balks no differently than they had in the past. There may have been one exception. On May 3, they called the Yankees' Vic Raschi for four in a game against Chicago.

Boston added a run off reliever Don Johnson in the seventh on a single and three walks. They could have had more. With two outs and the bases loaded, catcher Matt Batts, subbing for the injured Birdie Tebbetts, drove a ball to deep right-center field. DiMaggio, who had been shading the right-hand hitting Batts to left, sprinted across the outfield and with his back to the plate made a glove-handed catch in front of the Yankees' bullpen. "I really got only about a quarter of the ball in my glove," DiMaggio said after the game. The play was truly sensational, and though it cost their team three runs, the Red Sox fans applauded it generously. DiMaggio, often out of the lineup on Opening Day, was having an outstanding game, which followed a productive and mostly healthy exhibition season. Besides his marvelous play in the seventh, DiMaggio made two other fine running catches and in the fourth inning he threw out Al Zarilla at third base. At the plate he had three hits, including a double and a triple. He even received a plaque from the Boston players, presented to him before the game by Doerr. The memento was to have been presented at Yankee Stadium on "Joe DiMaggio Day," October 1, 1949, but was not ready then.

Down 10–4, the Yanks began their memorable eighth inning with Berra's single to left. Swinging at a pitch out of the strike zone, he bounced it by shortstop Stephens. Johnson drew a walk, but Lindell went down on a fly ball for the first out. During the Yankees' uprising in the sixth, Stengel had tried to prolong it by pinch-hitting for his number eight and nine hitters, Coleman and Sanford. Oddly, he had used two left-handed batters against the left-hander Parnell. Both failed to deliver: Dick Wakefield struck out and Bobby Brown grounded out. Although he had the veteran Stirnweiss on the bench, Stengel used rookie Billy Martin to replace Coleman at second base. Martin had been with the Oakland Oaks of the Pacific Coast League for the past two seasons, the first one under Stengel, who was very fond of the fiery 21-year-old. Now, with two on and one out, Martin, in his first big-league at-bat, smacked a double off the left-field wall to score Berra. Stengel sent Johnny Mize, another left-handed hitter, up to bat for the pitcher. The Yankees had purchased Mize from the crosstown Giants for $40,000 last August because Stengel felt that—even at age 36—Mize could still hit and would be of help in the stretch drive. He was, and he also delivered hits in his two pinch-hitting appearances in the World Series against the Dodgers. He came through again today, doubling down the right-field line to score the two base runners and make the score, 10–7.

By now the fans were beginning to worry—and so was McCarthy, who replaced Parnell with Walt Masterson, a veteran right-hander. While Masterson made his way to the mound, Stengel sent Jackie Jensen in to run for Mize. It was the first big-league appearance for Jensen, a former All-American running back from the University of California. Masterson got Phil Rizzuto for the second out, but Henrich—bad knees notwithstanding—got his second triple of the game, which scored Jensen. Gene Woodling hit for Bauer, and while he was at bat, Masterson threw a wild pitch that allowed Henrich to score. New York now trailed by just one run. After Woodling drew a walk and DiMaggio singled, McCarthy brought in Earl Johnson, a left-hander, to face Berra. Yogi, batting for the second time in the inning, got a single to short on a slow grounder that Stephens did not play well. Stephens's defensive lapse confirmed a belief among the Yankees' players that McCarthy was playing Stephens and Pesky in the wrong positions. They believed the Sox would be stronger defensively with Pesky at short and Stephens at third. That may have been true; however, the Red Sox felt that defense was not their major weakness vis-à-vis the Yankees—it was not having a relief pitcher comparable to Joe Page. The man they hoped would fill that role was Al Papai, a 32-year-old right-hander who had pitched for the St. Louis Browns in 1949. With Billy Johnson at the plate, and the bases loaded, McCarthy brought Papai in to replace Earl Johnson. Papai ran the count full before the Yankees' third baseman lashed a two-run single to center that put his team ahead, 11–10. Following a walk to Lindell that reloaded the bases, Martin singled, also on a 3–2 pitch, to drive in two more runs.

(Martin is the first player ever to have two hits in an inning in his first big-league game.) With New York's lead at 13–10, right-hander Charley Schanz, also making his Red Sox debut, relieved Papai. Schanz got Jim Delsing, batting for Jensen, for the final out of the inning. The nine runs the Yankees scored in the eighth inning remains their opening-day one-inning best.

The Yanks picked up two more runs in the ninth against Dave Ferriss, a two-time 20-game winner pitching his final big-league game. A double by DiMaggio drove in one and Berra's third consecutive single scored the other. As if to prove the Red Sox analysis of the differences between the two teams correct, Page, in contrast to the ineffectual relief pitching by the home team, mowed down the Sox in one-two-three order in the eighth and ninth innings to preserve the victory. Don Johnson got the win, his final one as a Yankee. At the June 15 trading deadline, the Yanks sent him to the Browns in an eight-player trade that also included Stirnweiss, Delsing, and pitcher Duane Pillette. Page had not been pitching well, and general manager George Weiss made the deal so Stengel could get two relief pitchers he wanted: right-hander Tom Ferrick and left-hander Joe Ostrowski. New York also received two throw-ins whom they sent to the minors: pitcher Sid Schacht and third baseman Leo Thomas. Earlier, in May, the Yanks sold Lindell to the St. Louis Cardinals. Lindell, like Stirnweiss, had been with the Joe McCarthy Yankees, and Stengel was working to put his own stamp on the team.

Tuesday, April 18, 1950

New York	ab	r	h	po	a	e	Boston	ab	r	h	po	a	e
Rizzuto ss	4	1	0	1	1	0	D. DiMaggio cf	5	2	2	3	0	0
Henrich 1b	6	2	2	7	0	0	Pesky 3b	5	2	2	1	5	0
Bauer rf	4	1	1	2	0	0	Williams lf	3	3	2	2	0	0
eWoodling	0	1	0	0	0	0	Stephens ss	6	1	3	2	1	0
Mapes rf	1	0	0	0	0	0	Zarilla rf	5	0	2	2	0	0
J. DiMaggio cf	6	2	3	7	1	0	Doerr 2b	4	1	3	2	1	0
Berra c	5	3	3	6	0	0	Goodman 1b	4	1	1	10	0	0
B. Johnson 3b	4	3	2	2	1	0	Batts c	5	0	0	5	0	0
Lindell lf	2	0	1	1	0	0	Parnell p	2	0	0	0	2	0
Coleman 2b	2	0	0	1	2	0	Masterson p	0	0	0	0	0	0
aWakefield	1	0	0	0	0	0	E. Johnson p	0	0	0	0	0	0
Martin 2b	2	1	2	0	0	0	Papai p	0	0	0	0	0	0
Reynolds p	1	0	0	0	0	0	Schanz p	0	0	0	0	0	0
Sanford p	1	0	0	0	2	0	gStringer	1	0	0	0	0	0
bBrown	1	0	0	0	0	0	Ferriss p	0	0	0	0	0	0
D. Johnson p	0	0	0	0	0	0	Total	40	10	15	27	9	0
cMize	1	0	1	0	0	0							
dJensen	0	1	0	0	0	0							
fDelsing	1	0	0	0	0	0							
Page p	0	0	0	0	0	0							
Total	42	15	15	27	7	0							

aCalled out on strikes for Coleman in sixth inning.
bGrounded out for Sanford in sixth inning.
cDoubled for D. Johnson in eighth inning.
dRan for Mize in eighth inning.
eWalked for Bauer in eighth inning.
fFlied out for Jensen in eighth inning.
gGrounded out for Schanz in eighth inning.

New York	000	004	092–15
Boston	310	500	100–10

Runs batted in—Williams 2, Stephens 2, Doerr 2, Zarilla, Goodman 3, J. DiMaggio, Berra, Henrich, Bauer, B. Johnson 3, Lindell, 2, Martin 3, Mize 2. Two-base hits—Williams, Stephens, B. Johnson, Martin, Mize, J. DiMaggio. Three-base hits—J. DiMaggio, Henrich 2. Home run—Goodman. Double play—Sanford, Coleman, and Henrich. Left on bases—New York 9; Boston 13. Bases on balls—off Parnell 5, Reynolds 4, Sanford 1, D. Johnson 5, Masterson 1, Papai 1, Ferriss 1. Struck out—by Parnell 4, Reynolds 3, Page 1, Ferriss 1. Hits—off Reynolds 10 in 3 innings (pitched to four batters in fourth), Sanford 3 in 2, D. Johnson 2 in 2, Page 0 in 2, Parnell 8 in 7 ⅓, Masterson 2 in ⅓, E. Johnson 1 in 0 (pitched to one batter), Papai 2 in 0 (pitched to three batters), Schanz 0 in ⅓, Ferriss 2 in 1. Hit by pitcher—by Parnell (Berra). Wild pitch—Masterson. Winning pitcher—D. Johnson. Losing pitcher—Masterson. Umpires—McGowan, McKinley, Hurley, and Honochick. Time of game—3 hrs. 28 min. Attendance—31,822.

For the first time ever, four American League teams finished with more than 90 wins, but the Yankees (98–56) finished first, three games ahead of the Detroit Tigers. The Boston Red Sox were third despite setting a major-league record by scoring 625 runs at home. The Yanks swept the Philadelphia Phillies in the World Series, although three of the four wins were by one run. Phil Rizzuto had his finest season ever, batting .324 and winning the Most Valuable Player Award; Yogi Berra finished third. Berra's 192 hits set the American League record for most hits in a season by a catcher. Vic Raschi led the league in winning percentage with a .724 mark (21–8).

Tuesday, April 17, 1951
Yankee Stadium, New York
New York 5 Boston 0

O, young Lochinvar is come out of the West. —Sir Walter Scott

In the spring of 1951, three young minor-leaguers, none of who had played above the Double A level, graduated from Casey Stengel's first "rookie school" onto the Yankees' roster. The school, held during the Yankees' spring training in Phoenix (they had arranged a one-year swap of training sites with the New York Giants), resulted in the promotion of pitcher Tom Morgan, infielder Gil McDougald, and shortstop-turned-outfielder Mickey Mantle. The Yankees had invited the 20-year-old Morgan to spring training because of his impressive 17–8 record with the Class A Binghamton (New York) Triplets in 1950. To everyone's surprise, he emerged as the club's most effective pitcher during spring training, leading Stengel to select him to pitch the "presidential opener" in Washington. Morgan, in just his third year as a professional, would have been only the ninth pitcher in the twentieth century (and the first Yankee) to make his major-league debut as an opening-day starter. Unfortunately, bad weather canceled the game and his debut. Stengel had intended to follow Morgan with Vic Raschi in the home opener the next day against Boston, and despite the rainout he stayed with that design. Raschi's lifetime record against the Red Sox was only 7–7, but 7–3 in the last two seasons. Since his debut in September 1946, he had won 70 games for New York and lost only 28. His .714 winning percentage (minimum 50 games) was the best in the American League over that time period, and a year ago he led in that department with a .724 mark (21–8). This afternoon's performance was vintage Raschi. Pitching against baseball's best-hitting team, he scattered six singles and shut out the Red Sox, 5–0. The

Yankees took the lead on a two-run homer by Jackie Jensen in the third inning and then added three more in the sixth. Left-hander Bill Wight, one of the pitchers the Red Sox obtained from the White Sox to strengthen their staff, started and gave up all five runs.

Boston's two new pitchers (Ray Scarborough was the other) and the addition of short-stop Lou Boudreau—fired as the manager of the Cleveland Indians in spite of winning 92 games—made the Sox the preseason favorite to win the American League pennant—just as they had been in every season since the end of World War II. Steve O'Neill, who took over as manager following Joe McCarthy's retirement in June 1950, planned to use Boudreau at shortstop and move Vern Stephens to third base. O'Neill said he would platoon the right-hand hitting Stephens with the left-hand hitting Johnny Pesky, playing Stephens at Fenway Park and Pesky on the road. That supposedly was the idea, yet although this was a road game for the Sox against a right-handed pitcher, Stephens was starting at third base and batting clean-up. Stengel also had a decision to make at third base. He considered starting McDougald, but went instead with the veteran Billy Johnson. A month later he traded Johnson to the St. Louis Cardinals, continuing the purge of pre–Stengel Yankees. McDougald had been a second baseman at Beaumont in the Texas League in 1950, where he batted .336, won the league's Most Valuable Player Award, and became a favorite of man-ager Rogers Hornsby. He would play in 131 games for New York in 1951, splitting his time between third base, which he shared with Bobby Brown, and second base, which he shared with Jerry Coleman. At season's end McDougald, who batted .306, would win Rookie of the Year honors, but here on Opening Day all the talk was of the other rookie—Mickey Mantle.

Most baseball fans—at least those over the age of 12—have learned to treat stories about sensational young "phenoms" with a healthy dose of skepticism. This is especially true for New Yorkers, who pride themselves on that quintessential urban trait. They remem-bered that as recently as 1947 they had read tales coming from the Giants' training camp in Phoenix about a spectacular rookie named Clint Hartung. It seemed the only problem the Giants had with Hartung was deciding if they wanted him to become the next Mel Ott or the next Carl Hubbell. He would, of course, become neither. Four years later, the dateline remained the same—Phoenix—but the team and the player had changed. It was now the Yankees training in the Arizona desert, and the player earning the superlative reviews was Mantle. Mickey was just 19 years old, a baby-faced switch-hitter who had batted a league-leading .383 and won the Western Association's Most Valuable Player Award playing for the Class C Joplin (Missouri) Miners in 1950. The Yanks brought him to training camp, where he amazed all who saw him with his blazing speed and tremendous power from both sides of the plate. Stengel wanted to bring him to New York, but general manager George Weiss argued that Mantle was not ready for the big leagues and needed to play a year at Triple A. But when Mantle hit .402 with nine home runs in the preseason games, Stengel's view prevailed. The day before the season opened, the Yankees signed him to a major-league contract.

Mantle's sensational spring, which included a series of highly publicized games on the West Coast, had attracted national attention. Almost daily, fans around the country read accounts of the almost mythical-like abilities of the Yankees' new "wunderkind." However, not all the stories about Mantle were positive. Some people questioned why, with America at war in Korea, this obviously healthy young man was not in the army. The war was not going well, and President Truman had recently relieved General Douglas MacArthur of his command. Truman fired the general for insubordination, but MacArthur was an American icon and many in the press were castigating the president for his decision. On this day, MacArthur was returning to the United States after an absence of 14 years, and his countrymen were welcoming him with an affection that bordered on adulation. As Commander in Chief, Truman had every right to fire MacArthur; nevertheless, his action focused attention on the war and who was or wasn't fighting it. Mantle wasn't fighting it because he was 4-F, and he was 4-F because of osteomyelitis, a serious bone disease he had developed a few years earlier. But not many people had ever heard of osteomyelitis and suggested that Mantle was getting special treatment. It was not easy to convince the public that a 19-year-old who could run the way Mantle did was physically disabled. The Yankees realized they had to do something to quell the misgivings and to ease the pressure on this young man. On Friday, April 13, the day they returned home to play the Brooklyn Dodgers at the Stadium, the club flew Mantle to Oklahoma for a reexamination by his draft board. Once again the doctors declared him unfit for military service and he headed back to New York.

Mantle later described Opening Day 1951 as the worst day of his life. He said that after a sleepless night, "I began to tremble all over from the moment I reached Yankee Stadium … I was so scared." It would be his first game there, having missed the Friday exhibition game with Brooklyn. Mantle's debut, in fall-like weather, drew 44,860 fans to Yankee Stadium— the largest opening-day crowd at the Stadium since 1946. And while normally it is only the hard-core fans who pay close attention to pregame batting and fielding practice, that was not true today. From the time they entered the park, almost all of the early arrivals had their eyes on Mantle. The Yanks had assigned him uniform No. 6, which seemed designed to follow the progression of Yankee greats Babe Ruth (No. 3), Lou Gehrig (No. 4), and Joe DiMaggio (No. 5). On his left sleeve, Mantle was wearing a patch honoring the league's 50th birthday. All American Leaguers were wearing the patch this year, while National Leaguers were wearing patches celebrating the senior circuit's 75th birthday. Mantle had been a shortstop at Joplin, but his .903 fielding average convinced the Yankees his future was in the outfield. Now, while still learning to think like an outfielder, Mantle had the added burden of mastering the intricacies of right field at Yankee Stadium. To help him, the Yanks employed the best teacher possible: Tommy Henrich, retired as an active player and serving as a coach. Henrich was in right field with Mantle during fielding practice, instructing him on the proper way to play rebounds off the wall. Before the game, a reporter took an informal poll of fans who had one of the best views of Mantle—the ones in Section 27 in right field. Nine out of ten said the youngster had the look of a major-leaguer.

Arthur "Red" Patterson, the Yankees' promotions director, coordinated the pregame ceremonies, which began with Major Francis Sutherland leading the Seventh Regiment Band on the parade across the Stadium's lush green grass to the flagpole. The condition of the playing field appeared impeccable, as it should after the meticulous care applied to it by "turf consultant" Walter Grego. Along with the players from both teams, the marchers included: Police Commissioner Thomas F. Murphy, Fire Commissioner George P. Monaghan, Bronx borough president James J. Lyons, and Yankees co-owners Del Webb and Dan Topping. Lucy Monroe sang the national anthem as three United States marines raised the American flag. Then Stengel, by himself, raised the 1950 World Series banner. On their return to home plate, Dick Butler, representing Commissioner "Happy" Chandler, presented the Yankees' players with watches or rings to commemorate that triumph. Then came a series of individual awards. American League president Will Harridge presented the Kenesaw Mountain Landis award to Phil Rizzuto, the league's Most Valuable Player. Rizzuto also received *The Sporting News'* Player of the Year award, while Jerry Coleman, his double-play partner, collected the Babe Ruth Memorial Award as the outstanding player of the 1950 World Series. *The Sporting News* presented the Executive of the Year Award to Weiss, but the largest trophy, standing more than three feet tall, was the one they gave to Yankees' announcer Mel Allen, voted Broadcaster of the Year. In addition to radio, Allen's television broadcasts would be seen on two channels in 1951; WPIX-TV, Channel 11, was joining WABD-TV, Channel 5, in televising Yankees' baseball to the metropolitan New York area. Like WABD, WPIX would carry only home games, but they would have exclusive coverage of all night games.

Following the presentations, a soldier, wearing a glove on his right hand, emerged from the Yankees dugout and walked to the mound. Although Bob Sheppard, the new Yankee Stadium public address announcer, did not announce his name, the crowd immediately recognized him. It was the recently inducted Whitey Ford, a native New Yorker whose nine wins (9–1) after coming up from the American Association's Kansas City Blues in mid 1950 had greatly aided the Yankees pennant drive. The fans stood and cheered as Ford, with managers Stengel and O'Neill standing behind him, tossed the season's first pitch to Yogi Berra behind the plate. Ford then got the ball back and presented it to his new wife, Joan, seated in a box by the Yankees dugout. They had been married for three days.

Raschi's day would have been much more trying had it not been for a stellar play by Joe DiMaggio in the first inning. After Joe's brother Dom led off the game with a single, Billy Goodman hit a soft liner over second. Joe, playing in his final opener, raced in and made a spectacular shoestring catch. Dom, not suspecting older brother Joe still had the speed to catch up with the ball, was somewhere between second and third when he did. After making the catch, Joe flipped the ball to first baseman Johnny Mize for an easy double play. DiMaggio's play meant that Raschi would be pitching to Ted Williams with two out and the bases empty, instead of nobody out and runners at first and third—a huge difference. Williams singled, but Raschi got Stephens on a come-backer to end the inning. Over the next eight innings, the Red Sox got four more singles, but never again threatened. The Yankees got their first hit in the third inning, a leadoff single to left by Coleman. Raschi bunted Coleman over to second, which brought up Jensen, who was playing only because Hank Bauer had pulled a muscle in his left leg. A year ago, the Yankees had been high on Jensen, believing that he would be the eventual successor to DiMaggio in center field. However, he had been a major disappointment, batting just .171 in 45 games. Stengel was so upset at Jensen's failure to hit that, for a day or two during spring training, he had even contemplated making him a pitcher. "If he can't hit he can't play in the outfield for the Yankees," said their manager. Jensen, who struck out on three pitches in his first at-bat, let ball one go by before driving the next pitch, an outside fastball, four rows deep into the right center-field seats. Jensen also led the way when the Yanks scored their three sixth-inning runs. He opened with a double to right and reached third on a bunt by Rizzuto. Wight had fielded Rizzuto's bunt and thrown to third in an attempt to get Jensen. But Stephens had been playing in and did not get back in time and Jensen got to the base before he could make the tag. It was the second consecutive opener in which Stephens had fueled a Yankees' rally by his hesitant play in the field. Mantle, batting right-handed against Wight, then got his first hit as a Yankee—a liner to left that scored Jensen. DiMaggio's single to left scored Rizzuto, and Berra's single to center scored Mantle. That was all for Wight. Ellis Kinder came on and got Mize on a fly to right and Johnson on a double-play grounder. After rookie Charlie Maxwell hit for Kinder in the seventh, lefty Mickey McDermott pitched a perfect seventh and eighth innings for Boston. Raschi, aided by three double plays, allowed only two Boston runners to reach second and none to reach third. In the ninth, Walt Dropo led off with a single, the visitors' sixth hit; but Bobby Doerr flied to Mantle and then Boudreau grounded to Rizzuto, who turned it into a game-ending double play.

Tuesday, April 17, 1951

Boston	ab	r	h	po	a	New York	ab	r	h	po	a
D. DiMaggio cf	3	0	2	1	0	Jensen lf	4	2	2	3	0
Goodman rf	3	0	1	2	1	Rizzuto ss	3	1	0	1	4
Williams lf	3	0	1	1	0	Mantle rf	4	1	1	3	0
Stephens 3b	4	0	0	2	2	J. DiMaggio cf	4	0	1	2	1
Dropo 1b	4	0	1	10	0	Berra c	2	0	1	6	0
Doerr 2b	4	0	0	3	1	Mize 1b	3	0	0	8	0
Boudreau ss	4	0	1	1	3	Collins 1b	0	0	0	1	0
Rosar c	2	0	0	4	1	Johnson 3b	2	0	0	1	1
Wight p	2	0	0	0	2	Coleman 2b	3	1	2	2	2
Kinder p	0	0	0	0	0	Raschi p	2	0	0	0	1
ᵃMaxwell	1	0	0	0	0	Total	27	5	7	27	9
McDermott p	0	0	0	0	1						
Total	30	0	6	24	11						

ᵃFouled out for Kinder in seventh inning.

Boston	000	000	000–0
New York	002	003	00X–5

Error—Boudreau. Runs batted in—Jensen 2, Mantle, J. DiMaggio, Berra. Two-base hit—Jensen. Home run—Jensen. Sacrifices—Raschi, Rizzuto. Double plays—J. DiMaggio and Mize; Rizzuto, Coleman, and Mize; Rizzuto, Coleman and Collins. Left on bases—New York 2; Boston 7. Bases on balls—off Wight 2, Raschi 4. Struck out—by Raschi 6, Wight 1, McDermott 1. Hits—off Wight 7 in 5 innings, Kinder 0 in 1, McDermott 0 in 2. Winning pitcher—Raschi (1–0). Losing pitcher—Wight (0–1). Umpires—McGowan, McKinley, Honochick, and Soar. Time of game—2 hr. 12 min. Attendance—44,860.

Behind Vic Raschi (21–10), Ed Lopat (21–9), and Allie Reynolds (17–8), the Yankees (98–56) finished first again, five games ahead of Al Lopez's Cleveland Indians. In the World Series they faced the New York Giants for the first time since 1937 and beat them in six games. Yankee Stadium attendance (1,950,107) dropped below 2 million for the first time in six years. Yogi Berra won the Most Valuable Player Award and Gil McDougald was voted Rookie of the Year. Mantle, after getting off to a slow start, was sent down to Kansas City, but later returned to New York and finished strong. In December Joe DiMaggio, after batting just .263, officially announced his retirement.

Wednesday, April 16, 1952
Shibe Park, Philadelphia
New York 8 Philadelphia 1

You can't sit on the lead and run a few plays into the line....
You've got to throw the ball over the goddamn plate and give the other
man his chance. That's why baseball is the greatest game....—Earl Weaver

Vic Raschi, with ninth-inning help from Johnny Sain, began New York's 50th year in the American League with an easy 8–1 victory at Philadelphia's Shibe Park. Raschi, who blanked the Red Sox on Opening Day a year ago, became the first Yankees' pitcher to win consecutive openers since Lefty Gomez in 1932–1933. Hank Bauer and Mickey Mantle led New York's 14-hit attack against A's pitchers Alex Kellner and Carl Scheib. Bauer had two hits, including a fourth-inning home run, while Mantle—no longer the anxious rookie he had been in 1951—contributed three hits, two runs batted in, and a stolen base.

Mantle was playing right field this afternoon, just as he had last year. Manager Casey Stengel was giving Jackie Jensen the first opportunity to replace the retired Joe DiMaggio in center field. (DiMaggio was working as a television announcer for the club.) Stengel had considered Bob Cerv, a rookie who hit well during spring training, for the position, but decided that Cerv lacked the necessary speed to cover Yankee Stadium's vast center field. Jensen did have the necessary speed, but again he failed to hit. Two and a half weeks into the season, with his batting average at a lowly .105 (two hits in 19 at-bats), the Yankees gave up on him. On May 3 they traded Jensen, pitcher Frank Shea, outfielder Archie Wilson, and minor-leaguer Jerry Snyder to Washington. In return New York received Irv Noren, an excellent outfielder in his third big-league season, and a throw-in, journeyman shortstop, Tom Upton. Shortly after trading Jensen, Stengel moved Mantle to center field where he would remain for most of his career.

Following another last-place finish in 1950, Connie Mack had finally stepped down as manager of the Athletics. Jimmy Dykes, a former player and coach with Philadelphia, took over in 1951 and moved the A's up two spots, while winning 18 more games than Mack's club did the year before. Yet despite their better play and the many physical improvements to Shibe Park, the A's 1951 home attendance was only 465,469. Although that was a one-season jump of 50 per cent, it was still the second lowest in either league. Even more discouraging to the Athletics, their National League tenants, the fifth-place Phillies, drew twice that, attracting 937,658 fans to their games. When only 11,771 came out for Opening Day, the Mack family, which still owned the club, feared it might be an indication of their drawing power in 1952. They realized the franchise was in trouble if there was such a sparse turnout for an opener—especially against the Yankees, a team that traditionally made up a significant portion of Philadelphia's total season attendance. The crowd might have been a little larger for yesterday's scheduled opener, which was rained out, but not much. As it turned out, the Athletics fielded a competitive team in 1952, finishing fourth. Attendance increased to 627,100, but in each of the following two years the team's performance and their attendance would decline sharply, leading to their relocation to Kansas City in 1955.

The Philadelphia Band and the Police and Fireman's Band took turns entertaining the crowd before the game. After the Marine Color Guard performed the flag-raising ceremony, President James A. Finnegan of the City Council, substituting for Mayor Joseph S. Clark who was too busy to attend, threw out the first ball. Kellner, a 27-year-old left-hander, took the mound to start his first opener. He had followed a 20-win rookie season (20–12) in 1949 with a 20-loss sophomore season (8–20) in 1950. He led the league in losses that year, and again in 1951 when he was one of six American League pitchers to lose 14 games. Kellner pitched creditably this afternoon, allowing only three runs (two earned) in 7 ⅓ innings. His teammates pulled him out of several tight spots with double plays, something Philadelphia pitchers had come to depend upon. The Athletics, who had three today, had led the league for the last three seasons, executing more than 200 twin-killings in each. This was at a time when only one other club in major-league history—the 1949 Red Sox—had ever turned more than 200 double plays in a single season even once.

A double play rescued Kellner in the third after the Yankees loaded the bases with one out. Third baseman Billy Hitchcock started it on a ground ball hit by Jensen, the only Yankees' starter to go hitless on the day. The next inning, after Mantle led off with a single, Gil McDougald, batting clean-up, hit into an Eddie Joost to Pete Suder to Ferris Fain double play. The versatile McDougald was playing third base, a position he would play for most of this season. Veteran Bobby Brown would play third in 24 games before going off to the army, and 20-year-old rookie Andy Carey would see action there in 14 games. Brown and Carey had officially joined the club the Sunday before the opener. Brown, after completing his medical internship in San Francisco, arrived in time to appear as a pinch hitter in the final exhibition game against Brooklyn. Carey, signed out of St. Mary's College of California for a $60,000 bonus, had shown promise with the Triple A Kansas City Blues in 1951, batting .288 with 14 home runs and 72 runs batted in. After McDougald hit into the double play, Bauer homered to put the Yanks ahead, 1–0. It remained that way until the sixth when Mantle singled, stole second, and raced home on McDougald's single. Mantle appeared not to have lost any of his great speed after his off-season surgery to repair the knee he injured in the 1951 World Series.

The Yankees increased their lead to 3–0 with an unearned run in the eighth. With one out and Phil Rizzuto who had singled on first, Fain let Jensen's ground ball go through his legs for a two-base error. With runners at second and third, Dykes chose not to pitch to Mantle. He ordered Kellner to walk him intentionally, and then brought in right-hander Scheib to pitch to McDougald. Scheib, in his ninth season with the Athletics, had been a mere 16 years old when he made his debut with them back in 1943; he is still the youngest player ever to participate in an American League game. Scheib got McDougald to hit into another double play, although the Yanks got a run out of it. He grabbed McDougald's comebacker and threw to second baseman Suder for the force on Mantle as Rizzuto scored. Suder had no play on McDougald; but when he saw Jensen going too far around third, he threw to shortstop Joost covering the bag. That started a rundown (Scheib to Suder to Joost to Fain to Hitchcock), which completed the double play to end the inning.

The Yankees changed what had been a close game into a rout in the ninth, sending 11 men to the plate against Scheib and scoring five of them. The first four batters—Bauer, Johnny Hopp, Jerry Coleman, and Charlie Silvera—each singled, resulting in two runs and a 5–0 lead. Hopp, in his last big-league season, had entered the game as a runner for Johnny Mize in the seventh and then taken over defensively at first base. A longtime National Leaguer, Hopp, who began his career with the Cardinals in 1939, was with Pittsburgh when the Yankees bought his contract in September 1950. Silvera was catching Raschi because Yogi Berra was still nursing the sore left hand he injured in an exhibition game at Atlanta a week earlier. Silvera, a Yankee since September 1948, became the backup to Berra when the Yanks sold Gus Niarhos to the White Sox in June 1950. However, in the two seasons he filled the role, Silvera caught in only 33 games. With Coleman at second and Silvera at first, Raschi attempted to sacrifice, but failed as Scheib fielded his bunt and threw to third, forcing Coleman. But Rizzuto singled Silvera home to make the score, 6–0, and one out later Mantle lined a double to left center to score two more.

Entering the last of the ninth with an 8–0 lead, Raschi seemed a good bet to secure his second consecutive opening-day shutout. Over the last four years, he had been the Yankees' most reliable pitcher, with 82 wins and 71 complete games. And he had been in command all the way in this game, allowing only two hits—a looping double to right by Hitchcock leading off the fifth, and a single by Joost leading off the sixth. However, Raschi, who had not gone nine innings all spring, may have stiffened during the long top of the ninth. He did not appear quite as sharp as he walked Joost, the leadoff batter. Then he walked Fain, the American League's defending batting champion, who would win the title again in 1952. When the first two pitches to Elmer Valo were also wide, Stengel, obviously anxious to get the game over, went to his bullpen. In came Sain, another former National Leaguer, like Mize and Hopp, whom the Yankees picked up in a late-season deal—this one on August 30, 1951. However, unlike the other two, which were straight cash deals, in this one the Yankees included a player with the $50,000 they sent to the Boston Braves. His name was Lew Burdette and six years later, while pitching for the Milwaukee Braves, he would defeat the Yankees three times in the 1957 World Series.

Sain completed the walk to Valo, which was charged to Raschi. At season's end, the three men who had just walked—Joost, Fain, and Valo—would finish second, third, and fourth in walks behind the league-leader, Washington's Eddie Yost. For Joost, with 122, it would be his sixth consecutive season of drawing more than 100 walks. With the bases loaded and nobody out, Gus Zernial, the A's clean-up hitter, came to the plate. Philadelphia had obtained Zernial from the Chicago White Sox in a blockbuster three-way trade on April 30, 1951. As part of the deal, the Athletics got rookie Minnie Minoso from the Cleveland Indians (the other team involved), but sent him to the White Sox. Minoso went on to have a sensational year—many felt that he rather than McDougald should have been Rookie of the Year—but the A's were happy with their end of the trade. Zernial provided them with their first genuine slugger in years. He led the league in home runs with 33 and runs batted in with 129. The Athletics had not had a player lead the league in either of those departments since Jimmie Foxx in the early 1930s.

The fans were clamoring for Zernial to hit a grand slam that would cut the Yankees' lead in half. He could not quite manage that, but his slow roller to third went for an infield single, scoring Joost and keeping the bases loaded. For the Philadelphia fans still in the park—those who had not left after the Yankees five-run ninth—there was finally something to cheer about. So far this inning they had knocked out Raschi and spoiled the Yankees' shutout; who knew where this rally would lead? It would take a miracle finish to win the game, but this was baseball and anything could happen. The clock would not run out on the home team. Such finishes, unique to baseball, do happen from time to time. When they do, they live forever in the memory of fans, and are among those recollections of the game that get passed down from fathers to sons and give the game its special place in American culture. But, unfortunately for the fathers and sons of Philadelphia, this would not be one of those times. Sain ended their dreams—and the game, quickly—striking out former Yankee Allie Clark and Hitchcock and getting Suder on a pop to McDougald. The Yanks had their fifth consecutive opening-day triumph and 11th in the last 12. Their only opening-day loss since 1940 had come when the A's Phil Marchildon defeated them, 6–1, in 1947. For Raschi, who was 4–0 against Philadelphia in 1951, the victory extended his lifetime mark against the Athletics to an astonishing 21–2. It was his seventh win in a row against the A's since losing to them on August 13, 1950.

The Yankees (95–59) equaled the record of their 1936–1939 predecessors by winning their fourth consecutive world championship. In a close and exciting race, they won the pennant by two games over the preseason favorites, the Cleveland Indians. Down three games to two in the World Series, the Yanks won the final two at Brooklyn to once again frustrate the Dodgers. In his first full season, Mickey Mantle batted .311 with 23 home runs and finished second in the league in doubles (37), total bases (291), and slugging percentage (.530). Allie Reynolds (20–8) led the league in earned run average (2.06) and strikeouts

(160), and tied Cleveland's Mike Garcia for the most shutouts (6). Reynolds finished second to Philadelphia's Bobby Shantz in the Most Valuable Player voting, with Mantle third and Yogi Berra fourth.

Wednesday, April 16, 1952

New York

	ab	r	h	po	a
Rizzuto ss	4	2	2	0	2
Jensen cf	5	0	0	2	0
Mantle rf	4	1	3	4	0
McDougald 3b	4	0	1	3	5
Bauer lf	4	2	2	0	0
Mize 1b	3	0	1	5	0
ªHopp 1b	2	1	1	4	0
Coleman 2b	4	0	2	4	0
Silvera c	4	1	1	5	0
Raschi p	4	1	1	0	2
Sain p	0	0	0	0	0
Total	38	8	14	27	9

Philadelphia

	ab	r	h	po	a
Joost ss	3	1	1	1	5
Fain 1b	2	0	0	7	1
Valo cf	2	0	0	2	1
Zernial lf	3	0	1	2	0
Clark rf	4	0	0	2	0
Hitchcock 3b	4	0	1	2	2
Suder 2b	3	0	0	6	4
Tipton c	3	0	0	5	0
Kellner p	2	0	0	0	0
Scheib p	1	0	0	0	2
Total	27	1	3	27	15

ªRan for Mize in seventh inning.

New York	000	101	015–8
Philadelphia	000	000	001–1

Error—Fain. Runs batted in—Bauer, McDougald 2, Coleman, Silvera, Rizzuto, Mantle 2, Zernial. Two-base hits—Hitchcock, Mize, Mantle. Home run—Bauer. Stolen base—Mantle. Sacrifice—Suder. Double plays—Hitchcock, Suder, and Fain; Joost, Suder, and Fain; McDougald and Mize; Scheib, Suder, Joost, Fain, and Hitchcock. Left on bases—New York 7; Philadelphia 6. Bases on balls—off Raschi 6, Sain 0, Kellner 2, Scheib 2. Struck out—by Raschi 3, Sain 2, Kellner 4. Hits—off Raschi 2 in 8 innings (none out in ninth), Sain 1 in 1, Kellner 8 in 7Ω, Scheib 6 in 1π. Runs and earned runs—Raschi 1 and 1, Sain 0 and 0, Kellner 3 and 2, Scheib 5 and 5. Wild pitch—Scheib. Winning pitcher—Raschi (1–0). Losing pitcher—Kellner (0–1). Umpires—McGowan, Grieve, and Paparella. Time of game—2 hrs. 45 min. Attendance—11,771.

Tuesday, April 14, 1953
Yankee Stadium, New York
Philadelphia 5 New York 0

Rob the average man of his life-illusion, and you rob him of his happiness at the same stroke.—Henrik Ibsen

The March 1953 relocation of the Boston Braves to Milwaukee reminded fans that for owners the concept of loyalty went in one direction only. Because the Braves had become the "other team" in Boston, running a poor second to the Red Sox in popularity and attendance, their owners were losing money and wanted out. The fact that Boston had been part of the National League since the league began play back in 1876, and that they had won a pennant as recently as 1948, did not really matter to them. But Braves' fans were shocked. How, they asked, could the league violate the sacred bond that supposedly existed between a team and its loyal followers? Well, they could—and they did. And when they did, whatever remained of the pretense that baseball was "just a game" vanished forever.

Baseball had experienced an unbroken period of franchise stability since the American League transferred the defunct Baltimore franchise to New York 50 years earlier. However, beginning with World War II, the population of the United States had begun inexorably to shift from its northeast quadrant to the South and West. And as more and more Americans moved out of the nation's older cities, other owners began to look hungrily at new markets, sending shudders through their teams' longtime fans. Boston's loss of the Braves was especially foreboding to fans of the St. Louis Browns and the Philadelphia Athletics, aware that once the precedent had been set and the first franchise moved, others would follow. In St. Louis, where the Browns ran a very poor second to the Cardinals, their owners had talked of moving before. Now it seemed just a matter of where and how soon. In Philadelphia, where the once mighty Athletics had fallen behind the Phillies in local affection, A's fans also viewed the future anxiously. The fear in both St. Louis and Philadelphia was justified; the Browns would move to Baltimore in 1954 and the Athletics to Kansas City a year later

Aside from curiosity, the Braves moving from Boston to Milwaukee did not have much of an impact on baseball fans in New York. What had westward expansion to do with them, they asked? Who would ever want to leave New York, where the Yankees, Dodgers, and Giants were three of baseball's most storied and profitable franchises? New Yorkers were confident that for however long they played baseball, these teams would be in New York. No one could have imagined that five years from now, New York City would be a one-team town.

Milwaukee played its first league game in Cincinnati on April 13, which turned out to be the only game played that day. The Yankees, beginning their fifth season under manager Casey Stengel, were supposed to play the "presidential opener" in Washington, but rain canceled the game. Had it been played, it would have been without President Eisenhower. Ike, in his first chance at throwing out the first ball, had flouted tradition by skipping the scheduled opener to play golf with Ben Hogan in Augusta, Georgia. Because of the rainout, the Yankees opened at home against the Philadelphia Athletics and Alex Kellner, a pitcher whom they defeated six times in seven decisions in 1952. However, Kellner was a much different pitcher this bitterly cold afternoon. He limited the Yankees to just five singles in shutting them out, 5–0. The loss was the Yanks' first on Opening Day since 1947, and the first time they had been shut out in an opener since Washington's Bobo Newsom blanked them, 1–0, in 1936. Although no one knew it at the time, this would be the Yankees' final opening-day game against the *Philadelphia* Athletics. The next time they played the A's on Opening Day would be ten years later, and the game would be in Kansas City. Since inaugurating the 1908 season against the Athletics at Hilltop Park, the Yanks had played 15 openers against Philadelphia, winning nine of them.

Unlike the previous day in Washington, there was no rain today. However, with the temperature hovering around 40 degrees, and 35 mile-per-hour winds, game conditions at Yankee Stadium were extremely uncomfortable. They were even worse in nearby New England, where five people died in the heaviest April snowstorm to hit that area since 1888. None of the Stadium's 23,534 shivering fans wore shirtsleeves or spring outfits today. As usual, the Seventh Regiment Band, led by Major Francis Sutherland, entertained the crowd before the game. At 1:20 P.M. they led the parade to the center-field flagpole, where Lucy Monroe sang "The Star-Spangled Banner" as a U.S. Marine Corps color guard raised the flag. Co-owners Dan Topping and Del Webb placed wreaths on the monuments to Babe Ruth, Lou Gehrig, Jacob Ruppert, and Miller Huggins, after which Stengel raised the 1952

American League pennant and World Series flags. The crowd stood for a silent prayer for two men long associated with the Yankees who recently had passed away: James P. Dawson, who covered the team for many years as a sportswriter for *The New York Times*, and Charles McManus, superintendent of the Stadium ever since its opening in 1923. Topping and Webb, along with Bronx borough president James Lyons and Mayor Vincent Impellitteri, led the players on the parade back to home plate. Impellitteri had been New York's mayor since winning a special election in 1950 to serve the unexpired term of William O'Dwyer. The former mayor had come under investigation shortly after his reelection in 1949 for allegedly taking illegal payoffs. The leaders of Tammany Hall persuaded President Truman that in the best interests of the New York Democratic Party, this was the right time to find a position for O'Dwyer in his administration. This being an era when Tammany Hall still had a great deal of clout in Democratic administrations, Truman complied, appointing O'Dwyer as his ambassador to Mexico.

When the players got back to home plate, Mel Allen was waiting for them. Allen served as the master of ceremonies for the ritual handing out of the rewards that always come to successful teams. American League president Will Harridge presented each Yankee player with his World Series memento, and then *The Sporting News* handed out awards to George Weiss as the top executive of 1952 and Allen as the top broadcaster. Dan Daniel of the *New York World-Telegram and The Sun*, representing the New York baseball writers, presented Stengel with a scroll, and some of Casey's fans presented him with a floral wreath for good luck. The wreath of pink flowers was in the shape of the number five, representing the hopes of all Yankees fans for a fifth consecutive championship. Mayor Impellitteri made a little speech imploring the Yankees to do just that, and then tossed out the first ball.

Stengel had planned to pitch Allie Reynolds in the opener at Washington and use Vic Raschi against Philadelphia today. But with the rainout, he adjusted the rotation, opting to stay with Raschi today and pitch Reynolds tomorrow against Bobby Shantz, last season's Most Valuable Player. For Raschi, it was his third consecutive opening-day start, something no Yankees' pitcher had done since Red Ruffing in 1938–40; and it came against his favorite opponent. Before losing his final two decisions to the Athletics in 1952, he had beaten them ten consecutive times. Even with the two losses, Raschi's lifetime record against Philadelphia was 24–4. The matchup of Raschi and Kellner was a repeat of last year's opener at Shibe Park, when Raschi defeated Philadelphia 8–1. It had been almost 30 years since the same two pitchers had opposed each other in consecutive Yankees openers. New York's Bob Shawkey and Boston's Howard Ehmke were the starters in both the 1923 and 1924 openers, with the Yanks winning each time.

In last year's opener, the A's did not score a run against Raschi until the ninth inning. They matched that today after just four batters. The first two, Eddie Joost and Dave Philley, singled. Manager Jimmy Dykes had his number-three hitter, Allie Clark, sacrifice the runners to second and third. Eddie Robinson's fly ball to Hank Bauer in right was just deep enough to allow Joost to score. Robinson was playing his first game for Philadelphia since coming over from the Chicago White Sox in a five-player deal made in January. The key acquisition for Chicago was Ferris Fain, the two-time defending American League batting champion, and the best fielding first baseman in the league. Losing Fain, who was well liked by the fans in Philadelphia, made the trade very unpopular there.

The Athletics used the Yankees' favorite weapon, the long ball, to add three more runs in the fifth. Catcher Ray Murray, who had hit only two home runs in his previous 403 major league at-bats, opened the inning with a line drive into the left-field seats. Kellner followed with a long drive over Mickey Mantle's head in straightaway center that Mantle might have misjudged. He got a slow start, finally catching up with it and extending his glove, only to have the ball bounce out. Kellner had a double, and no doubt fans around the Stadium were saying, or thinking, "DiMag would have had it"—and he probably would have. However, it is possible Mantle's concentration was lacking. His thoughts may have been on his first child, born just two days earlier. His son's birth concluded a memorable spring for Mantle, one in which he batted .412 and unloaded several mammoth home runs. He also failed his army physical again—this time due to the damaged ligament in his right knee he incurred in the 1951 World Series.

Joost attempted to bunt Kellner over to third, but instead hit a little pop fly in front of the plate. Raschi, in his haste to catch it and possibly get a double play, dropped the ball. But catcher Yogi Berra alertly pounced on it and threw Kellner out at third. Raschi got the second out, getting Philley on a ground ball to first baseman Joe Collins. This would be Collins's fourth full season with New York and his first opening-day start. While he would never do as well again as he had in 1952 (.280 with 18 home runs), Collins would remain a valuable part of Stengel's platoon system through 1957. Joost was now at second with two out when Raschi grooved one to Clark, who drove it into the stands in left, and suddenly it was 4–0.

After Bob Cerv batted for Raschi in the sixth inning, Ray Scarborough came on to pitch for New York. Scarborough, whom the Yankees bought from the Boston Red Sox in August 1952, held Philadelphia scoreless in the seventh and eighth. He left for pinch-hitter Bill Renna, who flied out in his big-league debut, and Ewell Blackwell pitched the ninth inning. The side-arming Blackwell, once among the most feared pitchers in baseball, had also come to the Yankees the previous August. To get him, the Yanks sent $35,000 to Cincinnati, along with pitcher Johnny Schmitz and three minor leaguers: pitcher Ernie Nevel and outfielders Bob Marquis and Jim Greengrass. Blackwell was only 30 years old, but the sore arm that had plagued him in Cincinnati would soon end his career. Philadelphia reached him for an insurance run in the ninth, which Joost scored after he walked, went to third on Philley's single—his third hit of the game—and came home as Clark bounced out to third baseman Gil McDougald. For Joost it was his third run scored, and for Clark his third run batted in. Joost would replace Dykes as manager in 1954 but would last only one season, the A's final one in Philadelphia. Meanwhile, Dykes would become the first manager of the newly transplanted Baltimore Orioles.

Tuesday, April 14, 1953

Philadelphia	ab	r	h	po	a	New York	ab	r	h	po	a
Joost ss	4	3	2	2	7	Rizzuto ss	4	0	1	1	3
Philley cf	5	0	3	2	0	Collins 1b	4	0	0	7	1
Clark rf	4	1	1	2	0	Bauer rf	4	0	2	3	1
Robinson 1b	4	0	1	11	0	Mantle cf	3	0	1	3	0
Zernial lf	2	0	0	2	0	Berra c	3	0	1	4	3
Michaels 2b	3	0	0	3	4	Woodling lf	3	0	0	2	0
Suder 3b	4	0	0	0	0	McDougald 3b	2	0	0	1	4
Murray c	4	1	1	5	1	Martin 2b	3	0	0	5	3
Kellner p	3	0	1	0	2	Raschi p	1	0	0	0	1
Total	33	5	9	27	14	ªCerv	1	0	0	0	0
						Scarborough p	0	0	0	0	0

Philadelphia

	ab	r	h	po	a

New York

	ab	r	h	po	a
[b]Renna	1	0	0	0	0
Blackwell p	0	0	0	1	0
Total	29	0	5	27	16

[a]Flied out for Raschi in sixth inning.
[b]Flied out for Scarborough in eighth inning.

Philadelphia	100	030	001–5
New York	000	000	000–0

Error—Kellner. Runs batted in—Robinson, Murray, Clark 3. Two-base hits—Philley, Kellner, Robinson. Home runs—Murray, Clark. Sacrifices—Clark, Michaels. Double plays—Kellner, Joost, and Robinson; Joost and Robinson; Joost, Michaels, and Robinson. Left on bases—Philadelphia 9; New York 3. Bases on balls—off Kellner 1, Raschi 2, Scarborough 1, Blackwell 2. Struck out—by Kellner 5, Raschi 2, Blackwell 1. Hits—off Raschi 7 in 6 innings, Scarborough 1 in 2, Blackwell 1 in 1. Runs and earned runs—Raschi 4 and 4, Scarborough 0 and 0, Blackwell 1 and 1. Hit by pitcher—by Scarborough (Kellner). Winning pitcher—Kellner (1–0). Losing pitcher—Raschi (0–1). Umpires—McGowan, Paparella, McKinley, and Honochick. Time of game—2 hrs. 23 min. Attendance—23,534.

In pitching just the fourth shutout of his major-league career, Kellner used his curve ball to frustrate Yankees' batters all afternoon. Not even the new electric heaters management had installed in the home team dugout (but not in the visitors') could help them against the veteran left-hander. They seemed on the verge of a comeback in the seventh when Mantle and Berra singled with one out. The consecutive hits brought the fans to life, but the drama was short-lived as Joost turned Gene Woodling's grounder into an inning-ending double play. Kellner finished in style with two ninth-inning strikeouts, fanning Bauer—the only Yankee with two hits—for the final out.

Six seasons had now come and gone since Brooklyn's Jackie Robinson had reintegrated major-league baseball. While the acceptance of black players was often slow in coming, particularly in the South, there were hopeful signs. One came today when the directors of the Cotton States League reinstated the Hot Springs, Arkansas franchise, dropped a week earlier, for refusing to release its two black players. Attorney-General James P. Coleman of Mississippi said the two men would not be allowed to play in the league's four Mississippi cities. While most northerners shook their heads at such stories, both the Athletics, representing the "cradle of liberty," and the Yankees, representing the nation's most liberal city, continued to be entirely Caucasian. That would change for the A's later this season when they brought up pitcher Bob Trice after he had won 21 games for the Ottawa Athletics of the International League. For the Yankees, integration was still two seasons away.

Casey Stengel led New York (99–52) to an unprecedented fifth consecutive world championship. As in 1952, Cleveland, under Al Lopez, was second, although this time the margin was 8½ games. The Brooklyn Dodgers were again the World Series victims, succumbing in six games. Yogi Berra finished a distant second to Cleveland's Al Rosen in the voting for the league's Most Valuable Player Award. Home attendance was 1,537,811, the fifth consecutive year it had dropped from 1948's all-time high of 2,373,901, when the Bucky Harris-led Yankees finished third.

Tuesday, April 13, 1954
Griffith Stadium, Washington
Washington 5 New York 3 (10 Innings)

So purely white they were.—Edmund Spenser

When President Dwight Eisenhower elected to spend Opening Day 1953 golfing with Ben Hogan in Augusta, Georgia, the snub to baseball upset tradition-minded fans far beyond the nation's capital. The outcry was so great that when the game got rained out, Ike, on the advice of his political advisors (fans are also voters), hurried back to Washington to throw out the first ball at the rescheduled opener. So when the same option faced him in 1954—a Yankees-Senators opener in Griffith Stadium or golf with Hogan—Eisenhower wisely chose baseball. Moreover, the president not only participated in the pregame ceremonies, he and First Lady Mamie Eisenhower sat through the entire game, which lasted just under three hours. Yankees manager Casey Stengel helped make it so lengthy by using a total of 19 players, including five pitchers. The Senators finally won the marathon, 5–3, on Mickey Vernon's dramatic tenth-inning home run, after which Eisenhower signaled the hero to join him. Vernon, whose climactic blow off reliever Allie Reynolds thrilled the crowd of 27,160, broke loose from his teammates' congratulatory hugs and headed to the presidential box. Ike shook his hand and said, "Nice going. Wonderful, a wonderful home run."

It had been a wonderful day all around for Washington baseball fans. During the late morning and early afternoon, the Meyer Goldman Band entertained them, just as they had been doing on Opening Day here for more than 30 years. Then, precisely at 2:30, the United States Army Band marched onto the field and the pregame ceremonies began. At 2:45 the president entered the park as the band greeted him with "Hail to the Chief." Speaker of the House Joe Martin of Massachusetts led the parade to the flagpole. Eisenhower's decisive victory in 1952 had carried enough Republicans with him to wrest control of the House from the Democrats, which allowed Martin to replace Sam Rayburn as Speaker. (Rayburn had replaced Martin in 1949.) Marching with Congressman Martin were American League president Will Harridge and Senators vice president Calvin Griffith. Griffith was substituting for his father, Clark Griffith, who was skipping the parade for the first time since becoming the team's president in 1912.

The elder Griffith was sitting next to the Washington dugout in Box 16, between Ike and Mamie. Others seated in or near the presidential box were Secretary of Defense Charles E. Wilson and wife Jessie, Secretary of Agriculture Ezra Taft Benson, Major General Howard Snyder, the president's physician, and Sherman Adams, his special assistant. Griffith presented Ike with a brand new glove to wear while throwing out the first ball. It was a $28 Lefty Gomez model, although made for a right-hander. Eisenhower's throw was "too hot to handle" for several players, but Yankees pitcher Johnny Sain finally came up with it. The photographers asked the president if he would throw another one, and he obliged gladly. He threw the ball to rookie Senators pitcher Cholly Naranjo, who was standing in front of the Washington dugout. But, to the consternation of the Secret Service, Naranjo, a 19-year-old Cuban, tossed it back to Ike. The president appeared to enjoy this exchange of throws, and he flipped it back to Naranjo a final time. Then, when Washington manager Bucky Harris assigned Naranjo the task of sitting in front of the presidential box to protect against foul balls, Eisenhower—evidently confident that he was able to catch anything hit his way—waved Naranjo back to the Washington bench. The pregame attention focused on Naranjo was his "15 minutes of fame." After the game, the Senators sent him to their Chattanooga Lookouts farm team. His major-league career would consist of 17 games with the 1956 Pittsburgh Pirates.

Harris was in the fifth (and final) year of his third stint as Washington's manager. He had refused to announce his starting pitcher in advance, perhaps seeking any advantage he could find. He said it would be either right-hander Bob Porterfield or left-hander Chuck

Stobbs. "I don't know what Bucky is trying to prove," Stengel said when he learned of Harris's ploy. "It makes no difference to me whether he pitches a left-hander or a right-hander. I have men for all positions." Finally, an hour before game time, Harris named Stobbs. Last year, his first in Washington, Stobbs won nine of his last 12 decisions to finish 11–8. However, he gained the greatest notoriety of his career on April 17, 1953, when he yielded Mickey Mantle's memorable "tape-measure" home run here at Griffith Stadium. Meanwhile, Stengel, not needing any more advantages as a comparison of the two rosters would clearly show, had announced his starting pitcher two days earlier. To no one's surprise, it was Whitey Ford, who had come back from two years in the Army to win 18 games (18–6) in 1953. The always dependable Vic Raschi, who started the last three openers, was no longer with the team. Raschi, winner of many crucial games for the Yankees and possessor of a spectacular 120–50 (.706) win-loss record, had won only 13 games (13–6) in 1953. Moreover, he was one of several veteran Yankees who had balked at the 1954 contracts the club had offered. General manager George Weiss deemed the 35-year-old Raschi the most expendable, and in what many perceived as a message to the other holdouts, unceremoniously sold him to the St. Louis Cardinals for $85,000.

Stobbs set the Yankees down in order in the first inning, and when the Senators headed for their dugout the fans noticed something unusual. Each player was still holding his glove, the result of a new restriction that prohibited gloves from being left on the playing field. Thus, a charming custom, one that little boys had always tried to execute exactly as their favorite big leaguer did, was eliminated.

Ford had his wife Joan and his parents watching today, but they saw a pitcher who bore little resemblance to the 18-game winner he had been in 1953. After an easy first inning, he yielded two runs in the second, and then after the Yanks had tied it in the third, allowed the Senators to regain the lead in the fourth. Roy Sievers, in his first plate appearance as a Senator, singled to open the second. Sievers had played for five years with the St. Louis Browns, winning the American League's Rookie of the Year Award in 1949. But he had not been very productive since, and the newly minted Baltimore Orioles (relocated from St. Louis) traded him to Washington for Gil Coan. With center fielder Jim Busby at the plate, a passed ball charged to catcher Yogi Berra allowed Sievers to move to second. Busby, formerly of the Chicago White Sox, was an excellent outfielder but was not noted as a hitter. However, after coming to Washington he batted .312 in 150 games in 1953. In his first at-bat of 1954, he drilled one of Ford's pitches on a line into right center that easily scored Sievers. Busby would have another good year, a .298 average in 155 games; in fact, these two seasons with Washington would be by far the best of his 13-year career. A good play by right fielder Hank Bauer in cutting the ball off limited Busby to a double. After Pete Runnels sacrificed him to third, Ed Fitz Gerald followed with a slow grounder to first base. Joe Collins tried to get the out at the plate, but the speedy Busby beat the throw.

Down 2–0, second baseman Jerry Coleman led off the third with the Yankees' first hit, a single to left. Coleman had missed almost all the 1952 and 1953 seasons serving as a marine combat pilot in Korea. He was, with Ted Williams and Bob Kennedy, one of the three major-leaguers who saw action in both World War II and the Korean War. Although an armistice had been signed last July, Americans were still being drafted, and Coleman was replacing one of them. Billy Martin, who had replaced Coleman at second base in 1952, was now himself in the army. After Phil Rizzuto's single to center put runners at first and third, Ford hit a little squibber that Stobbs fielded, checked Coleman at third, and then threw to second. However, his throw was wide and all three runners were safe. Bauer's two-run single to left tied the score and left the Yanks with two runners on and nobody out. The heart of the order was coming up—Collins, Mantle, and Berra—but Stobbs got out of the inning without further scoring.

A fourth-inning error by Coleman helped Washington regain the lead and knock Ford out of the game. With one out, he bobbled Runnels's grounder, allowing the Senators' short-stop to reach base safely. Ford got Fitz Gerald for out number two, but he walked the weak-hitting Wayne Terwilliger. Stobbs, left-handed all the way, then put his team ahead by sin-gling to right field. When Ford walked Eddie Yost to fill the bases, Stengel brought in right-hander Tom Gorman to pitch to right-handed- hitting Tom Umphlett. A year ago, as a Red Sox rookie attempting to replace Dom DiMaggio, Umphlett hit a solid .283. Nevertheless, Boston, always looking for power hitters, traded him and pitcher Mickey McDermott to Washington for Jackie Jensen. Harris countered the insertion of Gorman by sending up Tom Wright, a veteran left-handed hitter, to bat for Umphlett. Wright, in his first at-bat as a Senator, fanned, but Washington still led, 3–2.

Stobbs's best work may have been in the fifth, when to maintain his one-run advantage he had to overcome three Washington errors. Vernon made the first one when he dropped the throw from Stobbs after the pitcher had fielded Rizzuto's come-backer. Bob Cerv, batting for Gorman, lifted a fly ball to left-center that the usually sure-handed Busby dropped for error number two. After Bauer, attempting to bunt, forced Rizzuto at third, Stengel sent Bill Skowron up to bat for Collins. Skowron had signed with the Yanks in 1950 out of Purdue University, where he had been a halfback on the football team. He was a standout hitter in the minors, and had made the conversion from an outfielder to a first baseman while with the Triple A Kansas City Blues. Skowron's solid spring training, along with the retirement of Johnny Mize, induced Stengel to bring him to New York. Now, in his first major-league at-bat, Skowron popped out to second baseman Terwilliger. Stobbs then got Mantle to ground to Runnels, who flipped the ball to Terwilliger for the ostensible force play on Bauer and final out of the inning. However, second-base umpire Jim Honochik called Bauer safe, saying Terwilliger had failed to touch second base. It was the Senators' third error of the inning and loaded the bases. Stobbs now had to face the always dangerous Berra, but he again got the routine ground ball to short. This time Runnels and Terwilliger executed the play cleanly, although Mantle, who was still recovering from two off-season knee operations, almost beat the force at second.

Bob Kuzava in the fifth and sixth innings and Johnny Sain in the seventh and eighth did superb relief work for the Yankees. Each pitched two scoreless and hitless innings. By keeping Washington from increasing their lead, the Yankees were able to tie the game with a run in the ninth. Coleman, whose error had paved the way for the Senators' third run, started the comeback with a one-out double, New York's first hit since the third inning. When Rizzuto followed with a bouncer to Runnels, Coleman foolishly tried to reach third, but Runnels throw to Yost cut him down. Stobbs was now one out away from victory. He got two strikes on pinch-hitter Eddie Robinson, but Robinson, in his first Yankees' at-bat, singled to right to send Rizzuto to third and keep the inning alive.

Robinson and pitcher Harry Byrd were the men the Yankees were after when they made their huge five-for-six trade with the Philadelphia Athletics in December 1953. Among those going to Philadelphia in that trade were Bill Renna and two very promising minor-leaguers, Jim Finigan and Vic Power. Finigan would hit .302 this year and finish second to the Yankees' Bob Grim in Rookie of the Year voting. Power, a dark-skinned Puerto Rican, had been one of the two blacks in their minor-league system considered most likely to eventually integrate the Yankees. The other was Elston Howard, an outfielder whom the Yanks had just sent to the Toronto Maple Leafs of the International League, where he would learn to be a catcher. Power was a fine hitter, an excellent first baseman, and a certain major-leaguer. However, he played with a flamboyance that was then uncommon in baseball and generally frowned upon—particularly by the Yankees. Power's "showboating" and his reputation as a potential "troublemaker" doomed his chances in New York. The Yankees had been slow in recruiting black ballplayers. But if the reason was that management believed seeing a black player in a Yankees' uniform would displease a specific segment of their clientele, then a man like Power surely would not be the first.

Following Robinson's single, he trotted off the field as Enos Slaughter, wearing Raschi's old No. 17, came in to run for him. Just two days before the opener, in what many believed was simply the second part of the Raschi deal, the Yanks traded three players to the St. Louis Cardinals for the 38-year-old Slaughter. (One of them was minor leaguer Bill Virdon, who would be the National League's Rookie of the Year in 1955.) After 13 years as a Cardinal, Slaughter had lost his job to rookie Wally Moon, who would be this season's National League Rookie of the Year. Slaughter entered the 1954 season second among active players in hits (to Stan Musial) and runs batted in (to Ted Williams). He later recalled he had played in Griffith Stadium only once before, with an industrial team way back in 1934.

After losing Robinson, Stobbs tried to end the game against Bauer, but again failed. Bauer got his third run batted in of the game with a single to center that sent Rizzuto home with the tying run. Harris, sensing the game was slipping away, brought in right-hander Sonny Dixon to pitch to Skowron. Stengel responded by pulling Skowron in favor of left-handed-hitting Irv Noren. Dixon got Noren on a fly to Sievers, and when the Senators came to bat in the last of the ninth, it was against Reynolds, who had evolved into the Yankees' best relief pitcher. Noren, normally an outfielder, replaced Skowron at first base, becoming New York's third first baseman of the day. Reynolds got through the ninth despite issuing a walk, and Dixon easily set the Yanks down in the tenth, getting Mantle, Berra, and Gil McDougald.

Yost led off the bottom of the tenth with a walk, his third of the day. Reynolds struck out Tom Wright, the third time Wright had fanned, and prepared to face Vernon. The defending American League batting champion (.337) had been hitless in his four previous at-bats. Actually, no Senators batter had gotten a hit since the fourth inning. Vernon swung at Reynolds's first pitch, driving it to deep right field where the ball just nicked a beer sign before disappearing over the wall. Just like that, the game was over. The sun-drenched fans erupted with joy, with President and Mrs. Eisenhower sharing in their delight, both vocally and physically. While Ike was congratulating Vernon, Mamie leaped to her feet and began kissing and hugging 84-year-old Clark Griffith. Hours after he finished celebrating Washington's victory, the president was on his way to Augusta for a golfing vacation. For the Yankees, beginning their pursuit of a sixth consecutive world championship, it was their first opening-day road loss since 1940. That 2–1 defeat at Shibe Park in Philadelphia also had gone ten innings.

Tuesday, April 13, 1954

New York	ab	r	h	po	a		Washington	ab	r	h	po	a
Bauer rf	5	0	2	1	0		Yost 3b	2	1	0	2	0
Collins 1b	2	0	0	5	0		Umphlett rf	2	0	1	1	0

New York

	ab	r	h	po	a
cSkowron 1b	2	0	0	2	0
gNoren 1b	1	0	0	1	1
Mantle cf	5	0	0	4	0
Berra c	5	0	0	9	0
McDougald 3b	3	0	0	0	0
Woodling lf	4	0	0	0	0
Coleman 2b	4	1	2	3	2
Rizzuto ss	4	2	1	3	2
Ford p	1	0	0	0	1
Gorman p	0	0	0	0	0
bCerv	1	0	0	0	0
Kuzava p	0	0	0	0	1
dCarey	1	0	0	0	0
Sain p	0	0	0	0	0
eRobinson	1	0	1	0	0
fSlaughter	0	0	0	0	0
Reynolds p	0	0	0	0	0
Total	39	3	6	28*	7

Washington

	ab	r	h	po	a
aWright rf	3	0	0	0	0
Vernon 1b	5	1	1	5	0
Sievers lf	4	1	1	3	0
Busby cf	4	1	1	7	0
Runnels ss	2	1	0	2	5
Fitz Gerald c	4	0	0	7	2
Terwilliger 2b	3	0	0	3	0
Stobbs p	3	0	1	0	1
Dixon p	1	0	0	0	0
Total	33	5	5	30	8

*One out when winning run scored.
aStruck out for Umphlett in fourth inning.
bSafe on Busby's error for Gorman in fifth inning.
cPopped out for Collins in fifth inning.
dStruck out for Kuzava in seventh inning.
eSingled for Sain in ninth inning.
fRan for Robinson in ninth inning.
gFlied out for Skowron in ninth inning.

New York	002	000	001	0–3
Washington	020	100	000	2–5

Errors—Stobbs, Coleman, Vernon, Busby, Terwilliger. Runs batted in—Busby, Fitz Gerald, Bauer 3, Stobbs, Vernon 2. Two-base hits—Busby, Coleman. Home run—Vernon. Sacrifice—Runnels. Double play—Collins (unassisted). Left on bases—New York 8; Washington 6. Bases on balls—off Ford 3, Stobbs 2, Reynolds 2. Struck out—by Stobbs 5, Ford 3, Gorman 1, Kuzava 3, Sain 1, Dixon 1, Reynolds 1. Hits—off Ford 4 in 3⅔ innings, Gorman 0 in ⅓, Kuzava 0 in 2, Sain 0 in 2, Reynolds 1 in 1⅓, Stobbs 6 in 8⅔, Dixon 0 in 1⅓. Runs and earned runs—Off Ford 3 and 2, Reynolds 2 and 2, Stobbs 3 and 3. Passed ball—Berra. Winning pitcher—Dixon (1–0). Losing pitcher—Reynolds (0–1). Umpires—McGowan, Paparella, Honochik, and Chylak. Time of game—2 hrs. 58 min. Attendance—27,160.

Although they won 103 games (103–51), their most wins under Casey Stengel, the Yankees finished second, eight games behind the Cleveland Indians. Despite their second-place finish, Yogi Berra (.307, with 22 home runs and 125 RBIs) was the league's Most Valuable Player, and Bob Grim (20–6) was the Rookie of the Year.

Wednesday, April 13, 1955
Yankee Stadium, New York
New York 19 Washington 1

*The Constitution does not provide for first
and second class citizens.*—Wendell Willkie

Only a weather-related balk by Whitey Ford prevented the Yankees from registering the major leagues' most one-sided opening-day shutout. Ford's misstep allowed that distinction to remain with Babe Adams and the Pittsburgh Pirates. In the 1911 opener, at Cincinnati's Palace of the Fans, Adams blanked the Reds, 14–0. (In 2016, the Los Angeles Dodgers set a new mark with a 15–0 shutout of the San Diego Padres.) However, New York's 18-run margin of victory in their 19–1 thrashing of the Washington Senators is an American League record and second only to the Buffalo Bisons' 23–2 shellacking of the Cleveland Infants in the 1890 Players League opener (at least for the winner; this was game number two for the Senators). The Yankees pummeled four Washington pitchers for 16 hits, including home runs by Mickey Mantle, Yogi Berra, and Bill Skowron and triples by Bob Cerv and Andy Carey. Ford, who had three hits on the day, drove in four runs as did Mantle and Cerv, while Skowron drove in three. When the Yankees jumped to a 9–0 lead after five innings, many in the sparse gathering of 11,251 headed for the exits. It was not that they had tired of seeing the home team score runs, they simply wanted to escape from weather that was wholly unsuited for baseball. It was damp, hazy, and chilly, with temperatures in the mid–40s and a steady drizzle that fell throughout the day. While the club was anxious to play following yesterday's rainout of the scheduled opener, the unpleasant conditions kept many fans away. The crowd was the smallest for an Opening Day at Yankee Stadium since 1944.

Ford, making his second opening-day start, fared much better than last year when Washington drove him from the mound in the fourth inning. Today the 26-year-old left-hander was in complete control. He allowed only two hits (one fewer than he had), fanned eight, and retired the last ten batters consecutively. Ford was now the leader of a thoroughly transformed Yankees' pitching staff. Of the three stalwarts that had anchored the rotation in manager Casey Stengel's early years, two were gone and one would be going soon. General manager George Weiss sold Vic Raschi before the 1954 season; Allie Reynolds retired after it; and at the end of July of this year, the Yanks would send Ed Lopat to the Baltimore Orioles. With the departure of the three veterans, Ford emerged as the staff leader, a position he would retain for most of the next ten years. Behind him were right-handers Bob Turley and Don Larsen, both of whom came to the Yankees in last November's gigantic 18-player trade with Baltimore. Although Turley (14–15) and Larsen (3–21) had losing records for the seventh-place Orioles in 1954, they quickly became winners in New York, proving—as Red Ruffing had 25 years earlier—the immediate benefits of putting on Yankee pinstripes. Among those going south in the trade with Baltimore were veteran outfielder Gene Woodling; pitchers Harry Byrd and Jim McDonald; and rookie catcher Gus Triandos.

Two other right-handers, Johnny Kucks and Tom Sturdivant, both rookies, had pitched impressively during the spring and made the club. Stengel was hoping for a repeat of 1954 when Bob Grim, a rookie just out of the army, won 20 games (20–6) and the Rookie of the Year Award. To round out their starting rotation, the Yankees reacquired Tommy Byrne, a left-hander who originally broke in with them back in 1943. After stints with the St. Louis Browns, the Chicago White Sox, and the Senators, Byrne went to the minors where he won 20 games (20–10) last season for the Pacific Coast League Seattle Rainiers.

Mayor Robert F. Wagner Jr. was at the stadium to throw out the first ball, just as his father—then New York's acting lieutenant governor—had done at the Yankees' 1914 opener. Coincidentally, the weather at the Polo Grounds that day had also been wet and chilly. The following day Wagner, a confessed Giants' fan, would throw out the first ball at the Polo Grounds when the world champions opened their home season against the Dodgers. "It's not that I dislike the Yankees or the Dodgers," Wagner said. "I just happen to be a Giant fan." Police commissioner Francis Adams, Bronx borough president James J. Lyons, and Frank Kridel, chairman of a committee of Bronx fans, joined the mayor in the pregame parade. Major Francis Sutherland and the Seventh Regiment Band provided the music, and Seaman First Class Everett Morrison, a sailor stationed at Brooklyn's Floyd Bennet Field, sang the national anthem. Morrison substituted for Lucy Monroe, who was en route from Tokyo but had missed her plane connections in San Francisco. Back at home plate, Mel Allen introduced the Yankees' players, but for the first time in six years there were no World Series souvenirs to disperse. However, two Yankees received individual awards: Berra, the MVP Award from Shirley Povich of the *Washington Post and Times-Herald*, and Grim, the Rookie of the Year Award from Lou Effrat of the *New York Times*. Povich was president of the Baseball Writers Association of America and Effrat was chairman of the New York chapter. Kridel presented Stengel with a huge floral horseshoe donated by the fans' group he represented. The Senators were wearing new road uniforms, which for the first time since 1909 had the word "WASHINGTON" on their jerseys. Since 1910, the Senators had either worn a "W" on the left breast of the jersey or kept the jersey blank and worn the "W" on the left sleeve. Now they were again wearing their city name, spelled out in block letters of blue trimmed in red.

Rookie Elston Howard was not in the starting lineup, but as the Yankees' first black player he attracted a great deal of pregame attention from newsmen, photographers, and fans. Howard would make his debut the following day, at Boston's Fenway Park. Although 1955 was one year after *Brown v. Board of Education*, eight years after Jackie Robinson, and ten years after World War II, racial segregation was still prevalent in America. And, as today's news from Washington foretold, it would not end easily. The Justice Department had joined several southern states in urging the Supreme Court not to issue a "forthwith" decree to end school segregation. For Howard, his life on the road would differ greatly from the other Yankees. In three cities—Baltimore, Chicago, and Kansas City (the Athletics had moved there from Philadelphia)—the club informed him that he would be unable to live in the same hotel or eat in the same dining room as his teammates. In Washington, the nation's capital, he could stay in the same hotel as the other players, but the dining room was off limits to him. Howard, a man of quiet dignity, acquiesced to these humiliating restrictions.

As the 1955 season began, Stengel and Al Lopez of Cleveland were the only remaining American League managers who had been at the helm of their clubs on Opening Day 1954. Each of the other six teams had a new leader: Marty Marion in Chicago (he had managed the last nine games in '54), Pinky Higgins in Boston, Bucky Harris in Detroit, Lou Boudreau in Kansas City, Paul Richards in Baltimore, and Charlie Dressen in Washington. Dressen, whose Dodgers teams Stengel had conquered in 1952 and 1953, was let go by Brooklyn following the '53 season in a contract dispute with Dodgers owner Walter O'Malley. After a successful year managing the Oakland Oaks of the Pacific Coast League, Clark Griffith brought him back to the major leagues to replace Bucky Harris. Dressen already had one win to his credit after the Senators crushed the Orioles 12–5 in their home opener. He had mostly veterans on his club with only one rookie in the starting lineup—Bobby Kline, the shortstop. Before the game Dressen chatted with an old Brooklyn friend, Red Barber, now a Yankees' broadcaster. Barber had joined the Yanks in 1954 after friction with O'Malley ended his unforgettable 15-year sojourn in Brooklyn.

Recognizing the conventional wisdom that it was best to pitch left-handers in Yankee

Stadium, Dressen chose Mickey McDermott as his starting pitcher. However, the conventional wisdom works best when it is accompanied by talent—a commodity McDermott would display sporadically, but not today. He did hold the Yanks scoreless in the first two innings, but over the next six they would accumulate 19 runs against him and three relievers. Third baseman Carey tripled home the first two runs after McDermott walked Phil Rizzuto and Gil McDougald in the third inning. Carey had batted a solid .302 in 1954 after winning the third-base job early in the season. His doing so allowed Stengel to shift McDougald from third to second where he replaced Billy Martin, who was in the army, and Jerry Coleman, whose career was beginning to fade. Carey's triple was the first of the 11 he would hit in 1955, tying him with Mantle for the American League lead. Rizzuto, batting eighth, was making his ninth consecutive and 11th total opening-day start at shortstop. Stengel had experimented with Coleman at the position during spring training, and even tried Billy Hunter, who had come in the trade with Baltimore. But on Opening Day it was Rizzuto, now wearing glasses, who was in his familiar spot.

The Yankees exploded for five runs in the fourth, scoring the first two against McDermott, who left with two runners on base. Dressen replaced him with Ted Abernathy, a right-hander making his big-league debut. One out later, Mantle welcomed the rookie with a tremendous home run deep into the right-field bleachers. Carlos Paula, a Cuban-born outfielder who became Washington's first black player when he joined them in September 1954, batted for Abernathy in the fifth. With the Yankees comfortably ahead, Dressen was taking the opportunity to get a look at two other rookie pitchers who were attempting to stick with the club. He used right-hander Bill Currie and left-hander Vince Gonzales for two innings apiece, and he could not have liked what he saw. The Yanks battered Currie for five hits and six runs in the two innings he pitched, and Gonzales for six hits and six runs in his two innings. Currie was on the mound when Berra (with a man on) and Skowron powered back-to-back home runs in the sixth.

Wednesday, April 13, 1955

Washington

	ab	r	h	po	a
Yost 3b	4	0	0	1	3
Busby cf	3	0	0	2	0
Vernon 1b	3	1	0	8	1
Runnels 2b	4	0	1	5	2
Sievers lf	3	0	1	2	0
Umphlett rf	3	0	0	1	0
Fitz Gerald c	2	0	0	2	0
Oldis c	0	0	0	1	0
Kline ss	3	0	0	1	1
McDermott p	1	0	0	0	1
Abernathy p	0	0	0	1	0
[a]Paula	1	0	0	0	0
Currie p	0	0	0	0	1
[b]Roig	1	0	0	0	0
Gonzales p	0	0	0	0	0
Total	28	1	2	24	9

New York

	ab	r	h	po	a
McDougald 2b	3	2	1	1	2
Coleman 2b	2	0	0	3	1
Carey 3b	6	1	2	1	0
Mantle cf	5	3	3	4	0
Berra c	4	2	1	10	0
Skowron 1b	6	2	3	7	0
Bauer rf	3	3	1	0	1
Cerv lf	5	2	2	0	1
Rizzuto ss	0	2	0	1	2
[c]Hunter ss	1	0	0	0	0
Ford p	5	2	3	0	2
Total	40	19	16	27	9

[a]Hit into forceout for Abernathy in fifth inning.
[b]Struck out for Currie in seventh inning.
[c]Struck out for Rizzuto in seventh inning.

| Washington | 000 | 001 | 000–1 |
| New York | 002 | 524 | 33X–19 |

Errors—McDermott, Berra, Kline. Runs batted in—Carey 3; Ford 4; Mantle 4; Berra 2; Skowron 3; Cerv 4. Three-base hits—Carey, Cerv. Home runs—Mantle, Berra, Skowron. Stolen base—Rizzuto. Left on bases—Washington 5; New York 9. Bases on balls—off Ford 5, McDermott 3, Currie 2, Gonzales 3. Struck out—by Ford 8, Abernathy 1, Currie 1, Gonzales 1. Hits—off McDermott 4 in 3⅓ innings, Abernathy 1 in ⅔, Currie 5 in 2, Gonzales 6 in 2. Runs and earned runs—McDermott 6 and 6, Abernathy 1 and 1, Currie 6 and 5, Gonzales 6 and 6, Ford 1 and 1. Wild pitch—Currie. Hit by pitcher—by McDermott (Mantle, Rizzuto), Currie (Cerv). Balk—Ford. Passed ball—Fitz Gerald. Winning pitcher—Ford (1–0). Losing pitcher—McDermott (0–1). Umpires—Berry, McKinley, Flaherty, and Chylak. Time of game—2 hrs. 54 min. Attendance—11,251.

Abernathy, one of baseball's rare submarine-style pitchers, would be the only one of the three rookie pitchers to eventually succeed. His big-league career, mainly as a reliever, would last until 1972, and three times he would lead his league in total appearances. The debut aftermaths of the other two were much different. Currie would pitch in two more games this season before disappearing from the major leagues, while for Gonzales this one game comprised his entire big-league career.

Ford lost his shutout—and his place in the record book—in the sixth inning. With one out, Jim Busby walked but was forced at second by Mickey Vernon. Pete Runnels singled, sending Vernon to third and keeping the inning alive. Then, while preparing to pitch to Roy Sievers, Ford caught his spikes on the wet, slippery mound. It was clearly a balk and plate umpire Charlie Berry immediately waved Vernon home. Eventually, Sievers (who had Washington's other hit) walked, but Tom Umphlett popped to Carey to end the inning.

Today's win gave New York a share of the American League lead with Cleveland and Boston, which of course is meaningless on Opening Day. Nevertheless, it was a good omen for the Yankees, who were in first place for only four days in 1954. It was also a good omen for Ford, who did not win his first game last year until May 15—and that in relief. Ford would win 18 games in 1955 (18–7), which tied him with Bob Lemon of Cleveland and Frank Sullivan of Boston for the league high (1955 was the first season in American League history in which there were no 20-game winners). Ford's 18 complete games also led the league, but again it was at the time the lowest league-leading total ever.

In an exciting three-way race, New York (96–58) won the pennant by three games over Cleveland and five over Chicago. After seven World Series losses, including the last five to the Yankees, Brooklyn won its first championship, defeating the Yanks in seven games. Mickey Mantle led the league in home runs (37), walks (113), and slugging percentage (.611). Yogi Berra won his third Most Valuable Player Award, having previously won in 1951 and 1954.

Tuesday, April 17, 1956
Griffith Stadium, Washington
New York 10 Washington 4

I have touched the highest point of all my greatness.—William Shakespeare

The Year the Yankees Lost the Pennant is author Douglass Wallop's fable of a spectacular young ballplayer who leads the lowly Washington Senators past the New York Yankees to win the American League pennant. Made into a successful musical, *Damn Yankees* was playing its 400th performance on Broadway the same day the real Yankees and Senators were opening the 1956 baseball season in Washington. And while at the Forty-Sixth Street Theater in New York the fictional Joe Hardy was leading the Senators to victory, at Griffith Stadium, Mickey Mantle—his real-life counterpart—was doing the same for the Yankees.

At 24 and in his sixth major-league season, Mantle was still seeking the level of greatness everyone had predicted for him. After a shaky rookie season in 1951, he had put together four excellent seasons and become the idol of millions of youngsters throughout America. However, Mantle had never completely satisfied some Yankees fans, particularly the older ones, who argued that to be the true successor to Joe DiMaggio you must be more than just a very good player—you must be a great one. In 1956, Mantle would become that great player. He would win the Triple Crown and gain universal recognition as a performer of transcendent ability. It began on Opening Day with two tremendous home runs that led the Yankees to a, 10–4, victory. Mantle's two mighty blows, both hit left-handed, came precisely three years after his memorable 565-foot home run here. That one, against left-hander Chuck Stobbs, had been hit right-handed.

In all, there were six home runs hit in the game as the batters took advantage of Griffith Stadium's new dimensions. Besides the two by Mantle, Yogi Berra also homered for New York, while for Washington rookie Dick Tettelbach hit one, and Karl Olson, formerly of the Red Sox, hit two. This was most unusual for Griffith Stadium, always among the most difficult parks in the league in which to hit home runs; the Senators and their opponents had combined to hit just 45 there last season. Making it easier to hit home runs was the idea of Calvin Griffith, who had succeeded his foster father, Clark Griffith, as the Senators' new president. The elder Griffith, New York's first manager when they entered the league in 1903 and a baseball institution in Washington since 1912, had died in October 1955. Calvin's motive in reducing the home run distances was to increase the productivity of his three right-handed sluggers: Jim Lemon, Roy Sievers, and 19-year-old Harmon Killibrew. Knowing also that home runs brought fans to the park, he installed a six-foot high, galvanized fence, stretching from the left-field foul line to the home team bullpen in right center. The revised outfield measurements, which shortened the distance required for a home run by up to 45 feet, were responsible for all of today's home runs except the two by Mantle.

Lost in all the talk of Mantle's heroics was a route-going pitching performance by Don Larsen. At spring training, the free-spirited Larsen survived a one-car automobile accident, losing only a cap on a front tooth, but likely realizing it could have been much worse. After incurring no disciplinary action, he pitched well enough during the rest of the exhibition season to win the opening-day assignment. Aside from giving up the three home runs, Larsen pitched a respectable game, allowing only six hits and striking out six.

The pregame ceremonies officially got underway when President Eisenhower arrived. A motorcade stretching for a block and a half, and including motorcycles and ten black limousines brought the president to the park. It took just ten minutes to get from the White House at Pennsylvania Avenue and 16th Street to Griffith Stadium at Florida and Georgia Avenues. For the rest of the crowd of 27,837, who came mostly by car or bus, presumably it took longer. Mamie Eisenhower and her mother, Mrs. John Doud, were to have accompanied Ike this afternoon, but may have been discouraged by the nippy 50-degree temperature. The president watched as the United States Army Band, managers Casey Stengel and

Charlie Dressen, Griffith, and Congressman Joe Martin marched out to center field. Following Republican losses in the 1954 mid-term elections, Martin was once again the House *Minority* Leader. Those losses were on the minds of several of Eisenhower's advisors, who suggested he find a new running mate should he choose to run for a second term in November. Aware of the rumors, Vice President Richard Nixon implied today he would be willing to step down if it would help President Eisenhower get reelected.

As the band played "The Star-Spangled Banner," Stengel and Dressen pulled the ropes that raised the American flag. While the marching and flag raising went on, the players lined up along the foul lines, with the Senators displaying a few colorful additions to their blue pinstriped uniforms. Along with the red and white horizontal stripe added to their stockings in 1948, the blue "W" on the left breast now had a red outline and was drafted to present a three-dimensional effect. Following the national anthem, Stengel and Dressen came over to greet Mr. Eisenhower as the players from both teams assembled in front of the presidential box to prepare for his opening toss. It actually turned out to be two tosses, with Gil McDougald catching the first and Washington's third-base coach Cookie Lavagetto the second. The balls used in the ceremony, replicas of baseballs from 1876, were to honor the 80th anniversary of the year that the A. G. Spalding Company started making baseballs for the new National League.

While the Senators had altered their uniforms only slightly, they had arranged for a largely new group of players to wear them. The changes in personnel were due primarily to three multiplayer trades: with the White Sox in June 1955, the Red Sox in November 1955, and the Yankees in February 1956. Among the veterans no longer with Washington were Mickey Vernon, Bob Porterfield, Johnny Schmitz, Mickey McDermott, Jim Busby, and Tom Umphlett. Pitcher Camilo Pascual was one of five of Washington's starters in this game appearing in their first major-league opener. Pascual, a Cuban-born right-hander with a devastating curve ball, was in his third season, but until now the Senators had used him primarily in relief. Though he had gone 2–12 in 1955 and would finish 6–18 in 1956, baseball people believed Pascual had the ability to be a first-rate pitcher. Eventually, when the Senators and later the Minnesota Twins became competitive teams, Pascual would justify that belief.

After Hank Bauer began the game by fouling out, Pascual struck out shortstop Jerry Lumpe in the rookie's first major-league at-bat. Lumpe was part of an outstanding group of minor-leaguers that the Yankees had invited to spring training. The best had been Norm Siebern, winner of the James P. Dawson Award, given to the top newcomer in camp. However, Siebern ran into an outfield wall on March 22, ruining his chance of opening the season in New York. Just before Opening Day, the Yanks sent him and two other top prospects—shortstop Tony Kubek and catcher Darrell Johnson—to their Triple A farm team, the Denver Bears. Lumpe was starting the opener because of an injury to McDougald. With Billy Martin back from the army to play second and Andy Carey set at third, McDougald was no longer needed at those positions. But Stengel, wanting him in the lineup, had shifted this most versatile infielder to shortstop. And had he not torn a tendon near his knee, that is where he would have been this afternoon. Phil Rizzuto, who had made 11 opening-day starts at shortstop, was now at the end of his career and sat on the bench. The club would officially terminate Rizzuto in August when they unceremoniously released him to make room for the reacquired Enos Slaughter.

Pascual, now with two out and no one on, got behind two-and-nothing on Mantle. On the next pitch, Mickey put the Yanks ahead by driving it over the 31-foot wall in center field. The ball continued across an alley where it landed temporarily on a roof before bouncing onto Fifth Street. Washington answered back with a home run in the bottom of the first, a one-out blast by left fielder Tettelbach. His drive, hit on a full-count pitch, landed beyond the new fence in left, although short of the bleacher wall. For Tettelbach, an ex–Yankee, it was the first major-league hit of the 12 he would accumulate, and his only home run. In 1955 he had gotten into two games with the Yanks before they included him in the February 1956 trade that brought Mickey McDermott to New York. Two other former Yankees' farmhands from that transaction—right fielder Whitey Herzog and catcher Lou Berberet—were also in Washington's starting lineup.

An error by shortstop Jose Valdivielso helped the Yanks to two third-inning runs and a 3–1 lead. His failure to handle Lumpe's easy ground ball allowed the rookie to reach first base. Mantle went down swinging on three pitches, but Berra lined a home run 390 feet into the new bleacher seats in center field. Yogi also drove in the fourth New York run with a fifth-inning single that followed walks to Bauer and Mantle.

Olson's first home run in the bottom of the fifth cut the lead to 4–2. The ball, like Berra's, landed in the new seats in center. President Eisenhower, wearing a tan overcoat, a wide-brimmed hat, and a muffler to protect against the cold, put down the peanuts he was munching to rise and applaud Olson's blast. However, just as Washington fans were beginning to contemplate a possible comeback victory, the Yankees answered back with a four-run sixth. Elston Howard, playing left field, led off with a single and moved to second on a single by Carey. Pascual foiled Larsen, who was attempting to sacrifice, by striking him out. Then he struck out Bauer as the crowd roared their approval. (Pascual finished with a total of nine strikeouts in his six innings of work.) But Lumpe, who had already fanned twice, singled Howard home with his first big-league hit. Mantle, the next batter, jumped on Pascual's first pitch and sent it soaring over the Senators' bullpen in center field into a grove of trees 20 feet on the other side of the wall. The smattering of New York fans in the crowd cheered lustily, while Senator rooters, including the president, sat staring in amazement. Mantle's power, especially for those who were seeing it for the first time, was awe-inspiring. Carey and Lumpe scored ahead of Mickey, and the Yankees now led, 8–2.

In the seventh, the Senators again halved New York's lead as Olson's second homer, with Pete Runnels aboard, made the score, 8–4. The barrage of long-ball hitting in this park might have appeared incongruous to plate umpire Ed Rommel. Here at Griffith Stadium 30 years earlier, on Opening Day 1926, Rommel, pitching for the Philadelphia Athletics, had lost a 15-inning, 1–0, duel to Walter Johnson.

After going out in order in the seventh against Bob Chakales, the Yankees got their final two runs in the eighth. Tex Clevenger, traded to Washington by the Red Sox, was now on the mound. Clevenger got the first two batters, but then gave up a single to Lumpe. The crowd was now applauding Mantle as he made his way to the plate. In addition to his two tremendous home runs, Mantle had made two scintillating catches in center field and the fans were showing their appreciation of his talent. No one had ever hit three home runs on Opening Day and many in the crowd were pulling for Mickey to become the first. Clevenger, however, would not cooperate, judiciously walking him. Berra followed by doubling off the base of the wall in center, driving in both Lumpe and Mantle. It capped an outstanding opener for Berra, who had four hits—including a double and a home run—and five runs batted in.

Tuesday, April 17, 1956

New York	ab	r	h	po	a		Washington	ab	r	h	po	a
Bauer rf	4	1	0	2	0		Yost 3b	2	0	0	0	4
Lumpe ss	5	3	2	0	2		Tettelbach lf	4	1	1	0	0
Mantle cf	3	3	2	3	0		Herzog rf	4	0	1	2	0
Berra c	4	1	4	6	0		Sievers 1b	4	0	0	8	0
Skowron 1b	5	0	2	5	3		Runnels 2b	4	1	1	2	2
Martin 2b	5	0	0	0	1		Berberet c	3	0	0	14	0
Howard lf	5	1	1	6	0		cWright	0	0	0	0	0
Carey 3b	5	1	1	2	0		Olson cf	4	2	3	1	0
Larsen p	4	0	0	3	1		Valdivielso ss	2	0	0	0	4
Total	40	10	12	27	7		aOravetz	1	0	0	0	0
							Snyder ss	1	0	0	0	0
							Pascual p	2	0	0	0	0
							Chakales p	0	0	0	0	0
							bKillebrew	1	0	0	0	0
							Clevenger p	0	0	0	0	0
							dCourtney	1	0	0	0	0
							Total	33	4	6	27	10

aFlied out for Valdivielso in seventh inning.
bStruck out for Chakales in seventh inning.
cRan for Berberet in ninth inning.
dGrounded out for Clevenger in ninth inning.

New York	102	014	020–10
Washington	100	010	200–4

Error—Valdivielso. Runs batted in—Mantle 4, Tettelbach, Berra 5, Olson 3, Lumpe. Two-base hits—Runnels, Berra. Home runs—Mantle 2, Tettelbach, Berra, Olson 2. Left on bases—New York 7; Washington 5. Bases on balls—off Pascual 3, Larsen 3, Clevenger 1. Struck out—by Pascual 9, Larsen 6, Chakales 1, Clevenger 2. Hits—off Pascual 10 in 6 innings, Chakales 0 in 1, Clevenger 2 in 2. Runs and earned runs—off Larsen 4 and 4, Pascual 8 and 6, Clevenger 2 and 2. Wild pitch—Clevenger. Winning pitcher—Larsen (1–0). Losing pitcher—Pascual (0–1). Umpires—Rommel, Stevens, Runge, and Tabacchi. Time of game—2 hrs. 38 min. Attendance—27,837.

President Eisenhower, who had never left an opening-day game before it ended, was still there eating peanuts as the Senators batted in the ninth. Some faint hope may have stirred in him when Berberet walked and Olson singled with one out. However, Larsen got shortstop Jerry Snyder and pinch-hitter Clint Courtney on ground balls to end the game. Larsen's complete game was one of only six he would have for the regular season. He did, of course, add a seventh with a perfect game against Brooklyn in the World Series.

The Yankees (97–57) won another pennant, finishing nine games ahead of the Cleveland Indians. They avenged the World Series loss of 1955, defeating the Dodgers in seven games. Whitey Ford (19–6) led the league in winning percentage (.760) and earned run average (2.47). He tied for third place in the voting for the first Cy Young Award, won by Brooklyn's Don Newcombe. (From 1956 to 1966 there would be only one Cy Young Award given, covering both leagues.) Mickey Mantle won the Triple Crown (.353, 52 home runs, 130 RBIs), and also led the American League in runs scored (132), slugging percentage (.705), and total bases (376). He was the unanimous choice as the league's Most Valuable Player.

Tuesday, April 16, 1957
Yankee Stadium, New York
New York 2 Washington 1

Can we ever have too much of a good thing?—Miguel de Cervantes

One of baseball's truisms is that good teams win one-run games and bad teams lose them. So, when the Yankees found themselves in a tense opening-day struggle with the visiting Washington Senators, few in the Yankee Stadium crowd of 31,644 doubted that the home team would win—which they did, 2–1, on Andy Carey's bases-loaded single in the last of the ninth. Whitey Ford was the winning pitcher and Chuck Stobbs the loser, although both left-handers pitched remarkably comparable games. Ford allowed six hits, walked one, struck out seven, and allowed a seventh-inning home run by Roy Sievers; Stobbs allowed seven hits, walked three, also struck out seven, and allowed a seventh-inning home run to Yogi Berra. It was Washington's second straight one-run defeat of the new season, having lost, 7–6, in 11 innings to the Baltimore Orioles yesterday at Griffith Stadium.

Washington had furnished the Yankees' opening-day opposition for each of the past four years. Ford and Stobbs had squared off in the first of them in 1954 at Griffith Stadium. New York lost that one, 5–3, in ten innings, though neither pitcher was involved in the decision. The next year Ford held Washington to two hits in a, 19–1, romp at the Stadium. The Yankees' ace was still battling a cold he picked up in spring training, but he would not let that deprive him of the chance to pitch the opener, particularly against Washington. His lifetime record against the Senators was 12–3, and he had beaten them twice in 1956 without a loss. Stobbs, meanwhile, was only 8–13 lifetime against the Yankees, but that was a respectable mark considering the quality of the teams for which he had pitched. Washington had won only five of the 22 games played against the Yankees in 1956, and Stobbs had won three of them, while losing four.

The Yankees (except for the pitcher's spot) were fielding the same team that won the seventh game of the World Series last October. Johnny Kucks had pitched that one, shutting out Brooklyn, 9–0. It was the seventh pennant and sixth world championship the Yanks had won in Casey Stengel's eight years as manager. Cries of "Break up the Yankees," heard intermittently since the days of Babe Ruth, were reaching a new crescendo. However, instead of being "broken up" the club appeared to be the strongest it had been during Stengel's tenure. General manager George Weiss, taking advantage of his relationship with Arnold Johnson, the new owner of the Kansas City Athletics, had negotiated a seven-for-six trade with the A's in February. In the deal, the Yanks lost Irv Noren, Billy Hunter and pitchers Tom Morgan, Mickey McDermott, and Rip Coleman; but they gained pitchers Bobby Shantz and Art Ditmar and third baseman Clete Boyer.

Stengel further strengthened the club with the addition of four rookies: pitcher Ralph Terry, outfielder Woodie Held, and infielders Bobby Richardson and Tony Kubek, all of whom had starred for the 1956 Denver Bears of the American Association. In June the Yankees would include Terry and Held in the deal that sent Billy Martin to Kansas City and brought them reliever Ryne Duren and their second black player, outfielder Harry Simpson. With Martin gone, Stengel replaced him at second base with Richardson. The highest rated of the four rookies was the left-hand hitting Kubek, a .331 batter and the American Association's All-Star shortstop in 1956. But Stengel was satisfied with Gil McDougald at shortstop and switched Kubek to left field, where he planned to platoon him with Elston Howard. Despite having to learn a new position, the 20-year-old Kubek won the James P. Dawson Award as the team's outstanding newcomer. Once the season began, he played infield and outfield, batted .297, and was a nearly unanimous choice as the league's best rookie.

With such an imposing lineup, it's understandable why the fans were confident of a third consecutive pennant. Adding to their sense of good cheer was the weather. Unlike several recent openers that had seemed more like late winter than spring, the day was bright and sunny. The pleasant weather, along with the traditional opening-day bunting and decorations, had the crowd in that happy, anticipatory frame of mind the return of baseball invariably brings. One of life's great joys was back. Groundskeeper Jim Thompson and his crew had planted all new Merion bluegrass that helped make the Stadium look exceptionally captivating to winter-weary New Yorkers.

Before the game, the Yankees paraded to the center-field flagpole, where they raised the 1956 world championship banner. Infielder Jerry Coleman, formerly a major in the marine corps, marched at the front of the assembly while attempting to keep the players in some semblance of military order. The U.S. Army's 42nd Infantry Division, under the direction of Patrick J. Austin, played *Yankee Doodle Dandy* at the flag raising, and then accompanied Lucy Monroe as she sang the national anthem. Commissioner Ford Frick, after presenting the players with their World Series trinkets, asked Phil Rizzuto to take a special bow. It was an appropriate gesture and the crowd appreciated it. The manner in which the club had dismissed Rizzuto in August 1956 shocked many longtime Yankees fans. "The Scooter" had always been very popular in New York, and had played a significant role in the Yankees' success since joining them in 1941. Therefore, New Yorkers felt he deserved better than the harsh "business-as-usual" release Stengel and Weiss had given him. In what may have been a conciliatory hiring, Rizzuto was now serving as a radio and television broadcaster for the team.

Each Opening Day, it seemed, one or more members of the Yankees was receiving a personal award; this year was no different. American League president Will Harridge presented Mickey Mantle with his Most Valuable Player Award, and Joe Trimble conferred on Don Larsen the Babe Ruth Memorial Award as the outstanding player in the World Series. Trimble, of the *New York Daily News*, was chairman of the New York chapter of the Baseball Writers Association of America. The Bronx Chamber of Commerce presented the team with a floral arrangement in the shape of a baseball, which Stengel accepted on its behalf.

Robert F. Wagner Jr., the mayor of New York, threw out the first ball. Wagner had been a responsible mayor who kept the city financially stable. This morning, Comptroller Lawrence E. Gerosa reported that New York was in sound fiscal condition and there was no need for any gimmick taxes to bring in additional money. Yet by now it should have been obvious to the mayor, to parks commissioner Robert Moses, and to all the rest of New York's politicians that a crippling blow to the city's health was looming. The threats by Dodgers owner Walter O'Malley and Giants owner Horace Stoneham that they would move their clubs out of New York were growing much more ominous.

Right from the beginning, Ford and Stobbs settled into a fast-moving pitching duel. A major reason for Stobbs's "success" against the Yankees in 1956 had been his ability to handle Mantle; he held Mickey to just three hits in 23 at bats—all singles. But with two out in the first inning, Mantle, in his first at-bat of the new season, doubled. He moved to third on a wild pitch, but Berra took a called third strike to end the inning. Berra protested the call vigorously (and futilely), while jumping up and down and screaming at plate umpire Ed Rommel. Yogi claimed that catcher Ed Fitz Gerald had interfered by touching his bat as Stobbs let go with the pitch.

However, the greatest excitement in the early innings came with Mantle batting in the third. A spectator threw a smoke bomb onto the field that landed between Senators second baseman Herb Plews and right fielder Jim Lemon. The umpires had to stop play while this device, which sent clouds of orange smoke into the air, played itself out. Evidently the police did not remove the person who committed this idiotic gesture, because in the eighth inning he struck again. This time the smoke bomb went off in the mezzanine behind home plate, much to the annoyance of the fans seated there. Perhaps somebody else was responsible for the second incident, although it is difficult to imagine there would be two such people in Yankee Stadium on the same day.

Ford ran into trouble in the fifth, due in part to an error by Mantle. With Lemon on first with a walk, Mickey dropped Karl Olson's liner to put runners at first and second. Washington failed to take advantage of the gift, and it was still a scoreless game when the Senators came to bat in the seventh. That changed when Sievers led off with a long home run into the left-field seats. Sievers was on his way to leading the league in two of the three triple crown categories this season—home runs (42) and runs batted in (114). (Ted Williams would lead in the third, batting average, with a .388 mark.) After Sievers's home run, Ford fanned Lemon but gave up singles to Fitz Gerald and Olson. With the pitcher batting, manager Charlie Dressen, attempting to avoid a double play, ordered Stobbs to bunt. He did, but Ford fielded it and threw to Carey to force Fitz Gerald at third. He then got shortstop Lyle Luttrell on a fly to Howard for the third out. The 1957 Senators can make a reasonable claim to being the slowest team in major-league history. Stolen bases is not the sole category by which to judge team speed, but Washington's season total of 13 is the major leagues' all-time low.

No sooner had the fans taken their seats following the seventh-inning stretch than the Yankees evened the score. Berra did it by himself with a smash over the auxiliary scoreboard and into the right-field bleachers. The score was still, 1–1, when Berra led off the ninth with a line-drive single to left. Bill Skowron, with instructions to hit rather than bunt, flied out, but McDougald doubled into the left-field corner for his third hit of the day and second double. The ball hit the railing and ricocheted sharply past left fielder Sievers. Berra was around third and might have scored, but third-base coach Frank Crosetti yelled for him to stop. Berra skidded to a halt and returned to third. Crosetti had seen Sievers make a quick recovery of the ball and chose not to chance having the potential winning run thrown out at home. However, as the play developed Berra could have scored easily; Sievers had to hurry his throw and Fitz Gerald was forced to field it halfway up the first base line. Had Berra continued home and scored, McDougald would have been credited with a triple. McDougald ended the season with nine triples instead of ten. That left him tied for the most in the American League with teammates Simpson and Hank Bauer, but it was the first time in major league history that no player had reached double figures in triples.

Faced with the winning run at third base, Dressen called time and convened a conference on the mound to discuss strategy. Washington decided to walk Howard and load the bases, even though Stobbs had already fanned him three times. It was percentage baseball, setting up a force at the plate, or a potential inning-ending double play. Howard took the four wide ones and trotted down to first base to discuss the situation with coach Randy

Gumpert, substituting for Bill Dickey. Gumpert was a former Yankees' pitcher who was now a manager in their farm system. He had hurried in from the team's minor-league training camp in Hattiesburg, Mississippi, to replace Dickey, who was ill.

Tuesday, April 16, 1957

Washington	ab	r	h	po	a	New York	ab	r	h	po	a
Luttrell ss	4	0	0	2	1	Bauer rf	4	0	0	1	0
Plews 2b	4	0	0	0	1	Martin 2b	4	0	0	1	3
Runnells 1b	3	0	0	5	0	Mantle cf	4	0	1	3	0
Yost 3b	4	0	1	0	2	Berra c	4	2	2	7	0
Sievers lf	4	1	1	3	0	Skowron 1b	4	0	0	9	0
Herzog cf	0	0	0	0	0	McDougald ss	4	0	3	2	3
Lemon rf	4	0	2	3	0	Howard lf	3	0	0	2	0
Fitz Gerald c	4	0	1	8	1	Carey 3b	2	0	1	2	1
Olson cf, lf	3	0	1	4	0	Ford p	3	0	0	0	2
Stobbs p	3	0	0	0	0	Total	32	2	7	27	9
Total	33	1	6	25*	5						

*One out when winning run scored.

Washington	000	000	100—1
New York	000	000	101—2

Errors—Lemon, Mantle. Runs batted in—Sievers, Berra, Carey. Two-base hits—Mantle, McDougald 2. Home runs—Sievers, Berra. Double play—Ford, McDougald, and Skowron. Left on bases—Washington 6; New York 8. Bases on balls—off Ford 1, Stobbs 3. Struck out—by Ford 7, Stobbs 7. Runs and earned runs—off Stobbs 2 and 2, Ford 1 and 1. Wild pitch—Stobbs. Winning pitcher—Ford (1–0). Losing pitcher—Stobbs (0–1). Umpires—Rommel, Stevens, Napp, and Rice. Time of game—2 hrs. 12 min. Attendance—31,644.

The next batter was Carey, whom Stobbs had walked intentionally twice earlier. After two mediocre years, Carey had come into spring training as the only Yankees' regular who had to fight to retain his job. He did so by batting a solid .304 in the exhibition season. As he prepared to bat, Dressen, seeking any possible edge, shifted the defensive alignment of his outfield. He removed Sievers, switched Olson from center field to left, and called Whitey Herzog off the bench to play center. Stobbs ran the count to two balls and two strikes on Carey as the tension mounted. Although Stobbs was reluctant to have the count go full, he would not give in. He kept throwing curves and sliders, and Carey kept fouling them off. After fouling off six consecutive 2–2 pitches, Carey lifted a long fly ball down the left-field line. It was well over the head of Olson, who was playing shallow because of the do-or-die situation, and landed gently on the turf. Yankee fans may have expected a win, but it had been a tight, hard-fought game, and as Berra trotted in with the winning run they cheered mightily. Ford, who threw only 109 pitches today, injured his shoulder in a subsequent start and would win just 11 games (11–5) in 1957. The Senators, now 0–2, would lose 16 of their first 20, resulting in third-base coach Cookie Lavagetto replacing Dressen as the manager.

Al Lopez, who had chased the Yankees while managing the Cleveland Indians, was now managing the Chicago White Sox. Again he finished second as Chicago trailed the pennant-winning Yankees (98–56) by eight games. In the World Series, former Yankee Lew Burdette won three games as the Milwaukee Braves defeated the Yanks in seven games. Mickey Mantle finished second in batting average (.365) and slugging percentage (.665) to Ted Williams, and second in total bases (315) to Roy Sievers. However, he led the league in runs (121) and walks (146) and won his second consecutive Most Valuable Player Award, the fourth in a

*row won by a Yankee. Tony Kubek won 23 of the 24 votes for Rookie of the Year. Frank
Malzone of Boston got the other one.*

Tuesday, April 15, 1958
Fenway Park, Boston
New York 3 Boston 0

Cursed be he that removeth his neighbor's landmark.—Deuteronomy

In the years immediately after World War II, at a time when the United States was at
the height of its power, New York City reached its own particular zenith. Surely there had
been other magnificent eras in the city's history, but never one like the period that began
with V-J Day and lasted for about ten years. New York was the Mecca for successful and
ambitious people in finance, communications, the arts, entertainment, fashion, and virtually
every other facet of American life. Of course, the city had its problems, but while not everyone prospered, very few of those already there wanted to leave. The quality of life for most
New Yorkers had never been better. However, by the mid–1950s conditions began to change
and residents of the city began to sense a general decline. As children of previous generations of immigrants came to maturity and entered the middle class, they left their apart-
ments in Brooklyn and The Bronx for houses in Westchester County and Long Island. A
new group of immigrants, many of them poor and unskilled southern blacks and Puerto
Ricans, moved in to take their places. Inevitably, with such dislocation neighborhoods
deteriorated and crime increased, driving even more middle-class taxpayers out of the city.
The downward cycle continued for several decades before it began to reverse course in the
mid-1990s. Yet no matter how much life in the city has improved, it is unlikely that the
extraordinary esteem in which it was held at mid-century can ever be replicated. Nor can
the pride people felt or the pleasure they received from living there ever again be as strong.

For many New Yorkers, part of that pride and pleasure derived from the city's three
baseball teams. Between 1947 and 1957, New York teams dominated the game. Of the 11
World Series played in those years, seven had involved two New York teams and three
others had involved one. Then, in 1958, it all ended. Walter O'Malley, owner of the Brooklyn
Dodgers, and Horace Stoneham, owner of the New York Giants, moved "their" teams from
New York to California. Adults cringed and children wept. It was a cold-hearted, cynical
breach of the public trust that the National League callously allowed to happen. Furthermore, it was a devastating blow to the prestige of a city already in the early stages of deterioration. To millions of New Yorkers, having a baseball team that not only represented
them but also—or so they believed—"belonged" to them, was an important part of their
lives. The defection of the Dodgers and Giants was a shock to their fans and a disillusionment they would never forget.

By abandoning New York, the National League would be starting a season without a
franchise in the nation's biggest city for the first time since 1882. The void led the Philadelphia Phillies—sensing an opportunity to widen their fan base and their revenue—to arrange
to televise 78 games into the New York area. Similarly, the Yankees signed a contract with
WPIX, worth more than a million dollars, to increase their 1958 television coverage to 140
games. However, if the goal of these expanded telecasts by the Phillies and Yankees was to

capture disaffected Dodgers and Giants rooters, it was a complete failure. The number of Dodgers and Giants fans who eventually became Yankees fans was minuscule, and those who became Phillies fans even fewer. Many continued to follow their old team in its California incarnation, while some, disenchanted and brokenhearted, abandoned the game forever. However, when the National League "rewarded" New York with an expansion team in 1962, the Mets, many former Dodgers and Giants fans switched their allegiance to the newcomers.

Any hopes the Yankees had of attracting hordes of disgruntled National League fans ended quickly. In 1958, the first year they had the only game in town, attendance at Yankee Stadium fell below that of 1957. However, the grievous events in New York did not affect the Yankees' ability to attract fans in other cities. When Don Larsen opened the new season with a 3–0 shutout against Pinky Higgins's Boston Red Sox, a crowd of 35,223 was at Fenway Park to see it. The attendance was the largest ever for a Red Sox home opener, bettering the previous mark of 33,955 set in 1949, also against the Yankees. Boston's Willard Nixon matched Larsen's scoreless pitching for six innings, but he weakened in the seventh when the Yankees scored their three runs. Yogi Berra's home run accounted for two, and doubles by Bill Skowron and Andy Carey the third.

For decades, the Yankees had concluded the exhibition season with a weekend series against the Dodgers. This year, with Brooklyn gone, they played a two-game home-and-home series with the Phillies instead. Then, after working out at the Stadium on Monday, the Yanks left for Boston on the 6 P.M. train. The Red Sox had finished third in 1957, their best showing in six years. In their only significant off-season move, they traded first baseman Norm Zauchin and rookie outfielder Albie Pearson to the Washington Senators for infielder Pete Runnels. Pearson would earn Rookie of the Year honors in 1958, but Runnels, who had slipped to .230 in 1957, hit .322 in his first year in Boston. That was good for second place behind teammate Ted Williams's .328. Runnels would later win two batting championships as a member of the Red Sox, in 1960 and 1962.

Williams had energized the baseball world in 1957 by batting .388, the game's highest average since his own .406 in 1941. The Red Sox rewarded him with a reported salary of $135,000, making him the highest-paid player ever. But to the disappointment of the huge gathering, he was still recovering from a case of food poisoning and was not in uniform today. Williams attributed his illness to some bad oysters he had eaten on the train that took the Red Sox from Richmond, Virginia, to Washington for yesterday's "presidential opener." He had missed that game too—a 5–2 Senators victory in the first game played under the new American League decree that required batters to wear a protective helmet. On the advice of his doctor, Williams would sit out another day, spending Boston's home opener not with his teammates at Fenway Park, but back at his hotel listening to the game on the radio. The Sox would be televising 51 games in 1958, but this was not one of them.

Red Sox owner Tom Yawkey was another notable absentee. Yawkey was at his home in Georgetown, South Carolina, attending to personal business. There were, however, several other sports celebrities present. A group of hockey players from the Montreal Canadiens was at the game, including Bernie "Boom Boom" Geoffrion, Doug Harvey, Bert Olmstead, and Dickie Moore. They watched batting practice and the first three innings before leaving to prepare for that night's game against the Boston Bruins at the Boston Garden. The Bruins would defeat the Canadiens, 3–1, tying the Stanley Cup finals at two games apiece.

The record crowd made for gigantic traffic jams in the narrow streets around Fenway Park and revived discussion in Boston of the need for a new stadium. When the fans with tickets finally got seated, they noticed an interesting name change in Fenway Park's familiar left-field scoreboard. In the slot reserved for the home team's inning-by-inning score, which had read "*BOSTON*" since the park opened in 1912, were the words "*RED SOX*." After the Harvard Band provided the pregame amusement by entertaining the crowd with songs from previous eras in Red Sox history, both clubs lined up along the foul lines in numerical order. (More correctly, it was near numerical order—Hank Bauer, No. 9, was standing between Mickey Mantle, No. 7, and Berra, No. 8. It was the only mistake the Yankees made all day.) Massachusetts Governor Foster Furcolo, standing on the mound, threw out the first ball. Behind the plate to receive Furcolo's toss was Boston mayor John Hynes and behind him, dressed as an umpire, was comedian Bob Hope who was in town for the premier of his latest picture, "Paris Holiday" but also took the time to raise money for United Cerebral Palsy.

As far back as December, at a banquet in California, Larsen had informed manager Casey Stengel that he planned to be the Yankees' opening-day pitcher. Evidently Larsen had become a more responsible person since getting married last winter. He went out and earned the opening-day assignment by reporting to training camp in good shape, something he had not always done in the past. He also pitched more spring training innings this year than he ever had before. As a member of the St. Louis Brown/Baltimore Orioles, Larsen had been 0–6 against the Red Sox, but since joining the Yankees in 1955, he had beaten them nine of 12 times. Larsen's turnaround against Boston was another illustration of the advantages of pitching for a good team, and in these years the Yankees were far more than just a good team. They entered the new season expecting to win another pennant, with their only concern being the status of Tony Kubek. Kubek was in New York being treated for a pulled hamstring in his left thigh, but it was not his injury that had the Yankees worried. The cause of their distress was a report emanating from Milwaukee that Kubek would be inducted into the army on May 24 to begin serving a six-month tour of duty. Stengel had decided to make him the regular shortstop this season, and if the rumor were true it would be a setback to their pennant hopes. Kubek's mother, back in Milwaukee, said it was a false rumor, which, as it turned out, it was. Gil McDougald subbed for Kubek this afternoon. McDougald, the regular shortstop in 1957, would play the 1958 season primarily at second base, a position Bobby Richardson was manning in the opener. Billy Martin (traded to the Kansas City A's) and Jerry Coleman (retired), both longtime Yankees' second basemen, were no longer with the club. The team had also lost two other veterans to retirement: first baseman Joe Collins and pitcher Tommy Byrne.

Nixon, a hard-throwing right-hander who had been with Boston since 1950, had a winning lifetime record (12–9) against the Yankees, which in this era made him a rarity. He remained true to form as a Yankees nemesis through six innings, allowing just one hit, a second-inning, leadoff single to Berra. Nixon began the seventh with two quick strikes on Mantle, leading off. But Mantle, who over the years had become a more selective hitter, laid off the next four pitches, all of which were out of the strike zone. Nixon then got ahead of Berra, 0–2, and followed with two pitches that may also have been strikes, but Yogi fouled them off. His next pitch was a fastball at chin level that Berra hit on a high lazy arc down the right-field line. The ball was curving, but the distance to the foul pole was only 302 feet, and before the ball could land in foul territory it hit against the pole for a two-run homer—the fourth consecutive season Berra had hit an opening-day home run. Skowron, the club leader in home runs and runs batted in during the exhibition season, followed with a drive into the wind that hit high off the wall in left center. Center fielder

Jim Piersall quickly retrieved the ball, holding Skowron to a double. After Elston Howard, playing left field today, sacrificed the runner to third, Carey scored him with a double that struck the wall at almost the exact spot that Skowron's smash had. Nixon got the next two batters, Richardson and Larsen, on ground balls, one to shortstop Don Buddin and one to third baseman Frank Malzone. On each, first baseman Runnels was forced to dig the ball out of the dirt to avoid a possible throwing error. Buddin, who would lead American League shortstops in errors this year and next, had played a full season at shortstop for Boston in 1956 but missed the entire 1957 season serving in the military.

Malzone, a Bronx native, had Boston's first hit, an infield single with one out in the second, the inning in which the Red Sox had their best scoring opportunity. After Malzone's hit, Larsen walked the next two batters, Piersall and second baseman Ken Aspromonte, to load the bases. But Carey fielded Boston catcher Pete Daley's slowly hit grounder to third and threw it to Richardson to start an inning-ending double play. The Red Sox managed three other singles, by Buddin, Piersall, and Nixon, but all came in different innings. Only one other Boston runner made it to second base; that was Nixon who was sacrificed there by Buddin after his single in the sixth. With Nixon at second, Larsen got Runnels on a line drive to Bauer but then walked Gene Stephens. That brought up Jackie Jensen, who had homered yesterday in Washington. Jensen hit the ball hard but right at Carey, who stepped on third for the inning-ending force out. Larsen needed only 97 pitches and just under two hours to secure his fifth consecutive win against Boston.

Tuesday, April 15, 1958

New York	ab	r	h	rbi		Boston	ab	r	h	rbi
Bauer rf	4	0	0	0		Buddin ss	3	0	1	0
McDougald ss	4	0	0	0		Runnels 1b	4	0	0	0
Mantle cf	2	1	0	0		Stephens lf	3	0	0	0
Berra c	4	1	2	2		Jensen rf	4	0	0	0
Skowron 1b	4	1	1	0		Malzone 3b	4	0	1	0
Howard lf	2	0	1	0		Piersall cf	2	0	1	0
cDel Greco lf	0	0	0	0		Aspromonte 2b	2	0	0	0
Carey 3b	4	0	1	1		Daley c	2	0	0	0
Richardson 2b	4	0	0	0		aKlaus	1	0	0	0
Larsen p	3	0	0	0		Fornieles p	0	0	0	0
Total	31	3	5	3		Nixon p	2	0	1	0
						bGernert	1	0	0	0
						White c	0	0	0	0
						Total	28	0	4	0

aStruck out for Daley in eighth inning.
bGrounded out for Nixon in eighth inning.
cRan for Howard in ninth inning.

New York	000	000	300–3
Boston	000	000	000–0

Error—Buddin. Assists—New York 12, Boston 11. Double plays—Buddin, Aspromonte, and Runnels; Carey, Richardson and Skowron; McDougald, Richardson, and Skowron. Left on bases—New York 5; Boston 5. Put outs—New York 27: Howard 4, Carey 1, Richardson 4, Skowron 10, Bauer 2, Berra 2, Mantle 2, McDougald 1, Larsen 1. Boston 27: Runnels 13, Malzone 1, Aspromonte 3, Daley 4, Piersall 5, White 1. Assists—New York 12: Skowron 1, McDougald 4, Carey 3, Richardson 2, Berra 1, Larsen 1. Boston 13: Runnels 1, Nixon 1, Buddin 7, Malzone 3, Aspromonte 1. Two-base hits—Skowron, Carey, Howard. Home run—Berra. Sacrifices—Buddin, Howard.

	IP	H	R	ER	BB	SO
NEW YORK						
Larsen (W, 1–0)	9.0	4	0	0	3	2
BOSTON						
Nixon (L, 0–1)	8.0	4	3	3	3	3
Fornieles	1.0	1	0	0	0	1

Umpires—Summers, Honochick, Soar, and Umont. Time of game—1 hr. 58 min. Attendance—35,223.

The Yankees (92–62) won their fourth straight pennant, finishing ten games ahead of the Chicago White Sox. They came back from a three-games-to-one deficit against the Milwaukee Braves to avenge their World Series defeat of 1957. Bob Turley (21–7), the league's only 20-game winner, won the Cy Young Award at a time when only one award was given to cover both leagues. Turley finished second to Jackie Jensen in the voting for the Most Valuable Player Award. Ryne Duren tied Dick Hyde of Washington for the league lead in saves (not yet an official statistic), with 19, and finished second to Albie Pearson as Rookie of the Year.

Sunday, April 12, 1959
Yankee Stadium, New York
New York 3 Boston 2

The first day of spring is one thing, and the first spring day is another.
The difference between them is sometimes as great as a month.—Henry Jackson van Dyke

Baseball poets like to remind us that the seasons of the game correspond to the seasons of the year, and ultimately, to the seasons of our lives. At the heart of this allegory is spring as a symbol of renewal, and Opening Day (to fans the true first day of spring) as a fresh beginning. No team has yet lost a game and all have a chance, however varying, at winning the pennant. Sometimes, however, the reality of April weather plays havoc with this cherished illusion. By the time the Yankees and the Boston Red Sox belatedly got their 1959 seasons underway, every other team in both leagues had already played at least once. The Chicago White Sox were leading the American League with a 2–0 record, while in the National League the Pittsburgh Pirates had lost three games and were in last place.

Rain in New York had postponed the first two attempts to play the opener, but on the third day the precipitation finally ended. However, although it was no longer raining, it was windy and unseasonably cold; the temperature was 42 degrees at game time and it would never get any higher. The outfield grass was still wet and slippery, and debris powered by wind gusts blew around the stadium all afternoon. It was just an uncomfortable day to be at the ballpark, but after losing two dates, management—which estimated the two postponements had cost the club $100,000—wanted this one played. Yankees' officials were reluctant to lose another big home crowd, especially on a Sunday when attendance is traditionally higher. Nevertheless, it was not very high today; because of the frosty conditions only 22,559 hardy fans turned out for the Yankees' first-ever Sunday opener. Those who came liked what they saw: a well-played game and a home team victory. Bob Turley pitched a brilliant two-hitter, and Norm Siebern (now wearing glasses) hit an eighth-inning home run to give the Yanks a, 3–2, victory. The fans left the Stadium certain that they had seen the first step toward a fifth consecutive pennant. Few suspected that 1959 would be the Yankees' poorest season in 34 years.

Presumably, the front office was also confident of winning another championship. The Yankees made no off-season trades, and co-owner Dan Topping, so sure the team needed no help, abolished the spring training instructional school as a way to save money. (That was the school started by Casey Stengel that had helped launch so many of the team's youngsters on their way to the major leagues.) However, as the regular season approached and a series of injuries hit the team, general manager George Weiss began looking for replacements. While he was unable to make a major deal, he did make a minor one with the Kansas City Athletics. On Opening Day, Weiss traded minor leaguers Russ Snyder and Tom Carroll to the Athletics for Bob Martyn and Mike Baxes, neither of who ever played in another major-league game. The Yanks had given Carroll, an infielder, a large bonus in 1954, and under the rules of the day had to keep him on the major-league roster for the entire 1955 and 1956 seasons. In those two seasons he got into a total of 50 games with only 24 plate appearances. Carroll had been the last significant player signed by the late Paul Krichell, the scout who signed Lou Gehrig, Tony Lazzeri, and Whitey Ford.

Unlike the Yankees, the Red Sox, who finished third in 1958, had made several changes. They traded Jim Piersall, who spent eight stormy years in Boston, to the Cleveland Indians for Gary Geiger, a rookie in 1958, and veteran first baseman Vic Wertz. Infielder Billy Klaus went to the Baltimore Orioles for outfielder Jim Busby, and rookie pitcher Jerry Casale, who would become Boston's leading winner this season. One change the Red Sox had not made was in the complexion of their personnel. On Opening Day 1959, Boston remained the lone major-league team that had never had a black player. They did get as far as bringing one to training camp this spring, an infielder named Pumpsie Green, but sent him back to the Minneapolis Millers of the American Association, their top farm team. However, after Green batted .320 in 98 games for the Millers, the Sox relented and recalled him in mid–July. Twelve years after Jackie Robinson appeared in his first game with Brooklyn, each of the 16 major-league teams had been racially integrated.

Shortly after leaving their spring training base in Scottsdale, Arizona, a mysterious virus had struck the Red Sox, temporarily incapacitating several players. The club doctor sent three of them back to Boston: outfielder Bill Renna and pitchers Frank Sullivan and Ted Bowsfield. A more consequential loss for manager Pinky Higgins was the absence of Ted Williams, who was still wearing a brace around his neck to ease the pain of a pinched nerve. After winning his fifth and sixth batting championships the previous two seasons, 1959 would be a terrible disappointment for the 41-year-old Williams and his millions of fans. He would play in only 103 games and bat a lowly .254, the only time in his distinguished career he batted below .300.

Cold weather or not, Opening Day would not be complete without the traditional pregame ceremonies. This year they included a special presentation by Major General J. F. R. Seitz, chief of staff of the First Army, to co-owners Topping and Del Webb. It was the First Army Appreciation Award, given to the Yankees for their years of allowing servicemen to attend games at Yankee Stadium free of charge. The Yankees had invited Chief Justice Earl Warren to attend the opener, which he had tried to do on each of the previous two days but was unable to do today. However, another invited guest was there: Captain Felipe Guerra Matos, a compatriot of Fidel Castro, the revolutionary Cuban leader who had come to power two months earlier.

The Sporting News recognized Turley's great 1958 season with two awards: Player of the Year and the Cy Young Award. The latter award was presented by Will Harridge, who had recently retired as president of the American League. His successor was Joe Cronin, a former star player and manager with the Senators and the Red Sox, who had signed a seven-year contract in January. Barney Kremenko of the *New York Journal-American*, chairman of the New York chapter of the Baseball Writers Association, presented the Babe Ruth Award to Elston Howard as the outstanding player of the 1958 World Series. Bronx businessman Frank Kridel gave manager Stengel a floral wreath from the fans, and Commissioner Ford Frick presented the Yankees with their World Series mementoes. Some were women's rings, requested by players who already had several World Series rings and wanted something for their wives. Harridge, who had held his post since 1931, was given the honor of throwing out the first ball.

As Turley warmed up on the mound, a message appeared on the new scoreboard informing the crowd that this would be his first opening-day start. The ultramodern scoreboard, a huge structure costing $250,000 that sat atop the bleachers in right-center field, was a welcome addition to the fans. They were pleased at the news and statistical information they would now be receiving.

The Yankees took a 2–0 lead in their first at-bat with four singles off Boston starter Tom Brewer. There were two outs when Yogi Berra's single sent Siebern, who had gotten the first hit, to second. Gil McDougald followed with a ground ball to the left of second baseman Pete Runnels that went under his glove and into right field, scoring Siebern. First baseman Marv Throneberry's single brought Berra home with the second run. Throneberry, the Minor-League Player of the Year with Denver back in 1956 (the same award Siebern won in 1957), was replacing the ailing Bill Skowron at first base. Skowron, who again led the club in batting during the exhibition season (he hit .466), was unable to play because of a strained sacroiliac. It was the most recent flare-up of a recurrent back problem that dated from September 1957, when he first injured it while lifting an air-conditioning unit at his home in Hillsdale, New Jersey.

Turley, who walked Don Buddin to lead off the game and got the next batter to hit into a double play, had faced the minimum 18 batters through six innings. But in the seventh, Buddin walked again, and Runnels followed with a blooper to the opposite field that went for a grounds-rule double; a soft fly that landed just off the left-field foul line and bounded into the stands. Moments later, Buddin, who had been forced to hold at third, scored Boston's first run as Gene Stephens was grounding out to Throneberry. Then, after Wertz walked, Jackie Jensen hit a fly ball to Siebern in left that brought Runnels home with the tying run.

Siebern's game-winning, eighth-inning home run, on a 2–2 pitch, was his third hit of the game. It was a high drive that just reached the corner of the right-center field bleachers adjacent to the Yankees bullpen. How satisfying the cheers of the crowd must have been for Siebern, and how different from the booing he heard in his most recent Stadium appearance, the fourth game of last year's World Series. Only the Yankees' dramatic sweep of the final three games had prevented Siebern from being the series "goat." Playing left field, the sun field at Yankee Stadium, he had encountered the same predicament that so many before him had faced. The angle of the sun in late September and early October and the haze that hung over the stadium made it difficult to pick up the trajectory of fly balls. Stengel predictably responded to Siebern's plight by benching him for the final three games.

Sunday, April 12, 1959

Boston	ab	r	h	rbi		New York	ab	r	h	rbi
Buddin ss	2	1	0	0		Bauer rf	4	0	1	0
Runnels 2b	3	1	1	0		Siebern lf	4	2	3	1
Stephens lf	4	0	0	1		Mantle cf	4	0	0	0
Wertz 1b	3	0	1	0		Berra c	3	1	1	0
aBusby	0	0	0	0		McDougald 2b	3	0	1	1
Jensen rf	3	0	0	1		Throneberry 1b	3	0	1	1
Malzone 3b	3	0	0	0		Carey 3b	3	0	1	0
Geiger lf	3	0	0	0		Richardson ss	3	0	0	0
White c	3	0	0	0		Turley p	3	0	0	0
Brewer p	3	0	0	0		Total	30	3	8	3
Total	27	2	2	2						

aRan for Wertz in ninth inning.

Boston	000	000	200–2
New York	200	000	01X–3

Errors—None. Assists—Boston 12, New York 12. Double plays—McDougald, Richardson and Throneberry. Caught stealing—Berra. Left on bases—Boston 3; New York 4. Two-base hit—Runnels. Home run—Siebern. Sacrifice fly—Jensen.

	IP	H	R	ER	BB	SO
BOSTON						
Brewer (L, 0–1)	8.0	8	3	3	1	4
NEW YORK						
Turley (W, 1–0)	9.0	2	2	2	4	4

Passed ball—White. Umpires—Rommel, Stevens, Napp, and Rice. Time of game—2 hr. 7 min. Attendance—22,559.

Mickey Mantle followed Siebern's blast by putting one in almost the same spot. However, it was a few feet short and to the right, allowing right fielder Jensen to lean back over the three-foot high gate to the Yankees bullpen and catch it. Nonetheless, Turley had a one-run lead as he went out to pitch the ninth. He got through it, but not without a struggle. After Runnels drew a one-out walk, Stephens drove a ball to right-center that would have tied the game had it gone through. It didn't. Mantle, using his great speed, ran it down and then threw back to Throneberry in an unsuccessful attempt to double Runnels off first. Mantle had injured his throwing arm in a game against Milwaukee on March 11 in a situation similar to this one. Therefore, when he stopped to rub his shoulder and swing his arm about, the Yankees held their collective breaths. Mantle later reassured them that he had not reinjured himself. "There is nothing wrong with the arm," he said. "Maybe the arm was a little stiff because I'd been standing out there in the cold a pretty long time. But nothing hurt when I cut loose with the throw."

With two out, Wertz collected Boston's second hit, a pop-fly single that fell in short right field and sent Runnels to third. The potential winning run was at first as Turley faced Jensen, the league's RBI king and Most Valuable Player. As snow began to fall, Turley ended the game by getting Jensen to hit a ground ball to Bobby Richardson, playing shortstop. Richardson smoothly picked it up and tossed it to McDougald for the force on Busby, running for Wertz. Richardson was at short because Tony Kubek had not gotten his military obligation completed until late March and was not fully ready to play.

Although he limited the Red Sox to just two safeties, neither of which was solidly hit, Turley's best effort of the season lay ahead of him. On July 4, in the second game of a doubleheader at Washington, he pitched a one-hitter in shutting out the Senators, 7–0. The one hit was a ninth-inning bloop single by Julio Becquer that fell at left fielder Siebern's feet. However, despite occasional well-pitched games, Turley would never again be the pitcher he had been. Bone chips in his elbow cost him his fastball, and his record slipped to 8–11 in 1959. He would hang on for another four years, through 1963, but win just 18 more games.

> *The Yankees failed in their attempt to win a fifth consecutive pennant. They won just 79 games (79–75), their lowest total since 1925, and finished in third place, 15 games behind the Chicago White Sox. In 11 years under Casey Stengel, New York had won nine pennants, and the two they lost were to teams managed by Al Lopez: Cleveland in 1954 and Chicago in 1959. Despite their poor season, the Yanks increased their home attendance by more than 100,000 to 1,552,030, their first sizeable increase after ten years of almost steady decline.*

VII

1960–1969

In 1960, Casey Stengel won his tenth pennant in 12 years, but after losing the World Series in seven games to the Pittsburgh Pirates the Yankees fired both Stengel and general manager George Weiss, the man who had hired him in 1949. Ralph Houk, a former Yankees' catcher, moved up from the club's Triple A team at Denver to replace Stengel and led the Yanks to three consecutive pennants. He stepped up to be the general manager after the 1963 season, and Yogi Berra became the manager. Berra won the Yankees' fifth straight pennant in 1964, but after they lost the World Series to the St. Louis Cardinals, Houk fired him.

Johnny Keane, the Cardinals' manager in 1964, became the Yankees' manager in 1965, only to be replaced early the next year by Houk. Houk would stay on as manager while the club's ownership moved from Dan Topping and Del Webb to the Columbia Broadcasting System and then to a partnership group headed by George Steinbrenner. The 1964 pennant would be the last for 12 years as the Yankees dynasty that began with Babe Ruth finally ended. In 1966, after CBS purchased them, the Yanks finished last. Because two teams had been added in 1961 that meant tenth place. Two more teams were added in 1969, and both leagues split into six-team divisions.

The Yankees of the early '60s, with Mickey Mantle, Roger Maris, Bill Skowron, Tony Kubek, Yogi Berra, Elston Howard, Bobby Richardson, and Whitey Ford, were a team comparable to the best in baseball history. But by the time the decade ended, all were gone, and the Yanks, despite some fine players like pitcher Mel Stottlemyre and outfielder Bobby Murcer, had become also-rans.

Tuesday, April 19, 1960
Fenway Park, Boston
New York 8 Boston 4

The best is yet to be.—Robert Browning

Forty years after Babe Ruth made his Yankees' debut, Roger Maris, a man whom the public would forever link to the Babe, made his. Both had come to New York at age 25 in off-season transactions with the Yankees' preferred trading partner of the time: Ruth from the Boston Red Sox and Maris from the Kansas City Athletics. Obviously, at the time of the trade, in December 1959, no one was thinking of Maris in Ruthian terms; nevertheless, astute observers were aware that the Yanks had added a player of great potential. And unlike Ruth, whose eighth-inning error led to a defeat at Philadelphia in his 1920 debut,

Maris began his Yankees career in spectacular fashion. Playing before a crowd of 35,162, the third-largest home-opening crowd ever at Fenway Park, Maris had four hits—including a double and two home runs—and four runs batted in. Bill Skowron also had four hits as the Yanks banged out a total of 17 against five Boston pitchers in drubbing the Red Sox, 8–4. Ted Williams provided the home crowd with their biggest thrill of the day when he connected for an eighth-inning home run, the 494th of his illustrious career.

Right-hander Jim Coates went the distance for New York, allowing Boston nine hits and three walks. Coates had been in the Yankees organization since 1952 and was the International League's Pitcher of the Year with Richmond in 1957. After fracturing his right elbow in 1958, a potentially career-ending injury, he recovered with the help of Virginians manager Ed Lopat and again became a successful pitcher. (Lopat, the Yankees ace left-hander of the early 1950s, was now their pitching coach, having replaced the fired Jim Turner.) As a rookie in 1959, Coates was 6–1 for the Yanks, mostly in relief, but he did make four starts, completing two. The six-foot-four sophomore earned the opening-day assignment by being the team's most effective Grapefruit League pitcher. Although this exhibition season was the first time in Casey Stengel's 12 years as manager that no pitcher had gone nine innings, Coates, with seven, had gone the longest. Still, no Yankees' pitcher had started an opener with fewer lifetime wins than Coates since Marty McHale in 1914. McHale had only two wins (2–6) when he defeated Joe Bush and the Philadelphia Athletics, 8–2 at the Polo Grounds.

The Yankees, seeking the players necessary to rebound from their disappointing third-place finish in 1959, once again got the help they needed from the lowly Kansas City Athletics. General manager George Weiss had specifically targeted Maris, a left-handed power hitter who had hit 58 home runs in his three years with Kansas City and Cleveland. Weiss surmised that he would do even better at Yankee Stadium, with its short right-field porch. To get Maris, the Yankees sent the A's three players they now considered expendable: Hank Bauer, Don Larsen, and Norm Siebern. Bauer had been a prominent member of the team for 12 seasons and was second only to Yogi Berra in length of service. He was a man of character and competence, but at age 37 his best years were behind him. Larsen, whose victory total had fallen to six in 1959 (6–7), had no substantive place in the team's plans, and Siebern had never sufficiently impressed Stengel despite his demonstrated ability. Joe DeMaestri, a shortstop, and Kent Hadley, a first baseman, accompanied Maris to New York.

Getting Maris had been the only positive event of an otherwise difficult off-season for the Yankees. Weiss was unhappy at not winning the pennant in 1959 and focused on Stengel as the probable cause of the collapse. He concluded that at 69, Casey was no longer as alert as he once had been and made plans to replace him, possibly after the 1960 season when his contract expired. The Yankees also had to deal with salary disputes, some so acrimonious they caused Whitey Ford and Mickey Mantle to stage abbreviated holdouts. Weiss, notoriously tight fisted in salary negotiations, usually got his way in an era when players had little or no recourse. He eventually signed Mantle for $65,000, seven thousand dollars less than Mickey had earned the year before. Weiss had wanted to cut his salary even deeper after Mantle's batting average dropped to .285 in 1959 with "just" 31 home runs and 75 runs batted in. New York's problems continued into spring training, where the team finished the exhibition schedule with a record of 11–21, the worst in the American League. On the weekend before the opener, they concluded the preseason by losing two uninspired games to the Red Sox at Yankee Stadium. Traditionally, both leagues begin their regular seasons at about the same time, but this year the National League was already playing league games, having opened their regular season a week earlier.

Fenway Park had been a difficult place for the Yankees in 1959. They won only three of the 11 games played there and lost the season series to the Red Sox (9–13) for the first time since 1948. Yet despite their troubles with Boston last year, the Yanks continued to do well against Tom Brewer, today's starter, holding a 14–6 lifetime advantage over him. Even so, Brewer was among the players the two teams were discussing for a possible multiplayer trade. The consensus was that Brewer and outfielder Gene Stephens would go to the Yankees for infielder/outfielder Hector Lopez and pitcher Bob Turley. None of the supposed participants had a very good Opening Day, which may be one reason the trade never happened. Turley did not play, but Brewer was hit hard, Stephens went hitless and dropped a fly ball, and Lopez was the only Yankee starter who failed to get a hit.

Appropriately, on this windy but bright Patriots Day, general manager Ed McKeever and head coach Lou Saban of the new American Football League's Boston Patriots were at the game. So too was the commissioner of the league, Joe Foss, a World War II hero and the former governor of South Dakota. Earlier in the day, the Patriots had unveiled their club symbol—an angry-looking Continental Army soldier taking the position of a football center. The new league would begin their challenge to the established National Football League in the fall. Also, earlier today, Paavo Kotila, a 32-year-old Finnish farmer, won the Boston Marathon with a time of 2:20:54. The Harvard Band entertained with a variety of songs before the game and later played "The Star-Spangled Banner." Oddly, when the announcer asked both teams to line up along the foul lines for the national anthem, the Yankees did so along the third base line, but the Red Sox never appeared. Mayor John Collins of Boston, with Massachusetts governor Foster Furcolo at his side, threw out the first ball. Collins, a polio victim, made the throw from his wheelchair to catcher Haywood Sullivan.

When the Yankees posted their lineup, it had Maris in right field and Lopez in left. During the exhibition season, including the final two games at the Stadium, Maris had played left field and Lopez right. However, at Fenway Park right field was the more demanding position, so Stengel switched them for the opener and would keep Maris in right field for most of the season. Despite some fielding problems in the weekend games, Maris was an exceptional outfielder and Lopez was an extremely poor one. Lopez, the American League's first player born in Panama, had come to the Yankees from Kansas City in May 1959 for Jerry Lumpe, Tom Sturdivant, and Johnny Kucks. New York also reacquired pitcher Ralph Terry in the deal.

Stengel shook up his batting order in an attempt to revive his sluggish offense. He moved Maris into the leadoff position (he had batted leadoff twice with Kansas City in 1959), put Bobby Richardson second, Gil McDougald third, Lopez in the clean-up spot, and dropped Mantle to fifth. McDougald, playing third base today, had announced that 1960 would be his final season. Last year, the versatile infielder had become the first Yankee ever to start at least 20 games at second base, third base, and shortstop in the same season.

The revamped batting order produced no runs through the first three innings, for which the Red Sox infield can take much of the credit. Led by third baseman Frank Malzone, who turned in several acrobatic plays, the Sox backed Brewer with two double plays in the first three innings and a total of four while he was pitching. Boston had given Brewer a 1–0 lead in the first on base hits by Pete Runnels and Malzone and a sacrifice fly to right by Stephens. But in the fourth, the Yankees moved in front, 2–1, on singles by McDougald and Skowron, a double by Mantle, and another single by Elston Howard. Mantle's blow was a high drive that sailed over the head of center fielder Bobby Thomson, the man who in 1951 hit the most dramatic home run in baseball history. After 14 years in the National League, Thomson was playing in his first American League game, as Red Sox manager Billy Jurges tried to adjust for the void left by Jackie Jensen's retirement. Jensen's fear of flying compelled him to leave the game even though he had been the league's runs batted in leader for each of the past two seasons. After sitting out the entire year, Jensen would return in 1961, play that one year, and then retire permanently.

Maris's first home run, a towering blast into the right-field bleachers, came in the fifth inning and followed a leadoff single by Coates. Then, after Richardson singled and McDougald grounded into a double play, Lopez hit a fly ball to right that Stephens dropped. The official scorer, disregarding the wind and bright sun, charged Stephens with an error. Following a walk to Mantle, Skowron chased both runners home with a long double and the Yankees led, 6–1. Jurges replaced Brewer with Frank Sullivan, and it took the battery of Sullivan and Sullivan three pitches to dispose of Howard and end the inning. In the bottom of the fifth, Boston got their first two men aboard on walks to pinch-hitter Marty Keough and Don Buddin. However, Coates got Runnels to hit a ground ball to shortstop Tony Kubek, who started a quick double play to defuse the rally. Although Kubek was beginning his fourth year with the club, this was his first opening-day appearance. Injuries and military commitments had caused him to miss the previous three. Keough, who went to third on the double play, scored on a double by Malzone, a low line drive that managed to get over Lopez's head.

Maris drove in the Yankees' final two runs. His single off Nelson Chittum scored Kubek in the sixth, and he hit his second home run of the day in the eighth. It came off lefty Ted Bowsfield and, like the first, landed in the right-field bleachers. Al Worthington, another former National Leaguer making his American League debut, held the Yankees scoreless in his 1⅔ innings.

Boston's pitching was getting off to a very poor start. The eight runs they gave up today followed the ten they gave up in the 10–1 loss in the "presidential opener" at Washington, a game in which Senators' pitcher Camilo Pascual fanned 15 Red Sox batters. Boston's lone run came on a home run by Williams, the 493rd of his career, tying him with Lou Gehrig for fourth place on the all-time list. Williams had played his first major-league game on Opening Day 1939 at Yankee Stadium, getting one hit—a double—in four at-bats against Red Ruffing. Playing first base for New York in that long-ago game was Gehrig, the only time that Williams and Gehrig played against each other. Gehrig had already accumulated his 493 lifetime home runs, which at the time trailed only Babe Ruth. But with his home run today, a liner into the seats in the right-field corner, Williams moved into sole possession of fourth place and dropped Gehrig to fifth. Still ahead of him were Babe Ruth (714), Jimmie Foxx (534), and Mel Ott (511). Williams would hit 27 more home runs in 1960—including one in the last at-bat of his career—for a season total of 29. At the time no one had hit more in his final season. (Dave Kingman of the Oakland A's would hit 35 in 1986 and Boston's David Ortiz would hit 38 in 2016.) Williams had a lifetime total of 521 home runs when he retired, trailing only Ruth and Foxx.

Tuesday, April 19, 1960

New York	ab	r	h	rbi	Boston	ab	r	h	rbi
Maris rf	5	2	4	4	Buddin ss	3	0	2	1
Richardson 2b	5	0	2	0	ᵈWebster pr	0	0	0	0

New York   Boston

	ab	r	h	rbi
McDougald 3b	5	1	2	0
Lopez lf	5	1	0	0
Hunt lf	0	0	0	0
Mantle cf	3	2	2	1
Skowron 1b	5	0	4	2
Howard c	5	0	1	1
Kubek ss	5	1	1	0
Coates p	3	1	1	0
Total	41	8	17	8

	ab	r	h	rbi
Runnels 2b	5	1	2	0
Malzone 3b	4	0	2	1
Stephens rf	3	0	0	1
Williams lf	4	1	1	1
Busby lf	0	0	0	0
Thomson cf	4	0	0	0
Jackson 1b	4	0	1	0
H. Sullivan c	4	1	1	0
Brewer p	1	0	0	0
F. Sullivan p	0	0	0	0
^aKeough	0	1	0	0
Chittum p	0	0	0	0
^bGeiger	1	0	0	0
Bowsfield p	0	0	0	0
Worthington p	0	0	0	0
^cWertz	1	0	0	0
Total	34	4	9	4

[a]Walked for F. Sullivan in fifth inning.
[b]Grounded out for Chittum in seventh inning.
[c]Flied out for Worthington in ninth inning.
[d]Ran for Buddin in the ninth inning

New York   000   241   010–8
Boston   100   010   011–4

Errors—Stephens, H. Sullivan, Hunt. Double plays—Buddin, Runnels, and Jackson; Malzone and Runnels; Runnels, Buddin, and Jackson; Malzone, Runnels, and Jackson; Kubek, Richardson, and Skowron. Left on bases—New York 12; Boston 7. Put outs—New York 27: Maris 6, Richardson 2, McDougald, Lopez 3, Hunt, Mantle 3, Skowron 4, Howard 4, Kubek 2, Coates. Boston 27: Buddin 2, Runnels 4, Malzone, Stephens 3, Williams 2, Thomson 3, Jackson 8, H. Sullivan 4. Assists—New York 7: Richardson, McDougald 2, Skowron, Kubek 3. Boston 12: Buddin 2, Runnels 4, Malzone 3, Brewer 2, Chittum. Two-base hits—Maris, Buddin, Mantle, Skowron, Malzone. Home runs—Maris 2, Williams. Sacrifice—Coates. Sacrifice fly—Stephens.

	IP	H	R	ER	BB	SO
NEW YORK						
Coates (W, 1–0)	9.0	9	4	3	3	2
BOSTON						
Brewer (L, 0–1)	4.2	11	6	4	2	0
F. Sullivan	.1	0	0	0	0	0
Chittum	2.0	3	1	1	0	1
Bowsfield	.2	3	1	1	1	2
Worthington	1.1	0	0	0	2	0

Wild pitch—Brewer. Passed ball—Howard. Umpires—Hurley, Soar, Flaherty, and Stewart. Time of game—3 hrs. 2 min. Attendance—35,162.

Boston scored their last run, an unearned one, in the ninth. Rookie Ken Hunt, taking Lopez's place in left for defensive purposes, bobbled Haywood Sullivan's single, allowing Sullivan to take second. Although he had appeared in eight games for Boston, spread over three years (1955, 1957, and 1959), Sullivan had been hitless in his 12 at-bats. After taking third on Howard's passed ball, he scored on Buddin's two-out single. Coates ended the game, getting Runnels on a fly ball to Hunt. Stengel and Lopat used Coates as a starter and reliever in 1960. His 13 wins (13–3) were second highest on the club to Art Ditmar's 15 (15–

9). After two seasons in the league, Coates had a win-loss record of 19–4, giving him an .826 winning percentage.

> *In this final season of the 154-game schedule in the American League, the Yankees (97–57), won their last 15 games to finish eight games ahead of their young challengers, the Baltimore Orioles. Although they outscored the Pittsburgh Pirates 55–27 in the World Series, Pittsburgh won in seven games. After the season the Yankees replaced Casey Stengel with Ralph Houk. Led by league-leader Mickey Mantle with 40 and runner-up Roger Maris with 39, the Yanks hit 193 home runs to break the American League record they had established in 1956. Maris led the league in runs batted in (112) and slugging percentage (.581) and narrowly beat out Mantle to capture the Most Valuable Player Award.*

Tuesday, April 11, 1961
Yankee Stadium, New York
Minnesota 6 New York 0

Is baseball a business? If it isn't, General Motors is a sport.—Jim Murray

With the beginning of the 1961 season, the basic structure of major-league baseball changed. That structure, two eight-team leagues with each team playing every other league member 22 times for a total of 154 games, had existed since shortly after the turn of the century. There were, to be sure, fans who could recall when the only major league was the National League, and a time in the 1890s when it consisted of 12 teams. Some old-timers even remembered the American Association, which existed from 1882 to 1891, or the short-lived 1884 Union Association and 1890 Players League, all of which had major-league status. However, for the overwhelming majority of fans, the configuration now ending was the only one they had ever known. For generations of baseball lovers it had seemed a perfect design. Nevertheless, by the late 1950s it was evident that baseball's geography was based on an America that no longer existed. Results of the 1960 U.S. Census, released today by Secretary of Commerce Luther Hodges, revealed that the new U.S. population center was in Centralia, Illinois, 57 miles west of the 1950 center. That confirmed what was already apparent: the growth of the country's population was almost entirely in the South and West.

Both leagues had agreed to expansion as a way to satisfy the desire of cities in those regions for major-league baseball. Another factor—the threatened establishment of a third league, the Continental League, helped speed the process. Under the new arrangement, the National and American leagues would each add two teams and play a 162-game schedule; the number of games against each league opponent would be reduced from 22 to 18. The National League added teams in Houston and New York, but the new entries would not begin play until 1962. The American League, with new teams in Washington and Los Angeles, chose to begin under the revised format in 1961. Many fans, recognizing this break with the established order was just a first step, worried that stability and continuity would no longer be a cherished feature of baseball. They were correct. The transformation of every facet of American life was accelerating and baseball would not be immune. Eventually the game would overhaul its entire organizational design, making millions of new fans but upsetting many they already had. Driven by their ever-growing subservience to television, the owners would justify these alterations as "progress" and claim they were "giving the fans what they want."

In awarding an expansion team to Washington, the American League was replacing its original Washington Senators franchise, moved by Calvin Griffith to Minnesota following the 1960 season. Baseball's establishment, attuned to the precariousness of the 1922 ruling by the Supreme Court that baseball was a business, but not "interstate commerce," and thus not subject to antitrust legislation, preferred not to upset Congress and other powerful interests in the nation's capital. A day earlier, with President John F. Kennedy throwing out the first ball, the new Senators had played their first game, losing to Chicago, 4–3. This afternoon, the old Senators, now the Minnesota Twins, made their official entry into the American League before 14,607 chilled fans at Yankee Stadium. For the Twins and their fans back in Minnesota, it would be a jubilant debut. Despite the bitterly cold weather, Cuban-born Pedro Ramos pitched an overpowering 6–0 shutout. He limited the Yankees to just three singles and a walk, a most improbable beginning for a team that would go on to amass a record-shattering 240 home runs this season.

For the first time since 1948, the Yankees were opening the season under a manager other than Casey Stengel, who had compiled a 10–2 record in openers. The 70-year-old Stengel had won ten pennants and seven world championships in his 12-year run, but the Yanks wanted a younger man to lead the club. They promoted first base coach Ralph Houk, 41, who as manager of their Triple A team at Denver (1955–1957), helped develop several players on the current roster. Before that, he had been a seldom-used catcher with the Yankees between 1947 and 1954. The players soon learned that Houk's managerial style differed sharply from Stengel's. He preferred a set lineup rather than Casey's platoon system, and he used a positive approach and words of encouragement, a refreshing change from Stengel's sarcasm and grumpiness. Stengel, after a year away from the game—he turned down an offer to manage the Tigers—would return to New York in 1962 as manager of the expansion Mets. There he would reunite with his old boss, George Weiss. After 29 years, the Yankees had also dumped Weiss, and the Mets immediately hired him to be their president.

Due primarily to the trade for Roger Maris, Weiss had earned *The Sporting News* award as Executive of the Year for 1960, the fourth time he had won that distinction. In the past, he had always received the award as part of the ceremonies preceding the Yankees' home opener. Although Weiss was no longer with the club, *Sporting News* publisher J. G. Taylor Spink asked that he be included in this year's pregame awards. The Yankees informed Spink that because Weiss now worked for the Mets, in the other league, they felt it would be inappropriate to honor him. Still, there were other awards to be distributed. American League president Joe Cronin and Yankees co-owners Dan Topping and Del Webb handed out the pennant souvenirs to the players. Each Yankee had a choice of a watch or a ring, with most selecting the ring. *Daily News* sportswriter Dick Young, chairman of the New York chapter of the Baseball Writers Association, presented Maris with his 1960 Most Valuable Player Award. And after years of presenting a good luck wreath to Stengel, Frank W. Kridel, representing fan groups from the Bronx, presented one to Houk.

The presentations followed the festivities at the center-field flagpole, which featured the Air Force R.O.T.C band, drill team, and color guard from Manhattan College. Singer Stuart Foster sang the national anthem. Mayor Robert F. Wagner was to have thrown out the first ball, but he was too ill to attend, so Bronx borough president James Lyons served as his proxy. Earlier, following the raising of the American flag and the 1960 pennant, the club raised the 1921 American League championship flag. That year, Babe Ruth's unprecedented slugging led the Yankees to their first World Series, which they lost to John McGraw's New York Giants. Now, 40 years after that first all–New York Series, the widows of Ruth and McGraw, Claire Ruth and Blanche McGraw, were here for the ceremony. They sat with Eleanor Gehrig, the widow of Lou Gehrig, in a box next to the Yankees dugout. When public address announcer Bob Sheppard introduced the three "grand old ladies" of New York baseball, the fans gave them a standing ovation. In response to a reporter's question, Mrs. McGraw revealed that despite the Giants abandoning New York for San Francisco, she still rooted for them. Joe DiMaggio, a more recent contributor to New York's glorious baseball history, was also at the game. DiMaggio and his former wife, actress Marilyn Monroe, sat with Topping and Webb in the Yankees' official box on the mezzanine.

Because there had been a long history of competition between the cities of Minneapolis and St. Paul, the Twins, not wanting to upset either locale, resolved to play their home games in neither one. Instead they would play at Metropolitan Stadium, built in a cornfield in Bloomington, Minnesota, equidistant from the rival cities. The Twins would also break with precedent by identifying themselves as the "MINNESOTA" Twins—the first major-league team to use a state rather than a city as their official name. However, it was not "MINNESOTA" that was on the front of their gray road jerseys this afternoon; it was "TWINS," in navy blue with red trim. The Twins' players also wore navy blue stockings and caps. On the caps, instead of the logical "M" for Minnesota, there was an interlocking white "T" and red "C" for Twin Cities. St. Paul had opposed the "M," fearing that the public would interpret it as representing Minneapolis. Another symbol of the Twin Cities, two players shaking hands across a river, appeared on a patch on the left sleeve of the Twins' uniforms.

Houk began the pursuit of his first pennant by leading with his ace, Whitey Ford. This was Ford's fourth opening-day start, with the previous three coming against this club when they were in Washington. Ford, starting his tenth year, was coming off a season (12–9, .571) in which his winning percentage had fallen below .600 for the first time in his career. Yet his lifetime record of 24–5 against this team made him the obvious choice to pitch the opener.

In their final season in Washington, the Senators had finished fifth, their best showing in seven years. Ramos (11–18), along with Camilo Pascual (12–8) and Chuck Stobbs (12–7), had won nearly half the team's 73 victories. Ramos had been the workhorse, leading the league in games started (36) and his 274 innings pitched was second to Detroit's Frank Lary by ⅓ of an inning. Ramos's 18 losses were the most in the league for the third consecutive year. He made a strong bid to be the Twins' opening-day pitcher with seven scoreless innings against the Yanks at St. Petersburg on April 1. However, a few days before the opener he had spoken of his duty to return to Cuba to fight against Fidel Castro. (The ongoing acrimony between the United States and Cuba would lead shortly to the Bay of Pigs invasion.) Had he done so, Pascual would have pitched the opener. But, once Twins manager Cookie Lavagetto was sure Ramos would be available to him, he elected to open the season with him and pitch Pascual in the second game. Lavagetto had been the club's third-base coach before he replaced Charlie Dressen in May 1957. Sam Mele, his third base coach, would replace him midway through this season.

Ramos temporarily put the liberation of his homeland aside and concentrated on the task at hand. He completely dominated the Yankees, allowing just three singles—all in the first five innings. Yogi Berra had one in the first and Bill Skowron one in the fourth, both with two outs. Ford got the third, an infield single in the fifth. He was the last Yankee to reach base as Ramos retired the final 13 batters consecutively. Only once, in the second inning, did the Yankees get a runner as far as third base, and they did it without a hit.

Maris led off with a pop fly that should have been an easy play for center fielder Lenny Green. But before Green could make the catch, left fielder Jim Lemon cut in front of him and then dropped the ball for a two-base error. After Skowron flied out and Tony Kubek walked, Clete Boyer flied to right fielder Bob Allison. The ball was hit deep enough for Maris to take third after the catch, but Ford, with a chance to put his team ahead, bounced out to third baseman Reno Bertoia. Boyer was the Yankees' full-time third baseman after sharing the position with the now retired Gil McDougald in 1960.

While Ramos had allowed only three hits through six innings, Ford had done even better, allowing just two. Therefore, his sudden disintegration in the seventh surprised the crowd, who no doubt felt Ford was on the way to his 25th lifetime victory against his favorite patsies. Allison, the American League's Rookie of the Year in 1959, led off the inning by hitting Ford's second pitch a few rows back into the lower deck in left field. Earl Battey followed with a double down the left-field line. After Ford walked Bertoia, veteran second baseman Billy Gardner moved the runners up with a well-placed bunt. The next batter was Ramos, a good-hitting pitcher who hit 15 home runs during his career. Ralph Terry was hurriedly getting ready in the Yankees bullpen, but Houk and Johnny Sain, his new pitching coach, chose to stay with Ford. It was the wrong decision. Ramos lashed a two-run single to center, making the score, 3–0, and finishing Ford.

A scattering of boos greeted Terry's arrival on the mound as some fans had yet to forgive his World Series-losing pitch to Pittsburgh's Bill Mazeroski last fall. The boos increased when shortstop Zoilo Versalles hit his first pitch for a single. Terry retired Green but walked Harmon Killebrew to load the bases before getting Lemon for the third out. Terry further displeased the crowd when the Twins added two more runs against him in the eighth on an Allison single and a Bertoia home run. Jim Coates took over in the ninth and yielded Minnesota's final run when Versalles walked, stole second and third, and scored on Killebrew's long fly to Hector Lopez in left. Coates, a pitcher easily irritated, evidently took exception to the Twins' stealing bases with a five-run lead. He hit the next batter, Dan Dobbek, a defensive replacement for Lemon. Dobbek responded by stealing second, but was left there.

When the Yankees fired Stengel, they also fired his pitching coach, Ed Lopat, who now was serving in the same capacity for the Twins. Lopat had been working all spring with Ramos, attempting to teach him two of the fundamentals of good pitching: getting ahead in the count and changing speeds. Ramos applied those lessons today, but still would finish the season with twenty losses (11–20), which was again the most in the American League. The following spring, the Twins traded him to the Cleveland Indians for first baseman Vic Power and pitcher Dick Stigman.

Despite losing the opener, Ford would have his greatest season. Starting more often under Houk than he had under Stengel (a career-high 39 times), he won 25 games and lost only four. In the World Series, against the Cincinnati Reds, he ran his consecutive scoreless-innings streak to 32, breaking the record Babe Ruth had established in 1918.

If a new era had opened in baseball, a much more significant one had opened for mankind. That evening, Yuri Gagarin, a 27-year-old Russian cosmonaut, in his spaceship *Vostok*, became the first man to orbit the Earth.

Roger Maris with 61 home runs and Mickey Mantle with 54 led a robust New York offense that accounted for 240 home runs. Maris's 61st, on the final day of the season, broke Babe Ruth's longstanding record of 60 set in 1927. Four other Yankees hit 20 or more home runs: Bill Skowron (28), Yogi Berra (22), Elston Howard (21) and Johnny Blanchard (21). The team won 109 games (109–53) to finish eight games ahead of the Detroit Tigers, and in the

World Series disposed of the Cincinnati Reds in five games. Maris, who won the Most Valuable Player Award by just three votes over Mantle (225–222) in 1960, won again in 1961 by four votes over Mickey (202–198). Whitey Ford, the leader in wins (25), winning percentage (.862) and innings pitched (283), won the Cy Young Award.

Tuesday, April 11, 1961

Minnesota	ab	r	h	rbi		New York	ab	r	h	rbi
Versalles ss	5	1	2	0		Richardson 2b	4	0	0	0
Green cf	5	0	0	0		Lopez lf	4	0	0	0
Killebrew 1b	2	0	1	1		Berra c	4	0	1	0
Lemon lf	4	0	0	0		Mantle cf	4	0	0	0
Dobbek lf	0	0	0	0		Maris rf	3	0	0	0
Allison rf	5	1	2	1		Skowron 1b	3	0	1	0
Battey c	4	2	1	0		Kubek ss	2	0	0	0
Bertoia 3b	2	2	1	2		Boyer 3b	3	0	0	0
Gardner 2b	3	0	1	0		Ford p	2	0	1	0
Ramos p	4	0	1	2		Terry p	0	0	0	0
Total	34	6	9	6		ªGonder	1	0	0	0
						Coates p	0	0	0	0
						Total	30	0	3	0

ªGrounded out for Terry in eighth inning.

Minnesota	000	000	321–6
New York	000	000	000–0

Error—Lemon. Double play—Versalles, Gardner, and Killebrew. Left on bases—Minnesota 8; New York 4. Put outs—Minnesota 27: Versalles 2, Green 2, Killebrew 10, Lemon, Allison 6, Battey 5, Gardner. New York 27: Richardson 7, Lopez 2, Berra 3, Mantle 3, Maris 2, Skowron 9, Kubek. Assists—Minnesota 10: Versalles 2, Bertoia 3, Gardner 4, Ramos. New York 13: Richardson 3, Berra, Kubek 5, Boyer 3, Ford. Two-base hit—Battey. Home runs—Allison, Bertoia. Stolen bases—Versalles 2, Dobbek. Sacrifice—Gardner. Sacrifice fly—Killebrew.

	IP	H	R	ER	BB	SO
MINNESOTA						
Ramos (W, 1–0)	9.0	3	0	0	1	5
NEW YORK						
Ford (L, 0–1)	6.1	5	3	3	3	3
Terry	1.2	3	2	2	1	0
Coates	1.0	1	1	1	0	0

Hit by pitcher—by Coates (Dobbek). Umpires—McKinley, Soar, Chylak, and Smith. Time of game—2 hrs. 27 min. Attendance—14,607.

Tuesday, April 10, 1962
Yankee Stadium, New York
New York 7 Baltimore 6

Show me a hero and I will write you a tragedy.—F. Scott Fitzgerald

Mickey Mantle had been the idol of younger fans almost from the day he joined the Yankees, becoming to his generation what Babe Ruth and Joe DiMaggio had been to theirs.

However, no matter what his accomplishments, many older fans had been reluctant to recognize his greatness, until now. After 11 injury-plagued years of heroics, Mantle seemed to have finally earned the love and appreciation of Yankees fans of every generation. He had also, not coincidentally, earned the second-most lucrative contract in the team's history; his 1962 salary of $90,000 trailed only the six-figure sums DiMaggio received in his final years. Mantle's 54 home runs in 1961 had raised his lifetime total to 374 and moved him past DiMaggio and Yogi Berra into third place on the all-time Yankees list (behind Ruth and Lou Gehrig), and eighth overall. Home run number 375 came on Opening Day 1962. Mantle's eighth-inning leadoff blast against Baltimore's Hal Brown tied the game and sent the crowd of 22,978 into a frenzy. Later in the inning, the Yanks added another run on a double by Elston Howard and a run-scoring single by Bill Skowron to go ahead, 7–6. When Baltimore got the tying run on in the ninth, manager Ralph Houk turned to Luis Arroyo, the chunky left-hander (five-foot eight, 190 pounds) who had become the club's relief ace. Before coming to New York, in July 1960, from Jersey City of the International League, Arroyo had spent four undistinguished seasons in the National League, both as a starter and reliever for the St. Louis Cardinals, Pittsburgh Pirates, and Cincinnati Reds. Casey Stengel had used him strictly in relief in 1960, and he contributed five wins (5–1) and seven "saves" down the stretch. In 1961, under Houk, Arroyo appeared in a league-leading 65 games, again all in relief, won 15 (15–5), and "saved" 29 more. His outstanding season earned him sixth place in the Most Valuable Player voting, seven points behind fifth-place finisher Whitey Ford, whose victories he often preserved.

Ford, despite his limited work at the team's new spring home in Fort Lauderdale, again had the honor of pitching the season opener. The Yanks had moved from St. Petersburg, on the Gulf of Mexico, eastward across Florida's Alligator Alley to Fort Lauderdale on the Atlantic Ocean. They had abandoned Al Lang Stadium, shared for many years with the St. Louis Cardinals, in favor of a brand-new complex that was theirs alone. Except for the war years of 1943–1945, when they trained on the Jersey shore, and the year in Phoenix in 1951, the Yanks had been coming to St. Pete every spring since 1925. New York's new entry in the National League, the Mets, under the leadership of former Yankees Stengel and George Weiss, replaced them there. Bill Stafford had been the team's most effective pitcher during the exhibition season, but three of Stafford's nine losses in 1961 (14–9) had come against the Orioles, a team he had yet to beat. Ford, on the other hand, had defeated Baltimore four times in five decisions last year, and had a commanding 31–11 lifetime record against them, which included their pre-1954 years as the St. Louis Browns.

As the fans filed into the Stadium and found their seats on this bright, breezy day, the George Sueffert Band added to their pregame pleasure by playing Broadway show tunes, which seemed to please even the teenagers present. Although today was not a school holiday, at least not a scheduled one, there were many children of school age in the crowd. They were an exuberant bunch, cheering all the Yankees' players—but especially Arroyo and Roger Maris when those two received awards in a pregame ceremony. American League president Joe Cronin presented Maris with his second consecutive Most Valuable Player Award, to which Maris responded, characteristically, with a one-sentence speech thanking the baseball writers who voted for him.

In 1960, the increasing importance of relief pitchers had inspired *The Sporting News* to create a separate award. They called it the "Fireman of the Year," and Arroyo was the American League winner for 1961. He accepted with a smile and a nod but, unlike Maris, without speaking. Then, Mrs. Babe Ruth threw out the first ball to catcher Howard. After seven years of double duty as a catcher and an outfielder, the Yankees would use Howard only behind the plate in 1962.

The Orioles came to bat wearing their orange-and-black-trimmed road grays, with "BALTIMORE," in cursive, on the jersey fronts. Ford retired them in order, the only time he would do so in his six innings of work. Rookie John "Boog" Powell made the third out, fanning on three pitches. Powell, only 20 years old, was an imposing six-foot-four, 230-pound left-handed hitter whom the Orioles had converted from a first baseman to an outfielder. He had been the spring's most discussed newcomer, called by the *Associated Press* the best prospect in the American League. Harry Brecheen, the Orioles' pitching coach and a veteran of many years in the game, said Powell was the best prospect he had ever seen. Little wonder that the Stadium fans watched closely as he took his batting practice swings. In a Florida exhibition game, Powell had reached Ford for two singles in two at-bats, but Ford was a different pitcher when the games counted. He would face Powell three times today, striking him out twice and once getting him on a pop fly to third baseman Clete Boyer. Later Ralph Terry would fan him a third time. Powell would eventually become an exceptional hitter, adding a strong bat to the Orioles' improving young team that recently had cast off the inept image of their predecessors, the St. Louis Browns.

Baltimore had made great strides under their innovative former manager, Paul Richards, finishing second in 1960 before slipping to third in 1961. Richards had since left to become general manager of the new Houston .45s, but left behind a corps of excellent young pitchers. Unfortunately for his successor, former American League infielder Billy Hitchcock, three of them—Steve Barber, Jack Fisher, and Milt Pappas—were unavailable to begin the season. Barber, the team's best left-hander, was in the Army; Fisher was on the 30-day disabled list; and Pappas was recovering from an appendectomy. With his choices limited, Hitchcock called on veteran left-hander Billy Hoeft, who had been among the better pitchers in the league in the mid–1950s when he was with the Detroit Tigers. Hoeft won 16 games (16–7) in 1955 and 20 (20–14) in 1956. However, since coming to the Orioles in 1959, he had been predominantly a reliever, starting just 12 of the 54 games he had been in over the last two years. This season, his last in Baltimore, he would appear in 57 games, all but four of them in relief.

Hoeft got into trouble immediately. After facing just four men, his chances of making it out of the first inning appeared doubtful. He walked the first two batters—Bobby Richardson and Tom Tresh. After getting Maris on a long fly to right, he walked Mantle to load the bases. But before the game got out of control, Hoeft found the strike zone; he struck out Howard and got Skowron on a pop-up to escape the inning without a score. Rookie Tresh had earned the shortstop job in spring training, beating out another rookie, Phil Linz. Linz outhit Tresh .348 to .302, but the reporters covering the Yankees voted Tresh the James P. Dawson Award as the best rookie in camp, and evidently Houk agreed. Linz and Tresh had staged a similar battle at Triple A Richmond in 1961, with Tresh winning that one too. The switch-hitting Tresh would have a superb rookie season. He batted .286, with 20 home runs and 93 runs batted in, and won Rookie of the Year honors, just as he had at Richmond. Although Tresh played most of the season at shortstop, replacing Tony Kubek who was on active duty with the National Guard, he moved to the outfield shortly after Kubek returned in August.

The Orioles also were playing without their regular shortstop. Ron Hansen, the American League's Rookie of the Year in 1960, was—like Kubek—in the Army. Jerry Adair, normally the team's second baseman, replaced Hansen at short, while veteran Johnny Temple took over at second. It was Adair who gave the Orioles a 2–0 lead in the second with a two-out double that scored Jim Gentile, who had singled, and Gus Triandos, who had walked. His drive to straightaway center got caught up in a brisk wind that carried it over Mantle's head. In the third, Temple, in his first game as an Oriole, homered against the foul pole in left to increase Baltimore's lead to 3–0.

Howard got New York's first hit when he singled with one out in the fourth. Skowron followed with a tremendous blast to the deepest part of center field. Jackie Brandt went back to the 461-foot sign and with his back to the wall jumped for the ball, but it hit above his outstretched glove and bounced away. By the time he recovered and got the ball on its way homeward, Skowron was across the plate with a rare inside-the-park home run. Ordinarily among the team's best Grapefruit League hitters, Skowron had failed to hit a home run in any of this year's preseason games. New York went ahead, 5–3, in the fifth when Richardson and Tresh singled and Maris hit a 1–2 pitch ten rows deep into the right-field seats. The crowd, including Mrs. Ruth, gave Roger a standing ovation. A year ago, Maris had been subjected to intense pressure by both the media and the fans as he successfully chased the Babe's cherished single-season home-run record. Now, the stress would begin anew. The press reported that Maris's home run put him ten games ahead of his 1961 pace. (He did not hit his first home run that year until the Yankees' 11th game.) Baltimore made it 5–4 in the sixth, scoring a run after two were out. Brooks Robinson dumped a fly ball down the right-field line that Maris, wary of running into the railing, dropped. Robinson, who was given credit for a single, moved to second on a walk to Triandos and scored on Adair's single.

Joe Pepitone made his major-league debut when he grounded into a double play as a pinch hitter for Ford in the sixth. Pepitone, an outfielder/first baseman, was one of three rookies who made the jump to New York after playing the 1961 season with the Yankees' Amarillo farm club in the Texas League. Linz—who went to Amarillo after Tresh beat him out at Richmond—and pitcher Jim Bouton were the others. The eventual addition of these three young men—Pepitone, Linz, and Bouton—would significantly change the future makeup, character, and personality of the Yankees. Terry replaced Ford, and after getting through the seventh surrendered the lead in the eighth. Back-to-back doubles by Gentile and Brandt tied the score, and after an infield out, Triandos put the Orioles ahead. His long sacrifice fly to Hector Lopez in left brought Brandt home with Baltimore's sixth run.

In the Yankee eighth, Mantle led off against Brown, a 37-year-old right-hander who had pitched two scoreless innings since replacing Hoeft in the sixth. Batting left-handed, Mantle drove a full-count pitch 400 feet into the right-centerfield bleachers to tie the score at 6–6. While the cheering crowd was still savoring his home run, Howard followed with a double to left. Hitchcock removed Brown and brought in veteran knuckleballer Hoyt Wilhelm. Skowron, the first man Wilhelm faced, ripped a single to left, and Howard raced home with the Yankees' seventh run. Russ Snyder, who had earlier replaced Powell in left, appeared to have a play on the slow-running Howard. However, he chose to throw to second base to prevent Skowron from getting into scoring position.

Tuesday, April 10, 1962

Baltimore	ab	r	h	rbi		New York	ab	r	h	rbi
Temple 2b	5	1	3	1		Richardson 2b	3	1	1	0
ᶜBreeding	0	0	0	0		Tresh ss	3	1	1	0

Baltimore

	ab	r	h	rbi
E. Robinson rf	5	0	0	0
Powell lf	4	0	0	0
Snyder lf	1	0	0	0
Gentile 1b	5	2	2	0
dNicholson	0	0	0	0
Brandt cf	5	1	1	1
B. Robinson 3b	4	1	2	0
Triandos c	1	1	0	1
Adair ss	3	0	3	3
Hoeft p	2	0	0	0
aWilliams	1	0	0	0
Brown p	1	0	0	0
Wilhelm p	0	0	0	0
Total	37	6	11	6

New York

	ab	r	h	rbi
Maris rf	4	1	1	3
Mantle cf	3	1	1	1
Howard c	4	2	2	0
Skowron 1b	4	1	2	3
Lopez lf	3	0	0	0
Boyer 3b	4	0	2	0
Ford p	2	0	0	0
bPepitone	1	0	0	0
Terry p	1	0	0	0
Arroyo p	0	0	0	0
Total	32	7	10	7

aLined out for Hoeft in sixth inning.
bGrounded into double play for Ford in sixth inning.
cRan for Temple in ninth inning.
dRan for Gentile in ninth inning.

Baltimore	021	001	020–6
New York	000	230	02X–7

Error—Richardson. Double plays—Gentile, Adair, and Gentile; Adair, Temple, and Gentile; Richardson, Tresh, and Skowron. Left on bases—Baltimore 8; New York 5. Put outs—Baltimore 24: Temple 2, E. Robinson 6, Powell 2, Gentile 10, Brandt, Triandos 2, Adair. New York 27: Richardson 2, Tresh 2, Maris, Mantle 2, Howard 8, Skowron 8, Lopez 2, Boyer, Ford. Assists—Baltimore 11: Temple 3, B. Robinson 4, Adair 3, Gentile. New York 9: Richardson 3, Tresh, Boyer 3, Ford, Arroyo. Two-base hits—Adair, Gentile, Brandt, Howard. Home runs—Temple, Skowron, Maris, Mantle. Sacrifice fly—Triandos.

	IP	H	R	ER	BB	SO
BALTIMORE						
Hoeft	5.0	6	5	5	3	1
*Brown (L, 0–1)	2.0	3	2	2	0	0
Wilhelm	1.0	1	0	0	1	0
NEW YORK						
Ford	6.0	8	4	4	2	4
#Terry (1–0)	2.0	3	2	2	1	3
Arroyo	1.0	0	0	0	0	0

*Faced two batters in eighth inning.
#Faced one batter in ninth inning.

Umpires—Paparella, Soar, Rice, and Kinnamon. Time of game—2 hrs. 28 min. Attendance—22,978.

___

The Yanks took their 7–6 advantage into the ninth, but when Temple led off with a single—he and Adair each had three hits—Houk promptly yanked Terry and brought in Arroyo. As an indication of how strong the Yankees were, the three pitchers that Houk used on Opening Day—Ford, Terry, and Arroyo—had a combined 1961 record of 56–12. Arroyo got Earl Robinson on a slow ground ball to Richardson, but Marv Breeding, running for Temple, moved into scoring position at second. Breeding held as Arroyo threw out Snyder for the second out, and when Gentile followed with a twisting ground ball to second, it looked to be the game-ender. But Richardson booted the ball; Gentile was safe and Breeding moved to third. Hitchcock sent in Dave Nicholson, a reserve outfielder, to run for Gentile. With Brandt at the plate, Arroyo threw a pitch in the dirt, but Howard made a superb block to keep Breeding, who represented the tying run, at third. Brandt then hit Arroyo's next pitch high in the air to the right side of the infield. Richardson, the Gold Glove winner in 1961, called for the ball, and this time squeezed it for the final out.

Mantle and Maris would spend the evening at the premiere of *Safe at Home!* the movie they made with William Frawley. In 1962 their combined home run total would fall from 115 to 63. Terry, the winning pitcher, would relieve in only three other games this season, but as a starter he would lead the league in wins (23), games started (39), and innings pitched (298.2).

> *Although their win total dropped from 109 to 96 (96–66), it was enough for the Yankees to finish five games ahead of the Minnesota Twins. They defeated the San Francisco Giants in seven games to earn their 20th world title in the last 40 seasons. Mickey Mantle won his third Most Valuable Player Award, although injuries to both legs limited him to just 123 games. Bobby Richardson, whose 209 hits led the league, finished second in the MVP voting, and Tom Tresh, in addition to being the Rookie of the Year, finished 12th.*

Tuesday, April 9, 1963
Municipal Stadium, Kansas City
New York 8 Kansas City 2

… the privilege of absurdity; to which no living creature is subject but man only.—Thomas Hobbes

The Yankees had been part of the American League for 60 years, yet had never played an opening-day game more than 250 miles from home. That was the approximate distance to Washington and Boston, which along with Philadelphia (90 miles) were the only away cities in which they had opened. However, expansion and the movement of franchises had ended that cozy little arrangement forever. To open the 1963 season, the schedule makers sent the New Yorkers more than a thousand miles away—to Municipal Stadium in Kansas City. Ralph Terry, who had won last year's opener in relief of Whitey Ford, got the start. Terry had gone on from that, 7–6, win over the Baltimore Orioles to win 23 games (23–12), the most in the American League. He capped his best season ever with a 1–0 victory over the San Francisco Giants' Jack Sanford in the seventh game of the 1962 World Series. Terry's past success against Kansas City (2–0 in 1962 and 7–2 lifetime) led manager Ralph Houk to award him the opening-day start against his former team, which he justified with a complete-game, 8–2, win. It was the first time that a Yankees' pitcher had won back-to-back openers since Vic Raschi in 1951–1952, but Terry is the only one to do it as a reliever in one year and a starter in the other.

The Yanks won this one easily, pounding A's pitching for 13 hits; only Hector Lopez among the starting position players failed to get one. Lopez was in right field today, subbing for Roger Maris who was out with a pulled hamstring in his left leg. Four Yankees got two hits apiece, but Kansas City's chief assailant was Joe Pepitone, with two home runs and a double. Last November, in the only significant off-season deal he made, general manager Roy Hamey traded veteran first baseman Bill Skowron to the Los Angeles Dodgers for pitcher Stan Williams. The trade cleared the way for the 22-year-old Pepitone to become the Yankees' regular first baseman. In 1962, as a rookie, Pepitone played half the season in New York, batting .239 with seven home runs in 63 games, and the other half with the

International League's Richmond Virginians. After he compiled a .315 batting average at Richmond and added eight more home runs, the club felt safe in dealing Skowron.

Since moving from Philadelphia in 1955, the Athletics had finished sixth once, seventh three times, and last twice. That was in the six years before the 1961 expansion. In the two years since the league had grown to ten teams, Kansas City finished ninth both times. They had drawn more than a million fans in their first two years, but then the reality of having a mediocre major-league team replaced the novelty of having *any* major-league team. As attendance declined, Charles O. Finley, who had owned the team since 1961, began thinking about moving them to yet another city. Finley was one of those owners who were unable to attract people to their ballparks with baseball, so he attempted to draw them with gimmicks. Therefore, it is difficult to estimate how many of the 30,976 who came out to Municipal Stadium for the opener were there to see the Yankees and the Athletics, and how many were there for the numerous giveaways Finley was offering. The crowd of primarily Midwesterners appeared well dressed—especially the women, most of whom wore bright spring coats with fancy hats. While there were many baseball fans at the game, the loudest cheering was for the between-inning announcements of the various prizes won by spectators. Gifts included a thousand pounds of dill pickles, a thousand pounds of fertilizer, thousands of gallons of ice cream, and assorted amounts of beer, bubble gum, and cigars.

Finley had distributed broad-brimmed green and gold hats to groups of people in the stands, while others, those who did not receive the free ones, were wearing green paper hats sold at the concession stands. Finley himself was wearing a gold coat and a Kelly green ten-gallon hat. This proliferation of green and gold was in tribute to the new green and gold uniforms he had designed for his ball club. The Yankees, tastefully dressed in their traditional gray road uniforms with the blue hats and blue trimming, stood in sharp contrast to the garishly clad Athletics.

Finley's green and gold theme was also evident on the playing field. Behind home plate there was a painted gold crescent, which stood out against the bright green grass. Even the groundskeepers fit the motif with their new uniforms of green hats, gold shirts, and white pants and shoes. To complete the circus-like atmosphere, Finley had sheep—wearing green and gold tailored blankets—grazing on a slope beyond the right-field fence. Before the game, there was a fireworks display and the launching of a thousand balloons (green or gold colored, naturally), each one carrying tickets to a future A's home game. Several balloons landed as far away as a farm outside Sedalia, Missouri, 90 miles southeast of Kansas City.

Once the mind-numbing noise from the fireworks subsided, H. Roe Bartle, the mayor of Kansas City, introduced former president Harry Truman. Truman, who lived in nearby Independence, Missouri, made a brief speech, including a wish that "we beat the Yankees and send them back to New York where they belong." Evidently Truman still had not forgiven New York City for failing to pile up a vote total large enough to prevent him from losing the state to its Republican governor, Tom Dewey in the 1948 presidential election. Following his little pep talk, Truman introduced a youngster named Eric Ensloe who threw out the first ball. Ensloe had been chosen for the honor by the Kansas City Easter Seal Society.

In Finley's two years of ownership, he had employed two managers, Joe Gordon and Hank Bauer. Each had spent the major portions of his career with the Yankees and must have found Finley's approach to baseball bizarre. His new manager was another ex–Yankee, Ed Lopat, who would last into June of 1964. During the pregame conference at home plate,

Lopat presented Houk with a green sombrero, which his former teammate good-naturedly wore until the meeting concluded.

Lopat's starting pitcher, Diego Segui, had won eight and lost five as a rookie in 1962. Used mostly in relief, he split two decisions with the Yankees. Segui retired the first four batters this afternoon, but then Pepitone put the Yanks on the board with his first home run of the day. He went after the first pitch, a low curve ball, sending it high up on the embankment in right field where it scattered the sheep. "When I left the dugout, I knew I was going to swing at the first pitch," Pepitone said after the game. "I didn't care where it was." In the fourth, Mickey Mantle got the first of his two singles, and Elston Howard followed with a home run to left to make it 3–0. An inning later, when the Yankees extended the lead to 7–0, it served as a signal to many of the spectators that they no longer had to pay much attention to the game; they were now free to visit and chat with like-minded folks on the concourse and at the food lines. Clete Boyer had opened the four-run fifth with a single, went to second on a Terry sacrifice, and came home on Tony Kubek's single. Bobby Richardson followed by tripling between center fielder Jose Tartabull and right fielder Gino Cimoli to score Kubek. With the A's trailing, 5–0, Lopat removed Segui and brought in Dave Wickersham to face Tom Tresh, now a full-time outfielder with the return of Kubek. Tresh lifted a sacrifice fly to Chuck Essegian in left, scoring Richardson. But the Yanks were not finished. Mantle lined a single to right and Pepitone followed with a ground ball past first baseman Norm Siebern that went for a double. Mantle had stopped at third, but when shortstop Dick Howser—in his first league game in the field since suffering a broken hand last June in Chicago—failed to handle Cimoli's throw-in, Mickey came home with the unearned run.

Through five innings, Terry had limited Kansas City to just one hit, a third-inning single by Bill Bryan. The A's got one-out back-to-back singles in the sixth by George Alusik, batting for Wickersham, and Howser, but Terry stranded them. (Alusik was having a great year as a pinch-hitter (9-for-19) when Pedro Ramos of the Cleveland Indians broke his wrist with a pitch on August 10.) Pepitone's second home run, a drive over the right-field fence, came in the eighth against veteran right-hander Bill Fischer. For Pepitone it was a continuation of his springtime slugging, when he led the club in home runs (he had nine) and runs batted in. The Yankees were now up, 8–0, but any hopes Terry had of pitching a shutout ended in the Kansas City eighth. He got the first batter, third baseman Wayne Causey (substituting for the injured Ed Charles), on a fly to Lopez, but "grooved" a pitch to Bryan. The rookie catcher powered it over the right-field wall for his fourth major-league home run. Bryan's second home run had also come against the gopher ball-prone Terry following his call-up by Kansas City in September 1962. Terry walked the next batter—Manny Jiminez, batting for Fischer—the only free pass he allowed in the game, but retired Howser and Tartabull.

After Orlando Pena pitched a scoreless ninth for Kansas City, Jerry Lumpe opened the home half with a single to left. The next batter, Siebern, grounded sharply to first where Pepitone fielded the ball and turned it into a quick 3–6–3 double play. However, Essegian kept the A's alive, if barely, with a long drive into the parking lot beyond left field. It was Essegian's first home run for Kansas City, who had gotten him from the Indians for pitcher Jerry Walker to do just that—supply them with power. Terry got the final out by getting Cimoli to fly to center, where Jack Reed, who had replaced Mantle in the seventh inning, pulled it down. Terry's complete game was the first of his 18 in 1963, which tied him with the Minnesota Twin's Camilo Pascual for the league lead. Still, his win total slipped to 17 (17–13), third best on the staff behind Ford (24–7) and Jim Bouton (21–7).

Ralph Houk won his third pennant in three years as the Yankees (104–57) finished 10½ games ahead of the Chicago White Sox. But in the World Series, the Yanks scored only four runs and were swept by the Los Angeles Dodgers. Whitey Ford (24–7) led the American League in wins and winning percentage (.774), but the Dodgers' Sandy Koufax won the Cy Young Award unanimously. (Individual Cy Young Awards for each league would not come until 1967.) Elston Howard was voted the league's Most Valuable Player, becoming the first black to win the award in the American League. Ford finished third, but neither Roger Maris, who won in 1960 and 1961, nor Mickey Mantle, who won in 1962, got a single vote. Both had missed large parts of the season with injuries, Maris playing in 90 games and Mantle only 65.

Tuesday, April 9, 1963

New York	ab	r	h	rbi	Kansas City	ab	r	h	rbi
Kubek ss	5	1	2	1	Howser ss	4	0	1	0
Richardson 2b	5	1	2	1	Tartabull cf	4	0	0	0
Tresh lf	3	0	1	1	Lumpe 2b	4	0	1	0
Mantle cf	4	2	2	0	Siebern 1b	4	0	0	0
Reed cf	1	0	0	0	Essegian lf	4	1	1	1
Pepitone 1b	5	2	3	2	Cimoli rf	4	0	0	0
Howard c	4	1	1	2	Causey 3b	3	0	0	0
Lopez rf	4	0	0	0	Bryan c	3	1	2	1
Boyer 3b	4	1	2	0	Segui p	1	0	0	0
Terry p	3	0	0	0	Wickersham p	0	0	0	0
Total	38	8	13	7	[a]Alusik	1	0	1	0
Fischer p	0	0	0	0					
[b]Jiminez	0	0	0	0					
[c]Pfister	0	0	0	0					
Pena p	0	0	0	0					
Total	32	2	6	2					

[a]Singled for Wickersham in sixth inning.
[b]Walked for Fischer in eighth inning.
[c]Ran for Jiminez in eighth inning.

New York	010	240	010–8
Kansas City	000	000	011–2

Error—Howser. Double play—Pepitone, Kubek, and Pepitone. Left on bases—New York 6; Kansas City 4. Put outs—New York 27: Pepitone 11, Richardson 1, Lopez 3, Boyer 2, Mantle 2, Reed 2, Howard 3, Kubek 3. Kansas City 27: Howser 1, Lumpe 1, Essegian 3, Cimoli 3, Siebern 15, Tartabull 2, Bryan 2. Assists—New York 8: Richardson 4, Kubek 2, Pepitone 1, Boyer 1. Kansas City 16: Howser 7, Lumpe 4, Siebern 1, Causey 2, Segui 1, Wickersham 1. Two-base hits—Boyer, Pepitone, Tresh. Three-base hit—Richardson. Home runs—Pepitone 2, Howard, Bryan, Essegian. Stolen base—Kubek. Sacrifice—Terry. Sacrifice fly—Tresh.

	IP	H	R	ER	BB	SO
NEW YORK						
Terry (W, 1–0)	9.0	6	2	2	1	2
KANSAS CITY						
Segui (L, 0–1)	4.1	7	6	6	0	1
Wickersham	1.2	2	1	0	0	0
Fischer	2.0	2	1	1	0	0
Pena	1.0	2	0	0	1	0

Umpires—McKinley, Rice, Chylak, and Valentine. Time of game—2 hrs. 21 min. Attendance—30,976.

Thursday, April 16, 1964
Yankee Stadium, New York
Boston 4 New York 3 (11 Innings)

The thrones are rocking to their fall—
It is the twighlight of the Kings!—Annie Johnson Flint

The birth of the New York Mets in 1962 had ended the Yankees' four-year monopoly on baseball in the city and meant they would again have to compete for the New York fans and their dollars. It seemed a one-sided battle, pitting baseball's most glamorous organization against a woefully weak expansion club. Yet in their first two seasons, the Mets had not only drawn well, they had emerged as the favorites of many in the local press. Sportswriters celebrated their image of loveable, bumbling losers, often comparing them favorably to the machine-like efficiency of the Yankees. For although the Yankees had long been associated with excellence and success, the country was entering a period when these traits were becoming less valued. Once considered admirable and worth striving for, they were now coming under attack by people extolling mediocrity and anti-elitism.

On the other hand, the Yankees had not always been the successful team they were today. Early in the century, as the freshly created Highlanders, they had been the "new kid in town," challenging the established Giants for supremacy in New York. Now, more than 60 years later, as the ultimate establishment team, it was they who were being challenged; and the Mets were raising the ante. They were moving out of the dilapidated old Polo Grounds, where they had played in 1962 and 1963, and into a sparkling new stadium in Queens, just down the road from the World's Fair that was scheduled to open in a week. Moving to Shea Stadium was sure to give the Mets a big boost in the attendance wars, especially when contrasted with the growing perception of crime and violence in the neighborhoods around Yankee Stadium.

Perhaps the principal reason the Mets received such excellent press in New York was the continuing popularity of Casey Stengel, their manager. Stengel was still the darling of the local media, much more so than Ralph Houk, his successor with the Yankees, even though Houk had won three pennants and two World Series in his three years as manager. That may have influenced Houk, who had stepped up to replace the retired Roy Hamey as general manager, in selecting Yogi Berra as his replacement. The Yankees had more than Berra's competence in mind; Yogi had been a fan favorite for almost two decades, which the club hoped would help them in the public relations battle with the Mets. Berra made his managerial debut at Yankee Stadium with an 11-inning 4–3 loss to the Boston Red Sox. Only 12,709 showed up for the twice-postponed opener, which the Yankees saw as a bad omen in the coming battle with their National League rivals. Possibly spurred by the opening of Shea, the Yanks had done some remodeling at the Stadium designed to increase the comfort of their customers. They introduced new food stations, which offered the fans greater variety, and increased the number of vendors in the stands. Automatic Canteen Company of America now controlled the concessions at Yankee Stadium, thus ending the team's long association with the Stevens family.

The day was clear and bright, but the two days of rain, which had cost the Yankees at the gate, continued to hurt them during the game. Even before it started, the Yankees' outfielders commented on the still-soft turf. "The outfield is terrible," said Mickey Mantle. "It's worse than that. It's not muddy, but it's soft. You sink in it up to your ankles," added Roger Maris. "This can mean trouble," Tom Tresh correctly predicted. Of course, the conditions were the same for both teams, but they worked to Boston's advantage this afternoon. Twice in the second inning, the soggy, recently resodded outfield contributed to the Red Sox offense. Whitey Ford, who had beaten Boston three times without a loss in 1963, was the hard-luck loser. The loss prevented him from joining a select group of pitchers who had won 200 major-league games. Ford's 24–7 record last year raised his lifetime mark to 199–78 and gave him a winning percentage (.7184), at the time the best in the twentieth century for pitchers with at least 100 decisions. Ford, who pitched a complete game, allowed 13 safeties, although several were less than hard-hit. This was his sixth opening-day start as a Yankee, tying Lefty Gomez's team record.

Because raising the most recent pennant and handing out championship mementos was an accepted part of Yankees openers, everyone involved in those rituals this afternoon performed them in a brief, well-organized way. American League president Joe Cronin handed out the souvenirs and also presented Elston Howard with his Most Valuable Player Award. To celebrate Berra's first day as manager, the Yankees presented each fan that entered the stadium with a button that featured his picture and read, "Welcome Yogi Day." Bronx borough president Joseph Periconi continued a long tradition when he presented the new manager with a beautiful floral horseshoe arrangement. In recognition of Berra's debut, the Yankees chose William Bracciodieta, a Columbia University pre-med student and the second winner of the Yogi Berra Scholarship Award, to throw out the first ball. In his college debut a few days earlier, Bracciodieta had pitched a seven-inning one-hitter against the University of Pennsylvania.

Ford set the Red Sox down in order in the first inning, but walked Frank Malzone to lead off the second. After Dick Stuart sent Malzone to third with a single to center, came the first instance in which the playing conditions influenced the game. Lou Clinton hit a blooper into short right field that Maris, slowed by the spongy turf, could not reach. The ball hit the ground and just lay there. Malzone scored easily, but Stuart held at second when Yankees second baseman Bobby Richardson hustled out to retrieve the ball. Up next was center fielder Tony Conigliaro, whose parents and two brothers had come down from Massachusetts to watch this precocious 19-year-old "phenom" play his first major-league game. Last year, his first year in professional baseball, Conigliaro batted .363 with 24 home runs for the Wellsville (New York) Red Sox of the Class A New York–Pennsylvania League. Now he was in the big leagues, but he still had much to learn. Conigliaro had caused a bit of a stir on the morning of the second rainout when he overslept and missed the team bus to the Stadium. Red Sox manager Johnny Pesky fined him ten dollars, which found its way into the Jimmy Fund, long the Boston team's favorite charity.

Conigliaro's first big-league at-bat barely missed being a memorable one. Batting with Clinton at first, Stuart at second, and nobody out, he grounded sharply to Clete Boyer at third. Boyer stepped on the bag to force Stuart and threw to Richardson at second, forcing Clinton. Richardson then fired to first in an attempt to complete the triple play, but Conigliaro just beat the throw. It kept the inning alive. Bob Tillman, who would plague Ford all afternoon, followed with another pop fly into short right that, like Clinton's, died on landing. By the time Richardson scooped it out, Conigliaro, running with two out, had scored Boston's second run. The Red Sox made it 3–0 in the third. Shortstop Eddie Bressoud opened with a scratch single off Boyer's glove. He moved to second as Carl Yastrzemski was grounding out to Ford and scored on Malzone's single to left.

New York came back to score two runs against Boston starter Bill Monbouquette in the bottom of the third. Monbouquette, 20–10 in 1963, had won four of the only six games that Boston took from the Yankees last season. A single by Boyer and a walk to Ford put runners at first and second with nobody out. On Phil Linz's medium-speed ground ball to Bressoud, the Sox got the force on Ford, but Linz was safe at first as Boyer moved to third. Linz was subbing at short for Tony Kubek, who was suffering from inflamed back muscles. As a utility infielder, Linz would get to play in 112 games in 1964, 55 of them at shortstop. Later in the season he and Berra would have a serious disagreement over the accepted way in which Yankees' players react to defeat. Richardson's infield single moved Linz to second and scored Boyer. Linz took third after Maris flied deep to Conigliaro and came home on Mantle's single to right. Monbouquette stranded Richardson and Mantle when he got Tresh to pop to Bressoud.

New York threatened in the fourth when they loaded the bases on walks to Joe Pepitone and Ford and a single by Howard. But there was one out, and Monbouquette got Linz to ground to third where Malzone started an inning-ending double play. After the Yanks failed to get a runner in the fifth and sixth, Boyer opened the seventh with a single to right. Ford bunted and Monbouquette threw him out, but in doing so, he slipped on the wet grass and landed on his pitching elbow. The fall forced Monbouquette to leave the game. However, Boston had the league's best relief pitcher, six-foot-six Dick Radatz, ready in the bullpen. Radatz got out of the inning without a score, but in the eighth, the Yankees got an unearned run to tie the game. Singles by Maris and Tresh put runners at first and third with one out. The out had come when Yastrzemski made a fine catch of Mantle's 440-foot liner to left center. Mickey's drive, which would have been a home run in any other major-league park, caused many fans to ponder A's owner Charles Finley's recent criticism of Yankee Stadium as a "home run-haven." Radatz got Pepitone to hit a pop fly into short center field that second baseman Chuck Schilling, running with his back to the infield, caught up with but could not hold. Maris scored the tying run and Tresh, the potential winning run, moved to second. While it had been a difficult play for Schilling, the official scorer felt it was a ball he should have caught and charged him with an error. Radatz kept Tresh at second by striking out Howard and getting Boyer on a fly to Conigliaro.

In the ninth, Bressoud tripled with two out for Boston, and Linz reached second with one out for the Yankees. But neither team could score, and the game—tied at 3–3—went into extra innings. Pepitone almost ended it with two out in the tenth, but his long drive into the seats went barely foul. He eventually drew a walk, and Howard followed with a single to left, but a fine throw by Yastrzemski and a diving tag by Malzone cut down Pepitone trying to reach third. Ford had not gone nine innings this spring (no Yankee pitcher had); nevertheless, Berra had confidence in his longtime battery mate and sent him out to pitch the 11th. Ford got the first batter, Conigliaro, but then Tillman, who already had three singles, hit a 450-foot triple over Mantle's head. Mantle had caught a drive by Yastrzemski to the same area in the ninth inning, but Tillman's blast was just out of his reach. Had the traction been better, it was a ball he likely would have caught. Pesky replaced the slow-footed Tillman with Roman Mejias and sent the veteran Dick Williams up to bat for Radatz. (Mejias and Williams were beginning their final active seasons as major-leaguers.) Berra, sensing that it was time for him to get into the strategy game, convened his first managerial mound conference. He cautioned Ford, who had been pitching in the big leagues since 1950, to be alert for a possible squeeze play. Pesky may have had a squeeze play in mind, but on Ford's second pitch to Williams, which he said later was a sinker but was probably a spitter, the ball bounced on home plate and skipped away from Howard. The speedy Mejias scored easily.

With the removal of Radatz and Tillman, the Red Sox had a new battery in the last of the 11th. Russ Nixon took over behind the plate and right-hander Bob Heffner, a second-year man, came on to pitch. Heffner had gotten some advice from Yastrzemski when he made his way in from the left-field bullpen. Because it was now after 5 P.M. and shadows had fallen across the field, Yastrzemski told him to forget the slow stuff and to throw only fastballs and sliders. Heeding Yastrzemski's advice, Heffner fanned the first two batters, Boyer and Johnny Blanchard, pinch-hitting for Ford. However, before Blanchard struck out, he excited the crowd with two long drives that landed in the foul portion of the right-field seats. Linz was the Yankees' last hope, but he hit an easy roller to Bressoud that ended the game and Boston's six-game, opening-day losing streak. The Yankees would go to Baltimore and lose two more extra-inning decisions before Berra got his first managerial win, against the Orioles on April 19.

In an exceedingly tight race, the Yankees (99–63) finished one game ahead of the Chicago White Sox and two games ahead of the Baltimore Orioles. It was New York's fifth consecutive pennant, tying the record established by the 1949–1953 Yankees. However, unlike that group, this one did not win five consecutive World Series. They had lost in 1960 and 1963 and lost again this year, to the St. Louis Cardinals in seven games; the first Yankees' team to lose consecutive World Series since 1921–1922. The Yankees drew 1,305,638, their third straight year of declining attendance. The Mets, who finished tenth for the third straight year, drew 1,732,597, outdrawing the Yanks for the first time. After the loss to St. Louis, Ralph Houk fired Yogi Berra and hired Johnny Keane, who had been the Cardinals' manager. Mickey Mantle and Elston Howard finished second and third in the voting for Most Valuable Player, won by Baltimore's Brooks Robinson. During the summer, CBS bought 80 per cent of the Yankees for $11,200,000 and would eventually buy the remaining 20 per cent. Dan Topping was retained as club president.

Thursday, April 16, 1964

Boston	ab	r	h	rbi		New York	ab	r	h	rbi
Schilling 2b	6	0	0	0		Linz ss	6	1	1	0
Bressoud ss	5	1	3	0		Richardson 2b	5	0	1	1
Yastrzemski lf	5	0	0	0		Maris rf	5	1	2	0
Malzone 3b	4	1	2	1		Mantle cf	5	0	1	1
Stuart 1b	5	0	1	0		Tresh lf	5	0	1	0
Clinton rf	5	0	2	1		Pepitone 1b	3	0	0	0
Conigliaro cf	5	1	1	0		Howard c	5	0	2	0
Tillman c	5	0	4	1		Boyer 3b	5	1	2	0
ªMejias	0	1	0	0		Ford p	1	0	0	0
Nixon c	0	0	0	0		ᶜBlanchard	1	0	0	0
Monbouquette p	2	0	0	0		Total	41	3	10	2
Radatz p	1	0	0	0						
ᵇWilliams	1	0	0	0						
Heffner p	0	0	0	0						
Total	44	4	13	3						

ªRan for Tillman in 11th inning.
ᵇGrounded out for Radatz in 11th inning.
ᶜStruck out for Ford in 11th inning.

Boston	021	000	000	01–4
New York	002	000	010	00–3

Errors—Schilling, Stuart. Double plays—Malzone and Stuart; Boyer and Richardson; Linz and Pepitone. Left on bases—Boston 9; New York 10. Put outs—New York 33: Pepitone 15, Linz 1, Howard 5, Boyer 1, Mantle 2, Maris 3, Tresh 3, Richardson 3. Boston 33: Conigliaro 5, Yastrzemski 4, Tillman 6, Nixon 2, Bressoud 3, Schilling 1, Clinton 1, Malzone 3, Stuart 7, Monbouquette 1. Assists—New York 16: Linz 8, Boyer 4, Richardson 1, Ford 3. Boston 9: Bressoud 2, Schilling 2, Malzone 2, Yastrzemski 1, Stuart 1, Monbouquette 1. Two-base hits—Malzone, Bressoud. Three-base hits—Bressoud, Tillman. Sacrifice—Ford.

	IP	H	R	ER	BB	SO
BOSTON						
Monbouquette	6.1	6	2	2	3	1
Radatz (W, 1–0)	3.2	4	1	0	1	4
Heffner	1.0	0	0	0	0	2
NEW YORK						
Ford (L, 0–1)	11.0	13	4	4	2	5

Umpires—Hurley, Flaherty, Haller and Carrigan. Time of game—3 hrs. 8 min. Attendance—12,709.

Monday, April 12, 1965
Metropolitan Stadium, Bloomington, Minnesota
Minnesota 5 New York 4 (11 Innings)

The melancholy days are come.—William Cullen Bryant

On Palm Sunday 1965, a day before the Yankees' season opener in Minnesota, a series of tornadoes navigated a devastating path through six midwestern states, killing more than 250 people. Minnesota had been spared the tornadoes but had to contend with its own nature-induced calamity. Flooding, caused by the breakup of months of accumulated ice and snow, led the federal government to declare the entire state a disaster area. The next day flood conditions were still so bad that the Twins had to hire a helicopter to bring Jim Kaat, their opening-day pitcher, to Metropolitan Stadium. Kaat, who lived in Burnsville, Minnesota, on the other side of the swollen Minnesota River, was airlifted to the park along with teammates Rich Rollins, Dick Stigman, and Bill Bethea. The sun came out just as the game began, but the Metropolitan Stadium surface remained soggy and slippery from the five inches of snow that had covered it a week earlier. Moreover, the temperature never got much above 40 degrees and a stiff breeze blew constantly throughout the afternoon. Nevertheless, the game went on—a poorly played, extremely sloppy game won by the Twins, 5–4, in 11 innings. Four of the nine runs were unearned as the teams combined to commit eight errors, five by the Yankees. It was the second year in a row the Yanks had lost in 11 innings on Opening Day.

Under manager Sam Mele, the Twins had won 91 games in 1962 and 1963 before slipping to 79 wins in 1964. The 91 wins represented the franchise's best showing since the pennant-winning year of 1933 when, as the Washington Senators, they won 99 games. This year, hopes for a pennant were running high in the Twin Cities, so high that 15,388 fans, including Minnesota governor Karl Rolvaag, the first-ball thrower, ignored the floods to attend the game. One Twins' fan not in attendance was owner Calvin Griffith, home in bed with phlebitis in his leg. Griffith claimed it was the first opener he had missed in 30 years.

To win the pennant, Minnesota would have to get past the Yankees, who had won the last five. And despite some apparent weaknesses and a new manager, forecasters were giving the Yanks a reasonable chance of making it six in a row. The new manager was Johnny Keane, the man who led the Cardinals to a seven-game victory over the Yanks in the 1964 World Series. After the Series, general manager Ralph Houk hired Keane to replace the fired Yogi Berra. However, the players who had loved Houk when he was the manager—and tolerated Berra—disliked Keane almost from the beginning. Difficulties between Keane and his players would persist throughout the season.

The Yankees seemed especially unprepared for today's winterlike conditions, having played their most recent exhibition games in Puerto Rico and Houston. Yesterday they had concluded a three-game weekend series in the Houston Astrodome (still called the Harris County Domed Stadium at the time of this game) against the newly renamed Astros—the first games played between two major-league teams in the just-completed indoor arena. According to the American Football League schedule released this morning, the first professional football game at the Astrodome would be played on September 12 between the Houston Oilers and the New York Jets. Eventually, when the Astros had trouble getting grass to grow under the dome, they would compound their original transgression against aesthetics by installing artificial grass for the 1966 season. Thus, to Houston goes the blame for introducing domed stadiums and make-believe grass, two of baseball's most lamentable additions.

Kaat, a hard-throwing left-hander, took a 4–3 lead into the ninth inning this afternoon, but was victimized by Twins third baseman Cesar Tovar. Tovar allowed New York to tie the score when he dropped an easy pop fly that would have been the final out. But the rookie went from "goat" to "hero" in the 11th when he won the game with a two-out, bases-loaded single. The Twins had taken the early lead, getting a first-inning run off Yankees' starter Jim Bouton without the benefit of a base hit. Bouton, the Yanks' leading winner (18–13) in 1964, had early control problems. After retiring leadoff batter Zoilo Versalles, he walked Jerry Kindall, one of the weakest hitters in the league, and Rich Rollins. With Tony Oliva at bat, Bouton threw a wild pitch that advanced the runners. Kindall scored as Oliva bounced out to second baseman Bobby Richardson. Oliva, who had won the American League batting title as a rookie in 1964, with a .323 batting average, would win it again this year, with a .321 average. He is one of only two players in major-league history to win batting crowns in each of his first two seasons. (Benny Kauff won the Federal League batting title in 1914 and 1915, his first two seasons.)

Two Yankees errors in the second inning led to the first of Minnesota's three unearned runs. Jimmie Hall, leading off, reached base when first baseman Joe Pepitone booted his easy ground ball. Bob Allison followed Hall's steal of second with a single to center, and when center fielder Tom Tresh failed to field the ball cleanly, Hall came around to score. Because of the treacherous footing, and Mickey Mantle's chronic leg problems, Mickey was playing left field today while Tresh played center. The Twins boosted their lead to 4–0 with two more runs in the fourth, one of which was unearned. First baseman Harmon Killebrew singled and took second as Bouton threw another wild pitch. The Twins had returned Killebrew to the infield after three years in the outfield, in each of which he had led the league in home runs. One out later Allison walked, putting Twins' runners at first and second. Catcher Jerry Zimmerman, substituting for the sore-armed Earl Battey, grounded sharply to Tony Kubek at shortstop. Kubek threw to Richardson to start the double play, but his throw was high and everybody was safe. Kaat, the next batter, helped himself by stroking a Bouton change-up into center field for a two-run single. Tresh committed his second error of the game by again letting the ball get away from him. Kaat took second on the error, but Bouton retired Versalles and Kindall, preventing any further scoring.

Elston Howard accounted for the Yanks' first run with a fifth-inning home run into the new bleacher pavilion in left-center field. The New Yorkers closed the gap to 4–3 in the seventh, with Howard again striking the key blow. His double, following a walk to Mantle, put runners at second and third with nobody out. Mantle scored on Pepitone's grounder to Kindall, and Howard scored on Clete Boyer's sacrifice fly to Oliva. Minnesota still led, 4–3, when Kaat got Roger Maris for the first out in the ninth. Mantle followed with a single to center and Keane sent Arturo Lopez, a 27-year-old rookie from Puerto Rico, in to run for him. Third baseman Tovar made a good play to throw out Howard for out number two as Lopez moved to second. Tovar had entered the game in the third inning as a replacement for Rollins, who left with a twisted knee. The Venezuelan native had come to the Twins from Cincinnati in an off-season trade for pitcher Gerry Arrigo. Kaat, needing one more out for the win, got Pepitone to lift an easy pop fly to the left side. Tovar waved off shortstop Versalles and was standing under the ball, waiting, when it hit his glove and bounced out. Lopez, running with two out, scored the tying run. Kaat retired Boyer for the third out, but he was finished for the day. No pitcher is happy about losing what looked like a certain win, but for Kaat the snatching away of this victory was particularly disheartening. Although he had gained his first major-league win against New York in 1960, he had not beaten them since, losing nine consecutive decisions. Meanwhile, Tovar's error took Bouton off the hook and allowed him to maintain his 6–2 lifetime advantage over Minnesota. After he left, having given up four runs in five innings, relievers Hal Reniff and Pete Mikkelsen efficiently silenced the Twins' offense. Each pitched two scoreless innings, Reniff allowing just a walk and Mikkelsen a walk and a hit. When Mikkelsen retired the Twins in the home ninth, the game went into extra innings. It was the fourth consecutive extra-inning game for New York, as all three exhibition contests against the Astros had gone into overtime.

Don Mincher had pinch-hit for Kaat in the ninth, so Jerry Fosnow, another left-hander, was the Twins' pitcher as the Yankees batted in the tenth. Minnesota had signed Fosnow in 1964 as a free agent following his release by the Cleveland Indians. He seemed to have profited from the advice of Twins pitching coach Johnny Sain, who had first worked with him in the Florida Winter League. Sain continued to tutor him during the exhibition season, and Fosnow allowed just one run and seven hits in 17 innings. However, he got into an immediate predicament when Kubek, leading off, hit a fly ball to left that Allison dropped for a two-base error.

Pedro Gonzalez, batting for Mikkelsen, bunted Kubek over to third. One out later Richardson walked and stole second, but Fosnow struck out Maris to end the threat. Kindall's error on Lopez's leadoff grounder had Fosnow in trouble again in the 11th. Lopez had taken over in left field for Mantle after pinch-running for him in the ninth inning. With Howard, his most effective hitter of the afternoon, at bat, Keane disdained the sacrifice. He ordered Howard to hit away, which he did, bouncing into a 6–4–3 double play.

Pedro Ramos, a former Twin, had come on to pitch for the Yankees in the tenth. Ramos, who came from Cleveland last September for pitchers Ralph Terry and Bud Daley and $75,000, did what the Yanks expected of him in that last month; he helped them win the pennant. Leading off the 11th, Allison hit a fly ball to left that Lopez, battling the sun and wind, overran and allowed to drop untouched. By the time he got the ball back in to the infield, Allison was at third on the three-base error. "I ran too hard, too fast," a dejected

Lopez explained. "Then the wind caught the ball a little and I couldn't recover. The stadium was okay and the sun was no trouble. It was just me."

Traditional baseball strategy dictated that the Yankees now load the bases. Keane, playing by the book, ordered Ramos to intentionally walk pinch-hitters Rich Reese (batting for Zimmerman) and Sandy Valdespino (batting for Fosnow). With the bases loaded and nobody out and the Yankees infield and outfield playing in, all the Twins needed to win the game was a long fly ball. It was the most difficult position a pitcher could be in, but Ramos almost escaped successfully. He got Versalles on a short fly to Lopez and struck out Kindall, temporarily keeping Allison at third. (Versalles, who this season would earn the league's Most Valuable Player Award, had a terrible Opening Day, going hitless in six at-bats.) Then, after Ramos ran the count on Tovar to a ball and two strikes, the right-hand hitting Tovar lined a fastball into short center field. It fell safely as Allison trotted home with the winning run. Tresh, who dove for the ball, came up waving, claiming he had made the catch. It was a nice try, but it didn't work. Umpire Bill Haller, who was close to the play, saw that Tresh had caught the ball on the short hop and gave the safe signal. Tresh registered no complaint. In the clubhouse, he explained: "When the ball left the bat I figured I could get it. But it sailed a little and must have landed about a foot in front of me when I dived. I trapped it."

Although Kaat did not get credit for today's victory, he would finish with 18 wins (18–11) in 1965, including the pennant clincher. On September 26, Kaat would defeat the Senators, 2–1, giving Minnesota its first league championship. Bouton, while avoiding the loss, would compile a 4–15 record this season, and would win only five more games in his three remaining years in New York. The 1965 Yankees, like their 1954 predecessors, would fail in their attempt to win a sixth straight American League championship. That, however, is the extent of the similarities between the two clubs. The 1954 Yankees finished second with 103 wins and came back to capture pennants the next four years. In 1965, the Yanks would finish sixth—with 77 wins—and usher in an 11-year pennant drought.

Monday, April 12, 1965

New York

	ab	r	h	rbi
Tresh cf	5	0	1	0
Richardson 2b	4	0	1	0
Maris rf	4	0	0	0
Mantle lf	3	1	1	0
cA. Lopez lf	1	1	0	0
Howard c	5	2	2	1
Pepitone 1b	5	0	0	1
Boyer 3b	3	0	0	1
Kubek ss	4	0	0	0
Bouton p	1	0	0	0
aLinz	1	0	0	0
Reniff p	0	0	0	0
bH. Lopez	1	0	0	0
Mikkelsen p	0	0	0	0
eGonzalez	0	0	0	0
Ramos p	0	0	0	0
Total	37	4	5	3

Minnesota

	ab	r	h	rbi
Versalles ss	6	0	0	0
Kindall 2b	4	1	0	0
Rollins 3b	1	0	0	0
Tovar 3b	4	0	2	1
Oliva rf	5	0	0	1
Killebrew 1b	3	1	1	0
Hall cf	5	1	0	0
Allison cf	4	2	2	0
Zimmerman c	4	0	0	0
fReese	0	0	0	0
Kaat p	3	0	1	2
dMincher	1	0	0	0
Fosnow p	0	0	0	0
gValdespino	0	0	0	0
Total	40	5	6	4

*Two out when winning run scored.
ªFouled out for Bouton in sixth inning.
ᵇStruck out for Reniff in eighth inning.
ᶜRan for Mantle in ninth inning.
ᵈGround out for Kaat in ninth inning.
ᵉSacrificed for Mikkelsen in tenth inning.
ᶠIntentionally walked for Zimmerman in 11th inning.
ᵍIntentionally walked for Fosnow in 11th inning.

New York	000	010	201	00–4
Minnesota	110	200	000	01–5

Errors—Tresh 2, A. Lopez, Pepitone, Kubek, Kindall, Allison, Tovar. Double plays—Howard and Boyer; Versalles, Kindall, and Killebrew. Left on bases—New York 5; Minnesota 11. Put outs—New York 32: Tresh 4, Howard 7, Pepitone 11, Maris 2, A. Lopez 1, Boyer 1, Mantle 4, Kubek 2. Minnesota 33: Oliva 3, Killebrew 17, Kindall 5, Kaat 1, Zimmerman 3, Hall 4. Assists—New York 11: Howard 1, Richardson 7, Kubek 2, Boyer 1. Minnesota 20: Versalles 5, Killebrew 1, Kindall 4, Kaat 3, Tovar 5, Fosnow 2. Two-base hit—Howard. Home run—Howard. Stolen bases—Hall, Tovar, Richardson. Sacrifices—Maris, Gonzalez. Sacrifice fly—Boyer.

	IP	H	R	ER	BB	SO
NEW YORK						
Bouton	5.0	4	4	2	3	3
Reniff	2.0	0	0	0	1	1
Mikkelsen	2.0	1	0	0	1	2
Ramos (L, 0–1)	1.2	1	1	0	3	1
MINNESOTA						
Kaat	9.0	5	4	3	1	2
Fosnow (W, 1–0)	2.0	0	0	0	1	1

Wild pitches—Bouton 2, Reniff. Umpires—Honochick, Chylak, Odom, and Haller. Time of game—3 hrs. 14 min. Attendance—15,388.

Injuries kept Elston Howard, Roger Maris, and Tony Kubek out of the lineup for extended periods as the sixth-place Yankees (77–85) finished 25 games behind the pennant-winning Minnesota Twins. It was New York's first losing season and first second-division finish in 40 years. In his first full season, Mel Stottlemyre (20–9) emerged as the ace of the staff, while leading the league in complete games (18) and innings pitched (291). Kubek, whose injuries limited him to just 106 games in 1964 and 109 in 1965, retired, though he was only 29 years old. In June, baseball held its first free-agent draft of amateur players. The draft permanently altered the way in which the Yankees and all other teams would acquire those players in the future.

Tuesday, April 12, 1966
Yankee Stadium, New York
Detroit 2 New York 1

But many who are first shall be last.—St. Matthew

Yankees fans, long accustomed to winning, had been shocked and disappointed at the team's sixth-place finish in 1965. Because it followed five consecutive American League pennants, some assumed it was just an anomalous off-year, the kind teams have from time to time. However, the more perceptive fans correctly suspected that the Yankees dynasty had reached its end. They recognized that the team had suddenly grown old and no longer had the endless supply of young talent to replace their aging stars. The Yankees' past reluctance to sign black players had left their farm system weak, while the recently instituted amateur player draft would spread all future talent more evenly among the teams. Therefore, it was with an enthusiasm tempered by apprehension that a crowd of 40,006 made their way to 161st Street and River Avenue in the Bronx to gauge the potential of the 1966 Yankees. Not since Mickey Mantle's debut 15 years earlier had there been a larger opening-day crowd at Yankee Stadium. For those who feared the glory days were over, their first look at this year's team acted to confirm those suspicions. It was not so much that they lost—it was the way they lost. Fans left shaking their heads after the Yankees left the potential tying and winning runs on base in the ninth inning, no doubt recalling past late-inning comebacks.

The frustrating ending to Detroit's, 2–1, victory gave only the slightest hint of the agonizing season that lay ahead. Few in the crowd, which included Mrs. Babe Ruth and Mrs. Lou Gehrig, could have suspected how thoroughly dreadful the newly begun season would be—a season in which the Yankees would lose 89 games and finish in last place. Furthermore, attendance, which had been declining steadily, would fall to its lowest total since World War II. People love winners, especially in New York. And surely no one could have anticipated that before another season rolled around, both opposing managers would be dead. Yet on Opening Day all the losses and bad news are still in the future. Every team shares first place and optimism abounds, whether deserved or not. Some of the optimism about the future of baseball might have been tempered had fans fully understood the implications of today's announcement that major-league players had chosen Marvin J. Miller as the Executive Director of the Major League Baseball Players Association. Miller, an economist for the United Steelworkers Union, signed a two-year contract at $50,000 per year. Miller would lead a revolution that would free the players from the control of the owners, the results of which would often times severely strain fan loyalty.

Over the last decade, much of the pomp and pageantry had gone out of opening-day ceremonies at major-league parks. The Yankees had at least livened the now-subdued festivities with the presentation of World Series mementos and individual awards. However, because there are no such awards for teams that finish sixth, broadcaster Phil Rizzuto had nothing to do but introduce the players. Rizzuto had taken over the master of ceremonies duties at Stadium events after the Yankees fired Mel Allen following the 1964 season. The Yanks would fire Red Barber, the other melodious southern voice that had captivated New Yorkers for more than a quarter-century, following this season. During the player introductions, the crowd gave Mantle and starting pitcher Whitey Ford the loudest applause, but ungraciously booed several players—most noticeably Roger Maris and Joe Pepitone. Maris, limited by injuries to only 46 games in 1965, had batted a paltry .239; Pepitone's production had dropped from 28 home runs and 100 runs batted in, to 18 home runs and only 62 runs batted in.

The booing even extended to Mayor John Lindsay, in office only three months, and baseball commissioner William Eckert, beginning his second year. Historically, booing had been uncommon at Yankee Stadium, a park long known for its almost too sedate and polite fans. However, the times were changing, as were the manner—and manners—of many people now attending games at the Stadium. Not only was the team in decline, but so too was the deportment of the fans and the quality of civility both in and around the Stadium. Particularly guilty were the younger fans—obviously not all, probably not even a majority, but still far too many. There were plenty of young people at the game today with the schools closed for the Easter vacation. Some were celebrating the return of baseball (as were some adults) by blowing the loud, terribly annoying horns that were beginning to appear in baseball parks across the country. When asked about this assault on people's ears, Bill Kane, the assistant to team vice president Bob Fischel, said that if the horn blowing got out of control the Yankees would ban them from the park.

Guy Lombardo and his band entertained the crowd during the pregame activities and then accompanied vocalist Vic Damone in the playing and singing of the national anthem. Mayor Lindsay threw out the first ball and this season of anguish got underway. Ford was making his seventh (and final) opening-day start, breaking Lefty Gomez's Yankees' record. Except for the first one, at Washington in 1954, all had come at home. This, naturally, would be the first against Detroit, a team the Yanks had never before played on Opening Day. Ford, now 37 years old, had a 21–11 lifetime mark against the Tigers, 3–2 in 1965. Despite winning 16 games in 1965, his 13 losses gave him a winning percentage of .552—his worst ever. It lowered his career mark from .720 to .705, which dropped him behind former Yankee Spud Chandler's .717 as the best ever mark for twentieth century pitchers with at least 100 decisions. In his final two seasons, Ford would win just four games and lose nine, lowering his winning percentage to .690.

Don Wert, the game's first batter, went out on a liner to left fielder Tom Tresh. However, seconds after Tresh caught the ball, Detroit manager Charlie Dressen came charging out of the dugout with the season's first objection. Dressen complained to plate umpire Jim Honochick that the plastic hot water bottle Ford kept in his pocket was an illegal "foreign substance," expressly banned by league rules. Ford had undergone surgery in 1964 to correct circulation problems in his left shoulder, a procedure that left him with little feeling in his pitching arm when the weather was cold. Although today was sunny, it was a cool 56 degrees, and the temperature would decrease as the game progressed. Ford was using the hot water bottle as a hand warmer, but despite his explanation Honochick upheld the ban on "foreign substances." Yankees manager Johnny Keane, who had come out to argue his pitcher's case, headed back to the dugout carrying the plastic bottle.

Ford later admitted that Dressen's complaint had "irritated" him. "He thinks his club is going to win the pennant this year," he said after the game. "But he's not going to win it by aggravating people." The lack of the hand warmer did not adversely affect Ford's pitching. Through the first four innings, he held the Tigers to just one hit, a leadoff single by Jerry Lumpe in the fourth inning. Meanwhile, his teammates had managed just two hits against his opponent, Mickey Lolich—a single by Maris and a double by Mantle. If Ford's reign as one of baseball's best left-handed pitchers was ending, Lolich's was just beginning. At 25 and in his fourth year in the league, he had won 18 games (18–9) in 1964 and 15 (15–9) in 1965, including two of three against New York.

Pepitone broke the scoring drought when he led off the fifth with a home run eight rows deep into the lower right-field seats. Detroit, a strong team with legitimate hopes of winning its first pennant since 1945, tied the score in the top of the sixth. Mickey Stanley, a young right-handed-hitting outfielder, led off by pulling a Ford pitch just inside the third-base bag and down the line. The left-field ball boy, thinking it was a foul ball or just not paying attention, picked it up. The umpires awarded Stanley a grounds-rule double, which led to another protest by Dressen. He claimed Stanley should be at third, the base he would have reached had the ball boy not interfered. This protest was disallowed, and Stanley had to stay at second. It made little difference, for after Lolich struck out, Wert singled off shortstop Ruben Amaro's glove and Stanley came home. Tony Kubek's forced retirement, at age 29, led the Yankees to acquire Amaro, a weak hitter, but an excellent fielder. They traded Phil Linz to the Phillies to get Amaro, though they planned to use him only until 19-year-old Bobby Murcer was ready to take over. Often, such plans don't work out. Amaro was hurt in a collision with Tresh in the first week of the season and played in only 14 games in 1966. Clete Boyer and Horace Clarke shared the shortstop position for most of the season, with the rookie Murcer and veteran Dick Schofield both playing some.

The Yankees missed an excellent chance to retake the lead in the sixth. Bobby Richardson singled to center to lead off. But as Tresh went down swinging after twice failing to sacrifice, Richardson was doubled-up attempting to steal second by catcher Bill Freehan to second baseman Lumpe. Maris followed with a walk and Mantle got an infield single, but with runners at first and second, Lolich got Boyer, the Yanks' top hitter in the Grapefruit League, on a fly ball to right fielder Al Kaline. Mantle's presence in the lineup was an unexpected bonus for the Yankees and for the fans. Keane had envisioned playing the first month of the season without him after he underwent surgery on his right arm. Mantle, playing in his 16th consecutive opener, was now more popular with the fans than he had ever been. In this time of uncertainty and transition for the team, it was reassuring to them to look out at center field and see him there. After Mantle's single, his second hit of the game, Keane sent Roger Repoz in to run for him as Mickey trotted off to a standing ovation.

Both pitchers breezed through the seventh and eighth, but Lolich led off the ninth with a soft single to center. It was not like Ford to allow a hit in this type of situation, especially to such a weak hitter as Lolich, who entered the season with 14 hits (all singles) in 186 at bats—an .075 average. As Wert, the next batter, stepped in, Boyer and Pepitone, anticipating a bunt, moved in a few steps. But instead of bunting, Wert swung and hit a high bouncer that Boyer attempted to backhand by reaching across his body. The ball hit off his glove and rolled into fair territory. As Lolich continued around second and headed for third, Amaro retrieved the ball and threw it to Boyer who put the tag on the less-than-speedy pitcher. Wert reached second on the play, putting the lead run in scoring position. Pedro Ramos was warming up in the bullpen, but with two left-handed hitters—Lumpe and Norm Cash—coming up, Keane chose to stay with Ford. Lumpe made the second out, grounding to Richardson as Wert moved to third. Ford needed one more out, but Cash, swinging at the first pitch, hit a broken-bat blooper into center field for a run-scoring single. None of the three hits Ford allowed this inning had been hit hard. Nevertheless, Keane removed him and brought in Ramos to face Kaline. Cash promptly took off for second, and when catcher Elston Howard's throw went into center field, Cash continued to third. Kaline drew a walk, but Ramos prevented any further damage by getting the dangerous Willie Horton on a pop to Richardson.

Everyone in the crowd realized that getting a run against Lolich, who already had struck out ten, would be difficult. They brightened when Lou Clinton, batting for Repoz, walked to lead off the last of the ninth. Clinton, acquired from Cleveland for catcher Doc Edwards, was making his first appearance as a Yankee. Keane decided to play for the tie and ordered Boyer to lay one down. He did, but the bunt was too strong, enabling Lolich to field it and throw to shortstop Dick McAuliffe for a force at second on Clinton. The fans came to life again when Pepitone's single to right sent Boyer around to third. They now had two opportunities to at least tie the score. Howard, hitless on the day, was first. He ran the count to two-and-two, but then popped out to McAuliffe. With Amaro the due batter, Keane sent up Roy White—a switch-hitting rookie outfielder—to pinch-hit. White had joined the Yankees in September 1965 after leading the Southern League in hits (168), runs

(103), and triples (13), while playing for the oxymoronically-named Columbus (Georgia) Confederate Yankees. He hit .333 in 14 games, and after an outstanding spring (he won the James P. Dawson Award) earned a place on the big-league roster. White would have a long career in New York, eventually playing in more games as a Yankee than all but six others, but as an anxious youngster he was no match for Lolich. He chased the first pitch and popped it in the air, where McAuliffe caught it to end the game.

Tuesday, April 12, 1966

Detroit	ab	r	h	rbi	New York	ab	r	h	rbi
Wert 3b	4	1	2	1	Richardson 2b	3	0	1	0
Lumpe 2b	4	0	1	0	Tresh lf	4	0	0	0
Cash 1b	4	0	1	1	Maris rf	3	0	1	0
Kaline rf	3	0	0	0	Mantle cf	3	0	2	0
Horton lf	4	0	0	0	aRepoz cf	0	0	0	0
Freehan c	3	0	0	0	bClinton rf	0	0	0	0
McAuliffe ss	2	0	0	0	Boyer 3b	4	0	0	0
Stanley cf	3	1	1	0	Pepitone 1b	4	1	2	1
Lolich p	3	0	1	0	Howard c	3	0	0	0
Total	30	2	6	2	Amaro ss	3	0	0	0
					cWhite	1	0	0	0
					Ford p	3	0	0	0
					Ramos p	0	0	0	0
					Total	31	1	6	1

aRan for Mantle in sixth inning.
bWalked for Repoz in ninth inning.
cPopped out for Amaro in ninth inning.

Detroit	000	001	001–2
New York	000	010	000–1

Errors—Amaro, Howard. Double plays—Lumpe, McAuliffe, and Cash; Freehan and Lumpe; Boyer and Pepitone; Ford, Amaro, and Pepitone; Ford and Pepitone. Left on bases—Detroit 3; New York 7. Put outs—New York 27: Amaro 2, Tresh 3, Pepitone 10, Howard 4, Ford 1, Boyer 3, Mantle 1, Repoz 1, Richardson 2. Detroit 27: McAuliffe 6, Freehan 11, Horton 1, Stanley 1, Lumpe 3, Wert 1, Cash 3, Kaline 1. Assists—New York 12: Amaro 2, Boyer 2, Richardson 2, Ford 6. Detroit 6: McAuliffe 2, Freehan 1, Lumpe 1, Wert 1, Lolich 1. Two-base hits—Mantle, Stanley. Home run—Pepitone. Stolen base—Cash.

	IP	H	R	ER	BB	SO
DETROIT						
Lolich (W, 1–0)	9.0	6	1	1	4	10
NEW YORK						
Ford (L, 0–1)	8.2	6	2	2	1	4
Ramos	.1	0	0	0	1	0

Umpires—Honochick, Umont, Kinnamon, and Neudecker. Time of game—2 hrs. 26 min. Attendance—40,006.

On May 7, after the Yanks lost 16 of their first 20 games, General manager Ralph Houk fired Johnny Keane and again became the team's manager. Keane died the following January of a heart attack, at age 55. Dressen, 71, suffered a heart attack on May 16, and coach Bob Swift replaced him. On August 10 Dressen had another attack, this one fatal. Swift became ill in July and was replaced by coach Frank Skaff. In October, Swift, 51, died of cancer.

Just two years removed from having won five consecutive pennants, the Yankees (70–89) finished tenth and last, 26½ games behind the Baltimore Orioles. It was the team's first last-place finish since 1912. Mel Stottlemyre (12–20) and rookie Fritz Peterson (12–11) led the club in wins with 12, the second-lowest leading total in team history.

Monday, April 10, 1967
D.C. Stadium, Washington
New York 8 Washington 0

The years keep coming and going, men will arise and depart.—Heinrich Heine

Late in the 1966 season, the Columbia Broadcasting System purchased Dan Topping's remaining 10 percent share of the Yankees and became the team's sole owner. Michael Burke, a CBS executive and former CIA operative, with little knowledge of baseball, replaced Topping as president and brought in Lee MacPhail to be the general manager. Ralph Houk, who had served as manager and general manager after succeeding Johnny Keane in May 1966, would now concentrate fully on his managing duties. MacPhail, the son of former Yankees president Larry MacPhail, had been with the Yanks before. He served as director of player personnel from 1948 to 1958, before leaving to become president and general manager of the Baltimore Orioles. At the winter meetings, MacPhail, who had built a championship team in Baltimore, began the process of rebuilding the Yankees. Within a ten-day period, he traded Clete Boyer to the Atlanta Braves for Bill Robinson, a promising young outfielder, and sent Roger Maris to the St. Louis Cardinals for much-traveled third baseman Charley Smith.

By the time the Yankees opened the 1967 season against the Senators in Washington, only catcher Elston Howard and left fielder Tom Tresh were in the same positions they played in the 1966 opener. Two others, Mickey Mantle and Joe Pepitone, were playing the position the other had played in '66. Pepitone, the first baseman a year ago, was in center field, while Mantle was playing the first game of his career at first base. Joining Mantle in the Yankees' reassembled infield were Horace Clarke at second, replacing the retired Bobby Richardson, Smith at third, and John Kennedy, obtained from the Dodgers a week earlier, at shortstop. Robinson started in right field, and Mel Stottlemyre, making his first opening-day start, was the pitcher. Stottlemyre, after winning 20 games (20–9) in 1965—his first full season—followed by losing 20 (12–20) last year. His 20 losses were the most in the American League, making him the first Yankees' pitcher to lead the league in losses since Sad Sam Jones lost 21 in 1925.

Since coming into the American League as an expansion team in 1961, the second edition of the Senators had carried on the long history of futility established by their predecessors. However, they had been making progress in the three years since Gil Hodges became their manager. Washington's "new" Senators had never finished higher than eighth, but in 1966 that was two positions above the Yankees. And while Washington had lost four consecutive openers and five of six since entering the league, Opening Day was still the highlight of the Washington baseball season—often the only highlight. The Yankees, playing in their first "presidential opener" since 1956, had their own opening-day losing streak: three straight, and all by one run. Obviously one of the two losing streaks would end today, and after New York scored seven runs in the third inning there was no doubt about whose it would be. Behind Stottlemyre's two-hit pitching, the Yanks coasted to an easy, 8–0, victory before 44,382 disappointed fans.

The Senators had played their first season at old Griffith Stadium before moving into the newly constructed District of Columbia Stadium in 1962. The symmetrically built, completely enclosed park was among the first of those specifically designed to house both baseball and football. D.C. Stadium, which was also the home of the Washington Redskins, was located two miles east of the U.S. Capitol building, alongside the East Capitol Street Bridge.

Opening Day in Washington almost always meant that the president would be at the opener to throw out the first ball and pretend to be just a regular citizen. However, of all the American presidents who had served since William Howard Taft originated the custom, none was less interested in baseball than the current occupant of the White House, Lyndon Baines Johnson. Although Johnson had attended previous opening-day games here, neither business manager Joe Burke nor anyone else in the Senators' front office knew for sure if he would be coming today. There was speculation that Vice President Hubert Humphrey, a genuine baseball fan, would substitute for Johnson. Humphrey had arrived from Europe at 9:30 that morning, and LBJ was at Andrews Air Force base to meet him. Finally, at 1:15 P.M., the White House informed the Senators that President Johnson would indeed be attending today's game. Ten minutes later the first motorcycle rider from the president's entourage reached the stadium. Word of Johnson's plans had evidently been passed on to security details earlier in the day. His prosecution of the war in Viet Nam had triggered anti-war demonstrations around the country; so by the time the motorcade reached D.C. Stadium, there were more than 150 D.C. policemen and more than 100 secret servicemen on duty inside and outside the park.

Baseball commissioner William Eckert greeted LBJ on his arrival, and at the first sight of the president the marine band struck up "Hail to the Chief." Johnson, hatless and wearing a blue suit, took his seat in the presidential box. Seated with him were Senator John Pastore of Rhode Island and Senator Margaret Chase Smith of Maine, wearing a bright red dress and hat and a pink rose. Johnson, always gregarious in public, immediately began to shake hands with all the politicians and officials seated nearby. There were quite a few, including Speaker of the House John McCormack, House Majority Leader Carl Albert, House Minority Leader Gerald Ford, Maine Senator Edmund Muskie, Postmaster General Lawrence O'Brien, American League president Joe Cronin, commissioner Eckert, and from the Senators, James M. Johnston, chairman of the board, and George Selkirk, the general manager. While Johnson was not a baseball fan, no one could remember a president with a stronger throwing arm, or one who threw out more first balls. He threw three. Senators outfielder Fred Valentine got the first one after it bounced off some Yankees players' gloves, and Yankees' pitchers Al Downing and Dooley Womack caught the next two.

Opposing Stottlemyre was Pete Richert, a left-hander with an excellent fastball. Richert had developed into the Senators' best pitcher, leading the club in victories in each of his two years here since coming from the Dodgers in December 1964. The deal that brought him to Washington also brought pitcher Phil Ortega, outfielder Frank Howard, third baseman Ken McMullen, and first baseman Dick Nen. All were still with Washington, and Howard, McMullen, and Nen were in today's starting lineup. To get these four, the Senators sent Claude Osteen, who *had* been their best pitcher, to Los Angeles along with present Yankees shortstop John Kennedy and $100,000. After going 0–4 against the Yanks in 1965, Richert beat them twice without a loss in 1966. Without Boyer and the retired Hector

Lopez—the two men who had been the most successful against Richert—the Yanks were anticipating another difficult afternoon against him today. Richert did look strong in the first two innings, holding New York hitless, but then came the third-inning deluge. After striking out Stottlemyre, Tresh ripped a double into the left-field corner, the first of six consecutive Yankees' hits. The next batter was Robinson, who had confessed before the game, "No one is more nervous than I am."

Robinson's bid for a home run in the first inning had gone just foul, but now he followed Tresh's double with a drive over the 381-foot sign in left. That kind of power was the reason the Yanks had traded for Robinson, a man they expected to play a prominent role in their rebuilding plans. He had batted 11 times for the Braves in 1966, but this was his first big-league home run, and it gave the Yanks a 2–0 lead. As he crossed the plate, waiting to greet him and shake his hand was Mantle, who was now only 495 home runs ahead of Robinson. Mantle had walked in the first inning, but this time he singled hard to left. Pepitone followed with a slicing fly ball toward the left-field corner that Frank Howard played into a triple. Mantle came around to score run number three, but as he rounded second, he reinjured his left thigh and had to leave the game. Ray Barker, a journeyman picked up from Cleveland in a May 1965 trade for Pedro Gonzalez, took his place. Mantle, beginning his 17th season, said after the game, "I'm as discouraged as I've ever been in my life. I pulled the same muscle a couple of weeks ago in an exhibition game, but I thought I was over it. Now this." Fortunately, Mantle's injury proved not too serious, and he would play in 144 games this year, the most games he had played since 1961.

Trailing 3–0, Hodges played the Washington infield up in an attempt to keep Pepitone from scoring. However, by doing so, it enabled Elston Howard's routine grounder to the right side to squeeze through for a run-producing single. After Hodges visited the mound for a brief conversation with Richert, Smith got the Yanks' sixth consecutive hit, beating out a ground ball to McMullen. Clarke flied to Valentine for the second out, but Kennedy doubled into the right-field corner, scoring Howard and Smith with New York's fifth and sixth runs. Right fielder Cap Peterson, who earlier had dropped an easy fly, let the ball get away, allowing Kennedy to go to third. Hodges went back to the mound, but this time when he left he took Richert with him. Left-hander Darold Knowles, whom the Senators got from the Phillies in a trade for Don Lock, came in to make his Washington debut. Stottlemyre, in his second at-bat of the inning, greeted him with a line-drive single to center. It was the Yankees' eighth hit of the inning and it scored Kennedy with the seventh run. Tresh ended the merry-go-round with a grounder back to Knowles for the third out. Because of a troublesome right knee, Tresh had played only one week during spring training, so after the fifth inning Houk removed him. Steve Whitaker went in to play right field, with Robinson moving to left. After their third-inning assault, the Yanks would get only six more hits and one run, a Howard homer into the Washington bullpen against Jim Hannan in the seventh.

Even if the game had been close, it is unlikely that it would have captured President Johnson's attention. The president spent almost his entire visit chatting with Senators Smith, Pastore, and Muskie, although he did find time to consume two hot dogs along with some ice cream, peanuts, and popcorn. Johnson left after the fifth inning, by which time it had become apparent that the home team was not likely to win this game and probably would not even score. Stottlemyre was at his best this afternoon, completely overpowering the Senators. He struck out only six, but his excellent sinking fastball got 18 outs on ground balls. Washington's best chance came in the first inning after Eddie Brinkman, the leadoff batter, reached base on an error by shortstop Kennedy. It would be the only error the Yankees would make today, after committing 62 in 30 spring training games. Brinkman went to second as Bernie Allen grounded out to Mantle unassisted. Mickey bobbled the ball momentarily in his first chance at the new position, before recovering in time to make the play. A walk to Valentine put two runners on, but Stottlemyre struck out the dangerous Frank Howard on three pitches and got Nen on a comebacker.

Peterson, playing his first game for the Senators, led off the second with Washington's first hit. Clarke fielded his high bounder over the mound, but as he did he collided with shortstop Kennedy and could not make a throw. The Senators' next hit would not come until the ninth inning—a solid leadoff single to right by Valentine. Stottlemyre retired the next three, Howard, Nen, and Peterson, all on ground balls, and because this was the only American League game played today, the Yanks had sole possession of first place for the first time since 1964.

Monday, April 10, 1967

New York	ab	r	h	rbi		Washington	ab	r	h	rbi
Tresh lf	4	1	1	0		Brinkman ss	4	0	0	0
Whitaker rf	1	0	1	0		Allen 2b	4	0	0	0
Robinson rf,lf	4	1	2	2		Valentine cf	3	0	1	0
Mantle 1b	1	1	1	0		F. Howard lf	4	0	0	0
Barker 1b	3	0	0	0		Nen 1b	4	0	0	0
Pepitone cf	5	1	2	1		Peterson rf	3	0	1	0
E. Howard c	5	2	2	2		McMullen 3b	3	0	0	0
Smith 3b	5	1	1	0		Camilli c	3	0	0	0
Clarke 2b	4	0	2	0		Richert p	1	0	0	0
Kennedy ss	3	1	1	2		Knowles p	0	0	0	0
Stottlemyre p	4	0	1	1		ªChance	0	0	0	0
Total 39 8	14	8				Hannan p	0	0	0	0
						ᵇKing	1	0	0	0
						Lines p	0	0	0	0
						Total	30	0	2	0

ªWalked for Knowles in fifth inning.
ᵇGrounded out for Hannan in eighth inning.

New York	007	000	100–8
Washington	000	000	000–0

Errors—Kennedy, Peterson 2. Double plays—Allen and Nen. Left on bases—New York 7; Washington 6. Put outs—New York 27: Mantle 4, E. Howard 6, Stottlemyre 3, Clarke 1, Barker 10, Robinson 1, Kennedy 1, Pepitone 1. Washington 27: Brinkman 2, Nen 11, Allen 3, Peterson 1, Camilli 6, Valentine 1, Knowles 1, F. Howard 2. Assists—New York 16: Stottlemyre 3, Clarke 4, Barker 3, Kennedy 5, Smith 1. Washington 14: Brinkman 4, Nen 1, Allen 4, Peterson 1, Knowles 2, Hannan 1, McMullen 1. Two-base hits—Tresh, Kennedy, Whitaker. Three-base hit—Pepitone. Home runs—Robinson, E. Howard.

	IP	H	R	ER	BB	SO
NEW YORK						
Stottlemyre (W, 1–0)	9.0	2	0	0	3	6
WASHINGTON						
Richert (L, 0–1)	2.2	7	7	7	1	1
Knowles	2.1	3	0	0	2	3
Hannan	3.0	4	1	1	0	1
Lines	1.0	0	0	0	0	1

Umpires—Stevens, Stewart, Valentine, and Springstead. Time of game—2 hrs. 33 min. Attendance—44,382.

After a one-year stay in last place, the Yankees showed slight improvement (72–90), finishing ninth, 20 games behind the pennant-winning Boston Red Sox. The team batted .225, its lowest average ever (to that point), and its 1,043 batter strikeouts led the league. Two more stars of the glory years departed: Whitey Ford, the greatest pitcher in Yankees' history, announced his retirement after appearing in just seven games, and Elston Howard, a Yankees' mainstay since 1955, was traded to Boston in August for minor-league pitchers Ron Klimkowski and Pete Magrini.

Wednesday, April 10, 1968
Yankee Stadium, New York
New York 1 California 0

It is impossible, in our condition of society,
not to be sometimes a snob.—William Makepeace Thackeray

The announcement that Martin Luther King's funeral would be held on April 9 presented a dilemma for major-league baseball. Should they go ahead and play the season openers scheduled that day, or postpone them 24 hours as a gesture of respect for Dr. King? The owners had to weigh the revenue losses and schedule disruptions they would suffer by not playing against the negative publicity they would receive by playing. It was not an easy decision, but rising above their customary lack of wisdom and sensitivity, they chose to cancel all games scheduled for the 9th.

While many Americans had objected to King's methods, and some even to his cause, this was still a country that could be shocked and outraged by political assassination. Sadly, King's murder on April 4 was only the beginning of what would be America's most divisive year since the Civil War. Before it was over, the nation would grieve over another assassination—that of Senator Robert Kennedy—and suffer through antiwar riots over Vietnam and political riots at the Democratic National Convention. Civility and meaningful discourse would be under constant assault by such domestic terrorists as the Weathermen and the Black Panthers. Even as the baseball season began, scores of unorganized thugs, using King's death as a pretense, were continuing to burn and loot in cities and towns across the country. In some of those cities, including the nation's capital, officials feared for the safety of fans attending opening-day games. At the Washington Senators-Minnesota Twins game, where Vice President Hubert Humphrey threw out the first ball, combat-clad soldiers patrolled the streets around D.C. Stadium and armed troops guarded the nearby Capitol Building. In riot-torn Baltimore, the Orioles had to get army approval before they could play their game against the Athletics, who were playing their first game since moving from Kansas City to Oakland. New York City had been spared much of this barbarism thanks to the calming efforts of responsible black leaders and Mayor John Lindsay's strong relationship with the city's black population. Nevertheless, with Yankee Stadium located in an area that fans now viewed as unsafe, it was not surprising that despite the relative calm of the city, only 15,744 (including Mrs. Babe Ruth) showed up for the opener.

Historians remember 1968 as "the year of the riot," a tense explosive time when all established wisdom was being challenged and the very foundation of the nation appeared to be collapsing. Baseball fans, on the other hand, remember 1968 as "the year of the pitcher," a time of low-scoring games, weak hitting, and many shutouts. The precedent was set on Opening Day when four of the ten games ended in shutouts, including Mel Stottlemyre's 1–0 victory over the California Angels. Stottlemyre was the first Yankee pitcher ever to throw back-to-back opening-day shutouts, but unlike 1967 when he had eight runs to work with, this time he had just one. Frank Fernandez, his rookie battery mate, provided it with a second-inning home run. Fernandez's blast made a loser of California starter George Brunet, who did not find the lack of run support unusual. Of the veteran left-hander's league-leading 19 losses (11–19) in 1967, the Angels had scored two or fewer runs in 15 of them. Fernandez, six days short of his 25th birthday, had won the hearts of the crowd even before his home run with a spontaneous kiss of first-ball-thrower Marianne Moore. Yankees president Mike Burke had bypassed the usual politicians and asked the famed American poet if she would do the honors. The 80-year-old Miss Moore, a baseball fan and former Brooklyn Dodgers' rooter, accepted. As she got ready to make the throw, catcher Fernandez considerately moved closer to Miss Moore's box to receive the ball. After catching it knee-high, he handed it back to her and then leaned over and kissed her on the cheek. "I just did it on the spur of the moment," he later confessed.

Fernandez was the first Yankee other than Yogi Berra and Elston Howard to start behind the plate on Opening Day since Charlie Silvera back in 1952. But Berra was now a coach with the New York Mets, and Howard, who had started for the past six years, was with the Boston Red Sox. Manager Ralph Houk's plan was to platoon the right-handed-hitting Fernandez and the left-handed- hitting Jake Gibbs. With the left-hander Brunet on the mound for the Angels, Fernandez, who had played well during spring training, got today's start. The Staten Island native had made his big-league debut last September, batting .214 in nine games. Fernandez's home run was one of only three hits Brunet allowed; the other two were singles by first baseman Mickey Mantle. This was Mantle's 18th consecutive opener, and though neither he nor his fans knew it at the time, his last. Before the game he was presented with a plaque commemorating his 500th home run, hit off Baltimore's Stu Miller on May 14, 1967. The fans, aware that Mantle's career was nearing its end, cheered him vigorously, and continued to do so all afternoon. The plaque later would be placed ten rows back in the right field grandstand, near where that 500th home run had landed.

Stottlemyre, showing no sign of the arm problems that bothered him all spring, was in complete control. He allowed the Angels only four hits, struck out six, and never had to pitch with more than one runner on base. From the second inning through the sixth, he set the side down in order, part of a stretch in which he retired 18 in a row. He did not walk a man, nor did Brunet nor Tom Burgmeier, who pitched the eighth for California. In fact, Brunet and Burgmeier were so effective that only three Yankees reached base and only one runner was left—Mantle in the first inning. This rare early-season efficiency by the three pitchers made for a snappily played game that consumed only a brief hour and 43 minutes. And that included a minor brouhaha in the eighth when Stottlemyre ran afoul of the new rules concerning pitchers putting their hands to their mouths.

After yielding a two-out single to Mantle in the first, Brunet had retired the first two Yankees in the second and gotten ahead of Fernandez one ball and two strikes. However, on the next pitch, a high fastball, Fernandez pulled it into the left-field seats (newly painted blue) 400 feet away. Following the home run, the Yanks did not get another base runner until Mantle led off the seventh with a single to center. Tom Tresh was next, and although Tresh batted just .219 in 1967 and was coming off knee surgery, he was the clean-up hitter. So, while the situation might have called for a sacrifice bunt, Houk ordered Tresh to hit away. Tresh connected, driving the ball a long way to center field, but Roger Repoz caught it for the first out. When Bill Robinson struck out swinging on a busted hit-and-run play, Mantle was doubled-up—catcher Bob Rodgers, to second baseman Bobby Knoop, to first baseman Don Mincher. Robinson, who batted a disappointing .196 in 1967 with just seven home runs in 342 at-bats, had hit well this spring; however, the Yankees were not overly impressed, remembering he had also hit well in the spring of 1967. Nor would they be impressed with his 1968 season. For although Robinson would raise his average to .240, he hit only six home runs in the same number of at-bats (342), and again frustrated team officials with his weak hitting and lack of power.

Repoz led off the Angels' eighth with the third hit off Stottlemyre, a single to right. Mincher in the first and Chuck Hinton in the seventh had the previous two. With Angels manager Bill Rigney suffering from intestinal flu and back in his hotel watching the game on TV, coach Bob Lemon was running the team. Lemon called for the bunt, but Rodgers failed to deliver, popping out to Fernandez in foul territory. Jay Johnstone batted for Knoop, and it was after Stottlemyre threw him a called strike that the fireworks began. Al Salerno, umpiring at first, charged Stottlemyre with ball one, saying the pitcher had wet his fingers while still on the dirt part of the mound. A new rule decreed that a pitcher could not be on the 18-foot dirt circle that surrounds the rubber when he puts his fingers to his mouth. Just the day before, retired umpire Charlie Berry, who now worked for the American League, and ballpark superintendent George Stallings had inspected and approved the Stadium's rebuilt mound.

Stottlemyre claimed he was on the grass when he blew on his fingers, leading Houk to charge out of the dugout to support his pitcher. Houk confronted home-plate umpire Larry Napp, but Napp informed him it was a judgment call and therefore neither manager nor player could dispute it. Although he realized he had no legitimate reason for doing so, Houk announced that he was playing the game under protest. Stottlemyre then threw two more balls to Johnstone before eventually getting him on a fly ball to center fielder Joe Pepitone. Jimmie Hall, batting for Brunet, grounded to third baseman Mike Ferraro, whose throw to second was low, but Horace Clarke made a good pickup to force Repoz for the third out. Ferraro, the winner of the James P. Dawson Award, given to the best rookie in camp, had been having problems with his throwing all day. On the very first play of the game he made a nifty backhanded grab of Paul Schaal's ground ball, but then threw it over Mantle's head at first.

Wednesday, April 10, 1968

California	ab	r	h	rbi		New York	ab	r	h	rbi
Schaal 3b	4	0	0	0		Clarke 2b	3	0	0	0
Fregosi ss	4	0	1	0		Ferraro 3b	3	0	0	0
Mincher 1b	4	0	1	0		Mantle 1b	3	0	2	0
Hinton rf	4	0	1	0		Tresh lf	3	0	0	0
Reichardt lf	3	0	0	0		Robinson rf	3	0	0	0
Repoz cf	3	0	1	0		Pepitone cf	3	0	0	0
Rodgers c	3	0	0	0		Fernandez c	3	1	1	1

California   New York

	ab	r	h	rbi			ab	r	h	rbi
Knoop 2b	2	0	0	0		Michael ss	3	0	0	0
ᵃJohnstone	1	0	0	0		Stottlemyre p	2	0	0	0
Satriano 2b	0	0	0	0		Total	26	1	3	1
Brunet p	2	0	0	0						
ᵇHall	1	0	0	0						
Burgmeier p	0	0	0	0						
Total	31	0	4	0						

ᵃFlied out for Knoop in eighth inning.
ᵇGrounded into force out for Brunet in eighth inning.

California   000   000   000–0
New York   010   000   00X–1

Error—Ferraro. Double plays—Rodgers, Knoop, and Mincher. Caught stealing—by Fernandez (Schaal); by Rodgers (Mantle). Left on bases—California 4; New York 1. Put outs—New York 27: Clarke 2, Tresh 1, Michael 4, Pepitone 4, Fernandez 8, Mantle 5, Stottlemyre 3. California 24: Knoop 3, Schaal 2, Repoz 3, Rodgers 2, Reichardt 2, Fregosi 2, Mincher 8, Hinton 1, Burgmeier 1. Assists—New York 10: Clarke 2, Ferraro 3, Michael 1, Fernandez 1, Mantle 2, Stottlemyre 1. California 9: Knoop 1, Rodgers 1, Fregosi 5, Mincher 1, Burgmeier 1. Two-base hit—Fregosi. Home run—Fernandez.

	IP	H	R	ER	BB	SO
CALIFORNIA						
Brunet (L,0–1)	7.0	3	1	1	0	2
Burgmeier	1.0	0	0	0	0	0
NEW YORK						
Stottlemyre (W, 1–0)	9.0	4	0	0	0	6

Umpires—Napp, Salerno, Haller, and Neudecker. Time of game—1 hr. 43 min. Attendance—15,744.

California got the tying run to second in the ninth when shortstop Jim Fregosi hit a one-out double to left. However, Stottlemyre got Mincher on a grounder to Clarke and Hinton on a grounder to ex–Dodger Gene Michael at short to nail down the first of the 21 (21–12) victories he would have in 1968. The final pitch to Hinton was his 94th of the afternoon, but because of Salerno's call he was charged with 95.

The Detroit Tigers won the American League's last pure pennant race—before the adoption of divisions in 1969. The Yanks (83–79) had their first winning season in four years and moved up to fifth place. Still, they finished 20 games out of first place, the same as in 1967 when they finished ninth. Stan Bahnsen (17–12) won the Rookie of the Year Award. Mickey Mantle batted just .237 in his final season, which dropped his lifetime average from .302 to .298. He ended his career with 536 home runs, which put him third on the all-time list behind only Babe Ruth and Willie Mays. The American League set the record for lowest batting average (.23011) in a season, which still stands. The Yankees, at .214 (their all-time low), were the league's worst-hitting team.

Monday, April 7, 1969
Robert F. Kennedy Stadium, Washington
New York 8 Washington 4

The old order changeth, yielding place to new.—Alfred, Lord Tennyson

Following Senator Robert Kennedy's assassination in June 1968, Washington's District of Columbia Stadium was renamed in his honor. Kennedy had been shot to death in Los Angeles as he campaigned for the Democratic presidential nomination, a prize that Vice President Hubert Humphrey eventually won. However, vitriolic attacks from the left wing of his party weakened Humphrey, and he lost the presidency in a three-way race to the former vice president, Republican Richard M. Nixon. Former Alabama governor George Wallace of the American Independent Party finished third. As a result, it was Nixon and not Humphrey who was the guest of honor at the 1969 "presidential opener" in Robert F. Kennedy Stadium. The new president was part of a crowd of 45,113 that watched the Yankees thump the Senators, 8–4, on a beautiful spring afternoon. Bowie Kuhn, the former National League lawyer who had replaced William Eckert as the commissioner of baseball, was also part of the gathering that was the largest ever for a Washington opener. Kuhn was no stranger to baseball in Washington; as a boy here he had helped work the scoreboard at old Griffith Stadium.

Kuhn took office as professional baseball, beginning its second century, was transforming the basic structure of the major-league pennant races. Each league had expanded again, adding two teams and raising the total of league members from ten to 12. But realizing that a pennant race involving 12 teams would be unwieldy, the owners voted to split each league into an Eastern and Western Division. The National League placed a team in San Diego and a team in Montreal, the first non–American team admitted to the big leagues. American League owners awarded one franchise to Seattle and one to Kansas City, which had lost the Athletics to Oakland the year before. Current competitive balance was the National League's guide in making their division assignments. They put one expansion team in each division, the Montreal Expos in the East and the San Diego Padres in the West, but otherwise ignored geography. The American League, emphasizing geographical consistency, placed both expansion teams, the Kansas City Royals and the Seattle Pilots, in the Western Division with Chicago, Minnesota, Oakland, and California. The Yankees and Senators were in the East, along with Boston, Baltimore, Cleveland, and Detroit. The owners reasoned that with more teams involved in pennant contention, it would keep interest alive in those cities and, they hoped, result in higher attendance. What was lost, obviously, was that the team in each league with the best record would no longer automatically be the league champion. Under the divisional system, the two division winners would meet in a best-of-five league championship series to decide the league's representative in the World Series. Excellence established over a 162-game schedule could now be wiped out by a three-day slump.

With no other American League teams scheduled this day, this would be the league's first game under the new format. It also would be the Senators' first under their new ownership. Robert Short, a Minnesotan who served as the national treasurer of Humphrey's presidential campaign, had spent $9 million to purchase the club. He immediately endeared himself to baseball fans by luring Ted Williams out of retirement to manage his lackluster team. Not surprisingly, Williams received the biggest cheers during the pregame introductions, exceeding even those given to local hero Frank Howard. To show his appreciation, the new manager tipped his cap, something he had been criticized for not doing in his years as a player with the Boston Red Sox. In keeping with their advertised new look, the Senators had dropped the pinstripes from their home uniforms, which were now all white with red trimming. Their hats, sleeves, stockings, and belts were red, as was the script "Senators" across their jersey fronts. They wore, as did all major-league teams in 1969, a patch on their left sleeve commemorating professional baseball's centennial.

Before the game, Williams, a strong Nixon supporter, went over to the presidential box to chat with the president and those around him. With Nixon were Short, Kuhn, and Bud Wilkinson, the former University of Oklahoma football coach who was Nixon's friend and advisor. There were also six youth-league baseball players from the Washington area, guests of the president and seated in his box. Among other Washington dignitaries seated nearby were Chief Justice Earl Warren, FBI Director J. Edgar Hoover, Secretary of Defense Melvin Laird, and Secretary of Agriculture Clifford Hardin. Also at the game was former Green Bay Packers coach Vince Lombardi, recently hired to revive the fortunes of this city's other perennial loser, the Washington Redskins. When asked if he was nervous, Williams said: "All ballplayers get butterflies on Opening Day. You never lose it no matter how long you've been around—me, Joe DiMaggio, Stan Musial, Willie Mays—we all get it." Nevertheless, Williams seemed relaxed as he chided Nixon about the seal on the presidential box where the word "President" had been misspelled to read *Presidnt*.

When it came time to throw out the first ball, Nixon, a very knowledgeable fan, made three tosses, all of which were caught by Washington players. Both managers, Williams and the Yankees' Ralph Houk, were opening with their respective aces, Camilo Pascual and Mel Stottlemyre. Stottlemyre, 21–12 in 1968, was making his third consecutive opening-day start, the first Yankee to do so since Vic Raschi in 1951–1953. He had pitched shutouts in each of the previous two, including a two-hitter against the Senators here in 1967. Washington had given Stottlemyre trouble earlier in his career, but he had come back to win nine of his last ten against them and was 12–6, lifetime. Pascual, who broke in with the original Senators in 1954 and went with them to Minnesota in 1961, had led the team in wins in each of the two years since he returned to Washington. His 36 shutouts were more than any other active American League pitcher, and the only active pitchers in either league with more career strikeouts were Jim Bunning and Don Drysdale. Pascual, who had a 1–4 record in six starts on Opening Day, had pitched one opener against the Yankees, losing, 10–4, in 1956. His one win came in 1960 when he struck out 15 in defeating the Red Sox, 10–1. Boston's lone run that afternoon had come on a home run by Pascual's new manager, Ted Williams.

Five weeks earlier, Mickey Mantle had announced his retirement after 18 glorious seasons. His departure left a gaping hole in the heart, soul, and mystique of the Yankees. Mantle was the last link to New York's dynasty of the '50s and early '60s, and his loss would be felt throughout baseball. There was a poignant reminder of his absence this afternoon when a sign on the message board in right field greeted him with "Hello Mickey Mantle, wherever you are." But sentimentality does not win baseball games. Houk, ever the realist, looked at his roster and announced he would build this year's club around speed and defense. Speed would be a new weapon for the Yankees, a team that had personified power since the days of Babe Ruth. To Houk's delight, his club used both this afternoon—first speed and then power to subdue the Senators. They routed Pascual in the third inning and had eight runs before the Senators could score their first. Stottlemyre gave up 14 hits, but for the third straight opener he pitched a complete game.

The Yanks showed their speed early. Roy White, who last year became the team's regular left fielder, led off the second inning with a walk. White, whose 20 steals in 1968 tied Horace Clarke for the team lead, quickly stole second. After Joe Pepitone, back playing first base, flied to center fielder Del Unser, White stole third. He scored on shortstop Tom Tresh's single to right. Houk had moved Tresh back to short in 1968, but after 45 games this season, when he was batting just .182 (following a .195-season in 1968), the Yankees traded him to Detroit for outfielder Ron Woods. Tresh had never fulfilled the promise of his rookie year, and 1969 would be his last season. Bill Robinson forced Tresh, and then he too stole second. Pascual had a high leg kick and a slow delivery to the plate, and the Yankees runners were taking advantage of it. Catcher Jake Gibbs singled to left and Robinson scored the Yanks' second run.

In the third inning, youngsters Jerry Kenney and Bobby Murcer displayed the power component of the Yankees' attack when they slugged back-to-back home runs. Kenney hit a fast ball over the right-field wall, and Murcer blasted a change-up into the mezzanine in right. Kenney had played 18 games at shortstop for the Yanks in 1967 but missed 1968 because of military service. Now they were attempting to make him a center fielder. He hit only .234 in the Grapefruit League, yet it was good enough to earn him a share of the James P. Dawson Award, given to the best rookie in camp. Kenney's co-winner—this was the first time the voting had ended in a tie—was pitcher Bill Burbach. Today's Yankees' outfield was an indication of how much America, and baseball, had changed. With Kenney in center, White in left, and Robinson in right, the Yanks, one of the last major-league teams to use black players, were opening the season with an all–black outfield. The experiment with Kenney in center field would be short-lived, as he would spend most of the season—and his major-league career—as a third baseman.

Murcer, like Kenney, had spent some time with the Yankees previously—also as a shortstop—for 11 games in 1965 and 21 in 1966, 18 as a shortstop. He had spent the last two years in the army and also was attempting to learn a new position: third base. This experiment, too, was brief. Murcer had problems with ground balls, so little more than a month into the season he and Kenney switched positions. The Yanks expected that Murcer, who like Mantle came from Oklahoma and was signed by Tom Greenwade, would succeed Mickey as their next great player. They moved him to center field to encourage the process and even gave him Mantle's old locker.

After the two home runs and a ground out by White, Pepitone ripped a double to right center, prompting Williams, down 4–0, to make his first pitching change. He removed Pascual and brought in Bob Humphreys, a veteran right-hander. Humphreys got the third out, but ran into trouble in the fourth, an inning that featured Williams's first managerial argument with an umpire. Following a leadoff walk to Robinson, Gibbs hit a pop fly down the right-field line. After a long chase, second baseman Tim Cullen caught the ball, but then dropped it as he fell. First-base umpire Hank Soar ruled Cullen had not held the ball long enough, and therefore the runner was safe. As the fans booed and Cullen argued, Williams came out to talk to Soar, who had now been joined by plate umpire Jim Honochick. Williams, who as a player had a reputation for never arguing, claimed that Cullen had caught the ball, and then dropped it while trying to make the throw. The umpires disagreed, and the Yanks had runners at first and second. One out later, after Stottlemyre's bunt resulted in Robinson being forced at third, Clarke singled Gibbs home with the first of the league-leading 146 singles he would get this year. Kenney made the second out, but Murcer singled to right to score Stottlemyre, and when the ball got away from right fielder Ed Stroud, Clarke also scored and Murcer went to third. Dick Bosman replaced Humphreys and wild-pitched Murcer home for the Yankees' fourth run of the inning, all of which were unearned because of Cullen's error.

The Senators were promoting this season's team with a new slogan, "It's a whole new ballgame in 1969." There were signs proclaiming this hoped-for rebirth everywhere, even on lapel buttons that many people were wearing, including Justice Warren. However, when

Sherm Brody restated it over the public address system before the bottom of the third inning, with the Yankees leading, 4–0, those fans who did not greet the announcement with boos did so with sardonic laughter.

Washington pushed across a run in the fifth, ending Stottlemyre's string of opening-day scoreless innings at 22. With one out, Unser singled to left, his third consecutive hit, and moved to second on Stroud's single to center. Stottlemyre fanned Howard, the defending home-run champion, on three pitches, but first baseman Mike Epstein singled to left to score Unser. Ken McMullen hit into a force play, Gene Michael to Clarke, to end the threat. Michael had taken over at shortstop in the fifth inning, replacing Tresh who left with a sore throat. Washington added a run in the eighth on one of Cullen's three singles, a ground out by shortstop Eddie Brinkman, and a single to center by catcher Paul Casanova. Bernie Allen, batting for pitcher Casey Cox, also singled, but Unser stranded the two runners by grounding out to Clarke.

Monday, April 7, 1969

New York	ab	r	h	rbi		Washington	ab	r	h	rbi
Clarke 2b	5	1	1	1		Unser cf	5	1	3	0
Kenney cf	5	1	2	1		Stroud rf	5	1	2	0
Murcer 3b	5	2	2	3		Howard lf	5	1	1	2
White lf	4	1	0	0		Epstein 1b	4	0	1	1
Pepitone 1b	4	0	1	0		McMullen 3b	4	0	0	0
Tresh ss	3	0	1	1		Higgins p	0	0	0	0
Michael ss	1	0	0	0		cH. Allen	1	0	0	0
Robinson rf	3	1	0	0		Cullen 2b	4	1	3	0
Gibbs c	4	1	2	1		Brinkman ss	5	0	2	0
Stottlemyre p	3	1	0	0		Casanova	4	0	1	1
Total	37	8	9	7		Pascual p	0	0	0	0
						Humphreys p	1	0	0	0
						Bosman p	1	0	0	0
						aHolman	1	0	0	0
						Cox p	0	0	0	0
						bB. Allen	1	0	1	0
						Total	41	4	14	4

aFlied out for Bosman in sixth inning.
bSingled for Cox in eighth inning.
cGrounded out for Higgins in ninth inning.

New York   022 400 000–8
Washington   000 010 012–4

Errors—Cullen, Stroud. Left on bases—New York 5; Washington 12. Put outs—New York 27: Gibbs 5, Stottlemyre 1, Clarke 1, White 4, Kenney 1, Robinson 1, Michael 1, Pepitone 13. Washington 27: Unser 7, McMullen 3, Cullen 2, Howard 1, Epstein 7, Stroud 1, Casanova 6. Assists—New York 16: Murcer 4, Stottlemyre 3, Clarke 6, Michael 2, Pepitone 1. Washington 6: Brinkman 2, McMullen 1, Humphreys 1, Cullen 2. Two-base hits—Gibbs, Kenney, Pepitone, Unser, Brinkman. Home runs—Kenney, Murcer, Howard. Stolen bases—White 2, Robinson.

	IP	H	R	ER	BB	SO
NEW YORK						
Stottlemyre (W, 1–0)	9.0	14	4	4	2	4
WASHINGTON						
Pascual (L, 0–1)	2.2	5	4	4	1	0

	IP	H	R	ER	BB	SO
Humphreys	1.0	2	4	0	1	0
Bosman	2.1	0	0	0	0	2
Cox	2.0	2	0	0	1	3
Higgins	1.0	0	0	0	0	1

Wild pitch—Bosman. Umpires—Honochick, Soar, Umont, Haller, and Luciano (LF). Time of game—2 hrs. 47 min. Attendance—45,113.

About half the crowd had left when Washington batted in the ninth. However, President Nixon was still there telling those around him, as he had all afternoon, that Howard would hit a ninth-inning home run. He proved to be prophetic. Howard followed Stroud's leadoff single with a long drive into the Washington bullpen in left center field, making the score 8–4. Nixon, who had remained seated for the entire game—except for the seventh-inning stretch—jumped to his feet and stood applauding until Howard had made his way around the bases. The home run was the 14th hit of the game off Stottlemyre and it got the Yankees' bullpen, which had been active since the fifth, to throw a little harder. After retiring the next two batters, Stottlemyre walked Cullen, but he got Brinkman to fly to White for the final out. It was not a very artistic complete game—Washington stranded 12 runners—but it did help Stottlemyre to lead the league in 1969. His 24 complete games were one more than Detroit's Denny McLain.

Although Williams lost in his managerial debut, the seventh consecutive year that Washington had lost its opener, 1969 did turn out to be "a whole new ballgame" for the Senators. They had their first-ever winning season, with 86 victories (86–76).

> *In response to 1968's lack of offense, the rules committee lowered the mound from 15 inches to ten for 1969, and also reduced the strike zone. The American League's batting average increased by 16 points, with the Yankees going from .214 to .235. However, with only 94 home runs, the Yanks fell below 100 for the first time since 1945. In this first year of division play, New York (80–81) finished fifth in the six-team Eastern Division, 28½ games behind the Baltimore Orioles. Attendance at Yankee Stadium continued to decline, falling to 1,067,996.*

VIII

1970–1979

In January 1973 the Columbia Broadcasting System sold the Yankees to a group headed by Cleveland shipbuilder George Steinbrenner. Under CBS's ownership, the value and prestige of the Yanks had declined so much that they sold the club for less money than they paid for it. Steinbrenner vowed to return championship baseball to New York, and he did. He also brought chaos. Manager Ralph Houk lasted one season under Steinbrenner and Bill Virdon a season and a half before Billy Martin took over in early August 1975. The Yanks won three consecutive pennants (1976–1978) and two world championships (1977–1978) under Martin and Bob Lemon, who replaced Martin in July 1978. Then Martin replaced Lemon during the 1979 season, setting off Steinbrenner's ridicule-inspiring managerial changes of the 1980s.

Leading the Yankees' resurgence was a solid group of players obtained in trades: Graig Nettles, Lou Piniella, Willie Randolph, Sparky Lyle, Bucky Dent, and Chris Chambliss. The farm system produced catcher Thurman Munson and pitcher Ron Guidry, and the new free-agency rules allowed Steinbrenner to bring Reggie Jackson, Goose Gossage, and Catfish Hunter to New York.

The Yanks moved in as tenants of the Mets in Shea Stadium for the 1974–1975 seasons as Yankee Stadium underwent renovations. They returned in 1976 to a Stadium with a reduced seating capacity. Nevertheless, the Yanks went over the 2 million mark for the first time since 1950 and in 1979 broke their one-season attendance record.

Tuesday, April 7, 1970
Yankee Stadium, New York
Boston 4 New York 3

Perhaps my name too will be linked with theirs.—Ovid

After a turbulent decade, one that began with five straight pennants but included a last-place finish just two years later, the Yankees entered the 1970s with hopes for a return to glory. The 1969 season had ended on a high note, with five consecutive victories, but 1970 began all too familiarly, with a one-run loss. Unable to overcome Boston's early four-run lead, the Yanks fell to the Red Sox, 4–3. It was a discouraging outcome for the 21,727 at Yankee Stadium, many of whom recalled that 29 of the team's 81 losses in 1969 had also been by a single run. New York's run production was the second lowest in the league in 1969, a weakness that inspired general manager Lee MacPhail to engineer three trades at

264

the winter meetings. In each he secured a veteran hitter: outfielder/first baseman Curt Blefary from the Houston Astros, for Joe Pepitone; first baseman Danny Cater from the Oakland Athletics, for pitcher Al Downing and catcher Frank Fernandez; and utility player Pete Ward from the Chicago White Sox, for minor-league pitcher Mickey Scott. They added one more veteran just before the start of spring training, purchasing infielder Ron Hansen from the White Sox. Hansen and Blefary (1965) had reached the major leagues with the Baltimore Orioles, and each had won the Rookie of the Year Award (1960 and 1965 respectively). Overall there were only 14 holdovers on the Yankees' roster, with Bill Robinson, the opening-day right fielder for the past three seasons, not among them. Robinson had failed to live up to the club's expectations, and shortly before the season began they sent him to the Syracuse Chiefs of the International League. He would not play in the major leagues again until 1972, with the Philadelphia Phillies.

Two of the Yankees' new acquisitions, Blefary in right field and Cater at third base, were in their revamped opening-day lineup. So too were a pair of rookies—John Ellis at first base and Thurman Munson behind the plate. Ellis, 21, and Munson, 22, had come up through the Yankees' organization as catchers, each reaching the big leagues for a brief period in 1969. Ellis had shown the most promise of all the rookies in camp this spring. He batted .368 with 18 runs batted in, and won the James P. Dawson Award, beating Munson and pitcher Ron Klimkowski. However, because Munson was much the superior receiver, the Yanks were trying Ellis at first base, even though he had never played the position in his professional career. Before the game, Ellis received a telegram of encouragement from Eleanor Gehrig, sent through former Yankees president Larry MacPhail. "For thirty years I've been looking for Lou's successor (if not better), and I'm rooting for you," she wrote. If that message from Mrs. Gehrig did not put enough pressure on Ellis, manager Ralph Houk had him batting in the clean-up position. Houk did not believe that he had another Lou Gehrig in Ellis, but he did hope the rookie would at least play well enough to be his everyday first baseman. However, as with many preseason designs, it did not work out as planned. When Ellis struggled, Houk replaced him with Cater, who had been platooning with Jerry Kenney at third base.

To make today's opener more accessible to school-age youngsters, the Yankees pushed the starting time back to three o'clock. Attending baseball games was still affordable for young people, and even for entire families when compared to other forms of entertainment. While prices of tickets had risen in recent years, they remained reasonable. Box seats at Yankee Stadium were only four dollars, and you could still sit in the bleachers for 75 cents. (Bleacher seats would rise to a dollar next season.) Club officials were offering several new foods at the concession stands this season, including pizza rolls, knishes, and Chinese egg rolls. Team president Mike Burke was clearly trying everything possible to change the aristocratic image of his team. In an age of encroaching egalitarianism, the Yanks were no longer the "top banana" in New York. The Mets had not only drawn twice as many fans as the Yankees in 1969, their World Series upset victory over Baltimore had raised the spirits of the entire city. New Yorkers no longer thought of the Mets as buffoons, and now that they had the city's better team, their share of younger fans was sure to increase.

With Ellis leading their reconstituted lineup, the Yanks had enjoyed one of their best springs ever, winning 18 of 27 Grapefruit League games. The strong showing excited the fans, sophisticated enough to be suspicious of Grapefruit League results, but nonetheless anxious to get a look at all the recent additions. The new season got underway following a rousing rendition of the national anthem, sung by Metropolitan Opera baritone Robert

Merrill and accompanied by the Flushing High School Band. Whitney Young, president of the National Urban League, made it "official" by throwing out the first ball.

Despite their lack of success in recent seasons, the Yankees had made Houk baseball's highest-paid manager, signing him to a three-year contract at $65,000 per year. In contrast to Houk, who was in his second tour as Yankees' manager, Eddie Kasko of the Red Sox was making his major-league managerial debut. Kasko was replacing Dick Williams, fired late in 1969 less than two years after he won a pennant and took his team to the seventh game of the World Series. Weak pitching had hurt Boston last year, so in their only significant off-season deal they sent two minor-leaguers to the White Sox for veteran left-hander Gary Peters. Peters, the American League's Rookie of the Year in 1963, had twice led the league in earned run average, in 1963 and 1966. But a sore arm had limited him to a combined total of 14 wins over the past two seasons and Chicago made him available. Peters had been by far Boston's best pitcher this spring. In 32 exhibition-game innings he allowed no earned runs and held the opposition scoreless in 31 of those innings. Therefore, although Peters had lost his last six decisions to the Yankees and had not beaten them since May 5, 1968, Kasko named him to start the opener.

Houk, as he had done in each of the three previous seasons, gave the ball to Mel Stottlemyre. Only two other Yankee pitchers had started four consecutive openers: Jack Chesbro, in 1903–1906, and Lefty Gomez, who started six straight from 1932 through 1937. Stottlemyre had a string of three consecutive complete-game, opening-day victories; the first two had been shutouts, and in none of the three had the Yankees ever been behind. That latter distinction ended quickly. Boston broke on top with a run in the second inning and never relinquished the lead. Tony Conigliaro led off the inning with a single to right, but not before the fans greeted him with a warm ovation. In August 1967, a fastball from the California Angels' Jack Hamilton had severely damaged Conigliaro's left eye, causing him to miss the rest of that season and the entire 1968 season. He returned in 1969 to hit 20 home runs, with 82 runs driven in, an achievement that earned him the Comeback Player of the Year Award.

After rookie third baseman Luis Alvarado forced Conigliaro at second, catcher Jerry Moses singled to left. Alvarado went around to third, but Moses, trying to reach second, was out on a relay from left fielder Roy White to shortstop Gene Michael to second baseman Horace Clarke. Peters, among baseball's best hitting pitchers, followed with a liner to deep right field that Blefary started back on, but he staggered and fell on the recently resodded turf. The ball sailed over his head and landed on the yellowish-looking grass before bouncing into the Yankees bullpen. It was a grounds-rule double and it scored Alvarado. Blefary, who was a defensive liability at whatever position he played, blamed the field conditions for his failure to catch the ball. "The ground was soft out there," he reminded everyone. "Otherwise, I catch that ball."

Boston made it 2–0 in the third on Carl Yastrzemski's infield hit, George Scott's single to left, and Rico Petrocelli's double, lined to Cater's right just inside the foul line. They added two more in the fifth, assisted by Blefary's continuing problems in right field. Blefary lost Scott's leadoff liner in the sun, allowing the ball to bounce by him for a triple. Petrocelli scored Scott with his second double of the game, which again went between Cater and the foul line. Moses singled Petrocelli home, but evidently not content to hit singles, he again tried for second and again White's throw cut him down.

The Yankees kept pecking away at Peters, but through five innings he had kept them scoreless. Clarke had a single in the first and Bobby Murcer and Michael had singles in the second, but their best opportunity to score came in the third. After Clarke's single and Munson's walk put two runners on with nobody out, Peters escaped by fanning White, getting Ellis on a force out, and Cater on a fly to Yastrzemski. White's out started a string of ten consecutive batters that Peters retired, ending when he got White leading off the sixth. It was the last out he would get. Ellis got aboard when one of Peters's pitches grazed his uniform, and after Cater walked, Murcer dropped a single into short left. Yastrzemski tried to get Ellis at the plate, but his throw went astray; Ellis scored, and Cater and Murcer each moved up a base. The official scorer (making $35 per game this year, a raise of five dollars) charged Yastrzemski with an error. Blefary's grounds-rule double to left, which scored Cater and Murcer, cut Boston's lead to 4–3 and drove Peters from the game.

Kasko called in Bill Lee, a 23-year-old left-hander from the University of Southern California who pitched in 20 games for Boston in 1969. Lee seemed nervous and agitated on the mound; however, it did not affect his performance. Following a walk to Michael, he retired pinch-hitter Hansen on a liner to center fielder Reggie Smith, and got Clarke, who already had two singles, on a come-backer. Hansen was batting for Klimkowski, who had replaced Stottlemyre at the start of the sixth and pitched a one-two-three inning. Joe Verbanic came on to pitch a scoreless seventh and eighth, and Jack Aker followed with a scoreless ninth, keeping Boston's lead at one run. However, the Yankees could not mount a serious challenge against Lee, who fiercely protected his one-run advantage over the next three innings. He allowed only two runners in that span: Ellis, who singled with two out in the seventh, and Michael, who drew a two-out walk in the eighth. Facing the top of the order in the ninth, Lee got Clarke, Munson, and White on ground balls to end the game and save the victory for Peters. The save was now part of baseball's official statistics, having become so in 1969. It was the first save of Lee's career and his only one of the year. After appearing in 11 games, he entered the Army on June 5 and missed the remainder of the season.

Tuesday, April 7, 1970

Boston	ab	r	h	rbi	New York	ab	r	h	rbi
Andrews 2b	4	0	0	0	Clarke 2b	5	0	2	0
Smith cf	5	0	1	0	Munson c	3	0	0	0
Yastrzemski lf	5	1	2	0	White lf	5	0	0	0
Scott 1b	4	1	2	0	Ellis 1b	3	1	1	0
Petrocelli ss	5	1	2	2	Cater 3b	3	1	0	0
T. Conigliaro rf	2	0	1	0	Murcer cf	4	1	2	1
Alvarado 3b	3	1	0	0	Blefary rf	4	0	1	2
Moses c	3	0	2	1	Michael ss	2	0	1	0
Peters p	3	0	1	1	Stottlemyre p	1	0	0	0
Lee p	1	0	0	0	[a]Woods	1	0	0	0
Total	35	4	11	4	Klimkowski p	0	0	0	0
					[b]Hansen	1	0	0	0
					Verbanic p	0	0	0	0
					[c]Ward	1	0	0	0
					Aker p	0	0	0	0
					Total	33	3	7	3

[a]Fouled out for Stottlemyre in fifth inning.
[b]Flied out for Klimkowski in sixth inning.
[c]Struck out for Verbanic in eighth inning.

```
Boston       011    020    000—4
New York     000    003    000—3
```

Errors—Munson, Yastrzemski. Left on bases—Boston 10; New York 9. Put outs—New York 27: Clarke 4, Michael 2, Cater 4, Munson 4, Ellis 7, Murcer 6. Boston 27: Andrews 3, Petrocelli 2, Scott 10, Smith 2, Alvarado 1, Moses 6, Yastrzemski 3. Assists—New York 12: Clarke 1, Munson 1, Michael 4, Ellis 1, White 2, Cater 3. Boston 11: Andrews 2, Petrocelli 2, Alvarado 4, Peters 1, Lee 2. Two-base hits—Peters, Petrocelli 2, Blefary. Three-base hit—Scott. Stolen base—Yastrzemski. Sacrifices—Munson, Alvarado.

	IP	H	R	ER	BB	SO
BOSTON						
Peters (W, 1–0)	5.1	6	3	3	2	4
Lee S.1	3.2	1	0	0	2	1
NEW YORK						
Stottlemyre (L, 0–1)	5.0	10	4	4	3	1
Klimkowski	1.0	0	0	0	0	0
Verbanic	2.0	0	0	0	2	2
Aker	1.0	1	0	0	0	0

Hit by pitch—By Peters (Ellis). Umpires—Honochick, Umont, O'Donnell, and Maloney. Time of game—2 hrs. 19 min. Attendance—21,727.

By winning 93 games, the Yankees (93–69) had their best season since 1964, when they won the pennant. Nevertheless, their 93 wins were good for only second place, 15 games behind the Baltimore Orioles in the American League East. The Yanks also finished a distant second in the New York attendance race. Although they were up slightly at 1,136,879, the Mets drew a record-setting 2,697,479 to Shea Stadium. No New York team had ever had a higher one-season attendance. Thurman Munson won the Rookie of the Year Award with 23 of the 24 votes; Roy Foster of the Cleveland Indians got the other one.

Tuesday, April 6, 1971
Fenway Park, Boston
Boston 3 New York 1

I gave my life for freedom—This I know:
For those who bade me fight had told me so.—William Norman Ewer

Bostonians say the bitter feelings started in 1920, when the Red Sox sold Babe Ruth to the Yankees. New Yorkers trace it all the way back to the last day of the 1904 season, when Jack Chesbro's ninth-inning wild pitch allowed the Americans to edge the Highlanders (as the teams were then called) for the pennant. But whatever its origin, the rivalry between the Yankees and the Red Sox grew into the fiercest in the American League, with the enduring hostility between them among the most vehement in all of sports. Even the cultures of these two great cities (America's Sparta and Athens) had become an integral part of the antagonism between New York and Boston. There was a mutual dislike of each other's team, each other's fans, and each other's style that gave a special significance to every Yankees-Red Sox confrontation. Therefore, when Boston's Ray Culp opened the 1971 season with a 3–1 triumph over the New Yorkers, it brought joy not only to the 34,517 who braved the cold at Fenway Park, but to Red Sox lovers everywhere. They were especially pleased with the pugnacious manner in which their heroes earned the victory. Red Sox players revealed a newfound assertiveness on the base paths that contributed as much to their success as their batting and pitching skills. Pinch-runner John Kennedy and catcher Duane Josephson each made a hard, aggressive slide that prevented the Yankees from completing a double play; and Josephson showed fortitude and tenacity in the way he blocked the plate to keep the Yanks' Jim Lyttle from scoring the tying run. Boston's hard-nosed truculence was a welcome change for Red Sox fans whose team had a long history of playing a more easygoing, laid-back brand of baseball. As expected, Yankees manager Ralph Houk and his players were upset at Boston's physical style of play. It so disturbed them that late in the game, during between-innings warmups, first baseman Danny Cater allowed several hard throws to go unimpeded into the Boston dugout.

Houk had been anxious for a good start. His club had won only eight of their 31 exhibition games and endured losing streaks of seven and 12 games, the seven-game streak coming in their final seven preseason games. None of the regulars had hit well except Bobby Murcer, who at .310 was the only Yankee to hit above .300. Meanwhile, Culp was coming off an outstanding spring, one in which he compiled a 1.33 earned run average and allowed only 12 hits in 27 innings. Culp was Boston's best pitcher and had been since coming over from the National League in 1968. He was 5–5 against the Yankees: 3–2 at Fenway and 2–3 at Yankee Stadium. This afternoon, Culp made it four-out-of-six at Fenway with a complete-game five-hitter. Yankees starter Stan Bahnsen was not as effective as Culp; still, he turned in a creditable performance. In his first opening-day appearance, he held the hard-hitting Red Sox to just two runs in seven innings. Bahnsen was New York's number-three starter, but Houk used him because this was a one-game series and he preferred to use a right-hander at Fenway Park. Mel Stottlemyre was right-handed, but a stiff shoulder had adversely affected his preparation this spring; and Fritz Peterson, the Yanks' leading winner (20–11) a year ago, was a left-hander. Bahnsen had pitched 30 innings in the Grapefruit League, with a 3.60 earned run average. The onetime Rookie of the Year was 8–4 against Boston in his career, 3–3 at Fenway.

Rene Rancourt, singing the national anthem, and Bruce Bakaian, a marine wounded in Viet Nam who threw out the first ball, highlighted the subdued pregame activities on this 40-degree day. The spring of 1971 was not a very happy or convivial time in America—at least anywhere those emotions were not drug-induced. Most of the discontent centered on the growing bitterness and divisiveness over the war in Viet Nam; divisiveness exacerbated by the mixed messages Americans continued to get from their leaders, like those coming out of Washington today. In the Senate, Vermont's George Aiken predicted President Nixon would announce in tomorrow's TV speech a schedule that would lead to the removal of all U.S. forces from Vietnam next year. Meanwhile, in the House, four Democratic Party "doves" (Bella Abzug of New York, Parren Mitchell of Maryland, John Conyers Jr. of Michigan, and Ron Dellums of California) announced plans to conduct informal hearings into "command responsibility for U.S. atrocities in Vietnam" following the conviction of Lieutenant William Calley for the My Lai massacre.

The Red Sox wasted no time in showing their new aggressiveness. Luis Aparicio and Reggie Smith led off the first inning with singles, but Aparicio was thrown out trying for second and Smith was out on an attempted steal. Aparicio was making his Red Sox debut this afternoon, as were Josephson and second baseman Doug Griffin. The Sox had traded infielders Mike Andrews and Luis Alvarado to the Chicago White Sox to get Aparicio, a future Hall-of-Famer who was beginning his 16th major-league season. Josephson had also come from the White Sox, but Boston's biggest off-season deal was with the California Angels. The

Sox traded the immensely popular Tony Conigliaro, along with catcher Jerry Moses and pitcher Ray Jarvis, to the Angels for pitcher Ken Tatum, outfielder Jarvis Tatum, and Griffin.

After the singles by Aparicio and Smith, Bahnsen retired the next eight men. Four were on strikeouts, including three in the second inning. But after getting Aparicio leading off the fourth, back-to-back doubles by Smith to right and Carl Yastrzemski to left produced Boston's first run. Smith, who had three hits this afternoon, would lead the American League in both doubles (33) and total bases (302) this season. Yastrzemski had narrowly missed winning his fourth batting championship in 1970, losing by .0004 to the Angels' Alex Johnson. The Red Sox rewarded him with a three-year deal that would pay him a total of $500,000. Before long, utility infielders would be making half a million dollars *per year*, but in 1971 Yastrzemski's contract was the most lucrative ever for a player. Again, putting this in perspective, back in New York today the Uniformed Firefighters Association reached a tentative contract agreement with the city that would raise firemen's salary—including fringe benefits—to between $15,000 and $16,000 per year. Yastrzemski had begun earning his salary immediately, making a spectacular catch on the first play of the game. Horace Clarke hit a looping fly ball to left that Yastrzemski, angling to his right, slid and caught before skidding across the foul line. Despite his status as the game's highest-paid player, Yastrzemski would have his worst season to date in 1971, batting just .254.

Boston had shown their aggressiveness on the bases from the beginning, but the first instance of their belligerence on the base paths came in the fifth inning. Josephson, a former quarterback at University of Northern Iowa, slid hard into third, causing third baseman Jerry Kenney to do a complete flip before landing on his back. That play did not lead to a Boston run, but a similar play in the seventh inning did. Singles by George Scott and Josephson put runners at first and second with nobody out. Billy Conigliaro—Tony's younger brother—laid down an excellent sacrifice bunt to move them along. Griffin was the next batter, but manager Eddie Kasko sent in left-handed hitter Joe Lahoud to pinch-hit. With the pitcher due up next, Houk ordered Bahnsen to intentionally walk Lahoud to load the bases and set up the potential inning-ending double play. When Culp followed with a ground ball to shortstop Gene Michael, it appeared the Yankees' strategy had worked. Michael fielded the ball cleanly and tossed it to Clarke for the force on Kennedy, running for Lahoud. However, Clarke hesitated for a split second on the relay, just long enough for Kennedy to come smashing into him and prevent him from throwing to first. Kennedy's "takeout" of Clarke negated the double play and allowed Scott to score with Boston's second run. "I wasn't trying to hurt him but I had to break up the double play," Kennedy said after the game. "If I had slid, I couldn't have done it."

Culp now had a two-run lead to work with, which in the late innings is significantly greater than a one-run lead because of the strategic limitations it puts on the opposing manager. As the Yankees came to bat in the eighth, they still had just one hit—Thurman Munson's little tapper in the fourth that died on the grass between Culp and third baseman Rico Petrocelli. The Red Sox had moved Petrocelli to third base after getting Aparicio, who had won nine Gold Gloves at shortstop. Culp had retired all 11 batters since Munson's hit when Cater led off the eighth with a single to center. Lyttle also singled to center, and for the first time in the game the Yanks had two runners on base. When Kennedy, who replaced Griffin at second base, booted Kenney's ground ball, the bases were loaded. The Yankees' next two scheduled hitters were Michael and Bahnsen, so Houk went to his bench for two left-handed pinch hitters. The first was Frank Tepedino, a youngster whom the Yankees thought a lot of, but one whom they nonetheless kept returning to their Triple A team at

Syracuse. Culp got Tepedino on a pop to Aparicio and then struck out the second pinch hitter, Jake Gibbs. That brought up Clarke and led to the key play of the game. Clarke came through with a sharply hit single to right, easily scoring Cater. Lyttle, carrying the tying run, tried to score from second and seemed to have the throw from right fielder Smith beaten. However, Josephson had the plate blocked, and although Lyttle slid into him before he caught the ball, when Josephson applied the tag home plate umpire John Flaherty called Lyttle out. Lyttle and Houk argued that Josephson had blocked the plate without the ball, and furthermore that Lyttle had touched the plate. Flaherty answered that the rules permitted Josephson to block the plate when he was in the act of receiving the throw, and that he had brushed Lyttle aside and never let him reach the plate. Instead of a tied game and two runners still on base, Josephson's play ended the inning with the Yankees still trailing by a run. The crowd cheered their new catcher, who earlier had endeared himself with two singles—and would later add a third.

Afterwards, Lyttle said: "I slid against the edge of the plate, but didn't go across it, and that's why the umpire called me out. On top of that he was blocking the plate without the ball, which he isn't allowed to do." But Houk, a former catcher, disagreed. "He's got to knock the catcher out on a close play like that," the manager said. "Very seldom can a catcher keep you off the plate if you beat the play." Houk and coach Elston Howard, another former catcher, acknowledged that Josephson did have the right to block the plate, and that if there was anyone to blame it was Lyttle. When the catcher was blocking the plate without the ball, they claimed, it was the runner's job to bowl him over. Both cited the Pete Rose–Ray Fosse incident in last year's All-Star game.

Tuesday, April 6, 1971

New York	ab	r	h	rbi	Boston	ab	r	h	rbi
Clarke 2b	4	0	1	1	Aparicio ss	4	0	1	0
Munson c	4	0	2	0	R. Smith rf	4	1	3	0
White lf	4	0	0	0	Yastrzemski lf	4	1	2	1
Murcer cf	4	0	0	0	Petrocelli 3b	4	0	1	0
Cater 1b	4	1	1	0	Scott 1b	3	1	1	1
Lyttle rf	3	0	1	0	Josephson c	4	0	3	0
Kenney 3b	3	0	0	0	B. Conigliaro cf	3	0	0	0
Michael ss	2	0	0	0	Griffin 2b	1	0	0	0
[b]Tepedino	1	0	0	0	[a]Lahoud	0	0	0	0
Baker ss	0	0	0	0	J. Kennedy 2b	0	0	0	0
Bahnsen p	2	0	0	0	Culp p	3	0	0	1
[c]Gibbs	1	0	0	0	Total	30	3	11	3
Aker p	0	0	0	0					
Total	32	1	5	1					

[a]Intentionally walked for Griffin in seventh inning.
[b]Popped out for Michael in eighth inning.
[c]Struck out for Bahnsen in eighth inning.

New York	000	000	010–1
Boston	000	100	11X–3

Error—J. Kennedy. Double play—Clarke, Michael and Cater. Caught stealing—by Munson (R.Smith). Left on bases—New York 4; Boston 7. Put outs—New York 24: Cater 6, Munson 5, Clarke 5, White 2, Kenney 1, Murcer 1, Michael 4. Boston 27: Yastrzemski 2, Josephson 7, Scott 9, Culp 1, Aparicio 2, R. Smith 3, Griffin 1, B. Conigliaro 2. Assists—New York 15: Clarke 2, Michael 5, Kenney 2, Cater 2, Munson

1, Baker 1, Bahnsen 2. Boston 9: Culp 1, Aparicio 2, Griffin 3, Petrocelli 1, J. Kennedy 1, R. Smith 1. Two-base hits—R. Smith, Yastrzemski. Stolen base—Munson. Sacrifice—B. Conigliaro. Sacrifice fly—Scott.

	IP	H	R	ER	BB	SO
NEW YORK						
Bahnsen (L, 0–1)	7.0	8	2	2	2	5
Aker	1.0	3	1	1	0	0
BOSTON						
Culp (W, 1–0)	9.0	5	1	0	0	5

Umpires—Flaherty, DiMuro, Kunkel, and Luciano. Time of game—2 hrs. 19 min. Attendance—34,517.

The Red Sox added an insurance run against Jack Aker in the bottom of the eighth on a sacrifice fly by Scott. It scored Yastrzemski, who had singled and gone to third on Petrocelli's single. Still, when Munson singled to lead off the ninth, the Yanks—with the heart of the order coming up—needed just a home run to tie. But Culp retired Roy White, Murcer, and Cater to send the Boston fans home chilled but happy. Yet it was not to be a happy season for the dissension-ridden Red Sox. After the season ended, they traded, among others, Billy Conigliaro, Scott, Lahoud, and pitchers Sparky Lyle and Jim Lonborg. Nor would either of today's Yankees' pitchers have a future in New York. In December 1971, the Yanks traded Bahnsen to the White Sox for infielder Rich McKinney, and in May 1972 they sent Aker to the Chicago Cubs as the player-to-be-named in the January trade for outfielder Johnny Callison.

After winning 93 games and finishing second in 1970, the Yankees (82–80) retrogressed, finishing fourth, 21 games behind the Eastern Division champion Baltimore Orioles. Bobby Murcer had a superb year, batting .331 to finish second in the batting race to the Minnesota Twins' Tony Oliva (.337). Murcer hit 25 home runs, batted in and scored 94 runs, and finished seventh in the Most Valuable Player voting. Roy White set an American League record with 17 sacrifice flies, a statistic that had been in place since 1954. Bobby Bonilla of the Orioles tied White's record in 1996.

Sunday, April 16, 1972
Memorial Stadium, Baltimore
Baltimore 3 New York 1 (7 Innings)

And one man in his time plays many parts.—William Shakespeare

There has never been a player more popular and beloved in the city in which he played than Brooks Robinson was in Baltimore. In 1972, Robinson was beginning his 18th season as an Oriole, and in all those years—even during his worst slumps—he had never heard anything but cheers at Memorial Stadium. But after a 13-day player strike, which for the first time ever had shut baseball down, no one directly involved in the dispute was immune from the fans' wrath; and in Baltimore, the booing by disgruntled hometown fans included even Robinson. Opening-Day crowds in all the major-league parks were letting both the players and the owners know how they felt about the strike. Robinson was the Orioles' player representative and therefore an easily identifiable target for the fans' frustration. Nonetheless, fans are fans. Once the game began they forgot their animosities concerning monetary and labor negotiations and concentrated on baseball. Before the day was over, they would be cheering their great third baseman as he knocked in two runs to lead the

Orioles to a rain-shortened, 3–1, victory over New York. Robinson said afterwards, "I thought the fans overall were just great. The reaction they gave us all was very good."

The strike, which delayed the start of the season for nine days, had wiped out 86 major-league games, including six for the Yankees. They were to have opened with four games at home against the Orioles before traveling to Detroit for two against the Tigers and then here to Baltimore. When rain wiped out the rescheduled opener yesterday, the Yanks and Orioles elected to play a doubleheader today so as not to lose any more games. However, the rain continued today, twice causing delays and finally leading the umpires to end the game in the seventh inning. Game two was postponed to the following evening. The rain and lingering resentment about the strike cast a gloomy pall over the normally festive atmosphere of Opening Day. Baltimoreans even booed their popular mayor, William Donald Schaefer, when he was introduced before throwing out the first ball. However, that expression of opinion more than likely had to do with local politics and not with baseball. After Schaefer made the ritual toss to catcher Elrod Hendricks, the crowd of 11,995, including Orioles' owner Jerold C. Hoffberger, cheered the mayor's effort. Club president Mike Burke and general manager Lee MacPhail were here representing the Yankees and were equally pleased to see the long-awaited season finally get underway.

Over the past few years, the Orioles had been far-and-away the best team in the American League, and probably the best in both leagues. The 1969–1971 Orioles were only the third team in major-league history to win 100 games or more for three straight seasons, joining Connie Mack's 1929–1931 Philadelphia Athletics and Billy Southworth's 1942–1944 St. Louis Cardinals. Yet despite the Orioles' accomplishments, *The Sporting News* continued to overlook their manager, Earl Weaver, when voting for the Manager of the Year. Baltimore had won three pennants in the last three years, but TSN had given the award to Gil Hodges of the New York Mets, Danny Murtaugh of the Pittsburgh Pirates, and Charlie Fox of the San Francisco Giants. (It would not be until 1983 that each league would have its own Manager of the Year Award voted by the Baseball Writers Association of America.) Perhaps they continued to bypass Weaver because they appreciated what an excellent team he had to work with. Unfortunately, that appreciation seemed not to extend to the Baltimore fans as the Orioles continued to struggle at the gate. In each of their three pennant-winning seasons, they had drawn barely more than a million people to Memorial Stadium.

Baltimore's on-field success looked likely to continue in 1972. They were the choice of most forecasters to win a fourth straight pennant, even without slugging outfielder Frank Robinson, their team leader whom they had traded to the Los Angeles Dodgers. Chief among the Orioles' many strengths was a pitching staff that a year ago had produced four 20-game winners, something that only the 1920 Chicago White Sox had ever done before and no team has done since. Weaver had intended to use the youngest of those 20-game winners—26-year-old Jim Palmer—to pitch the opener, but the rainout caused him to reshuffle the rotation. He switched from Palmer to Pat Dobson, another member of that distinguished quartet. Dobson, a 30-year-old right-hander with an excellent curve ball, had broken in with Detroit in 1967. The Tigers traded him to the San Diego Padres in December 1969; but the next season the Padres dealt him to Baltimore, where he joined Palmer and left-handers Dave McNally and Mike Cuellar. Those three had all won 20 games in 1970 and repeated in 1971, joined by Dobson who went 20–8. Four of Dobson's wins and two of his losses in '71 came against New York.

The one-day postponement did not change Yankees manager Ralph Houk's pitching plans. Whenever that first game was played, he would start Mel Stottlemyre. After leading or tying for the team lead in wins from 1965 to 1969, Stottlemyre had finished second to Fritz Peterson in 1970. He came back to lead again in 1971 with 16 wins (16–12)—the sixth time that he had led the Yankees in wins. That tied him with Lefty Gomez for second place in team history, behind only Red Ruffing, who led seven times. Stottlemyre, with two victories and one defeat, was the only Yankees' pitcher who had a winning record against Baltimore in 1971.

Third baseman Rich McKinney, acquired from the White Sox in an off-season trade for Stan Bahnsen, got the first hit of the game, a one-out single in the top of the first. Dobson got the next two batters, Bobby Murcer and Roy White, but by then the rain that had been falling intermittently was now hard enough for home plate umpire John Flaherty to stop play and order the infield covered. The delay lasted 24 minutes, after which the Orioles scored their first run. With one out, Merv Rettenmund hit a little tap in front of the plate that went for a hit when Stottlemyre and catcher Thurman Munson collided as they went to field it. Boog Powell followed with a similar tap, but this time Stottlemyre did field it and threw Powell out as Rettenmund moved to second. The next batter was Robinson, and as public address announcer Rex Barney introduced him, there was a small smattering of jeers. Robinson's involvement in the negotiations between the owners and the union had kept him idle for 16 days. That combined with an exhibition season in which he batted a lowly .196 had made it an extremely difficult spring for him. Nevertheless, Weaver had him in the clean-up spot, and Robinson, with his penchant for rising to the occasion, quickly silenced his few critics by hitting Stottlemyre's first pitch for a run-scoring single.

Baltimore scored an unearned run in the second, but a double play prevented the inning from being even more damaging for New York. After Paul Blair and Davey Johnson opened the inning with singles, Mark Belanger's assignment was to move them up a base. Belanger took a strike and then bunted to the left side. It was extremely well placed, and Munson did a good job even getting to the ball. But he had to hurry his throw, and the ball sailed over first baseman Ron Blomberg's head and into right field. Munson's error allowed Blair to score, Johnson to go to third, and Belanger to reach second. Belanger got credit for a single, the first of his three hits. With Dobson up, runners at second and third, and no one out, Houk ordered the Yankee infield to play in. Dobson grounded to Blomberg for the first out, with the runners forced to hold. Houk ordered Don Buford walked intentionally to load the bases—a move that worked to perfection as Rettenmund bounced into an inning-ending double play, Stottlemyre to Munson to Blomberg.

Blomberg, 23, had been the first pick in the June 1967 Free Agent Amateur Draft, a pick the Yankees had "earned" after their last-place finish in 1966. Although he had played some games at first base with the Johnson City (Tennessee) Yankees of the Appalachian League in 1967, Blomberg had been primarily an outfielder as he made his way through the Yankees' system. He made a positive impression on Houk when he came up from the International League's Syracuse Chiefs in the second half of 1971 and batted .322 in 64 games. And now that the trade of Danny Cater to Boston had opened a spot at first base, Houk intended to platoon the left-hand hitting Blomberg there with the right-handed-hitting veteran, Felipe Alou.

Murcer's fourth-inning bloop double to left and Blomberg's single to center cut Baltimore's lead to 2–1, but second baseman Bernie Allen's error in the fifth led to another unearned run for the Orioles. Allen, who played last year with the Washington Senators (now playing their first season as the Texas Rangers), bobbled Powell's ground ball as he tried to flip it to shortstop Jerry Kenney. Allen's misplay allowed Rettenmund, who had walked with one out, to reach second. Rettenmund scored when Robinson came through with his second run-producing single, a grounder between third baseman McKinney and shortstop Kenney. Kenney, who started the 1969 opener in center field and the 1971 opener at third base, was playing his third different opening-day position in four years. He joined among others Roy Hartzell, Babe Ruth, Ben Chapman, Gil McDougald, Mickey Mantle, and Tom Tresh as Yankees who started openers at three or more different positions.

Blomberg, working on a perfect afternoon (Dobson hit him with a pitch in the second), walked to lead off the seventh. Johnny Callison followed with a pop-fly to short left that Belanger, the league's best defensive shortstop, raced after and caught. Callison was also making his Yankees' debut, after coming from the Chicago Cubs in a trade for pitcher Jack Aker. Munson was at the plate with a count of one strike when Flaherty again ordered the ground crew to cover the infield. Pat Santarone's crew did an outstanding job, taking only three minutes to get the rain-soaked tarpaulin in place. This delay lasted an hour and 17 minutes, and when play resumed the Orioles sent a new pitcher to the mound. Dobson had thrown just 71 pitches, but after cooling off for such an extended period, pitchers sometimes lose their stuff, or even worse: they hurt their arms. Weaver, unwilling to risk either possibility, replaced Dobson with 21-year-old Doyle Alexander. As a Dodgers' rookie in 1971, Alexander made 17 starts and compiled a record of 6–6. The pitching-rich Dodgers let him get away to Baltimore in the Frank Robinson trade.

Munson ripped Alexander's first American League pitch for a single to left, moving Blomberg to second. Allen hit a slow ground ball to third on which Robinson had only one play—at first base. He made the out there as the runners moved up. With the tying runs in scoring position, Houk sent Rusty Torres up to bat for Stottlemyre. Torres, a switch-hitting outfielder, had made a spectacular debut with the Yankees after they recalled him from Syracuse late last September. In nine games, he had ten hits in 26 at-bats for a .385 average. The count went to two balls and two strikes on Torres. He took the next pitch, which was very close, but Flaherty called it ball three. Alexander came back with a full-count slider that did not appear to be as good a pitch as the previous one, and Torres again took it. However, this time Flaherty bellowed strike three, ending the inning and stranding the two runners.

Powell was batting against Lindy McDaniel in the home seventh, with Rettenmund at first and one out, when the rains came again. Flaherty immediately waved his arms to signal that the game was over. It was 5:37 P.M.; three and a half hours had elapsed since the first pitch, although actual playing time was only an hour and 49 minutes. Everything that preceded the final cancellation became part of the official record. Coincidentally, Dobson (16–18) and Stottlemyre (12–18), today's starting pitchers, ended the season tied for the American League lead in losses. Stottlemyre, who also led the league in losses in 1966, is the only Yankee ever to lead more than once in that category.

After three straight division titles, the Orioles finished third, and following the season they traded Dobson, second baseman Johnson, pitcher Roric Harrison, and catcher Johnny Oates to Atlanta for catcher Earl Williams and infielder Taylor Duncan.

As a result of losing the four home games with Baltimore to the strike, the Yankees failed to draw a million (966,328) for the first time since 1945. They again finished in fourth place (79–76), but only 6½ games behind the Eastern Division champion Detroit Tigers. The Tigers edged the Boston Red Sox by a half game, helped by the decision to not make up any strike-canceled games. Detroit played one more game than Boston and won it. Bobby Murcer had another strong year. His batting average dropped to .292, but he led the league in runs (102) and total bases (314) and was second in home runs (33) and third in runs batted in (96). He finished fifth in the voting for the Most Valuable Player Award.

Sunday, April 16, 1972

New York	ab	r	h	rbi		Baltimore	ab	r	h	rbi
Kenney ss	3	0	0	0		Buford lf	3	0	0	0
McKinney 3b	3	0	1	0		Rettenmund rf	3	2	1	0
Murcer cf	3	1	1	0		Powell 1b	3	0	0	0
White lf	3	0	0	0		Robinson 3b	3	0	2	2
Blomberg 1b	1	0	1	1		Hendricks c	3	0	0	0
Callison rf	3	0	0	0		Blair cf	3	1	1	0
Munson c	2	0	1	0		Johnson 2b	3	0	1	0
Allen 2b	3	0	1	0		Belanger ss	3	0	3	0
Stottlemyre p	1	0	0	0		Dobson p	3	0	0	0
ªTorres	1	0	0	0		Alexander p	0	0	0	0
McDaniel p	0	0	0	0		Total	27	3	8	2
Total	23	1	5	1						

*One out in seventh inning when game was called.
ªStruck out Stottlemyre in seventh inning.

New York	000	100	0–1
Baltimore	110	010	0–3

Errors—Munson, Allen, McDaniel. Double plays—Johnson and Powell; Stottlemyre, Munson, and Blomberg; Blomberg (unassisted). Caught stealing—by Hendricks (Munson). Left on bases—New York 5; Baltimore 7. Put outs—New York 19: Blomberg 9, Munson 3, White 4, Kenney 1, Murcer 1, Callison 1. Baltimore 21: Powell 10, Belanger 3, Johnson 2, Hendricks 2, Rettenmund 1, Blair 2, Buford 1. Assists—New York 9: McKinney 1, Stottlemyre 3, Munson 2, Kenney 3. Baltimore 11: Powell 1, Belanger 1, Johnson 4, Hendricks 2, Robinson 2, Dobson 1. Two-base hit—Murcer. Sacrifice—Stottlemyre.

	IP	H	R	ER	BB	SO
NEW YORK						
Stottlemyre (L, 0–1)	6.0	8	3	1	2	2
McDaniel	.1	0	0	0	0	0
BALTIMORE						
Dobson (W, 1–0)	6.1	4	1	1	2	1
Alexander S.1	.2	1	0	0	0	1

Hit by pitch—By Dobson (Blomberg). Umpires—Flaherty, Haller, Neudecker, and Kunkel. Time of game—1 hr. 49 min. Attendance—11,995.

Friday, April 6, 1973
Fenway Park Boston
Boston 15 New York 5

The remedy is worse than the disease.—Francis Bacon

In the still air of the clubhouse, after the Red Sox had bombed his Yankees, 15–5, in the season opener at Fenway Park, manager Ralph Houk said: "I never saw a game affected by the wind so much. The ball was blowing all over the place, today. It was ridiculous some of the time." It truly was. The wind, which blew at a steady 25 miles per hour with gusts of up to 50, combined with a very bright sun to make it extremely difficult for fielders to judge correctly any ball hit in the air. Several times players settled under balls only to see the wind carry them more than 60 feet away. It was too bad, because—except for the blustery gales—it was great weather for an opener. Temperatures were in the mid–50s, which made for a pleasant day for the crowd of 32,882. And, of course, the Red Sox made it even more pleasant with a 20-hit assault on Yankees starter Mel Stottlemyre and two relievers. The Boston attack included three home runs: Carl Yastrzemski, who was moving from the out-field to first base this season, had one, and catcher Carlton Fisk had two—one a grand slam. Second baseman Doug Griffin had four hits and third baseman Rico Petrocelli and left fielder Tommy Harper each had three. Every Boston starter hit safely except Orlando Cepeda, the designated hitter, who went hitless in six tries.

Boston had signed Cepeda in January, shortly after the American League agreed to adopt the new rule allowing a "designated hitter" to bat for the pitcher. It was the first instance in which a team added a player specifically to fill that new position. Cepeda batted .324 as the Red Sox's designated hitter during spring training, and he would serve in that role in all his 142 games during the season, batting .289 with 20 home runs. The American League owners had voted to make this drastic departure from baseball tradition, first sug-gested by National League president John Heydler 45 years earlier, as a way to reverse the league's deteriorating offense. The owners believed there was a strong correlation between the declines in batting averages and run scoring and their league's falling attendance. It was to be a three-year experiment, with a new vote taken following the 1975 season. National League owners, whose attendance remained strong, chose not to go along. By turning base-ball from a nine-man game into a ten-man game, the American League was introducing the twentieth century's most extreme departure from existing major-league playing rules.

All 12 American League teams were opening their seasons today, but four of the games were at night, and the Milwaukee Brewers playing at Baltimore had a later start. Therefore, the Boston-New York game, the 1,472nd between the Red Sox and the Yankees in their 70-year rivalry, would be the first played under the new rules. But even beyond that, this afternoon's game would have special significance for the entire Yankees' organization. A group of partners, headed by Cleveland shipbuilder George Steinbrenner, now owned the club, and today would be game one of the "Steinbrenner era." The partnership group had purchased the team from the Columbia Broadcasting System in January 1973 for a reported $10 million. Under CBS ownership, the Yankees had won no pennants and attendance at Yankee Stadium had plum-meted; and when they sold the club, it was for less money than they had paid to buy it—some-thing that has not happened in the sale of a major-league club since. Steinbrenner, whose sports background was mainly in football, made two promises to the New York fans: first, that he would not take an active interest in running the club, and second, that he would bring the best players that he could to New York. He would keep the second promise.

The new owners selected Gabe Paul, an experienced baseball executive, to replace Michael Burke as the club's president; but the Yankees had begun to make personnel changes even before Paul took over. In a six-player deal with the Cleveland Indians the previous Novem-ber, they traded Jerry Kenney, John Ellis, Rusty Torres, and Charlie Spikes to the Indians for third baseman Graig Nettles and catcher Jerry Moses. Earlier in the week, another trade brought veteran outfielder Matty Alou from the Oakland A's for infielder Rich McKinney and pitcher Rob Gardner. The Alou brothers (newcomer Matty at .339 and holdover Felipe at .333) led the Yankees' batters in spring training, and Matty in right field and Felipe at first base were part of the team's first ten-man lineup. New York's first official designated hitter was Ron Blomberg. But unlike Boston, who signed Cepeda for the sole purpose of serving as their designated hitter and had used him there throughout the exhibition season, the Yankees had not used Blomberg at DH in any of their Grapefruit League games. He would fill the position 56 times this season, but Jim Ray Hart, whom the Yanks purchased from the Giants on April 17, would be their primary designated hitter in 1973.

Following Rene Rancourt's singing of "The Star-Spangled Banner," there was a bittersweet first-ball ceremony. At tonight's openers in Anaheim and Oakland, former Viet Nam prisoners of war were scheduled to throw out the first ball. However, although the Red Sox also had POWs as their guests—five of them from different areas around New England—they gave the honor instead to a young man named Ed Folger. Folger had been a player in Boston's minor-league system before having his leg amputated as the result of a farming accident last September.

Both teams were wearing the new style double-knit uniforms, although aside from the fabric, the Yankees' road-grays remained essentially unchanged. There were two minor additions—a blue stripe around each sleeve and white trim around the letters and numbers. Later in the month, the Yanks would add a patch to the left sleeve commemorating the 50th anniversary of the opening of Yankee Stadium. Nineteen seventy-three would be the last year of baseball in the original Stadium. Following the season, renovations would begin that would not be completed until 1976. This morning Mayor John Lindsay reported the cost to New York City of those renovations, including making the necessary highway improvements, had jumped $7 million over last year's original estimate to $27.9 million.

The Red Sox had begun wearing their redesigned home uniforms during the 1972 season. The new style featured a pullover jersey and sash belt. It had red and blue striping on both the vee-neck of the jersey and the belt, and the shoes were no longer black but red. Not to be outdone in this time of sartorial innovation, the American League umpires were wearing their new uniforms, which now included maroon jackets along with the traditional blue pants. Boston, which narrowly missed winning the Eastern Division in strike-shortened 1972 (they finished half a game behind Detroit), was opening with Luis Tiant. The Sox had rescued Tiant after the Minnesota Twins released him following the 1970 season. After going a disappointing 1–7 in 1971, he bounced back with a brilliant season in 1972, going 15–6 with a 1.91 earned run average, the lowest in the league. Tiant's lifetime record against New York, compiled mostly with Cleveland in 1964–1969, was ten wins and seven losses.

Stottlemyre, the Yankees' starter, had been a much better pitcher in 1972 than his league-leading 18 losses would suggest. He lost four games by one run, and in five of his losses the Yankees were shut out. Now in his tenth major-league season, Stottlemyre had a 16–13 career record against the Red Sox. The Yanks, who many were picking to win the Eastern Division title, got off to a great start this afternoon. Horace Clarke opened the game with a single to left. However, when he attempted to steal second on a pitch Roy White took for strike three, Fisk, despite soreness in his right shoulder, threw him out. The double play turned out to be most consequential because the next five Yankees reached base, and three of them scored. With two out and the bases empty, Matty Alou got a double when right fielder Reggie Smith lost his fly ball in the sun and wind. Possibly unnerved, Tiant walked the next two batters, Bobby Murcer and Nettles. Then Blomberg stepped in as the American League's first designated hitter, and he too walked to force in a run. (After Blomberg batted in the first inning, his bat was appropriated and shipped to the Hall of Fame.) Two more runs scored on Felipe Alou's double, a pop-fly to the right side that got caught up in the wind and blew away from second baseman Griffin.

Trailing 3–0, Boston got one back in the bottom of the first on Yastrzemski's tremendous home run into the center-field bleachers. It was a good sign for the Red Sox. Last season, Yastrzemski had not hit his first home run until July 22, and he finished the year with a total of only 12. In the second, the Sox scored four runs to take a 5–3 lead. The big blow was Fisk's first home run, a two-run blast that tied the score at 3–3. Singles by Griffin and Luis Aparicio and an error by Nettles accounted for the other two runs. Both Griffin and Aparicio's hits were routine pop-ups that the wind carried away from waiting Yankees' infielders. Nettles homered in the third to make it 5–4, but Boston came back in the home third to knock out Stottlemyre with three runs on four singles and a double by Fisk. Two of the singles, by Harper and Dwight Evans, were against Lindy McDaniel, but Stottlemyre was responsible for all three runs. Evans, Boston's right fielder, was just 21 years old, and the only rookie in either starting lineup. He had appeared briefly for the Red Sox in 1972, batting .263 in 18 games; that was after a season at Louisville in which he led the International League in runs batted in. One of the few Boston batters to have hit well in spring training, Evans won his position by beating out veteran Danny Cater and another highly touted youngster, Ben Oglivie.

While all the Red Sox hitters had struggled at the plate during the spring, none had been less productive than Fisk. Following an excellent rookie season in 1972 (he was the unanimous choice as the American League's Rookie of the Year), Fisk batted a feeble .107 in the Grapefruit League, with just three extra-base hits in 56 at-bats. This afternoon, it took him only three at-bats to get three extra-base hits. He had already homered in the second and doubled in the third when he tagged McDaniel for a fourth-inning grand slam that extended Boston's lead to 12–4. The drive, helped a bit by the wind, landed in the Yankees bullpen and followed a leadoff single by Yastrzemski, a double by Smith, and an intentional walk to Petrocelli. Fisk later said that although this was his first two-home-run game ever, the six RBIs he had was not his best. He claimed he had once driven in eight runs in a game when he was with Louisville.

Boston added their final three runs in the sixth against Casey Cox. During his three-inning stint, Cox hit two batters, Fisk and Smith. Perhaps it was wildness, or perhaps it was a message. Red Sox base runners were relaying catcher Thurman Munson's signs to the batters from second base, and Munson was informing them that he resented it. Although Tiant settled down after his first-inning wildness, at one point in the eighth inning he seemed on the verge of being replaced. Manager Eddie Kasko went to the mound with two runners on and one out, but Tiant was successful in pleading his case to continue. He retired the next two batters and got the Yanks in order in the ninth to earn the 129-pitch complete game victory.

Friday, April 6, 1973

New York	ab	r	h	rbi	Boston	ab	r	h	rbi
Clarke 2b	5	0	1	0	Harper lf	6	1	3	1
White lf	5	0	0	0	Aparicio ss	6	0	1	1
M. Alou rf	5	2	2	0	Yastrzemski 1b	4	2	2	2
Murcer cf	3	1	0	0	Smith cf	5	2	2	0
Nettles 3b	2	2	1	2	Miller cf	0	0	0	0
Blomberg dh	3	0	1	1	Cepeda dh	6	0	0	0
F. Alou 1b	4	0	3	2	Petrocelli 3b	4	3	3	0
Munson c	3	0	0	0	Fisk c	4	4	3	6
Michael ss	4	0	0	0	Griffin 2b	5	2	4	1
Total	34	5	8	5	Evans rf	5	1	2	1
					Total	45	15	20	13

New York   301   010   000–5
Boston   143   403   00X–15

Errors—Nettles, Michael. Double play—Fisk and Aparicio. Caught stealing—by Fisk (Clarke). Left on bases—New York 7; Boston 11. Put outs—New York 24: F. Alou 13, Munson 4, M. Alou 2, White 3, Murcer 1, Michael 1. Boston 27: Yastrzemski 11, Harper 3, Fisk 2, Griffin 2, Aparicio 3, Petrocelli 1, Smith 2, Evans 2, Miller 1. Assists—New York 12: Michael 2, Nettles 2, Stottlemyre 1, Clarke 4, McDaniel 2, Cox 1. Boston 7: Fisk 1, Griffin 3, Aparicio 1, Petrocell1 2. Two-base hits—M. Alou 2, F. Alou, Fisk, Smith, Evans, Harper. Home runs—Yastrzemski, Fisk 2, Nettles. Stolen bases—Yastrzemski, Griffin. Sacrifice fly—Yastrzemski.

	IP	H	R	ER	BB	SO
NEW YORK						
Stottlemyre (L, 0–1)	2.2	8	8	6	0	1
McDaniel	2.1	7	4	4	1	2
Cox	3.0	5	3	2	1	0
BOSTON						
Tiant (W, 1–0)	9.0	8	5	5	5	2

Hit by pitches—by Cox (Fisk, Smith). Umpires—Umont, Denkinger, Anthony and Deegan. Time of game—2 hrs. 57 min. Attendance—32,882.

The Yanks lost three straight at Fenway Park and another one in Cleveland before finally winning their first game. Neither of the Alou brothers, who had five of the Yankees' eight hits this afternoon, finished the season with New York. Both were sold to National League teams on September 6, Felipe to the Montreal Expos and Matty to the St. Louis Cardinals. Roy White, who went hitless in five at-bats, had now batted 22 times on Opening Day without a hit.

Following three consecutive winning seasons, the Yankees (80–82) fell below .500 and finished in fourth place in the Eastern Division, 17 games behind the Baltimore Orioles. Despite their third straight fourth-place finish, attendance in this last year of the original Yankee Stadium increased by nearly 300,000 over 1972, its highest level since the pennant-winning year of 1964. Ralph Houk, complaining of meddling by new owner George Steinbrenner, resigned at the end of the season, and 11 days later signed to manage the Detroit Tigers. Under the new designated hitter rule, batting averages and home runs for the American League increased significantly, from .239 and 1,175 HRs in 1972 to .259 and 1,552 HRs in 1973.

Saturday, April 6, 1974
Shea Stadium, New York
New York 6 Cleveland 1

I have been a stranger in a strange land.—Exodus

One day, back in March 1971, two seemingly unrelated stories appeared in the New York newspapers. In one, the Board of Education reported that because of a lack of money they were being forced to drop 6,500 teachers from the city's public schools. In the other, Mayor John Lindsay announced that the city planned to spend more than $20 million to refurbish Yankee Stadium. An obvious first reaction would be that a municipal government that lays off teachers while spending millions on a baseball park should reexamine its priorities. However, Mayor Lindsay, like state and local officials everywhere, had learned how important a major-league baseball team was to the economic vitality and self-esteem of a city. Losing a team meant not only the loss of millions of dollars in revenue; it was also a damaging blow to civic pride and spirit. New Yorkers were fully aware of the harm done to their city by the loss of the Dodgers and Giants in 1958. To give the Yankees any reason to even consider leaving New York was unthinkable. Work on the stadium and several highways leading to it began after the 1973 season. Not surprisingly, the estimated costs of the project continued to rise and now had passed $60 million. Meanwhile, the Yankees would play their home games at the park of their National League rivals, just as they had done from 1913 to 1922 when they played at the Polo Grounds. For the next two years they would share Shea Stadium with the Mets, using the locker room and offices of Shea's other tenants, the National Football League's New York Jets. Hoping to make new fans in Mets territory, the Yankees plastered the surrounding area with outdoor advertising announcing their arrival. The club also made sure the public knew it was not the Yankees but the city that bore responsibility for the 10 percent rise to $1.65 in Shea Stadium's parking fees.

The Yankees inaugurated their two-year stay in Queens with a 6–1 win over the Cleveland Indians before a small but highly partisan crowd of 20,744 Yankee rooters on a chilly, less than spring-like Saturday afternoon. Mel Stottlemyre went the distance for the win and Cleveland starter Gaylord Perry took the loss. Perry had won the Cy Young Award in 1972 on the strength of a 24–16 record, but had slipped to 19–19 for the Eastern Division cellar-dwellers a year ago. In both years, his first two in the American League, Perry had pitched well against the Yanks, winning four of five in '72 and four of six in '73. By contrast, Stottlemyre had always had difficulties with the Indians. Even after winning three of four against them in 1973, his lifetime mark against Cleveland (13–14) was still below .500.

In addition to a new "home," the Yankees also had a new manager: Bill Virdon, the 20th manager in the club's history. George Steinbrenner's first choice to succeed the departed Ralph Houk had been ex–Oakland A's manager Dick Williams, but A's owner Charlie Finley still had Williams under contract. When Finley refused to let him go without compensation, Steinbrenner went to Virdon. The former Pirates' manager was available because Pittsburgh had fired him late in 1973, one season after he led them to the National League's Eastern Division title.

This year's opening ceremonies were especially moving, and demonstrated baseball's ability to transcend age barriers. Fans seldom get the chance to let political leaders know what they think of them. So when a politician takes part in opening-day festivities, they often take the opportunity to make their feelings known—often, sadly, with boos. Not today. When New York mayor Abe Beame and Massachusetts senator Ted Kennedy walked to the mound to throw out the first ball, they heard only cheering and applause. However, the cheers were neither for the mayor nor the senator. They were for Kennedy's young son, Teddy Jr., who walked between them with the aid of a metal cane. There were no Yankees' rooters in this group of three. Although Beame had once been Phil Rizzuto's English teacher at Richmond Hill High School, the mayor had grown up a Dodgers' fan, while both Kennedys, naturally, rooted for their hometown Boston Red Sox. The cheering and applause had to do with something other than baseball. The entire country had read about Teddy Jr.'s brave struggle against the cancer that eventually led to the amputation of his left leg. New Yorkers were standing in for people everywhere in simply letting him know how much they admired his courage. Standing at the front of the mound, the 68-year-old Beame handed the ball to the 12-year-old Kennedy. Photographers surrounded Thurman Munson, standing behind home plate to receive the ball, almost hiding him from view, but Kennedy's high, arcing toss landed right in the catcher's glove. Munson trotted out to the mound and gave the ball to the youngster, who was wearing a Yankees jacket for the occasion.

Among those applauding this timeless ritual was William Shea, the New York lawyer for whom the Mets had named the ballpark. Shea had played a significant role in the successful effort to bring National League baseball back to New York following the desertion of the Dodgers and Giants. When the Mets opened their new stadium in 1964, the city showed its appreciation by naming it for him. Other notables who made the trek to Queens this afternoon included New York's former mayor, Robert F. Wagner Jr., New Jersey governor Brendan Byrne, band leader Lionel Hampton, former Yankees president Mike Burke, and almost-manager Dick Williams. Mrs. Lou Gehrig, as she so often did, attended the game as a guest of the Yankees. Also there as a guest of the club was 86-year-old Jack Martin, who played for the Yanks in 1912 and was their oldest living alumnus. Notably absent, however, was Steinbrenner, who a day earlier had been indicted for making illegal contributions to Richard Nixon's 1972 campaign for re-election and chose not to attend. As he had done so often at Yankee Stadium, opera star Robert Merrill sang the national anthem.

Perry and Stottlemyre kept the game scoreless until the Yankees broke through in the fourth. Munson led off with New York's first hit, a single to left. After Bobby Murcer fouled out and Ron Blomberg forced Munson at second, Graig Nettles homered to give the Yanks a 2–0 lead. Nettles picked on Perry's first pitch, driving it the opposite way, over the 371-foot sign in left. The Yankees' right-handed hitters took notice. Nettles's drive, while well hit, would have been just a long out in Yankee Stadium's cavernous left field.

Seemingly no game pitched by Gaylord Perry would be complete without a complaint by the opposition that he was throwing spitballs. Virdon and the Yankees' bench had been shouting those accusations all afternoon, until they finally bore fruit. In the sixth, on a 2–2 pitch to Nettles that dipped crazily, plate umpire Marty Springstead called it an automatic ball and then warned Perry about illegal pitches. The warning was significant. Under a new rule, umpires could issue such a warning even if they were unable to find evidence of a "foreign substance" on the ball. If a pitcher received two such warnings in a game, it meant automatic ejection. Perry and Cleveland manager Ken Aspromonte maintained that the pitch in question was Perry's forkball, but the warning stood. Springstead later explained: "In my opinion he threw an illegal pitch. I know what different pitches do, and it was an illegal pitch." Perry's next pitch was ball four, putting Nettles on base and giving the Yankees two base runners. Earlier in the inning, Murcer had singled and stolen second. Following the walk to Nettles, an infield single by designated hitter Bill Sudakis loaded the bases. (The Yanks had purchased Sudakis, a versatile switch-hitter, from the Texas Rangers last December.) Second baseman Gene Michael's fly ball to right fielder Charlie Spikes scored Murcer with New York's third run.

Michael, the Yankees' shortstop for the last five seasons, had moved to second to replace Horace Clarke. Clarke had been the team's second baseman since 1967, but had always had problems in making the double play. The Yankees had tried throughout the offseason to trade for a second baseman; when they were unsuccessful, Virdon switched Michael to second and put Jim Mason, also purchased from the Rangers last December, at shortstop. Eight weeks into the season, the Yanks sold Clarke to San Diego. Virdon's emphasis on defense was also the reason Mike Hegan was starting at first base. A cash acquisition from Oakland in August 1973, Hegan displayed his outstanding defensive abilities during spring training and won the position. Virdon vowed that part-time first baseman Blomberg, whom he had in right field today, would never play the position again as long as he was the manager. Three weeks into the season, the Yankees' first-base situation would change dramatically as the result of club president Gabe Paul's seven-player trade with Cleveland.

Paul had taken over Lee MacPhail's general manager duties after MacPhail succeeded Joe Cronin as president of the American League. On April 27 he sent pitchers Fritz Peterson, Steve Kline, Fred Beene, and Tom Buskey to Cleveland for pitchers Dick Tidrow and Cecil Upshaw and first baseman Chris Chambliss. Two weeks later, Paul sold Hegan to Milwaukee and Chambliss, the 1971 Rookie of the Year, settled in for a very successful six-year stay as the Yankees' first baseman. Blomberg never played another game at first base for New York, though he did play seven games there for the 1978 Chicago White Sox.

Cleveland threatened in the sixth on singles by Oscar Gamble and John Ellis, but third baseman Nettles killed the rally with a sensational play on Spikes's ground ball, turning it into an inning-ending double play. The Yankees then added three runs in the seventh to boost the lead to 6–0. Roy White opened the inning with a single to left, his first hit in 25 opening-day at-bats. White had earned today's start after holding off a strong challenge from Lou Piniella, whom the Yanks got from the Kansas City Royals in a trade for Lindy McDaniel. White took second on Hegan's sacrifice and third on Munson's infield single. With three left-handed hitters—Murcer, Blomberg, and Nettles—due up, Aspromonte removed Perry and brought in Tom Hilgendorf, a left-hander. Hilgendorf got Murcer to hit a ground ball to Buddy Bell behind the bag at third, but the Yanks got a break when Bell, an excellent fielder, made a mental error. As White raced home, Bell, evidently forgetting there was no runner at second, stepped on third base for what he thought was a force out. The time wasted in doing so made his hurried throw to first too late to get Murcer. Virdon sent the right-hand hitting Elliott Maddox—yet another player whom the Yanks had bought from Texas since the end of the 1973 season—up to bat for Blomberg. Maddox singled to center to score Munson, after which Hilgendorf walked Nettles and Michael to force Murcer across with run number six. After Mason struck out to end the inning, many in the crowd began chanting "We're number one," which prompted Yankees coach Whitey Ford to remark, "The crowds are livelier here than they were in the Stadium." Whether or not they were livelier, there was no doubt they were here to root for the Yankees. They had demonstrated that during the seventh-inning stretch by cheering loudly when the scoreboard posted the Mets' 5–4 loss at Philadelphia.

Stottlemyre had thrown 40 shutouts in his 11-year career, tying him with Red Ruffing for second place on the Yankees' all-time list. Only Ford, with 45, had more. When he retired Ellis to open the ninth, Stottlemyre seemed a good bet to get number 41. But Spikes put the shutout in jeopardy when he hit a 400-foot triple, a drive that landed at the base of the center-field wall. When Chambliss (still the Indians' first baseman) followed with a ground ball to shortstop Mason, Spikes came in to score. Bell grounded to Michael for the final out and the Yanks had their first opening-day win since 1969. For Stottlemyre this was the seventh opener he had started (tying him with Ford) and the fourth he had won, still the most ever by a Yankee. However, in what would be his final season, he won only five more games (no shutouts) and finished a disappointing 6–7. A rotator cuff injury led the Yankees to release him in the spring of 1975, ending his big-league career. Perry followed his opening-day loss with 15 consecutive wins to tie Johnny Allen's one-season club record set in 1937.

Saturday, April 6, 1974

Cleveland	ab	r	h	rbi	New York	ab	r	h	rbi
Lowenstein lf	4	0	1	0	White lf	4	1	1	0
Gamble dh	4	0	1	0	Hegan 1b	3	0	1	0

Cleveland	ab	r	h	rbi
Hendrick cf	4	0	0	0
Ellis c	3	0	1	0
Spikes rf	4	1	2	0
Chambliss 1b	4	0	1	1
Bell 3b	4	0	0	0
Duffy ss	3	0	0	0
Hermoso 2b	3	0	1	0
Total	33	1	7	1

New York	ab	r	h	rbi
Munson c	5	1	2	0
Murcer cf	4	2	2	1
Blomberg rf	3	1	0	0
aMaddox rf	2	0	1	1
Nettles 3b	2	1	1	2
Sudakis dh	3	0	1	0
Michael 2b	2	0	0	2
Mason ss	3	0	0	0
Total	31	6	9	6

aSingled for Blomberg in seventh inning.

Cleveland	000	000	001–1
New York	000	201	30X–6

Errors—Chambliss, Munson. Double play—Nettles, Michael, and Hegan. Left on bases—Cleveland 6; New York 11. Put outs—New York 27: White 4, Michael 3, Hegan 12, Munson 4, Murcer 1, Nettles 1, Mason 2. Cleveland 24: Lowenstein 1, Hendrick 2, Ellis 8, Spikes 3, Chambliss 2, Bell 1, Duffy 2, Hermoso 4, G. Perry 1. Assists—New York 14: Nettles 5, Michael 4, Mason 3, Stottlemyre 2. Cleveland 6: Chambliss 1, Bell 2, Hermoso 1, G. Perry 2. Two-base hits—Hermoso, Hegan. Three-base hit—Spikes. Home run—Nettles. Stolen bases—Munson, Murcer 2, Hegan. Sacrifices—White, Hegan. Sacrifice fly—Michael.

	IP	H	R	ER	BB	SO
CLEVELAND						
G. Perry (L, 0–1)	6.1	6	5	5	4	4
Hilgendorf	.2	2	1	1	2	2
Upshaw	1.0	1	0	0	1	1
NEW YORK						
Stottlemyre (W, 1–0)	9.0	7	1	1	1	4

Umpires—Springstead, Goetz, Denkinger, and Morgenweck. Time of game—2 hrs. 40 min. Attendance—20,744.

After staying in the race for the entire season, the Yankees (89–73) finished second, two games behind the Baltimore Orioles. It was the closest they had come since winning their last pennant ten years earlier, and it earned Bill Virdon The Sporting News Manager of the Year Award. At the conclusion of the season, Commissioner Bowie Kuhn suspended owner George Steinbrenner from baseball for two years after the Yankee owner was convicted of making illegal campaign contributions to President Nixon in 1972. The Yanks drew 1,273,075 to their temporary home, half a million fewer than the Mets.

Tuesday, April 8, 1975
Cleveland Stadium, Cleveland
Cleveland 5 New York 3

See, the conquering hero comes!—Thomas Morell

Ever since the founding of the National League in 1876, 427 different men had served as big-league managers. Some had been good. Some had been bad. All had been Caucasians. That particular coincidence ended on major-league baseball's 100th Opening Day when Frank Robinson, a black man, managed the Cleveland Indians to a 5–3 victory over the

New York Yankees. To make the day even more memorable, manager Robinson hit a storybook home run in his first at-bat. The 39-year-old outfielder, nearing the end of a great playing career, had come to Cleveland on waivers from the California Angels late in the 1974 season. On October 3, following a sixth consecutive losing season, the Indians fired manager Ken Aspromonte and named Robinson to replace him. As a still-active player, he became baseball's first player/manager since Hank Bauer of the 1961 Kansas City A's and the first in Cleveland since Lou Boudreau. It was under shortstop/manager Boudreau, in 1948, that the Indians last won the World Series. Al Lopez succeeded Boudreau in 1951 and won a pennant in 1954, but since then 10 different managers had tried and failed to bring another championship to Cleveland.

During his big-league career, now entering its 20th year, Robinson had established a reputation as a leader of men, black and white. And although his playing career was not yet over, Robinson did have managerial experience; for the past five seasons he had managed Santurce in the Puerto Rican winter league. General manager Phil Seghi's selection of Robinson had been immensely popular with Indians' fans, generating anticipation for the new season that had been lacking in Cleveland for a long time. The excitement of Robinson's history-making debut attracted a crowd of 56,204 to Cleveland Stadium on a bitterly cold day. When he was introduced before the game, the crowd rose to give him a prolonged standing ovation. Robinson removed his cap and waved it to the crowd, with a special wave to his family seated behind the Indians dugout. Frank's wife Barbara and their two children had flown to Cleveland from their home in Los Angeles for this momentous occasion. Robinson's introduction to the fans was just one in a series of thrills that made this among Cleveland's most unforgettable Opening Days ever. From an emotional standpoint, the afternoon's most powerful moment came when Rachel Robinson, Jackie's widow, threw out the first ball. Before she did, Mrs. Robinson spoke to the cheering crowd of her pride in being there and how much this would have meant to her late husband. She congratulated the Indians and the city of Cleveland for taking this historic step. Commissioner Bowie Kuhn and Mayor Ralph Perk also spoke of the importance of this day to Cleveland and to baseball and wished the Indians good luck. The fans booed them both. Former Indians pitcher Jim "Mudcat" Grant sang the national anthem.

Only one Cleveland player, pitcher Gaylord Perry, had challenged Robinson's authority during spring training. The two had squabbled on the first day of camp and again later. Nonetheless, both men were professionals, and because Perry was Cleveland's best pitcher, to no one's surprise Robinson chose him to pitch the opener. Perry had opened against the Yankees last year, losing, 6–1, at Shea Stadium. He then reeled off 15 straight wins before dropping 12 of 18 to finish 21–13. After losing to the Yanks three times in four decisions in 1974, his lifetime record against the New Yorkers was still a creditable 9–6.

Yankee manager Bill Virdon had Jim "Catfish" Hunter available to oppose Perry, but bypassed last year's Cy Young Award recipient for 19-game winner George "Doc" Medich. Hunter won the Cy Young while pitching for the Oakland A's, but became a Yankee after the season when A's owner Charlie Finley neglected to make a contractual payment to the pitcher's life insurance fund. The case went to an arbitrator, Peter Seitz, who declared Hunter a free agent. On New Year's Eve, the Yanks signed him to a five-year $3.75 million contract. Hunter, who earned $100,000 in 1974, was now making three times the salary of any other major-league player. But Medich, with a 0.77 earned run average, had been the team's best pitcher all spring, and Virdon rewarded him with the opening-day assignment. During a Grapefruit League season in which the Yankees won just 14 of their 31 games, he had won five of them without a loss. A part-time medical student at the University of Pittsburgh, Medich was beginning his third season with New York. In 1973 he had been the only rookie to make the team, even though he finished second in the voting for the James P. Dawson Award. The sportswriters had chosen Otto Velez as the team's most promising newcomer, but on Opening Day, Velez was with the Syracuse Chiefs in the International League and Medich was with the Yankees. He won 14 games and lost nine, and followed that with last season's 19–15 mark.

In addition to Hunter, the Yanks had added another big name from the Bay area. They traded the popular Bobby Murcer to the San Francisco Giants for speedy, power-hitting Bobby Bonds. During the '74 season, Virdon had moved Murcer from center field to right, replacing him with Elliott Maddox, a faster man. Maddox responded with his best year to date, but was unavailable for the opener because of an injured hand. Bonds, a right fielder with the Giants, started in center, with Ron Blomberg taking over in right. Roy White's thumb injury had not healed sufficiently for him to swing a bat, so Lou Piniella was in left. Ed Herrmann, a left-handed-hitting catcher obtained from the Chicago White Sox, was the designated hitter. In the infield, second baseman Sandy Alomar, purchased from the California Angels last July, combined with shortstop Jim Mason, third baseman Graig Nettles, and first baseman Chris Chambliss to give the Yankees their best inner defense in years. Nettles and Chambliss were among the eight Yankees on the opening-day roster who were former Indians.

As the Cleveland players, wearing their outlandish, new all-red home uniforms, took the field to begin the game, the temperature was a frigid 36 degrees. Perry set the Yankees down in the top of the first, and then was the first man out of the dugout to greet Robinson after his dramatic home run in the bottom of the inning. "He was so excited when he came in the dugout, his knees were shaking," Perry said. "I wanted to let him know I was with him. I was probably more happy for him than he was for himself." Serving as the designated hitter and batting second, Robinson connected on a 2–2 fastball, low and away, and drove it over the left-field fence. It was the 575th home run and 2,901st hit of Robinson's distinguished career. As he rounded the bases, the shivering crowd shed their blankets to give their new manager his second standing ovation of the day. After he crossed the plate, Robinson again took off his cap and waved to the crowd. This time they returned the salute by waving the Indians' pennants management had provided to each fan entering the park. The home run was the eighth Robinson had hit in an opening-day game, breaking the record of seven, held jointly by Babe Ruth, Eddie Mathews, and Willie Mays. (The record has since been tied by Ken Griffey Jr. and Adam Dunn.) "It was a great moment," Robinson said, while accepting congratulations after the game. "But you had to wait till the end, till the game was over. Now it's even more gratifying."

The Yankees scored their three runs in the second inning, enabling them to take a temporary 3–1 lead. Chambliss's double drove in Blomberg and Nettles, both aboard on singles, and Thurman Munson's base hit to left brought Chambliss home. Activity began in the Indians' bullpen, and Robinson later said Perry was one hit away from coming out. Undoubtedly aware of his precarious situation, Perry got Mason to hit into a force play and then threw a third strike past Alomar. After their four-hit second inning, the Yanks got only five more the rest of the way, with Chambliss's double the only one going for extra bases.

Second-inning singles by Boog Powell and John Ellis and Jack Brohamer's sacrifice fly gave the Indians their second run. Powell, who had been Robinson's teammate for six years in Baltimore, was making his debut as an Indian. The Orioles decided they no longer needed him after getting first baseman Lee May in a big off-season trade with the Houston Astros. So, after having spent 14 years as one of their best and most popular players, they traded him to Cleveland with pitcher Don Hood for catcher Dave Duncan. As if to prove to the Orioles that he could still play, Powell was having a big day. Although he later said that because of the cold he had no feeling in his feet from the fifth inning on, he was the hitting star of the game. He had three hits in three at-bats, drove in two runs, and scored three. In the fourth, it was Powell's homer to right center that tied the game at 3–3. In the sixth, he put the Indians ahead with a double that scored George Hendrick, who had walked and stolen second. When Brohamer later singled to center, Powell scored a very important insurance run. Following Brohamer's hit, Virdon replaced Medich with left-hander Rudy May.

Powell was also a key figure in the eighth inning, when the Indians threatened but failed to score. He led off the inning against new pitcher Sparky Lyle by drawing a walk. On a hit-and-run play, Ellis's perfectly placed ground ball to the right side hit the slow-moving Powell. Ellis got credit for a single, but Powell, because of the ball hitting him, was automatically out. Instead of runners at first and third with no one out, the Indians had a runner at first with one out. The next batter was Buddy Bell, Cleveland's excellent young third baseman whose dad, former major-league star Gus Bell, was at the game. Bell hit a bouncer back to the mound that Lyle fielded, but in his haste to make the double play, he threw wildly to second. Both runners were safe, and when Brohamer dropped a bunt along the third-base line and beat it out, the bases were loaded. Here the improved Yankees defense came to Lyle's rescue. Ed Crosby, playing shortstop for the injured Frank Duffy, pulled a ground ball to the right side. Chambliss made a diving stop and then threw home to force Ellis. Oscar Gamble followed with a long drive to center, but Bonds, using his great speed, caught up with it for the third out.

There was more drama to come in the Yankees' ninth. Nettles flied to Charlie Spikes for the first out, but Herrmann got aboard with a single to left. As Chambliss stepped in, Virdon sent White out to run for Herrmann. In his three previous at-bats Chambliss, a dangerous left-handed hitter, had reached Perry for a double and two singles. Robinson had a left-hander warming up but elected to stay with his ace. Nonetheless, he went to the mound to remind Perry—who was 36 years old and in his 14th big-league season—not to give Chambliss a pitch that he could pull for a game-tying home run. Robinson returned to the frosty dugout, but remained standing with his foot on the top step. (The pipes had frozen the night before, preventing the dugout heaters from working.) Seconds later, he watched as Chambliss drove a ball to deep right field. The crowd, which had been standing since the inning began, roared itself hoarse when Spikes, backed up against the fence, made the catch. Powell, Indians coach Jeff Torborg, and several other veteran Cleveland players and coaches said they had never seen such fan involvement. They continued to stand and roar until Perry got Munson on a come-backer for the final out. As Perry walked off the mound, the first man out of the dugout to congratulate him was Frank Robinson, who did so with a big hug.

Perry's victory was the 199th of his major-league career, but in June, with his record at 6–9, the Indians traded him to the Texas Rangers for three pitchers and $100,000. Today's win was the best and most exhilarating day of the year for the Indians who, despite the change in managers, had their seventh consecutive losing season. Attendance was also a disappointment. Last season, Cleveland had gone over the million mark for the first time since 1959, but even today's huge crowd and Robinson's history-making appointment could not prevent 1975 attendance from again falling below a million.

> *At the beginning of August, the Yankees, with a record of 53–51, fired last season's Manager of the Year, Bill Virdon, and replaced him with Billy Martin. They won 30 of their 56 games under Martin for a combined season record of 83–77, good for third place, 12 games behind the Boston Red Sox. Attendance in this second and final year at Shea Stadium was 1,288,048, essentially unchanged from 1974. Bobby Bonds, in his one season in New York, joined Ken Williams of the 1922 St. Louis Browns and Tommy Harper of the 1970 Milwaukee Brewers as the only American Leaguers to have at least 30 home runs and 30 stolen bases in the same season. Bonds hit 32 home runs and stole 30 bases. Catfish Hunter (23–14) led the league in complete games (30) and innings pitched (328), while tying the Baltimore Orioles' Jim Palmer for the most wins. He finished second to Palmer in the voting for the Cy Young Award.*

Tuesday, April 8, 1975

New York	ab	r	h	rbi		Cleveland	ab	r	h	rbi
Alomar 2b	2	0	0	0		Gamble lf	5	0	1	0
aJohnson	1	0	0	0		Robinson dh	3	1	1	1
Stanley 2b	0	0	0	0		Hendrick cf	3	1	0	0
Piniella lf	4	0	0	0		Spikes rf	4	0	0	0
Bonds cf	4	0	0	0		Powell 1b	3	3	3	2
Blomberg rf	4	1	2	0		Ellis c	3	0	2	0
Nettles 3b	4	1	1	0		Bell 3b	4	0	0	0
Herrmann dh	4	0	1	0		Brohamer 2b	3	0	2	2
bWhite	0	0	0	0		Crosby ss	4	0	1	0
Chambliss 1b	4	1	3	2		Total	32	5	10	5
Munson c	4	0	2	1						
Mason ss	3	0	0	0						
Total	34	3	9	3						

aStruck out for Alomar in seventh inning.
bRan for Herrmann in ninth inning.

New York	030	000	000–3
Cleveland	110	102	00X–5

Error—Lyle. Double play—Perry, Crosby and Powell. Caught stealing—By Ellis (Alomar); By Munson (Crosby). Left on bases—New York 5; Cleveland 8. Putouts—New York 24: Munson 4, Nettles 1, Blomberg 2, Chambliss 6, Mason 2, Alomar 3, Bonds 2, Medich 1, Piniella 2, Stanley 1. Cleveland 27: Ellis 6, Crosby 3, Gamble 3, Bell 1, Powell 9, G. Perry 1, Spikes 3, Hendrick 1. Assists—New York 12: Munson 1, Nettles 4, Chambliss 2, Mason 3, Alomar 1, Stanley 1. Cleveland 13: Ellis 1, Crosby 2, Bell 2, Powell 1, G. Perry 4, Brohamer 3. Two-base hits—Chambliss, Powell. Home runs—Robinson, Powell. Stolen base—Hendrick. Sacrifice fly—Brohamer.

	IP	H	R	ER	BB	SO
NEW YORK						
Medich (L, 0–1)	5.2	8	5	5	2	2
May	1.1	0	0	0	1	1
Lyle	1.0	2	0	0	1	0
CLEVELAND						
G. Perry (W, 1–0)	9.0	9	3	3	1	6

Passed ball—Munson.

Umpires—Chylak, McCoy, Brinkman and Cooney. Time of game—2:43. Attendance—56,204.

Thursday, April 8, 1976
County Stadium, Milwaukee
Milwaukee 5 New York 0

A man not old, but mellow, like good wine.—Stephen Phillips

Over the past few years, Hank Aaron had removed three of baseball's most revered names from their places at the top of selected all-time leader lists. In that stretch, Aaron had replaced Ty Cobb as the leader in games-played and at-bats, Stan Musial in extra-base hits, and Babe Ruth in home runs and runs batted in. He continued his assault on the major league record book on Opening Day 1976, driving in three runs to raise his lifetime RBI total to 2,265. Aaron's batting backed the shutout pitching of Jim Slaton and led the Milwaukee Brewers to a 5–0 win over the Yankees at Milwaukee's County Stadium. Slaton, a 25-year-old right-hander, allowed the visitors just four hits in registering his 14th major league shutout. He also walked three batters, but needed just 112 pitches on this uncomfortably cold day to hand New York its first opening-day shutout in 15 years. Because of his efficiency, the game lasted just two hours and nine minutes, sending an appreciative crowd of 44,868 chilled fans home early. Catfish Hunter suffered the loss as the Yankees began their first full season under manager Billy Martin.

Slaton had pitched the Brewers' opener a year ago, but lasted only into the third inning in Milwaukee's 5–2 loss to the Red Sox at Boston. After struggling through several poor early-season efforts, he righted himself and for much of June and July was among the best pitchers in the American League. But as pitchers sometimes do, Slaton temporarily lost whatever it was that had made him successful. During the last two months of the season he won just one of nine decisions and finished with an 11–18 record.

The Brewers had returned major league baseball to Milwaukee in 1970, one year after beginning life as the Seattle Pilots. However, as an expansion team, they had suffered through six consecutive losing seasons under managers Dave Bristol and Del Crandall. Although losing teams lose because of the abilities of their players, it's always been easier to replace the manager than to acquire better players. In keeping with that baseball axiom, the Brewers fired Crandall and hired Alex Grammas, a former big-league infielder whose major-league managerial experience consisted of leading the Pittsburgh Pirates for the last five games of the 1969 season. Along with a new manager, the Brewers were introducing a new mascot—Bonnie Brewer—that for the fans proved to be the best part of the brief pre-game festivities. The ceremonies concluded with Milwaukee County Executive John Doyne throwing out the first ball, and Ms. Joey English singing the national anthem.

Milwaukee's chilly weather (it was 44 degrees at game time) felt especially harsh contrasted with the warmth of Florida that the Yankees had enjoyed until yesterday. Training camp for all teams had opened late because of a labor dispute, which led to an owners' lockout of the players. It was not until mid-March, when Commissioner Bowie Kuhn ordered the camps opened, that spring training finally got started. The Yankees, 10–7 in the Grapefruit League, had made significant personnel changes and more than most teams would have benefitted from a full training period. Three off-season deals, including two major trades on December 11, 1975, brought six new players to New York. Pitcher Ed Figueroa and outfielder Mickey Rivers came from the California Angels for outfielder Bobby Bonds, and pitchers Dock Ellis and Ken Brett and rookie second baseman Willie

Randolph came from the Pirates for pitcher Doc Medich. Earlier, on November 22, the Yanks acquired Oscar Gamble, a left-handed-hitting outfielder with a "Yankee Stadium swing," from the Cleveland Indians for pitcher Pat Dobson. Gamble would have his first opportunity in the renovated Stadium next week when the Yanks opened their home season against the Minnesota Twins. The distance to right field in the new stadium was not as short as it had been in the old one; nevertheless, it was still an inviting target for left-handed hitters like Gamble.

Adding Rivers, Randolph, and Gamble to a lineup that already had Chris Chambliss, Graig Nettles, Roy White, Lou Piniella, and Thurman Munson, gave New York an offense equal to that of any in the American League East. And, inserting Ellis and Figueroa into the pitching rotation made the Yanks strong contenders to win their first pennant in 12 years. Five of the six additions would prove to be instrumental in the team's success this season—all but Brett, although even he contributed in a way. In May, the Yanks traded Brett and outfielder Rich Coggins to the Chicago White Sox for Carlos May, a valuable out-fielder. Of all the new Yankees, Randolph would have the most lasting impact. He got off to an impressive start as the unanimous winner of the James P. Dawson Award, and con-tinued to be a dependable player for the next 13 years. After leaving the Yankees in 1989, he would play four more seasons, for four different teams, before returning as a coach in 1994.

Martin, a disciple of Casey Stengel's strategy of platooning players, wanted to use as many left-handed batters as he could against Slaton. So, although Piniella had the best spring of all the Yankees, batting a prodigious .476, because he batted right-handed he was on the bench for the opener. White, a switch hitter started in left field, despite having been in a spring-long batting slump. Rivers and Gamble, both left-handed hitters, opened in center and right respectively. Another outfielder, Elliott Maddox, was on the disabled list with a knee injury that would limit him to just 18 games this season. But while Maddox, a right-handed hitter, would not have started anyway, injuries to two other Yankees—Ron Blomberg and Munson—did affect Martin's lineup. Blomberg, a left-handed hitter, damaged his right shoulder in the last exhibition game in Florida and was unable to play. The Yanks considered the injury a potentially serious one and were sending Blomberg back to New York to have it examined by the team-physician, Dr. Edward Crane. (Blomberg would play in only one game this season.) Munson had a broken index finger on his right hand, which prevented him from throwing but not from swinging the bat. Martin used him as the des-ignated hitter, with Rick Dempsey—who had gotten into 71 games in 1975—mostly as a pinch hitter, behind the plate.

After Rivers opened the game with a bloop single to center, Slaton easily retired the next three batters, White, Munson, and Chambliss. The Yankees would not get another hit until the sixth inning, by which time the Brewers had the game well in hand. Milwaukee had already scored five runs in the first two innings against Hunter, who was uncharacter-istically wild. He went to a full count on six batters in the first inning, and all of them reached base. Hunter got the leadoff hitter, Charlie Moore, but gave up a double to left by Don Money. He then walked the next two batters, George Scott and Darrell Porter, to load the bases and bring up Aaron, the designated hitter. This was Aaron's 23rd year in the big leagues and the 22nd opening-day game in which he had played. It was his second season in the American League, and he had already announced that it would be his last. Aaron, at $240,000 per season, was among the game's highest paid players, but by Opening Day 1977 he would be 43 years old and was expected to be working as a Brewers' executive.

Aaron, who had gone hitless in seven at-bats against Hunter in 1975, singled sharply to left on his first at-bat of '76. The hit scored Money and Scott and sent Porter to second. Following Sixto Lezcano's infield hit that reloaded the bases, Bill Sharp bounced a routine ground ball to shortstop Jim Mason. Had Mason fielded it cleanly, it might have been an inning-ending double play; instead he booted the ball and Porter came home with Milwaukee's third run. The bases remained full; but Hunter prevented any further scoring by getting 20-year-old shortstop Robin Yount on a pop to third and fanning second baseman Pedro Garcia. It had taken him a total of 51 pitches to get through the first inning.

Hunter, with a lifetime 16–4 record against Seattle/Milwaukee, later complained that his wildness was due to the flatness of the County Stadium mound. Sparky Lyle, who pitched a scoreless eighth for New York, concurred. Both agreed that while the height of the mound appeared to be the prescribed ten inches, it did not slope downward sharply enough. "What happens is that you go through your motion and your foot hits the mound before it's supposed to. So you throw high," Hunter said. "There's no way Hunter's going to walk that many guys," added Lyle. Manager Martin said he would ask the umpires to allow Figueroa, who was starting the second game of this series, to take his pre-game warmup pitches from the mound to better adjust to it.

In the Milwaukee second, Moore walked and scored on Porter's two-out double. Aaron followed with a run-scoring single to left. "I feel better than I did last year, I'm more relaxed," Aaron said after the game. "There's no pressure this year." Hunter retired the next ten batters and allowed only two hits and no walks over the next 5 ⅓ innings, but the damage had been done. Trailing 5–0, the Yankees were never able to mount a serious threat against Slaton, who said he had found no problems with the mound. After Rivers's first-inning single, he yielded just three more hits: a leadoff single by Mason in the sixth, a one-out single by Gamble in the seventh, and a two-out single by Gamble in the ninth. Only in the seventh, when Nettles followed Gamble's single with a walk, did the Yanks get two runners on in the same inning.

The last time New York had been shut out on Opening Day was 1961, when Pedro Ramos of the Twins beat them, 6–0. Yet, as traveling secretary Bill Kane prophetically said after the game, the Yankees did go on to win the pennant that year. They would again this year, but would have to climb from last place to do it. Because the Yanks and Brewers were opening a day earlier than the other American League clubs, the standings after today's game showed Milwaukee in first place and New York in last. Those positions would be reversed at season's end.

Slaton pitched another shutout in his next start, against the Detroit Tigers, on his way to a 14–15 season, decent enough for a team that finished in last place. For Hunter, who started openers for the Oakland A's in 1966, 1968, 1973, and 1974, this was his fourth loss in five opening-day decisions. He had also lost his first start as a Yankee a year ago (not the opener) before going on to win 23 games. Actually, he had lost his first three starts in 1975 and did not get his first win until April 27. Hunter, who was celebrating his 30th birthday today, would win only 17 games this year (17–15), ending his streak of five consecutive 20-win seasons. Barry Bonds would eventually pass Aaron in home runs; Pete Rose and Carl Yastrzemski would pass him in games-played; and Rose would pass him in at-bats. Aaron remains the lifetime leader in runs batted in and extra base hits.

The Yankees (97–62) won the East by 10½ games over the Baltimore Orioles. Then they won the fifth and deciding game of the American League Championship Series against the Kansas City Royals to capture their first pennant since 1964. In the World Series, the

National League champion Cincinnati Reds swept them in four games. Graig Nettles led the league in home runs (32), Roy White scored the most runs (104) and Sparky Lyle had the most saves (23). Thurman Munson, whom back in April Martin had appointed as the team's first captain since Lou Gehrig, batted .302, with 17 home runs and 105 runs-batted-in. He won the Most Valuable Player Award; Mickey Rivers finished third and Chris Chambliss fifth. In their first year back at Yankee Stadium, attendance soared to 2,012,434. Although the Stadium's seating capacity had been greatly reduced, it was the first time the Yankees had drawn more than two million since 1950.

Thursday, April 8, 1976

New York	ab	r	h	rbi	Milwaukee	ab	r	h	rbi
Rivers cf	4	0	1	0	Moore lf	3	1	0	0
White lf	3	0	0	0	Thomas cf	0	0	0	0
Munson dh	4	0	0	0	Money 3b	4	1	2	0
Chambliss 1b	4	0	0	0	Scott 1b	3	1	0	0
Gamble rf	4	0	2	0	Porter c	3	2	1	1
Nettles 3b	3	0	0	0	Aaron dh	3	0	2	3
Randolph 2b	2	0	0	0	ªBevacqua	0	0	0	0
Dempsey c	3	0	0	0	Lezcano cf,lf	4	0	1	0
Mason ss	3	0	1	0	Sharp rf	4	0	1	1
Total	30	0	4	0	Yount ss	3	0	0	0
					Garcia 2b	3	0	0	0
					Total	30	5	7	5

ªRan for Aaron in eighth inning.

```
New York     000    000    000–0
Milwaukee    320    000    00X–5
```

Error—Mason. Caught stealing—By Dempsey (Money). Left on bases—New York 6; Milwaukee 6. Put outs—New York 24: Randolph 4, Nettles 1, Rivers 3, Chambliss 8, Mason 1, White 3, Dempsey 4. Milwaukee 27: Garcia 2, Yount 3, Scott 11, Sharp 4, Lezcano 1, Slaton 1, Moore 3, Porter 1, Money 1. Assists—New York 10: Randolph 2, Nettles 2, Mason 4, Dempsey 2. Milwaukee 12: Garcia 4, Yount 3, Scott 1, Slaton 3, Money 1. Two-base hits—Money, Porter. Stolen base—Rivers. Sacrifice—Yount.

	IP	H	R	ER	BB	SO
NEW YORK						
Hunter (L, 0–1)	7.0	7	5	5	3	2
Lyle	1.0	0	0	0	1	2
MILWAUKEE						
Slaton (W, 1–0)	9.0	4	0	0	3	1

Passed ball—Porter.

Umpires—Goetz, Maloney, McKean, and Bremigan. Time of game—2:09. Attendance—44,868.

Thursday, April 7, 1977
Yankee Stadium, New York
New York 3 Milwaukee 0

Of all the affections which attend human life, the love of glory is the most ardent.—Sir Richard Steele

Yankee heroes were everywhere when the American League champions opened the 1977 season with a 3–0 shutout of the Milwaukee Brewers. Catfish Hunter pitched a masterful seven innings before an injury forced him to leave the game, and Sparky Lyle came on for the final two innings to preserve the shutout. There was newcomer Jim Wynn, whose mammoth second-inning home run got the Yankees their first run of the year. Nonetheless, putting the worthy contributions of Hunter, Lyle, and Wynn aside, this Opening Day belonged to Reggie Jackson. Making his Yankees' debut, the flamboyant Jackson thrilled a raucous, rambunctious crowd of 43,785 at Yankee Stadium with his skills at the plate, on the bases, and even in the field. Additionally, the win pleased everyone connected with the Yankees, although in reality they were happy just to see the new season begin. This had been a turbulent, chaotic off-season for the organization. In the five-and-a-half months since getting swept in the World Series, the Yanks had been through holdouts by Lyle, Chris Chambliss, and Roy White, bitter accusations against them by Mickey Rivers and Dock Ellis, and threats of departure from Graig Nettles. The discord had continued into spring training when George Steinbrenner, who had a limited understanding of baseball, and manager Billy Martin, clashed over the importance of winning exhibition games.

That was the negative side of the off-season. There also had been a positive side, as Steinbrenner spent a great deal of money trying to fulfill his promise to bring an "All-Star" team to New York. Taking advantage of the newly created free-agent reentry draft, Steinbrenner signed the Cincinnati Reds' fine young left-hander, Don Gullett, and Jackson, the most highly prized of all the free agents. Jackson had played for the Baltimore Orioles in 1976, after A's owner Charlie Finley traded him there following nine years in Oakland. The trade was completed just before the start of the season, and Jackson immediately became unpopular in Baltimore by holding out. Eventually he signed and had a solid year; he hit 27 home runs and his .502 slugging percentage led the league. However, when the Orioles refused to meet his salary demand for 1977 (he was asking for $250,000) Jackson became a free agent and the Yankees grabbed him. On the positive side, too, was the club's relatively injury-free training camp. The only player seriously hurt was Ron Blomberg, who tore cartilage in his left knee running into a wall in a game at Winter Haven, Florida. Blomberg had played only one game in 1976 because of a damaged shoulder, and now because of his knee injury, the Yanks expected him to miss the first two months of this season. As it turned out, the one game Blomberg played in '76 was his last in a Yankees uniform. He did not play at all in 1977, and following the season he signed as a free agent with the White Sox.

At the start of spring training, the Yanks felt they were weak at only one position—shortstop. Fred Stanley had played there most of the previous season after taking over for Jim Mason. But Stanley was a poor hitter, and Martin was not content to go into the season with him as an everyday player. He saw a possible solution in rookie Mickey Klutts, up from the Syracuse Chiefs of the International League. Klutts had batted .319, with 24 home runs and 80 RBI's in 1976, and the Yankees were hoping he would play well enough during the exhibition season to displace Stanley. However, Klutts broke a finger on early in spring training, and the club spent the entire spring trying to trade for a shortstop. Two days before the opener, they finally got one, obtaining 25-year-old Bucky Dent from the Chicago White Sox. To get Dent, among the best young shortstops in the league, they sent Oscar Gamble, minor league pitchers LaMarr Hoyt and Bob Polinsky, and $200,000 to Chicago. The consensus throughout baseball was that this team of outstanding players, with their big salaries and big egos, was the best that money could buy and should win the pennant—especially since the American League had spread the talent even thinner by adding two new teams, the Toronto Blue Jays and the Seattle Mariners. Still, no one expected the Yankees' road to victory would be smooth—not with a volatile mix of players, an interfering owner, and an unstable manager.

This would be the first true Opening Day at Yankee Stadium since 1970. The renovated Stadium had opened a year earlier, but the Yanks began that season in Milwaukee. Clearly, something had been lost in the transition from old to new; the new Stadium lacked the majesty and splendor of its predecessor, but still it was an exquisite ballpark. And with the flags and bunting, the autumn-like weather, and the exuberance of the crowd, there was even that World Series atmosphere so reminiscent of the old Stadium. Perhaps it was the influence of attending games at Shea Stadium for two years, or maybe just part of the general deterioration in common courtesy, but when public address announcer Bob Sheppard introduced the Brewers before the game, the crowd booed them all except Sal Bando. They made an exception for the former Oakland star, whom Milwaukee had signed as a free agent, and greeted him warmly. After presenting the visitors, Sheppard began his introduction of the Yankees. He got no further than "And now ladies and gentlemen, the defending—" before the roar of the crowd made it impossible to hear anything that came after. The loud and prolonged cheering for the home team made a strong impression on the Brewers. Bando and Milwaukee's starting pitcher, Bill Travers, later marveled at the level of support Yankees fans gave their players. "You're almost a forgotten entity in this park if you're not a Yankee," Bando said.

The pre-game activities, which were the most festive in recent years, included an unusual prayer by Reverend William Kalaidjian, a Congregational minister and New York City Police Department chaplain. In his invocation, Reverend Kalaidjian asked God, "We pray this year that from your great heaven we receive the world championship." Evidently not everyone believed that Steinbrenner had done enough to guarantee the Yankees a successful season. Mayor Abraham Beame, who would be the host of a post-game Welcome Home party for the team at Gracie Mansion, was at the game but would not be throwing out the first ball. Marketing manager Barry Landers had come up with the idea of giving the honor to "a typical Yankee fan," and it was Landers who selected Vince Pallitto, as the West Orange, New Jersey, hairdresser was passing through the turnstiles. Pallitto, who was there with his wife and two sons, had already paid $24 for four tickets, $1.50 for the toll on the George Washington Bridge, and $3.00 to park his car. However, he was glad to exchange his seats for the ones near the home team dugout Landers provided. Pallitto said he saw nothing unusual in the "typical Yankee fan" being a resident of New Jersey. He suspected that more Yankee fans lived there than in New York. That was highly unlikely, at least then, but it was the type of comment that would eventually threaten the Yankees' continued existence in the Bronx. When it came time to throw out the first ball, Pallitto strode to the mound and made his toss to the league's Most Valuable Player, catcher Thurman Munson. To complete the New Jersey theme of the day, the Westwood (NJ) High School Band entertained the crowd. In a break with tradition, they played *America the Beautiful* to start the game, instead of *The Star-Spangled Banner*.

Hunter had made five starts against the Brewers in 1976, winning three and losing two. One loss had come in the opener at Milwaukee when the Brewers took advantage of a rare streak of wildness to score five runs in the first two innings. They won that game, 5–0, but Hunter was a much different pitcher today. He permitted the Brewers only three hits and walked no one in his seven innings of work. Martin removed him only because Von Joshua's sixth-inning line drive had struck Hunter on the instep of his left foot, and the injury was becoming increasingly painful. Milwaukee manager Alex Grammas was opening with Travers, a six-foot-four left-hander, only because Jim Slaton, who beat Hunter in the opener a year ago, had the flu. Travers had been among the league's best pitchers in the first half of 1976, with a 10–6 record and a 1.91 ERA. Then, after the All-Star game (for which he was selected but did not play) he suffered a serious illness and fell off badly, finishing the year 15–16. He did win two of his five decisions against the Yankees, which gave him a lifetime 4–5 record against New York.

The fans did not have to wait long for the season's first dramatic confrontation. It came in the first inning when Travers faced Jackson with two runners on and two men out. Three of the first four Yankees had reached base safely. Rivers opened with a single to center but was out on an attempted steal. Then, after White popped to Bando, Munson walked and Chambliss singled him to second. The large crowd cheered as Jackson, wearing No. 44, stepped in for his first at-bat as a Yankee. He had worn No. 20 in spring training, but switched to 44 to honor the just retired Hank Aaron. From the moment he made his first appearance, Jackson was clearly the focus of attention from both the media and the fans. Being a player who relished the spotlight, he seemed inspired by the crowd's enthusiastic reception. He fouled off the first two pitches, and after Travers wasted one, lined another pitch foul. On Travers's next delivery, he flied easily to Joshua in center.

Unlike Jackson, Wynn, the designated hitter, made his first Yankees' at-bat a memorable one. The Yanks had purchased Wynn from the Atlanta Braves on November 30, the day after they signed Jackson, and therefore his arrival received little notice. But, with one out in the second, he connected on Travers's 2–1 fastball, sending it over the fence in straightaway center field. In the Stadium's former configuration, the drive—estimated at 450 feet—probably would have landed among the monuments. It was the 291st home run of Wynn's career, and also the last. The Yankees released him in July (he was batting .143) and although the Brewers signed him, 1977 would be his final big-league season.

Jackson got his first hit as a Yankee in the fourth, when he led off with a single to left. With Nettles at the plate, Martin signaled for the hit-and-run. Jackson took off for second base as Nettles looped a short fly into center field. After hesitating momentarily at second to make sure that nobody would catch the ball, Jackson went into third base with a headfirst slide, losing his cap in the process. The crowd was on its feet cheering. After Wynn popped out to shortstop Robin Yount, Martin called for the suicide squeeze. Willie Randolph executed the bunt perfectly as Jackson, running on the pitch, slid home past catcher Charlie Moore, again losing his cap. At that moment, there was not a fan in Yankee Stadium who did not believe Reggie was worth every cent of his multiyear $3.5 million dollar contract. Jackson, who had often played before meager crowds in Oakland, and whose flashiness blue-collar Baltimoreans failed to appreciate, was basking in his newfound glory. He even heard the cheers of the fans while in the field, specifically in the top of the third inning when he dove unsuccessfully for a double by Joshua. Jackson's fielding would not always earn such plaudits. Later in the season, in a June game at Boston, Martin accused him of not hustling on a fly ball, pulled him out of the game, and the two came close to a fistfight in the Yankees dugout. Today, however, Jackson could do no wrong. He scored the Yankees' third run in the sixth after leading off with a single and eventually coming home on a wild pitch. As he approached the plate to lead off the eighth, a chant of "Reggie, Reggie" began from the seats behind third base and quickly spread throughout the park. Nobody could remember such a thing ever happening at Yankee Stadium, which was more a reflection of the types of crowds now attending games at the Stadium than it was of the quality of the players who had preceded Jackson. "I feel like I've found a home," Jackson said after the game. He concluded his auspicious Yankee debut by grounding out to first baseman Cecil Cooper.

Thursday, April 7, 1977

Milwaukee	ab	r	h	rbi		New York	ab	r	h	rbi
Joshua cf	4	0	3	0		Rivers cf	4	0	2	0
Yount ss	4	0	0	0		White lf	4	0	1	0
Cooper 1b	4	0	1	0		Munson c	3	0	1	0
Bando 3b	4	0	0	0		Chambliss 1b	4	0	1	0
Lezcano rf	4	0	0	0		Jackson rf	4	2	2	0
Money 2b	3	0	1	0		Nettles 3b	4	0	1	0
Quirk dh	2	0	0	0		Wynn dh	3	1	2	1
[a]Brye	1	0	0	0		Randolph 2b	3	0	1	1
Wohlford lf	3	0	0	0		Dent ss	3	0	0	0
Moore c	3	0	0	0		[b]May	1	0	0	0
Total	32	0	5	0		Stanley ss	0	0	0	0
						Total	33	3	11	2

[a]Flied out for Quirk in eighth inning.
[b]Popped out for Dent in eighth inning.

Milwaukee	000	000	000–0
New York	010	101	00X–3

Errors—None. Double play—Yount, Money and Cooper. Caught stealing—By Moore (Rivers). Left on bases—Milwaukee 5; New York 9. Put outs—New York 27: Dent 1, White 5, Munson 6, Chambliss 11, Jackson 3, Rivers 1. Milwaukee 24: Moore 1, Yount 3, Cooper 10, Joshua 2, Money 4, Bando 2, Lezcano 2. Assists—New York 9: Dent 2, Nettles 1, Randolph 3, Hunter 2, Lyle 1. Milwaukee 10: Moore 1, Yount 3, Money 1, Bando 2, Travers 3. Two-base hit—Joshua. Home run—Wynn. Stolen base—Randolph. Sacrifice—Randolph.

	IP	H	R	ER	BB	SO
MILWAUKEE						
Travers (L, 0–1)	7.2	11	3	3	2	1
Castro	.1	0	0	0	0	0
NEW YORK						
Hunter (W, 1–0)	7.0	3	0	0	0	5
Lyle S. 1	2.0	2	0	0	0	0

Wild pitch—Travers.

Umpires—Springstead, Barnett, Evans, and Voltaggio. Time of game—2:16. Attendance—43,785.

While Jackson was executing his heroics, Hunter was sailing through the Brewers' lineup. He retired eight consecutive batters following Joshua's game-opening single, and nine straight after Don Money's single leading off the fifth. Lyle ran the streak to 12 straight with a perfect eighth, but did run into some trouble in the ninth. Joshua opened the Brewer's last chance with an infield single, his third hit of the day. Yount flied to Jackson, but Cooper singled to right, bringing Bando, the potential tying run to the plate. Lyle retired him on a fly to right, but still had to face Sixto Lezcano, another dangerous right-handed hitter. Working carefully, Lyle got Lezcano on a pop to first baseman Chambliss ending the game. Hunter's career-record against Seattle/Milwaukee improved to 20–6; however, the injury to his foot from Joshua's drive put him on the disabled list for a month. He never regained his form and had only nine victories (9–9) for the year.

As expected, rumors of disharmony surrounded the Yankees all season, and several times George Steinbrenner seemed on the verge of firing Billy Martin. Despite all that, the Yanks (100–62) won 40 of their last 53 games, and won the East by two and a-half games over the Baltimore Orioles and the Boston Red Sox. They again defeated the Kansas City Royals in the five-game American League Championship Series to win a second consecutive American League pennant. The Yankees then won their first World Series since 1962, defeating the Los Angeles Dodgers in six games. Sparky Lyle appeared in a league-leading 72 games, then the most ever by a Yankees' pitcher. He won 13 (13–5), saved 26, had an earned run average of 2.17, and became the first American League relief pitcher to win the Cy Young Award.

Saturday, April 8, 1978
Arlington Stadium, Texas
Texas 2 New York 1

Fortune may have yet a better success in reserve for you,
and they who lose today may win tomorrow.—Miguel De Cervantes

A heady sense of confidence gripped Dallas-Fort Worth area baseball fans as the 1978 season began—a confidence that seemed more rooted in reality than the vague optimism usually associated with Opening Day. Folks in this part of Texas felt certain that six months from now their Rangers would supplant this afternoon's visitors from New York as world champions. The 1977 season had been the Rangers best ever, although it had taken four managers to make it so. Frank Lucchesi was first, but he was fired in late June. Then came Eddie Stanky, who managed for one game and quit. After coach Connie Ryan filled in for six games, the Rangers selected Billy Hunter, who led them the rest of the way. Under Hunter, Texas played at a sensational .645 pace (60–33) and finished second in the West to Kansas City. Their 94 wins (94–68) were the most in franchise history, but the Rangers were not content with a second-place finish. During an expensive but productive off-season, they succeeded in bolstering both their pitching and their hitting. Two of those new additions, pitcher Jon Matlack and right fielder Richie Zisk, paid immediate dividends. Matlack pitched a complete game, and Zisk hit a tie-breaking ninth-inning home run as the Rangers came away with a thrilling, 2–1, victory.

Zisk, formerly of the Chicago White Sox, had signed with Texas as a free agent, while Matlack had come from the New York Mets as part of a huge multiplayer trade that also involved the Atlanta Braves and Pittsburgh Pirates. Texas further enriched themselves in that December 8 trade by acquiring Pittsburgh outfielder Al Oliver, who for a decade had been among the National League's most consistent hitters. Of the players leaving the Rangers, only right-hander Bert Blyleven appeared to be a significant loss. Texas also relinquished Gaylord Perry, in a trade with the San Diego Padres, but compensated for the loss of Blyleven and Perry by adding two other right-handed starters, Doc Medich and Ferguson Jenkins.

With all the comings and goings of players in Texas, only one original Ranger remained—third baseman Toby Harrah, who had now played in every one of the team's seven openers. By contrast to the wheeling and dealing in Texas, the Yankees' off-season had been a fairly quiet one. Only three players on the opening-day roster had not spent time with the club previously: pitchers Goose Gossage and Rawley Eastwick, and first base-man Jim Spencer. Veteran pitcher Andy Messersmith was also new, but Messersmith, who pitched well during the spring, hurt his shoulder just before the opener and would miss almost the entire season. The Yankees had made an important change in the front office. Al Rosen was the new president, with Gabe Paul again assuming the presidency of the Cleveland Indians.

From the time the American League announced its 1978 schedule, the Rangers and their fans had been looking forward to this opening three-game series. The Yankees were the world champions, and though they won only ten of their 23 Grapefruit League games played against major league opposition, they were still the team to beat in the American League. By making a strong showing against them, the Rangers could further authenticate their own legitimacy as a pennant contender. With that in mind, a near capacity crowd of 40,078 packed newly expanded Arlington Stadium for the opener. Majority owner Brad Corbett was so confident Texas would be hosting its first World Series, he had added approx-imately 5,400 seats to the park, bringing the capacity to 41,000. The Rangers had prepared for a big crowd; nevertheless, there remained a massive traffic jam in the parking lots and on the roads leading to the park shortly before the scheduled 3:15 p.m. start. A spirited group of spectators made up this rare sellout at Arlington Stadium, and while the weather was not especially warm (for April in Texas), three people had to be treated for heatstroke. The crowd cheered wildly at popular country singer Charley Pride's lively rendition of the national anthem, but greeted Governor Dolph Briscoe with a mixed reception when he threw out the first ball. One of those who applauded the incumbent governor was Ray Hutchison, a potential opponent. Hutchison sat a few rows behind Briscoe, with his wife of three weeks, Kay Bailey Hutchison, a future U.S. Senator. One somber note took place during the pre-game proceedings when the crowd stood for a moment of silence in memory of Dick Risenhoover. The Rangers' radio-TV broadcaster had died of cancer at age 51 that morning.

After Matlack retired the Yankees in order in the first inning, left-hander Ron Guidry took the mound for New York. Guidry was making his first opening-day start, but eventually he would make seven, tying Whitey Ford and Mel Stottlemyre for the most ever by a Yan-kees' pitcher. He had been up briefly with the Yanks in 1975 and '76, appearing in a total of 17 games. Then, in 1977, he blossomed, winning 16 games (16–7) and emerging as the Yankees' best pitcher. Like most of his teammates, Guidry had endured a lackluster spring. He pitched only 15 innings, and while he had 19 strikeouts in those 15 innings, his earned run average was a mediocre 4.80. Based on what he had done in 1977, Guidry was now the ace of the staff, and a most effective pitcher against the Rangers. A year ago, he had defeated Texas twice, 1–0 and 2–1, while holding them to a .118 batting average. The Rangers would have better success today, getting six hits in the first three innings before Guidry settled down. After that, he held them hitless for the next four before leaving for Gossage. The only run Guidry allowed came in the first inning. Leadoff batter Mike Hargrove singled, moved to second on Bert Campaneris's sacrifice, to third on Oliver's single, and scored on Zisk's single. Center fielder Mickey Rivers saved the Yanks from a possible big inning by throwing out Oliver as he tried for third on Zisk's hit.

The Yankees had been remarkably successful against left-handers in 1977. They com-piled a 49–27 record against lefties that included an amazing 26–4 mark against them after July 22. Yet, they could do very little today against left-hander Matlack. Through the first four innings, they had only two base runners: Reggie Jackson, whom Matlack hit leading off the second, and Bucky Dent, who had a two-out single in the third. This was not one of Jackson's better days. After Matlack hit him (on the left hand), catcher Jim Sundberg threw him out attempting to steal. Then, in the ninth, after he led off with a single, Matlack picked him off. While Matlack had his good stuff today, he also benefited from a very brisk wind that kept from one to four long blows (depending on whom you asked) from being home runs. Everyone agreed that Graig Nettles's seventh-inning drive against the right-field wall would have gone out on a less windy day, but Martin felt that there were others, too. "We should have had five runs or more," the Yankees' characteristically ungracious manager said. "The balls that [Willie] Randolph, [Lou] Piniella, Nettles, and [Cliff] Johnson, hit should have been home runs, but the wind kept them in. The wind beat us the ball game."

Piniella's drive in the fifth, which hit off the top of the left field wall for a triple, led to New York's only run. Chris Chambliss, who in 1977 failed to drive in a single run against the Rangers, scored Piniella with an infield hit. An inning later the Yanks seemed on the verge of driving Matlack from the game, but failed to get the needed big hit. They had runners at second and third with one out after Dent and Randolph led off with singles and Rivers sacrificed them over. Rivers, with a .383 average had been the team's best hitter in spring training, while Thurman Munson, the designated hitter and next batter, had been the worst, batting .233 with three runs-batted-in. However, manager Hunter, knowing that Munson was a much better hitter when the game was on the line, ordered Matlack to walk him intentionally. The Yankees were in excellent position; they had the bases loaded and two extremely dangerous hitters, Jackson and Piniella, coming up. Matlack was equal to the challenge. He got Jackson to hit a high pop that got caught up in the wind, but shortstop Campaneris stayed with it for the second out. Piniella followed with another long drive to left, but this time Oliver ran it down for out number three.

Guidry, who had not pitched more than five innings during spring training, told Martin before the seventh inning began that he thought it should be his last. Martin had Sparky Lyle, last year's Cy Young Award winner available, but chose to bring in Gossage to pitch the eighth. Gossage, signed as free agent from the Pirates, quickly fanned Hargrove and got Campaneris on a fly to right. Oliver got on with a single off Dent's glove, but when he tried to steal second, catcher Johnson's throw to Randolph nailed him. Johnson, not noted for his defensive ability, had earlier thrown out Campaneris when he attempted to steal second.

Matlack suffered cramping in his left forearm after retiring the Yanks in the eighth, but informed Hunter he was able to pitch the ninth. After getting the first out (the pick off of Jackson who had singled), he walked Piniella. Hunter went to the mound intending to bring in right-hander Len Barker who was warming in the bullpen, but Matlack assured his manager that he felt fine and wanted to continue. Hunter acquiesced, but later said that had there been a tenth inning, Barker would have been the pitcher. Matlack got Johnson and Chambliss on fly balls and the game remained tied at 1–1.

The first batter to face Gossage in the Rangers' ninth was Zisk, left at the plate when Oliver was caught stealing for the third out in the eighth. Zisk, who had 30 home runs and 101 RBI's with the White Sox in 1977, had struggled in his first spring with Texas, batting a disappointing .138 with just two home runs. Oddly, these two future millionaires, Gossage ($2,748,000 for six years) and Zisk ($2,955,000 for ten years) had once been traded for each other. That was in December 1976 when Zisk and pitcher Silvio Martinez went from Pittsburgh to the White Sox for Gossage and pitcher Terry Forster. Gossage quickly got ahead, no balls and two strikes, as Zisk swung and missed on a slider and then fouled off a fastball. His next pitch was intended to be a waste pitch, but Gossage made it too good. Zisk connected with the waist-high slider and hit a low line drive into the left field seats. It may have been the most exciting finish in Rangers' history and the jubilant fans reacted accordingly. So did Zisk. He threw both arms in the air as he rounded first base and by the time he reached home plate the entire Rangers' team was there to greet him. "Personally, it was very gratifying for me," Zisk said in the clubhouse. "A lot is expected of me." Meanwhile, Gossage took a philosophical approach: "I can't let this get me down," he said. "I've been around long enough where something like this isn't going to bother me tomorrow."

Happiest of those greeting Zisk at home plate was Matlack who had taken the first step in what would be a fine comeback season. Matlack was coming off his worst year ever, a year in which he had won only seven games, lost 15, and missed close to six weeks with a sore arm. But if the Rangers had been concerned about the condition of Matlack's left arm when they made the trade, today's performance did much to reassure them. Matlack went on to win 15 games (15–13) in 1978, and his 2.27 earned-run-average was second in the league to Guidry's.

In spite of this rousing start, Texas finished in a second-place tie with the California Angels, five games behind the Kansas City Royals. Hunter's failure to win the Division title cost him his job. The Rangers fired him on the next-to-last day of the season and hired Pat Corrales in his place. Guidry, after getting a no-decision in this game, won 13 consecutive games on his way to a 25–3 season—the most spectacular year a Yankees' pitcher has ever had. Gossage, the losing pitcher, finished with ten wins (10–11) and a league-leading 27 saves.

On July 17, the Yankees were in fourth place, 14 games behind the Boston Red Sox. One week later, owner George Steinbrenner fired Billy Martin, who had been feuding with both him and Reggie Jackson. After one game under Dick Howser, Bob Lemon took over and led the Yankees to the greatest comeback in American League history. They went 47–20 under Lemon to tie the Red Sox (99–63) for first place. Then they defeated Boston in a one-game playoff at Fenway Park to win the Eastern Division title. For the third consecutive year, the Yanks defeated the Kansas City Royals in the League Championship Series, this time in four games. They lost the first two games of the World Series to the Los Angeles Dodgers, but won the next four to win their second straight Series. Lemon, who had managed the Chicago White Sox earlier in the season, became the first manager ever to take over a team in mid-season and lead it to a World Series title. Guidry led the American League in wins (25), winning percentage (.893), earned run average (1.74), and shutouts (9). The .893 winning percentage is the highest in major league history for a pitcher with at least twenty wins. His nine shutouts tied the league record for a left-hander set by Babe Ruth in 1916. Guidry's 248 strikeouts were second to Nolan Ryan (260), but broke Jack Chesbro's Yankee record of 239 set in 1904 and remains the most ever by a Yankees' pitcher. He was the unanimous winner of the Cy Young Award and finished a close second to Boston's Jim Rice as the league's Most Valuable Player.

Saturday, April 8, 1978

New York	ab	r	h	rbi	Texas	ab	r	h	rbi
Randolph 2b	4	0	1	0	Hargrove 1b	3	1	2	0
Rivers cf	3	0	0	0	Campaneris ss	2	0	0	0
Munson dh	3	0	0	0	Oliver lf	4	0	2	0
Jackson rf	3	0	1	0	Zisk rf	4	1	3	2

New York	ab	r	h	rbi
Piniella lf	3	1	1	0
Johnson c	4	0	0	0
Chambliss lf	4	0	2	1
Nettles 3b	3	0	1	0
Dent ss	3	0	2	0
Total	30	1	8	1

Texas	ab	r	h	rbi
Harrah 3b	3	0	0	0
Bevacqua dh	3	0	0	0
Beniquez cf	3	0	0	0
Wills 2b	2	0	1	0
Sundberg c	3	0	0	0
Total	27	2	8	2

*Nobody out when winning run scored

New York	000	010	000–1
Texas	100	000	001–2

Error—Rivers. Double play—Wills, Campaneris and Hargrove. Caught stealing—By Sundberg 2 (Jackson, 2); By Johnson 2 (Campaneris, Oliver). Left on bases—New York 6; Texas 5. Put outs—New York 24: Guidry 1, Randolph 5, Nettles 2, Rivers 1, Johnson 3, Chambliss 8, Jackson 4. Texas 27: Beniquez 2, Oliver 4, Campaneris 2, Wills 5, Hargrove 7, Sundberg 6, Harrah 1. Assists—New York 13: Guidry 2, Randolph 1, Nettles 4, Rivers 1, Johnson 2, Dent 3. Texas 14: Oliver 1, Campaneris 6, Wills 1, Matlack 2, Hargrove 1, Sundberg 2, Harrah 1. Three-base hit—Piniella. Home run—Zisk. Sacrifices—Campaneris 2, Rivers.

	IP	H	R	ER	BB	SO
NEW YORK						
Guidry	7.0	6	1	1	2	2
*Gossage (L, 0–1)	1.0	2	1	1	0	1
TEXAS						
Matlack (W, 1–0)	9.0	8	1	1	2	6

*Pitched to one batter in ninth inning.

Hit by pitch—By Matlack (Jackson).
Umpires—Springstead, Barnett, Evans and Merrill. Time of game—2:11. Attendance—40,078.

Thursday, April 5, 1979
Yankee Stadium, New York
Milwaukee 5 New York 1

On Opening Day the world is all future, no past.—Lou Boudreau

Midway through the Yankees' 1979 season-opener with Milwaukee, Ron Guidry was pitching a perfect game. He had retired the Brewers in order through the first five innings, and the fans at Yankee Stadium were abuzz with the possibilities. There had been only one opening-day no-hitter in the major leagues, Bob Feller's back in 1940, and there had never been an opening-day perfect game. Nor, as it turned out, would there be one today. For after retiring Robin Yount, leading off the sixth, it all came crashing down on Guidry: the perfect game, the no-hitter, the shutout, and even the victory. Gorman Thomas broke the spell with a single to left, and before the inning was over the Brewers had driven Guidry from the mound, scored four runs, and were on their way to a, 5–1, win. Milwaukee's attack on Guidry, and the sudden loss of both the no-hitter and the lead, stunned the crowd of 52,719 at the Stadium, the largest crowd for a Yankees home opener since 1946. Bob Sheppard's announcement of Guidry's name during the pregame player introductions had generated thunderous applause, and as the sensational left-hander retired each successive Milwaukee batter the decibel level increased. But in Mike Caldwell, who went the distance for Milwaukee, the Yankees were up against the league's toughest pitcher for them to beat. It was Caldwell who had ended Guidry's season-opening 13-game winning streak last year with a, 6–0, victory on July 7—one of the three shutouts he pitched against the Yanks in 1978. His earned run average for rhe season against New York was 0.99.

Because of recently begun construction activity on a Bronx segment of the Major Deegan Expressway, the traffic problems for those fans driving to the stadium were even worse than usual. The project, which was expected to last at least two years, involved removing and replacing all the roadway concrete between 138th Street and 167th Street. Once the fans reached the Stadium, those approaching certain entrances had to pass through a picket line, one that included American League umpires Al Clark and Marty Springstead. All the major league umpires were on strike over what they felt was insufficient compensation, and substitute umpires were replacing them until they settled the dispute. (The strike would be settled on May 15.) As a safety precaution, New York City had 130 police officers on duty outside the Stadium; however, the only problems the police had were those created by the heavy traffic. Just about everything at Yankee Stadium, from ticket-prices to food, would cost a little more in 1979 as the expense of attending a baseball game continued its upward spiral. Box seats had gone up 50 cents, to $7, and reserved seats up 25 cents, to $5.25. The price of general admission ($2.50) and bleacher seats ($1.50) were unchanged, but the parking fee was now $3, and the price of a scorecard had increased to 75 cents.

George Steinbrenner had thoughtfully invited the two great voices of New York baseball—Mel Allen and Red Barber—to return to Yankee Stadium and raise the large red-and-white flag symbolizing the Yankees' 1978 World Series victory. Standing near the plaques and monuments to the great Yankees of the past, Allen and Barber, both without topcoats in the 53-degree weather, jointly raised the club's 22nd championship banner. Also present as guests of the Yankees were ten survivors of a reconnaissance patrol that played an important role in the 1944 Battle of the Bulge. As part of the tribute to these lesser-known American heroes, the Yanks awarded one of them the honor of throwing out the first ball. As Mayor Ed Koch, New York governor Hugh Carey, and New Jersey governor Brendan Byrne applauded her, Lucille James, the widow of a soldier who did not survive, made the toss to Thurman Munson and then kissed the Yankees' catcher on his cheek. Team captain Munson also got a pregame hug from Mrs. Lou Gehrig, wife of the former Yankees' captain. Robert Merrill, as usual, sang the national anthem.

Last summer, at Old-Timers Day, Steinbrenner had announced that Billy Martin, fired less than a week earlier, would be back to lead the team in 1980, which was still a year away. Meanwhile, Steinbrenner expected Bob Lemon, his current manager, to provide him with nothing less than another championship this year. To that end, he and team president Al Rosen had spent the winter bringing even more talent to the defending champions. They signed free agent pitchers Luis Tiant from the Boston Red Sox and Tommy John from the Los Angeles Dodgers, and engineered a five-for-five trade with the Texas Rangers. A disgruntled Sparky Lyle went to Texas, with the Yankees getting outfielder Juan Beniquez and left-hander Dave Righetti, the best pitcher in the Rangers' farm system, in return.

While the Yanks and Red Sox were engaged in their great 1978 pennant struggle, rookie manager George Bamberger had quietly led Milwaukee to its first winning season ever (93–69), and a very respectable third-place finish. The Brewers had strengthened their pitching during the off-season, trading for Reggie Cleveland and reacquiring free-agent Jim Slaton, and were now considered the Yankees' strongest challenger. However, their success would depend on another successful season by Caldwell. Under the tutelage of Bamberger, a former Baltimore Orioles' pitching coach, the veteran left-hander won the American League's 1978 Comeback Player of the Year Award and finished second to Guidry in the Cy Young Award voting. Caldwell's task would be a little easier this afternoon because of the absence of veterans Reggie Jackson and Lou Piniella from the Yankees lineup. Jackson was still battling a stomach virus, and Piniella was home in Tampa, Florida, with his wife who had recently given birth to their third child. Lemon replaced them with Paul Blair in right field and Roy White in left. White, a quietly efficient player, was beginning his 15th and final major league season, all with the Yankees. At his retirement, he ranked in the Yankees' top ten in games, at-bats, runs, hits, doubles, and stolen bases.

The Yanks got right after Caldwell. Their first three batters, Mickey Rivers, Willie Randolph, and Munson each singled, although only Randolph hit the ball hard. With the bases loaded and nobody out, the Yankees had Caldwell in deep trouble, but failed to press their advantage. They allowed him to escape with just one run, which scored on designated hitter Cliff Johnson's sacrifice fly. Caldwell got out of the inning by retiring Chris Chambliss and Graig Nettles, and held the Yanks to just four more hits and no further scoring the rest of the way. "I got psyched up when they ran the World Series flag up," Caldwell said later in explaining his dominating performance.

Meanwhile, Guidry, whose earned run average in the Grapefruit League was a bloated 6.65, was mowing down the Milwaukee hitters with regularity. Normally, his slider was his most effective pitch, but today he was getting the hitters out using mostly fastballs. He needed just 40 pitches to get through the first five innings, only ten of which were not strikes. The fans had given Guidry a standing ovation when he retired Sal Bando to end the fifth, and were roaring again when he faced Yount leading off the sixth. Yount took the count to three-and-two before lining out to shortstop Bucky Dent. But Thomas followed by lining a full-count fastball to left for Milwaukee's first hit. After the perfunctory booing of Thomas, the crowd again rose, applauding and cheering Guidry's valiant effort. Charlie Moore was next, and Guidry, perhaps upset at losing the no-hitter, walked him, again on a 3–2 pitch. Then he walked designated hitter Paul Molitor to load the bases. Guidry's sudden control problems were a result of his sudden loss of ability to keep his pitches down in the strike zone. He was consistently wild-high, and missing by enough that although a substitute umpire (Al Forman, a former National League umpire) was behind the plate, neither Guidry nor new pitching coach Tom Morgan complained about the calls.

Don Money put the Brewers ahead with a single to left that scored Thomas and Moore. "I was looking for a fast ball," Money said after the game. "If it was a slider, I would have let it go. But it was a fast ball right down the middle." Cecil Cooper's ground ball single to right brought Molitor home with the third run, and after Larry Hisle flied out, Sixto Lezcano singled to center scoring Money and extending the Brewers' lead to 4–1. That was all for Guidry, who had gone through the entire 1978 season without ever allowing more than three runs in any one inning. Guidry left to another standing ovation, as right-hander Dick Tidrow took his place on the mound. Tidrow got Bando for the third out, but was touched for Milwaukee's fifth run in the seventh on a single by Yount, a sacrifice by Thomas, and a single by Moore. Goose Gossage pitched a scoreless ninth.

After failing to capitalize on their first-inning rally, the Yankees had just two singles against Caldwell from the second to the sixth. They excited the crowd in the home seventh when Chambliss and Nettles led off with back-to-back singles to right. White tried to bunt his way on, but got credit for a sacrifice when Caldwell fielded his bunt and threw him out. The Yanks had two runners in scoring position but Caldwell kept them there. He got Blair on a grounder to third, the runners holding, and Dent, the Most Valuable Player of last year's World Series, on a comebacker to the mound. Caldwell had no more trouble in the final two innings of this speedily played game that took just two minutes more than two hours to complete. From there, he went on to have another outstanding season, winning 16 games (16–6) and a .727 winning percentage that was second best in the American League. The Brewers won 95 games but fell short, finishing in second place, eight games behind the Orioles.

For Guidry, it was a rare loss, only his fifth since August 10, 1977, making his record since that date an astounding 33–5. He seemed to take it in stride. "It's a long season," he said in the Yankee clubhouse. "I'm sure I'll win one or two. Now I don't have to wait until July 7 to lose the first one."

Four of the players that Lemon used in the opener, and Lemon himself, would be gone before the season ended. The Yanks traded Rivers, Johnson, and Tidrow, and tragically lost Munson in a plane crash. The Yankees' captain died on August 2 while trying to land his plane at an airport in Canton, Ohio. Steinbrenner fired Lemon in mid-June, and replaced him with Martin, although Martin was not supposed to return until the start of the 1980 season. Then, after Martin got involved in an off-season barroom brawl, Steinbrenner named Dick Howser to be the manager in 1980. The owner's revolving-manager policy was getting into full swing.

Following three successive pennants, the Yankees (89–71) under Bob Lemon (34–31) and Billy Martin (55–40), dropped to fourth place 13½ games behind the Baltimore Orioles. Ron Guidry, while not as spectacular as he had been in 1978, nevertheless won 18 games (18–8) and for the second consecutive year compiled the league's best earned run average (2.78). He had 201 strikeouts, again second to Nolan Ryan, and finished third in voting for the Cy Young Award. Tommy John, in his first year as a Yankee, finished second to the winner, Baltimore's Mike Flanagan. John was second in the league in wins (21–9), earned run average (2.97), innings pitched (276⅓), and complete games (17). Ron Davis, pitching only in relief, had a 14–2 record and a league-leading .875 winning percentage. The Yankees drew 2,537,765, breaking their all-time attendance record.

Thursday, April 5, 1979

Milwaukee	ab	r	h	rbi	New York	ab	r	h	rbi
Molitor dh	3	1	0	0	Rivers cf	4	1	1	0
Money 2b	4	1	1	2	Randolph 2b	4	0	1	0
Cooper 1b	4	0	1	1	Munson c	4	0	1	0
Hisle lf	4	0	0	0	Johnson dh	3	0	0	1
Lezcano rf	4	0	1	1	Chambliss 1b	4	0	1	0
Bando 3b	3	0	0	0	Nettles 3b	4	0	2	0
Yount ss	3	1	1	0	White lf	3	0	0	0
Thomas cf	3	1	1	0	Blair rf	3	0	0	0
Moore c	3	1	1	1	Dent ss	3	0	1	0
Total	31	5	6	5	Total	32	1	7	1

```
Milwaukee    000    004    100–5
New York     100    000    000–1
```

Error—Cooper. Double play—Money, Yount, and Cooper. Left on bases—Milwaukee 4; New York 6. Put outs—New York 27: Randolph 3, Dent 2, Blair 4, White 2, Munson 6, Chambliss 9, Rivers 1.

Milwaukee 27: Yount 5, Hisle 3, Cooper 12, Thomas 4, Lezcano 3. Assists—New York 11: Dent 4, Nettles 1, Tidrow 1, Randolph 4, Gossage 1. Milwaukee 13: Caldwell 2, Yount 4, Money 5, Bando 2. Sacrifices—Thomas, Yount, White. Sacrifice fly—Johnson.

	IP	H	R	ER	BB	SO
MILWAUKEE						
Caldwell (W, 1–0)	9.0	7	1	1	0	0
NEW YORK						
Guidry (L, 0–1)	5.2	4	4	4	2	3
Tidrow	2.1	2	1	1	0	1
Gossage	1.0	0	0	0	1	1

Umpires—Forman, Spenn, Dunne and Lazar. Time of game—2:02. Attendance—52,719.

IX

1980–1989

The New York Yankees won more games than any other major-league team in the 1980s, yet for the first time since the period before 1920, they went through a decade without winning a World Series. The Yankees won division titles in 1980 and 1981, but only one pennant (1981), a year split into two half-seasons as the result of 60 days lost due to a players' strike. The labor unrest that started during the 1970s continued throughout the 1980s and would culminate in the devastating strike of 1994–1995. Moreover, the owner-player battles and escalating salaries began to affect the way longtime baseball fans looked at the game.

George Steinbrenner used nine different men in making 12 managerial changes during the decade. Billy Martin was hired for a third, fourth, and fifth time, and in only five years was the Yankees' opening-day manager still there at the end of the season. Steinbrenner's behavior often put the Yankees in the unfamiliar position of being a baseball "laughingstock" and reversed a 60-year tradition of making the Yanks the team of choice for most players. He was able to bring stars like Dave Winfield, Don Baylor, Bob Watson, Rickey Henderson, and Ken Griffey Sr. to New York, but many others refused to play there. And of those that did, several were unhappy playing for Steinbrenner and expressed relief at leaving.

There were some bright spots. Ron Guidry, Tommy John, Dave Righetti, and Goose Gossage provided outstanding pitching, and first baseman Don Mattingly came along to take his place with previous Yankee greats. The club set its all-time home-attendance record in 1980 and then broke it in 1988.

Thursday, April 10, 1980 (N)
Arlington Stadium, Texas
Texas 1 New York 0 (12 Innings)

The worst is yet to come.—Alfred, Lord Tennyson

To the dismay of baseball fans everywhere, the 1980 season joined the growing list of seasons tarnished by the now familiar rancor and acrimony between players and owners. In 1980, as it had so often in the 1970s, labor-management struggles dominated the news throughout spring training. Fans attempting to follow the progress of their teams in Florida and Arizona read less about promising rookies and returning veterans than about disagreements relating to salaries and free agency. The conflict resulted in the cancellation of the

306

last eight days of training camp and the loss of 92 exhibition games. As the players disappeared from view, the fans were left to watch Marvin Miller for the players and Ray Grebey for the owners argue the merits of their clients' cases. Eventually, Miller and Grebey reached a temporary agreement that allowed the regular season to begin on time. The fans, as they always did when Opening Day arrives, overlooked all the unpleasant bickering and concentrated on baseball. However, while the fans forgave and forgot, the players did not. They warned that unless the owners consented to their demands by May 22, they would strike.

The Yankees, in their first night opener ever, began the season with a third consecutive opening-day loss. Playing at Texas, the Yanks bowed to the Rangers, 1–0, in a 12-inning thriller that was their longest opener—by innings—in 70 years. Texas's Jon Matlack and New York's Ron Guidry treated the 33,196 spectators at Arlington Stadium to a classic pitching duel. Both left after nine innings, but relievers kept the game scoreless for two more innings. The Rangers finally scored the game's only run with one out in the last of the 12th when ex–Yankee Mickey Rivers scored on a Goose Gossage wild pitch. Another former Yankee, Sparky Lyle, got the win while new Yankee Tom Underwood took the loss. Although Matlack and Guidry, both of who pitched superlative games, were not around for the finish, the two left-handers later jokingly vowed never to pitch against each other in an opener again. They had faced each other on Opening Day here two years ago in a game that Texas won, 2–1. That one ended dramatically, with Gossage pitching to Richie Zisk—and oddly, so would this one. Zisk ended the 1978 opener with a leadoff ninth-inning home run, but today he never got the bat off his shoulder. Gossage's first pitch to him—his first pitch after entering the game—was wild, allowing Rivers to score from third base with the game-winner.

Matlack had been on the disabled list for much of the 1979 season, winning only five games (5–4), which made today's effort particularly welcome to manager Pat Corrales and the Texas organization. Following postseason surgery to remove bone chips and spurs from his left elbow, Matlack had been outstanding this spring. He pitched 27 innings with a 1.17 ERA; nevertheless, the Rangers believed the true test of his recovery would begin tonight. Without him the Rangers finished third in 1979, but only five games off the lead. They hoped that with a healthy Matlack and the addition of veteran Rusty Staub to their lineup they could overtake the two teams that finished ahead of them—the California Angels and Kansas City Royals. Corrales had resigned himself to Matlack being a seven-inning pitcher, at least for the early part of the season, and specifically for the opener. Yet when the seventh inning ended and Matlack, who had not thrown many pitches, was working on a shutout, Corrales allowed him to continue. After nine, he had still thrown only 103 pitches; nevertheless, Corrales brought in Jim Kern to pitch the tenth.

Guidry too came out after nine, as Dick Howser, the Yankees' new manager, chose not to risk overworking his best pitcher. Most of the Yankees had remained in Florida during the strike, but Guidry received permission to work out on his own from Howser, general manager Gene Michael, and pitching coach Stan Williams. He did so at his home in Lafayette, Louisiana, arriving in Arlington a day before the opener after driving from Lafayette with his father. Guidry had faced the Rangers seven times in his career and had a 6–0 record against them; only in that 1978 opener had he not come away with a win. His earned run average against Texas was a phenomenal 1.29, and the Rangers combined batting average against him was just .207.

Before the game, Clayton Moore, who once played the Lone Ranger on television and in the movies, rode around the field on a white horse entertaining fans and players alike.

Because of a dispute over "ownership" of this fictitious character, a judge had barred Moore from wearing his famous black mask, so he wore Foster Grant wraparound sunglasses instead. Singer Kelly Garrett offered a pleasant rendition of "The Star-Spangled Banner," and former Rangers owner Brad Corbett threw out the first ball. (Corbett had sold the team in March to a group headed by Eddie Chiles of Fort Worth.)

Manager Howser had taken over a team that had more uncertainty about it than any Yankee club of recent years. Reggie Jackson, Graig Nettles, Lou Piniella, and Tommy John, players who would have to have good years for the Yanks to win, were all well into their 30s. Furthermore, the club would play this season without three men who had been team leaders both on the field and in the clubhouse: Thurman Munson was dead, Catfish Hunter had retired, and Chris Chambliss was in Toronto. The trade of Chambliss to the Blue Jays had fetched Underwood, along with catcher Rick Cerone, who would replace Munson. To take Chambliss's place at first base, they signed Bob Watson, a free agent from the Boston Red Sox. Left-hander Rudy May, traded to the Baltimore Orioles in a ten-player deal four years earlier, had returned to New York via free agency from the Montreal Expos. The Yankees had also acquired outfielder Ruppert Jones (from the Seattle Mariners) and third baseman Eric Soderholm (from Texas), both of whom were in the starting lineup. Besides Jones, the center fielder, and Soderholm, the designated hitter, first baseman Watson and catcher Cerone were also playing their first games in a Yankees uniform.

Two of the three hits the Yanks would get against Matlack came in the first inning. With two men out, Watson and Jackson singled. Watson made it to third on Jackson's hit, but Matlack got Piniella on a fly to right for the third out. In the fourth, Watson got a leadoff single to center and reached second on Jim Sundberg's passed ball. However, neither Jackson, Piniella, nor Soderholm could deliver him. From the fourth inning through the ninth, it was three-up and three-down as Matlack retired the last 18 batters and 25 of the last 26.

Most fans like high-scoring games with lots of hitting, but for the minority who love great pitching, this was a game to savor. As good as Matlack was, Guidry was better. Neither pitcher issued a walk, but while Matlack allowed three hits, Guidry allowed only two, both to Sundberg. He retired the last 12 Rangers and in his nine innings faced only two batters above the minimum 27. While his record against Texas remained at 6–0, he reduced his earned run average against them to 1.11, and their batting average against him slipped to a paltry .189.

Kern came on for Texas in the tenth, and after getting Jackson, put the next two men on base. Both were pinch hitters as Howser went to his bench for left-handed hitters against the right-hander Kern. Oscar Gamble, batting for Piniella, got on when Kern hit him with a change-up, and Jim Spencer, batting for Soderholm, drew a walk. With Nettles—another left-handed hitter—up next, Corrales, playing the percentages, removed Kern and brought in Lyle. Kern had been among the best relief pitchers in the league in 1979, while Lyle had been a major disappointment to the Rangers. However, this time Lyle made Corrales look good by striking out Nettles and getting Cerone on a force play grounder to third. When the Yankees took the field in the bottom of the tenth, Underwood, another left-hander, was on the mound. Had Rudy May not been on the disabled list, it is likely that he would have been Guidry's replacement. But since May was not due back for another two weeks, Underwood was getting his opportunity—and he made the most of it. He looked very strong in retiring three dangerous hitters—Al Oliver, Buddy Bell, and Zisk—in order. Then he got the first two batters in the 11th before Sundberg doubled for his third hit of the game.

Sundberg was the potential winning run, but Staub, batting for shortstop Pepe Frias, stranded him by grounding to Randolph. New York got a runner into scoring position with two out in the 12th, but Spencer popped out to second baseman Bump Wills.

Gossage was warmed and ready in the bullpen as Texas came to bat in the bottom of the 12th; however, Howser elected to stay with Underwood. Rivers opened the inning with a sharply hit grounder to third. Nettles knocked it down, but conscious of Rivers's speed he made a hurried off-balance throw to first. The ball got by Watson, as Rivers steamed into second. The error was the second of the game for Nettles, although the official scorer could easily have charged him with a third on Sundberg's third-inning single. Wills moved the winning run to third base with a sacrifice bunt that Watson handled unassisted. Howser ordered Underwood to walk Oliver and Bell, loading the bases and setting up the possibility of a double play or a force at home. Then he brought Gossage in to pitch to Zisk, the designated hitter.

Gossage had missed two months of the 1979 season after suffering a thumb injury in a clubhouse fight with Cliff Johnson. Still, he led the club with 18 saves and was clearly the pitcher Howser wanted in this kind of situation. After taking his warmup pitches and getting the sign, Gossage threw his first pitch—and suddenly the game was over. His fastball, low and away, hit off Cerone's glove and continued to the backstop as Rivers trotted home easily. Although it was scored a wild pitch, Cerone blamed himself for not stopping the ball after he had gotten his glove on it. "I should have caught the ball," he said. "I got my glove on it. I tried to backhand it. It was a tough pitch, but I'm a major-league catcher and I should have caught it." Gossage disagreed, saying, "The ball got away from me. I don't know what else to say. It's just one of those things." However, Gossage and Cerone did agree that it was a disadvantage to have worked together for only one inning because of this year's shortened spring training.

The Rangers' win stretched their opening-day winning streak to five, but it was not to presage a good year for Texas. Kern and Lyle had terrible seasons, which doomed the Rangers to a fourth-place finish, nine games below .500 and 20½ games behind the Royals. After the season's last game, the Rangers fired Corrales and signed Don Zimmer to manage the team in 1981. For the Yankees, the loss was the ninth in their last 11 openers and the seventh straight loss on the road. They had not won an away opener since Mel Stottlemyre's victory at Washington in 1969. There was no player strike during the 1980 season. The owners and players came to an agreement that permitted the entire season to be played without interruption. However, there were some issues that remained unresolved that would surface with disastrous results in 1981.

Thursday, April 10, 1980

New York	ab	r	h	rbi		Texas	ab	r	h	rbi
Randolph 2b	5	0	0	0		Rivers cf	5	1	1	0
Jones cf	5	0	0	0		Wills 2b	4	0	0	0
Watson 1b	5	0	3	0		Oliver rf	4	0	0	0
Jackson rf	5	0	1	0		Bell 3b	4	0	0	0
Piniella lf	3	0	0	0		Zisk dh	4	0	0	0
aGamble lf	1	0	0	0		Ellis 1b	3	0	0	0
Soderholm dh	3	0	0	0		Putnam 1b	1	0	0	0
bSpencer dh	1	0	0	0		Sample lf	4	0	0	0
Nettles 3b	4	0	0	0		Sundberg c	4	0	3	0

New York	ab	r	h	rbi		Texas	ab	r	h	rbi
Cerone c	4	0	0	0		Frias ss	3	0	0	0
Dent ss	4	0	0	0		ᶜStaub	1	0	0	0
Total	40	0	4	0		Norman ss	0	0	0	0
						Total	37	1	4	0

*One out when winning run scored.
ᵃHit by pitch for Piniella in tenth inning.
ᵇWalked for Soderholm in tenth inning.
ᶜGrounded out for Frias in eleventh inning.

New York	000	000	000	000–0
Texas	000	000	000	001–1

Errors—Nettles 2. Double play—Randolph and Watson. Left on bases—New York 6; Texas 5. Put outs—New York 34: Cerone 6, Watson 15, Guidry 1, Dent 1, Randolph 4, Jones 4, Nettles 1, Jackson 2. Texas 36: Oliver 4, Bell 2, Wills 2, Ellis 6, Putnam 4, Sundberg 9, Sample 3, Matlack 2, Frias 2, Rivers 2. Assists—New York 15: Randolph 6, Watson 1, Nettles 4, Dent 4. Texas 10: Ellis 1, Bell 5, Frias 2, Wills 2. Two-base hit—Sundberg. Sacrifice—Wills.

	IP	H	R	ER	BB	SO
NEW YORK						
Guidry	9.0	2	0	0	0	4
Underwood (L, 0–1)	2.1	2	1	1	2	1
#Gossage	0.0	0	0	0	0	0
TEXAS						
Matlack	9.0	3	0	0	0	5
Kern	.1	0	0	0	1	0
Lyle (W, 1–0)	2.2	1	0	0	0	3

#Pitched to one batter in twelfth inning.

Hit by pitch—By Kern (Gamble). Wild pitch—Gossage. Passed ball—Sundberg. Umpires—Springstead, Brinkman, Bremigan, and Merrill. Time of game—2 hrs. 39 min. Attendance—33,196.

Dick Howser led the Yankees (103–59) to their fourth Eastern Division title in five years, by three games over the Baltimore Orioles. New York's 103 wins were the most in either league. However, after having beaten Kansas City three straight times in the ALCS in 1976, 1977, and 1978, the Yanks lost to the Royals, who won the pennant in a three-game sweep. Reggie Jackson had his most productive season as a Yankee. He batted .300, with 111 RBIs, and his 41 home runs tied the Milwaukee Brewers' Ben Oglivie for the most in the American League. Rudy May led the league with a 2.46 earned run average, and Goose Gossage tied Kansas City's Dan Quisenberry for the most saves (33). Jackson and Gossage finished second and third in the Most Valuable Player voting behind the winner, George Brett. The Yanks' home attendance climbed to 2,627,417, breaking their team record established a year earlier and the league record established by the Cleveland Indians in 1948. They also drew 2,452,240 on the road, breaking the major-league record in that department. Nevertheless, despite the record-breaking attendance and winning the most games in either league, owner George Steinbrenner was upset at the loss to Kansas City and pressured manager Howser to resign.

Thursday, April 9, 1981
Yankee Stadium, New York
New York 10 Texas 3

I awoke one morning and found myself famous. —Lord Byron

Like all American institutions, the "national pastime" had not survived the iconoclasm and anti-intellectualism of the late 60s and early 70s unscathed. Along with the more serious charges of being racist and sexist (at a time when these words still had meaning), critics claimed that baseball lacked action; that it was "too slow" to attract younger fans. They said that football, a violent game that did not require much thought from its fans and was more easily adaptable to television, would soon replace baseball as America's favorite game. But baseball had been through this before, and as it always had, the game resuscitated itself. The thrilling 1975 World Series between the Boston Red Sox and the Cincinnati Reds seemed to revitalize fan interest, which had been growing ever since. The abilities and personalities of a new generation of players contributed to increased popularity and rising attendance, and it seemed everyone connected with the game was making lots of money. Yet despite the soaring revenues, or perhaps because of them, the ongoing conflict between owners' "rights" and players' "freedoms" intensified. Both sides had put off the question of free agent compensation in 1980 so they could start the season on schedule; but when they failed to reach a resolution by June of 1981, the players called for a strike. It was an action that the average American found extremely difficult to understand—or sympathize with. Driven by free agency, the average major-league salary had risen to $193,000, far higher than the salaries earned by all but a handful of fans.

The results of the strike were extremely destructive, not only for the 1981 season but for the disillusionment it fostered in millions of baseball lovers. There was a 60-day stoppage of play, canceling 712 games and resulting in the first major-league split season since 1892. First- and second-half winners led to an extra tier of playoff games and a mostly unsatisfying postseason. Everybody concerned lost money because of the strike: owners, players, the many businesses that depended on baseball, and the people working in those businesses. The Yankees missed 55 games, with the 30 at Yankee Stadium responsible for a revenue loss estimated at $7.1 million. While their insurance policies would allow most teams to eventually recoup their financial losses, it would take some fans a long time to "forgive" baseball. Some never would.

The strike interrupted what had been to that point an excellent season for the Yankees. It had begun splendidly, with some old heroes and one new one, leading them to an opening-day 10–3 victory over the Texas Rangers. Playing before 55,123 cheering fans, the largest crowd ever to see an opener at the new Yankee Stadium, Dave Winfield's splendid debut (two singles and two walks) and home runs by veteran Yankees' Bucky Dent and Bobby Murcer backed the steady pitching of 37-year-old Tommy John. Winfield was especially pleased to get that first game behind him after a Grapefruit League season in which he hit just .212 with no home runs. Asked later if he could now relax, Winfield said: "Can't relax around here. Today there was excitement. I wanted to do well and look good. All I did was try my best and things worked out." Before signing as a free agent with the Yankees, Winfield had played for eight years with the National League's San Diego Padres. Playing in the relative obscurity of San Diego, he had never gotten the recognition he deserved as one of the game's best players. But now that he was in New York, lack of recognition would no longer be a problem. After signing a ten-year, $21 million contract that made him the game's highest-paid player, the six-foot-six slugger was the new "favorite" of the local media. Winfield got a small taste of what that meant when hordes of reporters and photographers besieged him as he took pregame batting practice. Although Winfield was one of eight players on the Yankees' opening-day roster who had not been with the club in 1980, only he and center fielder Jerry Mumphrey were in the starting lineup. Mumphrey was the newest Yankee, having come over ten days earlier from San Diego, along with pitcher John Pacella. Ruppert Jones and three youngsters—outfielder Joe Lefebvre and pitchers Tim Lollar and Chris Welsh—went to the Padres.

Texas was supplying the opening-day opposition for the third time in four years, and for the third time a different pair of managers was opposing each other. In 1978 it had been Billy Hunter for Texas and Billy Martin for New York, and last year Pat Corrales led the Rangers and Dick Howser led the Yankees. Corrales and Howser now were gone, replaced by Don Zimmer in Texas and Gene Michael in New York. Zimmer, after four and a half years of managing the Red Sox, was trying to bring Texas its first American League pennant. Michael, the former Yankees' shortstop and general manager, got the job when Howser found working for owner George Steinbrenner unbearable. The two previous Yankees-Rangers openers had been well-pitched contests between Texas's Jon Matlack and New York's Ron Guidry. Both games were in Texas, with the Rangers winning each time in their final at-bat. Zimmer was staying with Matlack, but Michael was opening with John, who had led the club in wins the last two years, going 21–9 in 1979 and 22–9 in 1980.

Cheryl Howard and Elston Howard Jr., children of the late Yankees catcher Elston Howard, played major roles in the opening ceremonies. Cheryl sang the national anthem and Elston Jr., from the mound, threw out the first ball to catcher Rick Cerone. Howard, who broke the Yankees' color line in 1955 and went on to win the American League's Most Valuable Player Award in 1963, had died of heart failure in December 1980. A light rain that began as the U.S. Marine Drum and Bugle Corps played during the pregame activities continued into the game's early innings. Texas took the lead in the second when Billy Sample, after being hit by a pitch, reached second on a walk, third on a wild pitch, and scored on an infield single by Jim Sundberg. Dent's homer in the bottom of the second, with Graig Nettles and designated hitter Dennis Werth aboard, put the Yanks ahead, 3–1. The ball, which just cleared the fence in left and landed in the second row, undoubtedly evoked unpleasant memories for Zimmer. It was Dent's three-run blast in the 1978 playoff game that had snatched the pennant away from Zimmer's Red Sox. The three second-inning runs were one more than the Yankees' offense had gotten in their last three openers combined.

An error by Mumphrey led to Texas scoring an unearned run in the third, making it a one-run game at 3–2. Mumphrey let Bump Wills's leadoff single get by him, allowing Wills to go to second. Mickey Rivers's grounder to second baseman Willie Randolph moved Wills to third, and Al Oliver's grounder to shortstop Dent scored him. Mumphrey came back to lead off the home third with an infield single, and one out later he stole second. After Bob Watson walked and Lou Piniella forced Mumphrey at third for the second out, Cerone brought Watson and Piniella home with a double to left to put the Yankees ahead, 5–2. A Rangers' run in the fifth had reduced the lead to 5–3 as the Yanks came to bat in the seventh. Right-hander Steve Comer, who relieved Matlack an inning earlier following two-out singles by Dent and Randolph, was pitching. Comer escaped that threat by getting Mumphrey on a fly ball to Johnny Grubb, but in the seventh the Yankees pounded him for five runs. Winfield, Watson, and Piniella, the first three batters, each singled to produce one run. After Cerone's sacrifice bunt moved Watson to third and Piniella to second, Comer walked Nettles intentionally to load the bases. Werth, a right-handed hitter, was the due batter, but, as expected, Michael went to his bench for a left-handed hitter. Oscar Gamble seemed the obvious choice, or even Jim Spencer, but Michael chose neither. Instead he made his first pinch-hitting selection one to remember by choosing Murcer, back for his second tour with the Yankees. Michael later explained that he preferred to keep Gamble and Spencer in reserve for possible use later.

The Yankees once believed that Murcer would be the heir to Mickey Mantle, just as Mantle had been the heir to Joe DiMaggio. Their expectations had been too high for Murcer, who never achieved that exalted level. Nevertheless, he did have some excellent years in New York before the Yanks traded him to the San Francisco Giants for Bobby Bonds in October 1974. After two seasons with the Giants, he moved on to the Chicago Cubs before returning to the Yankees in June 1979. Murcer, now 34, had not hit well during the exhibition season, which jeopardized his chances of making the club. He was on the opening-day roster only because the Yankees were forced to put Reggie Jackson on the disabled list with a torn tendon in his right calf. Like everyone else in the Stadium, Murcer assumed that Gamble would be batting for Werth, so he still had his jacket on when Michael motioned for him to go up to hit. When the crowd spotted him removing his jacket and heading for the bat rack, they responded with a standing ovation. Murcer, waiting patiently, ran the count full before smashing a Comer fastball beyond the 353-foot sign in right field for the sixth grand slam of his career. Because he was extremely popular with both the fans and his teammates, Murcer's blast set off a jubilant celebration in the stands and in the Yankees dugout. In the clubhouse after the game, Murcer, sitting in his rocking chair, said: "When I came out the fans were a little more jubilant than I anticipated. It was the inspiration I needed; it got me going. It was like they cared I was here. I cared that I was here." Randolph followed Murcer's home run with a triple, which led Zimmer to yank Comer for Charlie Hough, who got the third out. The game was now safely out of reach, but Michael allowed John to pitch another inning. He came out after the eighth, having allowed only seven hits and two earned runs. Tom Underwood, whom the Yanks would trade to Oakland in May, set the Rangers down in the ninth. The win was the 215th of John's career and raised his lifetime record against Washington/Texas to 11–9. Matlack, the loser, got off poorly in '81, dropped out of the starting rotation, and finished with a 4–7 record. Despite his ineffectiveness today, Comer replaced Jim Kern as the Rangers' best relief pitcher, winning eight (8–2) and saving six.

Thursday, April 9, 1981

Texas	ab	r	h	rbi	New York	ab	r	h	rbi
Wills 2b	5	1	1	0	Randolph 2b	4	0	2	0
Rivers cf	4	1	0	0	Mumphrey cf	5	0	1	0
Oliver dh	5	0	1	1	Winfield lf	3	1	2	0
Bell 3b	5	0	2	0	Watson 1b	4	2	2	0
Sample lf	2	1	0	1	Piniella rf	4	2	2	1
Grubb rf	3	0	1	0	Cerone c	4	0	1	2
Putnam 1b	4	0	2	0	Nettles 3b	4	2	0	0
Sundberg c	3	0	1	1	Werth dh	2	1	0	0
Mendoza ss	2	0	0	0	aMurcer	1	1	1	4
bEllis	1	0	0	0	Dent ss	4	1	3	3
Wagner ss	0	0	0	0	Total	35	10	14	10
Total	34	3	8	3					

aHomered for Werth in seventh inning.
bFlied out for Mendoza in eighth inning.

Texas	011	010	000–3
New York	032	000	50X–10

Error—Mumphrey. Double play—Putnam (unassisted). Caught stealing—by Sundberg (Dent). Left on bases—Texas 10; New York 9. Put outs—New York 27: Piniella 6, Randolph 2, Dent 1, Mumphrey 6, Winfield 1, Cerone 2, Watson 8, Nettles 1. Texas 24: Putnam 5, Rivers 3, Bell 2, Grubb 4, Sundberg 3, Wills 5, Mendoza 2. Assists—New York 11: Randolph 5, Dent 2, John 1, Nettles 3. Texas 12: Bell 4, Sundberg 1, Wills 2, Putnam 1, Rivers 1, Mendoza 3. Two-base hits—Piniella, Grubb, Cerone. Three-base hit—Randolph. Home runs—Dent, Murcer. Stolen base—Mumphrey. Sacrifice—Cerone. Sacrifice fly—Sample.

	IP	H	R	ER	BB	SO
TEXAS						
Matlack (L, 0–1)	5.2	8	5	5	4	2
Comer	1.0	5	5	5	1	0
Hough	1.1	1	0	0	2	1
NEW YORK						
John (W, 1–0)	8.0	7	3	2	4	2
Underwood	1.0	1	0	0	0	0

Hit by pitch—by John (Sample). Wild pitches—John (2). Umpires—Phillips, Neudecker, McCoy, and Merrill. Time of game—2 hrs. 48 min. Attendance—55,123.

On June 12, the day the strike went into effect, the Yankees had a two-game lead over the Baltimore Orioles. When they finally settled it, the leagues instituted a format that divided the season into halves, with the winner of each half moving on to the playoffs. The Yankees and the other prestrike leaders were retroactively declared the winners of the first half. However, when the Yanks struggled in the second half, won by the Milwaukee Brewers, Steinbrenner fired Michael and again called on Bob Lemon to manage the team.

The Yankees finished with a combined 59–48 record, consisting of a 34–22 first-place finish in the first half, and a 25–26 sixth-place finish in the second half. After beating the Milwaukee Brewers three games to two in the East Divisional Series, the Yanks swept the American League Championship Series from Billy Martin's Oakland A's in three games. After winning the first two games of the World Series, they lost the next four to the National League champion Los Angeles Dodgers. Newcomers Dave Winfield (.294, 13 home runs, 68 runs batted in) and Jerry Mumphrey (.307, six home runs, 32 runs batted in) were the team's leading hitters of the shortened season, while Ron Guidry (11–5) and Tommy John (9–8) were the biggest winners. Rookie of the Year Dave Righetti made a big contribution after he came up from the Columbus Clippers of the International League—where he had been 5–0—with an 8–4 record and an earned run average of 2.06.

Sunday, April 11, 1982
Yankee Stadium, New York
Chicago 7 New York 6 (12 Innings)

It was a Sunday afternoon, wet and cheerless.—Thomas De Quincey

On the morning of April 6, 1982, Opening Day at Yankee Stadium, New York City lay under a foot of snow. The surprise spring blizzard disrupted the entire metropolitan area and, of course, canceled the Yankees' season opener with the Texas Rangers. So much snow and ice covered the field that the club was forced to cancel both games scheduled with the Rangers and the first two games of a series against the Chicago White Sox. It took head groundskeeper Jimmy Esposito and his crew five days of hard, tedious work to melt the snow and remove it from the field and the stands. By April 11, Easter Sunday, the stadium was ready and the Yanks and White Sox, the only teams yet to play in 1982, finally began their seasons. To make up for one of the games missed with Chicago, the Yankees scheduled a doubleheader for Opening Day; it was their first-ever opener against the White Sox and the first time they would play both games of an opening-day doubleheader. (The Yanks were supposed to play a doubleheader on Opening Day 1972 at Baltimore, but rain wiped out the second game.)

As part of the pregame ceremonies, the club showed its gratitude for the ground crew's outstanding work. They brought 16 members of the crew to the mound, where they watched as their boss, Esposito, threw out the first ball. The 31,008 fans in the stadium also displayed their appreciation for Esposito and his crew by giving them a standing ovation. The crowd was far below that of recent Opening Days at the Stadium, many of which had been sellouts. Not even the opportunity to see a doubleheader—a treat that had all but vanished from the big leagues—could induce more fans to spend their Easter Sunday at Yankee Stadium. While the bleachers were full, primarily with younger people, vast patches of empty blue seats were visible in other parts of the stadium. Springtime weather in New York is notoriously erratic, and Tuesday's raging snowstorm was already a memory. This Easter morning, amid strong winds that would menace the hats and bonnets of paraders along Fifth Avenue, it was 52 degrees and the sun was shining. However, as the afternoon progressed into early evening the temperature dropped steadily. In the fifth inning it drizzled briefly and the sun disappeared, and by the seventh it had gotten so cloudy they turned on the lights. The weather grew more dismal with each passing inning, and when Chicago won both games, the first 7–6 in 12 innings and the second 2–0, it capped a terrible day for Yankees fans.

Among the inducements for this afternoon's doubleheader was the opportunity to get a first look at the Yankees' ten new players. George Steinbrenner had pushed ahead with his plan to revamp the offense by subtracting power and adding speed. The names identifying the Yankees since Babe Ruth joined them more than 60 years earlier, names like "Murderer's Row," the "Bronx Bombers," and "Five o'clock lightning," all had signified power. Yet Steinbrenner thought he had a better idea for 1982. His major subtraction was Reggie Jackson. After five years in New York, Jackson was again a free agent, but Steinbrenner did not seriously attempt to re-sign him. Jackson signed instead with the California Angels, and the Yanks added two speedy former Cincinnati outfielders, Ken Griffey (in a trade for two minor-leaguers) and Dave Collins (as a free agent) to replace him. And while they could not have known it then, the club traded away a youngster who would develop into the type of player Steinbrenner seemed to have in mind. In a little-noted deal, the Yankees sent minor-league outfielder Willie McGee to the St. Louis Cardinals for left-handed pitcher Bob Sykes. McGee, a speedster, would go on to win two batting championships and a Most Valuable Player Award with the Cardinals, while Sykes never again pitched in the major leagues. In a pair of spring training trades, the Yanks reacquired veteran pitchers Doyle Alexander (from the San Francisco Giants) and added Shane Rawley from the Seattle Mariners, while losing young pitchers Bill Caudill, Andy McGaffigan, and Gene Nelson.

Just one day before the rescheduled opener, the club sent relief specialist Ron Davis to the Minnesota Twins for shortstop Roy Smalley. Manager Bob Lemon said he planned to use the switch-hitting Smalley against right-handed pitchers and occasionally to spell

Graig Nettles at third. Smalley's arrival upset incumbent shortstop Bucky Dent. However, when Dent protested at being platooned, the Yanks pointed out that since he had been with them his average against right-handed pitchers was a lowly .216. Still, Dent feared that Smalley's arrival meant that his stay in New York would soon be over. It was. In August, with Dent batting .169, the Yanks traded him to the Texas Rangers for Lee Mazzilli.

Because of the strike in 1981, the White Sox played only 106 games; nevertheless, at 54–52 it was their first winning-season since 1977. Over the winter they had strengthened their offense substantially, which, they believed, made them legitimate pennant contenders. New to Chicago were outfielders Steve Kemp and Rudy Law, infielder Vance Law, and first baseman Tom Paciorek. Also new were their uniforms; the White Sox had changed looks again, something they seemed to do more often than any other major-league team. Since 1976 they had worn a dark blue jersey on the road, sometimes with the same color pants and sometimes with white pants. Their new uniform was even less traditional. It featured a red-blue-red stripe on the sleeves and jersey front, with the word *SOX* in white displayed across the blue middle stripe of the jersey.

The first-game pitchers were a pair of veteran left-handers, Ron Guidry for the Yankees and Jerry Koosman for the Sox. Guidry was making his fourth opening-day start, but had yet to win one. Koosman, who at 39 was two years older than his manager Tony LaRussa, had come to Chicago from the Twins last August. His combined 13 losses in strike-shortened 1981— nine with Minnesota (3–9) and four with Chicago (1–4)—tied Juan Berenguer and Luis Leal for the league high. Guidry started by retiring seven Chicago batters in a row before third baseman Jim Morrison's home run to left produced the game's first run. Then, in their half of the third, the Yanks came back to score four runs against Koosman. They quickly loaded the bases on singles by Nettles, Rick Cerone, and Dent. Willie Randolph walked to force Nettles home, and Jerry Mumphrey singled to right to score Cerone. The Yanks now were ahead, 2–1, and had the bases loaded, still with nobody out. However, Koosman, who had been a big-league pitcher since 1967, kept his composure. He got Griffey to hit a ground ball to short that Bill Almon turned into a double play. Dent scored on the play and when Dave Winfield followed with an infield hit, Randolph came home. Despite the rally-killing double play, it had been a productive inning for the Yankees who now led, 4–1.

With Guidry—who had gone 3–0 against Chicago in '81—on the mound, it seemed an imposing lead. But in the very next inning, after their first two batters went down, the White Sox rallied for three runs to tie the game. A single by Paciorek, a walk to catcher Carlton Fisk, and a double by Harold Baines led to one run and base runners at second and third. Here Guidry, unlike Koosman, seemed to lose his composure. He committed a balk, which scored Fisk and sent Baines to third, and on his next delivery he threw a wild pitch that brought Baines home with the tying run. Chicago scored two more in the fifth against right-hander George Frazier to go ahead, 6–4. Almon greeted him with a single and then rode home on Ron LeFlore's triple. LeFlore scored on Tony Bernazard's long sacrifice fly to Mumphrey. Frazier, loser of three games in last year's World Series, was making the first of his team-leading 63 appearances this season, all in relief.

Koosman set the Yanks down in order in the fourth and fifth innings, but began the sixth by walking Griffey. Winfield brought the Yankees even again when he reached for a low outside fastball and hit it just beyond Baines's reach into the seats in right. Two outs later, after Nettles doubled, LaRussa relieved Koosman with right-hander Dennis Lamp, who ended the inning by fanning Cerone on a disputed checked-swing call. Left-hander Rawley made his Yankee debut in the seventh, holding the Sox scoreless before giving way to Goose Gossage with two out in the ninth. Lemon called on his ace with LeFlore at the plate, and Baines, the potential tie-breaking run, at second. Gossage retired LeFlore on a ground ball to Dent, and when the Yanks went out in order in the last of the ninth, the game proceeded into extra innings. Lamp and Gossage breezed through the tenth, but both faced serious threats in the 11th. Chicago had runners at first and second and only one out when Jerry Hairston came up to pinch-hit for Morrison. Hairston lined the ball hard, but it was right at first baseman Dave Revering who snared it and stepped on the bag for an unassisted double play. Griffey got the Yankees' only hit against Lamp when he singled to lead off the last of the 11th. He took second on a rare sacrifice by Winfield. With left-handed hitters Revering and Oscar Gamble due up, LaRussa replaced Lamp with left-hander Kevin Hickey. Hickey fanned Revering, but then Lemon made his own lefty/righty switch, replacing Gamble with the veteran right-hand hitting Lou Piniella. Hickey foiled that bit of strategic maneuvering by walking Piniella intentionally and then striking out Nettles.

Almon, Chicago's number-nine hitter, surprised everyone when he led off the 12th with a booming 400-foot-plus triple to left center, his third hit of the game. "That's as far as I can hit one," confessed Almon about his first career hit against Gossage. Lemon played the infield in, but LeFlore, who also had three hits today, poked a single to left that sent Almon across with what would be the game-winner. Hickey, a former softball player, easily disposed of Cerone, Smalley (batting for Larry Milbourne), and Randolph in the home 12th to nail down his first major-league victory. In the second game, a fine effort by Tommy John went to waste as Britt Burns and Salome Barojas shut out the Yankees on five hits. Midway through the game, the frustrated fans expressed their opinion of the club's purported switch from power to speed with chants of "Reggie, Reggie, Reggie." Steinbrenner had no comment.

Sunday, April 11, 1982 (1G)

Chicago	ab	r	h	rbi	New York	ab	r	h	rbi
LeFlore cf	6	1	3	2	Randolph 2b	4	1	1	1
Bernazard 2b	5	0	1	1	Mumphrey cf	5	0	1	1
Kemp lf	6	0	2	0	Griffey rf	4	1	1	0
Luzinski dh	6	0	0	0	Winfield lf	4	1	2	3
Paciorek 1b	5	1	3	0	Revering 1b	5	0	0	0
cR.Law	0	0	0	0	Watson dh	3	0	0	0
Squires 1b	0	0	0	0	aGamble dh	1	0	0	0
Fisk c	4	1	0	0	ePiniella	0	0	0	0
Baines rf	4	1	2	1	Nettles 3b	5	1	2	0
Morrison 3b	4	1	1	1	Cerone c	5	1	1	0
dHairston	1	0	0	0	Dent ss	3	1	1	0
Rodriguez 3b	0	0	0	0	bCollins	1	0	0	0
Almon ss	5	2	3	0	Milbourne ss	0	0	0	0
Total	46	7	15	5	fSmalley	1	0	0	0
					Total	41	6	9	5

aFlied out for Watson in ninth inning.
bGrounded out for Dent in tenth inning.
cRan for Paciorek in eleventh inning.
dLined into double play for Morrison in eleventh inning.
eWas intentionally walked for Gamble in eleventh inning.
fPopped out for Milbourne in twelfth inning.

Chicago	001	320	000	001–7
New York	004	002	000	000–6

Errors—None. Double plays—Almon, Bernazard, and Paciorek; Almon, Bernazard, and Paciorek; Revering (unassisted). Caught stealing—by Fisk (Randolph); by Cerone 3 (LeFlore, LeFlore, Kemp). Left on bases—Chicago 6; New York 4. Put outs—New York 36: Randolph 3, Griffey 1, Dent 1, Revering 10, Guidry 1, Milbourne 1, Mumphrey 5, Winfield 3, Cerone 11. Chicago 36: Almon 1, Fisk 6, Bernazard 4, Paciorek 14, LeFlore 3, Morrison 1, Baines, 1 Kemp 3, Lamp 1, Squires 2. Assists—New York 12: Randolph 3, Guidry 1, Cerone 2, Frazier 1, Dent 2, Rawley 1, Nettles 2. Chicago 19: Almon 7, Koosman 2, Fisk 1, Lamp 1, Bernazard 5, Paciorek 1, Morrison 2. Two-base hits—Baines, Paciorek, Nettles, Bernazard. Three-base hits—LeFlore, Almon. Home runs—Morrison, Winfield. Stolen base—R. Law. Sacrifice—Winfield. Sacrifice fly—Bernazard.

	IP	H	R	ER	BB	SO
CHICAGO						
Koosman	5.2	8	6	6	2	2
Lamp	4.2	1	0	0	1	2
Hickey (W, 1–0)	1.2	0	0	0	1	2
NEW YORK						
Guidry	4.0	4	4	4	1	5
Frazier	2.0	4	2	2	0	0
Rawley	2.2	3	0	0	0	3
Gossage (L, 0–1)	3.1	4	1	1	1	1

Balk—Guidry. Wild pitch—Guidry. Passed ball—Cerone. Umpires—Springstead, McCoy, Brinkman, and Cousins. Time of game—3 hrs. 24 min. Attendance—31,008.

This would be a season of innumerable roster changes for the Yankees. Before it was a month old, they traded Bob Watson, Milbourne, and Revering in a trio of deals that brought first baseman John Mayberry, catcher Butch Wynegar, and pitcher Roger Erickson to New York. Later that summer, besides trading Dent to Texas, they traded John to the California Angels for pitcher Dennis Rasmussen. These deals, and the seemingly endless shuttle of players back and forth from the Triple A Columbus Clippers, made for a very unsettling season. To add to the confusion, the team had to adjust to playing under three different managers. Fourteen games into the season, Steinbrenner fired Lemon and brought back Gene Michael, the man that Lemon had replaced last September. Then on August 3, following another White Sox doubleheader sweep at the Stadium, Steinbrenner again fired Michael and replaced him with Clyde King. The owner also used the stadium's public address system that day to inform the fans of *his* displeasure with the team.

Playing under three managers for the first time since 1946, the Yankees (79–83) finished fifth, 16 games behind the Milwaukee Brewers. It was the team's lowest finish since 1969 and their worst record since 1967. They were 6–8 under Bob Lemon, 44–42 under Gene Michael, and 29–33 under Clyde King. Dave Winfield had a solid season, batting .280 with 106 runs batted in. His 37 home runs were third best in the league.

Tuesday, April 5, 1983 (N)
Kingdome, Seattle
Seattle 5 New York 4

When I lose a ballgame I can't eat. Sometimes I can hardly sleep.
If you're in love with the game, you can't turn it on and off like a light.—Billy Martin

Billy Martin began his third tour as the Yankees' manager in typical Billy Martin fashion. He snarled at and argued with the umpires all evening, and then blamed them for his team's 5–4 loss to the Seattle Mariners. Martin was returning to New York—where he was very popular with a particular segment of New Yorkers—after three years of managing the Oakland Athletics. (Three years with a team was Martin's usual tenure before he wore out his welcome.) The New York press featured the volatile manager's Kingdome tirades prominently in the next day's newspapers, which is perhaps what George Steinbrenner had in mind when he rehired him. To hear Martin tell it, Steve Henderson, Richie Zisk, and Bill Caudill were not primarily responsible for his team's defeat this night; second-base umpire Dan Morrison was. "If there was a hex tonight," Martin said of Morrison, "he was in blue, he wasn't in white. He had a bad night. Maybe he's a bad umpire." The hex whose influence Martin was denying was the Kingdome, a place where the Yankees had never done well. In their previous 32 games at this indoor arena, which, if not the worst, was among the worst major-league parks ever built, the Yanks had lost 20.

The Mariners entered the season having won a franchise-record 76 games (76–86) in 1982. But their hopes for '83 had suffered a double blow during the off-season when they lost Floyd Bannister, their best pitcher, and Bruce Bochte, one of their best hitters. Bannister, a free agent, went to the Chicago White Sox, and Bochte, though only 32, retired. (In 1984 he would return with the Oakland Athletics.) Nevertheless, manager Rene Lachemann, who led them to last season's fourth-place finish, also a franchise high, remained confident. He predicted Seattle would do better this season, maybe even reach .500 for the first time. Lachemann, who had replaced Maury Wills early in the '81 season, was starting Gaylord Perry, the first right-hander to start an opener against the Yankees in seven years. The 44-year-old Perry, the oldest player in the major leagues, had won his 300th big-league victory against the Yanks here in the Kingdome last May. It was one of his ten 1982 wins (10–12), which raised his lifetime total to 307 (307–251) and tied him with Mickey Welch for 12th place on the all-time list. Perry was making his ninth opening-day start, and in doing so, he became the first major-league pitcher ever to start an opening-day game for five different teams (In 1990, Bert Blyleven would become the second). Perry, who previously pitched openers for the San Francisco Giants, the Cleveland Indians, the Texas Rangers, and the San Diego Padres, had four wins, three losses, and one no-decision on Opening Day. When he was with Cleveland, he had pitched back-to-back openers against the Yankees in 1974 and 1975, losing the first and winning the second. Overall, he had beaten New York 14 times and lost to them 12 during his years in the American League.

Opposing Perry was Ron Guidry, trying for the fifth time to get his first opening-day win. Despite Seattle's terrible record since coming into the league, Guidry had never found them an easy team to beat. It took two wins without a loss in 1982 to raise his career mark against the Mariners to 5–2. Guidry's 14 wins (14–8) in '82 led the club, yet despite a great start, it was not one of his better seasons. He was 8–1 after beating the Boston Red Sox on June 14, but struggled for most of the second half, winning six and losing seven with a 4.47 earned run average. However, he had looked like the old Guidry this spring, winning his only two decisions and compiling a 2.57 earned run average with 13 strikeouts in 16 innings. It had been a good spring (16–8) for many of the Yankees, much to the delight of Steinbrenner, who thought his team should never lose. The Yankees' owner continued to spend money freely, and this season there were two more expensive free agents added to the roster: Don Baylor from the California Angels and Steve Kemp from the White Sox. Both had signed multimillion-dollar five-year contracts, and both were in this evening's starting lineup, Baylor as the designated hitter and Kemp in right field. Ken Griffey Sr., who played right field last season and had been an outfielder throughout his ten-year major-league career, was playing his first major-league game at first base.

The Mariners featured two local children in the pregame ceremonies: seven-year-old Kirsten Ostrom, who sang the national anthem, and eight-year-old Patrick Lopez, who threw out the first ball. Patrick was recovering from leukemia at the Fred Hutchinson Cancer Research Center in Seattle.

Trying to determine baseball's worst owner would be difficult but fans in the Northwest could make a strong case for the Mariners' boss, George Argyros. Since buying the team in 1981, Argyros's reluctance to spend money and his poor personnel decisions made an already shaky franchise even worse. It was bitterness toward Argyros that caused Bochte to leave baseball, because after sitting out a year he would return to play for Oakland in 1984. The Mariners would draw just 813,537 this season, their lowest attendance ever—excepting strike-shortened 1981. Only one other crowd would top the 37,015 that came out this evening (by a few hundred), and many—if not most—of them came for the Beach Boys concert that followed the game. Yet as bad as Argyros and some of his fellow owners were, one could make a strong case that Steinbrenner was worse. His constant publicity seeking and often buffoon-like behavior had severely damaged the universal respect that the Yankees had once commanded. There was a time, not that long ago, when the Yankees were known for conducting their business with pride and distinction and rarely complaining, at least publicly. However, those days were slowly receding from memory. Under Steinbrenner—and Martin when he was the manager—the organization developed a much different reputation. Steinbrenner, who criticized everybody, often targeted the umpires, while Martin appeared to whine about any decision that went against him.

This evening Martin wasted no time in confronting umpire Morrison. After Willie Randolph opened with a base hit and Roy Smalley forced him at second, Dave Winfield singled to left. Smalley went to third easily, but Winfield, trying to make second, was out on Henderson's throw to Cruz. (That was left fielder Steve Henderson to second baseman Julio Cruz; not to be confused with center fielder Dave Henderson and shortstop Todd Cruz who were also in the Mariners' starting lineup.) Martin, claiming that Winfield was safe, got right in Morrison's face, but the 35-year-old umpire stuck to his call. Consequently, when Kemp followed with a single to right, the Yanks went ahead, 1–0, rather than 2–0.

Martin made his next appearance in the third inning. Julio Cruz, who with pitcher Glenn Abbott were the only original Mariners still in Seattle, started the inning with a long fly to left. Winfield went to the wall and jumped but could not reach it, and Cruz had a double. Out came Martin to argue that a fan had leaned over and touched the ball and therefore Cruz should be out because of interference. Again Morrison held to his decision. (Midway through the game, the Yankees announced that they would submit films of the two controversial plays to American League president Lee MacPhail.) After Cruz went to third on Butch Wynegar's passed ball, he scored on Manny Castillo's force-play grounder. Guidry got the next batter, Al Cowens, on a fly to center, but it would be the last out he would get. Zisk, who had a history of hurting the Yankees on Opening Day, did it again by smacking a two-run homer into the left-field seats. Seattle extended the lead to 4–1 when Dave Henderson followed with a single and new first baseman Pat Putnam doubled him home. That was it for Guidry. He had lasted just 2⅔ innings, his quickest opening-day exit ever. Martin called on Roger Erickson, a right-hander whom the Yanks had placed on the roster only two days earlier. Erickson, who said he would retire before returning to the minor leagues, earned the roster spot when Lou Piniella went on the disabled list.

The Yanks drove Perry out in the sixth, getting three runs to tie the score. The runs came on back-to-back home runs by Winfield, who followed Smalley's leadoff single with a home run to left, and Kemp, who hit Perry's next pitch—and his last—into the seats in right. Kemp, who batted .450 in the exhibition season, had singled twice earlier, and would draw a walk in his final at-bat. His perfect day was in sharp contrast to his fellow free agent, Baylor, who went hitless and struck out twice. Roy Thomas, who last pitched in the major leagues with the St. Louis Cardinals in 1980, relieved Perry. He got Baylor to pop out, but after Griffey singled, Lachemann went to his bullpen again. Left-hander Bryan Clark came in and induced Graig Nettles to hit into a double play. Nettles was beginning his 11th and final year in New York, and was the senior Yankee in length of service. Only he, Piniella, and Randolph remained from the team that opened the 1976 season.

Steve Henderson led off the Seattle seventh with a single to right, his third hit of the night. Martin replaced Erickson with George Frazier, and while Frazier was working on Castillo, Henderson stole second. Once again Martin was out to dispute Morrison's ruling, claiming that Henderson had overslid the base. And once again the umpire held his ground against the bullying Yankees' manager. Castillo got Henderson to third by directing a ground ball to second baseman Randolph, and Cowens got him home with a fly to Winfield. It was a manufactured run—single, steal, grounder to the right side, sacrifice fly—and it proved to be the game-winner. Erickson, who put the winning run aboard, took the loss.

Tuesday, April 5, 1983

New York	ab	r	h	rbi		Seattle	ab	r	h	rbi
Randolph 2b	5	0	1	0		S. Henderson lf	3	1	3	0
Smalley ss	4	2	1	0		Moses lf	0	0	0	0
Winfield lf	4	1	2	2		Castillo 3b	3	1	0	1
Kemp rf	3	1	3	2		Cowens rf	3	0	1	1
Baylor dh	3	0	0	0		Zisk dh	4	1	1	2
Griffey 1b	3	0	1	0		D. Henderson cf	4	1	1	0
[a]Robertson	0	0	0	0		Putnam 1b	4	0	2	1
Nettles 3b	4	0	0	0		T. Cruz ss	4	0	0	0
Mumphrey cf	4	0	0	0		Bulling c	3	0	0	0
Wynegar c	3	0	1	0		J. Cruz 2b	3	1	1	0
[b]Gamble	1	0	1	0		Total	31	5	9	5
Total	34	4	10	4						

[a]Ran for Griffey in ninth inning.
[b]Singled for Wynegar in ninth inning.

New York   100   003   000–4
Seattle   004   000   10X–5

Errors—Cowens, Griffey. Double plays—T. Cruz, J. Cruz, and Putnam; J. Cruz, T. Cruz, and Putnam. Caught stealing—by Wynegar (S. Henderson). Left on bases—New York 6; Seattle 5. Put outs—New York 24: Randolph 2, Wynegar 7, Nettles 1, Griffey 8, Mumphrey 3, Winfield 2, Erickson 1. Seattle 27: J. Cruz 2, Putnam 12, Perry 1, Cowens 1, Bulling 6, T. Cruz 3, S. Henderson 2. Assists—New York 13: Guidry 2, Randolph 2, Smalley 3, Wynegar 1, Nettles 3, Griffey 2. Seattle 15: J. Cruz 7, Putnam 1, Castillo 1, Perry 2, T. Cruz 3, S. Henderson 1. Two-base hits—Putnam 2, J. Cruz. Home runs—Zisk, Winfield, Kemp. Stolen base—S. Henderson. Sacrifice fly—Cowens.

	IP	H	R	ER	BB	SO
NEW YORK						
Guidry	2.2	7	4	4	1	4
Erickson (L, 0–1)	3.1	2	1	1	1	1
Frazier	2.0	0	0	0	0	2
SEATTLE						
Perry	5.0	8	4	4	0	2
Thomas	.1	1	0	0	0	0
Clark (W, 1–0)	2.0	0	0	0	0	1
Caudill S.1	1.2	1	0	0	2	3

Perry faced three batters in the sixth inning

Hit by pitch—By Perry (Baylor). Passed balls—Wynegar, Bulling. Umpires—Brinkman, Bremigan, Morrison, and McClelland. Time of game—2 hrs. 53 min. Attendance—37,015.

Clark began the Yankees' eighth by striking out Smalley, but after he did, Lachemann replaced him with Bill Caudill, a free-spirited right-hander. Caudill, one of those players who earned additional money by keeping within club-imposed weight goals, had emerged as the Mariners' stopper in 1982 when he saved a team record 26 games. He would match that mark this year, but save number one did not come easy. He sandwiched a walk to Kemp between a Winfield flyout and a Baylor whiff in the eighth, but then walked Griffey leading off the ninth. Andre Robertson, a young infielder, ran for Griffey. Robertson would soon win the shortstop job from Smalley, but then have to surrender it following an August auto accident. Caudill struck out Nettles and Jerry Mumphrey looking, but Oscar Gamble, batting for Wynegar, singled to center. That sent Robertson to second and kept the Yankees' hopes alive. The cheering Mariners fans were now on their feet and showing rare enthusiasm. Caudill sent them happily into the night and secured the win for Clark by getting Randolph on a game-ending fly ball to Cowens. Caudill, who felt that he still had to prove himself in spite of his excellent 1982 season, later conceded: "It was probably the most pumped up I've been in my life. It's such a big year for us, especially me. I had the year I had last year and all it did was raise questions about my ability."

The hoped-for "big year" in Seattle would have to wait. They would struggle through a terrible season, losing 102 games (60–102) and returning to their accustomed place at the bottom of the Western Division. In late June, following eight straight losses, Argyros fired the popular Lachemann and replaced him with onetime Milwaukee Brewers manager Del Crandall. Before the season was over, the team released or traded Perry, Abbott, Todd Cruz, and Julio Cruz. In November they traded Caudill to Oakland.

Martin continued his out-of-control behavior toward umpires, which led to MacPhail suspending him twice. Throughout the season there were rumors that Steinbrenner would fire him, but Steinbrenner kept him on and instead fired Art Fowler, Martin's pitching coach and longtime drinking buddy. Shortly before Christmas, though, Steinbrenner moved Martin to the front office and hired Yogi Berra for his second go as manager.

In spite of outstanding seasons by Dave Winfield and Ron Guidry, the Yankees (91–71) could do no better than third place, seven games behind the Baltimore Orioles. Don Baylor also had a fine year, but Steve Kemp, his great opener notwithstanding, hit only .241. Bobby Murcer retired in June and the Yanks recalled rookie outfielder/first baseman Don Mattingly from the International League's Columbus Clippers to take his place. Mattingly, who had won the James P. Dawson Award in the Spring, batted .283 in 91 games.

Tuesday, April 3, 1984
Royals Stadium, Kansas City
Kansas City 4 New York 2

Man is a pliable animal, a being who gets accustomed
to everything!—Fyodor Dostoyevski

"Everyone likes to win the opener, start off on the right foot if you can," said manager Yogi Berra after the Yankees' 4–2 opening-day loss at Royals Stadium. Nevertheless, Berra seemed unruffled by the defeat. He made the usual comments about it being a "long season," expressed disappointment that starter Ron Guidry had been unable to get his first opening-day win, and found encouragement in Jay Howell's excellent work in relief. But, of course, Berra—beginning his second tour as manager of the Yankees—had been through it all before. Twenty years earlier, in 1964, he led them to a pennant but lost the World Series in seven games to Johnny Keane's St. Louis Cardinals. After the Series, general manager Ralph Houk fired him and hired Keane. Berra went on to manage the Mets for four years (1972–1975) and since 1976 had been on the Yankees' coaching staff. Now, at age 58, he was again in a position where anything less than a world championship was considered a failure, a predicament he no doubt discussed with Kansas City Royals manager Dick Howser the night before the opener. Berra had dinner with his onetime boss, another casualty of owner George Steinbrenner's "win it all, or else" philosophy. Like Berra, Howser also had managed the Yankees for one season. In 1980 he led the club to the Eastern Division title, but when the Royals swept the Yanks in the ALCS, Steinbrenner forced him to resign. Howser was not out of work for long. He replaced Jim Frey in Kansas City in late 1981 and brought the Royals home second in 1982 and 1983.

Yet in spite of their two consecutive second-place finishes, the Royals were not a very good team. Finishing second in the American League West, baseball's weakest division, was no great accomplishment. Last season's second-place Royals had a losing record (79–83) and lagged 20 games behind the division-winning Chicago White Sox. And now, after a traumatic off-season, 1984 looked to be strictly a rebuilding year. Kansas City had been the big losers in last November's investigation into drug use in baseball. Four of their players were in prison, sentenced to three months each for attempting to buy cocaine. The Royals released or traded three of them: outfielder Jerry Martin, first baseman Willie Mays Aikens, and pitcher Vida Blue. They kept outfielder Willie Wilson, but like the others, he remained suspended until May 15. Also gone was Amos Otis, signed by the Pittsburgh Pirates after 14 years in Kansas City. In all, only ten players remained from the Kansas City team that opened the 1983 season. Pat Sheridan, replacing Wilson in center field, was the Royals' only opening-day outfielder with significant major-league experience. Right fielder Darryl Motley had played in only 61 big-league games before today, and left fielder Butch Davis was a 25-year-old rookie. Nor, except for second baseman Frank White, was there much experience in the Royals' infield. Former Yankees farmhand Steve Balboni, traded here with pitcher Roger Erickson, was at first base replacing Aikens, while on the left side Onix Concepcion was at shortstop and Greg Pryor at third base. Concepcion won the job from U. L. Washington, and Pryor was substituting for George Brett. The All-Star third baseman sustained a knee injury in the final preseason weekend that figured to keep him out of the lineup for up to eight weeks. On the mound for the Royals was Bud

Black, a 26-year-old left-hander, starting his first major-league opener. Black had a career record of 14–13, with only one decision against New York, a loss in August 1982. His catcher was Don Slaught, who earned the start by outhitting Kansas City's other catcher, John Wathan.

While turmoil was new to the Royals, it had become very familiar to the Yankees. Hardly a week passed during the winter (or a day in spring training) when Yankees fans didn't read about some new conflict between owner and player, owner and manager, player and manager, or even player and player. Every season now began with at least one player complaining about his salary or about the way the team was using him. Manager Berra had his own problems. Before he managed his first game, Steinbrenner was already dictating who should play where and when. At one point in the spring, Steinbrenner ordered his new manager to move Ken Griffey Sr. from the outfield back to first base and to play Omar Moreno—acquired from the Houston Astros for Jerry Mumphrey last August—in center field. An unhappy Griffey asked the Yanks to trade him, preferably to the National League. Steinbrenner did not grant Griffey his wish, but he did eventually accommodate shortstop Roy Smalley, who also wanted out, sending him to the White Sox in July. Steinbrenner also had to deal with veteran third baseman Graig Nettles, who was upset at the arrival of Toby Harrah from the Cleveland Indians (in a trade for pitcher George Frazier). Harrah was also a third baseman, and Nettles was unwilling to be a platoon player, even at 39. Three days before the scheduled opener the Yankees traded Nettles to the San Diego Padres for Dennis Rasmussen, a left-handed pitcher who previously had been Yankees property. Nettles's exit was perhaps expedited after Steinbrenner saw an advance copy of his book, *Balls*, which was highly critical of the owner. During his 11 years in New York, Nettles slugged 250 home runs, which at the time placed him sixth on the club's all-time home run list. He trailed only Babe Ruth, Mickey Mantle, Lou Gehrig, Joe DiMaggio, and Berra. Since then Nettles has fallen to tenth place, as Alex Rodriguez, Bernie Williams, Jorge Posada, and Derek Jeter have all passed him.

Frazier's departure and the loss of Goose Gossage—signed as a free agent by the Padres—left a huge hole in the Yankees' relief corps. The off-season addition of another starter, 45-year-old free agent Phil Niekro, solved the dilemma. It allowed Berra to move Dave Righetti out of the rotation and into the bullpen. Steinbrenner opposed the move and so did Righetti, but Berra believed the hard-throwing left-hander was the stopper he needed to replace Gossage.

The opener was to have been played the day before, but rain washed that out. And though today came up crisp and sunny, the forecast of possible snow helped limit the crowd to just 10,006. That was the second-lowest opening-day crowd in Royals history and about 25,000 below what the Royals expected yesterday. Even with the one-day postponement, playing on April 3 was the earliest the Yankees had ever begun a new season. This was the second time they had opened in Kansas City; in 1963 the Yanks beat Charlie Finley's Kansas City Athletics (now the Oakland Athletics), 8–2, at Municipal Stadium. However, this was their first opener at Royals Stadium, a park that opened in 1973 and had the American League's first fully artificial playing surface. Unlike the A's, the Royals were a successful franchise that generally drew well. Kansas City also had the best-behaved fans in the league, a reputation they reinforced by giving polite applause to the Yankees during the pregame introductions. One of those hearing his name announced for the first time in a major-league park was 18-year-old pitcher Jose Rijo, the youngest player in the team's history. But of all the Yankees, only the announcement of Berra stirred much emotion in the fans. They gave Yogi a warm welcome, while perhaps wondering how long he would last in his precarious new position.

The high school drill team scheduled to take part in yesterday's pregame ceremonies was missing today, unable to get another excused absence. However, the 1950s-era pop group The Platters returned this afternoon to sing the national anthem, and so did stage and screen star Yul Brynner, who threw out the first ball. After getting the ball back, Brynner, who was appearing here in a production of *The King and I*, gave the souvenir to Douglas Klais, a 12-year-old boy who played his son on stage. Brynner seemed grateful at being chosen for the first-ball honor. "Baseball is special to me," he said. "When I first came to the United States I learned baseball before I learned English. My first words of English were home run, strike and ball. It was very difficult learning the game before I could speak the language. I love it."

After Black retired the Yankees in order in the first inning, Concepcion delighted the crowd by hitting Guidry's first pitch over the fence in left. It came on a belt-high fastball and was his first major-league home run after 168 games and 439 at-bats. One out later, White doubled. Then, after designated hitter Hal McRae grounded to new Yankees shortstop Tim Foli, Balboni scored White with a single to right. A fourth-inning leadoff triple by Motley—a drive that glanced off left fielder Lou Piniella's glove and hit the wall—led to a third Royals run. Piniella had replaced starter Steve Kemp in the second inning after Kemp aggravated a spring training groin injury. Motley scored on Slaught's sacrifice fly to Dave Winfield.

The Yanks came to bat in the fifth, trailing, 3–0, and still looking for their first base runner. Leadoff batter Don Baylor finally ended Black's streak of consecutive batters retired at 12, when he singled to center. Winfield followed with a home run, the third straight opener in which he had hit a two-run homer. However, a Yankees' error helped the Royals get one of those runs back in the bottom of the fifth. One man was out when White hit a fly ball to deep left center. After a tentative chase, center fielder Moreno dropped the ball, allowing the speedy White to reach third base. The three-base error—Moreno later said he feared running into the wall—quickly turned into a run on McRae's sacrifice fly. Moreno's misplay was the more damaging one, but coincidentally, both he and Griffey—playing the positions chosen for them by Steinbrenner—each made an error in the opener.

After Winfield's home run, Black had walked Harrah but then set down the next nine in a row. Nevertheless, Howser removed him after seven innings and brought in Dan Quisenberry, the league's premier relief pitcher. Quisenberry, with a then major-league record 45 saves in 1983, extended the number of Yankees who had gone down consecutively to 14 by retiring the first five batters he faced. But before Quisenberry could get the final out, Don Mattingly, batting for Piniella, singled. Mattingly, the odd man out in Steinbrenner's spring shuffling, would get the break he needed from Kemp's injury. After the game, Berra announced that during Kemp's absence Mattingly would play left field against right-handers, with Piniella playing against lefties. Baylor, the designated hitter, followed Mattingly's single with a hard smash between short and third, but Concepcion made a great play on the ball. The slick-fielding shortstop, who had taken a hit away from Baylor in the seventh, went into the hole to make a backhanded grab and get the game-ending force at second. Black had the first of his team-leading 17 wins (17–12) and Quisenberry had the first of his league-leading 44 saves. Kansas City, despite the early-season injury to Brett, was on its way to a surprise division title.

Tuesday, April 3, 1984

New York	ab	r	h	rbi	Kansas City	ab	r	h	rbi
Moreno cf	4	0	0	0	Concepcion ss	4	1	1	1
Randolph 2b	4	0	0	0	Davis lf	4	0	0	0
Kemp lf	1	0	0	0	White 2b	4	2	1	0
Piniella lf	2	0	0	0	McRae dh	3	0	1	1
ªMattingly	1	0	1	0	Balboni 1b	4	0	1	1
Baylor dh	4	1	1	0	Motley rf	4	1	1	0
Winfield rf	3	1	1	2	Slaught c	2	0	2	1
Harrah 3b	2	0	0	0	Sheridan cf	3	0	0	0
Griffey 1b	3	0	0	0	Pryor 3b	3	0	2	0
Cerone c	3	0	0	0	Total	31	4	9	4
Foli ss	3	0	0	0					
Total	30	2	3	2					

ªSingled for Piniella in ninth inning.

New York	000	020	000–2
Kansas City	200	110	00X–4

Errors—Moreno, Griffey, Balboni. Double play—Foli and Griffey. Caught stealing—Davis. Left on bases—New York 2; Kansas City 5. Put outs—New York 24: Griffey 8, Kemp 1, Harrah 2, Moreno 1, Cerone 3, Winfield 5, Foli 4. Kansas City 27: Pryor 3, White 3, Balboni 13, Davis 2, Concepcion 1, Slaught 4, Sheridan 1. Assists—New York 8: Randolph 1, Foli 3, Griffey 1, Harrah 2, Howell 1. Kansas City 18: Pryor 3, White 1, Balboni 2, Concepcion 9, Black 3. Two-base hit—White. Three-base hit—Motley. Home runs—Concepcion, Winfield. Sacrifice fly—Slaught, McRae.

	IP	H	R	ER	BB	SO
NEW YORK						
Guidry (L, 0–1)	5.0	8	4	3	0	1
Howell	3.0	1	0	0	0	2
KANSAS CITY						
Black (W, 1–0)	7.0	2	2	2	1	3
Quisenberry S.1	2.0	1	0	0	0	1

Umpires—Barnett, Ford, Kaiser, and Roe. Time of game—2 hrs. Attendance—10,006.

Howell pitched the final three innings for New York, allowing just one hit—a single by Slaught. Nineteen eighty-four would be Howell's finest big-league season; he appeared in 61 games (all but one in relief), winning nine and losing four. Although he had only seven saves, he served as an efficient setup man for Righetti, who, after overcoming his reluctance, became an excellent stopper, responsible for 31 saves.

The loss dropped Guidry's career record to a still-brilliant 122–52, including 10–3 against Kansas City. His opening-day log now read no wins, two losses, and four no-decisions; and the Yanks had lost each of the six openers he started. In previous seasons, Guidry recovered from opening-day disappointments to have excellent seasons, but not in 1984. He would win only ten games (10–11).

The Detroit Tigers got off to a 35–5 start and won the Eastern Division by 15 games over the Toronto Blue Jays. The Yankees (87–75) had a poor first half, but recovered to finish third, 17 games behind. Without a pennant race, attendance dropped to 1,821,815, the first time the Yanks had fallen below 2 million (except for the strike year of 1981) since 1975. Don Mattingly and Dave Winfield battled for the batting championship all season before Mattingly won it on the last day. He was the Yankees' first batting champion since Mickey

Mantle in 1956. Mattingly batted .343 with 23 home runs and 110 runs batted in. He led the league in doubles (44) and hits (207), and finished second in slugging percentage (.537). Winfield had 19 home runs and 100 runs batted in to go with his .340 batting average. Mattingly finished fifth in the voting for the Most Valuable Player Award, won by Detroit reliever Willie Hernandez, who also won the Cy Young Award.

Monday, April 8, 1985
Fenway Park, Boston
Boston 9 New York 2

Tell him his pranks have been too broad to bear with.—William Shakespeare

When they split into two divisions in 1969, the American and National leagues abandoned the long tradition of each team playing every other team in its league the same number of games. Because they now were competing for division titles first, it made sense for teams to play more games against their division rivals than against teams in the other division. While this new schedule lacked the metaphysical pureness of the old system, it seemed a reasonable compromise. This arrangement held until a few years after the American League's expansion to 14 teams in 1977, when some Western Division owners complained they were losing lucrative home dates with the "glamour teams" like the Yankees and the Boston Red Sox. The American League responded by switching to a "balanced schedule," which served to reduce the number of games between the league's traditional rivals. Chief among those suffering reductions was the rivalry between those same Yankees and Red Sox, who now met in only four series a year, two in New York and two in Boston; and the schedule makers usually set their first series in June.

Since the Yankees entered the league in 1903, the Red Sox had been their most frequent opening-day opponent. Yet before today's Boston-New York season opener at Fenway Park, 12 years had passed since the last one, the longest interlude ever. Back in 1973, the Red Sox won, 15–5, in the Yankees' first game under George Steinbrenner's ownership, and the first game played under the American League's new designated hitter rule. At one time, after winning the 1960 opener, the Yanks led the opening-day series, 16–5 (the 1910 game ended in a tie). But Boston had won the last four to cut the margin to 16–9, and they would win again today. Led by the pitching of Dennis "Oil Can" Boyd and three home runs, the Red Sox coasted to an easy 9–2 victory.

This rare April meeting between the Yankees and Red Sox attracted national attention. As part of a feature on the return of baseball, the early-morning ABC-TV show *Good Morning America* was in the Red Sox dugout to interview managers Yogi Berra and John McNamara. Three inches of snow had fallen on Boston overnight. Nevertheless, at 7 A.M. Berra and McNamara were in Fenway Park to fulfill their obligation. During the interview, sporadic snow flurries filled the air, making it appear very unlikely that the game, scheduled for 2:20 P.M., would be played. That it was played is a credit to Joe Mooney's ground crew and Jackie DiAngelis's cleaning crew. Aided by a bright sun and temperatures that climbed to 48 degrees, they did an extraordinary job in removing the snow from both the field and the stands. Evidently, Bostonians were confident that despite the snow there would be a game. By 10:35 A.M., a steady stream of traffic flowed down Brookline Avenue, and long lines of fans waited at the ticket gates on Lansdowne Street and Yawkey Way. Eventually all the tickets were sold and 34,282 hardy fans, many wearing Yankees regalia, made their way into the park. There was always a sizable contingent of fans rooting for the Yankees when they played in Fenway, mostly New York–area college students who were attending school in the Boston area.

McNamara was managing his first game for Boston after earlier stints with the Oakland A's, San Diego Padres, Cincinnati Reds, and the previous two seasons with the California Angels. The team he inherited from the retired Ralph Houk was one with a lot of power but questionable pitching. How far Boston would go this year depended on three right-handers—Boyd, Al Nipper, and Roger Clemens—all of whom had shown great promise in 1984. These youngsters would have to take some of the burden from veteran left-handers Bruce Hurst and Bob Ojeda for the Sox to challenge in the East—a race that figured to be much closer than 1984, when the Tigers got off to a sensational start and breezed the rest of the way. Still, the defending champions were not the favorites. The Yankees had assumed that role with two more multimillion-dollar additions, pitcher Ed Whitson and outfielder Rickey Henderson. While Steinbrenner had his detractors in the press and among the fans, and deservedly so, no one could question his willingness to spend money. He steadfastly continued to pursue, and usually get, the best available players for the Yankees, and therefore expected them to win the pennant every year. But Steinbrenner's problem was that he did not understand the chemistry of baseball any more than he understood its rhythms. He failed to comprehend that you cannot just put together an "All-Star" team and assume it will win. All winning teams have certain characteristics in common, but having the "best player" at each position is not necessarily one of them. Steinbrenner, of course, had another problem; his constant interference prevented his baseball people from doing their jobs.

Whitson proved to be one of Steinbrenner's worst mistakes. He had been a mediocre major-league pitcher for seven years before winning 14 games (14–8) for last season's pennant-winning Padres. He was now a free agent, and based on that one good year Steinbrenner signed him for $4.4 million. Whitson would spend one and a half bitter, unhappy seasons in New York before the Yankees traded him back to San Diego. Henderson, on the other hand, was a different story. In six years with Oakland, he had used his speed and power to establish himself as a potent offensive threat, while gaining recognition as baseball's best leadoff hitter ever. He had led the league in stolen bases for each of the past five years, including a modern major-league record 130 in 1982. And he was still only 26 years old. New York gave up reliever Jay Howell and some fine young players, including Stan Javier, Eric Plunk, and Jose Rijo to get Henderson, but Steinbrenner believed he was well worth it. However, Henderson had a sprained left ankle and was sitting out the opener. Oscar Moreno, whose 24 hits led the Yanks in spring training, started in center field, flanked by Ken Griffey Sr. in left and Dave Winfield in right. Outfielder Steve Kemp, signed as a free agent in 1982, was now with the Pittsburgh Pirates. Kemp had recovered from a poor first season in New York to bat .291 in 94 games in '84; nevertheless, the Yanks traded him to the Pirates. Infielder Tim Foli also went to Pittsburgh in the deal, which brought Dale Berra, Yogi's son, and minor-leaguers Alfonso Pulido, a pitcher, and Jay Buhner, an outfielder, to New York. Both Pulido and Buhner began the season in the minor leagues: Pulido with the Columbus Clippers of the International League, and Buhner with the Ft. Lauderdale Yankees of the Florida State League. Berra, the third man in the trade, was on the bench today, but his dad planned to platoon him at third base with left-hand hitting second-year man Mike Pagliarulo.

Yogi had named Ron Guidry to pitch the opener, disregarding Guidry's opening-day history (six starts, six Yankee losses) and his subpar 1984 season. But four days earlier, Guidry had woken up with a stiff neck that still bothered him enough to pass up today's start. Berra turned to Phil Niekro, who at seven days past his 46th birthday was the second-oldest major-league pitcher ever to start an opener. (Jack Quinn was two months short of 48 when he started for the Brooklyn Dodgers in 1931.) Niekro had won 284 games in his 21 major-league seasons, which tied him with Ferguson Jenkins for 20th place on the all-time list. However, he had the dubious honor of having the worst opening-day record in history, having lost all six of his opening-day decisions when he pitched for the Atlanta Braves.

Niekro had been around so long that when he broke into the majors with the Braves (then in Milwaukee) back in 1964, Boyd, his mound opponent, was only four years old. Boyd was in just his third season in the league, but already had a reputation as a "hot dog." It was a reputation that the slender, six-foot-one, 150-pounder earned with the prancing, strutting, and "jive-talking" theatrics on the mound that antagonized opposing batters. Last year, following losses in his first three decisions, the Sox sent him back to the International League, but after several well-pitched games for the Pawtucket Red Sox, he returned to Boston and finished 12–12 for the season. He was 1–1 against the Yankees, losing to Niekro on June 13. McNamara selected him as his opening-day pitcher early in spring training, which Boyd justified by compiling a 2.40 earned run average in the Grapefruit League, with 23 strikeouts in 30 innings.

As part of the pregame festivities, the Red Sox paid homage to two longtime fans, allowing each to throw out an honorary first ball. Louis Capriccio and I. F. Giglio had been season ticket holders at Fenway Park since the mid–1930s. Suzyn Waldman, a member of the Red Sox booster club in New York, sang the national anthem. The Yankees actually led in this game, jumping off to a 2–0 lead in the second inning. There were two out with nobody on when Pagliarulo walked and catcher Butch Wynegar sent him home with a double to right. Dwight Evans had a possible play at the plate, but instead chose to throw to second to try to get Wynegar—a rare mistake for Boston's outstanding right fielder. Wynegar scored on shortstop Bobby Meacham's single to right. Meacham, who had endured a very difficult spring, batting .197 with five errors, was anxious to start well. A year ago he was on the opening-day roster, but after making a costly error against the Texas Rangers in the season's fourth game, Steinbrenner ordered him sent back to the minors. By mid–June when Andre Robertson showed that he had not fully recovered from his auto accident, Meacham came back to reclaim his position.

Boston needed just two batters in the last of the second to tie the score. Designated hitter Mike Easler singled and Tony Armas, the league's defending home run and runs batted in champion, homered on Niekro's first pitch. Armas connected on a knuckler down at his shoetops, driving it into the screen atop the wall in left field. Then, in the third inning, Niekro's control deserted him; he walked four men, including two with the bases loaded. With Evans, who had doubled, on second and one out, he passed Jim Rice and Easler to load the bases. Niekro was rarely effective on days when his knuckleball was not working well or he had difficulty controlling it. Today was one of those days. He got the second out with his best knuckleball of the game, striking out Armas looking, but then walked Bill Buckner and Rich Gedman to force in two runs. After the game, Niekro was unable to explain his wildness. "You don't like to start off the season not putting the ball over the plate when you were getting it over all spring," he said, pointing out that he had walked only six men in 27 innings this spring. "It's a bad feeling. Maybe I threw too hard. Maybe I rushed myself." Niekro departed after the fourth, but not before Evans blasted another of his knucklers over the Green Monster and onto Lansdowne Street for a solo home run.

Veteran left-hander Bob Shirley came on in the fifth and was touched for Boston's sixth run on singles by Easler, Buckner, and Gedman. An inning later, Jackie Gutierrez had a leadoff single and was at second with one out when Berra replaced Shirley with right-hander Joe Cowley. After struggling for eight years in the minors, Cowley had come up in midsummer last season and won nine games (9–2). His only two losses in '84 had been in relief, but with Evans and Rice due up, Berra was making the usual "lefty-righty" pitching change. This time it worked against him. Cowley walked Evans, and then Rice drove one of his fastballs into the center-field bleachers, making the score 9–2.

Even in Fenway, where big leads can disappear quickly, that was more runs than the Red Sox would need. The flashy Boyd easily handled the strength of the Yankees' batting order, especially Don Mattingly and Winfield, both of whom were hitless. Mattingly had batted against Boyd in the minors and didn't appear upset by his antics, but Winfield did. When he felt Boyd's pitches were too close to his chin during a third-inning walk, he let him know. The two exchanged words, but there were no further incidents. Bob Stanley, the ace of the Red Sox bullpen, relieved Boyd to start the eighth and retired five straight before Pagliarulo lined a double off the left-field wall. Pagliarulo, a native of nearby Medford, grew up as a Red Sox fan and recalled coming to Fenway Park openers as a child. A large group of his friends and family were here today, and now that the game was all but won, they cheered his hit lustily. When Stanley got Wynegar on a grounder to second baseman Marty Barrett for the final out, Boston had their first opening-day win since 1982.

For the Yankees, it was their fourth straight opening-day loss, and seventh of the last eight. Niekro's personal opening-day losing streak was now seven, but he did come back to win 16 games (16–12) for the Yankees in 1985. Number 16, an 8–0 shutout against Toronto on the last day of the season, was the 300th win of his career and made him the oldest major-leaguer ever to throw a shutout. (Jamie Moyer, of the Philadelphia Phillies became the oldest when he threw a shutout, at age 47, on May 7, 2010.) The Yankees lost all three games in Boston and were 6–10 on April 28 when Steinbrenner—despite his promise to Berra that no matter what happened this season he would not fire him—fired him. Billy Martin came back to serve his fourth term as manager.

After a slow start, the Yankees (97–64) got within a game and a half of the Toronto Blue Jays in mid–September, but were unable to catch them. They finished two games back. Although the Yanks did well under Martin (91–54), they were no doubt hindered by the strife and commotion that always surrounded him. After the season Steinbrenner once again fired Martin and appointed coach Lou Piniella as the manager for 1986. Ron Guidry rebounded from his poor 1984 season to lead the league in wins (22–6) and winning percentage (.786) and finish second to the Kansas City Royals' Bret Saberhagen in the Cy Young Award voting. Rickey Henderson had a splendid first season in New York. He batted .314 and led the league in stolen bases (80), setting a club record that surpassed Fritz Maisel's mark of 74 established in 1914. Henderson also scored 146 runs, the highest one-season total in the major leagues since Ted Williams scored 150 in 1949. By hitting 24 home runs, Henderson became the first American Leaguer to have more than 20 home runs and 50 stolen bases in a season. He finished third in voting for the Most Valuable Player Award, won by teammate Don Mattingly. Mattingly hit .324 with 35 home runs and a league-leading 145 runs batted in. He had 211 hits, 107 runs scored, and his 48 doubles were a league high.

Monday, April 8, 1985

New York	ab	r	h	rbi	Boston	ab	r	h	rbi
Moreno cf	4	0	1	0	Boggs 3b	5	0	1	0
Randolph 2b	3	0	0	0	Evans rf	4	3	2	1
Mattingly 1b	4	0	0	0	Rice lf	3	2	1	3
Winfield rf	3	0	0	0	Easler dh	3	2	2	0
Baylor dh	4	0	1	0	Armas cf	4	1	1	2
Griffey lf	4	0	1	0	Buckner 1b	2	0	1	1
Pagliarulo 3b	3	1	1	0	Gedman c	3	0	1	2
Wynegar c	3	1	1	1	Barrett 2b	4	0	0	0
Meacham ss	3	0	1	1	Gutierrez ss	4	1	1	0
Total	31	2	6	2	Total	32	9	10	9

```
New York   020   000   000–2
Boston     022   113   00X–9
```

Error—Gedman. Double plays—Meacham, Randolph, and Mattingly; Buckner (unassisted); Gutierrez, Barrett, and Buckner. Left on bases—New York 6; Boston 5. Put outs—New York 24: Meacham 2, Randolph 2, Mattingly 11, Wynegar 4, Griffey 2, Cowley 1, Pagliarulo 1, Winfield 1. Boston 27: Boyd 1, Buckner 10, Rice 3, Gedman 6, Gutierrez 2, Evans 2, Stanley 1, Barrett 2. Assists—New York 17: Meacham 5, Randolph 7, Mattingly 1, Wynegar 1, Pagliarulo 2, Winfield 1. Boston 12: Boyd 1, Buckner 2, Boggs 2, Gutierrez 4, Stanley 1, Barrett 2. Two-base hits—Wynegar, Pagliarulo, Evans. Home runs—Armas, Evans, Rice. Stolen base—Gutierrez.

	IP	H	R	ER	BB	SO
NEW YORK						
P. Niekro (L, 0–1)	4.0	5	5	5	5	3
Shirley	1.1	4	2	2	0	1
Cowley	1.2	1	2	2	1	0
Murray	1.0	0	0	0	0	0
BOSTON						
Boyd (W, 1–0)	7.0	5	2	2	4	5
Stanley	2.0	1	0	0	0	1

Passed ball—Gedman. Umpires—Phillips, Neudecker, McCoy, and Palermo. Time of game—2 hrs. 33 min. Attendance—34,282.

Tuesday, April 8, 1986
Yankee Stadium, New York
New York 4 Kansas City 2

For this relief much thanks.—William Shakespeare

Even before the 1986 season began, New Yorkers were already anticipating its end. With both the Yankees and the Mets coming off close second-place finishes in 1985, fans of both clubs fully expected that come October the city would have its first "subway series" in 30 years. On Opening Day, each club led with its ace and each came away with a victory. At Pittsburgh, the Mets—behind Dwight Gooden—defeated the Pirates, 4–2, to win their 15th opener in 17 years. Meanwhile, at Yankee Stadium, 55,602—the largest opening-day crowd since the Stadium reopened ten years earlier—watched Ron Guidry defeat the Kansas City Royals, also by a score of 4–2. For Guidry, the new Yankees' co-captain (with second baseman Willie Randolph), it was his first opening-day win after two losses and four no-decisions. The 35-year-old left-hander pitched only five innings before a strained calf muscle forced him to leave the game. New manager Lou Piniella then went to his bullpen for Rod Scurry and Dave Righetti, who held the Royals scoreless the rest of the way.

Everything appeared pleasant and festive during the pregame activities, including the weather, which was now sunny after a morning of drizzle and cloudiness. Metropolitan Opera baritone Robert Merrill sang the national anthem, as he so often did at Yankee Stadium, and this year the club gave the 68-year-old Merrill the additional honor of throwing out the first ball. Yet despite the general good feeling that always accompanies Opening Day, the fans were apprehensive. Concerned with owner George Steinbrenner's threat to leave Yankee Stadium for the New Jersey Meadowlands, they could only wonder how many future openers the Yankees would play on this hallowed site. While the thought of moving the Yankees out of Yankee Stadium, much less out of New York, appeared bizarre, those with long memories knew that it could happen. They also knew that the "Keep the Bombers the Bronx Bombers" buttons that fans were wearing would have no influence on Steinbrenner's decision. Neither would sentimental gestures, such as the black armbands the players were wearing on their left sleeves in memory of two Yankees' legends who had recently died: Roger Maris and Pete Sheehy, their longtime clubhouse man. Increasingly cynical fans had finally realized that sentiment in baseball went only so far. When it began to infringe on an owner's profits, then sentiment, history, and tradition were easily dispensable.

The visiting Royals were the world champions, the first defending champion opponent to open the season at Yankee Stadium in 61 years. The Washington Senators had dropped the 1925 opener at the Stadium to Urban Shocker, 5–1, after winning the only World Series in their history. Five years later, in 1930, the Yanks opened against the world champion Philadelphia Athletics, but that game was at Shibe Park. George Pipgras lost to Lefty Grove, 6–2, in Bob Shawkey's managerial debut. Shawkey lasted only the one year, serving as the link between Miller Huggins's 12 seasons as manager and Joe McCarthy's 16. However, given their recent history—the switch from Billy Martin to Piniella was the 14th managerial change in Steinbrenner's 14 years—no one thought it likely that Piniella would last anywhere near that long. He had been the team's hitting instructor, but had no prior managerial experience—none, not in the majors, not in the minors, not even in winter ball. That may have been the reason Steinbrenner kept two of his former managers close by: Gene Michael was coaching at third base, and Martin was making his debut in the broadcasting booth. Someone else who might have helped Piniella was Don Baylor, a veteran player who had been a stabilizing influence on the Yankees and seemed destined to be a future manager himself. But the Yanks had traded Baylor to the Boston Red Sox for left-hand hitting veteran Mike Easler in a swap of designated hitters. Easler was on the bench this afternoon against left-hander Bud Black as Gary Roenicke (traded from the Baltimore Orioles for infielder Rex Hudler and pitcher Rich Bordi) filled the DH spot.

Although Piniella, like Martin, was a volatile man, he had displayed a much more relaxed style of managing during spring training. Stepping up from player to manager often can cause problems for a new leader, but Piniella seemed to have the loyalty, respect, and admiration of his former teammates. However, the key question, as it had been with all of Steinbrenner's previous managers, would be how he would handle the owner's bluster and interference. All spring Steinbrenner had seemed unhappy while complaining about one thing or another. His constant criticism culminated in a fierce and uncalled for verbal attack on groundskeeper Jim Esposito at the Yankees' workout the day before the opener. Steinbrenner castigated Esposito in front of the players and the media, blaming him for the soft condition of the field, although a steady rain the night before had been responsible.

The Yankees began the new season confident of winning their first pennant in five years. They felt that the addition of pitcher Britt Burns to their starting rotation would enable them to make up last year's two-game deficit with the Eastern Division champion Toronto Blue Jays. But things did not work out in New York for Burns, a left-hander who had come from the Chicago White Sox last December in a trade for pitcher Joe Cowley and catcher Ron Hassey. An 18-game winner in '85, Burns injured his hip at spring training, an injury that doctors diagnosed as degenerative. Although he would attempt on several occasions to come back from his injury, Burns never pitched in another major-league game. However, as often happens in baseball—and in life—one man's misfortune is another man's opportunity. The loss of Burns, the trade of Cowley, and the release of Phil Niekro opened spots in the rotation that journeyman Dennis Rasmussen and rookies Doug Drabek and Bob Tewksbury (the James P. Dawson winner) filled.

Its world championship notwithstanding, Kansas City was a poor-hitting club, having finished next to last in the American League in batting average and runs scored. The Royals also had an especially poor record against the Yankees in recent years. They had lost 11 of the last 12 games played in New York, and 22 of the last 30 overall. Black had lost all three of his decisions against the Yanks in 1985 and was 2–6 lifetime against them. He had never won at the Stadium, nor would he today. He got through the first inning without allowing a runner, but walked Dave Winfield to lead off the second. Winfield remained at first as Roenicke struck out and left fielder Henry Cotto flied out. Third baseman Dale Berra was next. Berra, who seldom heard any cheers from the crowd a year ago, had gotten one quickly today when he leaped to make a one-handed catch of Lonnie Smith's leadoff line drive. Now, the fans cheered him again after his single to center sent Winfield to second. Berra was anxious to atone for a disastrous 1985 season in which he played only 48 games, batted a puny .229, and suffered through the repercussions of an earlier drug problem. However, he had a good spring, batting .344 in the Grapefruit League, and earned a spot on the roster. Berra's two-out single allowed catcher Butch Wynegar to bat and altered the course of the game. Wynegar, a switch-hitter batting right-handed, lashed a three-run homer into the lower left-field seats, scoring Winfield and Berra ahead of him. "I was screaming for it to go out," Wynegar said later. "I usually don't do that, but I was running to first screaming for the ball to get out."

Guidry sailed through the first three innings allowing only one hit, a double to Darryl Motley. But the Royals reduced the lead to 3–2 in the fourth when designated hitter Hal McRae followed a walk to George Brett with an opposite-field home run. McRae had been with the Royals since 1973, the first year of the designated hitter, splitting his duties for the first five years between DH and the outfield. He became Kansas City's full-time DH in 1978, and at his retirement in 1987 would hold many lifetime designated hitter records.

The Yanks got the game's final run, and the only one that was not the result of a home run, in the fifth. Shortstop Bobby Meacham singled, stole second, and scored on Randolph's bloop single to left. It was Meacham's second single of the game and his second steal. New York threatened to put the game out of reach in the eighth, but came up empty thanks to a questionable move by Winfield. Randolph and Don Mattingly had greeted new pitcher Dan Quisenberry with singles and were at first and second with nobody out. Winfield, the cleanup batter, who did not have even one sacrifice bunt in 1985, decided to move the runners over. He popped the first pitch in the air; Quisenberry grabbed it and threw to second baseman Frank White to double up Randolph. "I wanted to move the guys over," Winfield explained after the game. "I thought I'd attempt it on the first pitch. It was a good play," he said. "I popped up. So what?" Piniella agreed. "He was on his own," the manager said. "It was a good play. He just popped the ball up. But it was good baseball."

After the game, Brett and several other veteran Royals claimed that Guidry's pitches lacked their usual speed. Yet they managed only two hits against him in his five innings: McRae's home run and Motley's third-inning double. Guidry suffered the injury to his right leg after he fanned Motley for the first out in the fifth. It came while he was breaking toward first on Jim Sundberg's ground ball to first baseman Mattingly. The injury did not appear to be serious, and he struck out shortstop Angel Salazar for the third out, but Piniella was taking no chances with his best pitcher. He sent Scurry, a cash acquisition from the Pittsburgh Pirates last September, out to pitch the sixth. After a one-two-three inning, McRae singled to lead off the seventh, and one out later Steve Balboni walked; but Scurry stranded them, striking out Motley and Sundberg. In the eighth, after retiring pinch-hitter Lynn Jones, he hit Smith. Piniella went to Righetti, who had already accumulated 60 saves in his two seasons as a reliever. Righetti retired Willie Wilson before walking Brett, but escaped by getting the dangerous McRae on a force-out.

Tuesday, April 8, 1986

Kansas City	ab	r	h	rbi		New York	ab	r	h	rbi
Smith lf	4	0	0	0		Henderson cf	3	0	0	0
Wilson cf	4	0	0	0		Randolph 2b	4	0	2	1
Brett 3b	2	1	0	0		Mattingly 1b	4	0	1	0
McRae dh	4	1	2	2		Winfield lf	3	1	0	0
White 2b	4	0	1	0		Roenicke dh	3	0	0	0
Balboni 1b	3	0	0	0		bEasler dh	1	0	0	0
Motley rf	4	0	1	0		Cotto lf	3	0	1	0
Sundberg c	4	0	1	0		Berra 3b	3	1	1	0
Salazar ss	2	0	0	0		Pagliarulo 3b	0	0	0	0
aJones	1	0	0	0		Wynegar c	3	1	1	3
Biancalana ss	0	0	0	0		Meacham ss	3	1	2	0
cPryor	1	0	0	0		Total	30	4	8	4
Total	33	2	5	2						

aGrounded out for Salazar in eighth inning.
bFlied out for Roenicke in eighth inning.
cStruck out for Biancalana in ninth inning.

Kansas City	000	200	000–2
New York	030	010	00X–4

Errors—Brett, Meacham. Double plays—Salazar, White, and Balboni; Quisenberry and White. Caught stealing—by Sundberg (Henderson). Left on bases—Kansas City 8; New York 4. Put outs—New York 27: Berra 1, Meacham 1, Randolph 1, Mattingly 9, Cotto 1, Wynegar 10, Henderson 1, Winfield 1, Pagliarulo 1, Scurry 1. Kansas City 24: Brett 1, Balboni 8, Sundberg 3, Motley 2, Wilson 3, White 3, Smith 3, Quisenberry 1. Assists—New York 10: Berra 2, Meacham 4, Randolph 1, Scurry 2, Mattingly 1. Kansas City 11: Brett 1, Black 2, White 2, Balboni 1, Salazar 3, Sundberg 1, Quisenberry 1. Two-base hit—Motley. Home runs—Wynegar, McRae. Stolen bases—Meacham 2.

	IP	H	R	ER	BB	SO
KANSAS CITY						
Black (L, 0–1)	7.0	6	4	4	2	3
Quisenberry	1.0	2	0	0	0	0
NEW YORK						
Guidry (W, 1–0)	5.0	2	2	2	1	5
Scurry	2.1	1	0	0	1	3
Righetti S.1	1.2	2	0	0	1	2

Hit by pitch—By Scurry (Smith). Umpires—Garcia, Kosc, Reed, and Ford. Time of game—2 hrs. 26 min. Attendance—55,602.

Kansas City, which had won many games in their championship season with late-inning comebacks, was not through yet. White began the ninth with a single to left, bringing Balboni, with 36 home runs in 1985, to the plate as the tying run. He lined the ball hard, but right at shortstop Meacham for the first out. However, what had so far been an excellent day for Meacham almost turned around on the next play. He booted Motley's potentially game-ending double play grounder, and the Royals had the tying runs aboard. The play was reminiscent of Meacham's late-inning error that lost the Yanks a game in Texas early in 1984, the one that led to Steinbrenner's banishing him to the Columbus Clippers. Sundberg's single to center loaded the bases and brought up Buddy Biancalana, who had taken over at short after Jones batted for Salazar. Royals manager Dick Howser, aware of Biancalana's .194 lifetime batting average, replaced him with Greg Pryor, a much more disciplined batsman. Pryor was a contact hitter and therefore difficult to strike out; nevertheless, he went down swinging at a Righetti slider, low and away. By staying with his seemingly unhittable slider, Righetti fanned Smith for the final out. As the Yankees ran off the field with their first opening-day win in five years, Piniella celebrated by hugging everyone in sight.

Guidry had his first opening-day win and then won three of his next four. Yet 1986 would turn out to be Guidry's worst season. He missed most of July with a hand injury and finished 9–12 with a 3.98 earned run average. For Righetti—the only Yankee who actually lived in New York City—this was to be a memorable year. On the next-to-final day of the season, he saved both ends of a doubleheader in Boston, giving him 46 saves for the season and breaking the major-league record held jointly by Quisenberry and Bruce Sutter. (Bobby Thigpen of the White Sox broke Righetti's record with 57 saves in 1990.) The two appearances gave Righetti 74 for the year, tying the Yankees record he had set in 1985.

This would be a sadly tragic season for the Royals. In July, Howser had to leave the team after doctors discovered a tumor in his brain. Mike Ferraro took over, but the team never got over Howser's untimely departure and finished in fourth place. Howser was only 51 when he died the following June.

The Mets fulfilled their fans' expectations, winning the pennant and the World Series, but the Yankees (90–72) did not. Due mainly to erratic pitching, they finished second again, 5½ games behind the Boston Red Sox. Lou Piniella survived the season, but with a second place finish somebody had to go, and so George Steinbrenner replaced Sammy Ellis, Piniella's pitching coach, with Mark Connor. Don Mattingly continued to make his place among the all-time Yankee greats. He batted .352, second to Boston's Wade Boggs (.357), and led the league in slugging percentage (.573) and total bases (388). He also led in hits (238) and doubles (53), breaking club records set in 1927. Earle Combs had held the hit record, with 231, and Lou Gehrig the doubles record, with 52. Mattingly finished second in the Most

Valuable Player balloting to Red Sox pitcher Roger Clemens. Rickey Henderson again led the league in runs scored (130) and stolen bases. His 87 stolen bases broke his own club record.

Monday, April 6, 1987
Tiger Stadium, Detroit
New York 2 Detroit 1 (10 Innings)

Where there is no free agency, there can be no morality.—William H. Prescott

Jack Morris won 21 games (21–8) for the Detroit Tigers in 1986. He also led the American League in shutouts with six and was the only pitcher in either league to have won at least 15 games in each of the previous five years. Now, as a free agent at the peak of his career, the 31-year-old Morris was looking to cash in on his success. However, though he was one of the game's top pitchers, no other club seemed interested in signing him. Nor did clubs other than their own seem anxious to sign any other of this season's highly prized free agents—players such as Tim Raines, Andre Dawson, and Bob Boone. Morris and the others, aware of what was going on, accused the major-league owners of collusion. The Players Association agreed and in February 1987 filed a suit against the owners that they eventually won. Meanwhile, Morris took the Tigers to arbitration and won a contract for $1.85 million. His salary was the largest amount ever awarded a player through arbitration, but that distinction was short-lived. Four days later, Don Mattingly went even higher, receiving $1.975 million from the Yankees. Nevertheless, Morris's $1.85 million made him— along with Fernando Valenzuela of the Los Angeles Dodgers—the highest-paid pitcher in the game.

The Yankees were among the teams that could have had Morris. They simply had to agree to allow an arbitrator to determine his salary—but owner George Steinbrenner refused. Therefore, when the Yanks opened the 1987 season at Tiger Stadium, Morris was on the mound for the Tigers and not the Yankees. This was his eighth consecutive opening-day start for Detroit, and he had been extremely effective in the previous seven, winning six and losing only one. Morris's streak of consecutive opening-day starts would continue after he moved on to Minnesota and Toronto, and eventually reach 14, a still-existing major-league record. While he claimed no bitter feelings toward the Yankees, Morris undoubtedly took pleasure in his strong performance today. Although he was the losing pitcher in New York's 2–1 triumph, he clearly demonstrated just how much he could have helped the Yanks this season. He allowed no earned runs through nine innings before finally yielding the game-winner in the tenth. Of course, the Yankees were already familiar with Morris's capabilities. They had only six wins in 15 decisions against him, and last September 27 it had been his ten-inning, 1–0, victory that eliminated them from pennant contention.

The crowd of 51,315 booed Morris during the pregame introductions for his attempt to leave Detroit, but appeared ready to forgive him following his gritty effort. Nevertheless, after manager Sparky Anderson removed him, the fans' applause for Morris's ten innings of work on a very cold day failed to include the standing ovation they usually gave such efforts. Despite the cold and the storm clouds that hovered above, the convivial mood of Opening Day was present in and around red-white-and-blue-bedecked Tiger Stadium. You could even feel it in the surrounding neighborhoods, where free entertainment greeted the fans as they made their way to the 75-year-old park. It was a chilly 46 degrees when Michigan governor James Blanchard threw out the first ball to new Tigers catcher Orlando Mercado. Mayor Coleman Young was supposed to have been on the receiving end of Blanchard's throw, but Young was late in arriving. Bob Taylor, a local singer, sang the national anthem from in front of home plate, with the Yanks and Tigers lined up along the first- and third-base lines.

To the surprise of many, Lou Piniella was beginning his second season as the Yankees' manager. Piniella had done an excellent job in his rookie season, winning 90 games, but he had failed to win the division title. The necessity to win had become a part of the sporting life in New York, especially so for the Yankees under George Steinbrenner. But now, with their payroll up to $18.5 million and their recent failures exacerbated by the galling success of the world champion 1986 Mets, the ever-present pressure on the club and its manager was even more intense. The Steinbrenner Yankees, who had often traded promising youngsters for established players, had done it again following the '86 season. To get veteran pitchers Rick Rhoden, Cecilio Guante, and Pat Clements from the Pittsburgh Pirates, he sent the Pirates three of his best young pitchers: Doug Drabek, Brian Fisher, and Logan Easley. The principal figure in the deal was Rhoden, 15–12 in 1986 and long a successful starter in the National League for Pittsburgh and before that for Los Angeles.

Because of an arcane rule associated with free agency, Ron Guidry was among a group of players unable to re-sign with his team of a year ago until May 1. With Guidry unavailable and Rhoden still getting ready in Ft. Lauderdale, Piniella chose Dennis Rasmussen to pitch the season opener. Nineteen eight-six had been a breakthrough season for the six-foot-seven left-hander whose opportunity had come when Britt Burns suffered a career-ending injury. He capitalized on it by leading the team in wins with 18 (18–6), double the total of any other pitcher on the staff. Nevertheless, the Yanks remained skeptical about Rasmussen's ability to have another such season. After considering his pre–1986 lifetime record of 12–11, they gave him only a $75,000 raise, up to $175,000. Rasmussen had done nothing this spring to alter the Yanks' perception of him. In 26⅓ Grapefruit League innings, he had allowed 42 hits and had an ERA of 6.49.

The Tigers had also fared poorly this spring, suffering through 20 losses (9–20), the most in their 87-year history. Today's defeat further frustrated them, knowing that with perfect defense they would have come away with a nine-inning, 1–0 victory. New York's lone run in regulation time came in the fourth inning, the result of a two-out throwing error by third baseman Darnell Coles. With designated hitter Gary Ward at first, Dave Winfield hit a slow roller down the third-base line. Coles, whose throwing all spring had been erratic, fielded the ball while charging in and threw to first. His throw was to the outfield side of the bag and skipped past first baseman Darrell Evans—who attempted to backhand it—down into the right-field corner. Mike Heath, primarily a catcher, was playing right field. He retrieved the ball and made a good throw to the plate, but Ward slid in safely. Winfield got credit for a single; however, there was no RBI and the run was unearned. Ward, who had gotten on with the Yankees first hit, was batting fourth this afternoon despite having a .109 (5-for-46) lifetime batting average against Morris. New York signed him after the Texas Rangers let him go, and he won a job with his hot hitting in Florida. Ward would play mostly in the outfield this season, while also sharing the designated hitter slot with several others, including Mike Easler. The Yanks had traded Easler to the Phillies for pitcher Charles Hudson but then brought him back in a mid-season deal.

Detroit's failure to deliver the big hit was made more understandable by the absence of two of their best clutch hitters: catcher Lance Parrish, who was now with the Philadelphia Phillies, and outfielder Kirk Gibson, who was on the disabled list. Gibson, out with torn muscles in his rib cage, sat with several team doctors as he watched the game from the stands. Still, some credit for the Tigers being 0-for-7 with runners in scoring position in the first three innings—and 0-for-11 for the game—must go to the Yankees defense. It sparkled all afternoon, specifically in third baseman Mike Pagliarulo and left fielder Dan Pasqua, each of whom made two separate outstanding fielding plays.

After wasting a one-out triple by Larry Herndon in the first and a leadoff double by Coles in the second, the Tigers finally scored on Herndon's tremendous home run leading off the sixth. Rasmussen grooved a fastball, and Herndon drove it against the facing of the upper deck in center field. The ball was still rising when it hit, and had it not been interrupted likely would have traveled well over 500 feet. Center fielder Rickey Henderson started to chase it, but then stopped and stared in admiration. "It looked like it was going to go 600 feet," Henderson said in the Yankees clubhouse. "I had a great jump on the ball, and then it took off like there was a jet on it. I've never seen a ball with that much speed on it." Longtime Tigers watchers said it was the longest home run hit here since the days of Mickey Mantle.

Although Herndon's home run was the only runner that Rasmussen allowed from the fourth inning through the seventh, Piniella called in Dave Righetti to pitch the eighth. Catcher Mercado, whose career with the Tigers would last just ten games before they traded him to the Dodgers, greeted the Yankees' stopper with a single to left. After Lou Whitaker laid down a sacrifice bunt, moving Pat Sheridan, running for Mercado, to second, Righetti gave Herndon an "unintentional-intentional walk," passing him on four pitches. But both runners were left when Chet Lemon and Alan Trammell went out on fly balls. Trammell was having an especially difficult day at the plate. Anderson had moved him from his familiar number two position in the batting order to the cleanup spot, and three times he made the third out with runners in scoring position. Nonetheless, it was a record-setting day for Trammell and his second base partner, Whitaker, two of the most popular players in team history. The double-play combination of Trammell and Whitaker was beginning its tenth year with the same team, something that no other keystone pair had ever done.

Detroit had another chance to win the game for Morris in the ninth. Coles was on second after drawing a leadoff walk and moving to second on a sacrifice bunt by designated hitter Terry Harper. Evans, the next batter, would set major league home run (34) and American League runs-batted-in (99) records for players over 40 this season, but Righetti fanned him on three pitches. (Both records were later broken.) After walking Heath, Righetti ended the threat by fanning Tom Brookens, batting for substitute catcher Dwight Lowry. Righetti's walk to Heath was his third of the game, equaling his high for any game a year ago.

Monday, April 6, 1987

New York	ab	r	h	rbi	Detroit	ab	r	h	rbi
Henderson cf	4	0	2	1	Whitaker 2b	4	0	1	0
Randolph 2b	4	0	0	0	Herndon lf	4	1	2	1
Mattingly 1b	5	0	0	0	Lemon cf	5	0	0	0
Ward dh	4	1	1	0	Trammell ss	4	0	0	0

New York

	ab	r	h	rbi
Winfield rf	4	0	1	0
Pasqua lf	4	0	1	0
Pagliarulo 3b	4	0	1	0
Skinner c	2	0	0	0
ᶜWashington	1	1	1	0
Cerone c	0	0	0	0
Tolleson ss	4	0	2	0
Total	36	2	9	1

Detroit

	ab	r	h	rbi
Coles 3b	3	0	1	0
Harper dh	3	0	0	0
Evans 1b	4	0	0	0
Heath rf	2	0	0	0
Mercado c	3	0	1	0
ᵃSheridan	0	0	0	0
Lowry c	0	0	0	0
ᵇBrookens	1	0	0	0
Nokes c	0	0	0	0
Total	33	1	5	1

ᵃRan for Mercado in eighth inning.
ᵇStruck out for Lowry in ninth inning.
ᶜSingled for Skinner in tenth inning.

New York	000	100	000	1–2
Detroit	000	001	000	0–1

Error—Coles. Double plays—Trammell, Whitaker, and Evans; Lemon, Whitaker and Evans. Left on bases—New York 7; Detroit 8. Put outs—New York 30: Skinner 5, Randolph 2, Henderson 4, Cerone 1, Pasqua 5, Mattingly 8, Pagliarulo 2, Winfield 3. Detroit 30: Trammell 2, Whitaker 4, Herndon 2, Evans 12, Coles 1, Mercado 4, Heath 1, Morris 1, Lemon 3. Assists—New York 7: Randolph 3, Mattingly 1, Pagliarulo 1, Rasmussen 1, Righetti 1. Detroit 15: Trammell 6, Whitaker 4, Evans 1, Coles 2, Morris 1, Lemon 1. Two-base hits—Coles, Henderson. Three-base hit—Herndon. Home run—Herndon. Stolen base—Henderson. Sacrifices—Skinner, Whitaker, Harper.

	IP	H	R	ER	BB	SO
NEW YORK						
Rasmussen	7.0	4	1	1	1	3
Righetti (W, 1–0)	3.0	1	0	0	3	3
DETROIT						
Morris (L, 0–1)	9.2	9	2	1	2	4
Hernandez	.1	0	0	0	0	0

Umpires—Brinkman, Cooney, Reilly, and Welke. Time of game—3 hrs. 1 min. Attendance—51,315.

As the tenth inning began, Morris assured Anderson he still felt strong. Though complete games were becoming ever more infrequent, particularly on Opening Day, Sparky agreed to let his ace pitch another inning. Morris got the first two batters, but Claudell Washington, batting for catcher Joel Skinner, bounced a single between first and second. Washington, beginning his first full season with the Yankees, had come from the Atlanta Braves last June in a trade for Ken Griffey Sr. and Andre Robertson. Like Ward, he had little previous success against Morris, with just one hit in 13 at-bats. As shortstop Wayne Tolleson stepped in, Tiger relievers Willie Hernandez and Eric King were ready in the bullpen. Tolleson, too, came to the Yanks in a 1986 mid-season trade (with the Chicago White Sox), one that also brought Skinner and outfielder/DH Ron Kittle to New York. A former All-American wide receiver at Western Carolina University, Tolleson was at shortstop because Steinbrenner had again demoted Bobby Meacham to Columbus. He hit Morris's first pitch into right field, sending Washington to third. Hernandez and King began throwing even harder in the bullpen, but Anderson remained on the bench. "Jack Morris is always going to lose his game," his manager said later. "Nobody else is going to lose it for him." Henderson, with a walk and single in four previous appearances, was next. He took a ball and then a strike before ripping a double to right center, between Heath and

Lemon. It scored Washington with the go-ahead run and sent Tolleson to third. Then, after Morris walked Willie Randolph to load the bases, Anderson removed him (Morris had now thrown 120 pitches) and called in Hernandez. The former Cy Young winner got Mattingly, a .377 hitter with five home runs against Detroit a year ago, on a fly to center for the third out.

Rick Cerone, wearing No. 6, took over for Skinner behind the plate as Detroit batted in the tenth. Cerone had worn No. 10 in his first stint in New York (1980–1984), but the Yankees had since retired it in honor of Phil Rizzuto. Righetti, although he was pitching his third inning, simply overpowered the Tigers in the tenth. He easily retired Whitaker, Herndon, and Lemon to end what Anderson called the best-played opener he had seen in his 17 years as a manager. The Yanks had their first opening-day road win since Mel Stottlemyre beat the Washington Senators, 8–4, at Robert F. Kennedy Stadium in 1969, and their first extra-inning opening-day win since the 12-inning, 1–0, victory at Hilltop Park against the Philadelphia Athletics in 1908.

The Detroit Tigers recovered from a 9–16 start to sweep the final three games of the season from the Toronto Blue Jays and win the Eastern Division title on the last day of the season. New York (89–73) used a club record 48 players but still finished fourth, nine games back. Dennis Rasmussen was 9–7 when the Yanks traded him to the Cincinnati Reds for Bill Gullickson in late August. Injuries hurt the club, as Rickey Henderson, Don Mattingly, and Willie Randolph all had lengthy stays on the disabled list. In October, George Steinbrenner made Lou Piniella the general manager and grotesquely brought Billy Martin back for his fifth chance at managing the club.

Tuesday, April 5, 1988
Yankee Stadium, New York
New York 8 Minnesota 0

Every hero becomes a bore at last.—Ralph Waldo Emerson

An opening-day crowd of 55,802, the largest ever for a regular-season game in the "new" Yankee Stadium, turned out to welcome Billy Martin back to the Bronx. For reasons known only to him, owner George Steinbrenner decided that Martin, now almost 60 years old, should have one more crack at managing the Yankees—his fifth. To make room for Martin, Lou Piniella, who had been the manager for two full seasons, moved into the front office. Martin would last just 68 games before dissipating what was mercifully his final managerial opportunity, but today all was sweetness and light. Of course, with Rick Rhoden shutting out the world champion Minnesota Twins, 8–0, the normally disagreeable Martin had little to be disagreeable about. And while Rhoden was limiting Minnesota to just three hits, the Yankees were pounding out 11 against Twins ace Frank Viola and his successors, Keith Atherton and Tippy Martinez. Mike Pagliarulo and Rickey Henderson contributed home runs, and Panamanian-born rookie outfielder Roberto Kelly and veteran second baseman Willie Randolph each had three hits. Randolph was making his 13th consecutive opening-day start for the Yankees, but this would be his last season in New York until he returned as a coach in 1994. It would also be his worst season; a rib injury would limit Randolph to just 110 games and a .230 batting average.

Yet in spite of all these Yankee heroics, the loudest cheers of the day were for the embattled Dave Winfield, whom the fans rewarded with several ovations. New Yorkers were taking every occasion possible to let Winfield know that they sided with him in his ongoing battle with Steinbrenner and that they appreciated his desire to stay in New York. Winfield, who had the right to approve trades in which he was involved, had recently vetoed deals that would have sent him either to the Baltimore Orioles for Fred Lynn or to the Houston Astros for Kevin Bass. The crowd gave him his first ovation during the pregame introductions. When Bob Sheppard, beginning his 38th year as the stadium's public address announcer, called Winfield's name, it elicited the loudest applause of that ceremony. Among those cheering for Winfield on this warm, sunny day were New York State Attorney General Robert Abrams and James Fox, head of the FBI's New York office. In 1993, Fox would gain fame as the man who uncovered the perpetrators of the first World Trade Center bombing. Diane Munson and Arlene Howard, the wives of two former Yankees catching greats, shared in throwing out the first ball.

Winfield received an even louder cheer—accompanied by cries of "Dave, Dave, Dave"—when he took his place in right field to start the game. But even that paled when compared to the second-inning standing ovation that greeted his first plate appearance. The noise grew so deafening that Winfield was forced to step out of the batter's box to compose himself. "It was great, fantastic," he said. "The warmest welcome I've had." Viola struck him out in that first at-bat, but in the fourth Winfield drove in the season's first run. He lined a base hit to left that scored Randolph, who had doubled, and set off another thunderous outburst. Winfield would drive in 29 runs this month, tying the major-league record for April runs driven in. (Juan Gonzalez of the Texas Rangers holds the record with 35 in 1998.) Gary Ward, who had singled, moved to second on Winfield's hit, but when Kelly followed with another single and he tried to score, left fielder Dan Gladden's throw to catcher Tom Nieto nailed him. Ward was filling the designated hitter role today only because Jack Clark was still in Florida recovering from a torn tendon in his calf. Clark, acquired as a free agent from the St. Louis Cardinals to be the Yankees' DH, injured himself while hitting a home run against the Orioles in an exhibition game on St. Patrick's Day. He would return to the Yankees several days after the opener, play in 150 games, and lead the club in home runs with 27.

Winfield was at second and Kelly at first when Pagliarulo hit Viola's first pitch—a high fastball—for a three-run homer and a 4–0 Yankees lead. Center fielder Kirby Puckett went to the wall in deep right-center and leaped, but the ball ticked off the fingers of his glove and went over the fence. "I felt great," Pagliarulo said after the game. "I was floating around the bases. I had goose bumps." It was a rare home run against a left-handed pitcher for Pagliarulo, who had looked weak in striking out earlier. The season before, the left-handed-hitting third baseman hit only four of his 32 home runs against lefties; similarly, only five of the 29 home runs that Viola allowed in 1987 were to left-handed batters. Pagliarulo gave credit to manager Martin and batting coach Chris Chambliss, both of whom, he said, had told him to stand closer to the plate when facing southpaws.

Minnesota had squandered its best scoring chance in the top of the inning after reaching Rhoden for two of their three hits. It was the only inning in which they had more than one base runner; Rhoden, who did not walk a man, faced a total of only 30 batters. The Twins had gone out in order in each of the first three innings when Gladden led off the fourth with a long drive to center. It looked like a double or possibly a triple, but Kelly pulled it down with an excellent running catch. Still, after shortstop Greg Gagne followed with a double off the wall in left and Puckett beat out a high bouncer to third, Minnesota needed just a long fly ball to take the lead. But Rhoden kept the ball in the infield. He got the dangerous Kent Hrbek on a foul pop to third and the equally dangerous Gary Gaetti on a force-play grounder. Rhoden allowed only one more Twin to reach base: Tom Brunansky with a one two-out single in the eighth. Two weeks later Minnesota would trade Brunansky to the St. Louis Cardinals for second baseman Tommy Herr. Twins' general manager Andy MacPhail and manager Tom Kelly would later agree that it was a disastrous deal. Brunansky had been one of the Twins' finest players, while Herr was unhappy in Minnesota and wanted to go back to the National League. After the season MacPhail did trade Herr back to the National League, sending the disgruntled second baseman to the Philadelphia Phillies.

The Yanks got two more runs off Viola in the fifth when Henderson followed a walk to Rafael Santana by driving a two-nothing pitch deep into the seats in left. Not once this afternoon did Viola resemble the outstanding pitcher who defeated the Cardinals in the seventh game of the World Series last fall. Nor did he resemble the pitcher who defeated the Yanks two of three times in '87 with a 2.11 ERA. Nevertheless, Viola would recover from this poor opening-day effort to have the finest season of his career, winning 24 games (24–7) and the American League's Cy Young Award. He came out after five innings, replaced by right-hander Atherton. Don Mattingly's two-out seventh-inning double against Atherton drove in Randolph and put the Yanks ahead, 7–0. Mattingly had been hitless in three at-bats against Viola, which dropped his lifetime mark against the Twins' ace to 6-for-31.

New York's final run came in the eighth, an inning that featured a triple play by the Twins. Martinez, a former star reliever for the Orioles, had just taken over on the mound to begin what would be an unsuccessful attempt to resurrect his career. He had not pitched in the major leagues since 1986 and after three ineffective outings the Twins would give him his final release. He began the inning by walking Winfield. After Kelly singled, Martinez hit Pagliarulo to load the bases. Catcher Joel Skinner walked, forcing in a run and bringing shortstop Santana to the plate. Santana had become a historical footnote last December when the Yankees traded catcher Phil Lombardi to the Mets to get him. It was the first-ever deal between the two New York clubs that involved major-league players from both teams. Santana swung at a Martinez curve ball and grounded it sharply to third baseman Gaetti, who fielded it and stepped on third forcing Pagliarulo. Gaetti then threw to second baseman Steve Lombardozzi, forcing Skinner for the second out, and Lombardozzi threw to first baseman Hrbek to complete the triple play. It was the first—and still the only—opening-day triple play involving the Yankees, offensively or defensively.

When the Twins went quietly in the ninth, they had their first road loss of the new season, continuing the pattern established last season of success at home and failure on the road. Seldom if ever has a championship team played so poorly on the road as Minnesota did in 1987. They won the 1987 World Series by sweeping the Cardinals in the four games played at the Hubert H. Humphrey Metrodome, but in addition to losing the three Series' games played at St. Louis, the Twins lost 52 of their 81 regular-season games played outside the Metrodome. Minnesota would finish second this season, 13 games behind Oakland, but they were actually a better team than they were in their championship year. They would improve to 91–71 (they were 85–77 in '87) and would go 44–37 on the road.

Rhoden's shutout, the 17th of his big-league career and first in the American League, got the Yanks off to an excellent beginning. They won nine of their first ten games, but following a tough loss in Texas on May 6, Martin got into trouble again, this time in a nightclub brawl. Seven weeks later on June 23, Steinbrenner fired him and called Piniella out of the front office to replace the manager who had replaced him. The team was 40–28 at the time, but had just come off a road trip where they had lost seven of nine. Steinbrenner also reassigned two of Martin's coaches, Art Fowler and Clete Boyer. Five days after the season ended, Steinbrenner fired Piniella again and hired Dallas Green, former Philadelphia Phillies' manager and Chicago Cubs' farm director.

Fine offensive seasons by Dave Winfield, Don Mattingly, Rickey Henderson, Claudell Washington, and Jack Clark kept the Yankees (85–76) in the pennant race most of the way. They eventually fell to fifth, but only 3½ games behind the division champion Boston Red Sox. After going 40–28 under Billy Martin, they went 45–48 under Lou Piniella. Winfield, who batted .322 with 25 home runs and 107 runs batted in, finished fourth to Jose Canseco of the Oakland A's in voting for the Most Valuable Player. Henderson broke his own club record with 93 stolen bases as he led the league for the eighth time. After winning just five games in 1987 (5–8) and two (2–3) this season, Ron Guidry's great career ended with his retirement.

Tuesday, April 5, 1988

Minnesota	ab	r	h	rbi		New York	ab	r	h	rbi
Gladden lf	4	0	0	0		Henderson lf	4	1	1	2
Gagne ss	4	0	1	0		Randolph 2b	4	2	3	0
Puckett cf	4	0	1	0		Mattingly 1b	4	0	1	1
Hrbek 1b	3	0	0	0		Ward dh	4	0	1	0
Gaetti 3b	3	0	0	0		Winfield rf	3	2	1	1
Bush dh	3	0	0	0		Kelly cf	4	1	3	0
Brunansky rf	3	0	1	0		Pagliarulo 3b	3	1	1	3
Nieto c	3	0	0	0		Skinner c	3	0	0	1
Lowry c	0	0	0	0		Santana ss	3	1	0	0
Lombardozzi 2b	3	0	0	0		Total	32	8	11	8
Total	30	0	3	0						

Minnesota	000	000	000–0	
New York	000	420	11X–8	

Errors—None. Triple play—Gaetti, Lombardozzi, and Hrbek. Left on bases—Minnesota 3; New York 4. Put outs—New York 27: Randolph 4, Mattingly 6, Skinner 4, Henderson 1, Winfield 5, Kelly 4, Pagliarulo 3. Minnesota 24: Gladden 1, Nieto 6, Gagne 1, Hrbek 9, Gaetti 2, Puckett 2, Brunansky 2, Lombardozzi 1. Assists—New York 8: Pagliarulo 2, Santana 3, Rhoden 1, Randolph 2. Minnesota 9: Lombardozzi 1, Gladden 1, Nieto 2, Gagne 2, Gaetti 3. Two-base hits—Gagne, Randolph, Mattingly. Home runs—Pagliarulo, Henderson.

	IP	H	R	ER	BB	SO
MINNESOTA						
Viola (L, 0–1)	5.0	8	6	6	1	6
Atherton	2.0	2	1	1	0	1
Martinez	1.0	1	1	1	2	0
NEW YORK						
Rhoden (W, 1–0)	9.0	3	0	0	0	4

Hit by pitch—By Martinez (Pagliarulo). Umpires—Garcia, Bremigan, Reed, and Hirschbeck. Time of game—2 hrs. 23 min. Attendance—55,802.

Tuesday, April 4, 1989 (N)
Hubert H. Humphrey Metrodome, Minneapolis
New York 4 Minnesota 2

Fans are the only ones who care. There are no free-agent fans.
There are no fans who say "Get me out of here.
I want to play for a winner."—Dick Young

Major league baseball made two excellent appointments in the winter of 1988–1989. First, the owners elected National League president A. Bartlett Giamatti to be the new commissioner, succeeding Peter Ueberroth who had held the post since 1984. Giamatti, a former president of Yale University, had a true love of baseball and an appreciation of its place in the American culture. Then the owners chose Bill White to take Giamatti's place as National League president. White, a former All-Star first baseman and most recently a Yankees' broadcaster, became the first black man to preside over a professional sports league. Unfortunately, these positive developments were eclipsed by a series of reports of immoral and illegal behavior by a trio of the game's biggest names. Boston's Wade Boggs, the American League batting champion, confessed that he was involved in an extramarital affair; Oakland's Jose Canseco, the American League's Most Valuable Player, had several highly publicized driving mishaps; and worst of all, there were allegations that Cincinnati Reds manager Pete Rose illegally bet on sporting events.

Then too, there were the usual off-season battles between teams and players over money. Contractual disputes had always been a part of baseball, but over the last ten years the public had come to view them differently. In the past, when the owners held complete power, fans could sympathize and identify with players who were trying to get a few thousand dollars more from a club. However, in this age of free agency and multimillion-dollar contracts, it was difficult for them to identify with either players or owners. Every time someone threatened to leave for a new team because ownership failed to satisfy his desires, it reinforced the fans' conviction that players had no loyalty to the cities in which they played. The people in Minnesota were the latest to be subjected to such a threat. It was from Frank Viola, and it came just a few hours before he went out to pitch the season opener against the Yankees. Viola, the reigning Cy Young Award winner, announced that he was unhappy with Twins owner Carl Pohlad's offer of $7.9 million for three years and would become a free agent at the end of the season. To make his defection even less palatable to the locals, he spoke openly about signing with his hometown team, the Yankees. Supposedly, Viola was asking for $8.1 million, $200,000 more than Pohlad was offering. That was a relatively small difference, the fans felt, if Viola truly wanted to stay in Minnesota. But then Pohlad was using Opening Day to communicate his own sense of loyalty to a location. Earlier in the day, he announced that the Twins would be moving their Florida spring training home from Orlando to Fort Myers. That the Twins had been coming to Orlando since 1936, when they were still the Washington Senators, meant little to Pohlad. When he asked the city to spend $6 million to improve the training site and they offered to pay only $3 million, he abruptly ended the relationship.

While the crowd exhibited mixed feelings about Viola (some applause, some boos), they cheered vigorously for Twins coach Tony Oliva when he threw out the first ball. Oliva, a three-time batting champion, had spent his entire career in Minnesota, a career that ended just before the arrival of free agency. The Jets, a local rock group, performed the national anthem. These were heady days for the Twins. After winning their first world championship in 1987, they finished second in the Western Division in 1988, but improved their win-loss record by six games. Minnesota also became the first American League team to draw more than 3 million people when 3,030,672 paid their way into the Hubert H. Humphrey Metrodome last season. They made a good start toward bettering that mark when a near-capacity crowd of 52,394 showed up for tonight's opener. (They didn't, drawing just under 2.3 million in '89.) And while most fans entered the Metrodome discussing what they perceived as Viola's stubbornness and greed, they left marveling at his opponent Tommy John's endurance and tenacity. The 45-year-old left-hander held the Twins to two runs in seven innings in leading the Yankees to a 4–2 victory.

New York began the pennant chase after going through what was now an all-too-familiar period of off-season upheaval. There continued to be a constant flow of players in and out of pinstripes, and, of course, there was a new manager. To lead the Yankees in 1989, George Steinbrenner hired Dallas Green, who had last managed in 1981 with the Philadelphia Phillies. Steinbrenner also hired veteran baseball man Syd Thrift to run the front office. Jack Clark, the team leader in home runs a year ago, was gone after just one season, traded with Pat Clements to the San Diego Padres for pitchers Jimmy Jones and Lance McCullers and outfielder Stan Jefferson. Free agent Claudell Washington, another dependable hitter, left to join the California Angels, but three other free agents came to New York: pitchers Andy Hawkins from the Padres and Dave LaPoint from the Pittsburgh Pirates, and second baseman Steve Sax from the Los Angeles Dodgers. Sax's arrival led to the departure of Willie Randolph, who left the Yankees after 13 seasons to sign with the Dodgers.

During spring training the Yankees made two more deals, trading catcher Joel Skinner to the Cleveland Indians for outfielder Mel Hall and reacquiring Steve Balboni from the Seattle Mariners. The club hoped that newcomers Hall and Balboni would supply some of the power lost by the absence of Clark and Dave Winfield. Although the Yanks had resigned themselves to being without Winfield for three months while he recuperated from back surgery, the recuperation took longer than expected and Winfield would miss the entire season. Regular shortstop Rafael Santana injured his elbow in Florida and he too would miss the 1989 season. With Don Mattingly also out of the opening-day lineup—he was home in New Jersey nursing back spasms—Twins manager Tom Kelly declared: "That team doesn't look like the Yankee Yankees. Those names you expect aren't there. It doesn't seem the same." Kelly was right; this Yankees' lineup was indeed not one to inspire fear in managers or opposing pitchers. However, while it was lacking in offense, what it did have was Tommy John; and it was John's determination and pitching wisdom that made the difference this night.

At the start of spring training, Green had said he thought John was too old to pitch in the major leagues. But when John yielded only four runs in 24 innings in the exhibition season—and looked so impressive in doing it—he not only won a place on Green's pitching staff but also the honor of starting his fifth opener. John's previous opening-day assignments were for the Chicago White Sox in 1966, 1970, and 1971 and for the Yankees in 1981. At 45 years and 10 months, John was then the third-oldest pitcher ever to start a major-league opener, and the oldest ever to win one. Minnesota got to him for ten hits in his seven innings, and twice he seemed on the verge of destructing. In the fourth inning and again in the sixth, Minnesota had the bases loaded with two outs, but each time John retired the next batter. In the fourth, the Twins had taken a one-run lead on a single by Wally Backman (in his first game as a Twin), a force-play grounder by Kirby Puckett, and singles by Gary Gaetti and Kent Hrbek. Later in the inning, with Gaetti at third, Hrbek at second, and Carmelo Castillo, who had walked, at first, John got Gene Larkin on a routine grounder to Sax. Then in the sixth, after he retired the first two batters, Tim Laudner singled, Castillo doubled, and Larkin walked to again load the bases. But Greg Gagne, after fouling off three full-count pitches, went out on a liner to right fielder Gary Ward.

By that time the Yanks had taken a 2–1 lead with two runs in the fifth. Alvaro Espinoza, Santana's replacement at shortstop, started the uprising with a one-out single to center. Espinoza had spent parts of three different seasons with the Twins, but had primarily been a minor-leaguer during his eight-year career. The Yankees' Columbus Clippers farm team signed Espinoza as a free agent for the 1988 season. He hit only .246, but played a solid shortstop. When the Yanks lost Santana for the year, they gave Espinoza the opportunity to replace him. Roberto Kelly's double off the wall in left scored Espinoza with the tying run. Kelly took third on Rickey Henderson's infield single and scored the go-ahead run on Sax's sacrifice fly.

Except for Seattle's Kingdome, Minnesota's Metrodome was the most aesthetically unappealing park in baseball; but not to Viola—he loved it. At least he loved pitching there. Since May 27, 1987, he had won 23 games at the Metrodome while losing only twice. Nevertheless, when Espinoza and Kelly, the first two batters in the seventh, hit singles and Henderson walked, Viola was through for the night. Henderson's walk was on a 3–2 pitch, and before manager Kelly came out to get him, Viola yelled at home-plate umpire Jim Evans, whose calls he had questioned all evening. There was some applause and only a scattering of boos as Viola left, just as there had been at the pregame introductions. It was difficult to tell just how the Minnesota fans felt about their recalcitrant pitcher; perhaps they forgave him, or perhaps they just didn't care. The Twins' front office reacted differently. On July 31, when they realized they had no chance of keeping Viola, they traded him to the New York Mets—the first time a team had traded a Cy Young Award winner in the season after he won the award. The Mets got baseball's winningest pitcher over the previous five years in exchange for a group of youngsters that included pitchers Kevin Tapani, David West, and Rick Aguilera. Soon after moving to New York, Viola would learn that not all fans were so forgiving or uncaring as the ones he left.

Juan Berenguer inherited the bases-loaded-nobody-out situation and got out of it with only one run scoring, which was on Sax's force-play grounder. Berenguer held the score at 3–1 by striking out ex–Tiger Tom Brookens, the designated hitter in his Yankees' debut, and getting Balboni on a pop to second. Minnesota made it 3–2 in the home seventh, John's last inning, on singles by Dan Gladden and Backman and two ground balls. John departed, having taken part in a major-league game for a record-tying 26th season, a record Nolan Ryan would eventually break. To mark the occasion, he had autographed the first ball, which was then removed from play and sent to the Hall of Fame. Green had Dave Righetti available, but instead turned the game over to right-hander Dale Mohorcic, whom the Yankees had picked up late last season from Texas for Cecilio Guante.

Tuesday, April 4, 1989

New York	ab	r	h	rbi		Minnesota	ab	r	h	rbi
Henderson lf	3	0	2	0		Gladden lf	5	1	2	0
Sax 2b	4	0	0	2		Backman 2b	5	0	2	0

New York	ab	r	h	rbi
Brookens dh,3b	4	0	1	0
Balboni 1b	4	0	0	0
Ward rf	3	0	0	0
ªHall rf	1	0	0	0
Pagliarulo 3b	3	0	0	0
Mohorcic p	0	0	0	0
Slaught c	4	0	0	0
Espinoza ss	4	2	2	0
Kelly cf	4	2	4	2
Total	34	4	9	4

Minnesota	ab	r	h	rbi
Puckett cf	4	1	0	0
Gaetti 3b	4	0	1	1
Hrbek 1b	4	0	2	1
Laudner c	3	0	1	0
ᵇMoses	1	0	0	0
Harper c	0	0	0	0
Castillo rf	2	0	1	0
ᶜBush rf	1	0	0	0
Larkin dh	3	0	0	0
Gagne ss	4	0	1	0
Total	36	2	10	2

ªGrounded out for Ward in eighth inning.
ᵇLined out for Laudner in eighth inning.
ᶜFlied out for Castillo in eighth inning.

New York	000	020	101–4
Minnesota	000	100	100–2

Error—Backman. Double plays—Gladden and Laudner; Gaetti, Backman, and Hrbek; Slaught and Espinoza. Caught stealing—by Slaught (Gladden). Left on bases—New York 8; Minnesota 9. Put outs—New York 27: Espinoza 2, Balboni 12, Ward 1, Slaught 5, Kelly 4, Sax, 1 Mohorcic 1. Pagliarulo 1. Minnesota 27: Backman 5, Gladden 2, Gagne 2, Hrbek 5, Laudner 4, Harper 2, Puckett 4, Castillo 3. Assists—New York 10: Slaught 1, Espinoza 2, Pagliarulo 2, Sax 3, John 2. Minnesota 8: Backman 3, Gladden 1, Gagne 2, Gaetti 2. Two-base hits—Brookens, Kelly, Castillo. Home run—Kelly. Stolen bases—Hrbek, Gaetti, Kelly 2, Henderson 3. Sacrifice fly—Sax.

	IP	H	R	ER	BB	SO
NEW YORK						
John (W, 1–0)	7.0	10	2	2	2	3
Mohorcic S.1	2.0	0	0	0	0	2
MINNESOTA						
#Viola (L, 0–1)	6.0	8	3	3	4	1
Berenguer	3.0	1	1	1	0	4

#Viola pitched to three batters in the seventh inning.

Balk—Berenguer. Umpires—Evans, Shulock, Morrison, and Welke. Time of game—2 hrs. 53 min. Attendance—52,394.

Roberto Kelly's long home run to right off Berenguer in the ninth gave Mohorcic an insurance run. For Kelly, who missed two months of his 1988 rookie season with wrist and knee injuries, it gave him a perfect 4-for-4 night, and the first four-hit game of his career. He also stole two bases—the Yanks stole a total of five, with Henderson getting the other three. Three of Kelly's hits came off Viola, against whom he was now 7-for-9 lifetime. Between them, Kelly and Espinoza had six of the nine Yankees' hits, and scored all four runs.

Meanwhile, Mohorcic was perfect, retiring all six men he faced. Yet all the postgame talk was about John and his ability to pitch out of trouble. Manager Kelly's comments were typical. "Tommy John got the outs when he needed them," Kelly said. "We got quite a few hits, but the times it counted, when the ducks were on the pond, we couldn't get it." John's victory was the 287th of his career, but he would win only one more (while losing seven) before the Yankees released him on May 30. Some other Yankees who started today's opener would also be gone before long. Ward was first; the club released him two weeks after the opener. Then in June they sent Henderson back to the Oakland A's in exchange for outfielder Luis Polonia and pitchers Eric Plunk and Greg Cadaret. A few weeks later, third baseman Mike Pagliarulo went to the Padres for pitcher Walt Terrell. Finally, on August 18, claiming that hiring Green had been his biggest mistake in baseball, Steinbrenner fired him along with his four coaches. Former Yankees shortstop Bucky Dent, Steinbrenner's 11th different manager in 17 years, finished out the season.

With a 56–65 record under Dallas Green and an 18–22 mark under Bucky Dent, the Yankees (74–87) finished fifth, 14½ games behind the Toronto Blue Jays. It was the fourth consecutive year that their win total had declined. Attendance, which had increased in each of those years, fell by more than 460,000 to 2,170,485. Several times during the season the fans at Yankee Stadium showed their displeasure with owner George Steinbrenner, both vocally and with signs. But that did not deter him. Syd Thrift, hired in March as vice president of baseball operations, resigned on August 30 after Steinbrenner ordered the team's scouts to stop traveling to evaluate talent as a cost-saving measure. When general manager Bob Quinn resigned at the end of the season, Steinbrenner promised that he would now take a greater interest in the team's day-to-day operations. Steve Sax batted .315 with 205 hits, including a club record 171 singles. Roberto Kelly also had an excellent season, batting .302 with 35 stolen bases.

X

1990–1999

Six years after they began the new decade with one of their worst seasons ever, the Yankees and their fans, experienced one of their best. They had finished seventh and last in the Eastern Division in 1990 (the Yanks' first last-place finish since 1966), winning just 67 games, their fewest wins in a full season since 1913. The club improved steadily under Buck Showalter who took over as manager in 1992 and led the club for the next four seasons. Despite setting a longevity record for the George Steinbrenner era, Showalter's successful career in New York ended when Steinbrenner chose to let him leave following the 1995 season. But under the new management team of general manager Bob Watson and veteran National League player and manager Joe Torre, who succeeded Showalter, the 1996 Yankees won their first world championship since 1978. They followed with three more World Series titles in 1998, 1999, and 2000.

Throughout the 90s, baseball continued to alienate its fans with seemingly endless labor squabbles. The failure of the owners and players to settle their differences culminated in the worst strike in the game's history—one that wiped out much of the 1994 season, including the World Series, and made for a shortened 1995 season. When the 1994 season ended on August 11, the Yankees were in first place in the newly revised Eastern Division. The owners had further diluted the pennant race by creating three divisions where there were two and adding a "wild-card" team, thus creating an additional round of play-offs. The strike delayed this new television-inspired gimmick for one year, but it went into effect in 1995. New York, by having the best second-place record in the league made the playoffs as the first wild card team, losing the Division Series to the Seattle Mariners in five games. Although this new set of playoffs was a contrivance that devalued the regular season, it was nevertheless an exciting series, and even allowed Don Mattingly finally to participate in "postseason" play before his retirement following the season.

Increasing salaries, free agency and the difficulties of "small-market" teams made for unprecedented movement among players during this decade. Among the former All-Stars who played for New York in the nineties were Wade Boggs, Paul O'Neill, Tim Raines, David Wells, Ruben Sierra, Danny Tartabull, Tino Martinez, Jimmy Key, David Cone, Roger Clemens, John Wetteland, Jack McDowell, Kenny Rogers, Dwight Gooden, Darryl Strawberry, and Cecil Fielder. Yet, as it was in the glory days, the Yankees' new dynasty was spearheaded by youngsters brought up in their farm system—men like center fielder Bernie Williams and pitcher Andy Pettitte, who established themselves as stars in 1995; pitcher Mariano Rivera and shortstop Derek Jeter, in 1996; and catcher Jorge Posada in 1998.

Thursday, April 12, 1990
Yankee Stadium, New York
New York 6 Cleveland 4

It's more than a game. It's an institution.—Thomas Hughes

Another year, another labor-management squabble, another work stoppage. This time it was over the owners' failure to reach a compromise on their "basic agreement" with the Players Association. Following a breakdown in negotiations, the owners used their favorite weapon: they locked the players out of their spring training camps. The lockout, which began on February 15 and lasted for 32 days, shortened spring training to three weeks and delayed Opening Day for one week. However, by making some slight adjustments, the leagues ensured that all teams would play their full 162-game schedules. Under the revised schedule, the Yankees were supposed to open with a two-game series in Cleveland beginning Tuesday, April 10, but both games were canceled because of weather. An all-day rain canceled the first one, and snow halted play the following night in the bottom of the fourth inning with the Yankees trailing, 2–1. On the original schedule, the one before the lockout, April 12 was supposed to be an off day for both teams. But the amended schedule was using this date to make up one of the three scheduled Yankee Stadium games between the two clubs canceled by the late start. So, following the two nights of bad weather in Cleveland, the Yankees and Indians moved to New York where they finally got their 1990 seasons started. On a cool, sunny afternoon at the Stadium, a spirited crowd of 50,114 saw the home team twice surrender two-run leads before coming away with an exciting, 6–4, win.

As was customary in the George Steinbrenner era, this year's opening-day manager (Bucky Dent) was different from last year's opening-day manager (Dallas Green). Actually, Dent had managed the club since taking over from Green last August, but this was his first time managing in an opener. His opponent, Cleveland's John McNamara, who had been a manager for 16 years, with the Oakland Athletics, the San Diego Padres, the Cincinnati Reds, the California Angels, and the Boston Red Sox, was managing his first game with the Indians. Both managers had chosen a veteran right-hander for last night's snowed-out game: McNamara selected Tom Candiotti, while Dent went with newly acquired Tim Leary. For this afternoon's contest, both managers stayed with veterans, but switched to left-handers, Bud Black for Cleveland and Dave LaPoint for New York. LaPoint had already pitched for seven different clubs by the time the Yankees got him as a free agent from the Pittsburgh Pirates in December 1988. He was a disappointing 6–9 for the Yankees before rotator cuff surgery ended his 1989 season on August 21. "I don't think anybody had it in their imagination that I would be the opening-day starter," LaPoint said. "I didn't figure Opening Day. I figured fourth or fifth starter. But by default, the weather and other things, there I was." Black, after struggling through three seasons in which he won a total of 17 games, had bounced back to win 12 (12–11) for the 1989 Indians. This would be his fourth opening-day start and third against the Yankees; as a member of the Kansas City Royals, he started against Ron Guidry in 1984 and 1986. Black won the '84 game, 4–2, but lost in '86 by the same score. He was 0–1 versus the Yanks in 1989 and 3–11 for his career.

Despite winning more games in the 1980s than any other major-league team (854), for the first time since 1910—1919, the Yankees had completed a decade in which they did not win a World Series. The 1980s had begun with two Eastern Division titles and a pennant, but then went downhill, concluding with consecutive fifth-place finishes in 1988 and '89. Yet to their everlasting credit, come Opening Day, baseball fans disregard things like lock-outs and lowly finishes and greet the new season with enthusiasm. Those who came to Yankee Stadium and to ballparks around the country were sadly beginning to accept periodic labor strife as part of the game, something they had to endure every few years. And as for lowly finishes, they no longer came as a shock to the generation of Yankees fans that grew up after the dynasty years. Of course, there was not much that could shock New Yorkers now. Even this morning's report that nearly 2,000 people were murdered in New York City in each of the past five years did not deter the fans from making their way through the dangerous neighborhoods around the Stadium. The alarming murder rate was further evidence—if anyone needed further evidence—of how much the quality of life (no pun intended) in New York had deteriorated. In 1951, Mickey Mantle's rookie year, the total number of murders in the city was 244.

The afternoon began on a bittersweet note when 25-year-old Billy Joe Martin threw out the first ball. Martin, from Lubbock, Texas, was the son of the late Yankees' manager who was killed in a drunk-driving accident last Christmas Day. Afterwards, Dent presented Martin with a Yankees jersey bearing the familiar No. 1 his father had worn both as player and manager. The crowd gave the young man polite applause, saving their largest ovations for Don Mattingly and Dave Winfield. Although they were pleased the 38-year-old Winfield was playing again—his first league game since 1988—some doubted that he could make a successful comeback. After missing the entire 1989 season recovering from back surgery, he had only one hit in 29 Grapefruit League at-bats this spring. Yet while a number of fans had misgivings about Winfield, Champ Summers, the team's batting coach, did not. When asked about Winfield's unproductive spring, Summers said that neither Winfield's poor hitting, nor that of Jesse Barfield (6-for-29 with no home runs) concerned him. Both, he felt, would be ready on Opening Day. Sure enough, Winfield was ready on Opening Day. He hit a run-scoring double in the snowed-out game, and then in his first at-bat this afternoon he doubled to left to lead off the second inning. Two outs later, Winfield was at third and Mel Hall at first when Black was undone by a pair of rookies. Catcher Bob Geren and third baseman Mike Blowers came through with base hits, scoring Winfield and Hall and giving New York a 2–0 lead. Black followed by walking Steve Sax to load the bases, but got Alvaro Espinoza for the third out.

Cleveland tied the score in the fourth on a two-run homer by Cory Snyder, only to have the Yanks regain the lead in the fifth. Mattingly's two-out single scored Blowers, who had walked to lead off the inning. Mattingly, the Yankees' most popular player began the 1990 season with a .323 lifetime batting average, 164 home runs, and 717 runs batted in. The day before the scheduled opener, he signed a five-year contract that would pay him $19.3 million.

Mattingly was baseball's "highest-paid player," and while that distinction did not last as long as it did in the days of Babe Ruth, Joe DiMaggio, and Mickey Mantle, for now at least it belonged to him. Mattingly had joined the Yankees in 1983, the same year the New York Mets acquired Keith Hernandez in a one-sided trade with the St. Louis Cardinals. Over the next seven years, New Yorkers had the pleasure of watching two of the finest first basemen ever. Naturally, they argued over which one was better. However, Hernandez was now nearing the end of his career and no one any longer compared him with Mattingly. He had signed on with Cleveland for this his final season, and was in today's starting lineup. Unfortunately, that allowed many younger "fans" in the stadium, remembering the rivalry with Mattingly but untutored in baseball mores, to jeer his every move.

Dent relieved LaPoint in the top of the sixth with right-hander Jeff Robinson, obtained from Pittsburgh in an off-season trade for Don Slaught. LaPoint, who had not pitched more than five innings all spring, threw 75 pitches, allowed five hits, did not walk anyone, and received a warm sendoff as he left the mound. Robinson entered the game with Mitch Webster on second and one out and retired two dangerous right-handed hitters, Candy Maldonado (a free agent from the San Francisco Giants) and Snyder.

Former Red Sox right-hander Al Nipper came on for Cleveland in the bottom of the sixth and gave up a run on a two-out single by Roberto Kelly and a double by Geren. It was Geren's second run batted in of the game and gave the Yanks a two-run lead. Geren had broken into organized baseball back in 1979, but didn't reach the majors until 1988. He caught ten games for the Yankees that year, 65 in 1989, and expected to be the regular catcher this season. Of his start today, Geren said it "was the first time I've been to an Opening Day, even as a fan."

Both teams had a base runner in the seventh, but failed to score; still, the best was yet to come. The game's last inning and a half were a fan's delight, loaded with strategy, action, and drama. In that stretch, the Indians retied the score before the Yanks again took the lead and then held off another Indian uprising in the ninth to preserve the victory. It all started when Indians catcher Sandy Alomar Jr. led off the eighth by drawing a walk. Alomar had come to Cleveland with outfielder Chris James and Carlos Baerga, a highly touted rookie infielder, as part of a major winter deal that sent the Indians' best player, outfielder Joe Carter, to the San Diego Padres. Ex-Yankee Rafael Santana was due to follow Alomar, but McNamara started the managerial maneuvering by sending Dion James, a left-handed batter, up to pinch-hit. Dent countered by pulling Robinson and bringing in left-hander Greg Cadaret to pitch to James. McNamara then called James back and substituted the right-hand hitting Joey Belle (later to be known as Albert Belle). After all the "deep thinking" ended, Cadaret got Belle on a pop to Blowers. Then he got Webster on a fly to Kelly, but second baseman Jerry Browne singled to keep the inning alive. With Maldonado coming up, Dent went to his bullpen again, this time for right-handed fastballer Eric Plunk. Plunk got Maldonado to hit a short fly ball, but Kelly, despite a great effort, could not quite reach it. Alomar scored easily, and Browne, running with two outs, also scored, beating Kelly's throw home. Maldonado tried to reach second but was out from Geren to Sax; still, Cleveland had tied the score.

McNamara brought in left-hander Jesse Orosco, like Hernandez a former Met, to pitch the last of the eighth. Orosco replaced Cecilio Guante, who had replaced Nipper an inning earlier. With two out, Kelly was on first, having forced Barfield who walked, when Geren singled for his third hit of the day. Geren's hit sent Kelly to third and McNamara to the mound. Out went Orosco and in came soft-throwing right-hander Doug Jones, Cleveland's best relief pitcher and saver of 69 games over the past two seasons. Dent answered by sending left-handed hitter Luis Polonia up to pinch-hit for Blowers. Polonia, anxious to wipe out the memory of last season's personal problems, poked the first pitch into center, scoring Kelly. His hit put the Yanks ahead, 5–4, and made Polonia the hero of the moment. (His heroics did not prevent the club from trading him to the Angels just 16 days later to reacquire Claudell Washington.) The Yanks got an insurance run when Geren scored from second as Browne threw wildly to first on Sax's slow ground ball. The official scorer ruled it a hit for Sax, but no run batted in, and the run was unearned.

Dent sent Plunk out to pitch the ninth, keeping his ace Dave Righetti in reserve. Plunk got the first batter, Snyder, on a grounder to Randy Velarde, Blowers's replacement at third base. Hernandez followed with a single, his first American League hit, and then went out for pinch-runner Tom Brookens. The tying run was at the plate, but Dent stayed with Plunk and had his faith rewarded. After wild-pitching Brookens to second, Plunk got Chris James on a grounder to Sax for the second out. Then he retired Brook Jacoby on a fly to Kelly, and the Yankees had their fifth consecutive opening-day victory—one that was especially satisfying. Cleveland had beaten them nine times in 13 games in 1989, the Yanks' worst winning percentage against the Indians since 1908, when they lost 16 of 22. But then, as Mattingly said after it was over, "Any win is a good win."

Dent lasted until June. The team was 18–31 when Steinbrenner fired him and brought Columbus Clippers manager Stump Merrill from the International League to New York. In August Steinbrenner dismissed general manager Harding Peterson and promoted Gene Michael to the post. Winfield's stay in New York ended on May 16, when the Yanks traded him to California for pitcher Mike Witt. Steinbrenner's long-running feud with Winfield had serious repercussions for the Yankee boss. While it was going on he hired Howie Spira, a known gambler, to try to find damaging information about Winfield. The arrangement between Steinbrenner and Spira greatly displeased Fay Vincent, who had become commissioner after Bart Giamatti's death in September 1989. Vincent ordered Steinbrenner to resign his position as managing general partner by August 20 and issued a lifetime ban against his involvement in the team's day-to-day operations. Steinbrenner chose one of his partners, Robert Nederlander, to succeed him.

Thursday, April 12, 1990

Cleveland

	ab	r	h	rbi
Webster cf	4	0	1	0
Browne 2b	3	1	1	0
Maldonado lf	4	1	2	2
Snyder rf	4	1	2	2
Hernandez 1b	4	0	1	0
dBrookens	0	0	0	0
C. James dh	4	0	0	0
Jacoby 3b	4	0	1	0
Alomar c	2	1	1	0
Santana ss	2	0	0	0
aD. James	0	0	0	0
bBelle	1	0	0	0
Fermin ss	0	0	0	0
Total	32	4	9	4

New York

	ab	r	h	rbi
Sax 2b	3	0	1	0
Espinoza ss	4	0	0	0
Mattingly 1b	4	0	2	1
Winfield dh	4	1	1	0
Hall lf	4	1	1	0
Barfield rf	3	0	0	0
Kelly cf	4	2	1	0
Geren c	4	1	3	2
Blowers 3b	2	1	1	1
cPolonia	1	0	1	1
Velarde 3b	0	0	0	0
Total	33	6	11	5

aAnnounced for Santana in eighth inning.
bPopped out for D. James in eighth inning.
cSingled for Blowers in eighth inning.
dRan for Hernandez in ninth inning.

Cleveland	000	200	020–4
New York	020	011	02X–6

Errors—Browne. Double plays—Espinoza, Sax, and Mattingly; Santana and Hernandez. Left on bases—Cleveland 3; New York 8. Put outs—New York 27: Geren 4, Mattingly 10, Barfield 1, Blowers 1, Sax 2, Kelly 6, Espinoza 2, Hall 1. Cleveland 24: Hernandez 8, Browne 3, Alomar 5, Santana 2, Webster 5, Fermin 1. Assists—New York 14: Geren 1, Mattingly 1, Barfield 1, Hall 1, Blowers 1, Sax 2, Kelly 1, Espinoza 4, LaPoint 1, Velarde 1. Cleveland 11: Black 1, Browne 2, Jacoby 4, Santana 2, Orosco 1, Fermin 1. Two-base hits—Winfield, Geren. Home run—Snyder. Sacrifices—Sax, Browne.

	IP	H	R	ER	BB	SO
CLEVELAND						
Black	5.0	6	3	3	2	1
Nipper	1.0	2	1	1	0	2
Guante	1.0	0	0	0	0	1
Orosco (L, 0–1)	.2	1	2	1	1	1
Jones	.1	2	0	0	0	0
NEW YORK						
LaPoint	5.1	5	2	2	0	4
#Robinson	1.2	1	1	1	1	0
Cadaret	.2	1	1	1	0	0
Plunk (W, 1–0)	1.1	2	0	0	0	0

#Robinson pitched to one batter in the eighth inning.

Hit by pitch—By Guante (Espinoza). Wild pitch—Plunk. Umpires—McCoy, Clark, Hirschbeck, and Phillips. Time of game—2 hrs. 59 min. Attendance—50,114.

The 1990 season was among the worst in the club's history. Under Bucky Dent (18–31) and Stump Merrill (49–64), they finished 67–95, seventh and last in the East, 21 games behind the Boston Red Sox. The last-place finish was their first since 1966, and not since 1913 had a Yankees team won fewer games in a full season. Don Mattingly's back problems led to his worst season. He played in only 102 games, batting .256, with just five home runs and 42 runs batted in. Rookie Kevin Maas replaced Mattingly at first base for much of the second half of the season, hitting 21 home runs in only 254 at-bats. Maas finished second to Cleveland Indians catcher Sandy Alomar Jr., who won the American League's Rookie of the Year Award unanimously.

Monday, April 8, 1991
Tiger Stadium, Detroit
Detroit 6 New York 4

When a man assumes a public trust, he should
consider himself as public property.—Thomas Jefferson

The 1991 baseball season began on schedule. There was a time when fans would take such an occurrence for granted, but now they saw it as a gift. Unlike last year, when an owners' lockout of the players shortened spring training and delayed the start of the season, this year there was peace—a temporary and uneasy peace, but still peace. Oh, there had been an umpires' strike—it seemed no season would be complete without some kind of labor conflict—but they had settled it by Opening Day. Still, the settlement came too late for the regular umpires to work the openers except for the Milwaukee Brewers-Texas Rangers game in Texas. Substitute umpires would handle the other games, including the Yankees' opener in Detroit, a city where the fans were in a state of turmoil. Even the Tigers' 6–4 win did little to alleviate the anger they felt at the recent actions and statements by team owner Tom Monaghan and team president Bo Schembechler. For starters, Monaghan wanted to leave Tiger Stadium, which he claimed was too old, and build a modern new ballpark in the suburbs. He pointed out that when the new Comiskey Park opened next week in Chicago, the only remaining major-league parks built before Tiger Stadium would be Fenway Park and Wrigley Field. Detroit, he added, had become "one of the worst baseball cities" in America, with a stadium located in an "unsafe part of an unsafe city." [Monaghan's chronology was a bit off. Tiger Stadium and Fenway Park opened in 1912 and Wrigley Field in 1914.]

Monaghan's assessment was in sharp contrast to Detroit's longstanding reputation as one of the great baseball cities. Yet it was true that attendance had been slumping, falling from a record high of 2,704,794 in the championship 1984 season, to just over half that in 1990. Adding to Detroit's attendance problems was the racial makeup of the crowds at Tiger Stadium. They were overwhelmingly white, as they now were at all major-league parks, and white people were continuing to leave Detroit for the suburbs. The lead story in this morning's *Detroit Free Press* confirmed the exodus, reporting that the percentage of black residents in Detroit had increased sharply during the 1980s and so had segregation. With many remaining fans reluctant to make the trip to Tiger Stadium for safety reasons, Monaghan was pushing to be in a new suburban stadium by Opening Day 1995. If there had ever been a feeling of sentiment attached to owning a baseball team, it no longer existed—anywhere. For even though there is more prestige in owning the Detroit Tigers than in owning Domino's Pizza (the source of Monaghan's fortune), a businessman expects each of his enterprises to make money. And unquestionably, a new suburban stadium, with the now ubiquitous skyboxes, would be a moneymaker for Monaghan and the Tigers.

Schembechler was another story. A former football coach at the University of Michigan, he seemed intent on alienating the fans. What particularly outraged them was his treatment of Ernie Harwell, the Tigers' beloved radio and TV announcer. Harwell had been in Detroit for 31 years, but Schembechler told him that because the Tigers were trying to appeal to a younger audience, this season would be his last. Not surprisingly, the crowds heading toward the entrance gates passed groups of pickets who were protesting both Harwell's firing and the plans for a new park. Opening Day is often a sellout in Detroit, but there were several thousand empty seats today. Still, a crowd of 47,382 turned out on a drizzly, 70-degree day, the warmest Opening Day in Detroit since 1960. They were in for another surprise. Two weeks earlier, Schembechler's disregard for the Tigers' adult fans led him to fire Steve Schlesing, the longtime organist at Tiger Stadium, and replace him with piped-in rock music. So between innings of this afternoon's opener, in a lovely old ballpark where fans once cheered Ty Cobb, Hank Greenberg, and Al Kaline, they were now assaulted by the sounds of Madonna's "Into the Groove."

All around baseball today, the host cities were including a tribute to Persian Gulf War veterans in their Opening Day ceremonies. Americans were feeling extremely patriotic in April 1991, principally because of the recently concluded war. The victory over Iraq had been much less costly in American lives than anticipated, although pundits continued to question President George Bush's decision to allow Iraqi dictator Saddam Hussein to remain in power. Nevertheless, the president's efforts in coordinating the military alliance against Iraq had given him the highest approval ratings of his presidency and seemed to assure his reelection in 1992. Air Force Captain Steven Tate, a Michigan native who during the war shot down the first Iraqi jet, threw out the first ball. Tate threw the ball from the mound with his wife and two young children looking on. Management, in an attempt to appease the fans and show its "warm and fuzzy" side, used onetime Tigers' fan-favorite Mark Fidrych and manager Sparky Anderson's young grandson to bring the ball out to Captain Tate. Michigan's new governor, John Engler, was at a funeral and unable to attend the game, but Mayor Coleman Young was there and as usual heard the boos of the crowd. Bob Taylor sang the national anthem, the 22nd time he had done so at Tiger Stadium. Anderson had been the Tigers' manager since 1980, and in every one of those years Jack Morris had been his opening-day pitcher. But with Morris now in Minnesota, Anderson turned to Frank Tanana, a veteran left-hander with a 17–17 lifetime record against New York, including 10 wins in his last 14 decisions. This was not a new experience for Tanana; he had been the California Angels' opening-day pitcher from 1976 through 1979.

A year ago, when Commissioner Fay Vincent issued his lifetime ban against George Steinbrenner's involvement in the Yankees' day-to-day operations, Steinbrenner selected Robert Nederlander to replace him. The new managing general partner had a different approach to the game than his predecessor. Nederlander stressed fiscal responsibility and an emphasis on rebuilding the team through its farm system. As a result, three of the Yankees' most promising youngsters were in the opening-day lineup. The three—designated hitter Kevin Maas, left fielder Hensley Meulens, and third baseman Mike Blowers—combined to drive in all four Yankee runs. Meulens, the first major-leaguer born in Curacao, drove in the first one in the first inning when he lined a two-out single to right center. It scored Don Mattingly, who had singled and reached second with a rare stolen base. The 23-year-old Meulens had earned International League Player of the Year honors with the Columbus Clippers in 1990 and was the first rookie to open the season in left field for the Yankees since Hank Bauer in 1949. Detroit answered back in its half of the first, taking a 2–1 lead against Yankees starter Tim Leary. Alan Trammell followed Lloyd Moseby's one-out double by driving a one-nothing pitch deep into the left center-field seats.

Manager Stump Merrill looked upon Leary as the ace of the staff, and had named him to pitch the opener more than a week earlier. Despite his league-leading 19 losses last year, Leary's nine wins were the most by a Yankees' starter (reliever Lee Guetterman had 11), making 1990 the first time in the team's history that no starter won at least ten games. Moreover, he had never lost to the Tigers; he was 4–0, including two wins here a year ago.

A two-out, two-run homer by Maas, following another single by Mattingly (whom Merrill had batting second), gave the Yanks a 3–2 lead in the third. Maas, playing with a pulled thigh muscle, drove Tanana's first pitch into the upper deck in right. Last season, left-handers had held Maas to a paltry .164 batting average and surrendered only three of his 21 home runs. Blowers made his contribution, leading off the fourth. He homered on a 2–1 pitch to give the Yanks a 4–2 lead. New York threatened again in the sixth against Dan Petry and in the seventh against Paul Gibson, but in both innings Trammell started double plays to end the rallies. Trammell was doing it all for Detroit. His fifth inning, two-run double into the left-field corner—his third and fourth runs batted in of the afternoon—had tied the score at 4–4. It was a great start for the Tigers' shortstop after just two extra-base hits and no home runs in 62 spring training at-bats.

Leary had struck out nine through six innings; but after yielding five hits, three walks, and four runs, Merrill took him out. Left-hander Greg Cadaret came on in the seventh and gave up a single to Milt Cuyler and a walk to Tony Phillips. He got Moseby to pop up his sacrifice-bunt attempt, but with right-handed hitters Trammell and Cecil Fielder due up, Merrill called in right-hander Eric Plunk. Anderson ordered a double steal to get the runners into scoring position and reduce the possibility of a double play. However, Cuyler, a rookie, failed to get a good jump and stopped between second and third. The textbook play in this situation is for the catcher (Matt Nokes) to run at the base runner until he commits himself. Instead, Nokes threw to second, allowing Cuyler to cruise easily into third.

"I was thinking he was far enough off second to pick him off, but I should have been thinking I could run at him," Nokes said later. Mattingly, the newly appointed team captain, was solicitous. "I'm sure he'd like to do it differently," he said. "You look at those things constructively, and you learn." Plunk then got Trammell to foul out to Nokes for what should have been the third out. However, it was only the second, and it allowed Fielder to bat. Fielder was the American League's defending home run and runs batted in leader. His 51 home runs last season made him the first American Leaguer to top 50 since Roger Maris and Mickey Mantle in 1961. Plunk kept him in the park, but the big man's double into the left-field corner scored Cuyler and Phillips to give Detroit a 6–4 lead. Fielder would go on to win the league's home run (tied with Jose Canseco) and runs batted in titles for a second consecutive season, something no American Leaguer had done since Jimmie Foxx in 1932–1933. After the game, a reporter asked Merrill if he had thought about walking Fielder—second base was open—and pitching to Tony Bernazard. Bernazard had replaced Lou Whitaker at second base in the fourth inning after Alvaro Espinoza spiked Whitaker in the right arm on a steal attempt by the Yankees' shortstop. "I didn't consider it," Merrill said. "Plunk had struck out Fielder three of the five times he'd faced him before." Bernazard followed Fielder's double with a single to right, but Jesse Barfield's throw to the plate retired the lumbering Fielder for the third out.

Gibson, saved by Trammell's fine defense in the seventh, also pitched a scoreless eighth and got the win. Mike Henneman gave up a one-out single to Steve Sax in the ninth, but retired Mattingly and Roberto Kelly to earn the save. Cadaret was the loser as the Yankees' opening-day winning streak ended at five. "We gave them an extra out in the inning," said Merrill about Nokes's mental error. "That's what killed us. In these kind of games, you have to execute if you want to win." Interestingly, Nokes didn't enter the game until the sixth inning when he pinch-hit for starting catcher Jim Leyritz. It is interesting because earlier in the week, Merrill and general manager Gene Michael had expressed their anger over stories that the Yankees' pitchers preferred having Bob Geren behind the plate, rather than Leyritz or Nokes. Geren did get into the game, catching the eighth inning after Randy Velarde batted for Nokes, as Merrill used every non-pitcher on the roster except outfielder Scott Lusader. Nokes rebounded from his embarrassing start to have a solid year. He hit a team-leading 24 home runs, knocked in 77 runs, and showed great improvement defensively. Merrill, the first Yankees' manager to last a full season since Lou Piniella in 1987, was fired the day after it ended and succeeded by Buck Showalter, one of his coaches.

Monday, April 8, 1991

New York	ab	r	h	rbi	Detroit	ab	r	h	rbi
Sax 2b	5	0	1	0	Phillips dh	3	1	0	0
Mattingly 1b	5	2	2	0	Moseby lf	4	2	1	0
Kelly cf	4	0	1	0	Trammell ss	4	1	2	4
Maas dh	2	1	1	2	Fielder 1b	3	0	1	2
Meulens lf	4	0	2	1	Whitaker 2b	0	0	0	0
Barfield rf	4	0	1	0	Bernazard 2b	3	0	1	0
Leyritz c	2	0	0	0	Deer rf	4	0	0	0
ᵃNokes c	1	0	0	0	Tettleton c	3	0	1	0
ᶜVelarde ph, 3b	1	0	0	0	Fryman 3b	3	1	1	0
Blowers 3b	2	1	1	1	Cuyler cf	3	1	1	0
ᵇLovullo 3b	1	0	0	0	Total	30	6	8	6
Geren c	0	0	0	0					

New York

	ab	r	h	rbi
Espinoza ss	3	0	1	0
[d]Hall	1	0	0	0
Total	35	4	10	4

[a]Reached on an error for Leyritz in sixth inning.
[b]Intentionally walked for Blowers in sixth inning.
[c]Flied out for Nokes in eighth inning.
[d]Fouled out for Espinoza in ninth inning.

New York	102	100	000–4
Detroit	200	020	20X–6

Errors—Espinoza, Bernazard. Double plays—Trammell, Bernazard, and Fielder; Trammell, Bernazard, and Fielder. Caught stealing—by Tettleton (Kelly, Espinoza); by Geren (Tettleton). Left on bases—New York 8; Detroit 8. Put outs—New York 24: Leyritz 8, Espinoza 1, Meulens 2, Kelly 2, Nokes 4, Mattingly 3, Sax, 2, Barfield 1, Geren 1. Detroit 27: Deer 5, Tettleton 4, Cuyler 2, Whitaker 1, Fielder 9, Moseby 1, Trammell 2, Bernazard 2, Gibson 1. Assists—New York 6: Sax, 1, Barfield 1, Blowers 1, Lovullo 1, Velarde 1, Geren 1. Detroit 14: Tanana 1, Tettleton 1, Whitaker 2, Fielder 2, Trammell 4, Bernazard 2, Fryman 2. Two-base hits—Moseby, Trammell, Fielder. Home runs—Maas, Blowers, Trammell. Stolen bases—Mattingly, Fryman, Cuyler.

	IP	H	R	ER	BB	SO
NEW YORK						
Leary	6.0	5	4	4	3	9
Cadaret (L, 0–1)	.1	1	2	2	1	0
Plunk	1.1	2	0	0	3	1
Farr	.1	0	0	0	1	0
DETROIT						
Tanana	5.0	8	4	4	2	2
Petry	1.0	0	0	0	1	0
Gibson (W, 1–0)	2.0	1	0	0	1	1
Henneman S.1	1.0	1	0	0	0	1

Umpires—Deegan, Arata, Harvey, and Knauss. Time of game—3 hrs. 15 min. Attendance—47,382.

It was another dismal season for the Yankees; they finished in fifth place (71–91), 20 games behind the Toronto Blue Jays. Their combined win-loss mark for 1989–1991 of 212–273 was the club's worst three-year record since the 1913–1915 period. Scott Sanderson, in his first year with the club, had an outstanding season, winning 16 games (16–8) for a team that won only 71. He was the Yankees' lone representative on the American League All-Star team, but did not play. It was the first time ever that the Yankees did not have a player take part in the All-Star game.

Tuesday, April 7, 1992
Yankee Stadium, New York
New York 4 Boston 3

Where have you gone, Joe DiMaggio?—Paul Simon

A crowd of 56,572 saw the Yankees defeat the Boston Red Sox 4–3 in the season opener at Yankee Stadium. Perhaps some of them also took part in the New York State presidential primaries held that day; but if they did, they were part of a small minority. The turnout was an embarrassingly low 27 per cent, which pundits blamed on New Yorkers' unfamiliarity with the major Democratic contenders. The total vote was far less than in 1984 and 1988 when the controversial Jesse Jackson was on the ballot. Depending on which wing of the Democratic Party one belonged to, Jackson was either a unifying force or a divisive one, yet everyone agreed that his absence robbed the race of much of its passion and enthusiasm. After an insufferably dull campaign, Arkansas governor Bill Clinton won with 41 percent of the vote, well below the combined total of former Massachusetts senator Paul Tsongas and former California governor Jerry Brown, who finished second and third. The Republican contest inspired even less excitement with President George Bush easily defeating his challenger, right-wing newspaper columnist Pat Buchanan. However, if passion and enthusiasm were missing from politics this day, they could be found in abundance at the Stadium, as they could at any renewal of baseball's fiercest rivalry. And with Joe DiMaggio throwing out the first ball and potential Hall-of-Famers Roger Clemens, Wade Boggs, and Don Mattingly in the starting lineups, there was certainly no lack of name recognition.

Politics, at least of the local variety, did make an appearance (or nonappearance) at the opener. Mayor David Dinkins, New York's first-ever black mayor, chose not to attend the game. To do so, the mayor would have had to cross a picket line set up by the striking Yankee Stadium ushers, and "politically correct" politicians—particularly those in New York City—did not cross union picket lines. Meanwhile, Scott Sanderson, the Yankees' starting pitcher, clearly belonged at the opposite end of the "politically correct" spectrum. On joining the club last year, Sanderson announced that he would not speak to the news media in the locker room if women were present. "It's not a constitutional issue, it's a moral issue," he said. "I don't believe women belong where men are dressing, and I don't believe men belong where women are dressing." Before today's game, Sanderson revealed (presumably to all reporters) that he had never in his career started an opener, not even in high school or college. Nevertheless, the 35-year-old Sanderson was New York's best pitcher and the obvious opening-day choice for new manager Buck Showalter. Sanderson had established himself as the staff ace in 1991 with his 16 wins (16–10), more than twice the total of any other Yankees' starter. By contrast, this was the fifth straight year that Clemens had opened for the Red Sox. He was 2–0 in the previous four, with a 2.93 earned run average.

With Showalter, a Yankees' coach the past two seasons, now at the helm, it marked the sixth consecutive season that a different manager was leading the Yankees on Opening Day. Between Lou Piniella in 1987 and Showalter in 1992, there had been: Billy Martin in '88, Dallas Green in '89, Bucky Dent in '90, and Stump Merrill in '91. Showalter, who at 35 was the youngest manager in the major leagues, had spent his entire career in the Yankees organization. In his five seasons managing in the minor leagues, all at Double A or lower, he had four first-place finishes and twice earned his league's Manager of the Year Award. Before that he played for seven years in the minors, ending with the International League Columbus Clippers in 1983. Another member of that Columbus team, Butch Hobson, was also making his big-league managerial debut today. Hobson, who managed against Showalter in the Eastern League in 1989, was replacing Joe Morgan, whom the Sox had let go after four consecutive winning seasons.

This afternoon's crowd, the largest for a regular season game since the Stadium reopened in 1976, began the day in high spirits and remained that way throughout. In the clubhouse after the game, right fielder Jesse Barfield said, "It was magical out there. The fans were with us from the very first pitch. It would be great if they came back again for the second game." However, to many in the crowd, especially the older fans, the only "magical" moment was seeing Joe DiMaggio on the field at Yankee Stadium again. For them it recalled a time when the Yankees were not only baseball's best team, but also its proudest and most majestic. But such qualities do not attach themselves to teams that ask people like John Goodman, the actor who played Babe Ruth in a dreadful movie biography of the Babe, opening later in the month, to throw out the first ball. Yet that is what would have happened if Yankees vice president Barry Halper had not stepped in. Halper saved the club another blow to its dignity when he prevailed upon DiMaggio, a friend, to do the honors instead. After public address announcer Bob Sheppard introduced the players, Robert Merrill sang the national anthem—the 23rd consecutive year the Metropolitan Opera baritone had done so at the Yankees home opener. Meanwhile, the 77-year-old DiMaggio waited in the Yankees dugout. He exchanged greetings with Merrill after the great opera star returned, and then moved to the top of the steps. Sheppard announced, "At the area near the pitcher's mound, baseball's greatest living player (a description he always demanded be made) will throw out the first ball, Joe DiMaggio." The crowd yelled and applauded as DiMaggio, dressed impeccably as he always was, trotted out waving both hands. He stopped near the mound and tossed the ball to catcher Matt Nokes. Then he shook hands with Nokes and returned to the dugout, eventually heading to the owner's box where he watched the game with sportscaster Howard Cosell. How much had baseball changed since DiMaggio retired? His salary in 1951, his final season, was $100,000 per year, then considered astronomical. Now the *average* salary for a major-leaguer had passed the $1 million mark, and the Yankees, at $1.7 million per player, were leading the way.

Showalter, anxious to get started, had arrived at the park at 7:30 A.M., though he did not complete his lineup card until shortly before game time. The cause of the delay was the questionable physical condition of newly acquired free agents Danny Tartabull (strained right wrist) and Mike Gallego (bruised right heel). Tartabull, a right fielder, had developed into one of the league's best hitters, batting .316 with 31 home runs and 100 runs batted in for the 1991 Kansas City Royals. His slugging percentage, a league-leading .593, was the highest in the American League in four years. Eligible for free agency, he chose to leave Kansas City and sign a $25.5 million, five-year contract with the Yankees. Tartabull's injured wrist had prevented him from playing in the last five exhibition games; but after declaring that he felt well enough to swing a bat, Showalter put him in the lineup as the designated hitter.

Gallego, however, would not be in today's lineup. The former Oakland second baseman had enjoyed a terrific spring, batting .422 with a .536 on-base percentage. Like Tartabull, he wanted very much to play in the opener, despite the heel injury that had bothered him for the past ten days. But after watching him jog before the game in a pair of specially made spikes, the Yankees put him on the 15-day disabled list. Yet even without Gallego, players who were not with the club on Opening Day a year ago were manning three of the four infield positions; first baseman Mattingly was the lone repeater. At third base was Charlie Hayes, acquired from the Philadelphia Phillies in a trade for rookie pitcher Darrin Chapin. And with Steve Sax traded to the Chicago White Sox for pitchers Melido Perez, Bob Wickman, and Domingo Jean, Pat Kelly, a mid-season call-up in 1991, was at second. Showalter had planned to use Gallego at shortstop and bat him in the leadoff spot, but when he went on the disabled list, it opened places for two men—Andy Stankiewicz and Randy Velarde. Stankiewicz, a six-year minor-leaguer, took Gallego's place on the roster, and Velarde took his place at shortstop and in the leadoff slot. Velarde, a .361 hitter in the Grapefruit League (22-for-61), made the most of his opportunity today; twice he led off an inning by getting on and both times he scored. In the first inning, he walked, went to third on Mattingly's single, and came home as Roberto Kelly was bouncing into a force play. The Yanks had a, 1–0 lead, but not for long. Sanderson had retired the Sox one-two-three in the first, but in the second, Boston's two young left-handed power hitters, Phil Plantier and Mo Vaughn, touched him for solo home runs. With one out, Plantier drove a 2–0 pitch deep into the seats in right center, and then after veteran slugger Jack Clark fanned, Vaughn hit a 3–2 pitch into the lower deck in right.

Now Clemens had a 2–1 lead, and he protected it by sailing through the middle innings in mid-season form. After yielding Mattingly's first-inning single, he retired the next 12 batters in order. Nokes had a single in the fifth, and so did Hayes, but Barfield, batting between them, hit into a double play—one of four the Sox turned in the game. Velarde opened the sixth by grounding a single to center. The Yankees got a break when Mattingly singled on a grounder to third that hopped erratically and seemed to confuse third baseman Boggs. Roberto Kelly followed by ripping a double into the gap in left center that scored both runners. That gave Kelly three runs batted in for the day and put the Yanks ahead, 3–2. The next batter, Mel Hall, grounded out to second baseman Jody Reed, as Kelly moved to third. In this tightly pitched game, Hobson chose to play his infield in against Tartabull to prevent another run from scoring. Tartabull swung at a fastball in on his fists and hit a little pop fly toward second base that would have been an easy out with a normal infield alignment. Instead, the ball just eluded the fielders' pursuit and fell safely for a run-producing single. It was not much of a hit, although Tartabull, who previously was 6-for-36 against Clemens, said, "I thought it looked great." Clemens viewed it differently, "Things were pretty bizarre in the sixth," he said. "They found a way to get things in there."

With a two-run lead, Showalter went to his bullpen, getting one inning apiece from Greg Cadaret, John Habyan, and Steve Farr. Boston got one run back against Cadaret in the seventh. They loaded the bases with one out on walks to Tony Pena and Luis Rivera and Boggs's infield single. Reed, a .500-hitter (27-for-54) against the Yankees in '91, scored Pena with a sacrifice fly, but Cadaret fanned Mike Greenwell for the third out. Habyan took over in the eighth and gave up a leadoff single to Ellis Burks. Any of the next three batters, Plantier, Clark, and Vaughn, could have put Boston ahead with one swing, but Habyan did not allow the ball to leave the infield. He struck out both Plantier and Clark and got Vaughn on an easy grounder to Mattingly to maintain the Yankees' 4–3 lead. Despite Habyan's strong performance, Showalter brought on his stopper, Farr, to pitch the ninth. Farr had 23 of the team's 37 saves in 1991, his first season in New York, and would have 30 of their 44 saves this year. Pena greeted him with a single, which again put the tying run aboard. At this point, with the light-hitting Rivera at the plate, everybody in the park knew he would attempt to sacrifice Pena to second base. The obvious bunt situation gave Mattingly an opportunity to show why he was a consistent Gold Glove winner. By twice interspersing feinted charges to the plate with returns to the bag to handle pickoff attempts, Mattingly greatly reduced Pena's lead off first. Therefore, Rivera's well-placed bunt, which should have gotten Pena to second, turned into a force play. Mattingly charged in and threw to Velarde, with the ball getting to second base just ahead of the runner. As umpire Vic Voltaggio made the out sign, the crowd came to their feet and cheered in recognition of what Mattingly had done. Mattingly's style and ability, reminiscent of past Yankees' greats, had earned him enormous admiration and respect in New York, even among those fans too young to remember that glorious past.

Tuesday, April 7, 1992

Boston	ab	r	h	rbi		New York	ab	r	h	rbi
Boggs 3b	5	0	1	0		Velarde ss	3	2	1	0
Reed 2b	4	0	1	1		Mattingly 1b	4	1	3	0
Greenwell lf	4	0	0	0		R. Kelly cf	4	1	1	3
Burks cf	4	0	1	0		Hall lf	3	0	0	0
Plantier lf	3	1	1	1		Tartabull dh	3	0	1	1
Clark dh	4	0	0	0		Nokes c	3	0	1	0
Vaughn 1b	3	1	1	1		Barfield rf	3	0	0	0
Pena c	3	1	1	0		Hayes 3b	2	0	1	0
Rivera ss	3	0	1	0		P. Kelly 2b	3	0	0	0
Total	33	3	7	3		Total	28	4	8	4

```
Boston       020   000   100–3
New York     100   003   00X–4
```

Errors—None. Double plays—Rivera, Reed, and Vaughn; Reed, Rivera and Vaughn; Rivera and Vaughn; Rivera, Reed, and Vaughn. Left on bases—Boston 8; New York 2. Put outs—New York 27: Mattingly 7, Nokes 12, Barfield 1, Hayes 2, R. Kelly 1, Velarde 2, Hall 2. Boston 24: Reed 3, Rivera 3, Greenwell 1, Vaughn 10, Plantier 1, Burks 1, Pena 5. Assists—New York 7: Mattingly 1, Hayes 3, Velarde 1, P. Kelly 1, Sanderson 1. Boston 14: Reed 6, Rivera 7, Boggs 1. Two-base hits—Reed, R. Kelly. Home runs—Plantier, Vaughn. Stolen base—R. Kelly. Sacrifice fly—Reed.

	IP	H	R	ER	BB	SO
BOSTON						
Clemens (L, 0–1)	8.0	8	4	4	1	5
NEW YORK						
Sanderson (W, 1–0)	6.0	4	2	2	2	5
Cadaret	1.0	1	1	1	2	2
Habyan	1.0	1	0	0	0	2
Farr S.1	1.0	1	0	0	0	1

Hit by pitch—By Clemens (Hayes). Umpires—McKean, Kaiser, Voltaggio, and Johnson. Time of game— 2 hrs. 46 min. Attendance—56,572.

The crowd remained on its feet, encouraging Farr as he slipped a third strike past Boggs and got Reed to foul out to Hayes. Whatever joy Showalter felt at his first major-league win, he chose to mask it, remaining in the dugout as the players congratulated one another. "That was their moment," he said. "I had nothing to do with the way they played." The win, New York's 17th in their 28 openers against Boston (1910 was a tie), ended a five-game opening-day losing streak against the Red Sox that began in 1964. Beating Clemens made it particularly rewarding. Over the course of his marvelous career, Clemens had beaten the Yankees 14 times, with this being only his sixth loss. Last season, when he captured his third Cy Young Award, Clemens was 3–1 against the Yanks with a 2.18 earned run average. One of those wins came against Sanderson, a 2–0 shutout at Fenway Park on September 20. It was Sanderson's only loss to Boston in four decisions in '91, a season in which his earned run average against the Sox was a very impressive 0.96.

The Red Sox would make only one more visit to New York this season, and not until August 6, four months hence. That, of course, was because of the American League's senseless "balanced schedule," another "improvement" by the owners that made baseball less appealing to its longtime fans.

After getting off to a 6–0 start, the Yankees (76–86) found their true level. They tied the Cleveland Indians for fourth place in the Eastern Division, 20 games behind the Toronto Blue Jays. Attendance fell to 1,748,737, the lowest (excluding the 1981 strike year) since the Stadium's renovation in 1976. In August, Commissioner Fay Vincent told George Steinbrenner he would lift the suspension against him and allow him to resume control of the club's everyday operations in 1993. A month later, under pressure from the owners, Vincent resigned. No one took his place, but Milwaukee Brewers owner Bud Selig became the acting commissioner.

Monday, April 5, 1993
Cleveland Stadium, Cleveland
New York 9 Cleveland 1

Some things don't need changing ... moonlight doesn't need changing, azaleas don't need changing, baseball doesn't need changing.—Ted Turner

Through wars, depressions, and even the death of a president, Opening Day has always offered baseball fans a temporary diversion from the gravity of "real-life" events. But occasionally, the circumstances surrounding Opening Day intertwine with a "real-life" event; and when they do, an afternoon at the ballpark becomes more of a catharsis than an escape. Such was the case for the 73,290 chilled fans at Cleveland Stadium who saw the Indians lose the 1993 season opener to the Yankees. For while the details of the 9–1 loss would soon fade, they would never forget the emotional tributes to Indians' relief pitchers Tim Crews and Steve Olin that preceded it. The ceremonies helped bring closure to a city still grief-stricken over the March 22 boating accident in Clermont, Florida, that killed Crews, 31, and Olin, 27, and seriously injured pitcher Bob Ojeda. The memorial service began shortly before game time. As the scoreboard showed a likeness of the memorial patch that the Indians would wear this season, the players from both teams took their places along the first- and third-base foul lines. Then, as the huge crowd stood with heads bowed, the remaining members of the Indians' bullpen contingent—Ted Power, Derek Lilliquist, Eric Plunk, and Kevin Wickander—escorted Crews's and Olin's wives and parents onto the field. Public address announcer Tom Glasenapp introduced Crews's wife Laurie and his parents, Jim and Martha Crews; then Olin's wife Patti and his parents, Gary and Shirley Olin. Glasenapp told them, "The thoughts and prayers of all of Cleveland will be with you forever." Few in the large crowd—the second-largest American League opening-day crowd ever—remained dry-eyed. The sense of bereavement grew even greater when Indians general manager John Hart and manager Mike Hargrove presented Laurie Crews and Patti Olin with their late husbands' jerseys.

Players from both sides said they expected this to be a heartrending afternoon and had prepared for it, but none more than Yankees' starting pitcher Jimmy Key. Having started and won three openers with the Toronto Blue Jays, Key was familiar with the tumult surrounding Opening Day. So, although he had warmed up before the memorial service, when it concluded he returned to the bullpen to throw some more pitches. Key was making his Yankees' debut this afternoon, having come as a free agent in December. That was just two months after he concluded nine years in Toronto by winning two games against the Atlanta Braves in the World Series, including the clincher. He got the opening-day start when manager

Buck Showalter's first choice, Melido Perez, suffered a hip injury. Actually, Key seemed a better choice. He had been the Yanks' best pitcher this spring (3–0 with an 0.67 ERA) and had a superb 12–4 career record against the Indians.

Key was not the only new face on the 1993 Yankees. Turnover on the club had been unusually high, even by the standards of the free agent era. Five players from the Yanks' 1992 opening-day lineup were no longer with the club, including the entire starting outfield: Roberto Kelly, Mel Hall, and Jesse Barfield. Kelly went to the Cincinnati Reds in a trade for Paul O'Neill, and Hall and Barfield signed to play in Japan. Scott Sanderson, who pitched and won last year's opener, signed as a free agent with the California Angels, and third baseman Charlie Hayes was the Colorado Rockies' second pick in the National League's expansion draft. (In addition to the Rockies, the NL had added a team in Miami to be called the Florida Marlins.) Joining Key as new Yankees were left-handed pitcher Jim Abbott and three players who were in today's starting lineup: third baseman Wade Boggs, shortstop Spike Owen, and left fielder O'Neill. Boggs from the Boston Red Sox and Owen from the Montreal Expos came via free agency, but New York had to send three promising minor-leaguers—first baseman J. T. Snow and pitchers Jerry Nielsen and Russ Springer—to the Angels for Abbott.

With much of its manufacturing base gone, the city of Cleveland had been losing business and population for a long time. But recently, thanks to strong political leadership, they had begun to revitalize the downtown area, the goal being to bring people—and money—from the suburbs back into the city. The planned centerpiece of the new downtown Cleveland would be a magnificent baseball-only stadium, patterned after Baltimore's highly successful Camden Yards. Meanwhile, the Indians, who had not won a pennant since 1954 and had never even won a divisional title, were undergoing a resurrection of their own. Hart had put together a team of exciting young players, many of whom he signed to long-term contracts—players such as Kenny Lofton, Carlos Baerga, Albert Belle, Sandy Alomar Jr., and Paul Sorrento. The deaths of Crews and Olin had cast a pall over Cleveland baseball, but like all things, it would pass. This would be the Indians' 62nd and final season at Cleveland Stadium (the new park would open in 1994), so before long, nostalgia would replace grief as the dominant emotion in Cleveland. More than 2 million fans would come out to see the Indians in 1993, the first time the club had drawn that many since 1949. Yankees' owner George Steinbrenner, who grew up in the Cleveland area, was already nostalgic. He recalled his father taking him to games as a boy, at League Park and at Cleveland Stadium. Steinbrenner had been back in baseball's good graces since March 1, the date former commissioner Fay Vincent had designated as the end of his suspension.

The Indians chose their legendary former pitcher, 74-year-old Bob Feller, to throw out the first ball. Feller, wearing an Indians' jacket bearing his old No. 19 (game-time temperature was only 36 degrees), walked to the mound and threw a strike over the inside corner. He left, hearing the cheers he had heard so often here, and Charles Nagy, the current ace of the Indians' staff, took his place. The Yankees had beaten Nagy twice early in his career, which began in 1990, but he had become a much better pitcher since then. Last season, when he won 17 games (17–10) for the fourth-place Indians, Nagy compiled a 1.37 earned run average against the Yanks in beating them three times without a loss. Today, however, he was no match for Key who allowed the Indians just one run, three hits, and no walks in his eight innings. Key had thrown only 71 pitches, but when his shoulder began to tighten, Showalter brought in John Habyan to pitch the ninth. Key's efficiency contributed to a playing time of less than two and a half hours, despite the Yankees' nine runs and 16 hits. "He works very fast," said shortstop Owen. "He moves the ball around the plate and he knows what he is doing out there. On a day like today, you don't want to be standing out there for 15 minutes." Hargrove, while disappointed at losing, had nothing but praise for Key's performance. "What you saw out there was a veteran pitcher with good control, and a young club that was aggressive and overanxious at the plate. You put those two things together and the pitcher wins every time."

The game was tight for five innings, before the Yanks erupted for five runs in the sixth. Danny Tartabull gave New York a 1–0 lead when he led off the second inning with the first of his three hits, a long home run to right center. This was an encouraging beginning for Tartabull, who made two trips to the disabled list in 1992 and went homerless in this year's exhibition games. Cleveland tied the score in the third on Carlos Martinez's double, Glenallen Hill's single, and Alomar's sacrifice fly. After Key set the Indians down in order in the fourth, he gave up a one-out double to designated hitter Reggie Jefferson in the fifth. However, Jefferson would be Cleveland's last base runner; Key retired the last 11 batters he faced, and Habyan got the three he faced in the ninth.

The Yanks had gone ahead, 2–1, in the top of the fifth on a single by Owen and a double by Pat Kelly. They blew the game open in the sixth, scoring five runs on seven hits and driving Nagy from the game. Catcher Matt Nokes provided the first three runs when he homered with Don Mattingly and O'Neill aboard. Nokes, like Tartabull, had not hit a home run all spring and before this at-bat was 1-for-17 lifetime against Nagy. After designated hitter Kevin Maas made the second out—he was the only Yankee to go hitless— singles by Owen, Kelly, and Bernie Williams loaded the bases. Although Williams, a switch-hitter, was still only 24, he had been in the Yankees' organization since 1986, splitting the last two seasons between New York and the Columbus (Ohio) Clippers of the International League. His growth and development as a player convinced the Yankees that he was finally ready to become their full-time center fielder and allowed them to trade Roberto Kelly. Williams's hit finished Nagy, and Hargrove called in Wickander to face Boggs. The five-time American League batting champion stepped in against Wickander looking for his first hit as a Yankee. He had gone hitless in three at-bats against Nagy, a right-hander, but against left-hander Wickander he slapped a single up the middle; Owen and Kelly scored, and the Yanks led, 7–1.

Owen's double and Kelly's home run, the third hit for each, accounted for the Yankees' final two runs against left-hander Dennis Cook in the eighth. Kelly had withstood a challenge for his position from Mike Gallego, winning it with his superior defense and a Grapefruit League batting average of .333, compared to Gallego's .167. Nevertheless, he did not learn from Showalter that he would be the opening-day second baseman until the day before the game. Both Kelly and Gallego would have good seasons in 1993. As the regular second baseman, Kelly batted .273, while Gallego, filling in at second, short, and third, hit a career-high .283. Kelly's home run was the Yankees' third of the game; the first time they had hit three home runs on Opening Day since Elston Howard hit one and Joe Pepitone hit two at Kansas City in 1963. The last time that three *different* Yankees homered in an opener was in 1962, when Mickey Mantle, Roger Maris, and Bill Skowron connected against the Baltimore Orioles at Yankee Stadium.

After the game, Showalter said he was extremely pleased with his team's performance. "I'm proud of our club today," he said. "It was a lot of fun as far as the game was concerned. It was a tough emotional day." For the Indians, it would be a tough, emotional *season*. They never fully recovered from their springtime disaster, finishing the season 76–86, the same as in 1992. Nagy underwent shoulder surgery in May that kept him out of action until he started against the Chicago White Sox on the last day of the season. Meanwhile, Ojeda recovered from his injuries and returned to the team in August, but was granted free agency at the end of the season and signed with the Yankees for 1994.

In September, the owners voted to "improve" baseball by approving another round of "play-offs" to precede the World Series. To get this additional playoff series, which would begin next season, each league would abandon its two-division setup and reconstitute itself into three divisions. The three division winners would then advance to the first round of the playoffs, along with a fourth team. That fourth team, or "wild-card," would be the team that finished in *second place* in one of the three divisions, but had a better record than the other two second-place finishers. Now one of the many reasons that baseball has always existed at a level far above other team sports is the way it determines its champions. There are no second chances in baseball. A team cannot stumble through the regular season, then hit a postseason "hot streak" and emerge a winner. Nothing so identifies the game and accounts for its unique place in American life as does the "pennant race," that grueling day-by-day struggle by which, no matter the margin, one team establishes its superiority. But now the owners, with their "profits-above-all" mentality, had destroyed that uniqueness. And then, to add insult to injury, they—and their allies in television—told the fans that another round of playoffs was not only inevitable (true) and desirable (doubtful), it was needed to save baseball (an outright lie). From what were they "saving" it, these self-appointed saviors who gave us designated hitters, artificial turf, domed stadiums, scoreboards that tell you when to cheer, and league championship and World Series games that for much of the country end after midnight? Tradition is a concept not much in fashion anymore, but it remains an inseparable part of baseball. For many fans, getting used to wild-card teams would take a long time indeed.

Monday, April 5, 1993

New York	ab	r	h	rbi		Cleveland	ab	r	h	rbi
Williams cf	5	0	1	0		Lofton cf	4	0	0	0
Boggs 3b	4	0	1	2		Fermin ss	3	0	0	0
Mattingly 1b	5	1	2	0		[a]Howard	1	0	0	0
Tartabull rf	5	1	3	1		Baerga 2b	3	0	0	0
O'Neill lf	5	1	2	0		Belle lf	3	0	0	0
Nokes c	5	1	1	3		Sorrento 1b	3	0	0	0
Maas dh	4	0	0	0		Jefferson dh	3	0	1	0
Owen ss	5	3	3	0		Martinez 3b	3	1	1	0
Kelly 2b	4	2	3	3		Hill rf	3	0	1	0
Total	42	9	16	9		Alomar c	2	0	0	1
						Total	28	1	3	1

[a]Grounded out for Fermin in ninth inning.

New York	010	015	020–9
Cleveland	001	000	000–1

Errors—None. Double plays—Baerga, Fermin, and Sorrento; Kelly, Owen, and Mattingly. Left on bases—New York 8; Cleveland 1. Put outs—New York 27: Williams 2, Tartabull 3, Kelly 1, O'Neill 2, Nokes 3, Mattingly 13, Key 2, Owen 1. Cleveland 27: Fermin 1, Belle 4, Baerga 2, Sorrento 10, Lofton 2, Hill 3, Alomar 5. Assists—New York 12: Kelly 1, Boggs 1, Key 2, Owen 6, Habyan 1, Mattingly 1. Cleveland 9: Nagy 1, Fermin 4, Baerga 4. Two-base hits—Martinez, Tartabull, Kelly, Jefferson, Owen. Home runs—Tartabull, Nokes, Kelly. Sacrifice fly—Alomar.

	IP	H	R	ER	BB	SO
NEW YORK						
Key (W, 1–0)	8.0	3	1	1	0	3
Habyan	1.0	0	0	0	0	0
CLEVELAND						
Nagy (L, 0–1)	5.2	11	7	7	1	3
Wickander	0.1	1	0	0	0	0
Cook	1.1	4	2	2	1	1
Plunk	0.2	0	0	0	0	0
Lilliquist	1.0	0	0	0	0	1

Umpires—Barnett, Kosc, Clark, and Morrison. Time of game—2 hrs. 18 min. Attendance—73,290.

New York (88–74) had its first winning season in five years and finished in second place, seven games behind the Toronto Blue Jays. Under the three-division format planned for 1994, the Yankees would have been the wild-card team. Buck Showalter finished second to Gene Lamont of the Chicago White Sox in voting for the American League's Manager of the Year. Jimmy Key was third in the American League with a .750 winning percentage, and his 3.00 earned run average was the league's third lowest. He won a career-high 18 games (18–6) and finished fourth in voting for the Cy Young Award. Danny Tartabull led the Yankees in home runs (31) and runs batted in (102), but his 156 strikeouts set a new club record.

Monday, April 4, 1994
Yankee Stadium, New York
New York 5 Texas 3

A plague on both your houses!—William Shakespeare

Under the Major League's new three-division format, the Yankees had two possible paths into the American League's expanded playoffs. They could either win the newly shrunken Eastern Division, a five-team entry consisting of the Yanks, the Boston Red Sox, the Baltimore Orioles, the Detroit Tigers, and the Toronto Blue Jays; or they could finish second, but with a better record than the second-place teams in the Central and Western Divisions. Having accomplished either of the two, they then would have to survive a best-of-five Division Series and a best-of-seven League Championship Series to win the pennant. For obvious reasons, the extra round of playoffs reduced the likelihood that a league's best team would make it to the World Series. Nevertheless, the Yanks fully expected they would get there for the first time in 13 years, their longest Series absence since they played in their first one back in 1921. Although recent Yankees' clubs had proved the highest-paid teams are not necessarily the best teams, it was still reasonable to expect that with a payroll of about $45 million they would at the very least be a strong contender. The primary reason for the Yankees' seven-game deficit with Toronto in 1993 had been their bullpen, and they had strengthened that. Steve Farr had departed, but they signed free agent Jeff Reardon from the Cincinnati Reds and traded pitcher Domingo Jean and infielder Andy Stankiewicz to the Houston Astros for Xavier Hernandez. Manager Buck Showalter was counting on Hernandez to be the stopper in '94, and that is exactly what he looked like on Opening Day. He came on in the ninth inning and retired three batters in a row to preserve the

5–3 win against the Texas Rangers. After that impressive debut, the fans left Yankee Stadium even more assured this would be the Yankees' year. The pitching of the two men who preceded Hernandez, Jimmy Key and Bob Wickman, was further reason for optimism. Left-hander Key started and pitched into the eighth inning before leaving with one out and a runner at second. Showalter called on right-hander Wickman, who prevented any further scoring, and then turned it over to Hernandez in the ninth.

Although the Yankees won and the crowd of 56,706 set a new attendance record for a regular season game at the remodeled stadium, owner George Steinbrenner was not completely happy. With new ballparks opening this year in Texas and Cleveland, it gave him an opportunity to voice his oft-repeated criticisms of both Yankee Stadium and the Bronx. Steinbrenner's lease with the Stadium would expire in 2002, and he was continuing to make his case for a new place to play. He seemed to prefer Manhattan, along the west shore by the Hudson River, but as always there was the veiled threat of a move to New Jersey.

Before the game, the Yankees honored two Americans who had won medals at the recently concluded Winter Olympics at Lillehammer, Norway: Cathy Turner, who won a gold medal in Short Track Speedskating, and Picabo Street, who took the silver in Alpine Skiing. The cast from the Broadway revival of *Damn Yankees* entertained the crowd with their rendition of "You Gotta Have Heart," and old standby Robert Merrill of the Metropolitan Opera sang the national anthem. However, the highlight of the pregame ceremonies was the appearance of 79-year-old Joe DiMaggio to throw out the first ball. Almost forty-three years had passed since DiMaggio played his last game here, but to millions of New Yorkers he remained the archetypal Yankee. Dressed in a navy blue suit with a white shirt, blue silk tie, and black shoes, DiMaggio waved to the crowd and from the mound threw the ball on the fly to catcher Mike Stanley.

In his 13 years with the Yankees, DiMaggio played under three managers (not counting the two interim managers in 1946), a much different scenario from the past 13 years when 10 different men had managed the club. Showalter, managing his third consecutive opener, was the first to do that since Billy Martin in 1976–1978. And at 38, he was still the youngest manager in the major leagues, two years younger than Texas manager Kevin Kennedy. Kennedy was in his second season with the Rangers after leading them to a second-place finish in 1993, their best showing in seven years. He bested Showalter nine games to three in their teams' head-to-head meetings, continuing a recent pattern of Texas dominance against New York. The Rangers had now won 36 of the last 53 games played, and the season series for each of the last six years. Kevin Brown, this afternoon's starting pitcher, defeated the Yankees three out of four last season, raising his lifetime mark against them to 11–2. His .846 winning percentage was the best ever for any pitcher with at least ten decisions against the Yankees, and his career earned run average against the New Yorkers was a formidable 2.39. Key, on the other hand, had only a 6–6 record against Texas, including a win with no losses as a Yankee.

Along with their shoddy relief pitching, a lack of speed had hurt the Yanks in '93. To partially rectify that shortcoming, they signed speedy free agent outfielder Luis Polonia. Like Hernandez, Polonia paid immediate dividends. Batting leadoff, he began his second stay in New York with a first-inning single and moved to second on a single by Wade Boggs. Normally, Polonia would have reached third on Boggs's hit, but he slipped rounding second and had to go back. Don Mattingly, needing one more RBI to reach 1,000, flied out. With designated hitter Danny Tartabull at the plate, Polonia took off for third. He made it safely, just beating the throw from catcher Ivan Rodriguez as Boggs cruised easily into second.

The steal by Boggs was his first as a Yankee and only his 17th since reaching the major leagues in 1982. Tartabull's sacrifice fly brought Polonia home with the game's first run. "It was perfect," Polonia said after the game. "It was exactly as I was thinking when I was coming here today. I wanted to get on base, steal, and score a run." Paul O'Neill followed with a ground single to left, but left fielder Juan Gonzalez threw Boggs out at the plate for the final out of the inning. Boggs, who had four hits on the day—the 51st four-hit day of his career—talked of the emotion of Opening Day. "It's very stressful, very intense," he said. "It eats at you. Now you can relax and get on with the season." Although Boggs had a .338 lifetime batting average when he joined the Yankees in 1992, his average at Yankee Stadium was only .276. He improved upon that immediately when he hit .314 there in '93.

In the third, O'Neill's base-loaded double scored Boggs and Mattingly, both aboard with singles, to give the Yanks a 3–0 lead. Brown walked Stanley intentionally to reload the bases but escaped further scoring by retiring Bernie Williams and Mike Gallego. Williams opened in center field even though shoulder and groin injuries had prevented him from playing in the outfield all spring. Texas scored a run in the fourth when Chris James and Will Clark led off with doubles, cutting the lead to 3–1. The tying run was at the plate with three of the best home-run hitters in the league coming up. But in what he would later call "the turning point" of the game, Key got Gonzalez, Jose Canseco, and Dean Palmer, stranding Clark at second base. Clark, signed as a free agent by the Rangers, was playing his first American League game following seven splendid seasons with the San Francisco Giants.

Key got some breathing room in the fifth when Tartabull and Stanley hit solo home runs to extend New York's lead to 5–1. Both hit 0–1 pitches deep into the left-field seats. Stanley, a backup for most of his career (six years in Texas and 1992 with the Yanks), had become the team's first-string catcher in 1993, batting .305 with 26 home runs and 84 runs batted in. Brown came out after the fifth, replaced by James Hurst, who pitched one inning in his first big-league appearance, and then Cris Carpenter, who worked the seventh and eighth. The Yankees failed to score against either one. Meanwhile, Texas picked up a run in their half of the seventh on a double by Palmer, an infield single by Rodriguez, and a sacrifice fly by second baseman Doug Strange. An inning later, when David Hulse led off with a long double to right and scored on Clark's ground-rule double to left, Showalter called for Wickman. Six times in Key's ten no-decision games in 1993, he left with a lead that the Yankees' bullpen eventually surrendered; but this was a new season. First, Wickman got Gonzalez, the American League home-run leader for each of the past two seasons, to ground out to third baseman Boggs. Then, after falling behind Canseco and eventually walking him, he ended the threat by getting Palmer to ground into a force play.

As the Yanks were batting in the last of the eighth, Showalter told Wickman that if his teammates could score another run, he would allow him to pitch the ninth. But when they failed to add to their 5–3 lead, Showalter called on Hernandez. The Astros had used the Texas-born right-hander mainly as a setup man, but Showalter was giving him the opportunity to be a closer. Hernandez had not done well in that role during spring training, but he was flawless today. He retired the Rangers in order, striking out the last two batters, Strange and Manny Lee, to save the victory for Key. It made Key, who defeated Cleveland on Opening Day 1993, the first Yankees' pitcher to win consecutive openers since Mel Stottlemyre won three straight in 1967–1969.

With the lovely spring weather and a home team win, it should have made for a pleasant day at the ballpark. Yet many serious fans left the Stadium saddened by what they had seen—not the game, but much that surrounded it. The rotating advertisements on the stands behind home plate did not rotate today, but only because ESPN had the television rights to the game. The fans knew that with the shot looking in from center field so prominent in baseball telecasts, from now on they would be forced to look at those ads every time they watched a Yankees' game on local TV. Moreover, knowledgeable fans continued to lament the ear-shattering music that blared out from the speakers between innings and prevented any meaningful discussion of the game. They shook their heads in disbelief at the additions of mindless diversions such as "subway races" played out on the scoreboard. There just seemed to be more people at ballgames (and not only in New York) who came for some purpose other than watching baseball. What other explanation was there for all the drinking and fighting that went on in the stands this afternoon?

After losing both fans and prestige for 15 years, baseball finally hit bottom in 1994. On August 12, after a seemingly endless period of negotiations between players and owners failed to produce a basic agreement, the players went on strike. During a previous strike in 1981, Yale president Bart Giamatti wrote an op-ed piece in the *New York Times* asking both sides "to remember that you are the temporary custodians of an enduring public trust." Those words, which went unheeded in 1981, had even less impact in 1994 as both sides were now more determined than ever to "win." But, of course, nobody would win. The strike wiped out the remainder of the season, including—for the first time since 1904— the World Series. The premature ending of the season was particularly unfortunate for the Yankees. They were in first place, playing well, and seemed a good bet to appear in their first World Series since 1981. When the season ended, the Yankees (70–43) were leading the Eastern Division by 6½ games over Baltimore. Texas, despite being ten games under .500 (52–62), was leading in the West.

Jimmy Key had another excellent season, going 17–4 and winning The Sporting News' American League Pitcher of the Year Award. He finished second to the Kansas City Royals' David Cone for the Cy Young Award. Paul O'Neill won the batting championship with a .359 average, the highest by a Yankee since Mickey Mantle's .365 in 1957. O'Neill finished fifth and Key sixth in the voting for the Most Valuable Player Award. Xavier Hernandez did not provide the relief pitching expected of him. He had only six saves, a 5.85 earned run average, and the Yankees elected not to retain him for 1995. Wade Boggs batted .342, fifth-best in the league and the highest ever for a Yankees' third baseman. Buck Showalter, the first Yankee manager under George Steinbrenner to finish three full seasons, won the Manager of the Year Award.

Monday, April 4, 1994

Texas	ab	r	h	rbi	New York	ab	r	h	rbi
Hulse cf	4	1	1	0	Polonia lf	5	1	1	0
James rf	4	1	1	0	Boggs 3b	5	1	4	0
Clark 1b	4	0	2	2	Mattingly 1b	4	1	1	0
Gonzalez lf	4	0	1	0	Tartabull dh	1	1	1	2
Canseco dh	3	0	0	0	O'Neill rf	4	0	2	2
Palmer 3b	4	1	1	0	Stanley c	3	1	1	1
Rodriguez c	4	0	1	0	B. Williams cf	3	0	1	0
Strange 2b	3	0	0	1	Gallego ss	3	0	0	0
Lee ss	4	0	0	0	Kelly 2b	4	0	0	0
Total	34	3	7	3	Total	32	5	11	5

Texas	000	100	110–3
New York	102	020	00X–5

Errors—Gallego. Caught stealing—by Rodriguez (B. Williams). Left on bases—Texas 6; New York 9. Put outs—New York 27: Stanley 3, Mattingly 12, Boggs 1, Kelly 4, Polonia 4, O'Neill 2, B. Williams 1. Texas 24: Gonzalez 3, Clark 11, James 1, Rodriguez 4, Lee 4, Hulse 1. Assists—New York 12: Gallego 5, Stanley 2, Boggs 3, Key 2. Texas 16: Gonzalez 1, Lee 4, Rodriguez 1, Brown 1, Strange 7, Hurst 1, Carpenter 1. Two-base hits—Hulse, James, Clark (2), Palmer, O'Neill, B. Williams. Home runs—Tartabull, Stanley. Stolen base—Polonia, Boggs. Sacrifice fly—Tartabull, Strange.

	IP	H	R	ER	BB	SO
TEXAS						
Brown (L, 0–1)	5.0	10	5	5	3	1
Hurst	1.0	1	0	0	1	0
Carpenter	2.0	0	0	0	1	1
NEW YORK						
Key (W, 1–0)	7.1	7	3	3	0	2
Wickman	0.2	0	0	0	1	0
Hernandez S.1	1.0	0	0	0	0	2

Umpires—McKean, Joyce, Craft, and Hickox. Time of game—2 hrs. 36 min. Attendance—56,706.

Wednesday, April 26, 1995
Yankee Stadium, New York
New York 8 Texas 6

He too serves a certain purpose who only stands and cheers.—Henry Adams

No one really knows how far the owners would have gone with their scheme to subvert the players' strike with the use of replacement players for the 1995 season. Fortunately, we never found out. On March 31, U.S. District Court Judge (and future Supreme Court Justice) Sonia Sotomayor, responding to a request by the National Labor Relations Board, issued an injunction against the owners that effectively ended the strike. Spring training began again, this time with legitimate major-league players and prospects. Opening Day was pushed back to the end of April, which gave each team three and a half weeks to prepare. Because of the late start and the extra week needed for the new best-of-five division series, the regular season was shortened to 144 games. Baseball was not yet willing to begin the World Series in November.

Now that the strike had ended and all the scheduling was taken care of, an essential question remained. Did the American public any longer care? The strike had affected baseball fans profoundly, and only time would tell how many it had driven away permanently. Surely, none would ever think of the game in quite the same way. It was more than just the length of the strike, or even that it cut short what had been a marvelous season, leaving no record-setting performances, no pennant winners, and no World Series. The strike would stay with the fans—perhaps forever—in the words and actions of the people who governed the game and those who played it. They (not all, but far too many) had revealed themselves as men who had no sense of baseball's history, its traditions, or its place in American life.

As Opening Day approached, millions of fans remained alienated. From every major-league city there came stories of longtime ticket holders who had vowed never to come back to baseball. Still, in the end, most would; they loved the game too much to stay away. However, the degree of emotional commitment with which they came back was not the same as before, at least at the beginning of the season; that would take a while to regain its former high level. The club owners, more concerned with the fans' *financial* commitment than their emotional commitment, offered varying propositions to appease them. Some took the unprecedented step of lowering prices. The Yankees' peace offering was to invite the public to their pre-opening-day workout at the Stadium, free of charge. As an added inducement, they threw in a complimentary hot dog, soda, and bag of peanuts; still, only slightly more than 6,300 fans showed up. The following day there were more than 6,000 empty seats for the opener with Texas, and some of those that came either held up signs showing their displeasure, or did so vocally.

Although the crowd of 50,245 was among the day's best, it was the smallest for a Yankee Stadium opener since 1990, another season that started late because of labor difficulties. Yet for the most part, the crowd acted like opening-day crowds always do. A new season was beginning under a bright blue sky, and they were here to enjoy it. And enjoy it they did. The Yankees pounded out 14 hits in defeating the Rangers, 8–6, and generally played like the Eastern Division favorites that they were. Jimmy Key, coming off shoulder surgery, pitched five innings for the win, and newly acquired stopper John Wetteland earned his first American League save. It was New York's ninth win in their last ten openers and the fourth in a row for manager Buck Showalter. But above all, the Yankees' players were happy just to be back playing baseball. They also expressed relief at the fans' reception of them. "We had 50,000 here," Key said, speaking of the big crowd. "That says a lot about true base-ball fans in New York." Don Mattingly, the only Yankees' starter without a hit, said, "I'm glad they're back. You never know as a player how much damage you've done." Danny Tartabull, whose second-inning home run got the Yanks started, added, "The welcome from the fans was incredible, and we gave them a show." Only Showalter seemed less than pleased with the fans' reaction, and that was because he thought they were *too* forgiving. "I'm never surprised by the intensity of New York fans and their zest and emotion," he said. "But at the same time, there's a part of you that wishes they'd make it a little bit tougher so we don't go through that again."

Seemingly forgotten by most major-league players were their previous statements of union solidarity and the plight of the "working man." Their strike was over (though the problems that caused it remained), but the one by the major-league umpires was not. So while the players may not have liked beginning the season with replacement umpires, not one of them refused to cross the picket lines set up by members of the Major League Baseball Umpires Association. (The umpires' strike would end in a few days.)

Joe DiMaggio graced the day by throwing out the first ball and Robert Merrill sang the national anthem. DiMaggio got the ovation he always received at Yankee Stadium, which was not true of Governor George Pataki and Mayor Rudy Giuliani, who threw out the "second" and "third" balls. It did not seem to matter that Pataki, who had only recently taken office, had vowed to keep the Yankees in New York, nor that Giuliani seemed on his way to being an extremely effective mayor; the crowd booed both of them. Pataki's vow may have been meaningless, but with George Steinbrenner continuing to talk about mov-ing the club to New Jersey, it was nonetheless reassuring to hear. The crowd did not boo George Steinbrenner, but then Steinbrenner was not in the stadium. Recent surgery for a detached retina prevented him from flying, so he stayed at home in Tampa, watching the game on ESPN. Also home watching on TV was Johnny Oates, the Rangers' new manager. Oates was in Virginia tending to his ailing wife, Gloria, while Jerry Narron, a coach, ran the club.

Key was making his third consecutive opening-day start for the Yankees, something no pitcher had done since Ron Guidry in 1982–1984. He was coming off a magnificent 17–4 season (or partial season), but had since undergone surgery on his left shoulder. The Yanks had bolstered their pitching staff when they acquired former Cy Young Award winner Jack McDowell from the Chicago White Sox in an off-season trade; still, a full recovery by Key appeared critical to their pennant hopes. The veteran left-hander departed with no one out in the sixth—having thrown 83 pitches—but said later he felt no pain in his shoulder. Key had surrendered three runs on seven hits, but he was leading, 5–3, thanks to the hitting of his teammates. They had pummeled Texas starter Kenny Rogers for four runs and added one against John Dettmer. For Dettmer, who pitched one-third of an inning in the fourth, today's appearance would be the last in his big league career. Rogers, a left-hander, had beaten the Yankees five-of-six in his career, lasted only three innings. He gave up a home run to Tartabull leading off the second, a blast that came after Showalter gave his cleanup batter the hit sign on 3–0. Rogers threw a fastball that Tartabull drove over the fence in left center, making it the third straight year he had hit an opening-day home run. The Yanks reached Rogers for three hits and three runs in the third, an inning in which he threw 44 pitches. The key hit was a single by Wade Boggs, a career .458-hitter against Rogers (11-for-24). Pat Kelly, who had singled, was on first when Rogers and Boggs got into one of those fascinating batter-pitcher confrontations. They had battled through ten pitches with lots of foul balls and neither man giving in. Finally, on the 11th pitch, Showalter called for a hit-and-run. Boggs delivered, slapping the ball past the spot shortstop Benji Gil had just vacated. Rogers recouped to get Jim Leyritz on a line out to center, but walked defending batting champion Paul O'Neill and Tartabull to force Kelly home. Mattingly's force-play grounder scored Boggs and then catcher Mike Stanley's infield single scored O'Neill.

When the inning ended, Rogers was finished; but he would bounce back to have his finest season. He won a career-high 17 games (17–7), and then, as a free agent, signed to pitch for the Yankees in 1996. Narron sent Dettmer, 0–6 in '94, out to pitch the fourth and the Yanks got a quick run against him on singles by Tony Fernandez and Kelly, and a sacrifice fly by Boggs. Fernandez, signed as a free agent from the Cincinnati Reds, was here to be the Yankees' shortstop until young Derek Jeter proved he was ready to play at the major-league level. Jeter was on the opening-day roster and would play in 15 games with the Yanks this year, but spend most of the season with the Columbus Clippers of the International League.

Texas had scored a run in the third inning, so as Key took the mound in the sixth, he had a 5–1 lead. However, after the first three men batted, the Rangers had narrowed the gap to 5–3 and Key was gone. A single by Otis Nixon (obtained from the Boston Red Sox in a trade for Jose Canseco), a double by Jeff Frye, and a two-run single by Will Clark finished him. Showalter did not want Key to face designated hitter Mickey Tettleton, a switch-hitter who had five career home runs against him. Knowing when to change pitchers may be the most important strategic decision a manager must make, and this time Showalter made the right move. Right-hander Bob Wickman got Tettleton to bounce sharply to second baseman Kelly, who started a snappy double play. Then Wickman got catcher Ivan Rodriguez on a fly ball to Tartabull to end the inning. In the last of the sixth, facing left-handed rookie Terry Burrows, the Yankees got the two runs back. Following a leadoff home run by Bernie Williams, Fernandez lined a double to right and eventually came home as Boggs was grounding into a double play.

However, Texas, playing without Juan Gonzalez—their leading home-run threat—was not finished. They answered back with a three-run seventh, a rally that began with Wickman hitting the leadoff batter. After he plunked Dean Palmer and gave up a double to Rusty Greer that sent Palmer to third, Narron sent switch-hitter Mark McLemore up to bat for right-hand hitting Billy Hatcher. Both McLemore and Hatcher were playing their first games for Texas, as were Tettleton and Nixon. McLemore brought both runners home with a single to right, cutting the lead to 7–5. Later in the inning it became 7–6 when McLemore scored on a ground ball by Nixon.

Veteran left-hander Steve Howe replaced Wickman in the eighth and survived a very shaky outing. He loaded the bases on two walks and a single before getting McLemore on a fly to center fielder Williams. Tartabull's run-scoring single in the last of the eighth gave the Yanks an insurance run, and then Showalter gave the ball to Wetteland. New York had taken advantage of the Montreal Expos' weak financial position to "steal" Wetteland in a so-called trade on April 5. Montreal, in the process of getting rid of all their good young talent before their salaries got too high, received a minor-league player and much-needed cash in return. Baseball had talked about but had yet to solve the problems created by the growing disparity between its big-market and small-market teams—a disparity illustrated by the 1995 average salary for the two team's players. For Montreal it was $411,142 and for the Yankees it was over $2 million—the highest in history. Wetteland entered the game to a prolonged ovation, which continued throughout the inning. He was perfect in his Yankees' debut, getting pinch-hitter Mike Pagliarulo on a fly ball, Nixon on a grounder, and then finishing with a flourish by striking out Frye. After saving 105 games for Montreal over the last three years, Wetteland now had his first as a Yankee.

Key raised his opening-day record to 6–0, while becoming the first Yankee to win three consecutive openers since Mel Stottlemyre in 1967–1969. However, after the opener things went downhill for Key, as they did for another of today's heroes—Tartabull. Key was 1–2 when he reinjured his shoulder in May and missed the rest of the season. And Tartabull, whom Steinbrenner had said would have to have a big year for the Yankees to win, didn't. He was hitting .224 with six home runs when the Yanks traded him to the Oakland Athletics on July 28 for outfielder Ruben Sierra. The same day, the club obtained David Cone from the Toronto Blue Jays in a trade for three minor-leaguers. Cone went 9–2 the rest of the way in helping the Yanks become the American League's first-ever wild-card team.

Major League attendance was sharply down in 1995, an average of just over 6,000 per game, as fans in many cities took their time in coming back to baseball. The Yankees drew just 1,705,263 in 72 home dates.

A 79–65 record landed the Yankees in second place in the East, seven games behind the Boston Red Sox. However, because their record was better than those of the second-place teams in the other two divisions, the Yanks earned the wild-card spot. They lost the Division Series to the Seattle Mariners in an exciting five-game playoff. Yet as exciting as it may have been, it was still a series between teams with the league's third- and fourth-best records. After starting the year at Columbus in the International League, left-hander Andy Pettitte came up and won 12 games (12–9) to finish third in voting for Rookie of the Year. Wade Boggs (for the 13th time in 14 seasons), Paul O'Neill, and Bernie Williams all hit .300 or better. Don Mattingly finally got to play in a postseason game, but George Steinbrenner did not re-sign him for 1996. Mattingly said he would sit out the season, but would not rule out coming back in 1997. Steinbrenner also chose not to re-sign Buck Showalter. Showalter signed with the Arizona Diamondbacks, scheduled to begin play in 1998, and Joe Torre signed to manage the Yankees in 1996.

Wednesday, April 26, 1995

Texas	ab	r	h	rbi
Nixon cf	4	1	2	2
Frye 2b	5	1	1	0
Clark 1b	4	0	1	2
Tettleton dh	4	0	1	0
ᵇHare	0	0	0	0
Rodriguez c	4	0	1	0
Palmer 3b	2	1	0	0
Greer rf	3	1	2	0
ᶜFox rf	0	0	0	0
Hatcher lf	2	1	1	0
ᵃMcLemore lf	2	1	1	2
Gil ss	2	0	0	0
ᵉPagliarulo	1	0	0	0
Total	33	6	10	6

New York	ab	r	h	rbi
Boggs 3b	4	1	1	1
Leyritz dh	5	1	2	0
O'Neill lf,rf	3	1	1	0
Tartabull rf	3	1	2	3
ᵈG. Williams lf	0	0	0	0
Mattingly 1b	5	0	0	1
Stanley c	4	0	2	1
B. Williams cf	3	1	1	1
Fernandez ss	4	2	2	0
Kelly 2b	4	1	3	0
Total	35	8	14	7

ᵃSingled for Hatcher in seventh inning.
ᵇRan for Tettleton in eighth inning.
ᶜWalked for Greer in eighth inning.
ᵈRan for Tartabull in eighth inning.
ᵉFlied out for Gil in ninth inning.

Texas	001	002	300–6
New York	013	102	01X–8

Errors—Greer. Double plays—Gil, Frye, and Clark; Palmer Frye, and Clark; Frye, Gil, and Clark; Kelly, Fernandez, and Mattingly. Caught stealing—by Stanley (Nixon). Left on bases—Texas 5; New York 9. Put outs—New York 27: O'Neill 1, Tartabull 4, Mattingly 6, Stanley 5, B. Williams 4, Fernandez 1, Kelly 3, Key 2, Wickman 1. Texas 24: Nixon 2, Clark 6, Hatcher 1, Rodriguez 6, Frye 4, McLemore 1, Gil 2, Greer 2. Assists—New York 9: Stanley 2, Mattingly 1, Fernandez 2, Kelly 2, Key 1, Wickman 1. Texas 9: Rogers 1, Frye 3, Palmer 2, Gil 3. Two-base hits—Frye, Rodriguez, Greer, Hatcher, Fernandez. Home runs—Tartabull, B. Williams. Sacrifices—Nixon, Gil. Sacrifice fly—Boggs.

	IP	H	R	ER	BB	SO
TEXAS						
Rogers (L, 0–1)	3.0	5	4	4	2	3
Dettmer	0.1	2	1	1	0	0
Burrows	2.1	5	2	2	1	1
Whiteside	2.0	1	1	1	1	2
*Oliver	0.0	0	0	0	1	0
R. McDowell	0.1	1	0	0	0	0
NEW YORK						
#Key (W, 1–0)	5.0	7	3	3	0	3
Wickman	2.0	2	3	3	0	0
Howe	1.0	1	0	0	2	1
Wetteland S.1	1.0	0	0	0	0	1

#Pitched to three batters in sixth inning.
*Pitched to one batter in eighth inning.

Hit by pitch—By Wickman (Palmer). Wild pitches—Wickman, Oliver. Umpires—Deegan, Harvey, Walding, and Klein. Time of game—3 hrs. 10 min. Attendance—50,245.

Tuesday, April 2, 1996
Jacobs Field, Cleveland
New York 7 Cleveland 1

If we open a quarrel between the past and the present,
we shall find that we have lost the future.—Winston Churchill

As baseball began what fans anticipated would be its first full season in three years, there was a guarded sense of optimism surrounding the game, a feeling that baseball had finally bottomed out and would now start to reclaim its traditional place as America's national pastime. The renaissance had begun last September with Cal Ripken breaking Lou Gehrig's consecutive-games-played streak. Interest in Ripken's quest was extremely high nationwide, and the graceful way in which the Baltimore Orioles' veteran shortstop responded warmed the hearts of fans everywhere. An exciting set of playoffs and a World Series between two excellent teams—the Atlanta Braves and the Cleveland Indians—further reminded fans why they loved this game. This spring, the stories coming out of the training camps in Florida and Arizona were mainly of baseball, a welcome change from the past few years. True, the game still had neither a labor agreement nor a commissioner. (Milwaukee Brewers owner Bud Selig was serving as the acting commissioner.) Nevertheless, it seemed the owners had begun to recognize at long last what it was they had to do to win back their old fans and make new ones. There were so many superb players in the game, and so many young ones verging on greatness, that one could not help but be enthusiastic. Baseball had survived so many crises in the past and come back stronger and more popular than ever, there was no reason to think it would not do so again.

In New York, along with talk of a bright future for the Yankees built around the team's young stars, there remained the overriding question of where the team would play when their lease at Yankee Stadium expired in 2002. The State of New Jersey was actively courting owner George Steinbrenner to move the club to the Meadowlands, while Mayor Rudy Giuliani spoke for all New Yorkers when he said the Yankees belonged in New York. That they belonged there was without question. New York was making its own comeback: the most recent wave of immigrants was beginning to establish their place in the economy, and the crime rate was down drastically. But like all American cities, New York had major budgetary problems and had to decide what cost it would be willing to bear to keep the Yankees. On Opening Day 1996, Steinbrenner was considering three options: (1) once again renovating Yankee Stadium, (2) moving to the West Side of Manhattan, or (3) moving to New Jersey. That the plans for the Manhattan site (the most expensive) called for a multipurpose, domed stadium, while New Jersey offered an outdoor, grass-field, baseball-only park made the problem even more vexing.

The Chicago White Sox and Seattle Mariners opened the 1996 season at Seattle's Kingdome on Sunday evening, March 31, the first time a major league game had been played in March. The Yankees were scheduled to open the next day, but three inches of snow in Cleveland forced a postponement. By the following afternoon, Jacobs Field's head groundskeeper Brandon Koehnke and his crew had cleared the field, and although the temperature at game time was only 38 degrees, 42,289 dedicated Indians fans showed up. They cheered themselves hoarse when owner Richard Jacobs handed the players their American League championship rings, but that little ceremony would be the highlight of their afternoon. Playing in their earliest opener ever, the Yankees scored five runs in the last two innings to turn a tight pitchers' duel into a 7–1 rout. Starter David Cone went seven innings to pick up the win, raising his lifetime record against Cleveland to 4–3. Meanwhile, Cleveland's Dennis Martinez saw his career mark against the Yanks fall to a dismal 2–14. Martinez had not beaten New York since way back on June 11, 1982, when he pitched for Baltimore. The 41-year-old right-hander had a strong outing, allowing just two runs and five hits in his seven innings. "I did the job I was supposed to do," he said. "I got people out. But when you don't take advantage of the other pitcher when he's struggling, and the pitcher is the caliber of David Cone, you're going to be in trouble when he finds his groove."

Cleveland, a city that had revived its love affair with the Indians, was eager for Opening Day. Last season's post-strike decline in baseball attendance and enthusiasm had affected most franchises, but not this one. The Indians drew 2,842,745 to set a team record, breaking the mark set by the 1948 Indians, who played in a park that had 30,000 more seats than Jacobs Field. For 1996, the club had taken the unprecedented step of selling every seat in the park before the season even began. There would be no deciding at the last minute to take the family out to see a ballgame in Cleveland this year. The reason for all the excitement was an Indians' team that was among the best in recent memory. After winning their first American League pennant in 41 years, winning 100 games in the abbreviated 144-game schedule, they won the five-team Central Division by 30 games, a major-league record for a first-place finisher. They followed with victories over Boston and Seattle in the play-offs before losing the World Series in six games to Atlanta. Now, the Indians were overwhelming favorites to repeat in the American League—something they had never done before. In fact, each time Cleveland had won the pennant in the past—in 1920, 1948 and 1954—the Yankees had succeeded them as champions the following year.

Of course, the Yanks had won those pennants in an eight-team league. Now the New Yorkers would have to get through the defending Eastern Division champion Red Sox and the much-improved Orioles to even get a shot at the Indians. And, for the first time since 1992, they would be doing it under new leadership. Bob Watson had replaced Gene Michael as general manager, and he in turn had named Joe Torre the new field manager. Torre, fired by the St. Louis Cardinals last June, had 32 years of big-league experience as a player and manager, all in the National League. That was quite a different résumé than his predecessor, Buck Showalter, who had never played or managed in the major leagues before he became the Yankees' manager in 1992. Showalter had done an excellent job in his four years, but George Steinbrenner had chosen to let him move on. When Steinbrenner failed to re-sign him, Showalter joined the expansion Arizona Diamondbacks, a team that would not even begin play until 1998. Besides Showalter, Steinbrenner had also let some valuable players get away, players who had contributed to the Yankees' 1995 wild-card finish but were now free agents. Catcher Mike Stanley signed with the Red Sox, infielder Randy Velarde with the California Angels, and pitcher Jack McDowell with the Indians. Darryl Strawberry, rescued from oblivion by Steinbrenner in 1995, failed to hook on with any big-league club. To varying degrees the Yankees would miss them all, but mostly they expected that they would miss Don Mattingly, who decided to retire when Steinbrenner showed no apparent interest in keeping him.

Mattingly's place in Yankees' history and in their record book was secure. At his retirement, only six others had played in more games as a Yankee, and only four had more at-bats. Mattingly was second all-time in doubles (442), fifth in hits (2,153), seventh in batting average (.307) and home runs (222), and eighth in runs batted in (1,099) and runs scored

(1,007). He also held the Yankees' record for most hits (238) and most doubles (53) in a season, setting both records in 1986. To replace Mattingly, the Yanks completed a major trade with Seattle for first baseman Tino Martinez, a 28-year-old left-handed hitter who had 31 home runs and 111 runs batted in for the Mariners in 1995. They believed Martinez would do even better at Yankee Stadium, although well aware that he would have a difficult task as the successor to a very popular player. Reliever Jeff Nelson and rookie pitcher Jim Mecir also came to New York in the trade, but the Yanks lost two very promising youngsters, third baseman Russ Davis and pitcher Sterling Hitchcock. Two other trades brought catcher Joe Girardi from the Colorado Rockies and veteran outfielder Tim Raines (beginning the season on the disabled list) from the White Sox. From the free agent market, the Yankees signed infielder Mariano Duncan and pitchers Dwight Gooden and Kenny Rogers. Gooden, the former New York Met, was attempting to come back from a suspension related to substance abuse, while Rogers had been deemed one of this year's free agent prizes. Steinbrenner was forced to outbid several teams to get the 31-year-old left-hander, who had gone 17–7 for Texas last year. However, the owner's major off-season move was re-signing Cone, a free agent whom the Orioles were also actively pursuing. Cone, 9–2 for the Yanks last year after coming over from the Toronto Blue Jays (18–8 overall), was among the game's best pitchers and the presumptive anchor of the Yankees' staff. At the start of the season only he and Andy Pettitte (based on his strong rookie year in 1995) appeared to be dependable starters. No one knew how well Rogers would do in New York, Gooden's past made him questionable, and Jimmy Key and Melido Perez were coming off arm injuries. Taking all the permutations and combinations of his pitching staff into consideration, Torre announced the first day of spring training at the Yanks' new complex in Tampa that Cone would pitch the opener. Cone had opened twice before—for the Mets in 1992 and for the Blue Jays last year. For Martinez, starting on Opening Day was routine; he had done it ten times previously, more than any other active major-league pitcher.

Along with the disbursement of the players' championship rings, there was a pregame moment of silence for National League umpire John McSherry. The stadium flag sat at half-mast for McSherry, who died on the field at Riverfront Stadium in Cincinnati yesterday. Dave Winfield, who finished his 22-year big-league career with the Indians last season, was to have thrown out the first ball but couldn't make it back to Jacobs Field today. Cleveland manager Mike Hargrove did the honors, and then after Rocco Scotti sang the national anthem, Martinez and Cone took over. They each pitched two scoreless innings before the Yankees scored the game's first run on Duncan's single and Paul O'Neill's double. It was the second double of the game for O'Neill, now a lifetime .365 hitter against Martinez. (The first had raised his opening-day consecutive-game batting streak to eight.) Duncan, whom the Yanks obtained to be a utility infielder, was opening at second base because Pat Kelly and Tony Fernandez were on the disabled list. Watson had considered dealing for a second baseman, but backed off when the other clubs asked for pitching in return. The club was reluctant to give up either Scott Kamieniecki or sophomore Mariano Rivera in case any of their frontline starters faltered.

Duncan's double-play partner this afternoon was 21-year-old Derek Jeter, the first rookie to start an opener at shortstop for the Yankees since Tom Tresh in 1962. Martinez had struck him out in his first at-bat, but in the fifth Jeter homered over the 19-foot wall in left to put the Yankees ahead, 2–0. That was another first for Jeter: the first opening-day home run by a Yankees' rookie since Jerry Kenney's blast off Washington's Camilo Pascual at RFK Stadium in 1969. The Yanks, who had used a different shortstop in each of their last six openers, were expecting Jeter to fill the position for many years. They had even given him uniform No. 2, one of only two single-digit numbers the club had not retired. (Torre wore the other one, No. 6.) Jeter, the club's first draft choice in 1992 (out of high school), had quickly progressed through the system. After beginning 1994 with Tampa of the Florida State League, he moved up to Albany of the Eastern League and then to Columbus of the International League. He hit above .300 at each stop (.329, .377, .349) and won *The Sporting News'* Minor League Player of the Year Award. Last season, after playing in 15 games with the Yankees, Jeter went back to Columbus where he batted .317 and led the league with 96 runs scored. However, he also led in errors (29), which led Torre to wonder whether the young man was ready to play shortstop in the major leagues. Jeter's performance this afternoon allayed his manager's fears. "He was everything you could ask for today," Torre said. Jeter made several outstanding defensive plays, but the best one—and the most important—came in the seventh inning. The score was still 2–0 at the time, and Sandy Alomar Jr., who had doubled, was on second with two out. Omar Vizquel hit a looping fly ball that Jeter, with his back to the plate, caught in short left field to end the inning. "That was a big play for them," Vizquel said. "I thought it was going to drop." But Jeter felt he had it all the way. "I thought I had a good chance on that play," he said. "It was hit kind of high and I figured I had a chance. I was just as proud of that play as the home run."

After Jeter's catch, Cone's work for the day was done. He came out having yielded just two hits in his seven innings—Alomar's double and Julio Franco's single that ended Cone's bid for a no-hitter an inning earlier. (Franco, who played in Japan in 1995, took over the Indians' first-base job made vacant when Cleveland granted free agency to Paul Sorrento.) Cone did have some problems with his control, walking a total of six. In the first inning he walked Franco and Albert Belle, but got Eddie Murray on a fly ball to center. Then Murray and Jim Thome walked with two out in the fourth, prompting a visit to the mound from Girardi and new pitching coach Mel Stottlemyre. Cone threw three straight balls to the next batter, the free-swinging Manny Ramirez, before running the count full. His 3–2 pitch was a high fastball that Ramirez drove to deep right, but O'Neill caught up with it at the warning track. "Getting out of that was huge," Cone said after the game.

Bob Wickman relieved Cone in the eighth and gave up a leadoff single to Kenny Lofton. Lofton, the American league's stolen base leader the past four seasons, stole second, and after Franco walked, he stole third. Lofton scored on Carlos Baerga's ground ball to give Cleveland their lone run of the day. But by then they were down by four because the Yanks had scored three runs in the top of the eighth. Switch-hitting Bernie Williams accounted for all three with his first right-handed at-bat of the season. Williams, an emerging star, unloaded on left-hander Alan Embree's 2–0 pitch for a 410-foot home run, scoring O'Neill and Ruben Sierra ahead of him. O'Neill, who walked, was on third and Sierra, who singled, was on second, but Hargrove declined to walk Williams intentionally despite his .409 batting average against Cleveland last year. Had Hargrove done so, he would have then brought in right-hander Eric Plunk to pitch to right-handed-hitting Gerald Williams. The reason he stayed with Embree, Hargrove explained, was to avoid putting Plunk in the position of having to face his first batter of the season with the bases loaded. Plunk did come on in the ninth, when the Yanks added two more runs against him and Paul Assenmacher on a single by Girardi, an intentional walk to Duncan, a single by O'Neill, and a double by Sierra.

Steve Howe had replaced Wickman with one out in the eighth, but Torre sent his closer, John Wetteland, out to pitch the ninth. Wetteland set the Indians down in order, and the Yankees had their fifth consecutive opening-day win and the tenth in their last 11. Their record at Jacobs Field was now 7–2, making New York and Texas the only two visiting teams to have winning records there. This win was New York's 990th against Cleveland (990–800) since the two teams started playing each other in 1903. Torre had his first American League win, but his boss was not there to see it. Steinbrenner was in California filming an episode of the comedy show *Seinfeld* in which he would appear as himself. The scenes were cut and never shown on home TV, but were part of the DVD version.

Tuesday, April 2, 1996

New York

	ab	r	h	rbi
Boggs 3b	5	0	0	0
Duncan 2b	4	2	1	0
O'Neill rf	4	1	3	2
Sierra dh	5	1	2	1
T. Martinez 1b	4	0	1	0
B. Williams cf	4	1	1	3
G. Williams lf	4	0	0	0
Girardi c	3	1	1	0
Jeter ss	4	1	1	1
Total	37	7	10	7

Cleveland

	ab	r	h	rbi
Lofton cf	4	1	1	0
Franco 1b	2	0	1	0
Baerga 2b	4	0	0	1
Belle lf	2	0	1	0
Murray dh	3	0	0	0
Thome 3b	2	0	0	0
Ramirez rf	4	0	0	0
Alomar c	3	0	1	0
aBurnitz	1	0	0	0
Vizquel ss	4	0	0	0
Total	27	1	4	1

aGrounded out for Alomar in ninth inning.

New York	001	010	032–7
Cleveland	000	000	010–1

Errors—None. Double plays—T. Martinez, Jeter, and Cone; Duncan, Jeter, and T. Martinez. Left on bases—New York 7; Cleveland 8. Put outs—New York 27: Girardi 6, Boggs 1, G. Williams 1, Jeter 4, O'Neill 2, B. Williams 4, T. Martinez 8, Cone 1. Cleveland 27: Vizquel 2, Franco 8, Alomar 8, Ramirez 1, Lofton 5, Belle 3. Assists—New York 8: Jeter 3, Duncan 4, T. Martinez 1. Cleveland 9: Baerga 5, Vizquel 2, D. Martinez 2. Two-base hits—O'Neill (2), Sierra, Alomar. Home runs—Jeter, B. Williams. Stolen bases—Girardi, Murray, Lofton (2).

	IP	H	R	ER	BB	SO
NEW YORK						
Cone (W, 1–0)	7.0	2	0	0	6	4
Wickman	.1	2	1	1	1	0
Howe	.2	0	0	0	0	0
Wetteland	1.0	0	0	0	0	1
CLEVELAND						
D. Martinez (L, 0–1)	7.0	5	2	2	2	5
Embree	1.0	2	3	3	1	2
Plunk	0.1	1	1	1	0	1
Assenmacher	0.2	2	1	1	1	0

Umpires—Phillips, Merrill, Roe, and Scott. Time of game—3 hrs. 8 min. Attendance—42,289.

Two of this afternoon's starters, Gerald Williams and Ruben Sierra, and two of the relief pitchers, Bob Wickman and Steve Howe, would not finish the season in New York. The Yanks would release Howe and trade the other three in deals that brought slugger Cecil Fielder (from the Detroit Tigers) and pitchers Ricky Bones and Graeme Lloyd (from the Milwaukee Brewers) to the Yankees. Wetteland would lead the league with 43 saves and earn the World Series Most Valuable Player Award, then leave the Yankees and sign with the Texas Rangers. Cone was 4–1 when he underwent surgery in early May to repair an aneurysm in his pitching arm. He returned on September 2 to boost the slumping Yankees with seven no-hit innings at Oakland in a game the Yanks won, 5–0.

> *Under the imperturbable leadership of Joe Torre, the Yankees (92–70) won the Eastern Division title by four games over the Baltimore Orioles and then defeated the Western Division champions, the Texas Rangers, three games to one in the Division Series. They faced Baltimore in the American League Championship Series, the Orioles having "earned" their place in the ALCS by winning the wild-card race and then defeating the Central Division champion Cleveland Indians. After splitting two games in New York, the Yanks won three straight at Camden Yards to reach the World Series for the first time in 15 years. They capped the year, one of the most satisfying in team history, by winning their first world title since 1978. After losing the first two games at the Stadium to the heavily favored Atlanta Braves, the Yankees won the next four, including a three-game sweep in Atlanta. Derek Jeter was the unanimous choice as the American League's Rookie of the Year, and Andy Pettitte finished second to the Toronto Blue Jays' Pat Hentgen in one of the closest-ever votes for the Cy Young Award. Torre shared Manager of the Year honors with Texas' Johnny Oates. The Yanks drew 2,250,124 in 78 home dates, far below Baltimore and Cleveland, and trailing even Texas, Seattle, Toronto, and Boston.*

Tuesday April 1, 1997 (N)
Kingdome, Seattle
Seattle 4 New York 2

Rejoice, O young man in thy youth.—Ecclesiastes

Baseball had added a new scheduling gimmick for the 1997 season, one designed to entice fans, who they mistakenly assumed needed such gimmicks. As part of the December 1996 Basic Agreement between the owners and the players, this season would feature a one-year experiment where American and National League teams would play 15 or 16 inter-league games.

For the first time, the Yankees would play regular season games against the Mets, their New York neighbors, the Atlanta Braves, the Montreal Expos, and the Florida Marlins. As with other recent innovations, like the designated hitter and wild cards, acceptance by the fans was mixed. Mostly—but by no means always—it split between younger fans in favor and older fans opposed.

Not so with another tweak to the schedule, which met with almost universal approval, especially when a winter storm warning was issued for New York and other Northeastern cities. In a move seemingly long overdue, opening day games would be played in as many domed stadiums and warm-weather sites as possible.

"It looks like we made the right decision for a day or so," said Katy Feeney, the senior vice president of the National League. "We're going to prove to be very smart with the warm-weather schedule we have this year," boasted Derek Irwin, the vice president of the American League.

The Yankees were beginning the defense of their twenty-third world championship in the Seattle Kingdome against the West Division runner-up Mariners. Yankees manager Joe Torre chose David Cone as his starter. Cone was 7–2 in 1996, but spent much of the season on the disabled list after undergoing surgery to remove an aneurysm from under his right armpit. Mariners skipper Lou Piniella chose left-hander Jeff Fassero as his starter. Fassero, who had spent his entire six-year career with the Montreal Expos, was coming off a 15–11 season. Seattle had acquired him in a five-player trade in October 1996.

Torre's lineup was largely unchanged from the one that opened the 1996 season, including Cone, the winning pitcher in the Yankees' 7–1 victory at Cleveland. The changes were in left field and in the designated hitter spot. Former Mets slugger Darryl Strawberry was in left, replacing Gerald Williams, traded to the Milwaukee Brewers in mid season. And Cecil Fielder was the designated hitter in place of Ruben Sierra. The Yanks had traded Sierra to the Detroit Tigers for Fielder at the July 31 deadline last year.

The Yankees still had bitter memories of the Kingdome, where they had lost to the Mariners in the 1995 Division Series. After winning the first two games at home, they went to Seattle needing only one win, but lost three straight games. Cone still lamented his failure to hold the lead in the deciding game of that '95 Division Series, though he did see a bright side. "It came at such a dark time in baseball history," he said, referring to the strike that had ruined the 1994 season. "That series helped revive baseball from the doldrums," he proclaimed. "It probably saved baseball here in Seattle."

One result of the series was the start of a rivalry between the teams. The bad feelings peaked in a brawl on August 28, 1996, ignited by Paul O'Neill's reaction to a pitch coming too close to his head. "I don't expect any problems," O'Neill said when asked if he expected manager Piniella to instruct his pitchers to come in tight on him. "If there are, there are," he answered.

Seattle centerfielder Ken Griffey Jr. had emerged, at age 27, as the best all-around player in the game. Despite a wrist injury that caused him to miss 20 games in 1996, he slugged 49 home runs and drove in 140 runs. Griffey started the new season in spectacular fashion hitting home runs in his first two at-bats to lead the Mariners to a 4–2 win. It was the Yankees first opening-day loss in six years, but the 13th loss in their last 16 games with the Mariners.

This season marked the 50th anniversary of Jackie Robinson's 1947 debut with the Brooklyn Dodgers. In honor of this civil rights milestone, baseball had decreed Robinson's number 42 be retired by all clubs. Players currently wearing the number would be allowed to continue wearing it, but it would never again be issued to a new player. Pitcher Mariano Rivera, who wore the number for the Yankees, would be the last player to wear number 42 when he retired following the 2013 season. In honor of the occasion, Sharon Robinson, Jackie's daughter, threw out the ceremonial first ball.

The Yankees scored a run against Fassero in the top of the first inning. Fielder's sacrifice fly scored Wade Boggs who had singled and moved to third on Bernie Williams's double. Griffey's two-out 421-foot home run in the home half of the inning tied the score. The Yanks regained the lead in the second on second baseman Mariano Duncan's double and catcher Joe Girardi's two-out, two-strike single. Cone again surrendered the lead when third baseman Russ Davis, a former Yankee, led off the Seattle third with a home run down the left-field line to tie the score, 2–2.

Cone retired the next two batters, but Alex Rodriguez reached on an infield hit. The 21-year-old shortstop, judged a "can't-miss" player since his high school days in Miami, had been the Mariners' first pick in the 1993 amateur draft. In 1996, his first full season, he led the American League in batting (.358), runs scored (141), and doubles (54), validating all the scouting reports and his lofty draft selection.

Rodriguez's single kept the inning alive and brought Griffey to the plate for his second at-bat of the season. Cone, pitching carefully, fell behind, 3–0 before bringing the count full. Griffey connected on the next pitch, sending a high fly to right field. Initially, O'Neill seemed to have it in range, but the ball carried into the first row of seats for a two-run homer. It was Griffey's 22nd multi-homer game and his 22nd career home run against the Yankees. "He is the best player I've ever seen," Piniella said in the winner's clubhouse.

Cone held the Mariners scoreless from the fourth inning through the sixth, as did relievers Brian Boehringer, Mike Stanton, and Jeff Nelson in the seventh and eighth. Meanwhile, Fassero now with a two run lead, limited the Yankees to one additional hit—a sixth-inning single by Fielder—over the next five innings. Bobby Ayala and Norm Charlton protected the lead, giving Fassero a win in his American League debut.

Ayala, a right-hander, pitched a scoreless eighth and retired Fielder leading off the ninth. With the next three Yankees' batters left-handed swingers, Piniella replaced Ayala with left-hander Norm Charlton. Tino Martinez greeted Charlton with a single to right. Next up was O'Neill, Charlton's former teammate with the 1990 world champion Cincinnati Reds, managed by Piniella. O'Neill also singled to right, putting the tying run aboard. Pat Kelly ran for O'Neill as the dangerous Darryl Strawberry stepped in as the potential winning run.

With the count at 2–2, Strawberry hit a sharp ground ball to second baseman Joey Cora who turned it into a 6-4-3 game-ending double play. As 57,586 fans in the Kingdome breathed a big sigh of relief, Charlton had the first of what would be his team-leading 14 saves this season.

Seattle, which reached 90 wins (90–72) for the first time, won the American League West Division title. Ken Griffey Jr. had his greatest season, leading the American League in home runs (56), runs (125), runs batted in (147), slugging percentage (.646), and total bases (393). He won the Most Valuable Player Award unanimously. The Mariners also set a new team attendance record, drawing more than 3 million for the first time.

Sparked by interleague play, overall major league attendance was up by 4.6 percent over 1996, reaching its second highest total ever. Attendance for interleague games averaged 33,407, which was 20 percent higher than it was for intraleague games. The dramatic increases all but guaranteed that the one-year "experiment" would continue into 1998 and very likely beyond.

The Yankees (96–66) finished second in the American League East, two games behind the Baltimore Orioles. As the wild-card team, they led the Cleveland Indians two games to one in the five-game Division Championship Series, but lost the next two at Cleveland, each by one run. Cleveland lost in the World Series to the Florida Marlins as the Marlins became the first wild card team to win the Series. In the voting for the American League's Most Valuable Player Award, Tino Martinez finished second to Ken Griffey Jr., who got all 28 first-place votes. Mariano Rivera replaced the departed John Wetteland as the Yankees' closer. He recorded 43 saves with a 1.88 earned run average and was named the American League's Fireman of The Year by The Sporting News.

Tuesday, April 1, 1997

New York	ab	r	h	rbi	po	a	Seattle	ab	r	h	rbi	po	a
Jeter ss	4	0	0	0	0	4	Cora 2b	3	0	0	0	0	4
Boggs 3b	4	1	2	0	1	2	Rodriguez ss	4	1	1	0	2	4
Williams cf	4	0	1	0	2	0	Griffey cf	4	2	2	3	1	0

New York	ab	r	h	rbi	po	a
Fielder dh	3	0	1	1	0	0
T. Martinez 1b	4	0	1	0	8	0
O'Neill rf	3	0	1	0	1	0
aKelly	0	0	0	0	0	0
Strawberry lf	4	0	0	0	2	0
Duncan 2b	3	1	1	0	2	2
Girardi c	3	0	1	1	8	1
Cone p	0	0	0	0	0	0
Boehringer p	0	0	0	0	0	1
Stanton p	0	0	0	0	0	0
Nelson p	0	0	0	0	0	0
Total	32	2	8	2	24	10

Seattle	ab	r	h	rbi	po	a
E. Martinez dh	4	0	1	0	0	0
Buhner rf	3	0	0	0	3	0
Sorrento 1b	3	0	1	0	11	4
Wilson c	3	0	1	0	6	0
R. Davis 3b	3	1	1	1	0	0
Tinsley lf	3	0	0	0	1	0
Fassero p	0	0	0	0	2	5
Ayala p	0	0	0	0	1	0
Charlton p	0	0	0	0	0	0
Total	30	4	7	4	27	17

```
New York    110    000    000—2
Seattle     103    000    00X—4
```

aRan for O'Neill in ninth inning.

Errors—None. Double plays—Girardi and Duncan; Cora, Rodriguez, and Sorrento. Caught stealing—Girardi, Cora. Left on bases—New York 5; Seattle 4. Two-base hits—Williams, Duncan, Wilson. Home runs—Griffey (2), R. Davis. Sacrifice Fly—Fielder.

	IP	H	R	ER	BB	SO
NEW YORK						
Cone (L, 0–1)	6.0	7	4	4	2	8
Boehringer	1.0	0	0	0	0	0
Stanton	.1	0	0	0	0	0
Nelson	.2	0	0	0	0	0

Wild pitch—Cone.

	IP	H	R	ER	BB	SO
SEATTLE						
Fassero (W, 1–0)	7.0	5	2	2	1	6
Ayala	1.1	1	0	0	0	0
Charlton S.1	0.2	2	0	0	0	0

Umpires—HP, Drew Coble; 1B, Tim McClelland; 2B, Mark Johnson; 3B, Gary Cederstrom. Time of game—2:46. Attendance—57,586.

Wednesday April 1, 1998 (N)
Edison Field, Anaheim
Anaheim 4 New York 1

There is nothing permanent except change.—Heraclitus

Once again a baseball season opened under a set of organizational conditions different from those in place the previous season. This time it was the Division structure that had changed as a result of expansion and realignment. After much wrangling, the owners and interim commissioner Bud Selig—the interim would be removed in July—decided on the placement of the two new teams. The Arizona Diamondbacks were assigned to the National League's West Division and the Tampa Bay Devil Rays to the American League's East Division.

In addition, the Detroit Tigers moved from the American League East to the American League Central, and the Milwaukee Brewers moved from the American League Central to the National League Central, becoming the first team in the 20th century to switch leagues.

Milwaukee's switch gave the National League 16 teams and the American League 14, the first time the leagues had a different number of teams since the expansion of the American League to ten teams in 1961.

One of those two expansion teams was the Los Angeles Angels, who used that name through the 1964 season. From 1965 to 1996 they were known as the California Angels, before switching to the Anaheim Angels in 1997. Consequently, when the Yankees opened the 1998 season in Anaheim, it was against the Anaheim Angels.

The Yankees had added several new players in the off-season. They acquired second baseman Chuck Knoblauch from the Minnesota Twins and third baseman Scott Brosius from the Oakland A's in trades, and signed designated hitter Chili Davis as a free agent.

Gone were third baseman Charlie Hayes, designated hitter Cecil Fielder, and pitcher Kenny Rogers. Gone too was general manager Bob Watson, who had resigned in early February and was replaced by Brian Cashman. The 31-year-old Cashman's first move, just three days after taking the position, had been to trade the team's number one draft pick from 1996, pitcher Eric Milton, (among others) to the Minnesota Twins for Knoblauch.

Exhibition game's statistics generally do not mean much, still the Yanks were encouraged by their play this spring, which included a combined .314 batting average over 31 games. Particularly effective were Knoblauch, who reached base in every game and had a .561 on-base percentage, and Derek Jeter, their budding superstar, who batted .394, with a .789 slugging percentage. They were anxious to get the season started, even if it was on a field that an El Nino weather pattern had soaked with rain. The wet weather and a Disney-inspired pre-game fireworks display delayed the opening by an hour. Game-time temperature was a very un-Southern California-like 53 degrees.

Ninety-year-old Gene Autry, the Angels' original owner, threw out the first ball. Autry was accompanied by former Angels' stars Rod Carew, Jim Fregosi, Bobby Grich, and Reggie Jackson. Two of the best left-handers in the game were the opposing starters: Anaheim's Chuck Finley, 13–6 in 1997, and the Yankees' Andy Pettitte, 18–7.

Perhaps it was caused by the cool weather, or the one-hour rain delay, but Finley was uncharacteristically wild. He walked six batters in the first five innings, but he was able to work around them. Catcher, Matt Walbeck, came to his rescue in the second inning when he threw out Davis and Chad Curtis on steal attempts. The Yankees got their first hits in the fourth on leadoff back-to-back singles by Paul O'Neill and Bernie Williams. But Finley was able to get out of the two-on, nobody-out jam without being scored on. He struck out Tino Martinez and Davis then got Curtis on a force out.

Pettitte matched Finley for three innings before the Angels broke through with a four-run fourth. Fielder, who had signed with Anaheim as a free agent after an often-tempestuous two seasons in New York, opened the inning with a single. He had always had success against Pettitte—6 hits in 11 at-bats—and had won a 10-pitch at-bat in the first inning by drawing a two-out walk that loaded the bases. Pettitte escaped by striking out Garrett Anderson on his 27th pitch of the inning.

Norberto Martin followed Fielder's leadoff single in the fourth with a one-out liner down the right field line that sent the lumbering Fielder to third. The next batter was Walbeck, hitless in six career at-bats against Pettitte. He connected with a fastball driving it just to the left of center fielder Bernie Williams. In attempting to cut it off, Williams slipped and fell on the wet grass as the ball skipped by him. Fielder and Martin scored as Walbeck wound up on third with his first triple in nearly three years.

Pettitte hung a curve to the next batter, Gary Disarcina, that Disarcina ripped inside the third-base line for a run-scoring double. Darrin Erstad then singled to right, which scored Disarcina with the Angels fourth run. It was more than enough as Finley and two relievers held the Yankees to one run in a 4–1 victory. Finley, who won his last ten decisions in 1997, now had an 11-game winning streak.

New York's lone run came in the sixth. Williams led off with his second hit of the day—he would have-three—and took third on a single by Martinez. But again, Finley limited the damage. He induced Davis to ground into a double play, with Williams scoring, and retired Curtis on a ground ball. Overall the Yankees had five hits and seven walks against Finley and relievers Mike Holtz and Troy Percival, but failed several times to deliver with runners on base. Davis alone failed three times with runners in scoring position.

It was a disappointing loss for Joe Torre and his players. The Yankees payroll was now a gargantuan $72 million, and owner George Steinbrenner was expecting that to translate into another world championship. It was an especially upsetting outing for Pettitte, who allowed nine hits, three walks and struck out only three in his six innings. The week before the season began he had said it was "sickening" how good this team can be. Torre, beginning his third season as manager, was also aware of how good a team he had, yet he remained cautious in his optimism. "You don't play the damn thing on paper, unfortunately, but if they did, we'd have a pretty good shot at this thing," he said.

Pettitte finished with 16 wins (16–11), which was third on the club to David Cone (20–7) and David Wells (18–4). Mariano Rivera had 36 saves and three in the World Series. Over the course of the season, Jorge Posada replaced Joe Girardi as the team's number one catcher. Posada joined Pettitte, Rivera, Bernie Williams, and Derek Jeter as the core group that would lead the Yankees into the 21st century. All had come out of the Yankees' minor league system.

The Yankees more than lived up to preseason expectations by winning an American League record 114 games (114–48), since eclipsed by the 2001 Seattle Mariners, who won 116. They won the Eastern Division by 22 games over the runner-up Boston Red Sox. After sweeping the Texas Rangers in three games to win the Division Championship Series, they defeated the Cleveland Indians in six games to win the League Championship Series. Having captured their 35th American League pennant, the Yankees swept the San Diego Padres to claim their 24th world championship. Bernie Williams won the American League's batting title with a .339 average, and Joe Torre was named the American League's Manager of the Year. While talk of replacing 75-year-old Yankee Stadium continued, the club drew just under three million.

Wednesday, April 1, 1998

New York							Anaheim						
	ab	r	h	rbi	po	a		ab	r	h	rbi	po	a
Knoblauch 2b	2	0	0	0	0	2	Erstad 1b	5	0	1	1	7	0
Jeter ss	4	0	0	0	0	1	Edmonds cf	4	0	0	0	1	0
O'Neill rf	3	0	1	0	5	0	Hollins 3b	2	0	1	0	2	3
Williams cf	4	1	3	0	1	0	Salmon rf	3	0	1	0	3	0
Martinez 1b	3	0	1	0	11	1	Fielder dh	3	1	2	0	0	0
Davis dh	3	0	0	0	0	0	Anderson lf	4	0	0	0	1	0
Curtis lf	3	0	0	0	2	0	Martin 2b	4	1	1	0	2	2

New York

	ab	r	h	rbi	po	a
Brosius 3b	4	0	0	0	1	2
Girardi c	2	0	0	0	3	0
ªRaines	1	0	0	0	0	0
Pettitte p	0	0	0	0	1	2
Holmes p	0	0	0	0	0	0
Lloyd p	0	0	0	0	0	0
Total	29	1	5	0	24	8

Seattle

	ab	r	h	rbi	po	a
Walbeck c	4	1	2	2	8	2
Disarcina ss	4	1	3	1	3	2
Finley p	0	0	0	0	0	0
Holtz p	0	0	0	0	0	0
Percival p	0	0	0	0	0	0
Total	33	4	11	4	27	9

ªFlied out for Girardi in ninth inning.

New York	000	001	000–1
Anaheim	000	400	00X–4

Errors—None. Double plays—Martinez; Martin, Disarcina, Erstad. Caught stealing—Davis, Curtis. Left on bases—New York 8; Anaheim 9. Two-base hits—Martin, Disarcina, Salmon. Three-base hits—Walbeck.

	IP	H	R	ER	BB	SO
NEW YORK						
Pettitte (L, 0–1)	6.0	9	4	4	3	3
Holmes	1.2	2	0	0	0	0
Lloyd	0.1	0	0	0	0	0
ANAHEIM						
Finley (W, 1–0)	7.0	4	1	1	6	7
Holtz	1.0	1	0	0	1	0
Percival S.1	1.0	0	0	0	0	1

Hit by pitches—by Pettitte (Hollins) Umpires—HP, Jim Evans; 1B, Larry McCoy; 2B, Mark Johnson; 3B, Chuck Meriwether. Time of game—2:52. Attendance—43,311.

Monday April 5, 1999 (N)
Network Associates Coliseum, Oakland
Oakland 5 New York 3 (8 Innings)

Maybe baseball does not cleanse the world of all sin.
But for millions of people, it comes awfully close.—Clyde Haberman

The exciting 1998 home run race between the St. Louis Cardinals' Mark McGwire and the Chicago Cubs' Sammy Sosa had excited the nation and done much to counter the labor disputes between the owners and the players union that had alienated fans in recent years. McGwire had won that race, with 70 home runs to Sosa's 66, as he shattered Roger Maris's major league record of 61 set in 1961.

If one significant economic problem remained in baseball, it was the increasing gulf between the rich teams and the poor ones. Of the 13 teams with payrolls above $48 million in 1998, only three had a losing record. Of the 17 teams below $48 million, only three had a winning record. As one example of the disparity, the Los Angeles Dodgers were paying one player, pitcher Kevin Brown, $15 million, which is slightly less than the $17 million the Montreal Expos were paying its entire team. (The Yankees, as usual, had the highest payroll at $85 million.)

Maris had broken Babe Ruth's record of 60 home runs, set in 1927. But because he did it in the first year of American League expansion, when the schedule increased from 154 games to 162, many older fans resisted accepting Maris's record. There was no such resistance to McGwire (or Sosa), but there would be some years later when it was revealed that both men had taken performance-enhancing drugs.

Given the varying circumstances under which Ruth, Maris, and McGwire set their records highlights the futility of comparing players across eras. Yet, fans love to do it. Similarly, whenever the discussion gets around to the best team ever, three Yankees' clubs are generally included—those from 1927, 1939, and 1961. Yet none of those clubs, or any other major league club, had won as many games as the 1998 Yankees. After a then American League record 114 regular season wins, they won three in the Division Series, four in the League Championship Series, and four more in the World Series, for a major league record 125 wins.

The Yankees were already the overwhelming favorites to repeat in 1999, when news out of their Tampa spring training site, on February 18, further solidified those expectations. The Yankees had pulled off a trade that sent pitchers David Wells and Graeme Lloyd, and infielder Homer Bush to the Toronto Blue Jays in exchange for Roger Clemens, who even at age 36 was baseball's premier pitcher.

After 13 seasons with the Boston Red Sox, during which he won a franchise record 192 games (tied with Cy Young) and three Cy Young Awards, the Sox let him leave as a free agent after the 1996 season. Clemens signed with Toronto, where in his two seasons with the Blue Jays he won two more Cy Young Awards. He also won the pitchers' Triple Crown in both years, leading the league in wins, strikeouts, and earned run average. Clemens had finished his exceptional 1998 season with a flourish, winning his last 15 decisions.

But of course Clemens's accomplishments and the Yankees record-breaking season were in the past. They would start the 1999 season even with every other team in the league. "Last year is history," said general manager Brian Cashman. "We won the 1998 World Series, but this is 1999. We hope Roger can take us to the next level this year, which is winning this year's Series."

The Yankees would begin the season without their manager, Joe Torre, who was still recovering from prostate cancer surgery. Don Zimmer, his trusted aide and bench coach, would manage the club in the interim. "You keep hearing the Yankees are a cinch. There is no such thing," Zimmer said the day before the opener. "We're just trying to go out and win the Eastern Division. That's our first goal. This is a good team, it will win a lot of games," added Zimmer, who was already feuding with owner George Steinbrenner about how to run the team.

Overall it had not been a good spring for the Yankees. The club had lost 14 of 20, including nine of their last 11, and Steinbrenner had reacted in his usual way to his team losing games, no matter what the circumstances.

Zimmer had dismissed the spring training results, as most baseball people did. His focus was on the regular season and not surprisingly for his first game as the Yankees' manager he went with his ace. Clemens, a six-foot-four, 230-pound right-hander, would attempt the first step toward that higher level Cashman had spoken of against the Oakland A's at Oakland's Network Associates Coliseum. This was the second season the stadium bore that corporate name after being the Oakland-Alameda County Stadium since the team arrived from Kansas City in 1969.

Art Howe, in his fourth season as manager of the A's, had planned to open with his ace, left-hander Kenny Rogers, but Rogers had begged off saying he was not yet in shape. Howe's second choice was Gil Heredia, a 33-year-old right-hander who had never won more than six games in any of his nine previous big league seasons. By contrast, Clemens, beginning his 16th major league season, had accumulated 233 victories, the most among active pitchers. He ranked 10th all-time in strikeouts (3,153) and had led the league with the lowest earned run average six times.

The A's were a team on the rise, but it was a past glory that was celebrated in the pregame ceremonies. The honorees were a group of players from the 1989 Oakland team that swept their Bay Area rivals, the San Francisco Giants, ten years earlier in the earthquake-interrupted World Series of 1989. Among them was bullpen star Dennis Eckersley who threw out the first ball. Despite the weather on this wet and chilly night, a sellout crowd of 46,380 turned out and was rewarded with a 5–3 Oakland win.

"I'm pretty jacked up for every start," said Clemens, as intense a competitor as the game has ever seen. "I get excited out there." By the time he got "out there," the Yankees had staked him to a 1–0 lead on a single by Derek Jeter, an error by A's second baseman Tony Phillips, and a run-scoring single by Bernie Williams. The Yankees loaded the bases in each of the first two innings but Heredia was able to prevent them from any additional scoring.

Clemens retired the first two batters he faced, before walking left-handed sluggers Jason Giambi and Matt Stairs. The right-handed-hitting John Jaha flied to center to end the threat, and in the second, Clemens retired the side in order. It had been raining hard through the first two innings, which led home plate umpire Jim Evans to suspend play for 47 minutes between the second and third innings.

Chili Davis's third-inning home run gave the Yankees a 2–0 lead that Clemens protected through four. The only hit he had allowed was a two-out, bunt single by Jason McDonald in the third. Clemens retired the first two batters in the Oakland fifth and thought he had struck out Miguel Tejada for the third out. But Evans called his 3–2 pitch a ball. The next batter was Phillips, who made amends for his error by smashing a 1–1 fastball over the right-field wall to tie the game at 2–2.

T.J. Mathews, who would appear in 362 games in his eight-year career, all in relief, replaced Heredia in the seventh. He retired the first two batters he faced—Chuck Knoblauch and Joe Girardi—before surrendering a home run to Jeter, the young shortstop's third hit of the day.

Clemens again had the lead, 3–2, but again, he could not keep it. He walked Phillips with one out in the seventh, his 107th pitch on this chilly night. Not willing to risk an injury to his ace, Zimmer sent pitching coach Mel Stottlemyre to the mound to remove Clemens. His replacement was veteran left-hander Mike Stanton, another career reliever. (He would appear in 1,178 games in a 19-year career, with just one start.) Within the space of three batters, Stanton turned a one-run New York lead into a one-run Oakland lead. McDonald singled Phillips to third and took second as Williams threw to third in an attempt to cut down Phillips. It was a mental error by Williams, whose throw had no chance of beating the speedy Phillips to the bag. Giambi's slow grounder to Jeter scored Phillips with the tying run, and a single to right by Stairs scored McDonald with the lead run. Right-hander Jeff Nelson replaced Stanton and was touched for a double by Jaha that scored Stairs, giving Oakland a 5–3 lead.

Neither team scored in the eighth, and as the Yankees came to bat in the ninth a heavy rain began pouring down. Evans ordered the tarpaulin back on the field and after waiting an hour and 21 minutes canceled the final inning at 12:27 a.m. local time. It was unlikely that many fans back in New York, where it was 3:27 a.m., were still watching. Although disappointed with the loss, Zimmer said Evans made the right decision after waiting long enough to see if the rain would stop.

> Don Zimmer served as an interim manager for the season's first 36 games while Joe Torre recovered from surgery. Under his leadership the Yankees won 21 and lost 15. They went 77–49 after Torre returned to finish first in the East Division, four games ahead of the Boston Red Sox. The Yanks swept the three-game Division Series from the Texas Rangers and defeated the Red Sox four games to one in the League Championship Series. For the second consecutive season they won the World Series in four games, this time over the Atlanta Braves. Derek Jeter batted .349 and led the league in hits with 219. The Yankees went over the 3 million mark in attendance for the first time, drawing 3,292,736 fans to the Stadium.

Monday, April 5, 1999

New York	ab	r	h	rbi	po	a	Oakland	ab	r	h	rbi	po	a
Knoblauch 2b	3	0	0	0	3	2	Phillips 2b	3	2	1	2	0	1
Jeter ss	3	2	3	1	0	2	McDonald cf, lf	3	2	2	0	3	0
O'Neill rf	3	0	0	0	1	0	Giambi dh	3	0	1	1	0	0
Williams cf	4	0	1	1	2	0	Stairs rf	3	1	1	1	1	0
Martinez 1b	4	0	0	0	6	1	Jaha 1b	4	0	1	1	6	2
Davis dh	2	1	1	1	0	0	ᵃChristenson pr, lf	0	0	0	0	0	0
Ledee lf	4	0	0	0	2	0	Grieve lf	4	0	1	0	2	0
Brosius 3b	3	0	0	0	0	1	Saenz 1b	0	0	0	0	2	1
Girardi c	3	0	0	0	8	0	Chavez 3b	4	0	0	0	0	0
Clemens p	0	0	0	0	1	1	Hinch c	4	0	0	0	6	1
Stanton p	0	0	0	0	0	0	Tejada ss	3	1	0	0	2	3
Nelson p	0	0	0	0	1	1	Heredia p	0	0	0	0	1	2
Total	29	3	5	3	24	8	Mathews p	0	0	0	0	1	0
							Total	31	5	7	5	24	10

ᵃRan for Jaha in seventh inning.

New York	101	000	10–3
Oakland	000	020	30–5

Errors—Phillips. Stolen bases—McDonald. Caught stealing—Jeter. Left on bases—New York 7; Oakland 7. Two-base hits—Jaha. Home runs—Davis, Jeter, Phillips.

	IP	H	R	ER	BB	SO
NEW YORK						
Clemens	6.1	4	3	3	5	8
Stanton (L, 0–1)	0.1	2	2	2	0	0
Nelson	1.1	1	0	0	0	0
OAKLAND						
Heredia	6.0	4	2	1	3	6
Mathews (W, 1–0)	2.0	1	1	1	1	0

Hit by pitches—by Heredia (Jeter). Umpires—HP, Jim Evans; 1B, Larry McCoy; 2B, Chuck Meriwether; 3B, Dale Ford. Time of game—2:40. Attendance—46,380.

XI

2000–2009

The Yankees began and ended the first decade of the new millennium by winning the World Series. And twice—in 2001 and 2003—they won the pennant but lost in the World Series. They made the playoffs in nine of the ten seasons—missing only in 2008—but lost in the Division Series four times and in the League Championship once. Joe Torre managed the team through the 2007 season before leaving to become manager of the Los Angeles Dodgers. Joe Girardi replaced him in 2008 and led the team the rest of the decade. In 2009, the Yankees moved into a new Yankee Stadium, built across the street from the original one.

Of the team's five core players, three—shortstop Derek Jeter, catcher Jorge Posada, and pitcher Mariano Rivera—played the entire decade. But center fielder Bernie Williams left unceremoniously after the 2006 season when the team failed to resign him, and Andy Pettitte signed as a free agent with the Houston Astros in 2004, before returning as a free agent in 2007.

While the farm system developed only one new major star—Robinson Cano–trades and free agency brought many top players from other teams to New York. Foremost among them were pitchers Mike Mussina, Randy Johnson, and CC Sabathia, and position players Jason Giambi, Hideki Matsui, Johnny Damon, Mark Teixeira, and Alex Rodriguez.

Monday April 3, 2000 (N)
Edison Field, Anaheim
New York 3 Anaheim 2

The time is out of joint.—William Shakespeare

For years, governments, businesses, and individuals had worried that the computers everyone depended on would malfunction at midnight on December 31, 1999. But to everyone's relief, the great "Y2K scare," proved to be just that—a scare. The new millennium arrived without the apocalypse so many had feared. On January 1, 2000, the world went on as usual, as did baseball, although the new century ushered in a significant, if not widely noted, organizational change. The National League and the American League, which had been separate legal entities for 100 years, merged into a single organization—Major League Baseball (MLB)—led by the Commissioner.

The most visible manifestation of this consolidation was in the umpiring crews. The days of American League umpires and National League umpires were over. Beginning with the 2000 season all crews would consist of a mix of umpires from both leagues.

For the Yankees, opening their season in Anaheim, it made little difference who was umpiring the game. To a man, they had one goal—a third consecutive world championship. No team had won the World Series in three consecutive seasons since the 1972–1974 Oakland Athletics; and no Yankees' team had done it since Casey Stengel's club won five straight from 1949 through 1953. Two veterans who had played key roles in the previous two championship seasons gave their perspective on what the winning of a third straight title would mean.

"If you win three straight, you put an asterisk by those teams," said outfielder Paul O'Neill. "I'd love to be part of one of those, and associated with one of those. I don't care how long your career is—you could play 15 years, but if you could play on a team that wins three championships, that's how you're going to be remembered."

Pitcher David Cone had an interesting take on how these Yankees teams were perceived by fans in other cities. "We're both very proud of what's gone on here, and we're both fiercely proud of the run we've had. I like what's being said about the Yankees—it's a throwback team, a selfless group, a likable group. I just feel good when I hear people say this is a team that's tough to hate. That says a lot, because the Yankees are very easy to hate."

The opening in Anaheim marked the fifth consecutive year the Yanks had opened on the road and the fourth consecutive year they had opened with a night game on the West Coast. As it was for each of the last four seasons, the games would come on in New York at 10:35 p.m. Youngsters who had been waiting for opening day since the end of the previous season would see at most an inning or two of the game. Only the most devoted adults would be able to see the entire game. Night games draw better than day games, but opening day is special and something is lost when a team's fans can't be a part of it, even vicariously via radio or television.

Joe Torre was back to lead the Yankees for his fifth season, unlike the Angels who had a new manager. Mike Scioscia, a longtime catcher for the Los Angeles Dodgers was moving up after only one year of minor league experience. Scioscia, 41, had managed the Albuquerque Dukes, the Dodgers Pacific Coast League affiliate in 1999.

Orlando Hernandez, affectionately known in New York as El Duque, was Torre's obvious choice to pitcher the opener. The 34-year-old right-hander, a defector from Cuba in 1998, had compiled a sparkling 29–13 record in his two seasons with the Yankees. He was the team's leading winner in 1999 (17–9) and had been Torre's choice to pitch Game One of the Division Series, the League Championship Series, and the World Series.

Moreover, he had been the Yanks best pitcher this spring, with a 1.17 ERA in five starts. Opposing Hernandez would be Ken Hill, also a 34-year-old right-hander. Hill had won 16 games in a season three times—for the Montreal Expos in 1992 and 1994, and for the Texas Rangers in 1996—but with a mediocre 4–11 record in 1999, he was clearly on the downside of his career.

The Angels took a 1–0 lead on a second-inning home run by Tim Salmon, their slugging outfielder. Salmon had hit 23 or more home runs for six consecutive seasons (1993–1998) before an injury limited him to 98 games and just 17 home runs in 1999. Three hits and a pair of uncharacteristic mental errors by the Yankees threatened to increase Anaheim's lead in the fifth inning, but Hernandez escaped without a run scoring.

With one out, singles by Scott Spezio and Gary Disarcina put Angels' runners at first and second. Hernandez got the dangerous Darin Erstad to hit a weak fly ball to short left field. Shortstop Derek Jeter, drifted back onto the grass, but then stopped, assuming left fielder Shane Spencer would make the catch. Meanwhile Spencer, assuming Jeter would make the catch, pulled up short. The breakdown in communication resulted in a gift single for Erstadt and loaded the bases.

After a visit to the mound by pitching coach Mel Stottlemyre, Hernandez faced Adam Kennedy, who hit a looping pop fly to third baseman Scott Brosius. Again Hernandez's defense failed him. Kennedy's pop fly was not high enough for the umpires to invoke the infield fly rule and Brosius unthinkingly caught it for the second out. He either ignored or did not hear Hernandez screaming at him to let the ball drop. Had he done so, he almost certainly could have picked it up and thrown home or to second base to start a double play, as Kennedy had barely moved from the batter's box.

Instead of being out of the inning, Hernandez had to face Mo Vaughn, a powerful left-handed batter. After a very successful career with the Boston Red Sox that included a Most Valuable Player Award in 1995, Vaughn left as a free agent after the 1998 season. In 1999, his first year in Anaheim, he had 33 home runs and 108 runs batted in.

Hernandez, who had already struck out Vaughn twice, once on a fastball and once on a curve ball, struck him out again—this time on a change up. If games have momentum-changing moments, Hernandez's strikeout of Vaughn to leave the bases loaded was the momentum changer this evening.

After surviving the bottom of the fifth, Jeter led off the Yankees' sixth with a single, just the third hit Hill had allowed. But he had walked three, and the Yanks had forced him to throw many pitches—57 in the first three innings alone. The first 14 batters for the always patient Yankees had taken the first pitch.

Hill's pitch count was now well into the 90s. O'Neill followed Jeter's hit with a drive that sailed over the center field wall, an estimated 430 feet from home plate. The home run, along with a single and a walk, enhanced O'Neill's reputation as one of baseball's best ever opening-day performers. His batting average for his 14 career openers was .426, with two home runs and 10 runs batted in.

Hill, now trailing, 2–1, retired Bernie Williams, after which, Scioscia brought in Kent Mercker who got the final two outs. Spencer's seventh-inning, leadoff home run off Mercker upped New York's lead to 3–1, but Anaheim did not go down easily. They had the tying run either on base or at the plate in each of the final three innings, but failed to get the big hit. Overall, they left 11 runners on base. The Angels had a runner at first base with two outs in the seventh, but Hernandez retired Vaughn on a ground ball to first baseman Tino Martinez. In the eighth, Jeff Nelson, who replaced El Duque, issued a two-out walk to Troy Glaus. Spezio followed with a drive to left that Spencer grabbed to rob him of an extra-base hit.

Spencer was playing left field because Williams had a sore right arm and was being used as the designated hitter. Ricky Ledee, normally a left fielder, took Williams's place in center, while Spencer took Ledee's place in left. Spencer was the defensive star of the game, as he also made a sliding catch in the second inning that took a hit away from Garret Anderson.

As everyone in the crowd of 42,704 knew he would, Torre brought in Mariano Rivera to pitch the ninth inning. The game's premier closer was not as sharp as usual. He gave up a one-out single to Disarcina, a walk to Erstadt, and a two-out run-scoring single to Vaughn.

The run snapped his streak of 31 ⅓ consecutive innings without allowing an earned run compiled at the end of the 1999 season. Rivera earned his first save of the 2000 season by getting the dangerous Tim Salmon on a fly ball to O'Neill. In ending their three-game losing streak on Opening Day, the Yankees were now 56–41-1 in their 98 openers, and 16–9 in openers as defending World Series winners.

The Yankees' win total slipped to 87 (87–74) but it was sufficient for them to finish 2½ games ahead of the Boston Red Sox in the Eastern Division race. They defeated the Oakland A's three games to two in a hard-fought Division Series and won the League Championship Series in six games over the Seattle Mariners. When the Yanks defeated the New York Mets in five games, they had won their third consecutive world championship and 26th overall. It was also their 11th win in the 14 World Series played between the Yankees and a National League team based in New York City.

Monday, April 3, 2000

New York	ab	r	h	rbi	po	a	Anaheim	ab	r	h	rbi	po	a
Knoblauch 2b	4	0	1	0	2	1	Erstad lf	4	0	3	0	3	0
Jeter ss	4	1	1	0	2	2	Kennedy 2b	5	0	1	0	1	4
O'Neill rf	3	1	2	2	4	0	Vaughn 1b	5	0	1	1	13	2
Williams dh	4	0	0	0	0	0	[b]Clemente	0	0	0	0	0	0
Martinez 1b	4	0	1	0	7	0	Salmon rf	5	1	1	1	1	0
Ledee cf, lf	4	0	0	0	1	0	Anderson cf	4	0	0	0	1	0
Posada c	3	0	0	0	6	1	Glaus 3b	2	0	1	0	0	4
Spencer lf	4	1	1	1	4	0	Spezio dh	2	0	1	0	0	0
Kelly cf	0	0	0	0	0	0	Molina c	3	0	0	0	3	2
Brosius 3b	2	0	0	0	1	1	[a]Palmeiro	1	0	0	0	0	0
Hernandez p	0	0	0	0	0	0	Disarcina ss	4	1	2	0	3	3
Nelson p	0	0	0	0	0	0	Hill p	0	0	0	0	1	1
Rivera p	0	0	0	0	0	0	Mercker p	0	0	0	0	0	0
Total	32	3	6	3	27	5	Petkovsek p	0	0	0	0	1	0
							Total	35	2	10	2	27	16

[a]Struck out for Molina in ninth inning.
[b]Ran for Vaughn in ninth inning

New York	000	002	100–3
Anaheim	010	000	001–2

Errors—Vaughn. Double plays—Martinez. Caught stealing—Knoblauch, O'Neill, Glaus. Left on bases—New York 5; Anaheim 11. Two-base hits—Kennedy. Home runs—O'Neill, Spencer, Salmon.

	IP	H	R	ER	BB	SO
NEW YORK						
Hernandez (W, 1–0)	7.0	8	1	1	3	4
Nelson	1.0	0	0	0	1	1
Rivera S.1	1.0	2	1	1	1	1
ANAHEIM						
Hill (L, 0–1)	5.1	4	2	2	3	2
Mercker	2.2	2	1	1	0	1
Petkovsek	1.0	0	0	0	0	0

Umpires—HP, Tim McClelland; 1B, Terry Craft; 2B, Paul Schrieber; 3B, Phil Cuzzi. Time of game—3:02. Attendance—42,704.

Monday, April 2, 2001
Yankee Stadium, New York
New York 7 Kansas City 3

One generation passeth away, and another generation cometh.—Ecclesiastes

Major-league teams had long since ceased the practice of spending the last two weeks of spring training by "playing their way North." Rather than playing games in towns and cities throughout the South and Midwest, they now preferred to complete the training period in the warmth of Florida or Arizona. A downside of the change was the teams having to adjust to going from temperatures in the 70s and 80s to those in the 40s and 50s.

Such was the case on Opening Day 2001, when the Yankees hosted the Kansas City Royals at a cold, cloudy, and misty Yankee Stadium. Cold weather tends to favor pitchers, particularly fastball pitchers, and in Roger Clemens, the Yankees had one of the fastest ever. Clemens, beginning his 18th major league season, expected to not only win this afternoon's game, but also to accomplish a personal milestone. He needed only five strikeouts to break Walter Johnson's American League record of 3,508.

The Yankees had not re-signed David Cone following his 4–14 season in 2000, yet they had upgraded their pitching staff by signing Mike Mussina, the longtime ace of the Baltimore Orioles. A starting quartet of Clemens, Mussina, Andy Pettitte, and Orlando Hernandez, along with Mariano Rivera, baseball's best closer, gave the Yankees the best pitching in the league. They also had the strongest starting lineup in the league, making them the favorites to win a fourth consecutive world championship. Not since the 1949–1953 Yankees won five consecutive World Series had any team won as many as four in a row. And it was more difficult now. Those Casey Stengel teams simply had to win the pennant and they were in the Series. Joe Torre's teams had to first win two sets of playoffs to get there.

Opening day financial data indicated the Yankees were no longer number one in total team payroll. That title now belonged to the Boston Red Sox, at $111.5 million, with the Yankees ($109.8 million) and the Los Angeles Dodgers ($109 million) close behind. (The following day, a recalculation based on the value of outfielder Manny Ramirez's contract lowered the Red Sox total and bumped the Yankees into their customary top spot.) The Red Sox, in addition to signing David Cone, had added Ramirez and pitcher Hideo Nomo, giving them by far the largest increase in the three payrolls, a whopping 43 percent over their 2000 opening-day payroll of $77.9 million. The Yankees were up nearly 19 percent over their major league-high $92.5 million a year ago.

The ever-increasing cost of attending a major league baseball game showed no letup this season. The Yankees had the second-highest ticket prices this year, an average of $28.90 The Red Sox, at $36.08 per average ticket were number one. The Yankees were also No. 2 in the Fan Cost Index, a survey that rated how much money fans spend at the park. They found that a family of four attending a game at Yankee Stadium could expect to spend $192.60 for tickets, parking, four hot dogs, six drinks, two programs and two caps this year, up 10.3 percent from last year.

Three former Yankees, Hall-of-Famers all, took part in the pregame ceremonies. Yogi Berra and Phil Rizzuto helped Dave Winfield raise New York's 26th championship flag. The now obligatory recording of Frank Sinatra's "New York, New York" was played and baritone Robert Merrill, as he had done so often, sang the national anthem.

The emotional highlight of the ceremonies came when pitching coach Mel Stottlemyre, diagnosed last year with multiple myeloma (cancer of the bone marrow), was given a thunderous ovation when he threw out the first ball. Stottlemyre, who made seven opening day starts with the Yankees, had a stem cell transplant on September 11 and did not return to fulltime duty for the rest of the season.

Now cancer free, Stottlemyre said he had chills as he threw the ball to a misty-eyed

Joe Torre, who had called him almost every day during his absence. "Have you ever tried to catch a ball with tears in your eyes?" asked Torre, a former catcher.

"I had chills going up my back," Stottlemyre said, aware of the significance of throwing out the first ball at a Yankee Stadium opener. "It was a big day for me, a tremendous honor. I've seen who usually throws out the first pitch at Yankee Stadium. .. It was always the legends, someone like DiMaggio or Mantle or Whitey. Someone like that."

When the Yankees took the field, their double play combination was different from the one they had used the last three seasons. Utility infielder Luis Sojo was at shortstop, instead of Derek Jeter, and 25-year-old Alfonso Soriano was at second base, instead of Chuck Knoblauch.

A day earlier, the Yankees had placed Jeter, outfielder Shane Spencer, and pitcher Ramiro Mendoza on the 15-day disabled list, retroactive to March 22. Jeter would remain at the team's training complex in Tampa, Florida, until later in the week, rehabilitating a strained thigh. Now the team leader and the most popular player with the fans, he had started the last five openers at shortstop and would miss only one more (2013) until his retirement following the 2014 season.

Knoblauch's defense as a second baseman had been more than adequate in his seven years with the Minnesota Twins (1991–1997) but started to deteriorate after he joined the Yankees. His errors doubled from 13 in 1998 to 26 in 1999, and in 2000 he began to have difficulty making accurate throws to first base. Torre was moving him to left field, where Knoblauch would became the 11th different Yankee to start in left field in the past 13 season openers. He would have only one chance in this game, catching a routine third-inning fly ball by Carlos Beltran that the fans greeted with a good-natured standing ovation.

New York took a 1–0 lead on Tino Martinez's fourth inning home run off Royals right-hander Jeff Suppan. Kansas City tied the score in the fifth on singles by catcher Hector Ortiz and second baseman Carlos Febles that sandwiched a ground out by shortstop Rey Sanchez. A solo home run by Jermaine Dye in the top of the sixth put the Royals ahead, 2–1, but the Yankees exploded in the home half as their first five batters of the inning accounted for five runs.

Paul O'Neill led off the inning with a single, and Bernie Williams, batting left-handed, followed by hitting a 3–0 pitch for a home run, putting the Yanks ahead, 3–2. "I had a green light my first at-bat," Williams said, "but I chose not to take it. This time I had a good idea of what he was throwing and I felt a little more comfortable hitting with three balls and no strikes. I was just looking for something in the vicinity of the strike zone that I could put a good swing on."

A shaken Suppan, who had yet to walk a batter, then walked the next two: Martinez and David Justice, the latter acquired from the Cleveland Indians in a June 29, 2000 trade. The next batter was Jorge Posada, a switch-hitter who was considered a better batter from the right side: a .241 average in his career against right-handers, and a .324 hitter against left-handers. Nevertheless, Royals manager Tony Muser replaced Suppan with left-hander Tony Cogan. Muser was hoping that by making Posada bat right-handed, it would be easier to get a ground ball double play.

Cogan, making his major league debut, fell behind, 3–1. His next pitch to Posada, an excellent low-ball hitter, was a low fastball. Posada drove it over the left-center field fence to extend the Yankees' lead to 6–2. (This would be Cogan's only major league season.) An inning later, Posada got his third hit and fourth run batted in of the game when he doubled against Kris Wilson to score Justice.

Meanwhile, Clemens had allowed just the two runs and struck out four through eight innings. His strikeout of Beltran in the eighth was number 3,508 of his career, tying Johnson's 74-year-old league mark. Clemens had thrown only one complete game in 2000, but he wanted very much to break Johnson's record today. Opening Day complete games had mostly vanished from baseball, but given the circumstances, and a five-run lead, Torre allowed him to come out for the ninth inning.

The first batter, Dye, doubled to left—his third hit of the game—and took third on a wild pitch to Joe Randa. When Clemens eventually fanned Randa for strikeout 3,509, breaking Johnson's record, his day's work was done. Torre replaced him with Todd Williams, as Clemens left the mound to standing ovation. Unlike the one given laughingly to Knoblauch earlier, this one was in recognition of Clemens's great career.

When pitcher Williams erred on a ball hit by Mark Quinn, Dye scored to cut the lead to 7–3. Torre wasted no time in replacing Williams with Mariano Rivera, who got the final two outs, preserving the first of Clemens's 20 wins this season.

The 2001 season was interrupted by the horrific attacks of September 11, causing the schedule to be interrupted for seven days and the season to be extended for a week. The Yankees (95–65–1) finished 13½ games ahead of the Boston Red Sox to win their fourth consecutive East Division title. They defeated the Oakland A's three games to two in another hard-fought Division Series and won the League Championship Series in five games over the Seattle Mariners, a team that had won 116 regular season games. Their attempt to win a fourth consecutive World Series was thwarted by the Arizona Diamondbacks, who by scoring two runs against Mariano Rivera in the last of the ninth inning of Game Seven, won their first Series with a 3–2 victory. The three Series games played in New York, the major site of the 9/11 attacks was marked by patriotic displays and attempts to heal the nation's spirits. Roger Clemens (20–3) won a record-setting sixth Cy Young Award and was named Pitcher of the Year by the Sporting News. Mariano Rivera led the league with 50 saves and was named Fireman of the Year by the Sporting News. Mike Mussina was second in the league in earned run average (3.15) and strikeouts (214).

Monday, April 2, 2001

Kansas City	ab	r	h	rbi	po	a	New York	ab	r	h	rbi	po	a
Febles 2b	4	0	1	1	2	1	Knoblauch lf	4	0	1	0	1	0
Beltran cf	4	0	1	0	2	0	Bellinger lf	0	0	0	0	0	0
Sweeney 1b	3	0	0	0	11	2	Soriano 2b	5	0	1	0	2	3
Dye rf	4	2	3	1	1	0	O'Neill rf	5	1	1	0	4	0
Randa 3b	4	0	0	0	0	1	B. Williams cf	4	1	2	2	4	0
Quinn lf	4	0	0	1	3	0	Justice dh	3	2	1	0	0	0
Brown dh	4	0	1	0	0	0	Martinez 1b	3	2	2	1	9	0
Ortiz c	3	1	1	0	2	2	Posada c	4	1	3	4	6	0
[a]Ibanez	0	0	0	0	0	0	Sojo ss	4	0	0	0	0	1
Sanchez ss	3	0	0	0	1	6	Brosius 3b	4	0	2	0	1	1
[b]Alicea	1	0	0	0	0	0	Clemens p	0	0	0	0	0	3
Suppan p	0	0	0	0	2	1	T. Williams p	0	0	0	0	0	0
Cogan p	0	0	0	0	0	0	M. Rivera p	0	0	0	0	0	0
Santiago p	0	0	0	0	0	0	Total	36	7	13	7	27	8
Wilson p	0	0	0	0	0	0							
Henry p	0	0	0	0	0	0							
Total	34	3	7	3	24	13							

[a]Walked for Ortiz in ninth inning.
[b]Grounded out for Sanchez in ninth inning.

| Kansas City | 000 | 011 | 001–3 |
| New York | 000 | 105 | 10X–7 |

Errors—T. Williams. Double plays—Sanchez, Febles, Sweeney; Soriano, Martinez. Stolen base—Beltran. Left on bases—Kansas City 6, New York 8. Two-base hits—Dye, Posada. Home runs— Dye, Martinez, B. Williams, Posada.

	IP	H	R	ER	BB	SO
KANSAS CITY						
Suppan (L, 0–1)	5.0	8	5	5	2	2
Cogan	0.1	2	1	1	1	0
Santiago	0.2	0	0	0	0	0
Wilson	1.0	3	1	1	0	1
Henry	1.0	0	0	0	0	0

Suppan pitched to four batters in the sixth inning

	IP	H	R	ER	BB	SO
NEW YORK						
Clemens (W, 1–0)	8.1	7	3	3	1	5
T. Williams	0.0	0	0	0	0	0
M. Rivera	0.2	0	0	0	1	0

WP—Clemens.

Umpires—HP, Tim Welke; 1B, Charlie Williams; 2B, Gary Cedestrom; 3B, Marvin Hudson. Time of game—2:56. Attendance—55,814.

Monday, April 1, 2002
Oriole Park at Camden Yards, Baltimore
Baltimore 10 New York 3

Big Brother is watching you.—George Orwell

The September 11, 2001 terror attacks on New York and Washington by radical Muslims had changed everyday life in America. Increased security, with all the intrusiveness, frustration, and aggravation-producing annoyances that went with it, was now the norm at airports, federal, state, and local government facilities, and most public events. Going to a baseball game would never again be the same—especially in New York City, which had suffered by far the most physical damage and the most loss of life from the attacks

The first game of the 2002 season in New York was at Shea Stadium, where the Mets were hosting the Pittsburgh Pirates. The fans "were not prepared for what greeted them," wrote the *New York Times*. The *Times* described "snaking lines similar to those at airports, with security guards and police officers searching fans as they entered the stadium and telling them to empty all bags that were not see-through."

The paper noted that the "increased security meant that some people, even some who arrived early, missed the first inning as they were subjected to complete searches.

It was all part of the new way of doing things after September 11, as opening day, a springtime rite for many die-hard fans, became yet another tradition altered by the "war on terror."

Meanwhile, the Yankees were opening their season against the Baltimore Orioles at

Camden Yards, where the new routine for spectators entering the park was much the same. The Yanks had made several significant additions this season, most notably 31-year-old first baseman Jason Giambi, signed as a free agent from the Oakland Athletics. Giambi had been the American League's Most Valuable Player in 2000, and a close runner up in 2001 to Ichiro Suzuki of the Seattle Mariners.

Also coming to New York via free agency were outfielder Rondell White, from the Montreal Expos, and pitchers David Wells, from the Chicago White Sox and Steve Karsay, from the Atlanta Braves. The club had filled the hole at third base left by the retired Scott Brosius by trading David Justice to the Mets for Robin Ventura. At 34 and coming off back-to-back poor seasons, Ventura was acquired to fill the gap at third until highly touted rookie Drew Henson was ready to take over.

Henson, a star quarterback at the University of Michigan who chose to pursue a professional career in baseball, proved to be a bust. His major league career consisted of three games in 2002 and five in 2003. He later played in the National Football League as a quarterback for the Dallas Cowboys in 2004 and the Detroit Lions in 2008.

Except for Wells, all the newcomers appeared in the opener. So too did rookie Nick Johnson, who served as the designated hitter, although none distinguished themselves in New York's 10–3 defeat.

The club's most noteworthy off-season loss was outfielder Paul O'Neill, who had retired. O'Neill's talent and intensity made him very popular in New York. In his nine years with the Yankees, he batted .303, and had won a batting championship with a .359 average in the strike-shortened 1994 season.

Retirement had also claimed Baltimore's most popular player, Cal Ripken, who watched the game from one of the team's luxury suites. For the first time since his debut in August 1981, Ripken, the face of the franchise and a future Hall of Famer, would not be on the Orioles roster.

A year ago, at Yankee Stadium, the first-ball thrower was pitching coach Mel Stottlemyre, in remission from bone marrow cancer. This year, in Baltimore, the honor went to Johnny Oates, the Orioles former manager (1992–1994) who was battling a brain tumor. (Oates would succumb to the disease, at age 58, in December 2004.)

Baltimore's current manager was Mike Hargrove, now in his third season. His Orioles had finished fourth in the five-team East Division in his first two seasons and would finish fourth again this year and next. Jason Johnson was their only pitcher who had won as many as 10 games in 2001; nevertheless, Hargrove chose veteran Scott Erickson to pitch the opener. Erickson had won 135 games in his career with Baltimore and before that with the Minnesota Twins. But an elbow injury had caused him to miss a good part of the 2000 season and all of 2001.

Erickson was the first pitcher to start an opener after not pitching in the major leagues the previous season since Alex Fernandez of the Florida Marlins in 1999. He was the first in the American League since Diego Segui pitched the first game for the expansion Seattle Mariners in 1977.

Unlike Hargrove, Yankees manager Joe Torre had several star pitchers from whom to choose. Along with Wells, who was in his second stint with the Yankees, he had Andy Pettitte, Mike Mussina, Orlando Hernandez, and Roger Clemens. As expected, he chose Clemens, the reigning Cy Young Award winner. For Clemens, 20 victories away from 300, this would be his 12th opening-day start.

The Yankees scored an unearned run in the first inning, on walks to Derek Jeter and

Giambi, a stolen base by Jeter and a throwing error by Orioles catcher Geronimo Gil. Ventura, in his first at-bat as a Yankee, ended any hopes of a big inning by grounding into a double play.

Clemens protected the lead by limiting the Orioles to a David Segui single through the first three innings, but his own mental mistake in the fourth changed the course of the game. With one out, David Segui hit a hard one-hopper headed up the middle that Clemens reached for with his bare hand. The ball smashed into the meaty part of his palm, under his pinkie.

Torre, pitching coach Stottlemyre, and trainer Gene Monahan rushed to the mound. They talked with Clemens and after watching him throw a few pitches, Torre decided to keep him in the game. A wild pitch moved Segui to second, after which Clemens walked Jeff Conine and Jay Gibbons to load the bases. The next batter was Tony Batista, whom the Orioles had picked up from the Toronto Blue Jays the previous June. Batista, who had the unenviable task of replacing Ripken at third, had battled Clemens through an eight-pitch at-bat in the second inning before flying out. This time he swung at the first pitch and drove it over the center-field fence for only the second opening day grand slam in Orioles history. (Eddie Murray had the first, against Kansas City in 1982 at Baltimore's Memorial Stadium.)

Fireworks erupted from near the spot where the ball landed, further exciting the crowd of 48,058, the largest opening day crowd to date at Camden Yards. Later in the inning, Gil's single scored Melvin Mora to make the score, 5–1.

The Yankees threatened Erickson when White led off the fifth with a single. Shane Spencer also singled, the second of his three hits. An unruffled Erickson retired the next two batters, but walked Jeter to load the bases. A grand slam would have tied the score, and with Giambi coming up, the Yanks had the batter they wanted in this situation. Erickson escaped by getting Giambi to ground out to second baseman Jerry Hairston.

When asked later how he felt about failing at that crucial point in the game, Giambi said, "Any four-letter word would work in that situation. It was a pitch I could hit. He just took enough off." Giambi would recover from his inauspicious debut to have an excellent first season with the Yankees. He batted .314, with 41 home runs and 122 runs batted in.

Mora's bases-clearing double in the home fifth raised Baltimore's lead to 8–1, and ended Clemens's day. He had faced 13 batters after his foolish attempt to stop Segui's bouncer with his bare hand, allowing eight runs, five hits, five walks, and throwing two wild pitches. After Jay Tessmer replaced him, Clemens was taken to nearby University Hospital where, to the great relief of Torre and the Yankees, X-rays of his hand were negative.

Erickson left after six innings having allowed just one run. Given his more than a year away, it had been a most impressive performance. His replacement, Rodrigo Lopez, pitched a scoreless seventh, but allowed a two-run homer to Jeter in the eighth. The Orioles used two hits and two walks against Steve Karsay in their half of the inning to match the two runs the Yanks had scored against Lopez. "It was just one of those days when I didn't pitch well," Karsay said after the game. "I'm not making excuses."

Jorge Julio pitched a scoreless ninth to nail down the Orioles' win. Several hours later, the University of Maryland defeated Indiana University to win its first NCAA basketball championship and make it an even more satisfying day for Maryland sports fans.

The Yankees (103–58) finished 10½ games ahead of the Boston Red Sox to win their fifth consecutive East Division title. However, their streak of playing in four consecutive World Series ended when they lost to the wild-card Anaheim Angels three games to one in the

Division Series. Alfonso Soriano led the league in hits (209) and runs scored (128). Clemens won 13 games (13–6) in 2002, leaving him seven wins short of 300.

Monday, April 1, 2002

New York	ab	r	h	rbi	po	a	Baltimore	ab	r	h	rbi	po	a
Soriano 2b	4	1	0	0	2	1	Hairston 2b	5	0	1	0	2	5
Jeter ss	3	2	1	2	1	0	Singleton cf	5	0	0	0	1	0
Giambi 1b	4	0	1	0	6	1	Segui dh	5	1	3	1	0	0
B. Williams cf	1	0	0	0	1	0	Conine 1b	2	2	0	0	14	0
Ventura 3b	3	0	0	0	0	3	Gibbons rf	3	2	1	0	1	0
Posada c	4	0	0	0	7	2	Batista 3b	3	2	1	4	1	3
White lf	4	0	1	0	5	0	Mora lf	2	2	1	3	1	0
Spencer rf	4	0	3	0	1	0	Gil c	4	1	2	2	4	3
Johnson dh	3	0	0	0	0	0	Bordick ss	3	0	0	0	3	4
Clemens p	0	0	0	0	1	0	Erickson p	0	0	0	0	0	1
Tessmer p	0	0	0	0	0	0	R. Lopez p	0	0	0	0	0	0
Lilly p	0	0	0	0	0	0	Ryan p	0	0	0	0	0	0
Karsay p	0	0	0	0	0	0	W. Roberts p	0	0	0	0	0	0
Total	30	3	6	2	24	7	Julio p	0	0	0	0	0	0
							Total	32	10	9	10	27	16

New York   100   000   020–3
Baltimore   000   530   02X–10

Errors—Ventura, Gil. Double plays-Bordick, Hairston, Conine. Stolen bases—Jeter, Mora (2). Caught stealing—Spencer, B. Williams. Left on bases—New York 9; Baltimore 5. Two-base hits—Spencer, Mora, Gil. Home runs—Jeter, Batista.

	IP	H	R	ER	BB	SO
NEW YORK						
Clemens (L, 0–1)	4.1	7	8	8	5	4
Tessmer	1.0	0	0	0	0	0
Lilly	1.2	0	0	0	0	2
Karsay	1.0	2	2	2	2	1

Wild pitches—Clemens (2)

	IP	H	R	ER	BB	SO
BALTIMORE						
Erickson (W, 1–0)	6.0	3	1	0	5	2
R. Lopez	1.0	2	2	2	2	1
Ryan	0.2	0	0	0	0	1
W. Roberts	0.1	0	0	0	0	0
Julio	1.0	1	0	0	1	0

Lopez pitched to four batters in the eighth inning

Hit by pitches—by Erickson (B. Williams). Umpires—HP, Jerry Crawford; 1B, Joe West; 2B, Brian Gorman; 3B, Phil Cuzzi. Time of game—3:15. Attendance—48,058.

Monday, March 31, 2003 (N)
SkyDome, Toronto
New York 8 Toronto 4

One more such victory and we are lost.—Pyhrrus

The usual joy that accompanies a victory was absent from the Yankees' clubhouse following their 8–4 opening night win in Toronto. It would be hard to imagine a comparably depressing win in the club's 101-year history. The six shutout innings by Roger Clemens, the grand slam by Alfonso Soriano, and the successful major league debut of Hideki Matsui were overshadowed by the shoulder injury to shortstop Derek Jeter. The third-inning injury threatened to keep the Yankees leader and best player out indefinitely.

Bothered by shoulder and thigh injuries, Jeter's batting average had "slumped" to .297 in 2002, the first time in five years he had failed to hit above .300. That led George Steinbrenner to criticize him during the offseason for his lifestyle and his lack of focus on his job. It was a typically ridiculous rant by Steinbrenner, perhaps motivated by the Yankees being eliminated, three games to one, by the Anaheim Angels in the Division Series, despite having led the league with 103 wins.

The definition of success for the New York Yankees had for almost a century been different from that of other teams. For owner Steinbrenner, manager Joe Torre, the players, and the fans, not winning the World Series constituted an unsuccessful season.

Todd Zeile, who was signed as a free agent after playing for nine other teams noticed the difference the first day of spring training. "You don't hear the clichés around here about having a good season or being happy to make the playoffs. The goal here is to win a championship."

His negative carping about Jeter aside, Steinbrenner had helped the club with a positive offseason acquisition, signing 28-year-old Japanese outfielder Hideki Matsui. Matsui, a left-handed hitter had played ten seasons for the Yomiuri Giants, winning three Most Valuable Player awards and collecting 332 home runs. There had been a reluctance by major league clubs to sign position players from the Japanese leagues, but the phenomenal success of outfielder Ichiro Suzuki, signed by the Seattle Mariners in 2000, had changed that mindset. In addition to Matsui, the Yankees had made another big splash internationally, winning the battle to sign 31-year-old Cuban right-hander, Jose Contreras.

"Everyone knows this is a tough place to work," Torre had said about playing the opener at the Skydome. It had been made even tougher by a SARS virus that had invaded Toronto. Moreover, there was the pressure on the Yankees to go all the way this year. That pressure, always present, was exacerbated because for the first time in the Torre era, the Yanks had endured two straight title-less seasons. Added to that, they had the league's highest payroll making the Yankees a prime target for every other team. "I don't have a problem with the expectations of winning it all," Jeter had said. "If you do, you shouldn't come here to play."

Roger Clemens for the Yankees and Roy Halladay of the Blue Jays, two of the league's best were the opposing pitchers. Clemens, 40, needed just seven wins to reach the 300 mark, while Halladay, 25, had blossomed in 2002 winning 19 games, with a 2.93 earned run average.

Canadian Lorne Michaels, the founder of the television show Saturday Night Live threw out the first ball. Michaels was not quite a native-born Canadian. He was born in Palestine in 1944 during the British Mandate, but his family moved to Toronto when he was an infant.

The Yankees, playing their first opening day game in March, scored a run in their first at-bat. A double by Jeter was followed by Matsui lining the first American League pitch he saw for a two-out, opposite field single. Matsui was starting in left field, the tenth different left fielder the Yankees had used in the last 10 openers. Fluctuation at the position was so common, no Yankee had started consecutive openers in left field since Rickey Henderson in 1988 and 1989. It was a good start for Matsui, whose appearance had attracted 100 members of the Japanese media and a great deal of booing by the Toronto fans.

A Toronto newspaper ad, crafted by the Blue Jays' marketing department, had encouraged fans to boo Matsui during each of his at-bats. As one New York newspaper wrote: "It was tactless and tasteless, and fed into a surge of recent Canadian anti-Americanism." While there was some booing of Matsui in each of his bats, there were also cheers. "I was a little relieved after the first at-bat," he said through an interpreter. "After that I didn't hit that well. Hopefully, I'll do better tomorrow."

Jeter suffered his injury in the third inning after reaching first with a one-out walk. He was running on a 0–1 pitch to Jason Giambi that Giambi bounced back to Halladay. With no chance to get Jeter, Halladay threw to first to retire the batter. But Jeter noticed that no one was covering third base and continued running. Catcher Ken Huckaby ran over to receive first baseman Carlos Delgado's throw, but the throw was high and Jeter, with a head first slide appeared to have beaten the tag. Umpire Paul Emmel gave the safe sign but reversed the call when Huckaby knocked Jeter off the bag with his left shin guard to complete the double play.

When Jeter failed to immediately jump up and run off the field, as would normally be the case, it became obvious he was seriously injured. Torre and trainer Gene Monahan ran to third where a writhing Jeter was surrounded by several of his teammates. Dr. Erin Boynton, a local orthopedist and Blue Jays team doctor Ron Taylor, a former Mets pitcher, examined Jeter before he was loaded into a cart and taken off the field, as Blue Jays fans gave him an ovation.

"I felt something pop, and I didn't know if I broke something," Jeter said later. His left shoulder, which had been dislocated, was popped back into place and now in a sling. He told Torre he'd be back the next day, but Torre knew the recovery would take weeks, if not months. When the Yankees took the field for the home third, Enrique Wilson was at shortstop.

The Yankees added two runs in the fourth inning, on a two-run homer by Robin Ventura, and then broke the game open in the sixth. They scored five runs on just two hits, the big blow being a grand slam by Alfonso Soriano. Halladay also walked two and was hurt by second baseman Orlando Hudson's error on a Matsui ground ball. Hudson's error made all five runs unearned.

Soriano had developed into one of the top players in the league in 2002, finishing third in the balloting for the Most Valuable Player Award. He led the American League in plate appearance (741), at-bats (696), runs (128), hits (209), steals (41) and was second in total bases (381) and third in doubles (51). He also hit .300 with 39 homers, 102 RBI and slugged .547.

With his team behind, 8–0, following Soriano's home run, manager Carlos Tosca replaced Halladay with Pete Walker. Tosca was beginning his first full season as manager of the Blue Jays, having replaced Buck Martinez a third of the way through the 2002 season.

Torre replace his starter, Clemens, after six innings, in which he allowed no runs, three hits, walked one, and struck out five. Jose Contreras, a 31-year-old right-hander made a spectacular impression in his much-anticipated debut in the seventh. Contreras had defected from Cuba in October 2002 when playing in the Americas Series in Mexico. He was touched for a leadoff double by Eric Hinske, the American League's reigning Rookie of the Year, but then struck out the next three batters: Hudson, Chris Woodward, and Ken Huckaby.

Contreras gave up a leadoff single to Shannon Stewart in the eighth, but after retiring the next two batters, he walked Carlos Delgado and Josh Phelps to load the bases. Due up was Hinske, who had doubled off Contreras the inning before and was a left-handed batter. That prompted Torre to go to his bullpen for left-hander Chris Hammond, signed as a free agent from the Atlanta Braves. Hammond, who was replacing the departed Mike Stanton as Torre's number one lefty reliever, got ahead of Hinske, 0–2, but on the next pitch, Hinske ripped a two-run double into right.

Hammond got the final out, and was replaced in the ninth inning by Jason Anderson, a 23-year-old right-hander, making his major league debut. Anderson faced just two batters, yielding pinch-hit singles to Tom Wilson and Greg Myers, and was gone. Torre quickly replaced him with yet another newcomer to his staff, veteran right-hander Juan Acevedo, signed as a free agent from the Detroit Tigers. A single by Stewart and a sacrifice fly by Vernon Wells accounted for two runs to make the final score, 8–4.

Neither Acevedo nor Anderson would finish the season with the Yankees. After they released Acevedo in June, he signed with the Blue Jays, and in July they traded Anderson to the Mets. Roy Halladay would bounce back from his opening-day loss to win a league-leading 22 games (22–7) and the Cy Young Award.

Derek Jeter would miss the next six weeks, returning to active duty on May 13. He batted .324 for the season, third in the American League. Enrique Wilson and Erick Almonte filled in at shortstop during his absence. The Yankees were 25–11 without Jeter and had a three-game lead over the Boston Red Sox when he returned. They repeated as East Division champions, finishing six games ahead of Boston. The Yankees reached the World Series by defeating the Minnesota Twins, three games to one in the Division Series, and the Red Sox, four games to three in the League Championship Series. A four games to two loss to the Florida Marlins in the World Series prevented them from winning their 27th championship.

Monday, March 31, 2003

New York	ab	r	h	rbi	po	a	Toronto	ab	r	h	rbi	po	a
Soriano 2b	5	1	2	4	0	2	Stewart lf	5	1	2	1	1	0
Jeter ss	1	1	1	0	0	1	Catalanotto rf	5	0	1	0	2	0
E. Wilson ss	3	0	0	0	1	1	Wells cf	4	0	1	1	5	0
Giambi 1b	5	0	0	0	6	1	Delgado 1b	3	1	1	0	11	3
Williams cf	2	1	0	0	2	0	Phelps dh	2	0	0	0	0	0
Matsui lf	4	0	1	1	3	0	Hinske 3b	4	0	2	2	0	1
Posada c	4	2	2	1	11	0	Hudson 2b	4	0	0	0	0	3
Ventura 3b	3	2	1	2	0	0	Woodward ss	3	0	0	0	2	4
Mondesi rf	2	0	0	0	3	0	T. Wilson ph	1	1	1	0	0	0
Johnson dh	4	1	0	0	0	0	Huckaby c	3	0	0	0	4	0
Clemens p	0	0	0	0	0	0	Myers ph	1	1	1	0	0	0
Contreras p	0	0	0	0	0	0	Halladay p	0	0	0	0	2	3
Hammond p	0	0	0	0	0	0	Walker p	0	0	0	0	0	0
Anderson p	0	0	0	0	0	0	Linton p	0	0	0	0	0	1
Acevedo p	0	0	0	0	1	0	Total	35	4	9	4	27	15
Total	33	8	7	8	27	5							

```
New York    100    205    000—8
Toronto     000    000    022—4
```

Errors—Hudson. Double plays-Delgado, Woodward, Halladay; Halladay, Delgado, Huckaby. Left on bases—New York 5; Toronto 9. Two-base hits—Jeter, Soriano, Wells, Hinske 2. Home runs—Ventura, Soriano. Sacrifice Fly—Wells.

	IP	H	R	ER	BB	SO
NEW YORK						
Clemens (W, 1–0)	6.0	3	0	0	1	5
Contreras	1.2	2	2	2	2	4
Hammond	0.1	1	0	0	0	0
Anderson	0.0	2	2	2	0	0
Acevedo	1.0	1	0	0	0	1

Wild pitches—Clemens
Hit by pitches-by Clemens (Phelps)

	IP	H	R	ER	BB	SO
TORONTO						
Halladay (L, 0–1)	5.2	7	8	3	4	2
Walker	1.1	0	0	0	1	0
Linton	2.0	0	0	0	1	0

Hit by pitches—by Halladay (Mondesi). Umpires—HP, Joe West; 1B, Jeff Kellogg; 2B, Bill Miller; 3B, Paul Emmel. Time of game—2:50. Attendance—50,119.

Tuesday, March 30, 2004 (N)
Tokyo Dome, Tokyo
Tampa Bay 8 New York 3

*Every man has a lurking wish to appear considerable
in his native place.*—Samuel Johnson

On Opening Day 1999, the Colorado Rockies defeated the San Diego Padres, 8–2, in Monterey Mexico in the first major league opener played outside North America. The following year, the Chicago Cubs defeated the New York Mets, 5–3, at Japan's Tokyo Dome in the first big league opener played in Asia.

The opening game in Japan, and a second game the next day, drew capacity crowds. Plans were made for a 2003 opener between the Oakland Athletics and the Seattle Mariners, which would serve as a homecoming for Ichiro Suzuki, a member of the Mariners since 2001. Many American observers had questioned whether Suzuki, the Japanese Pacific League's best player in his years with the Orix Blue Wave, would be able to cope with American League pitching. Suzuki (or Ichiro as most American fans called him) had proven the skeptics wrong, by leading the league with a .350 batting average and 242 hits and winning the Rookie of the Year and Most Valuable Player awards. He followed with a .321 average and 208 hits in his second season.

Japanese fans eagerly looked forward to the return of the conquering hero, but real life interfered. Major League Baseball canceled the games in early March because the United States seemed to be on the verge of going to war in Iraq. (The U.S. invaded Iraq on March 20.) This year, those fans would get a chance to cheer the return of another conquering hero, outfielder Hideki Matsui of the Yankees. Matsui had slugged 332 home runs and won three Most Valuable Player awards while playing for Tokyo's Yomiuri Giants (1993 to 2002), the country's most popular team.

The Yankees were opening the season at the Tokyo Dome against the Tampa Bay Devil Rays, who were designated the home team. The Yanks had arrived in Japan a few days earlier and gotten acclimated by playing exhibition games against the Yomiuri Giants (a win) and the Hanshin Tigers (a loss). The Yankees and Devil Rays had the baseball stage all to themselves. All the other major league clubs were opening from four to six days later.

Alex Rodriguez was foremost among the many new faces populating the Yankees' roster and uniformed staff this season. The 27-year-old shortstop was coming off a season in which he won his third consecutive home run title and was voted the league's Most Valuable Player. The Yankees had acquired him, along with a large chunk of his record-setting $252 million contract, in an offseason trade with the Texas Rangers in which Alfonso Soriano went to Texas. Although Rodriguez was by all measures a better defensive shortstop than Derek Jeter, the incumbent, the Yankees had decided to keep Jeter at short and move Rodriguez to third base.

Other newcomers added by trade or free agency, included outfielders Gary Sheffield and Kenny Lofton, starting pitchers Kevin Brown and Javier Vazquez, and bullpen veterans Paul Quantrill and Tom Gordon. Manager Joe Torre had added former Yankees players Don Mattingly, Luis Sojo, and Roy White to his coaching staff and shifted Willie Randolph, from third base coach to bench coach. Conversely, 16 players who made the Yankees' opening-day roster in 2003 were no longer with the team.

The expansion Devil Rays, under second-year manager Lou Piniella, were beginning their seventh season in the American League's East Division. They had finished fifth and last in each of the previous six. Their offense was led by outfielders Carl Crawford and Rocco Baldelli, third baseman Aubrey Huff, and first baseman Tino Martinez, the 36-year-old former Yankee. Martinez had come to the Rays in an offseason trade with the St. Louis Cardinals.

After Rudy Giuliani, the former mayor of New York City and an ardent Yankees fan, and Junichiro Koizumi, the Japanese Prime Minister, threw out the first ball (to Martinez and Matsui respectively) the game began. It was 7:14 p.m. in Tokyo, but only 5:14 a.m. in New York. Even in the city that never sleeps, only the most devoted fans were in front of their television sets at that hour. They were overjoyed to have baseball back, but an opener in Tokyo did not seem right to them; nor did it to many of the players.

Alex Rodriguez said he wouldn't believe his season had officially started until he played at Yankee Stadium. "It's Opening Day, but it won't feel like the real thing until we get to the big house."

Jason Giambi, who always saw the bright side of things, admitted there was something missing. "It's not Opening Day until you get to New York," Giambi said. "Nothing beats Opening Day in New York."

Victor Zambrano, the only Tampa Bay pitcher with a double digit win total in 2003 (12–10), got off to a rough start, yielding an opposite field two-run homer to Giambi. Matsui, who had doubled, scored ahead of him. Matsui had been the center of attention for the fans and the media before the game, it seemed all the 55,000 people in the stands were snapping pictures of him while he batted.

"I'm not really concentrating on the fans' cheering and what's going on," Matsui said through an interpreter. "I really try to leave that out and focus on the game."

Rodriguez, batting third, between Matsui and Giambi, had made his long-awaited Yankees' debut, by striking out. During spring training he had been asked frequently about the pressure of playing in New York. "I feel like I lived some of that in Seattle. Lou Piniella

(Rodriguez's manager with the Mariners) was an old Yankee, and he brought the old-time Yankee toughness. He wanted us to feel pressure like we were in New York."

Opening Day starts were nothing new to the Yankees' Mike Mussina, even if the venue was. Mussina started six openers when he pitched for the Baltimore Orioles and had a 3–2 record, including a win over the Devil Rays in 1999. This evening, he was attempting to become the 100th major league pitcher to reach 200 career victories. But pitchers are creatures of habit, and Mussina's pregame routine was shattered by jet lag. Normally he slept until 9 or 10 a.m. before a night game start, but this morning he had awoken at six. Yet he was able to preserve the two-run lead until Toby Hall's two-run single in the fourth inning tied the score.

Doubles by Rodriguez and Sheffield gave New York a 3–2 lead in the sixth, but it would be the end of the Yankees' offense, as Lance Carter (two innings) and Danys Baez (one inning) blanked them over the final three innings. Meanwhile, the Devil Rays would score the game's next six runs. Jose Cruz, making his Tampa Bay debut, erased the Yankees short-lived lead with a leadoff home run in the home sixth. After the next three batters—Martinez, Julio Lugo, and Hall—doubled to account for two more runs, Torre replaced Mussina with Paul Quantrill, the first of Quantrill's league-leading 86 appearances this season.

"I just didn't feel like I had my best stuff," Mussina said after the game. "I didn't have a pitch I could go with when I needed to. I just didn't pitch well." While calling the trip great for baseball, he admitted he had dreaded it and that his body clock refused to let him believe he had pitched a game that counted. "It didn't feel like opening day to me," he said.

The Devil Rays added three runs in the seventh off Quantrill and Felix Heredia, two coming on a Tino Martinez home run. Mussina had missed his potential milestone, a 200th win, but Martinez had reached one of his own. His two-run blast against Heredia made him the 99th player in baseball history to reach 300 home runs.

The Yankees had not played well and Derek Jeter, in his second year as team captain, was quick to acknowledge it.

"It was a poor showing," said Jeter who had gone hitless in five at bats. "That's not the way you want to open the season, but there is a long way to go."

"We lost, so, yeah, the jet lag got us," he said when asked if opening in Japan had played a part in the Yankees' terrible performance. "But it's there for both teams," he said stating the obvious. It's not like they flew out on a different day. I can't tell you everything about our team after one game."

Of course most teams did not panic over losing one game, but this was the George Steinbrenner Yankees. "I wonder if George has called a meeting yet," said one Yankees employee.

Not wanting to return home with an 0–2 record, there was some pressure on the team, especially pitcher Kevin Brown to win the next day. "We need a big win for the split and then get a few days off," said Giambi. (They did win the next day, 12–1).

The Yankees (101–61) won the East Division title, finishing three games ahead of the Boston Red Sox. It was the seventh consecutive season they had finished first in the East Division and the seventh consecutive season the Red Sox had finished second. The Yankees defeated the Minnesota Twins, three games to one in the Division Series. They won the first three games of the League Championship Series against the Red Sox, but Boston staged an unprecedented comeback to win the next four. The Red Sox then swept the St. Louis Cardinals to win their first World Series since 1918. The Yankees tied for first in the league in home runs and finished second in runs scored, but no Yankees batter hit .300 and no Yan-kees pitcher won more than 14 games. Mariano Rivera led the league with 53 saves and won The Sporting News Fireman of the Year Award.

Tuesday, March 30, 2004 (N)

New York	ab	r	h	rbi	po	a	Tampa Bay	ab	r	h	rbi	po	a
Jeter ss	5	0	0	0	2	5	Crawford lf	5	0	0	0	2	0
Matsui lf	4	1	1	0	1	0	Rolls 2b	5	0	2	0	2	1
Rodriguez 3b	4	1	1	0	0	2	Baldelli cf	4	1	1	0	1	0
Giambi 1b	4	1	2	2	11	0	Huff dh	5	1	2	1	0	0
Sheffield rf	2	0	2	1	2	1	Cruz rf	4	2	1	1	2	0
Posada c	4	0	0	0	3	2	Martinez 1b	3	3	3	2	10	0
Sierra dh	4	0	0	0	0	0	Lugo ss	4	1	1	1	3	2
Wilson 2b	4	0	0	0	1	2	Hall c	4	0	3	3	7	0
Lofton cf	3	0	1	0	4	0	Sanchez 2b	4	0	2	0	0	4
Mussina p	0	0	0	0	0	0	Zambrano p	0	0	0	0	0	2
Quantrill p	0	0	0	0	0	1	Carter p	0	0	0	0	0	0
Heredia p	0	0	0	0	0	1	Baez p	0	0	0	0	0	0
Total	34	3	7	3	24	14	Total	38	8	15	8	27	9

New York   200   001   000–3
Tampa Bay   000   203   30X–8

Errors—Heredia. Left on bases—New York 7; Tampa Bay 9. Stolen base-Cruz. Two-base hits—Matsui, Rodriguez, Sheffield, Giambi, Martinez, Lugo, Hall, Rolls. Three-base hits—Lofton. Home runs—Giambi, Cruz, Martinez.

	IP	H	R	ER	BB	SO
NEW YORK						
Mussina (L, 0–1)	5.0	10	5	5	2	2
Quantrill	1.0	1	1	1	0	0
Heredia	2.0	4	2	2	1	1

Mussina pitched to four batters in the sixth inning
Quantrill pitched to one batter in the seventh inning

TAMPA BAY						
Zambrano (W, 1–0)	6.0	6	3	3	1	4
Carter	2.0	1	0	0	1	1
Baez	1.0	0	0	0	1	1

Umpires—HP, Joe West; 1B, Brian Gorman; 2B, Jerry Meals; 3B, CB Bucknor. Time of game—2:45. Attendance—55,000.

Sunday, April 3, 2005 (N)
Yankee Stadium, New York
New York 9 Boston 2

Once more unto the breach dear friends, once more.—William Shakespeare

For much of baseball history, the site of the opening game of a new season belonged to the Washington Senators or the Cincinnati Reds. Now it was decided by ESPN, a television network. ESPN, in concert with the corporate entity, Major League Baseball, would pick a game they believed would draw the highest national viewership and move it from Monday, when most teams opened, to Sunday night. The choice for 2005 was an obvious one—the world champion Boston Red Sox against the New York Yankees at Yankee Stadium. The last time these two teams played was in Game Seven of last year's League Championship Series, a game won by Boston to complete their unprecedented comeback after having lost the first three games.

Over their now more-than- a-century old rivalry, the Red Sox had been the Yankees most frequent opening-day opponent. In their 28 previous meetings the Yankees held a 17–10 advantage, with one tie (1910). The Yankees were 9–3 at the Stadium, 6–4 at Fenway Park, 2–1-1 at Hilltop Park, and 0–2 at the Polo Grounds. In the two Polo Grounds open-ers—1917 and 1919—the Red Sox were the reigning World Series champions, as they were this year.

Boston manager Terry Francona's choice to pitch the opener was David Wells signed as a free agent from the San Diego Padres. Wells was a free-spirited lefthander who had been a fan favorite in two stints with the Yankees. Another newly acquired lefthander, Randy Johnson, whom the Yankees got in a January trade with the Arizona Diamondbacks, was manager Joe Torre's choice. Johnson was a five-time winner of the Cy Young Award (four with Arizona and one with the Seattle Mariners), and a nine-time league leader in strikeouts. He was among the most dominant pitchers ever and still very formidable at age 41.

The Yankees were opening at home for only the second time in the last ten seasons. The sellout crowd gave their usual hostile greeting to the visiting Sox during the pre-game introductions. Nine players from their American League Championship Series roster were gone so could not hear the especially loud booing directed at Curt Schilling, Bronson Arroyo, Johnny Damon, Manny Ramirez, and even Wells. The fans maintained a respectful moment of silence for Pope John Paul II, who had died a day earlier, loudly cheered beloved Hall of Famer Yogi Berra, who threw out the ceremonial first ball, before settling in for the battle.

Johnson was making his 13th opening day start, with a 5–2 record in the previous 12, for the Seattle Mariners and Arizona Diamondbacks. He recognized that pitching an opener for the Yankees against the Red Sox was much different. "I have never been part of a rivalry like I am about to be part of," he said. "But I just don't get wrapped up in it." Ignor-ing the frenzy surrounding him, he breezed through the first inning, retiring Damon on a ground ball to second baseman Tony Womack. Signed as a free agent, Womack would become a utility player in his one year in New York, after yielding second base to rookie Robinson Cano early in the season. Johnson then fired called third strikes past Edgar Renteria, in his Red Sox debut, and Ramirez. Often underrated, Renteria was one of the game's top shortstops. He had come to Boston as a free agent after nine successful seasons in the National League, three with the Florida Marlins and six with the St. Louis Cardi-nals.

The strikeouts of Renteria and Ramirez raised Johnson's career total to 4,163, behind only Nolan Ryan and Roger Clemens among the all time leaders. The Sox scored the first run of the 2005 season in the second inning on a double by David Ortiz and a single by Jay Payton, also making his Boston debut. Hideki Matsui made the play of the game when he took a home run away from Kevin Millar, who batted between Ortiz and Payton.

The Yankees tied the score in their half of the inning on singles by Matsui and Jason Giambi and Bernie Williams's sacrifice fly. They took a 4–1 lead in the third, as the 41-year-old Wells seemed to lose his composure. Derek Jeter led off with a double and scored one out later on Gary Sheffield's long double to left-center that would have been a home run in most other parks. Wells retired Ruben Sierra for out number two, but Matsui scored Sheffield with a line single to center.

After Jorge Posada reached on an infield single, Wells who pitched in short sleeves despite the 43-degree temperature and steady wind, began to struggle. He hit Giambi on the upper portion of his right arm with an 0–2 pitch to load the bases. It was not the kind of mistake that veteran pitchers make, and Wells compounded it by balking home a run. As he went into his full windup to deliver a 2–2 pitch to Williams, he stepped off the rubber with his left foot. Wells explained that he thought catcher Jason Varitek had put down a different sign, so he backed off the rubber.

By the time he got the third out, Wells had already thrown 57 pitches. He survived the fourth inning, despite singles by Womack and Alex Rodriguez, but ran into trouble again in the fifth. He fanned Matsui, the leadoff batter, but then allowed a double by Posada, hit Giambi again, and walked Williams to load the bases. Having seen enough, Francona replaced him with veteran reliever Mike Myers. It proved to be the right move, as Myers got Womack to hit into an inning-ending double play.

Wells had been warmly received when he returned to New York as a San Diego Padre after his first departure from the Yankees. He no doubt knew it would be different this time when he returned as a member of the hated Red Sox. He had been booed all night, and another loud chorus of boos accompanied his departure from the game.

"It is what it is, it's out of my control," Wells said of the booing. "The first game of the season is always a big game. I knew what I was up against. I had a bad night."

Johnson exited after six innings, having allowed one run and five hits, with six strikeouts. He retired the side in order only in the first, but came up big when it was needed. He held the Red Sox to one hit in eight at-bats with runners in scoring position. Sixty of his 95 pitches were strikes. "Things will get sharper as time goes on," Johnson said.

Tanyon Sturtze pitched a scoreless seventh and eighth, while Tom Gordon was touched for Boston's second run in the ninth. By that time, the Yankees had a 9–1 lead. They had scored two in the sixth (both unearned) against Blaine Neal and Alan Embree, and put the game out of reach with a three-run eighth against Matt Mantei, including a home run by Matsui, his third hit of the night.

Matsui, along with Johnson, was the star of the game. He had gone 3 for 5 with a home run and three runs batted in, and made the defensive play of the game robbing Millar of a home run. "You have to watch him every day to appreciate what he does," Torre said of his left fielder. "He approaches every spring training game like it's a regular-season game. He made a great play on Millar. That was a very important play." Francona agreed. "You just don't know how the game's going to turn if he doesn't make that catch."

The Yankees won the East Division title for the eighth consecutive season. They finished with a record of 95–67, the same record as the Boston Red Sox, but because they defeated Boston 10–9 in their regular season games, they were declared the East Division champions. It was also the eighth consecutive season the Red Sox had finished second. In the Division Championship Series, the Yankees lost to the Anaheim Angels in five games. Home attendance passed the 4 million mark for the first time in team history (4,090,696). Alex Rodriguez led the league in home runs (48), runs scored (124), slugging percentage (.610) and was voted the league's Most Valuable Player. Jason Giambi finished first in walks (108) and on base percentage (.440). Mariano Rivera and Joe Nathan of the Minnesota Twins were co-winners of The Sporting News Fireman of the Year Award.

Sunday, April 3, 2005 (N)

Boston	ab	r	h	rbi	po	a	New York	ab	r	h	rbi	po	a
Damon cf	4	0	0	0	2	0	Jeter ss	5	2	2	0	2	5
Renteria ss	4	0	0	0	1	4	A. Rodriguez 3b	6	1	2	1	0	2
M. Ramirez lf	4	0	0	0	3	0	Sheffield rf	4	2	1	1	1	0
Ortiz dh	4	1	1	0	0	0	Sierra dh	5	0	1	1	0	0
Millar 1b	2	1	0	0	4	0	Matsui lf	5	3	3	3	1	0
Varitek c	4	0	3	0	7	0	Posada c	4	0	2	0	10	0
Payton rf	3	0	1	1	3	0	Giambi 1b	2	0	1	0	7	0
[a]Nixon	0	0	0	1	0	0	Martinez 1b	0	1	0	0	1	1
Mueller 3b	3	0	0	0	0	3	Williams cf	2	0	0	1	2	0
Bellhorn 2b	4	0	1	0	4	1	[b]Crosby, cf	0	0	0	0	1	0
Wells p	0	0	0	0	0	0	Womack 2b	5	0	3	0	1	3
Myers p	0	0	0	0	0	0	Johnson p	0	0	0	0	0	0
Neal p	0	0	0	0	0	0	Sturtze p	0	0	0	0	1	0
Embree p	0	0	0	0	0	0	Gordon p	0	0	0	0	0	0
Timlin p	0	0	0	0	0	0	Total	38	9	15	7	27	11
Mantei p	0	0	0	0	0	0							
Halama p	0	0	0	0	0	0							
Total	32	2	6	2	24	8							

[a]Hit a sacrifice fly for Payton in ninth inning.
[b]Ran for Williams in eighth inning

Boston	010	000	001–2
New York	013	002	03X–9

Errors–Damon, Halama, Giambi. Double plays—Renteria, Bellhorn, Millar; A. Rodriguez, Womack, Giambi. Stolen base—Jeter, Womack. Left on bases—Boston 7, New York 14. Two-base hits—Ortiz, Varitek, Bellhorn, Jeter, Sheffield, Posada, Sierra. Home runs— Matsui. Sacrifice Fly—Nixon, Williams.

	IP	H	R	ER	BB	SO
BOSTON						
Wells (L, 0–1)	4.1	10	4	4	1	4
Myers	0.2	0	0	0	0	0
Neal	0.1	1	2	1	1	0
Embree	0.2	1	0	0	1	0
Timlin	1.0	1	0	0	0	1
Mantei	0.2	1	3	2	3	1
Halama	0.1	1	0	0	0	0

Hit by pitches—by Wells, 2 (Giambi, 2)

	IP	H	R	ER	BB	SO
NEW YORK						
Johnson (W, 1–0)	6.0	5	1	1	2	6
Sturtze	2.0	0	0	0	0	3
Gordon	1.0	1	1	1	1	1

Umpires—HP, Joe West; 1B, Brian Gorman; 2B, Mike DiMuro; 3B, Tom Hallion. Time of game—3:19. Attendance—54,818.

Monday, April 3, 2006 (N)
McAfee Coliseum, Oakland
New York 15 Oakland 2

*The Bostonian who leaves Boston ought to be
condemned to perpetual exile.*—William Dean Howells

Center fielder Johnny Damon had completed four very successful seasons with the Boston Red Sox, including 2004 when he helped lead Boston to its first World Series title since 1918. In addition, his long hair and beard had become symbolic of a happy-go-lucky carefree club whose players took pride in referring to themselves as "idiots." The facial hair worn by many of the Red Sox was in sharp contrast to the clean-shaven Yankees and accentuated the bitter rivalry between the two perennial contenders for the East Division title.

Thus it came as a bitter disappointment to Boston fandom when Damon decided to leave as a free agent after the 2005 season; that he signed with the Yankees, after rejecting a similar deal with the Sox, was considered almost treasonous. George Steinbrenner had offered him a four-year contract at 13 million dollars a year, a hefty increase over the 8 million the Red Sox had paid him in 2005. The addition of Damon, who had no trouble adapting to Steinbrenner's distaste for facial hair, gave manager Joe Torre one more weapon in an already loaded Yankees' offense. Damon gave them their first true leadoff hitter since Chuck Knoblauch occupied that position from 1998 through 2001.

Torre also had four new members on his coaching staff, all former major league managers: Tony Pena, Larry Bowa, Lee Mazzilli, and Joe Kerrigan. Two other Yankees' coaches had never managed, but were beloved players who had spent their entire careers with the Yankees; Don Mattingly, in this third year as hitting coach and someone Torre predicted (correctly) would be a big league manager before long, and Ron Guidry, who was replacing Mel Stottlemyre as the team's pitching coach. Stottlemyre had resigned following the 2005 American League Division Series loss to the Los Angeles Angels, citing personal disagreements with Steinbrenner among his reasons for leaving.

Five seasons had passed since the Yankees won their 26th World Series and the powerhouse team they had assembled for 2006 intensified the pressure on them to win that 27th title. A seemingly unnecessary reminder was waiting for them in the clubhouse after they finished their workout at Oakland's McAfee Coliseum the day before the opener. Draped over the back of each chair were two T-shirts—one gray and one blue.

The message on the back of the gray shirt was: "1 team, 1 mission." On the front was the interlocking NY over the number 27. On the blue shirt was "257 days, 37 weeks, nine months" above a printed schedule that started on the first day of spring training and ended with the last World Series game. "Win the 27th World Championship," general manager Brian Cashman said when asked what the mission was. "I don't need to explain it."

"Everyone in the room feels we can win a championship," said Damon. "If we don't win it, it will be a shame." Jason Giambi also clearly understood the mission. "When you walk into this clubhouse from day one, it's to win the World Series," he said. "It's not to be good or win the division. If we stay healthy, I like our chances. It's an All-Star team up and down."

The Athletics skipped the traditional first ball ceremony, but did pay tribute to Bill King by placing a ball on the chair of their late broadcaster.

Left-hander Barry Zito had been the workhorse of the Oakland pitching staff since his sophomore season in 2001. Three times he had led the league in games started and he would lead again this year. But Zito was no problem for the Yankees this night. He survived the first inning by striking out Giambi after issuing two two-out walks, but the Yanks drove him from the game with a seven-run second inning.

A still wild Zito walked the first two batters: Hideki Matsui and Jorge Posada, who was making a rare start behind the plate with Randy Johnson on the mound. Posada had not started a game with Johnson since last July 1 when the two had a difficult time working together. (Posada did catch Johnson when Johnson came on in relief during Game Five of the Division Series against the Angels.)

Bernie Williams's single to left scored Matsui, as Posada took second. The next batter, Robinson Cano, was coming off an outstanding first season, in which he finished second to A's pitcher Huston Street in the Rookie of the Year voting. Nevertheless, Torre had Cano lay down a sacrifice bunt. Catcher Jason Kendall fielded the ball and threw to third in an attempt to force Posada, but third baseman Eric Chavez had failed to cover the bag.

The short-haired, clean-shaven Damon, who had struck out in his first at-bat as a Yankee, snapped an 0-for-16 Opening Day slump by ripping an 0–2 pitch to right to score Posada. Derek Jeter's ground single to left, on a 3–2 pitch, brought Williams home with the third run. Cano went to third base on the hit and Damon to second.

Working with the bases loaded, Zito got the first out of the inning by fanning Gary Sheffield, but Alex Rodriguez homered deep into the left-field seats for the 12th grand slam of his career. It was just the fourth Opening Day grand slam by a member of the Yankees. The previous three were by Russ Derry in 1945, Bobby Murcer in 1981, and Alfonso Soriano in 2003.

Quickly down, 7–0, manager Ken Macha removed his ace and replaced him with journeyman Kirk Saarloos. The 1 ⅓ innings Zito pitched marked the shortest outing of his career, to date, but he went on to win 16 games (16–10) as Oakland won the Western Division championship.

"I felt unusually calm and poised," a happy Rodriguez said in the winner's clubhouse. "I'm usually more excited on Opening Day. I really enjoyed myself out there. I'm proud of the way the guys went out and swung the bats."

Future Hall-of-Famer Frank Thomas, signed as a free agent by the A's after a lengthy career with the Chicago White Sox got one run back when he homered in the bottom of the second. The blast moved Thomas into a tie for 28th place on the all-time home run list. It was the 449th of his career, tying him with Sheffield and Jeff Bagwell.

Thomas's home run would be the only run Johnson allowed in his seven innings. "You don't want to lose focus," Johnson said about pitching with a big lead. "You have to continue to make pitches and continue to not allow them to have big innings."

Tanyon Sturtze pitched a scoreless eighth and newcomer Ron Villone, who came in a trade with the Florida Marlins, allowed Oakland's second run in the ninth. Many of the 35,077 in the sellout crowd had long departed when Kendall's sacrifice fly scored Milton Bradley to make the final score, 15–2.

Meanwhile, the Yankees kept up the onslaught. Matsui's three-run homer off Saarloos highlighted a four-run fourth inning, and Matsui's run-scoring single and Williams's bases loaded walk against Brad Halsey in the fifth gave New York a 12-run lead. They added two more against Jay Witasick in the eighth on run-scoring singles by Jeter and Rodriguez.

Everyone in the Yankees' lineup contributed to the one-sided victory. Posada was the only starter to go hitless, but he had a walk and was twice hit by pitches. Matsui had four hits, including a home run, drew two walks and drove in four runs. Rodriguez had three hits, including his grand slam, and drove in five runs. Damon, 3-for-7 with two runs scored in his Yankees' debut, had said earlier, "You know, I think (this lineup) could be one of the best of all time."

The A's lost not only the game; they lost shortstop Bobby Crosby who left in the fifth inning. Cano's third inning slide at second base had bruised Crosby's left index finger. Despite his .239 batting average in 2004, Crosby had been named the American League's Rookie of the Year. In retrospect, the 2004 rookie class had been a poor one, with only Zack Greinke of the Kansas City Royals (4th) and Alex Rios of the Toronto Blue Jays (5th) going on to successful careers.

The Yankees (97–65) easily won the East Division title, finishing 10 games ahead of the Toronto Blue Jays. It was their ninth consecutive East Division title, but the first time a team other than the Boston Red Sox finished second. They won the first game of the Division Series from the Detroit Tigers, but were eliminated when the Tigers won the next three. Before the season, there was expectation that this powerful lineup might score 1,000 runs, something no Yankees' team had done since 1936. They did not quite make it, scoring 930. Derek Jeter finished second in runs scored (118) and third in hits (214) and close second to the Minnesota Twins' Justin Morneau in balloting for the Most Valuable Player Award. Second year pitcher Chien-Ming Wang finished second to Minnesota's Johan Santana in the race for the Cy Young Award. Wang and Santana tied for most games won (19).

Monday, April 3, 2006 (N)

New York	ab	r	h	rbi	po	a	Oakland	ab	r	h	rbi	po	a
Damon cf	7	2	3	1	6	0	Ellis 2b	4	0	1	0	1	2
Jeter ss	6	2	2	2	2	1	Kotsay cf	4	0	2	0	2	0
Sheffield rf	4	2	1	0	3	0	Bobby Crosby ss	2	0	0	0	1	0
Bubba Crosby rf	1	0	0	0	1	0	Perez ss	2	0	0	0	2	2
Rodriguez 3b	5	2	3	5	0	3	Chavez 3b	4	0	0	0	0	1
Giambi 1b	3	2	1	1	5	0	Thomas dh	3	1	1	1	0	0
aPhillips 1b	1	0	0	0	2	0	bD. Johnson dh	1	0	0	0	0	0
Matsui lf	4	2	4	4	2	0	Bradley rf	4	1	2	0	3	0
Posada c	3	1	0	0	3	0	Payton lf	4	0	1	0	2	0
Stinnett c	0	0	0	0	2	0	Kendall c	3	0	0	1	8	1
Williams dh	5	1	1	2	0	0	Swisher 1b	4	0	1	0	7	1
Cano 2b	5	1	2	0	1	2	Zito p	0	0	0	0	0	0
R. Johnson p	0	0	0	0	0	0	Saarloos p	0	0	0	0	0	0
Sturtze p	0	0	0	0	0	0	Halsey p	0	0	0	0	1	0
Villone p	0	0	0	0	0	1	Witasick p	0	0	0	0	0	0
Total	44	15	17	15	27	7	Calero p	0	0	0	0	0	0
							Total	35	2	8	2	27	7

aRan for Giambi in seventh inning.
bGrounded out for Thomas in ninth inning

New York	070	420	020–15
Oakland	010	000	001–2

Errors—Giambi, Bobby Crosby. Left on bases—New York 15; Oakland 7. Caught stealing -Cano. Two-base hits—Cano, Sheffield, Damon, 2. Home runs—Rodriguez, Matsui, Thomas. Sacrifice hit—Cano. Sacrifice Fly—Kendall.

	IP	H	R	ER	BB	SO
NEW YORK						
Johnson (W, 1–0)	7.0	5	1	1	0	3
Sturtze	1.0	1	0	0	0	1
Villone	1.0	2	1	1	0	1
OAKLAND						
Zito (L, 0–1)	1.1	4	7	7	4	3
Saarloos	3.1	7	5	4	0	2
Halsey	1.1	1	1	1	1	0
Witasick	2.0	4	2	2	3	1
Calero	1.0	1	0	0	1	2

Hit by pitches—by Saarloos, (Posada); by Halsey, (Posada, Giambi). Umpires—HP, Tim Welke; 1B, Kerwin Danley; 2B, Gary Cederstrom; 3B, Jim Reynolds. Time of game—3:14. Attendance—35,077.

Monday, April 2, 2007
Yankee Stadium, New York
New York 9 Tampa Bay 5

Nothing is so good as it seems beforehand.—George Eliot

In December 2004, following a season in which he won 18 games (18–8) with a 3.00 earned run average for the Florida Marlins, right-hander Carl Pavano signed as a free agent with the Yankees. The contract was for four years and would pay him just under $40 million. To say that the Yankees had not received what they expected from Pavano would be a gross understatement. As they entered the 2007 season, the signing of Pavano, now 31 years old with a 61–64-career record, was shaping up as one of general manager Brian Cashman's worst blunders.

A series of injuries had limited him to only 17 games and four wins (4–6) in 2005 and made him miss completely the 2006 season. During his time with the Yankees, he had been the target of scorn and ridicule from the fans and from a portion of the New York press. Even worse, some of his teammates had begun to question his dedication.

At spring training this year, pitcher Mike Mussina said he was not the only Yankee who believed Pavano had to prove to them he wanted to pitch for the team. "It didn't look good from a player's and teammate's standpoint," Mussina said of Pavano's injuries. "Was everything just coincidence? Over and over again? I don't know." Manager Joe Torre agreed Pavano had much to do to gain his teammates acceptance.

His road to redemption would begin when Torre named him to start the opener, at home, against the Tampa Bay Devil Rays. Pavano was the first Yankees' pitcher to start an opener after not having pitched in the major leagues the previous season since Jim Vaughn in 1910.

He had not been Torre's first choice; Chien-Ming Wang was. But Wang, who had emerged as the staff ace in 2006, had an injured hamstring; Andy Pettitte, back after three years with the Houston Astros, also was recovering from an injury; Mussina's pitching schedule made him unavailable; and Randy Johnson, a 17-game winner in '06, had been traded to the Arizona Diamondbacks for four players. Foremost among those coming from

Arizona to New York was Luis Vizcaino, a veteran reliever whose 359 relief appearances over the previous five years were the fifth most in the major leagues.

Also gone from the Yankees was Gary Sheffield, whose emotional explosiveness would not be missed, but whose explosive bat would be. However the biggest loss of all was popular outfielder Bernie Williams, perhaps no longer as a performer, but as one reporter said, for "leaving a gash in the club's soul." The parting with Williams, a Yankees' fixture for 16 seasons, had reminded fans yet again that baseball was a business with little room for sentiment.

The 37-year-old Williams's contract had expired at the end of the 2006 season. He realized he was no longer the player he had been, but he wanted to stay with the Yankees as a back-up outfielder and pinch hitter. The club offered him an invitation to spring training as a non-roster invitee, where he would have to compete for a job. A disappointed Williams chose instead to retire. The fans showed their displeasure at the unceremonious "dumping" of Williams, a proud and dignified man, with frequent chants of "We want Bernie" throughout the opener.

Yet heroes come and heroes go. Almost as a counterbalance to the absence of Williams, the sellout crowd of 55,035 had the opportunity to cheer and welcome the popular Bobby Murcer back to New York. Murcer, battling a brain tumor, was shown on the video scoreboard while broadcasting an inning with the YES Network television crew. The fans gave him a standing ovation, while the Yankees' players all came out of their dugout to applaud him.

Just before the August trading deadline in 2006, the Yankees had made an excellent trade in which they acquired pitcher Cory Lidle and outfielder Bobby Abreau from the Philadelphia Phillies and gave up very little in return. Lidle started nine games in the final two months of the season, winning four and losing three. Abreu proved to be the more valuable addition, batting .330 with 42 runs batted in.

Both were expected to be back this season. Abreu was, and in the starting lineup. But Lidle was not. On October 11, he and his copilot had been killed when the plane he was piloting crashed into a building at East 72nd Street on Manhattan's Upper East Side.

The Yankees used the pregame ceremonies to honor Lidle by playing a moving video tribute to the late pitcher. Jason Giambi, who had been Lidle's high school teammate and friend for nearly 20 years, stood with Lidle's widow, Melanie, and their son, Christopher, during the showing. Melanie Lidle threw out the ceremonial first pitch. The Yankees would further honor Lidle by having the players wear a black armband on their left sleeves for all of the 2007 season.

Tampa Bay' second-year manager Joe Maddon was opening with his ace, Scott Kazmir, a 23-year-old lefthander. Kazmir allowed two first-inning runs on Giambi's single that scored Johnny Damon and Abreu, who had also gotten on base with singles.

The Devil Rays got a run in the second with the help of two players making their major league debuts—28-year-old third baseman Akinori Iwamura, from Japan, and 22-year-old center fielder Elijah Dukes. Iwamura reached on an error by Derek Jeter, moved to second on a walk to Dukes, and scored the unearned run on B. J. Upton's single. Upton's hit was a grounder up the middle that, according to one New York writer, "just about any shortstop turns into the third out. But Jeter's range to his left is so poor that the ball eluded him even with a dive."

Jeter's error was one of three the Yankees made; the others were by third baseman Alex Rodriguez and first baseman Josh Phelps, whom the Yanks had acquired from the Baltimore Orioles in the 2006 Rule 5 Draft.

Jorge Posada's home run in the fourth inning gave the Yankees a 3–1 lead, which the speedy Rays erased with a four-run fifth. After Dukes led off with a home run, Upton singled, stole second, and scored on a Carl Crawford single. Crawford later scored on a single by Rocco Baldelli, which finished Pavano. While his replacement, Brian Bruney, was striking out Ty Wigginton, Baldelli stole second. Delmon Young's single scored Baldelli, to put Tampa Bay ahead, 5–3. With Iwamura at bat, Young took off in another attempt to steal second, but this time Posada's throw to Jeter retired him.

The Yankees bounced back to tie the score in the sixth on Jeter's two run single off Shawn Camp that scored Posada and Robinson Cano. They went ahead an inning later against Brian Stokes—the eventual loser—when Rodriguez singled, stole second, and came home on Giambi's single. It was the third run batted in for Giambi on what had been an emotional afternoon for him.

"That was probably one of the toughest things I've ever had to do in my life," he said after the game. "You want to win when you give a guy a big tribute. It meant a lot to me today to be a part of it. I'll always remember it."

Rodriguez's two run homer was part of a three-run Yankees' eighth that made the final score, 9–5. He drove the first pitch he saw from Juan Salas deep into the seats in left-center, making it the second consecutive opener in which he homered. The home run was the 465th of the 31-year-old Rodriguez's career, tying him with Hall of Famer Dave Winfield for 28th place.

Tampa Bay failed to score again after their fourth inning uprising, as Sean Henn, Vizcaino, Kyle Farnsworth, and Mariano Rivera each pitched one scoreless inning. Vizcaino was the winner, while Rivera excited the crowd by striking out the side in the ninth.

On April 9, Pavano made his second start. He went eight innings in defeating the Minnesota Twins, 8–2. Six days later, he was placed on the 15-day disabled list with what was described as an "elbow strain." He missed the rest of the season, but returned in 2008 to pitch in seven games, with a record of 4–2. The Yankees chose not to resign him for the 2009 season.

The Yankees (94–68) had their streak of nine consecutive East Division titles snapped when they finished two games behind the Boston Red Sox. Playing as the wild-card team, they lost in the Division Championship Series for the third straight year, this time in four games to the Cleveland Indians. Alex Rodriguez led the league in home runs (54), runs batted in (156), runs scored (143), and slugging percentage (.645). He won The Sporting News Player of the Year Award and was voted the league's Most Valuable Player. Joe Torre, who had managed the Yankees since 1996, left after the 2007 season to become the manager of the Los Angeles Dodgers. Joe Girardi replaced him. Torre's record in New York was a spectacular 1,173–767 (.605) and included six pennants and four World Series titles.

Monday, April 2, 2007

Tampa Bay	ab	r	h	rbi	po	a	New York	ab	r	h	rbi	po	a
Crawford lf	4	1	2	1	2	0	Damon cf	2	1	1	0	2	0
Zobrist ss	4	0	0	0	0	2	Cabrera cf	0	0	0	0	2	0
Baldelli dh	4	1	1	1	0	0	Jeter ss	4	0	1	2	2	3
Wigginton 1b	4	0	1	0	7	1	Abreu rf	5	2	2	1	1	0
Young rf	4	0	1	1	3	0	Rodriguez 3b	5	2	2	2	0	1
Iwamura 3b	3	1	1	0	0	2	Giambi dh	5	0	2	3	0	0
Navarro c	4	0	0	0	5	0	Matsui lf	3	0	0	0	2	0

Tampa Bay

	ab	r	h	rbi	po	a
Dukes cf	3	1	1	1	2	1
Upton 2b	4	1	2	1	4	0
Kazmir p	0	0	0	0	1	1
Camp p	0	0	0	0	0	1
Stokes p	0	0	0	0	0	0
Lugo p	0	0	0	0	0	1
Salas p	0	0	0	0	0	0
Total	34	5	9	5	24	9

New York

	ab	r	h	rbi	po	a
Posada c	4	2	2	1	8	1
Cano 2b	4	1	1	0	3	3
Phelps 1b	0	0	0	0	6	0
ªMientkiewicz 1b	1	1	1	0	1	0
Pavano p	0	0	0	0	0	1
Bruney p	0	0	0	0	0	0
Henn p	0	0	0	0	0	0
Vizcaino p	0	0	0	0	0	0
Farnsworth p	0	0	0	0	0	0
Rivera p	0	0	0	0	0	0
Total	33	9	12	9	27	9

Tampa Bay	010	040	000–5
New York	200	102	13X–9

ªSacrifice bunt for Phelps in sixth inning.

Errors—Jeter, Rodriguez, Phelps. Double plays—Dukes, Zobrist, Upton; Jeter, Cano, Phelps (2). Stolen base—Crawford, Upton, Baldelli, Damon, Abreu, Rodriguez. Caught stealing-Young. Left on bases—Tampa Bay 4, New York 8. Home runs—Dukes, Posada, Rodriguez. Sacrifice Hit—Mientkiewicz, Cabrera.

	IP	H	R	ER	BB	SO
TAMPA BAY						
Kazmir	5.0	6	5	5	4	5
Camp	0.1	1	0	0	0	0
Stokes (L, 0–1)	1.2	2	1	1	0	0
Lugo	0.1	1	1	1	0	0
Salas	0.2	2	2	2	0	0

Hit by pitches—by Kazmir (Jeter); by Camp (Cabrera)

	IP	H	R	ER	BB	SO
NEW YORK						
Pavano	4.1	6	5	4	2	2
Bruney	0.2	1	0	0	0	1
Henn	1.0	1	0	0	0	0
Vizcaino (W, 1–0)	1.0	0	0	0	0	0
Farnsworth	1.0	1	0	0	0	1
Rivera	1.0	0	0	0	0	3

Umpires—HP, Gary Darling; 1B, Larry Poncino; 2B, Jerry Meals; 3B, Bruce Dreckman. Time of game—3:01. Attendance—55,035.

Tuesday, April 1, 2008 (N)
Yankee Stadium, New York
New York 3 Toronto 2

Shrine of the mighty! can it be, that this is all remains of thee.—Lord Byron

A sense of beginnings and endings lent a special feel to the Yankees 2008 opener. For the first time in 12 years, a new manager was leading them; and this would be the start of their final season at the original Yankee Stadium, which opened in 1923. In 2009 they would begin play in a new Yankee Stadium, currently under construction across the street.

Joe Torre had left to manage the Los Angeles Dodgers. With 10 East Division titles and four world championships in his 12 seasons, Torre had earned his place alongside Miller Huggins, Joe McCarthy, and Casey Stengel as the Yankees' greatest managers. Joe Girardi, a former Yankees' catcher, coach, and broadcaster, who had managed the Florida Marlins in 2006, was replacing him. The Marlins fired Girardi after the season despite his winning the National League's Manager of the Year award. He had beaten out several other candidates for the manager's job, including Yankees coaches Don Mattingly, who chose to go to Los Angeles with Torre, and Tony Pena, who chose to remain.

Torre sent a pregame telegram of best wishes to Girardi, but much to the dismay of the fans already in the park, the new manager's debut, one that would kick off a season-long celebration for the old ballpark, was delayed by a day. A light rain was enough for the afternoon game to be postponed until the following night. Spectators who had come early sat through a delay of more than an hour before the game was officially called.

"It was misting, it wasn't raining," said one upset fan. "No one cares about the fans anymore; they could have played. I don't get it." Neither the fans nor the players failed to notice that the Blue Jays and the Tampa Bay Rays (they had dropped "Devil" from their name this season), who played in domed stadiums, were opening on the road. (The Rays had opened the night before in Baltimore.)

The Yankees chose to play the rescheduled game at night because the forecast for the afternoon included scattered rain showers. The only other time the Yanks had played a night home opener was in 2005, against the Boston Red Sox. Playing on what was originally an off day meant the Yankees would be scheduled to play 20 games in the next 20 days and 33 games in the next 34 days.

"It is what it is," said Alex Rodriguez, the American League's reigning Most Valuable Player. "You take one pitch at a time. The season has a lot of challenges to it, that's the first."

Chien-Ming Wang, one day past his 28th birthday, was Girardi's opening day choice; John Gibbons, Toronto's manager, chose Roy Halladay, possessor of a 10–4 lifetime record against New York. Wang, a native of Taiwan, had been the Yankees' leading winner in each of the past two seasons, with 19; similarly, Halladay led Blue Jays' pitchers in 2006 and 2007, with 16.

A full house was on hand to see the final opening day at Yankee Stadium. Hall-of-Famer Reggie Jackson, the team's former slugger and once and future advisor to the general manager, had the honor of throwing out the first ball. Making the ceremonial toss for the first time, Jackson's throw reached catcher Jose Molina's glove on the fly. "I was nervous about it, where the ball would go, what my throw would be like," Jackson said. "I had a little Mr. October working tonight."

Rodriguez staked the Yankees to a 1–0 lead in the first inning, when his two-out double to right-center field scored Bobby Abreu, who had singled. The Jays tied the score in the second. Frank Thomas led off with a single to left, took second on Lyle Overbay's infield single, and went to third on Aaron Hill's fly ball to right. Marco Scutaro hit a ground ball to first baseman Jason Giambi who threw to shortstop Derek Jeter to retire Overbay, but Jeter's return throw to first was too late to complete the double play and allowed Thomas to score.

Thomas, at the tail end of his Hall of Fame career, batted just .167 in 16 games for Toronto, who released him on April 20. Oakland signed him four days later, and he played his final 55 games for the A's, batting .263.

Scutaro led off the fifth with a walk, stole second, and eventually scored on a ground out by Shannon Stewart. The Yanks tied it at 2–2 in the sixth on Melky Cabrera's fly ball that just made it over the 314-foot marker in the right-field corner. "It was a patented Yankee Stadium home run," said Gibbons.

The 23-year-old Cabrera, batting ninth and playing center field, was the only Yankee regular who had never started a season-opener. But he had played in 150 games in 2007, batting .273 with eight home runs and 73 runs batted in, and was coming off a most impressive spring training. Cabrera also displayed his defensive prowess in the fourth inning by making sensational back-to-back catches on drives by Overbay and Hill.

Cabrera said he considered it "an honor" to be starting on Opening Day at Yankee Stadium at the most famous position in the team's history. Johnny Damon, the opening day center-fielder the previous two seasons was asked if he had talked to Cabrera about the significance of following men like Earle Combs, Joe DiMaggio, Mickey Mantle, and Bernie Williams.

Damon, the left fielder today, said he had not, but he had great confidence in Cabrera who, like Mantle and Williams, was a switch-hitter. Cabrera's range and his throwing arm had particularly impressed Damon. "The way he goes and gets balls, the way teams respect his arm, so that's all we want Melky to be able to do, is run, catch, throw the ball and whatever else he hits, it's a bonus for us."

Cabrera, with a diving attempt, came close to robbing Hill again in the seventh, but missed and Hill had a double. Giambi took a hit away from Scutaro and prevented a likely run with a leaping catch of Scutaro's liner. Wang then retired Gregg Zaun and David Eckstein on ground balls to end the inning. Relying heavily on his outstanding sinker, Wang got 13 of his 21 outs on the ground. "He (Wang) just gutted it out," Girardi said. "He made the pitches that he had to make."

The Yankees scored the tie-breaking and eventual winning run in the home seventh. A single by Rodriguez and a walk to Giambi put runners at first and second, with no outs. Girardi had moved Robinson Cano, an emerging star, up from the lower regions of the batting order to the number six spot. The 25-year-old second baseman batted .306 in 2007 while reaching career highs with 19 home runs and 97 runs batted in.

Halladay got Cano to ground out, allowing Giambi to reach second while Rodriguez took third. Manager Gibbons ordered Jorge Posada walked intentionally to load the bases. Hideki Matsui, batting eighth, hit what appeared to be an inning-ending, double play grounder to the right side. But second baseman Hill fumbled the ball and managed only the force out at second as Rodriguez scored the go-ahead run.

Torre had been successful using one or two pitchers as a bridge from his starter to his closer, a role filled by John Wetteland in 1996 and Mariano Rivera ever since. Girardi saw no reason not to follow that pattern. To pitch the eighth inning, he brought in Joba Chamberlain, a 22-year-old right-hander. Chamberlain had become a fan favorite in New York since the Yankees brought him to the big leagues last August 7. Using an overpowering fastball, he compiled a dazzling 0.38 earned run average in 19 games (24 innings).

Chamberlain issued a one-out walk to Alex Rios, but struck out Vernon Wells and Frank Thomas, the latter on a pitch clocked at 97 miles per hour. With his customary "Enter the Sandman" blasting on the PA system, Rivera set the Jays down in order to wrap up the Yankees' first win of the season and Girardi's first win as their manager. As Derek Jeter said of his postgame talk with Girardi: "I just told him, 'It's the first of many.'"

In Joe Girardi's first season, the Yankees failed to reach the postseason for the first time since 1993. (There were no playoffs in the strike-interrupted 1994 season.) The team won

89 games (89–73), but finished in third place, eight games behind the Tampa Bay Rays who won their first East Division title. Attendance in this final year at the original Yankee Stadium was a record 4,298,655. Mike Mussina ended his 18-year American League career with his first 20-win season (20–9). Alex Rodriguez led the league in slugging (.573).

Tuesday, April 1, 2008

Toronto	ab	r	h	rbi	po	a	New York	ab	r	h	rbi	po	a
Eckstein ss	4	0	0	0	3	5	Damon lf	4	0	1	0	0	0
Stewart lf	4	0	1	1	0	0	Jeter ss	4	0	1	0	1	6
Rios rf	2	0	1	0	1	0	Abreu rf	4	1	2	0	1	0
V. Well cf	4	0	0	0	1	0	A. Rodriguez 3b	3	1	2	1	0	3
Thomas dh	4	1	1	0	0	0	Giambi 1b	3	0	0	0	15	1
Overbay 1b	4	0	1	0	15	1	Cano 2b	3	0	1	0	2	5
Hill 2b	4	0	1	0	1	4	Posada c	2	0	0	0	5	0
Scutaro 3b	3	1	0	1	0	1	Matsui dh	3	0	0	1	0	0
Zaun c	3	0	1	0	3	1	Cabrera cf	3	1	1	1	3	0
Halladay p	0	0	0	0	0	3	Wang p	0	0	0	0	0	0
Downs p	0	0	0	0	0	1	Chamberlain p	0	0	0	0	0	0
Total	32	2	6	2	24	16	Rivera p	0	0	0	0	0	0
							Total	29	3	8	3	27	15

Toronto	010	010	000–2
New York	100	001	10X–3

Double plays—Overbay, Eckstein, Overbay; Eckstein, Hill, Overbay; Cano, Giambi. Stolen base—Scutaro (2), Rios. Caught stealing—Jeter. Left on bases—Toronto 6, New York 5. Two-base hits—Hill, A. Rodriguez. Three-base hits—Damon. Home runs—Cabrera.

	IP	H	R	ER	BB	SO	
TORONTO							
Halladay (L, 0–1)	7.0	7	3	3	2	3	
Downs	1.0	1	0	0	1	0	
NEW YORK							
Wang (W, 1–0)	7.0	6	2	2	2	2	
Chamberlain	1.0	0	0	0	1	2	
Rivera	S.1	1.0	0	0	0	0	1

Umpires—HP, Gary Darling; 1B; Jerry Meals; 2B Bill Miller; 3B, Paul Emmel. Time of game—2:31. Attendance—55,112.

Monday, April 6, 2009
Oriole Park at Camden Yards, Baltimore
Baltimore 10 New York 5

After all, tomorrow is another day.—Margaret Mitchell

The 2009 baseball season opened with the country suffering through its worst economic setback since the Great Depression of the 1930s. Professional sports had always considered themselves immune to recession, citing studies that showed since 1970 professional leagues in general grew more profitable in the face of economic downturns.

But the effect of this recession on consumers and corporations had hit the sports world like no other. According to the *Baltimore Sun*, NBA teams, many of which were losing money, had been forced to greatly reduce their ticket prices. Even the NFL, the behemoth of American sports, cut about 10 percent of its staff in December.

Baseball commissioner Bud Selig admitted he too was worried by the overall impact of unemployment in the country. "I used to think we were recession-proof," Selig said. "I really did. This is different."

In Baltimore, the Yankees were opening the season against the Orioles, a team that had endured 11 consecutive losing seasons and generally declining attendance. The Orioles, who had played at Camden Yards since 1992, slipped below the two million mark in 2008 for the first time. Yet fans are forever hopeful, especially on Opening Day, and for local fans there were reasons for optimism. Baltimore's two best players—right fielder Nick Markakis and second baseman Brian Roberts—were signed to long term contracts; center fielder Adam Jones was a budding star; and catcher Matt Wieters and pitchers Jake Arrieta, Chris Tillman, and Brian Matusz were among the game's most highly rated prospects.

The slowed economy and financial uncertainty seemed to have had a negative impact on most teams' aggressively pursuing of free agents. But not the Yankees, who signed three big ones: pitchers CC Sabathia and A. J. Burnett, and first baseman Mark Teixeira.

The Yankees and Boston Red Sox had long been the most popular draws at Camden Yards, but the composition of the crowds had shifted during the Orioles more than a decade of poor seasons. Boston and New York fans of those teams began to make up an increasing portion of those in attendance. It was less so today, as Baltimoreans had long treated Opening Day as a combined holiday and social event. Still, a sizeable contingent of Yankees' fans was part of the crowd of 48,607. No one expected the Orioles would draw a bigger crowd this season.

Following three games in Baltimore, the Yankees would play three against the Royals in Kansas City and three against the Rays in St. Petersburg, before playing their first game in the new Yankee Stadium. Nevertheless, the players were already wearing uniform patches on their left sleeve commemorating the new park.

The 2008 season had been an all-around disappointment to club officials, players, and fans alike. But the players had come to camp brimming with confidence and feeling very positive about the upcoming season. Spring training records are generally meaningless, yet the Yanks expected their 24–10–1 mark, their best Grapefruit League winning percentage in 48 years, was indicative of what was to come. Odds-makers had taken notice and made them the favorites to win their division.

The starting pitchers this afternoon—Sabathia for New York and Jeremy Guthrie for Baltimore—were familiar with one another. They had been teammates with the Cleveland Indians, and coincidentally had seen each other this past December, when both were in Las Vegas to watch the Oscar De La Hoya-Manny Pacquiao fight at the MGM Grand Garden Arena.

Sabathia, a former Cy Young Award winner, was the first black pitcher to start an Opening Day game for the Yankees. At 6 feet seven inches and 309 pounds, he may have been the only major league pitcher ever to weigh more than 300 pounds. Moreover, his size 56 jersey was likely the largest ever worn by a Yankee.

Centerfielder Brett Gardner scored the game's first run when he led off the third inning with a single and later came home on Johnny Damon's sacrifice fly. The speedy Gardner, a second-year player, had won the center field position in spring training after a fierce battle with Melky Cabrera.

Sabathia had survived a difficult 19-pitch first inning that included a leadoff single by Brian Roberts, a walk to Adam Jones, the number two hitter, and two wild pitches. Additionally, Sabathia, a big league pitcher since 2001 who had never thrown two wild pitches in an inning, did it in his first inning as a Yankee. It appeared he and catcher Jorge Posada were having problems getting in synch on pitch selections.

Baltimore retaliated with three runs in its half of the third inning; Jones drove home two with a triple and later scored on Markakis's sacrifice fly. Sabathia's disappointing debut worsened in the fifth inning, when the Orioles scored three more runs to take a 6–1 lead. Not that he was manhandled. Baltimore's four hits in the inning—by the first four batters—were a double by Roberts and infield singles by Jones, Markakis, and Melvin Mora. That accounted for three runs; the fourth came on a bases loaded walk to Luke Scott that finished Sabathia. Jonathan Albaladejo came in to pitch to Gregg Zaun with the bases still loaded. The Yankees avoided further damage when Gardner caught Zaun's fly ball and threw Mora out at the plate.

In 4⅓ innings, Sabathia allowed 8 hits, 6 earned runs, walked 5, and had no strikeouts. It was only the fifth time in 255 career starts that he had failed to record a strikeout. "I got behind too much," Sabathia said. "I think I threw only four first-pitch strikes. I couldn't throw my fastball for strikes and everything comes off my fastball."

Mark Teixeira's debut had also been disappointing. He went 0-for-4, with a walk, and stranded two runners in the eighth. Teixeira was a Maryland native and his bad day delighted the Baltimore fans, who jeered him at every opportunity. They had not forgiven him for joining the Yanks as a free agent rather than the Orioles. But Teixeira had two good reasons for his choice; New York's offer was for more years and more money than was Baltimore's.

The Yanks scored two in the sixth on Posada's home run, followed by a walk to Robinson Cano and a double by Xavier Nady, acquired in a July 26, 2008 trade with the Pittsburgh Pirates. They added two more in the seventh, against Chris Ray, on a Damon single and a Hideki Matsui home run.

Ray walked the next batter, Posada, and with the lead reduced to one run, and with the left-handed-hitting Cano due up, Orioles manager Dave Trembley replaced Ray with Jamie Walker, a left-hander. Cano singled to center moving Posada, the potential tying run, to second. Trembley yanked Walker and brought in right-hander Dennis Sarfate to pitch to Nady, a right-handed batter. This time his strategy worked. Nady hit a ground ball to third baseman Mora, who stepped on the bag for the force on Posada and threw to first baseman Aubrey Huff to complete the inning-ending double play.

The Yankees threatened again in the eighth against new pitcher Jim Johnson. Nick Swisher, batting for Cody Ransom started the inning with a double. (Ransom was playing third base while Alex Rodriguez continued to recover from his offseason hip surgery.) Ramiro Pena, making his big league debut as a runner for Swisher, moved to third on Gardner's bunt. With Derek Jeter at bat, the Orioles played the infield in to cut off the possible tying run. Trembley's move was again successful, as shortstop Cesar Izturis threw out Jeter while holding Pena at third. A walk to Damon brought Teixeira to the plate. It was a chance for Teixeira to silence the crowd, which continued to boo his every move. But his comebacker hit off Johnson's glove and went to second baseman Roberts who tossed it to Izturis for the force on Damon.

Baltimore added four runs in the home eighth to make the final score, 10–5. Izturis, signed as a free agent, accounted for two with a home run off Phil Coke, and the Orioles added two more against Brian Bruney. Izturis's home run, just his third in the past four seasons, barely made it over the left-field wall.

The Yankees asked for a ruling of fan interference after Damon claimed someone in the stands reached over and bumped him. "I thought I had it," Damon said. "I don't know what happened. I was definitely interfered with but the umpires ruled the ball was in the seats. It seems like that was a place for instant replay, no?"

The "no-call" capped what had been a most frustrating day for Girardi and the Yankees.

The Yankees justified their status as preseason favorites by winning 103 games (103–59) and finishing eight games ahead of the Boston Red Sox in the East Division. They defeated the Minnesota Twins, three games to none, in the Division Series and the Anaheim Angels, four games to two, in the League Championship Series. They followed winning their 40th pennant by winning their first World Series since 2000 and their 27th overall, by topping the Philadelphia Phillies in six games. Mark Teixeira and CC Sabathia recovered from their opening day flops to have successful seasons. Teixeira tied for the league lead in home runs (39), led in runs batted in (122), won a Gold Glove and a Silver Slugger Award, and finished second to Joe Mauer of the Minnesota Twins in voting for the Most Valuable Player Award. Sabathia won 19 games, tying him for the league lead and finished fourth in voting for the Cy Young Award. Mariano Rivera had 44 saves and won the Sporting News Fireman of the Year Award. The seating capacity of more than 52,000 at the new Yankee Stadium was only slightly less than that of the old stadium. Nevertheless, the attendance of 3,719, 358, was significantly lower than the record 4,298,655 the team had drawn in 2008.

Monday, April 6, 2009

New York	ab	r	h	rbi	po	a	Baltimore	ab	r	h	rbi	po	a
Jeter ss	5	0	3	0	3	5	Roberts 2b	4	2	3	0	1	2
Damon lf	3	1	2	1	2	0	Jones cf	3	3	3	3	6	0
Teixeira 1b	4	0	0	0	10	1	Markakis rf	4	2	2	2	1	0
Matsui dh	5	1	1	2	0	0	Mora 3b	3	0	1	0	4	1
Posada c	3	1	1	1	3	1	Huff 1b	5	0	1	3	6	0
Cano 2b	3	1	1	0	2	5	Wigginton dh	4	0	1	0	0	0
Nady rf	4	0	1	1	1	0	Scott lf	2	0	0	1	2	0
Ransom 3b	3	0	0	0	0	2	Pie lf	0	0	0	0	0	0
[a]Swisher	1	0	1	0	0	0	Zaun c	4	1	1	0	4	2
[b]Pena 3b	0	0	0	0	0	0	Izturis ss	4	2	2	2	3	3
Gardner cf	3	1	1	0	3	1	Guthrie p	0	0	0	0	0	1
Sabathia p	0	0	0	0	0	0	Ray p	0	0	0	0	0	0
Albaladejo p	0	0	0	0	0	1	Walker p	0	0	0	0	0	0
Coke p	0	0	0	0	0	0	Sarfate p	0	0	0	0	0	0
Bruney p	0	0	0	0	0	0	Johnson p	0	0	0	0	0	1
Marte p	0	0	0	0	0	0	Sherrill p	0	0	0	0	0	0
Total	34	5	11	5	24	16	Total	33	10	14	10	27	10

[a]Doubled for Ransom eighth inning.
[b]Ran for Swisher in eighth inning.

New York	001	002	200–5
Baltimore	003	030	04x–10

Double plays—Cano, Jeter, Teixeira; Gardner, Posada; Jeter, Teixeira; Mora, Huff. Left on bases—New York 11; Baltimore 8. Stolen bases—Izturis. Caught stealing—Roberts. Two-base hits—Nady, Swisher, Roberts, Zaun, Huff. Three-base hits—Damon, Jones. Home runs—Posada, Matsui, Izturis. Sacrifice hit—Gardner. Sacrifice Fly—Damon, Markakis.

	IP	H	R	ER	BB	SO
NEW YORK						
Sabathia (L, 0–1)	4.1	8	6	6	5	0
Albaladejo	1.1	2	0	0	0	0
Coke	1.2	2	2	2	1	2
Bruney	0.1	1	2	2	2	0
Marte	0.1	1	0	0	0	0
BALTIMORE						
Guthrie (W, 1–0)	6.0	7	3	3	3	3
Ray	0.1	2	2	2	1	0
Walker	0.0	1	0	0	0	0
Sarfate	0.2	0	0	0	0	0
Johnson	1.0	1	0	0	1	0
Sherrill	1.0	0	0	0	1	1

Hit by pitches—by Guthrie, (Posada). Umpires—HP, Randy Marsh; 1B, Mike Winters; 2B, Lance Barksdale; 3B, James Hoye. Time of game—3:31. Attendance—48,607.

XII

2010–2017

During the first few years of this decade three players who made their debuts in 1995 and spent their entire careers with the Yankees retired: Jorge Posada played his last game in September 2011, Mariano Rivera in September 2013, and Derek Jeter in September 2014. Each had been a major contributor to the team's success and each had taken his place in the Yankees' record book. Particularly Jeter, who ended his career as the team's all-time leader in games, plate appearances, at-bats, hits, singles, doubles, stolen bases, hit-by-pitch, times on base, strikeouts, double plays grounded into, and total outs made.

Also gone to retirement were Andy Pettitte, Alex Rodriguez, and Mark Teixeira. Robinson Cano, the best player to come out of the farm system since Derek Jeter, batted .309 in nine excellent seasons in New York before signing as a free agent with the Seattle Mariners following the 2013 season.

With the start of the 2017 season, Joe Giradi began his 10th season as manager. His teams had won only one pennant and World Series championship, in 2009, his second season. The Yankees' only postseason appearance from 2013 through 2016 was a one game wild-card loss to the Houston Astros in 2015.

Owner George Steinbrenner died in July 2010 and his sons Hal and Hank took over the ownership duties. The Yankees continued to trade for or sign veteran free agents, including Jacoby Ellsbury, Brian McCann, Aroldis Chapman, Carlos Beltran, Mashahiro Tanaka, and Curtis Granderson. But general manager Brian Cashman also began drafting and trading for talented youngsters like Tyler Austin, Dellin Betances, Greg Bird, Starlin Castro, Clint Frazier, Didi Gregorius, Aaron Hicks, Aaron Judge, Gleyber Torres, Ronald Torreyes, and Tyler Wade.

The change in approach brought hope for the future, hope that at least some of these youngsters would replicate the homegrown talent of the 1990s and lead the Yankees to yet another dynasty.

Sunday, April 4, 2010 (N)
Fenway Park, Boston
Boston 9 New York 7

Baseball is continuous, like nothing else among American things,
an endless game of repeated summers, joining the long generations
of all the fathers and all the sons.—Donald Hall

For the first time since 2001, the Yankees opened a season as the defending world champions. They would do so at Fenway Park, on a Sunday night, the first of 18 games they would play against the Boston Red Sox. ESPN, the all-sports network that had a contractual arrangement with Major League Baseball to have a say in scheduling, chose the battle between the bitter rivals to kick off the new season. While the intensity of the rivalry had lessened somewhat, ESPN executives knew Yankees-Red Sox games generally drew large television audiences. Boston and New York had been on national television so often fans in other cities had become almost as familiar with their players as they were with players on their local teams.

While the makeup of both teams' rosters remained mostly consistent, the offseason competition to strengthen themselves had become almost as fierce as the competition on the field. Especially so when both were after the same player, like the Texas Rangers' Alex Rodriguez, in 2004, and Japanese pitcher Daisuke Matsuzaka, in 2007.

This season, Red Sox general manager Theo Epstein had added right-handed pitcher John Lackey, third baseman Adrian Beltre, shortstop Marco Scutaro, and center fielder Mike Cameron, in whom the Yankees had also been interested.

"There was an awful lot of competition out there for Mike Cameron," Yankees general manager Brian Cashman said. "It got to be more than we wanted to pay, frankly. He had value in that market and the Red Sox clearly wanted him."

With the addition of Cameron, Jacoby Ellsbury, who played center in 2009, would move to left field, replacing the departed Jason Bay. (Ellsbury would miss most of the 2010 season after injuring his ribs in an April 11 collision with Beltre.)

Although losing out on Cameron, Cashman had made three major additions to the Yankees: right-hander Javier Vazquez, and outfielder Curtis Granderson, via trades, and free-agent first baseman Nick Johnson. Gone were Melky Cabrera, traded to the Atlanta Braves in the Vasquez deal, along with two fan favorites, the Yankees allowed to leave through free agency. Johnny Damon signed with the Detroit Tigers, and Hideki Matsui, the Most Valuable Player of the 2009 World Series, signed with the Los Angeles Angels.

Tonight's game marked the 30th time the teams had met in the opener, with the Yankees holding a decided 18–10-1 edge in the previous 29. It was also the 10th time the Yankees had opened the season against Boston as the defending champions— they were 8–1 in the previous nine.

Boston fans had been a long suffering group, but the years of weak Red Sox teams were long gone. Also gone was the general empathy and good will other fans felt toward them. They had already won two World Series in the new century to the Yankees one. "It's incredibly competitive because there's two teams with that kind of talent and the ability to win it all," said Alex Rodriguez. "When we get together, you know you're facing the best, and given that we won the World Series, we're going to feel like the hunted. Everybody is coming after us and giving it the best they can against us every time out."

The honor of throwing out the first pitch to open the Red Sox 110th season went to Pedro Martinez, one of the best pitchers ever to wear a Boston uniform. The still popular Martinez, wearing his old No. 45 jersey, threw the ball to his former catcher, the still active Jason Varitek. Ever the showman, Martinez had made his way to the mound from left field while blowing kisses and making hugging gestures to the fans. The only sour note for the fans came when he was intercepted by Alex Rodriguez, who gave him a hug. It was the only time during his trip to the mound that boos were heard.

Other former Boston favorites in the park were pitcher Curt Schilling and shortstop Nomar Garciaparra, analysts for ESPN, and the ever-popular 91-year-old Johnny Pesky. The crowd of 37,440, on a very pleasant 67-degree evening, marked Fenway Park's 551st consecutive sellout.

Sox manager Terry Francona opened with his ace right-hander, Josh Beckett, 17–6 in 2009. Becket breezed through the first inning and the first two batters in the second before yielding back-to-back home runs to Jorge Posada and Curtis Granderson. Posada's hit the "Pesky Pole" in right field, while Granderson's sailed over the Red Sox bullpen in right. Nick Swisher and Brett Gardner followed with singles, but Beckett retired Derek Jeter to end the inning. For Posada, it was the fourth Opening Day home run of his career. The only Yankee with more was Babe Ruth, with five.

A second-inning double by Kevin Youkilis off CC Sabathia and Beltre's sacrifice fly halved the Yankees lead. After pitching poorly in last year's opener at Baltimore, Sabathia, became the pitcher the Yanks hoped he would be, winning 19 games (19–8).

Robinson Cano led off New York's fourth inning with a double, but two outs later he had advanced only as far as third base. Beckett then walked Swisher and gave up a run-scoring single to Gardner. Jeter singled, scoring Swisher and sending Gardner to third. The Yankees then pulled off a rare (especially for them) double steal as the speedy Gardner stole home and Jeter stole second.

With a 5–1 lead and their best pitcher on the mound, a repeat of last season's 0–8 start against Boston seemed unlikely. But the Sox fought back, as they always did under Francona. A run in the fifth, on singles by J. D. Drew, Cameron, and Scutaro, was followed by a three-run sixth that tied the score and finished Sabathia.

The first runs came on Youkilis's triple to right, on a 3–0 pitch, that scored Dustin Pedroia and Victor Martinez. Joe Girardi allowed Sabathia to pitch to the left-handed-hitting David Ortiz, who grounded out without the run scoring. He then brought in David Robertson who gave up a game-tying single to Beltre.

Scott Schoeneweis had replaced Beckett in the fifth inning and Ramon Ramirez had replaced Schoeneweis in the sixth. But when Ramirez walked Mark Teixeira to lead off the seventh and then gave up a double to Rodriguez, Francona called on Hideki Okajima. Both runners would score: Teixeira on a ground out by Cano and Rodriguez on a single by Posada.

The Yankees, who had lost a two-run lead and a four-run lead, once more had a two-run lead. To hold it until they could get to Mariano Rivera in the ninth, they turned to Chan Ho Park. The Korean-born right-hander, signed as a free agent in February, was beginning his 17th major league season.

The singing of "God Bless America" before the home team batted in the seventh inning had become a ritual at many ballparks since the disaster of September 11, 2001. This evening, Steven Tyler, of the rock group Aerosmith performed his version.

When Boston came to bat in the home seventh, they needed only three batters to again tie the score—a single by Scutaro and a home run by Pedroia into the seats atop the Green Monster in left field.

When Youkilis followed with a double, Girardi replaced Park with Damaso Marte. With Ortiz at the plate, Youkilis advanced to third on a wild pitch by Marte and scored on a passed ball by Posada. The Red Sox now led, 8–7, and would add an insurance run against Joba Chamberlain in the eighth inning.

Before they did, Neil Diamond wearing a Red Sox cap and a seemingly out-of-place "Keep the Dodgers in Brooklyn" jacket, came out on the field to sing "Sweet Caroline." The recording of Diamond's "Sweet Caroline" had become a ritual at Fenway Park and the fans, delighted to see him in the flesh, greeted him with a warm reception.

Daniel Bard had pitched a scoreless eighth for Boston before Francona brought in his closer, Jonathan Papelbon. The 29-year-old right-hander was Boston's answer to the Yankees' Rivera. Pabelbon had 151 saves over the last four seasons and Rivera had 147. Papelbon retired the first two batters before Posada singled for his third hit of the game. That brought up Granderson, the potential tying run. He had homered in his first at-bat as a Yankee, but all he could manage this time was a routine ground ball to third.

A few days after this game, Josh Beckett would sign a lucrative four-year contract with Boston; however, injuries would limit him to only 21 starts this year, with a 6–6 record and a 5.78 earned run average

The Yankees finished second in the East Division, one game behind the Tampa Bay Rays. Their 95 wins (95–67) easily earned them entry into the postseason as the wild card team. They swept the Minnesota Twins in three games to win the Division Series but lost the League Championship Series in six games to the Texas Rangers, giving the Rangers their first American League pennant. CC Sabathia again recovered from a poor opening day outing to have a very successful season. He led the league with 21 wins (21–7), tied for the lead in games started (34), and finished second in innings pitched (237⅔). Mark Teixeira led the league with 113 runs scored, while Derek Jeter tied for the runner up spot, with 111. Robinson Cano's 200 hits were second in the league to the Seattle Mariners' Ichiro Suzuki. Owner George Steinbrenner died in July 2010; his sons Hal and Hank took over the ownership duties.

Sunday, April 4, 2010

New York	ab	r	h	rbi	po	a	Boston	ab	r	h	rbi	po	a
Jeter ss	5	0	2	1	2	0	Ellsbury lf	5	0	0	0	1	0
Johnson dh	3	0	0	0	0	0	Pedroia 2b	4	2	2	3	4	6
aWinn pr, dh	0	0	0	0	0	0	Martinez c	5	1	1	0	2	0
Teixeira 1b	4	1	0	0	10	1	Youkilis 1b	4	3	3	2	12	1
Rodriguez 3b	5	1	1	0	2	5	Ortiz dh	3	0	0	0	0	0
Cano 2b	5	1	2	1	0	3	Beltre 3b	3	0	1	2	0	3
Posada c	4	1	3	2	5	0	Drew rf	4	1	1	0	1	0
Granderson	4	1	1	1	3	0	Cameron cf	3	1	2	0	5	0
Swisher rf	3	1	1	0	1	0	Scutaro ss	3	1	2	1	1	4
Gardner lf	4	1	2	1	0	0	Beckett p	0	0	0	0	0	1
Sabathia p	0	0	0	0	1	0	Schoeneweis p	0	0	0	0	0	0
Robertson p	0	0	0	0	0	0	Ramirez p	0	0	0	0	0	0
Park p	0	0	0	0	0	0	Okajima p	0	0	0	0	0	0
Marte p	0	0	0	0	0	0	Bard p	0	0	0	0	1	0
Chamberlain p	0	0	0	0	0	0	Papelbon p	0	0	0	0	0	0
Total	37	7	12	6	24	9	Total	34	9	12	8	27	15

aRan for Johnson in eighth inning.

New York	020	300	200–7
Boston	010	013	31x-9

Errors—Gardner. Double plays—Rodriguez, Teixeira; Scutaro, Pedroia, Youkilis; Beltre, Pedroia, Youkilis. Passed ball—Posada. Left on bases—New York 9; Boston 6. Stolen bases—Gardner, Jeter. Two-base hits—Cano, Rodriguez, Youkilis (2), Martinez. Three-base hits—Youkilis. Home runs—Posada, Granderson, Pedroia. Sacrifice Fly—Beltre.

	IP	H	R	ER	BB	SO
NEW YORK						
Sabathia	5.1	6	5	5	2	4
Robertson	0.2	1	0	0	0	0

	IP	H	R	ER	BB	SO
Park (L, 0–1)	0.2	3	3	2	0	1
Marte	0.0	0	0	0	1	0
Chamberlain	1.1	2	1	1	1	0

Wild pitch—Marte

BOSTON						
Beckett	4.2	8	5	5	3	1
Schoeneweis	1.0	0	0	0	0	1
Ramirez	0.1	2	2	2	1	0
Okajima (W, 1–0)	1.0	1	0	0	1	0
Bard	1.0	0	0	0	1	0
Papelbon S.1	1.0	1	0	0	0	0

Wild pitch—Schoeenweis

Umpires—HP, Joe West; 1B, Angel Hernandez; 2B, Paul Schrieber; 3B, Rob Drake. Time of game—3:46. Attendance—37,440.

Thursday, March 31, 2011
Yankee Stadium, New York
New York 6 Detroit 3

It was the spring of hope.—Charles Dickens

After winning the World Series in 2009, the Yankees finished second in the East in 2010 and then lost to the Texas Rangers in the 2010 American League Championship Series. For almost every other team that would count as a successful season, but for the Yankees it was a disappointment. Redemption had been on their mind from the first day of spring training 2011, helped along by co-owner Hank Steinbrenner's accusation that they had not being hungry enough last season.

Steinbrenner had mentioned no names, but four players in particular felt the need to improve. Pitcher A. J. Burnett, 10–15 with a 5.26 earned run average, had been heavily criticized by the fans and the press and, at age 34, was out to win them back. That quest was scheduled to begin when he started the second game of the opening series.

First baseman Mark Teixeira, a notoriously slow starter, was determined to end his annual April struggles. "Last year was awful, it was embarrassing," Teixeira said of April 2010, when he batted .136 with two home runs and nine runs batted in in 22 games. The year before he batted .200 with three home runs and 10 runs batted in in 19 April games.

Alex Rodriguez, lighter and two years removed from hip surgery, felt ready to increase his home run total from the 30 he had hit in each of the past two seasons. And above all was Derek Jeter, whose .270 batting average was a full-season career low. In addition, Jeter, 36, and Rodriguez, 35, who made up the left side of the Yankees infield, had looked slow in the field. Both had looked much better this spring, and Rodriguez said he sensed the team was driven by "the bad taste in our mouths" from 2010.

Expanded playoffs had make picking the eventual World Series winner more difficult, but picking winners in the five-team Division was easier—not easy in most cases, but easier. In the American League, it was the improved Boston Red Sox getting the most attention, rather than the perennial champion Yankees or the defending champion Tampa Bay Rays.

Boston had added two of the game's top players in the offseason, signing free agent outfielder Carl Crawford and trading with the San Diego Padres for slugging first baseman Adrian Gonzalez. In addition, Dustin Pedroia, Kevin Youkilis and Jacoby Ellsbury were healthy again after missing significant chunks of time in 2010. The Las Vegas Hilton had the Red Sox listed at 10–17 to win the East and the Yankees at 2–1. For the World Series, the Phillies were 5–2, the Red Sox 4–1, and the Yankees 6–1.

"It sounds strange because of our talent level and the past that nobody is picking us," said CC Sabathia New York's Opening Day starter. "It's kind of funny, we won 95 games last year."

This was Sabathia's eighth career Opening Day start, the first five coming with the Indians. He became the 12th Yankees pitcher to make at least three Opening Day starts; the first since Roger Clemens made four (1999, 2001–2003; and the first left-hander to start three since Jimmy Key (1993–95).

The Yanks were opening at home against the Detroit Tigers, only the fourth time the Tigers had furnished the opening-day opposition and the first time in New York since 1966. It was the first March regular-season game ever played in the Bronx, and March was not going out like a lamb. With a game-time temperature of 42, the weather was more like winter than spring. Accompanying the cold was a light mist and wind, making it a most uncomfortable afternoon for the 48,226 in attendance, and for the players.

Before Sabathia took the mound, former Yankee Mike Mussina threw out the first ball. In 2008, Mussina had ended his 18-year American League career with his first 20-win season (20–9). During his years with Baltimore, he was the Orioles opening day starter six times, and he was the Yankees somewhat reluctant opening day pitcher in 2004. It was not the opening day assignment that bothered Mussina; it was playing the game in far-away Tokyo, Japan, which he felt adversely affected the players' body clocks.

Sabathia had won 19 and 21 games in his two seasons with the Yankees. But both excellent seasons had come after shoddy performances on Opening Day. Last year in Boston, the Red Sox scored five runs against him in 5 ⅓ innings, and in 2009, the Orioles scored six runs in 4 ⅓ innings. The Yankees lost both games.

After breezing through a one-two-three first inning, Sabathia got into immediate trouble in the second. Singles by Miguel Cabrera and Victor Martinez, and a walk to Ryan Rayburn loaded the bases with nobody out. Cabrera came home on Jhonny Peralta's sacrifice fly, but Sabathia prevented a big inning by retiring the next two batters with no advancement by the base runners.

Tigers' starter Justin Verlander (18–9 in 2010) was not only Detroit's best pitcher; he was among the two or three best pitchers in the league. In the six innings he pitched this afternoon, he allowed the Yankees just three hits and walked four, while striking out eight. His only mistake was the three-run homer Teixeira tagged him for in the third inning. It was a well-hit drive that landed in the upper deck in right, though just barely fair.

Meanwhile, Detroit scored single runs in the fourth and fifth innings against Sabathia to tie the game at 3–3. The run in the fifth, facilitated by second baseman Robinson Cano's error, was unearned.

Complete games had become a rarity in baseball, particularly on Opening Day. This afternoon was no different. Like Verlander, Sabathia left after six innings, as managers

Joe Girardi of the Yankees and Jim Leyland of the Tigers turned to their respective bullpens.

On December 8, 2009 the Yankees, the Tigers, and the Arizona Diamondbacks had engineered a three-team, seven player trade, that included pitcher Phil Coke and center fielder Austin Jackson going from the Yankees to the Tigers, and Tigers center fielder Curtis Granderson going from Detroit to New York. All three took part in this game, as did pitcher Dan Schlereth, who went from Arizona to Detroit. (The prize acquisition of this trade would turn out to be pitcher Max Scherzer, who also went from Arizona to Detroit.)

Joba Chamberlain pitched the seventh for the Yankees and retired the side in order. The first man he faced was Jackson, who went down looking. It was the third strikeout of the day for Jackson, whose high strikeout totals in the minor leagues was one reason the Yanks had traded him. As a rookie with Detroit in 2010 he led the league with 170 strikeouts. This season he would have 181.

Coke, a lefthander, was Leyland's choice to pitch the seventh. The first batter he faced was Granderson, who hit a 2–0 fastball for a home run to put the Yankees ahead, 4–3. Granderson had suffered an oblique strain during spring training and played in a minor league game a day earlier to see if he was at full strength. He proved he was with the home run and two terrific catches in the outfield.

"There were obviously questions on Tuesday how it was going to turn out," Girardi said of Granderson's minor league stint. "He looked great today—outstanding defense, big home run."

"To be in a situation where you didn't even know if he was going to be here for Opening Day, he had a big game," said Jeter. "Everyone knows how good Curtis is and what he's capable of doing, but more importantly we're happy that he feels good."

"I enjoyed watching him play with us," Verlander said of Granderson. "I can't say I enjoyed watching him today."

The Yanks added another run in the inning (unearned) off Coke and Ryan Perry to go up by two. Russell Martin reached on an error by third baseman Brandon Inge and was sacrificed to second. At this point Perry replaced Coke and threw a wild pitch moving Martin to third. He scored on Jeter's sacrifice fly to center. Jeter was officially 0-for-2 in the game and remained 74 hits shy of 3,000. In the eighth, Nick Swisher singled Rodriguez home to make the final score, 6–3.

Rafael Soriano, who had a league-leading 45 saves for Tampa Bay in 2010 retired the three men he faced in the eighth inning. The Yankees had signed him as a free agent with Soriano agreeing to serve as the setup man for Mariano Rivera, as he did today. Rivera pitched the ninth, and with the aid of Granderson's catch of Inge's long drive, he, like his two predecessors, pitched a perfect inning. Rivera's save was number 560 and left him 41 behind Trevor Hoffman's all-time record of 601.

According to Elias Sports Bureau, Rivera made a bit of history when he entered the game in the ninth. Along with Jeter and Jorge Posada, they became the first trio of teammates in MLB, NBA, NFL and NHL history to play together in each of 17 straight seasons. Posada was the Yankees' designated hitter in the game, as he would be for most of the season, as free agent signee Russell Martin took over as the everyday catcher.

This would be Posada's final season. He finished his career with a .273 batting average, 275 home runs, and 1,065 runs batted in. Of all the great catchers in Yankees' history, none had hit as many doubles or drawn as many walks as Posada, and only Yogi Berra had appeared in more games or had more home runs.

Led by Justin Verlander and Miguel Cabrera, the Tigers would go on to win the Central Division title this season. Verlander (24–5) won the Cy Young and Most Valuable Player awards, along with the pitchers' Triple Crown, and Miguel Cabrera won the batting championship with a .344 average.

The Yankees, with the best record in the league (97–65), won the East Division by six games over the Tampa Bay Rays, but lost to the Detroit Tigers in five games in the Division Series. Curtis Granderson led the league in runs (136) and runs batted in (119). His 41 home runs were two behind the Toronto Blue Jays' Jose Bautista. He was also third in the league in triples, with 10. Robinson Cano was second to Granderson in runs batted in (118) and tied for third in the league in doubles (46). Brett Gardner's 49 steals tied him for the league lead with the Oakland Athletics' Coco Crisp. Mariano Rivera had 44 saves and won the Sporting News Fireman of the Year Award. During the season, Rivera recorded his 602nd career save, making him the major league's all-time leader in that category.

Thursday, March 31, 2011

Detroit	ab	r	h	rbi	po	a	New York	ab	r	h	rbi	po	a
Jackson cf	4	1	1	0	2	0	Gardner lf	2	0	0	0	2	0
Rhymes 2b	3	0	0	0	4	1	Jeter ss	2	1	0	1	0	1
Ordonez rf	4	0	1	0	2	1	Teixeira 1b	3	1	1	3	3	1
Cabrera 1b	2	2	1	1	4	3	Rodriguez 3b	2	1	1	0	0	2
Martinez dh	4	0	1	0	0	0	Cano 2b	3	0	0	0	2	0
Raburn lf	3	0	1	0	3	0	Swisher rf	4	0	1	1	3	0
Peralta ss	3	0	0	1	0	3	Posada dh	4	0	0	0	0	0
Inge 3b	4	0	2	1	0	0	Granderson cf	3	1	1	1	7	0
Avila c	4	0	0	0	8	0	Martin c	3	2	1	0	10	0
Verlander p	0	0	0	0	1	0	Sabathia p	0	0	0	0	0	0
Coke p	0	0	0	0	0	1	Chamberlain p	0	0	0	0	0	0
Perry p	0	0	0	0	0	0	Sorianoa p	0	0	0	0	0	0
Schlereth p	0	0	0	0	0	0	Rivera p	0	0	0	0	0	0
Total	31	3	6	3	24	9	Total	26	6	5	6	27	4

```
Detroit     010   110   000–3
New York    003   000   21X–6
```

Errors—Inge, Cano. Stolen base—Martin. Left on bases—Detroit 6, New York 4. Doubles—Inge, Rodriguez. Home runs—Teixeira, Granderson. Sacrifice hit—Rhymes, Gardner (2). Sacrifice Fly—Peralta, Cabrera, Jeter.

	IP	H	R	ER	BB	SO
DETROIT						
Verlander	6.0	3	3	3	4	8
Coke (L, 0–1)	0.1	1	2	1	0	0
Perry	0.2	0	1	1	1	0
Schlereth	1.0	1	0	0	0	0
NEW YORK						
Sabathia	6.0	6	3	2	2	7
Chamberlain (W, 1–0)	1.0	0	0	0	0	1
Soriano	1.0	0	0	0	0	1
Rivera S.1	1.0	0	0	0	0	1

Wild pitch—Verlander, Perry, Schlereth.

Umpires—HP, Dale Scott; 1B; Jerry Meals; 2B CB Buckner; 3B, Dan Iassogna. Time of game—3:02. Attendance—48,226.

Thursday, April 6, 2012
Tropicana Field, St. Petersburg, Florida
Tampa Bay 7 New York 6

The day shall come, the great avenging day.—Homer

For the 11th time in the last 16 seasons, the Yankees were opening on the road.

This year it was at Tropicana Field, the dour, dismal indoor home of the Tampa Bay Rays. They had played here in the final regular season game of the 2011 season, which turned out to be the most memorable game in the Tampa Bay Rays brief history. After falling behind the Yankees, 7–0, the Rays had rallied to eventually tie the score in the ninth inning, and to win in the 12th on Evan Longoria's second home run of the day. While the game was meaningless to the Yankees, who had already clinched first place in the East and played a makeshift lineup; the win by the Rays allowed them to make the playoffs as the wild card team and contributed to *The Sporting News* selecting Joe Maddon the American League's Manager of the Year.

The Rays had memorialized the area where Longoria's game-winning homer in game 162 entered the stands by creating what they called the "162 Landing," a field-level picnic area situated just inside the left-field foul pole. Re-living that game and raising the wild card banner were the highlights of the pregame ceremonies.

Jimmy Dundee, the son of Hall of Fame boxing trainer Angelo Dundee, was the unusual choice to throw out the first pitch. Angelo, who had trained, among others, Muhammad Ali and Sugar Ray Leonard died in Tampa on February 1. However he had moved there from his longtime base in Miami just five years earlier to be closer to his children.

Two of the best pitchers in the American League were facing off in the 2012 opener: James Shields for Tampa Bay and CC Sabathia for New York. The two aces had opposed each other in two classic pitchers' duels during an 11-day span last July. Sabathia won the first, 1–0, at Yankee Stadium, and Shields won the second, 2–1, at Tropicana Field. "Big Game" James, as Shields was called, had lived up to that moniker in 2011, with 16 wins (16–12) and a 2.82 earned run average. He led the league in complete games (11), tied for the lead in shutouts (4), and was second in innings pitched (249⅓). In addition, he made the All-Star team for the first time and finished third in the voting for the Cy Young Award.

Sabathia (19–8), the first Yankees' pitcher to start four consecutive openers since Mel Stottlemyre (1967–1970), had led the club in wins in each of his first three seasons in New York. And he continued to be a workhorse, facing more batters than any other American League pitcher in 2011, while throwing at least 230 innings for the fifth straight season.

Sabathia had not looked sharp this spring, a condition that continued into the first inning of the first game that counted. He had walked Desmond Jennings and given up a single to Longoria, and with two outs they were on third and second respectively. The situation was hardly desperate as the due batter was Sean Rodriguez, a light-hitting shortstop with a .229 career batting average. But Rodriguez was a right-handed-hitter and the on deck batter, Carlos Pena, was left-handed. So 15 minutes into the season, Joe Girardi, no stranger to charges of over-managing, made his first strategic decision of the new season. He ordered Sabathia to intentionally walk Rodriguez and pitch to Pena.

Back in Tampa after one season with the Chicago Cubs, Pena had been the Rays most feared slugger from 2007 to 2010, when he hit 144 home runs. But Girardi had his reasons.

The notebooks he kept on batter-pitcher matchups showed Pena had not done well against Sabathia, 4-for-35 (.114) with two home runs and 19 strikeouts. The count went to 3-2 before Pena drove a 3-2 fastball 428 feet into the right-field seats for a grand slam. It was only the third opening-day grand slam ever against the Yankees; Boston's Carlton Fisk hit one off Lindy McDaniel in 1973; and Baltimore's Tony Batista hit one against Roger Clemens in 2002.

"Shields has been so tough against us," Girardi said after the game in an attempt to justify the move, "Normally I wouldn't do something like that in the first inning. But we were thinking about that." Sabathia came to the defense of his manager. "It was the right decision," he said. "If I make a better pitch, we aren't talking about any of this right now."

The Yankees came back with two in the second to cut the Rays lead in half. Alex Rodriguez led off with a double and Mark Teixeira was hit by a pitch. Both later scored; Rodriguez on a ground out by free agent signee Raul Ibanez, in his Yankees' debut, and Teixeira on a wild pitch. The Yanks threat for a big inning ended when Shields struck out Curtis Granderson with the bases loaded.

An inning later, the Yanks reached Shields for four hits and four runs to take a 6-4 lead. The big blow was a three-run home run by Ibanez, their 39-year-old designated hitter now in his 17th major league season. Longoria's home run in the home third cut the Yankees lead to 6-5. The teams had combined for 11 runs in three innings, before Shields and Sabathia settled down. After they departed, the bullpens took control.

Shields left after five innings, having given up six runs and nine hits. Over the past few years, Maddon had gained a reputation as baseball's best in-game strategist. However, what makes one manager an outstanding in-game strategist and another guilty of over-managing may be more perception than reality. In this case, Maddon apparently made all the right moves. He used six pitchers in the final four innings, and the six: J. P. Howell, Wade Davis, Burke Badenhop, Jake McGee, Joel Peralta, and Fernando Rodney allowed no runs and no hits.

Still, the Yankees had their chances. They left the bases loaded in the seventh and two on in the eighth. Overall, they went 2-for-11 with runners in scoring position, left 12 runners on, and left the bases loaded three times.

Sabathia left after six innings, with the Yankees ahead, putting him in line to win his first opener with New York. Girardi was following a pattern he and Joe Torre before him, had used hundreds of times—take the lead after six innings, hold it in the seventh and eighth, and then bring in Mariano Rivera to close it out.

Girardi used Rafael Soriano, who pitched a scoreless seventh, and David Robertson, who pitched a scoreless eighth, setting the stage for Rivera. The all-time saves leader, with 603, had been almost automatic against the Rays in his career, converting 60 of 61 save opportunities. (The one blown save had come on August 16, 2005, on a home run by the now-retired Eduardo Perez.)

Rivera's cutter ranked as one of the most effective pitches ever. It had been almost unhittable in spring training, but after getting ahead of leadoff hitter Jennings, he left a 1-2 cutter up in the strike zone and Jennings lined it to center to put the tying run on. The next batter, the underrated Ben Zobrist, lashed a triple to right-center to score Jennings with the tying run.

With the potential winning run at third, and nobody out, Girardi did the obvious. He had Rivera intentionally walk Longoria and Luke Scott to load the bases and set up a force play at home. He also replaced right fielder Nick Swisher with infielder Eduardo Nunez and positioned Nunez in front of second base. The other four infielders also played in with the hope of turning ground balls hit to them into force plays at the plate. The two remaining outfielders, Granderson and Brett Gardner were also compelled to play shallow.

Rivera, appearing unruffled, as he always did, fanned Sean Rodriguez and got ahead of Pena, 1–2. Aware that Pena struck out often, the Yankees' hopes for getting out of the inning had brightened. Not for long, though. Rivera's next pitch was again high in the strike zone and Pena drove it far over left-fielder Gardner's head. Zobrist trotted home with the game-winner, igniting a huge celebration among the sold-out crowd of 34,078.

With the loss, the Yankees were now 63–46–1 all-time on Opening Day, including a 28–32 mark when they opened on the road.

The Yankees (95–67) won the East Division title by two games over the rejuvenated Baltimore Orioles. They defeated the wild card Orioles in five games to win the Division Series before being swept by the Detroit Tigers in the League Championship Series. After appearing in just nine games, Mariano Rivera injured his knee on May 3 and missed the rest of the season. Rafael Soriano replaced him in the closer role and saved 42 games. Boone Logan led the league with 80 games pitched, and Derek Jeter led the league in hits, with 216. Curtis Granderson's 43 home runs tied him for second place with Josh Hamilton of the Texas Rangers. Both were one home run behind the Detroit Tigers' Miguel Cabrera who won the Triple Crown.

Friday, April 6, 2012

New York	ab	r	h	rbi	po	a	Tampa Bay	ab	r	h	rbi	po	a
Jeter ss	4	0	1	0	1	1	Jennings cf	4	2	2	0	0	0
Granderson cf	5	0	0	0	1	0	Zobrist rf, 2b	5	1	1	1	3	1
Cano 2b	5	1	2	0	3	0	Longoria 3b	3	2	3	1	1	0
A. Rodriguez 3b	3	2	2	0	1	3	Keppinger dh	3	0	2	0	0	0
Teixeira 1b	2	1	0	0	5	1	aScott ph, dh	1	0	0	0	0	0
Swisher rf	5	1	1	1	1	0	S. Rodriguez ss	2	1	1	0	3	6
Nunez rf	0	0	0	0	0	0	Pena 1b	5	1	3	5	11	1
Ibanez dh	5	1	1	4	0	0	Johnson 2b	3	0	0	0	1	2
Martin c	4	0	0	0	12	1	bVogt ph, lf	1	0	0	0	0	0
Gardner lf	4	0	2	0	1	1	Molina c	3	0	0	0	5	1
Sabathia p	0	0	0	0	0	1	Joyce lf, rf	4	0	0	0	1	0
Soriano p	0	0	0	0	0	0	Shields p	0	0	0	0	2	0
Robertson p	0	0	0	0	0	0	Howell p	0	0	0	0	0	0
Rivera p	0	0	0	0	0	0	Davis p	0	0	0	0	1	0
Total	37	6	9	5	25*	8	Badenhop p	0	0	0	0	0	0
							McGee p	0	0	0	0	0	0
							Peralta p	0	0	0	0	0	0
							Rodney p	0	0	0	0	0	1
							Total	34	7	12	7	27	12

*One out when winning run scored
aGrounded into a double play for Keppinger in seventh inning.
bStruck out for Johnson in eighth inning.

New York	024	000	000–6
Tampa Bay	401	000	002–7

Errors—Longoria. Double plays—Teixeira, Jeter; S. Rodriguez, Pena. Left on bases—New York 12; Tampa Bay 10. Two-base hits—A. Rodriguez. Three-base hits—Zobrist. Home runs—Ibanez, Pena, Longoria.

	IP	H	R	ER	BB	SO
NEW YORK						
Sabathia	6.0	8	5	5	3	7
Soriano	1.0	0	0	0	1	1
Robertson	1.0	1	0	0	1	3
Rivera (L, 0–1)	0.1	3	2	2	2	1
TAMPA BAY						
Shields	5.0	9	6	6	3	3
Howell	0.2	0	0	0	0	0
Davis	1.0	0	0	0	1	0
Badenhop	0.0	0	0	0	0	0
McGee	1.0	0	0	0	1	1
Peralta	0.1	0	0	0	2	1
Rodney (W, 1–0)	1.0	0	0	0	0	1

Hit by pitches—by Shields, (Teixeira)
Wild pitch—Shields

Umpires—HP, Joe West; 1B, Sam Holbrook; 2B, Andy Fletcher; 3B, Rob Drake. Time of game—3:44. Attendance—34,078.

Monday, April 1, 2013
Yankee Stadium, New York
Boston 8 New York 2

Ah! When will this long weary day have ended.—Edmund Spencer

A year ago, when Derek Jeter started at shortstop it was the 16th Opening Day he had done so, extending his franchise record. No shortstop had started 17 or more with the same club since Hall-of-Famer Barry Larkin with the Cincinnati Reds; nor would they today. Jeter, who had not missed an Opening Day since 2001, was rehabilitating in Florida. He had fractured his left ankle during the first game of the 2012 American League Championship Series against the Detroit Tigers, ending his season.

Unfortunately for the Yankees, the injury had not healed well, necessitating the extended recovery period. Jeter was accompanied on the disabled list by three other major contributors to the team's offense: center fielder Curtis Granderson, third baseman Alex Rodriguez, and first baseman Mark Teixeira.

After the 2011 season, the Red Sox, who had won 90 games that year, fired their manager, Terry Francona, and replaced him with Bobby Valentine. Under Valentine, who seemed to have lost control of the team, the 2012 Red Sox had their worst season since 1965 winning just 69 games. As a result, new general manager Ben Cherington fired Valentine and brought in John Farrell for the 2013 season. Farrell, a former major league pitcher, had served as a pitching coach under Francona and for the last two seasons had managed the Toronto Blue Jays.

Cherington also made numerous changes to his roster. Only eight players remained from the team that began the 2012 season. And one, slugger David Ortiz, was, like Jeter, in Florida rehabilitating an injured ankle. The Sox were also minus regular shortstop Stephen Drew, out most of the spring with a concussion after being hit in the head by a pitch. Taking his place was 23-year-old Jose Iglesias, an outstanding defender who had appeared in a total of 35 games in 2011–2012.

Three free agent signees were playing their first games in a Red Sox uniform this afternoon. At first base was Mike Napoli, from the Texas Rangers, with 20 or more home runs in each of the last five seasons. In right field was Shane Victorino, from the Los Angeles Dodgers, who had a career .275 batting average in his nine big league seasons, all in the National League. The designated hitter was Jonny Gomes, from the Oakland A's, a ten-year veteran who had 18 home runs for the A's in 2012.

However, the most talked about newcomer was left fielder Jackie Bradley Jr., an exciting 22-year-old who had never played above Double-A. But a sensational spring—a .419 batting average with eight extra base hits, including two home runs, and 12 runs batted in in 28 games—persuaded Farrell to add him to the roster.

This promised to be quite a day for baseball fans in New York. In addition to the Yankees opening against the Red Sox at the Stadium, the New York Mets were opening against the San Diego Padres at Citi Field in Queens. Never in the 51 years since the Mets entered the National League had the two New York teams opened a season at home on the same day and essentially at the same time.

Fans with long memories recalled that the last time two of the city's teams had played their home openers under similar circumstances was on April 18, 1957. On that long ago day the New York Giants played the Philadelphia Phillies at the Polo Grounds, and the Brooklyn Dodgers played the Pittsburgh Pirates at Ebbets Field. They also recalled it was the last season those two storied teams played their home games in New York. The well founded suspicion that this would be the case, no doubt contributed to the disappointing attendance at both parks—only 8,585 at the Polo Grounds and 11,202 at Ebbets Field. With game-time temperatures expected to be in the high 50s, and with no threat that the Yankees would be deserting the city after the season, the crowd of nearly 50,000 was two-and-a-half times larger than the combined crowds 56 years earlier.

New York's mayor, Robert Wagner, a Giants' fan, had thrown out the ceremonial first pitch at the Polo Grounds, while on the other side of the East River, the Dodgers were raising the 1956 National League pennant at Ebbets Field. Neither politicians nor pennants were present today, and it's likely the fans in both parks preferred the popular former stars of the two teams who did this year's first ball honors—Lou Piniella for the Yankees and Rusty Staub for the Mets. Broadway star Constantine Maroulis sang the national anthem at Yankee Stadium and television star Emmy Rossum performed the anthem at Citi Field.

CC Sabathia (15–6 in 2012) was starting his fifth consecutive opener for the Yankees. He had not done particularly well in the previous four, but as the team's ace, he was manager Joe Girardi's choice to try again. Sabathia did show some slight improvement; a year ago, the Tampa Bay Rays had score four runs against him in the first inning. This year the Red Sox waited until the second inning to score four. The massively built lefthander got through the first, including two strikeouts, and retired Will Middlebrooks to open the second.

The Sox were counting heavily on third baseman Middlebrooks, whom they had brought up last May. In 75 games, he batted .288 with 15 home runs and 54 runs batted in before his season ended when he broke a wrist on August 10.

Sabathia's troubles began when after retiring Middlebrooks he walked Jarrod Saltalamacchia. Gomes then singled off the glove of third baseman Jayson Nix, Rodriguez's replacement. Sabathia got ahead of Bradley, 1–2, and threw him a pitch he thought was strike three. But home plate umpire Ted Barrett called it a ball, and Bradley eventually walked to load the bases. After Iglesias's infield single scored Saltalamacchia, Ellsbury forced Gomes at the plate for the second out.

Needing one more out to avoid the big inning, Sabathia gave up a two-run single to Victorino and a single to Dustin Pedroia that brought home the fourth run.

"Anytime you get two outs, you're a pitch away," Sabathia said. "Just couldn't make that pitch." Although it appeared he had lost something off his fastball, neither he nor Girardi seemed concerned—at least outwardly. "Health-wise, I feel fine," said Sabathia, who had undergone surgery last fall to remove a bone spur from his left elbow. "Elbow, shoulder, and everything."

Boston lefthander Jon Lester, making his third opening day start, was taking the first step as he tried to come back from the worst season of his career—a 9–14 record (his first ever losing season) and a 4.82 earned run average. He worked five innings, allowing the Yankees two runs, the only two runs they would have this afternoon.

Catcher Francisco Cervelli's two-out, bases-loaded single in the fourth brought in Kevin Youkilis, who had doubled and Vernon Wells, who had walked. Both Youkilis and Wells were newcomers to the Yankees, Youkilis as a free agent and Wells via a trade. This would be the final major league season for each. Youkilis, a one-time Red Sox stalwart, played in just 28 games, with the final one on June 13. Wells played the whole season with New York, appearing in 130 games, but was released the following winter.

Boston made it 5–2 with a run off David Phelps in the seventh. The Yankees, who had gone down in order against Koji Uehara in the sixth, aroused the crowd when they started the home seventh by getting their first two runners aboard against Andrew Miller. The intimidating, although at times wild, Miller, walked Cervelli and Brett Gardner. Miller, a six-foot-six lefthander, who would strike out 48 batters in 30⅔ innings this season, suddenly found the plate. He followed the two walks by notching his first two whiffs of the season— Eduardo Nunez, Jeter's replacement at short, and Robinson Cano, now acknowledged as the Yankees' biggest offensive threat.

The next batter was Youkilis, whose best days were behind him. Nevertheless, he represented the potential tying run, and he batted right-handed. Farrell followed the book, and replaced Miller, his hard-throwing left-hander, with Andrew Bailey, a hard-throwing right-hander. Bailey's strikeout totals for the season would be much like Miller's; fanning 39 batters in 28⅔ innings. He struck out Youkilis with a 95 mph fastball. "Timely hitting is the key," Youkilis said after the game. "We just didn't have that today."

Any hope the Yankees had of coming back ended when the Sox scored three runs against Joba Chamberlain in the ninth. Chamberlain allowed three hits and walked two in just two-thirds of an inning. The Yanks chose not to re-sign the once promising right-hander after the season, and he signed with the Detroit Tigers.

Farrell replaced Bailey with Junichi Tazawa in the eighth and closed it out with Joel Hanrahan in the ninth. Boston had acquired Hanrahan in a December 2012 trade with Pittsburgh. Hanrahan had saved 76 games for the Pirates in 2011–2012, but was on the disabled list for most of this season, which would be his last.

Lester had his first Opening Day win and the first of 15 (15–8) of his comeback season. He also made some Opening Day history for the Red Sox. The last Sox pitcher to make three straight Opening Day starts was Pedro Martinez, who made seven (1998–2004). The last left-hander to make three straight Opening Day starts was Mel Parnell (1952–1954). The only other lefty to do it was Babe Ruth (1916–1918). No lefthander had won an Opening Day start for the Red Sox since Gary Peters did it at Yankee Stadium 43 years ago.

For the Yankees, it was the first time they had lost on Opening Day at home since a 7–6 loss to the Chicago White Sox in 1982.

After making the playoffs for four consecutive years, and 17 of the last 18, the Yankees finished in a third-place tie with the Baltimore Orioles. Their 85 wins (85–77) were the fewest in a season since they won 79 in 1995. The Boston Red Sox went from last in the East Division in 2012 to first in 2013 and went on to win the World Series. Mariano Rivera ended his 19-year career with a major league record 652 saves. He retired as the team's all-time leader in games pitched, with 1,115. Derek Jeter spent three separate stints on the disabled list and played in only 17 games, with a .190 batting average.

Monday, April 1, 2013

Boston	ab	r	h	rbi	po	a	New York	ab	r	h	rbi	po	a
Ellsbury cf	6	1	3	2	2	0	Gardner cf	4	0	1	0	1	0
Victorino rf	6	0	2	3	4	0	Nunez ss	4	0	0	0	3	3
Pedroia 2b	6	0	2	1	1	0	Cano 2b	4	0	1	0	0	3
Napoli 1b	5	0	0	0	4	0	Youkilis 1b 3b	4	1	1	0	7	2
Middlebrooks 3b	4	1	0	0	2	0	Wells lf	3	1	0	0	1	0
Saltalamacchia c	2	2	1	0	10	0	Francisco dh	1	0	0	0	0	0
Gomes dh	4	1	2	0	0	0	aHafner ph dh	2	0	1	0	0	0
Bradley lf	2	2	0	1	2	0	Suzuki rf	4	0	1	0	1	0
Iglesias ss	5	1	3	1	2	5	Nix 3b	2	0	0	0	0	2
Lester p	0	0	0	0	0	0	bOverbay ph, 1b	2	0	0	0	4	0
Uehara p	0	0	0	0	0	0	Cervelli c	3	0	1	2	10	0
Miller p	0	0	0	0	0	0	Sabathia p	0	0	0	0	0	1
Bailey p	0	0	0	0	0	0	Phelps p	0	0	0	0	0	0
Tazawa p	0	0	0	0	0	1	Logan p	0	0	0	0	0	1
Hanrahan p	0	0	0	0	0	0	Kelley p	0	0	0	0	0	0
Total	40	8	13	8	27	6	Chamberlain p	0	0	0	0	0	0
							Eppley p	0	0	0	0	0	0
							Total	33	2	6	2	27	12

aPopped out for Francisco in sixth inning.
bFlied out for Nix in sixth inning.

Boston	040	000	103–8
New York	000	200	000–2

Double plays—Tazawa, Iglesias, Napoli. Left on bases—Boston 13, New York 8. Two-base hits— Saltalamacchia, Youkilis. Three-base hits—Ellsbury.

	IP	H	R	ER	BB	SO
BOSTON						
Lester (W, 1–0)	5.0	5	2	2	2	7
Uehara	1.0	0	0	0	0	0
Miller	0.2	0	0	0	2	2
Bailey	0.1	0	0	0	0	1
Tazawa	1.0	1	0	0	0	0
Hanrahan	1.0	0	0	0	0	0
NEW YORK						
Sabathia (L, 0–1)	5.0	8	4	4	4	5
Phelps	1.1	1	1	1	2	0
Logan	0.2	1	0	0	0	0
Kelley	1.0	0	0	0	0	1

	IP	H	R	ER	BB	SO
Chamberlain	0.2	3	3	3	2	2
Eppley	0.1	0	0	0	0	0

Wild pitch—Lester, 2; Eppley.

Umpires—HP, Ted Barrett; 1B; Alfonso Marquez; 2B Mike DiMuro; 3B, Dan Bellino. Time of game—3:37. Attendance—49,514.

Tuesday, April 1, 2014 (N)
Minute Maid Park, Houston
Houston 6 New York 2

I have built a monument more lasting than bronze.—Horace

The Yankees failure to make the postseason in 2013 all but guaranteed that general manager Brian Cashman would have a busy offseason, and that it was. Four big name players were signed, at a cost of half-a-billion dollars, and two even bigger names were lost.

Coming to New York as free agents from other major league teams were catcher Brian McCann, from the Atlanta Braves; outfielder Carlos Beltran, from the St. Louis Cardinals; and outfielder Jacoby Ellsbury, from the Boston Red Sox.

The Yankees also outbid other clubs, most notably the Red Sox, to sign Masahiro Tanaka, the ace pitcher for the Tohoku Rakuten Golden Eagles of the Japan Pacific League. Tanaka had won 99 games and lost 35 in his seven seasons in Japan, including an amazing 24–0 record and 1.27 earned run average in 2013.

Leaving New York for the Seattle Mariners, who signed him to a $240 million contract, was second baseman Robinson Cano who had been their best player. The Yankees also would be without future Hall of Famer Alex Rodriguez in 2014. On August 5, 2013, following Major League Baseball's claim that they had undeniable evidence Rodriguez had obtained illegal performance-enhancing substances from a clinic in South Florida and then tried to interfere with their investigation, commissioner Bud Selig suspended the Yankees' third baseman for 211 games. That would cover the rest of the 2013 season and the entire 2014 season.

Rodriguez appealed the suspension through the Major League Baseball Players Association, whose lawyers brought the case to arbitration. In January 2014, arbitrator Fredric Horowitz reduced the suspension to 162 games—the length of the 2014 regular season. Even with the reduction, it is the longest drug suspension and the longest non-lifetime suspension in baseball history.

Aware it was impossible for them to adequately replace either Cano or Rodriguez the Yankees did the best they could. They signed Brian Roberts, a longtime Baltimore Oriole, to play second base, and veteran Kelly Johnson to play third base, despite Johnson having played only 16 big league games at that position.

The Yankees revamped lineup opened the 2014 season against the Houston Astros at Minute Maid Park in a game that matched the only two teams yet to play this season; the other 28 teams had all opened in March. Houston, which had entered the National League in 1962, along with the New York Mets, had been switched to the American League West Division in 2013. The move was made to balance the number of teams in each league at 15.

Since 1998, when the most recent expansion increased the total number of teams to 30, the National League had fielded 16 teams and the American League 14.

The Astros were coming off the three worst seasons in their history. After setting records for most losses in a season, with 106 in 2011, and topping that with 107 in 2012, they broke the record again in 2013. Playing their first season in the American League, Houston lost 111 games. Despite their horrendous showing, Bo Porter, their rookie manager in 2013, was back at the helm.

Porter had employed 26 pitchers in 2013, and only one—22-year-old Jordan Lyles—had won as many as seven games (7–9). But Lyles was no longer an Astro. After the season, he and outfielder Brandon Barnes were traded to the Colorado Rockies for outfielder Dexter Fowler. Houston had signed veteran right-hander Scott Feldman as a free agent during the offseason, and it was he whom Porter selected to pitch the opener. Feldman had a 12–12 record in 2013, split between the Chicago Cubs (7–6) and the Baltimore Orioles (5–6).

Yankees manager Joe Girardi gave the ball to CC Sabathia, the sixth consecutive season he had done so. That allowed Sabathia to tie Lefty Gomez (1932–1937) for the most consecutive opening day starts as a Yankee, though it was one short of the record seven total starts, shared by Whitey Ford, Mel Stottlemyre, and Ron Guidry.

Sabathia had not been particularly effective in most of his previous five opening day starts. The Yankees had won only one, with the win going to Joba Chamberlain.

Girardi and Sabathia believed the massive left-hander was in better physical condition than he had been in last year. "I feel unbelievable," Sabathia said the day before the opener. "My arm feels great, my knee feels fantastic. I have no complaints. I feel really strong and ready to start the season. Last year, I kind of had some doubts going into the year and not feeling strong [with] my elbow. This year, I don't feel anything to worry about."

The six-foot-seven left-hander, who had once weighed more than 300 pounds, had slimmed-down to 280; nevertheless, at age 33 his fastball was topping out at about 90 mph down from the 98 mph of his prime.

Fowler made his Houston debut by leading off the bottom of the first with a double. One out later, he scored on Jose Altuve's single to left. Altuve then stole second and went to third on a wild pitch.

Altuve's single and his stolen base were harbingers of things to come this season for the young second baseman. He would win the batting title (.341), while leading the league in hits (225) and stolen bases (56).

With Altuve at third, Yankees first baseman Mark Teixeira attempted to cut him down at the plate after fielding Jason Castro's ground ball. But his throw to catcher McCann was well off target. Altuve scored easily and Castro made it to first minus any play on him. Outfielder Jesus Guzman, a former San Diego Padre, made his Astros debut a memorable one by blasting Sabathia's first pitch to him for a two-run homer. The four runs allowed by Sabathia again had put his team in an early hole.

The hole got deeper in the second inning when L. J. Hoes led off with a home run on a Sabathia change up. The Astros increased their lead to 6–0 on Fowler's second double and Altuve's second run-scoring single. Houston failed to score against in Sabathia's final four innings, or in the one inning each pitched by Dellin Betances and Vidal Nuno, but their six runs were more than enough.

Meanwhile, Feldman had little difficulty with the punch-less Yankees, retiring 10 of the first 11 batters he faced. The one exception came in the first inning when he hit Derek Jeter on the left forearm with an 88 mph fastball. The sense of panic that gripped

Yankees at seeing their captain hit, passed quickly when Jeter trotted to first base apparently unharmed.

One of the most well-liked and respected players of his era, Jeter moved in different circles than his teammates. Before heading to Minute Maid Park, he had lunched with former president George H. W. Bush and former First Lady Barbara Bush at Katch 22. The upscale restaurant was owned by Kory Clemens, the chef son of Roger Clemens. That evening, when he took the field for batting practice, Houstonians greeted him with loud chants of "Let's go Jeter."

Jeter had announced this would be his last season, and the accolades for him from fans and opposing players would continue throughout the season.

Ellsbury, McCann, and Beltran failed to pick up the slack left by the departures of Rodriguez and Cano, going a combined 2-for-12, both singles. Additionally, the bottom four hitters in the lineup—Alfonso Soriano, Brett Gardner, Brian Roberts, and Kelly Johnson—combined to go 1-for-14.

The Yankees mounted their first threat in the seventh inning, when Feldman gave up a single to Teixeira, hit Gardner with a pitch, and walked Roberts, to load the bases. Two men were out, but with left-handed-hitting Johnson due to bat, Porter replaced Feldman with Kevin Chapman, a left-hander. Chapman induced Johnson to hit a comebacker to the mound, which he threw to catcher Castro to force Teixeira, ending the inning.

Porter replaced Chapman with Chad Qualls in the eighth, after Chapman walked the leadoff batter, Ellsbury. Singles by Jeter, and run-scoring singles by McCann and Teixeira accounted for two runs, but Qualls got Alfonso Soriano to hit into an inning-ending double play. Matt Albers pitched a scoreless ninth to send the 42,117 fans home happy.

Sabathia had now made 11 Opening Day starts in his career—six with the Yankees and five with the Cleveland Indians. His won-lost record for those appearances was 1–3 with a bloated 6.12 earned run average. In six Opening Day starts with the Yankees, he was 0–3 with a 7.71 earned run average. His three losses matched Ray Caldwell for the most opening day losses without a win by a Yankees' pitcher. He would never start another opener.

The Yankees 84–78 record was good for second-place in the East Division, 12 games behind the Baltimore Orioles but not good enough to make the playoffs. This was the second consecutive year missing the playoffs for New York, something that had not happened since the pre-wild card years of '92–'93 (excepting 1994 when there were no playoffs). A mostly lackluster season was marked by tributes to Derek Jeter in every city in which the Yankees played and capped by a game-winning, walk-off hit in his final Yankee Stadium at bat. The 2014 season was Jeter's 20th and last as a major-leaguer. He left the game holding franchise records in Games Played (2,747), At Bats (11,195), Hits (3,465), Singles (2,595), and Doubles (544).

Tuesday, April 1, 2014 (N)

New York	ab	r	h	rbi	po	a	Houston	ab	r	h	rbi	po	a
Ellsbury cf	4	1	0	0	1	0	Fowler cf	4	2	2	0	3	0
Jeter ss	3	1	1	0	0	2	Grossman lf	4	0	0	0	3	0
Beltran rf	4	0	1	0	2	1	Altuve 2b	4	1	2	2	2	4
McCann c	4	0	1	1	10	1	Castro c	4	1	1	1	4	0
Teixeira 1b	3	0	2	1	11	0	Guzman 1b	4	1	1	2	8	2
Soriano dh	4	0	0	0	0	0	Carter dh	4	0	1	0	0	0
Gardner lf	3	0	0	0	0	0	Dominguez 3b	4	0	0	0	1	1

New York   Houston

	ab	r	h	rbi	po	a		ab	r	h	rbi	po	a
Roberts 2b	3	0	0	0	0	4	Hoes rf	2	1	1	1	4	0
Johnson 3b	4	0	1	0	0	2	Villar ss	3	0	1	0	0	2
Sabathia p	0	0	0	0	0	1	Feldman p	0	0	0	0	1	0
Betances p	0	0	0	0	0	0	Chapman p	0	0	0	0	0	1
Nuno p	0	0	0	0	0	0	Qualls p	0	0	0	0	1	0
Total	32	2	6	2	24	11	Albers p	0	0	0	0	0	0
							Total	33	6	9	6	27	10

New York   000   000   020–2
Houston   420   000   00X–6

Errors—Beltran. Double plays—Dominguez, Altuve, Guzman. Left on bases—New York 8; Houston 4. Stolen bases—Altuve. Two-base hits—Johnson, Fowler (2). Home runs—Guzman, Hoes.

	IP	H	R	ER	BB	SO
NEW YORK						
Sabathia (L, 0–1)	6.0	8	6	6	1	6
Betances	1.0	0	0	0	0	2
Nuno	1.0	1	0	0	0	3

Wild pitch—Sabathia

	IP	H	R	ER	BB	SO
HOUSTON						
Feldman (W, 1–0)	6.2	2	0	0	2	3
Chapman	0.1	0	1	1	1	0
Qualls	1.0	3	1	1	0	0
Albers	1.0	1	0	0	0	0

Hit by pitches—by Feldman (2), (Jeter, Gardner).

Umpires—HP, Gerry Davis; 1B, Phil Cuzzi; 2B, Bran Knight; 3B, Quinn Wolcott. Time of game—2:51. Attendance—42,117.

Monday, April 6, 2015
Yankee Stadium, New York
Toronto 6 New York 1

Past and to come seems best; things present, worst.—William Shakespeare

Perhaps it would have been different if George Steinbrenner still owned the Yankees, rather than his sons Hal and Hank. Despite two consecutive seasons of missing the postseason, the club had extended general manager Brian Cashman's contract for three years.

An even sharper break with the George Steinbrenner years was the Yankees limited participation in the free agent market. Three of the game's best pitchers—Jon Lester, Max Scherzer, and James Shields—became free agents following the 2014 season, but Cashman, the Yanks' general manager since 1998, did not actively pursue them.

He did have one major free-agent signing, left-handed reliever Andrew Miller, who had pitched for the Boston Red Sox and the Baltimore Orioles in 2014. Miller would take over David Robertson's role as the team's closer. Robertson had saved 39 games last season but left to sign with the Chicago White Sox.

Cashman was, however, active in the trade market, adding two 25-year-olds in his quest to bring young talent to a mostly veteran team. To replace the retired Derek Jeter, the Yankees acquired shortstop Didi Gregorius from the Arizona Diamondbacks, in a December 5, 2014 trade that also involved the Detroit Tigers. Two weeks later, Cashman sent second baseman Martin Prado and pitcher David Phelps to the Miami Marlins for pitcher Nathan Eovaldi and two other players.

Neither Gregorius nor Eovaldi had a history that solicited more than a yawn from most New York fans. Eovaldi had a dismal 15–35 record in four National League seasons, including a 6–14 record and a league-leading 223 hits allowed for the 2014 Marlins. During spring training, pitching coach Larry Rothschild had tutored him on how to get better results from his raw talent.

Gregorius arrived with an excellent reputation as a defender, which made him an improvement over Jeter whose defense never had been his strong point. The Yankees were counting on Gregorius to be better offensively than his .243 batting average in 191 National League games would indicate. A likeable young man, he'd had a solid spring training, going 13-for-48 with five doubles and two triples.

"I don't feel pressure," said Gregorius. "I'm just looking forward to the opportunity. It's not about me replacing Jeter. It's about me playing baseball and playing well and being myself."

Other youngsters the Yankees were counting on for the future, first baseman Greg Bird, second baseman Rob Refsnyder, outfielder Aaron Judge, and pitcher Luis Severino, also made positive impressions this spring.

Much of the pregame excitement centered on 39-year-old Alex Rodriguez, who was returning after a one-year suspension for using PEDs and then lying about it. The New York fans, normally extremely judgmental in drug-related cases, seemed to have forgiven him, greeting the announcement of his name with a rousing ovation.

For years, the fans in the bleachers had conducted a roll call in the top of the first inning, calling out each Yankee position players' name—but never for the designated hitter. But today's designated hitter was Rodriguez, and to welcome him back, the fans made an exception and did call out his name.

"That's a first for me. That's pretty cool," Rodriguez said. "I love our Bleacher Creatures. That was a pretty neat experience."

When he led off the third inning with his first at-bat and the Yankees already down, 5–0, most of the fans stood up to cheer him, drowning out the few that booed.

Rodriguez batted seventh, the first time he had started a game that far down in the order in a regular-season game since 1996, when as a 20-year-old he batted eighth for the Seattle Mariners. (Former Yankees manager Joe Torre batted Rodriguez eighth against the Detroit Tigers in the 2006 postseason.)

CC Sabathia had started the last six Yankees' openers, five of which they lost. Manager Joe Girardi ended that streak by opening the season with his new ace, Masahiro Tanaka, 13–5 with a 2.77 earned run average in 2014.

Tanaka had been the Yankees best pitcher during the first half of 2014 before injuring his elbow. But after the All-Star break, he made only two late-September appearances. Tanaka had made his much anticipated, big-league debut against the Toronto Blue Jays in April 2014, winning, 7–3. He said he did not anticipate the same case of nervousness he had then when he faced the Blue Jays today. "Looking back at last year, I think there was a lot of attention for me on how I would pitch being my first year here," Tanaka said through his translator. "There were certain pressures, but this year I'm not feeling that. For now, I think I'm a little bit more relaxed." Tanaka, who had chosen not to undergo Tommy John surgery, readily admitted his velocity was down some this season.

Toronto starter, Drew Hutchison, was making his first Opening Day start, and his 44th major league start overall. He had won 11 and lost 13 in 2014, his first full season, but finished strong, posting a 3.32 ERA in his last seven starts. The 24-year-old right-hander became the Blue Jays youngest Opening Day starter ever.

Torre, a newly elected Hall-of-Famer and currently Major League Baseball's chief baseball officer, threw out the ceremonial first pitch. The West Point Band from the United States Military Academy performed the national anthem. The West Point Color Guard presented the colors as 75 Cadets unfurled a giant American flag.

In each of the previous three openers, all of which the Yankees lost, the opposition had reached Sabathia for four runs in the first or second innings. Tanaka ended that trend with two scoreless innings before the Blue Jays pounded him for five runs in the third.

After Kevin Pillar led off with a single, Tanaka walked second baseman Devon Travis, the number-nine hitter in his first big league at-bat. Manager John Gibbons had his leadoff batter, Jose Reyes, attempt to move the runners up with a sacrifice bunt. Third baseman Chase Headley fielded the ball, but threw wildly past first baseman Mark Teixeira, allowing Pillar to score, Travis to reach third, and Reyes to reach second. Both scored on Russell Martin's single to right, upping the Toronto lead to, 3–0. Martin, the former Yankees' catcher, had played the last two seasons for the Pittsburgh Pirates before signing with Toronto.

Tanaka retired the first of the Blue Jay's most dangerous batters, Jose Bautista (35 home runs in 2014) but could not get by the second, Edwin Encarnacion (34 home runs in 2014). With the count, 2–1, Encarnacion connected with a 90 mph sinker, driving it into the left-field seats to give the Blue Jays a five-run lead. Tanaka struck out three during a scoreless fourth, but the damage had been done

"He got behind a lot of hitters," Girardi said. "As we know this is a dangerous club if you're pitching from behind. The first two innings he was ahead in the count and looked really good. Then he got behind and made mistakes."

The Yankees only run came in the sixth inning on Brett Gardner's leadoff home run. Gardner's home run was the Yankees' 100th on Opening Day and the first since Raul Ibanez hit one in 2012.

Travis matched that with his first big league hit, a home run, off Chase Shreve in the seventh. Shreve was one of five pitchers Girardi used following Tanaka's departure. Like the others—Chris Martin, David Carpenter, Justin Wilson, and Esmil Rogers—Shreve had previous major league experience, and all but Rogers were making their Yankees' debuts. Travis's home run off Shreve was the only run they allowed, while contributing six strikeouts, which along with Tanaka's six, tied the Yankees' Opening Day record of 12. (Martin had three in his one inning of work, and Carpenter, Wilson, and Rogers each had one.)

The Yankees' offense did little to stir the sellout crowd of 48,469 until the eighth inning, and then only briefly. They put two men on against left-hander Aaron Loup, who had replaced Hutchison in the seventh. Both reached thanks to Loup's wildness. He hit the leadoff batter, Gregorius, on the right elbow, and two outs later he walked Carlos Beltran. With Teixeira due up, Gibbons replaced Loup with Miguel Castro, a 20-year old right-hander. Castro had been the talk of the Blue Jays training camp with a fastball that registered just under 100 mph and excellent control (12 strikeouts, no walks in 12⅓ innings).

But the Teixeira-Castro confrontation did not take place, at least not in the eighth. Gregorius put an abrupt ending to the mini-rally when he curiously took off for third base and was thrown out by catcher Martin by two feet.

The inning-ending mental error was an embarrassing moment for Gregorius, one that had the fans making unfavorable comparisons with the man he had replaced. "[Girardi] told me in that situation it's not the time to run," he said after the game. "I told him it was my mistake and I'll never do it again."

Later that day, Torre, who had managed the Yankees for 12 seasons, received the "Pride of the Yankees" award at the team's Welcome Home Dinner. The Yankees had made the playoffs in each of those 12 seasons under Torre, winning six pennants and four World Series.

The Yankees finished second in the East Division, six games behind the Toronto Blue Jays. Their 87-75 record qualified them for one of the two wild card spots, but they lost, 3–0, in the one-game playoff, to the other qualifier, the Houston Astros, and failed to move on. Masihiro Tanaka and Didi Gregorius recovered from their opening day mishaps to record decent seasons. Tanaka had a 12–7 record, with a 3.51 earned run average, while Gregorius batted a solid .265.

Monday, April 6, 2015

Toronto	ab	r	h	rbi	po	a	New York	ab	r	h	rbi	po	a
Reyes ss	3	1	0	0	0	0	Ellsbury cf	4	0	0	0	4	0
Martin c	4	1	1	2	5	1	Gardner lf	4	1	1	1	2	0
Bautista rf	5	0	0	0	8	0	Beltran rf	3	0	0	0	1	0
Encarnacion 1b	4	1	1	2	5	0	Teixeira 1b	3	0	0	0	6	0
Smoak 1b	0	0	0	0	1	0	McCann c	4	0	1	0	12	0
Donaldson 3b	4	0	0	0	3	0	Headley 3b	4	0	0	0	2	2
Navarro dh	4	0	1	0	0	0	Rodriguez dh	2	0	1	0	0	0
Pompey cf	3	0	0	0	1	0	Drew 2b	3	0	0	0	0	0
Pillar lf	4	1	2	0	3	0	Gregorius ss	2	0	0	0	0	3
Travis 2b	2	2	1	1	1	3	Tanaka p	0	0	0	0	0	0
Hutchison p	0	0	0	0	0	0	Martin p	0	0	0	0	0	0
Loup p	0	0	0	0	0	0	Shreve p	0	0	0	0	0	0
Castro p	0	0	0	0	0	0	Carpenter p	0	0	0	0	0	1
Total	33	6	6	5	27	4	Wilson p	0	0	0	0	0	0
							Rogers p	0	0	0	0	0	0
							Total	29	1	3	1	27	6

```
Toronto      005      000      100–6
New York     000      001      000–1
```

Errors—Headley. Left on bases—Toronto 6, New York 5. Stolen bases—Pillar, Pompey. Home runs—Encarnacion, Travis, Gardner. Sacrifice hit—Reyes.

	IP	H	R	ER	BB	SO
TORONTO						
Hutchison (W, 1–0)	6.0	3	1	1	2	3
Loup	1.2	0	0	0	1	1
Castro	1.1	0	0	0	0	1

	IP	H	R	ER	BB	SO
NEW YORK						
Tanaka (L, 0–1)	4.0	5	5	4	2	6
Martin	1.0	0	0	0	0	3
Shreve	1.1	1	1	1	0	0
Carpenter	1.2	0	0	0	0	1
Wilson	0.2	0	0	0	3	1
Rogers	0.1	0	0	0	0	1

Hit by pitches—by Loup, (Gregorius)

Umpires—HP, Fieldin Culbreth; 1B; Jim Reynolds; 2B Jerry Meals; 3B, Paul Schreiber. Time of game—2:59. Attendance—48,469.

Tuesday, April 5, 2016
Yankee Stadium, New York
Houston 5 New York 3

When shall I see those halcyon days.—Aristophanes

For the first time since 1992, when they defeated Roger Clemens and the Boston Red Sox, the Yankees opened the season at home against the reigning winner of the Cy Young Award. This time it was against left-hander, Dallas Keuchel of the Houston Astros.

A cold rain that had caused the game to be canceled the day before was gone, at least the rain was. The skies were clear and the sun was shining, but the weather remained frigid. Groundskeepers used blowers to remove the ice chunks that covered parts of the field, while heaters were going full blast in the dugouts and the bullpen. Even the bat racks were being warmed with blasts of hot air.

The temperature was 27 degrees when batting practice began; it had risen to 36 degrees by the time Yankees starter Masahiro Tanaka threw the first pitch, but that was still the coldest for any Yankees home game since 2003. Hideki Matsui, the popular former Yankees' outfielder threw out the first ball, but another tradition, the unfurling of a giant American flag across the field, fell victim to the cold and wind. Although the game was a sellout, with the official attendance listed as 47,820, at no point during the afternoon were the stands any more than half full.

Keuchel's league-leading 20 wins (20–8), along with his 2.48 earned run average and 216 strikeouts, had led to his earning 22 of the 30 Cy Young Award votes. (David Price, who split the season between the Detroit Tigers and the Toronto Blue Jays, had the other eight.) He had been particularly effective against the Yankees, with 22 consecutive scoreless innings against them during the season, including six in the wild-card playoff game, won by the Astros, 3–0. Of the 79 New York batters Keuchel faced in 2015, he allowed 11 singles, one double, walked two, and struck out 28.

Keuchel had made one start against the Yankees in 2014. He gave up three runs in the second inning but then blanked the Yanks for six consecutive innings. Consequently, he had a 29 consecutive innings shutout streak against them broken in the second inning of this game (6 in 2014, 16 in 2015, 6 in the 2015 wild-card play-in game, and 1 in 2016).

The Yankees had traded for two right-handed hitters during the off-season and both were in manager Joe Girardi's starting lineup. Starlin Castro, from the Chicago Cubs, was at second base, and Aaron Hicks, from the Minnesota Twins, was in left field. They and all the other Yankees' players were wearing a patch with the number 8 on it in memory of Yogi Berra, who had died the previous September.

The New Yorkers ended their scoring drought against Keuchel with two runs in the second inning. Castro, who would soon become a fan favorite, hit a two-run double to left in his first at bat as a Yankee that scored Carlos Beltran, who had singled, and Brian McCann, who had walked.

Tanaka had been touched for five, third-inning runs in losing the opener to the Toronto Blue Jays a year ago. He started much stronger against Houston, retiring the first nine batters. The Astros broke through in the fourth, benefitting from left-fielder Hicks playing leadoff batter Jose Altuve's line drive into a double. Altuve took third on George Springer's infield single and scored when Carlos Correa hit into a force play.

Tanaka got through the fifth and retired the first two batters in the sixth. But before he could complete the six innings Girardi had hoped for, Correa homered on a 1–0 splitter to tie the score, 2–2. When Tanaka walked the next batter, Colby Rasmus, Girardi brought in Chase Shreve to get the third out.

The yielding of home runs had become a problem for Tanaka. He had given up only 15 in 2014, his first season, but was touched for 25 in 154 innings last season, plus two more in the wild-card game.

With the score still tied, Dellin Betances came on for the Yankees in the eighth inning and walked the first man he faced, Altuve, who quickly stole second. One out later, Correa hit a squibber up the first base line that Betances moved over to field. Correa was racing to first in what appeared to be fair territory, blocking Betances's view of first baseman Mark Teixeira. Betances attempted to throw the ball over Correa's head but his throw was too high and sailed over Teixeira and into right field, allowing Altuve to come around with the lead run.

Girardi immediately raced out to object, claiming that Correa should be ruled out for interference and Altuve should be returned to second base. Home plate umpire Dana DeMuth permitted the Yankees' manager to make his case, but maintained that Correa had been in the base line and therefore would not change his decision. Girardi, who later said he was surprised he had not been ejected for continuing to argue, announced he was playing the game under protest, later disallowed.

When play resumed, Correa also attempted to steal second base, but umpire Ed Hickox called him out. Now it was the Astros turn to argue the call. Manager A. J. Hinch challenged the call and asked for the play to be reviewed. The challenge was successful as the review resulted in the out call being reversed. Colby Rasmus walked, and with two outs, he and Correa scored on Luis Valbuena's single, making the score, 5–2.

Shortstop Correa, who also made a spectacular play to take a hit away from Alex Rodriguez, was playing in his first major league opener. Called up at age 20 by Houston in June 2015, he batted .279, with 22 home runs in 99 games and was voted the American League's Rookie of the Year.

"Off the charts," said Rodriguez, when asked about Correa's talent level. "We're getting to see him too often these days. But [he's] a very special talent on both sides of the ball. Five tools, fun to watch."

Keuchel left after seven innings, having retired the last 11 batters he faced. His replacement, Ken Giles, gave up a home run to the first batter in the eighth, Didi Gregorius, to cut the lead to 5–3. But he retired the next three batters, as did Luke Gregerson, who pitched the ninth.

For the Astros, it was a club record fourth consecutive opening day win, while for the Yankees, the loss was their fifth consecutive on opening day, matching the franchise record set in 1934–1938.

The Yankees (84–78) finished fourth in the East Division, nine games behind the Boston Red Sox. Masahiro Tanaka (14–4) had his best season as a Yankee, with career highs in wins (14), innings pitched 199⅔, and strikeouts (165). For Alex Rodriguez and Mark Teixeira, 2016 was their final major league season. In his eight years as a Yankee, Teixeira had 206 home runs, 13th on the team's all time list. Rodriguez played 12 seasons with the Yankees, slugging 351 home runs, sixth on their all time list, behind Babe Ruth, Mickey Mantle, Lou Gehrig, Joe DiMaggio, and Yogi Berra.

Tuesday, April 5, 2016

Houston	ab	r	h	rbi	po	a	New York	ab	r	h	rbi	po	a
Altuve 2b	4	2	1	0	4	4	Ellsbury cf	4	0	0	0	1	0
Springer rf	5	0	1	0	0	0	Hicks lf	2	0	0	0	3	0
Correa ss	4	2	1	2	1	4	ᵇGardner ph, lf	1	0	0	0	1	0
Rasmus lf	2	1	0	0	1	0	Rodriguez dh	3	0	0	0	0	0
Gomez cf	4	0	0	0	2	0	Teixeira 1b	3	0	0	0	10	1
Valbuena 3b	4	0	1	2	1	1	Beltran rf	4	1	1	0	0	0
Tucker dh	2	0	1	0	0	0	McCann c	3	1	1	0	10	0
ᵃWhite ph, dh	1	0	1	0	0	0	Headley 3b	3	0	0	0	0	1
Gonzalez 1b	4	0	0	0	9	1	S. Castro 2b	3	0	1	2	1	4
J. Castro c	4	0	0	0	8	0	Gregorius ss	3	1	1	1	0	2
Keuchel p	0	0	0	0	0	1	Tanaka p	0	0	0	0	1	2
Giles p	0	0	0	0	0	0	Shreve p	0	0	0	0	0	1
Gregerson p	0	0	0	0	1	0	Betances p	0	0	0	0	0	0
Total	34	5	6	4	27	11	Barbato p	0	0	0	0	0	0
							Total	29	3	4	3	27	11

ᵃSingled for Tucker in seventh inning.
ᵇStruck out for Hicks in eighth inning.

Houston	000	101	030–5
New York	020	000	010–3

Errors—Betances. Double plays—Altuve, Gonzalez; Valbuena, Altuve, Gonzalez. Left on bases—Houston 6, New York 3. Stolen bases—Correa (2), Altuve, Rodriguez. Doubles—Altuve, Tucker, S. Castro. Home runs—Correa, Gregorius.

	IP	H	R	ER	BB	SO
HOUSTON						
Keuchel (W, 1–0)	7.0	3	2	2	4	5
Giles	1.0	1	1	1	0	2
Gregerson S.1	1.0	0	0	0	0	1
NEW YORK						
Tanaka	5.2	4	2	2	1	4
Shreve	1.1	1	0	0	0	2
Betances (L, 0–1)	0.2	1	3	0	2	1
Barbato	1.1	0	0	0	0	3

Hit by pitches—by Barbato, (White)

Umpires—HP, Dana DeMuth; 1B; Greg Gibson; 2B Ed Hickox; 3B, Mike Estabrook. Time of game—3:17. Attendance—47,820.

Sunday, April 2, 2017
Tropicana Field, St. Petersburg, Florida
Tampa Bay 7 New York 3

Almost everything that is great has been done by youth.—Benjamin Disraeli

In the week leading up to the annual August 1 trading deadline, the 2016 Yankees reversed their traditional position of making deals to strengthen themselves for the homestretch. Stuck in fourth place in the East Division, with little hope of making the playoffs, they became sellers rather than buyers. Gone in trades were outfielder Carlos Beltran, to the Texas Rangers, and two of the game's best relief pitchers, Andrew Miller and Aroldis Chapman: Miller to the Cleveland Indians and Chapman to the Chicago Cubs. (Chapman, a free agent. returned to New York for the 2017 season.) Two weeks later they released Alex Rodriguez, ending Rodriguez's tempestuous 12 years as a Yankee.

During that same time frame, general manager Brian Cashman began to fill the roster from a farm system *Baseball America* rated as baseball's' second best. He brought up outfielders Tyler Austin and Aaron Judge and recalled catcher Gary Sanchez. The transformation from veteran stars to young hopefuls had begun. The Yankees opening-day lineup in 2015 had been the oldest in baseball. Now it was among the youngest, with 17 players in their 20s and eight in their 30s. According to ESPN the average age of their 25-man roster was 28.1 years old, the team's youngest since 1969. (Outfielder Matt Holliday, 37, signed as a free agent, and pitcher CC Sabathia, 36, were the two oldest members of the team.)

The 2017 season opened on a Sunday with three games—an afternoon game, a late afternoon game, and a night game. ESPN, which televised all three, set the times for the games. The prime-time night game, which would draw the biggest audience, matched the Chicago Cubs, the media's new darlings, beginning the defense of their first world championship in 108 years against their arch rival, the St. Louis Cardinals. The Yankees, once a fixture for prime time telecasts, played the new season's first game against the Tampa Bay Rays at Tropicana Field.

The pregame ceremonies included four-star Army General Raymond A Thomas III, commander of the Joint Special Operations Command at MacDill Air Force base in Tampa, throwing out the ceremonial first pitch (from the mound), and Air Force Staff Sergeant Cherrelle Warren singing the national anthem.

After which, Rays' right-hander Chris Archer took the mound. It was Archer's third consecutive opening-day start, which tied the franchise record for consecutive opening day starts held by James Shields (2008–2010).

Archer had led the major leagues with 19 losses in 2016 (9–19); nevertheless, he was manager Kevin Cash's best pitcher, and already acknowledged as one of the best young pitchers in the American League.

When asked if he was putting last season behind him, Archer said no, he had used it as motivation and fuel during the entire offseason. Normally a hard worker, he had spent the offseason, spring training, and participation in the World Baseball Classic to prepare himself. He reflected on what had gone wrong in 2016.

"For the first couple months I was trying to do too much. I was trying to strike everybody out from pitch one. It's not a recipe for success no matter how good you are, how good your stuff is. It's just being Chris Archer. Not trying to strike out everybody. Not trying to be [Justin] Verlander and be [Max] Scherzer and be Price. Be Chris Archer. And it's plenty. It's plenty."

The 28-year-old Archer was facing a Yankees' lineup that included four 24-year-olds: catcher Gary Sanchez, first baseman Greg Bird, right fielder Aaron Judge, and shortstop Ronald Torreyes. It was the first time since 1932 that four players age 24 or younger started the Yankees' season opener. Hopes were high that Sanchez, Bird, and Judge were future stars and that for each, this opener would be the first of many in a Yankees uniform.

Torreyes was playing shortstop in place of Didi Gregorius, whose shoulder injury was expected to keep him out until May. Torreyes and newcomer Pete Kozma, a journeyman, would fill in until Gregorius returned. Moreover, the club had two promising shortstops in the minor leagues: Gleyber Torres and Tyler Wade, who would likely be in the Bronx before long.

The Yankees had played exceptionally well in spring training, compiling a 24–9 record, the best in both leagues. Pitcher Masahiro Tanaka's 0.38 earned run average (one earned run in 23⅔ innings) was the third lowest in the last 20 years among pitchers who worked at least 20 innings. Tanaka, making his third consecutive opening day start for Joe Girardi, became the 13th Yankees' pitcher to start three or more openers. He also tied Hideo Nomo for the most major-league Opening Day starts by a Japanese-born pitcher.

In his first three seasons in New York, Tanaka had become the Yankees' best pitcher, with a 39–16 record and a 3.12 earned run average. He had made 75 starts during that time and had never been as ineffective as he was today, when he was driven out after just two and two-thirds innings. It was the second-shortest start of his career, and the first time he had failed to last five innings since July 10, 2016, against the Cleveland Indians. He set a career high by allowing seven earned runs and lost to the Rays for the first time in nine career starts. (In the second game of a May 14, 2017 doubleheader, Tanaka allowed eight earned runs in a start against the Houston Astros.)

Tanaka's start was the shortest by a Yankee on opening day since 1983, when Ron Guidry also lasted two and two-thirds innings against the Mariners in Seattle. The only other Yankees' pitcher to record just eight outs in an opening day start was Mel Stottlemyre, against the Boston Red Sox at Fenway Park, in 1973.

The Rays went to work immediately on Tanaka, who later admitted through a translator he might have been "a bit hyped up." Leadoff batter Corey Dickerson hit a line-drive single on his second pitch, went to third on Kevin Kiermaier's double, and scored on Evan Longoria's sacrifice fly. After Brad Miller's single and Steven Souza's walk loaded the bases, Logan Morrison's single scored two to put the Rays ahead, 3–0.

The Yankees notched their first two runs of the season in the second on singles by Starlin Castro and Chase Headley, a double by Judge that scored Castro, and a ground out by Torreyes that scored Headley. That was the sum of their offense against Archer, who blanked them over the next five innings.

Longoria's two-run homer down the left-field line in the home second restored the Ray's three-run lead. Morrison's solo homer to right in the third gave the Rays a 6–2 lead. They added a seventh run on a double by Tim Beckham and a bunt by Mallex Smith that Sanchez threw into right field. Tommy Layne got the final out of the inning, and he, Adam Warren, Jonathan Holder, and Chase Shreve held the Rays scoreless the rest of the way.

Archer, with a 7–2 lead, had retired 14 of 15 before Castro led off the seventh inning with a single, his third hit. The Yankees eventually loaded the bases with two outs, but Archer retired Sanchez on a grounder to short. It was the last of his 108 pitches.

Danny Farquhar pitched a scoreless eighth for the Rays, but the Yanks loaded the bases with nobody out in the ninth against Austin Pruitt. Headley opened the inning with his third single. Judge hit a ground ball to third that Longoria erred on attempting a force at second. Aaron Hicks, who had batted for Torreyes in the seventh and stayed in the game, hit a liner that shortstop Beckham got his glove on but could not hold.

Manager Cash yanked the unlucky Pruitt and brought in his closer Alex Colome. Free agent signee Chris Carter, pinch-hitting for Pete Kozma who had replaced Torreyes at short, hit a run-scoring fly ball. The next two batters were Sanchez and Bird, who had gone 0–4 and 0–3 respectively. Colome handled them easily, striking out Sanchez and retiring Bird on a fly ball to center.

The loss was the Yankees eighth in their last nine openers and marked the first time they had lost six in a row. It dropped their all-time opening day record to 63 wins, 51 losses, and one tie.

Sunday, April 2, 2017

New York	ab	r	h	rbi		Tampa Bay	ab	r	h	rbi
Gardner lf	4	0	1	0		Dickerson dh	5	1	1	0
Kozma ss	0	0	0	0		Kiermaier	3	2	2	0
BCarter ph	0	0	0	1		Longoria 3b	4	1	2	3
Sanchez c	5	0	0	0		Miller 2b	5	1	2	0
Bird 1b	4	0	0	0		Souza rf	3	0	0	0
Holliday dh	4	0	0	0		Morrison 1b	4	1	3	3
Ellsbury cf	3	0	0	0		Beckham ss	4	1	1	0
Castro 2b	4	1	3	0		Smith lf	4	0	1	0
Headley 3b	4	2	3	0		Norris c	4	0	1	0
Judge rf	4	0	1	1		Archer p	0	0	0	0
Torreyes ss	2	0	0	1		Farquhar p	0	0	0	0
ᵃHicks ph lf	2	0	1	0		Pruitt p	0	0	0	0
Tanaka p	0	0	0	0		Colome p	0	0	0	0
Layne p	0	0	0	0		Total	36	7	13	6
Warren p	0	0	0	0						
Holder p	0	0	0	0						
Shreve p	0	0	0	0						
Total	36	3	9	3						

ᵃFlied out for Torreyes in seventh inning.
ᵇHit a sacrifice fly for Kozma in ninth inning.

```
New York     020    000    001–3
Tampa Bay    322    000    00x–7
```

Errors—Sanchez, Longoria. Left on bases—New York 9; Tampa Bay 9. Stolen bases—Kiermaier. Two-base hits—Judge, Keirmaier, Beckham. Home runs—Longoria, Morrison. Sacrifice Flies-Longoria, Carter.

	IP	H	R	ER	BB	SO
NEW YORK						
Tanaka (L, 0–1)	2.2	9	7	7	2	3
Layne	1.0	1	0	0	0	2
Warren	2.1	0	0	0	0	2
Holder	1.0	2	0	0	0	2
Shreve	1.0	2	0	0	1	1

	IP	H	R	ER	BB	SO
TAMPA BAY						
Archer (W, 1–0)	7.0	7	2	2	1	5
Farquhar	1.0	0	0	0	0	2
Pruitt	0.0	2	1	0	0	0
Colome S.1	1.0	0	0	0	0	1

Hit by pitches—by Farquhar, (Ellsbury)

Wild pitch—Shreve

Umpires—HP, Jerry Layne; 1B, Marvin Hudson; 2B, Dan Bellino; 3B, Mike Estabrook. Time of game—3:21. Attendance—31,042.

The Yankees finished a surprising second in the East Division, two games behind the Boston Red Sox. Their 91–71 record qualified them for one of the two wild card spots. After defeating the other qualifier, the Minnesota Twins, they defeated the Cleveland Indians, three games to two, in the Division Series but lost the League Championship Series to the Houston Astros in seven games. Aaron Judge led the American League with 52 home runs, a rookie record. He was the unanimous choice as Rookie of the Year and finished second to Houston's Jose Altuve in voting for the Most Valuable Player. After the season, the club announced that manager Joe Girardi would not return. Girardi had a .562 winning percentage in his 10 seasons, including a pennant and a world championship in 2009. In December, the Yankees hired 44-year-old Aaron Boone, a former player with no managerial experience, to replace Girardi. On December 11, they traded second baseman Starlin Castro and two minor leaguers to the Miami Marlins for outfielder Giancarlo Stanton, the 2017 National League's homerun (59) and runs batted in (132) leader.

2018 Postscript

Thursday, March 29, 2018
Rogers Centre, Toronto
New York 6 Toronto 1

On May 29, 2018, the Yankees opened their 116th American League season against the Toronto Blue Jays at Toronto's Rogers Centre. New Yankees manager Aaron Boone chose right-hander Luis Severino as his starting pitcher, while Toronto's John Gibbons chose J.A. Happ. The Yankees won, 6–1, as Severino pitched 5⅔ shutout innings. Chad Green, Dellin Betances, and Aroldis Chapman pitched in relief, with Betances yielding the Blue Jays' only run on Kevin Pillar's eighth-inning home run. Giancarlo Stanton, New York's prized off-season acquisition, made a spectacular debut, with two home runs, a double, and four runs batted in.

Bibliography

Anderson, Dave, Murray Chass, Robert Creamer, and Harold Rosenthal. *The Yankees: Four Fabulous Eras of Baseball's Most Famous Team.* New York: Random House, 1979.

Appel, Marty. *Pinstripe Empire: The New York Yankees from Before the Babe to After the Boss.* New York: Bloomsbury, 2012.

Allen, Maury. *Where Have You Gone, Joe DiMaggio?* New York: E. P. Dutton, 1975.

Allen, Mel, and Ed Fitzgerald. *You Can't Beat the Hours.* New York: Harper and Row, 1964.

Allen, Oliver E. *New York, New York.* New York: Macmillan, 1990.

Alexander, Charles C. *Our Game: An American Baseball History.* New York: Henry Holt, 1991.

_____. *Ty Cobb.* London: Oxford University Press, 1984.

_____. *Spoke: A Biography of Tris Speaker.* Dallas: Southern Methodist University Press, 2007.

Armour, Mark L. and Levitt, Daniel R. *Paths to Glory: How Great Baseball Teams Got That Way.* Dulles, Va.: Brassey's, 2003.

Baldassaro, Lawrence. *Beyond DiMaggio: Italian-Americans in Baseball.* Lincoln: University of Nebraska Press, 2011.

Barber, Red. *1947: When All Hell Broke Loose.* Garden City, NY: Doubleday, 1982.

Barra, Allan. *Yogi Berra: Eternal Yankee.* New York, W. W. Norton, 2009.

Barrow, Edward G., with James M. Kahn. *My Fifty Years in Baseball.* New York: Coward-McCann, 1951.

Chadwick, Bruce and David Spindel. *The Bronx Bombers.* New York: Abbeville Press, 1991.

Cohen, Robert W. *The Lean Years of the Yankees, 1965–1975.* Jefferson, N.C.: McFarland, 2004.

Coverdale, Jr., Miles. *Whitey Ford: A Biography.* Jefferson, N.C.: McFarland, 2006.

Cramer, Richard Ben. *Joe DiMaggio: The Hero's Life.* New York: Simon & Schuster, 2000.

Creamer, Robert W. *Babe: The Legend Comes To Life.* New York: Simon & Schuster, 1974.

_____. *Baseball in 1941: A Celebration of Baseball's Best Season Ever in the Year America Went to War.* New York: Viking, 1991.

_____. *Stengel: His Life and Times.* New York: Simon & Schuster, 1984.

Curran, William. *Big Sticks: The Batting Revolution of the Twenties.* New York: William Morrow, 1990.

Dewey, Donald and Nicholas Acocella. *The Biographical History of Baseball.* New York: Carroll & Graff, 1995.

DiMaggio, Dom, and Bill Gilbert. *Real Grass, Real Heroes.* New York: Kensington, 1990.

The DiMaggio Albums. Richard Whittingham, Editor. New York: G. P. Putnam, 1989.

Eig, Jonathan. *Luckiest Man: The Life and Death of Lou Gehrig.* New York: Simon & Schuster, 2005.

Encyclopedia of Major League Baseball Team Histories. Editor: Peter Bjarkman. Westport, CT: Meckler, 1991.

Fetter, Henry D. *Taking on the Yankees: Winning and Losing in the Business of Baseball.* New York: W. W. Norton, 2003.

Freedman, Lew. *DiMaggio's Yankees: A History of the 1936–1944 Dynasty.* Jefferson, N.C.: McFarland, 2011.

Frommer, Harvey. *Five O'Clock Lightning: Babe Ruth, Lou Gehrig and the Greatest Baseball Team in History, The 1927 New York Yankees.* Hoboken, NJ: John Wiley & Sons, 2008.

_____. *New York City Baseball.* New York: Macmillan, 1980.

_____. *A Yankee Century.* New York: Berkley Publishing Group, 2002.

Gallagher, Mark. *The Yankee Encyclopedia.* Champaign, Ill.: Sagamore, 1996.

Gershman, Michael. *Diamonds.* New York: Houghton Mifflin, 1993.

Gittleman, Sol. *Reynolds, Raschi and Lopat: New York's Big Three and the Great Yankee Dynasty of 1949–1953.* Jefferson, N.C.: McFarland, 2007.

Goldstein, Richard. *Spartan Seasons.* New York: Macmillan, 1980.

Golenbock, Peter. *Dynasty: The New York Yankees 1949–1964.* New York: Berkley, 1975.

Gomez, Vernona, with Lawrence Goldstone. *Lefty: An American Odyssey.* New York: Ballantine Books, 2012.

Graham, Frank. *Lou Gehrig: A Quiet Hero.* New York: Putnam, 1942.

_____. *The New York Yankees.* New York: G. P. Putnam's Sons, 1948.

Graham, Frank, Jr. *A Farewell to Heroes.* New York: Viking, 1981.

Halberstam, David. *Summer of '49.* New York: Morrow, 1989.

_____. *October 1964.* New York: Villard, 1994.

Helyar, John. *Lords of the Realm.* New York: Ballantine, 1994.

Henrich, Tommy, and Bill Gilbert. *Five O'Clock Lightning*. New York: Birch Lane, 1992.

Honig, Donald. *Baseball America: The Heroes of the Game and the Times of their Glory*. New York: Macmillan, 1985.

_____. *Baseball When the Grass was Real*. New York: Coward, McCann and Geoghegan, 1975.

Hubbard, Donald. *The Red Sox Before the Babe: Boston's Early Days in the American League, 1901–1914*. Jefferson, N.C.: McFarland, 2009.

Hynd, Noel. *The Giants of the Polo Grounds*. New York: Doubleday, 1988.

James, Bill. *The Bill James Historical Baseball Abstract*. New York: Villard, 1986.

Jennison, Christopher. *Wait 'til Next Year*. New York: Norton, 1974.

Jones, David, editor. *Deadball Stars of the American League*. Washington, D.C.: Potomac Books, 2006.

Jordan, David M. *The Athletics of Philadelphia: Connie Mack's White Elephants, 1901–1954*. Jefferson, N.C.: McFarland, 1999.

Kahn, Roger. *The Era, 1947–1957: When the Yankees, the Giants, and the Dodgers Ruled the World*. New York: Ticknor & Fields, 1993.

Kavanagh, Jack. *Walter Johnson: A Life*. South Bend, IN: Diamond Communications, 1995.

Kelley, Brent E. *They Too Wore Pinstripes: Interviews with 20 Glory-Days New York Yankees*. Jefferson, NC: McFarland, 1998.

Knorr, Charles P. *The End of Baseball As We Knew It: The Players Union, 1960–81*. Champaign: University of Illinois Press. 2002.

Koppett, Leonard. *Koppett's Concise History of Major League Baseball*. Philadelphia, Pa.: Temple University Press, 1998.

_____. *The New Thinking Man's Guide to Baseball*. New York: Simon & Schuster, 1991.

Kuklick, Bruce. *To Everything a Season*. Princeton, NJ: Princeton University Press, 1991.

Leavengood, Ted. *Clark Griffith: The Old Fox of Washington Baseball*. Jefferson, NC: McFarland, 2011.

Leavey, Jane. *The Last Boy: Mickey Mantle and the End of America's Childhood*. New York: Harper, 2010.

Leib, Fred. *Baseball as I Have Known It*. New York: Coward, McCann and Geoghegan, 1977.

_____. *The Boston Red Sox*. New York: Putnam, 1947.

Levitt, Daniel R. *Ed Barrow: The Bulldog who Built the Yankees' First Dynasty*. Lincoln: University of Nebraska Press, 2008.

Levy, Alan H. *Joe McCarthy: Architect of the Yankee Dynasty*. Jefferson, NC: McFarland, 2005.

Light, Jonathan Fraser. *The Cultural Encyclopedia of Baseball*. Jefferson, NC: McFarland, 1997.

Linn, Ed. *The Great Rivalry: The Yankees and the Red Sox 1901–1990*. New York: Ticknor & Fields, 1991.

Lowry, Philip J. *Green Cathedrals: The Ultimate Celebration of Major League and Negro League Ballparks*. New York: Walker & Company, 2006.

Lynch, Michael T. *Harry Frazee, Ban Johnson and the Feud that Nearly Destroyed the American League*. Jefferson, NC: McFarland, 2008.

Macht, Norman L. *Connie Mack: The Turbulent and Triumphant Years*. Lincoln: University of Nebraska Press, 2012.

_____. *Connie Mack and the Early Years of Baseball*. Lincoln: University of Nebraska Press, 2007.

Marshall, William. *Baseball's Pivotal Era, 1945–1951*. Lexington: The University Press of Kentucky, 1999.

Mayer, Ronald A. *The 1937 Newark Bears*. East Hanover, NJ: Vintage, 1980.

Mead, William B. *Even the Browns*. Chicago: Contemporary, 1978.

Meany, Tom. *The Yankee Story*. New York: RE. P. Dutton, 1960.

Montville, Leigh. *The Big Bam: The Life and Times of Babe Ruth*. New York: Broadway Books, 2006.

Moore, Jack B. *Joe DiMaggio: Baseball's Yankee Clipper*. New York: Praeger, 1986.

Mosedale, John. *The Greatest of All*. New York: Dial, 1974.

Murdock, Eugene C. *Ban Johnson: Czar of Baseball*. Westport, CT: Greenwood Press, 1982.

Neft, David S., Richard M. Cohen, and Michael Neft. *The Sports Encyclopedia: Baseball 2005*. 25th ed. New York: St. Martin's Griffin, 2005.

Neyer, Rob and Eddie Epstein. *Baseball Dynasties: The Greatest Teams of All Time*. New York: W. W. Norton, 2000.

Oakley, J. Ronald. *Baseball's Last Golden Age, 1946–1960: The National Pastime in a Time Of Glory and Change*. Jefferson, N.C.: McFarland, 1994.

Okkonen, Marc. *Baseball Uniforms of the 20th Century*. New York: Sterling, 1991.

Okrent, Daniel, and Harris Lewine, Editors. *The Ultimate Baseball Book*. Boston: Houghton Mifflin, 1979.

Pietrusza, David. *Judge and Jury: The Life and Times of Judge Kenesaw Mountain Landis*. South Bend, IN: Diamond Communications, 1998.

Povich, Shirley. *The Washington Senators*. New York: G. P. Putnam's Sons, 1954.

Reidenbaugh, Lowell. *Take Me Out to the Ball Park*. St. Louis: Sporting News, 1983.

Reisler, Jim. *Babe Ruth: Launching the Legend*. New York: McGraw-Hill, 2004.

Rice, Damon. *Seasons Past*. New York: Praeger, 1976.

Ritter, Lawrence S. *The Glory of Their Times*. New York: Macmillan, 1966.

Roberts, Selena. *A-Rod: The Many Lives of Alex Rodriguez*. New York: HarperCollins, 2009.

Robinson, Ray. *Iron Horse: Lou Gehrig in His Time*. New York: Norton, 1990.

_____, and Christopher Jennison. *Yankee Stadium: 75 Years of Drama, Glamour, and Glory*. New York: Penguin Studio, 1998.

Rosenthal, Harold. *The 10 Best Years of Baseball*. Chicago: Contemporary, 1979.

Seidel, Michael. *Streak: Joe DiMaggio and the Summer of '41*. New York: McGraw-Hill, 1988.

Seymour, Harold, and Dorothy Z. Seymour. *Baseball: The Golden Age*. New York: Oxford University Press, 1971.

Shatzkin, Mike. *The Ballplayers*. New York: Morrow, 1990.

Sowell, Mike. *July 2, 1903*. New York: Macmillan, 1992.

_____. *The Pitch That Killed*. New York: Macmillan, 1989.

Sparks, Barry. *Frank "Home Run" Baker: Hall of Famer*

and *World Series Hero*. Jefferson, NC: McFarland, 2006.

Spatz, Lyle. *Yankees Coming, Yankees Going: New York Yankee Player Transactions, 1903 through 1999*. Jefferson NC: McFarland, 2000.

_____, ed. *Bridging Two Dynasties: The 1947 New York Yankees*. Lincoln: University of Nebraska Press and the Society for American Baseball Research, 2013.

Spatz, Lyle, and Steve Steinberg. *1921: The Yankees, The Giants, and the Battle for Baseball Supremacy in New York*. Lincoln: University of Nebraska Press, 2010.

Stark, Benton. *The Year They Called Off the World Series: A True Story*. Garden City Park, NY: Avery, 1991.

Steinberg, Steve, and Lyle Spatz. *The Colonel and Hug: The Partnership That Transformed The New York Yankees*. Lincoln: University of Nebraska Press, 2015.

Stout, Glenn, and Richard Johnson. *Red Sox Century*. Boston: Houghton Mifflin Harcourt, 2004.

_____. *Yankees Century*. Boston: Houghton Mifflin Harcourt, 2002.

Sullivan, Neil J. *The Diamond in the Bronx: Yankee Stadium and the Politics of New York*. New York: Oxford University Press, 2001.

Surdam, David G. *The Postwar Yankees: Baseball's Golden Age Revisited*. Lincoln: University of Nebraska Press, 2008.

Thomas, Henry W. *Walter Johnson: Baseball's Big Train*. Washington, D.C.: Phenom Press, 1995.

Tofel, Richard. *A Legend in the Making: The New York Yankees in 1939*. Chicago: Ivan R. Dee, 2003.

Wagenheim, Kal. *Babe Ruth: His Life and Legend*. New York: Henry Holt, 1974.

White, G. Edward. *Creating the National Pastime: Baseball Transforms Itself, 1903–1953*. Princeton: Princeton University Press, 1996.

Williams, Joe. *The Joe Williams Reader*, edited by Peter Williams. Chapel Hill, NC: Algonquin, 1989.

Newspapers

Baltimore News American
Baltimore Sun
Boston Globe
Boston Herald
Boston Post
Chicago Tribune
Cleveland Plain Dealer
Dallas Morning News
Detroit Free Press
Detroit News
Kansas City Star
Los Angeles Times
Milwaukee Journal
Minneapolis Tribune
Newark Star Ledger
New York American
New York Daily News
New York Herald
New York Herald Tribune
New York Journal American
New York Post
New York Press
New York Sun
New York Times
New York Tribune
New York World
New York World Telegram
Philadelphia Bulletin
Philadelphia Inquirer
Philadelphia Press
Seattle Post-Intelligencer
Sporting News
Washington Evening Star
Washington Post

Index